SELF-CONSCIOUS EMOTIONS

SELF-CONSCIOUS EMOTIONS

The Psychology of Shame, Guilt, Embarrassment, and Pride

Edited by

JUNE PRICE TANGNEY
George Mason University

KURT W. FISCHER
Harvard University

Foreword by **JOSEPH CAMPOS**

THE GUILFORD PRESS
New York   London

© 1995 The Guilford Press
A Division of Guilford Publications,
72 Spring Street, New York, NY 10012

Printed in the United States of America

This book is printed on acid-free paper.

Last digit is print number: 9   8   7   6   5   4   3   2   1

Library of Congress Cataloging-in-Publication Data

Self-conscious emotions : the psychology of shame, guilt,
    embarrassment, and pride / edited by June Price Tangney
    and Kurt W. Fischer.
        p.   cm.
    Includes bibliographical references and index.
    ISBN 0-89862-264-6
    1. Emotions. 2. Affect (Psychology) I. Tangney, June Price.
II. Fischer, Kurt W.
BF511.S345   1995
152.4—dc20   94-31710
                                                            CIP

To Our Spouses,
John and Jane

Contributors

Patricia Adams, B.A., Department of Psychology, University of Tennessee, Knoxville, Tennessee

Karen Caplovitz Barrett, Ph.D., Department of Human Development and Family Studies, Colorado State University, Fort Collins, Colorado

Roy F. Baumeister, Ph.D., Department of Psychology, Case Western Reserve University, Cleveland, Ohio

Susan A. Burggraf, M.A., Department of Human Development, Bryn Mawr College, Bryn Mawr, Pennsylvania

Joseph de Rivera, Ph.D., Department of Psychology, Clark University, Worcester, Massachusetts

Robert N. Emde, Ph.D., Department of Psychiatry, University of Colorado School of Medicine, Denver, Colorado

Tamara J. Ferguson, Ph.D., Department of Psychology, Utah State University, Logan, Utah and University of Utrecht, Utrecht, The Netherlands

Kurt W. Fischer, Ph.D., Department of Human Development, Harvard University, Cambridge, Massachusetts

Sharon Griffin, Ph.D., Department of Education, Clark University, Worcester, Massachusetts

David W. Harder, Ph.D., Department of Psychology, Tufts University, Medford, Massachusetts

Todd F. Heatherton, Ph.D., Department of Psychology, Dartmouth College, Hanover, New Hampshire

Warren H. Jones, Ph.D., Department of Psychology, University of Tennessee, Knoxville, Tennessee

Shinobu Kitayama, Ph.D., Kyoto University, Faculty of Integrated Human Studies, Kyoto, Japan

Karen Kugler, Ph.D., Private Practice, Tulsa, Oklahoma

Michael Lewis, Ph.D., Institute for the Study of Child Development, Robert Wood Johnson Medical School, New Brunswick, New Jersey

Janice Lindsay-Hartz, Ph.D., Private Practice, Miami, Florida

Hazel Rose Markus, Ph.D., Department of Psychology, University of Michigan, Ann Arbor, Michigan

Michael F. Mascolo, Ph.D., Department of Psychology, Merrimack College, North Andover, Massachusetts

Hisaya Matsumoto, Ph.D., Department of Psychology, Kyoto University, Kyoto, Japan

Rowland S. Miller, Ph.D., Division of Psychology and Philosophy, Sam Houston State University, Huntsville, Texas

Kazuo Miyake, Ph.D., Department of Psychology, Faculty of Liberal Arts, University of the Air, Chiba, Japan

David Oppenheim, Ph.D., Department of Psychology, University of Haifa, Haifa Israel

JoAnn Robinson, Ph.D., Institute of Behavioral Genetics, University of Colorado, Boulder, Colorado

Thomas J. Scheff, Ph.D., Department of Sociology, University of California at Santa Barbara, Santa Barbara, California

Klaus R. Scherer, Ph.D., Professor of Psychology, University of Geneva, Geneva, Switzerland

Hedy Stegge, M.A., Department of Child Studies, Free University, Amsterdam, The Netherlands and Division of Developmental Psychology, University of Utrecht, Utrecht, The Netherlands

Arlene M. Stillwell, Ph.D., Department of Psychology, State University of New York at Potsdam, Potsdam, New York

Deborah Stipek, Ph.D., Graduate School of Education, University of California at Los Angeles, Los Angeles, California

June Price Tangney, Ph.D., Department of Psychology, George Mason University, Fairfax, Virginia

Patricia E. Wagner, Ph.D., Hutchings Psychiatric Center, Syracuse, New York

Harald G. Wallbott, Ph.D. Department of Psychology, University of Giessen, Giessen, Germany

Kosuke Yamazaki, M.D., Professor of Psychiatry, School of Medicine, Tokai University, Isehara, Japan

Carolyn Zahn-Waxler, Ph.D., National Institute of Mental Health, Laboratory of Developmental Psychology, Bethesda, Maryland

Foreword

This book deals with long-neglected emotions. Pride, shame, guilt, embarrassment, envy, and jealousy have always been the province of the poet and the novelist, but rarely of the social scientist. To the layperson this neglect constitutes an enigma: Why should emotions that are so prevalent, and so crucial for the human condition, be so elusive a phenomenon of scientific study?

The answer, in my opinion, rests in the philosophy of science. Researchers tend to gravitate to what they consider at a given time to be the study of the most basic phenomena—the processes that in combination with each other account for the more complex aspects of reality. Scientists also tend to study what is most measurable. Facial expressions of emotion seemed to fit both these criteria. First, facial expressions provided a limited set of "basic" emotions that were measurable by very specific rules of organization of the facial musculature. These basic emotions (sadness, joy, surprise, fear, anger, disgust, and perhaps contempt) also seemed closely linked to underlying physiology. For many years, few psychologists doubted that these seven or so emotions were indeed the "atoms of affect," and the proper object of study on emotion.

The use of the term "basic" to refer to the facially measurable emotions and the designation as "secondary" and "derived" of all other emotions (including pride, shame, guilt, and the other emotions discussed in this book) had powerful connotations and scientific consequences. Such terms ensured that self-conscious emotions would be deemed explainable only after a much deeper understanding of the basic ones. The existence of "palette theories" of emotion that attempted to explain secondary emotions as blends of the primary and discrete ones added to the attention devoted to some emotions, and to the neglect of others. To study "complex" emotions was as unwise to the student of emotion of the time as the study of information processing was to a behaviorist a few decades earlier. In both cases, the study of the complex was deemed premature.

In light of such considerations and their apparent persuasiveness, what forces accounted for the remarkable and recent upsurge of interest in all of the social sciences in emotions such as those deemed "self-conscious"? I propose three reasons.

First and foremost is the decline of basic emotions theories. Researchers studying facial expressions became disenchanted with the limitations of approaches that study the recognition of actor-posed facial displays across cultures. They instead began to investigate the facial movement patterns of real people in real life settings, using objective measurement procedures. In the process, such investigators made a disconcerting discovery: The facial patterns of the basic emotions were seen only rarely, in quite constrained contexts, usually only in situations eliciting extreme reactions, and perhaps only in a very narrow age window between the maturation of particular patterns of facial organization and the impact of socialization on facial displays. Suddenly, the basic emotions did not seem so basic anymore.

At almost the same time, researchers studying how emotions were elicited began to specify patterns of appraisal, or core-relational themes, as Richard Lazarus calls them. These themes predicted on an a priori basis the elicitation of many emotions besides the "basic seven." All of the self-conscious emotions were so predicted, and thus a new scheme for what constituted a "basic" emotion emerged. This scheme depended on the specification of different appraisal patterns for between fifteen and thirty emotions, and the list has been growing steadily. From the vantage point of appraisal theories, the "derived" emotions were not secondary at all, but as primary as the "basic" ones.

Another factor that broadened interest in emotions stemmed from a new theoretical approach to emotion–functionalism. This approach traces its philosophical roots to the articles written a century ago by John Dewey in the first two volumes of the *Psychological Review*. It stresses the importance of understanding emotions by studying their functional consequences, and not by investigating discrete behaviors—whether these behaviors appeared in the face or in instrumental behavior. Functionalism thus provided a new means for measuring emotions and, in the process, liberated the study of emotion from approaches emphasizing the former list of basic emotions. Conceptualizations of these functional consequences led to the postulation that many previously neglected emotions could be identified from the functional equivalence of morphologically quite different behaviors. For example, shame can be manifested either by hiding behaviors and cutting off social communication, or by a rapid increase in rate of speech and equally rapid shifts of speech content. Both the hiding behaviors and its apparent opposite—the increases in parameters of speech—share a similar functional consequence. They both direct the attention of a significant social other away from one's flawed behavior. Similar considerations about the functional consequences of emotions were extended to affects such as guilt, love, envy, jealousy, and desire. A new approach to emotion measurement was thus born.

These three recent trends—the dissatisfaction with facial expression measurement, the study of patterns of appraisal, and the rise of functionalist approaches—combined in the mid-1980s to create a shift in the *zeitgeist* for the study of emotion. One consequence of this shift is the publication of the present book, which is at the moment the best single compendium of the different approaches, the different findings, and the different implications for the social sciences, of what used to be called the "complex" emotions.

The inspiration for this volume came from a conference devoted to the emerging study of self-conscious emotions held at the Asilomar Conference Center in December, 1988. This conference was dedicated to the memory of Helen Block Lewis, a psychoanalyst who was years ahead of her time in stressing the importance of shame. The meeting, which was organized with the support of the Sloan Foundation and the John D. and Catherine T. MacArthur Network on Developmental Transitions, and chaired by Professor Kurt W. Fischer and me, highlighted the need to bring together what was known about the new studies of emotions once relegated to the realm of the poet and novelist. The result is the present volume.

The editors should be congratulated for the broad representation of topics in the book, their stress on diversity of theoretical and empirical approaches to the self-conscious emotions, and the cross-cultural contributions without which no understanding of self-conscious emotions would be complete. The book is timely, its contents excellent, and its impact likely to be great. Above all, this book should be to its editors the source of a wonderful self-conscious emotion: pride.

JOSEPH CAMPOS
Berkeley, California
May, 1994

Acknowledgments

The idea for this edited volume grew out of two pivotal conferences supported by the Sloan Foundation, the Social Science Research Council, and the MacArthur Network on Early Childhood. The first conference, on emotion and cognition in development, was held in Winter Park, Colorado in the summer of 1985. The second conference, on shame and other self-conscious emotions, was held in Asilomar, California, in December 1988. We are grateful for the generosity of these Foundations, which provided the opportunity for us and so many of the contributors to this volume to share with each other new ideas and discoveries, and to return to our labs with renewed enthusiasm and pride.

We owe a special debt to Joseph Campos, who played a key role in helping to organize these unique conferences and who provided us with much guidance and encouragement throughout the preparation of this book.

Work on this project was also supported, in part, by a grant from the National Institute for Child Health and Human Development to June Price Tangney, and grants from the Spencer Foundation and the MacArthur Network on Early Childhood and a fellowship from the Center for Advanced Study in the Behavioral Sciences and the MacArthur Foundation to Kurt Fischer.

Many thanks to Jennifer Sanftner, Jennifer Vaught, and Erma Larson for their invaluable assistance with various stages of coordination and manuscript preparation, and to David Lasky, our skillful, patient, and wise production editor at the Guilford Press.

Finally, we wish to thank our many graduate and undergraduate students and colleagues at George Mason University and Harvard University for teaching and learning with us about shame, guilt, embarrassment and pride.

Contents

IV. SELF-CONSCIOUS EMOTIONS AND SOCIAL BEHAVIOR

V. SELF-CONSCIOUS EMOTIONS AND PSYCHOPATHOLOGY

I

INTRODUCTION

1

Self-Conscious Emotions and the Affect Revolution: Framework and Overview

KURT W. FISCHER
JUNE PRICE TANGNEY

In the last 20 years, there has been a revolution in the study of emotion. Emotion—and, more broadly, affect—used to be treated as peripheral to the main business of the social sciences, epiphenomena to the proper focus on behavior and thought. If affect was considered important at all, it was only for the extremes of human behavior, such as psychopathology, or the outskirts of scientific endeavor, such as psychoanalysis. Now, with the emotion revolution, affect has moved to center stage, becoming a focus of new research and theory and a primary topic for graduate students' interest (a sure sign of where the field is headed).

Not only is affect at the center of mind and behavior in the emerging framework, but minds are no longer merely brains that happen to be in bodies. People are embedded: Our minds are parts of our bodies, and with our minds/bodies we act, think, and feel in a physical and social world (Barrett & Campos, 1987; Fischer, 1980; Lakoff, 1987; Wozniak & Fischer, 1993). The objects, events, and people we live with are parts of our actions, thoughts, and feelings (Gibson, 1979; Rogoff, 1993; Vygotsky, 1978). There is no mind—action, thought, or affect—without body and world. There is no mind without other people.

The centrality of other people is particularly evident in emotions. All the emotions are fundamentally social, but the emotions that are the focus of this book—the "self-conscious emotions"—are especially social. Emotions such as shame, guilt, pride, and embarrassment are founded in social relationships, in which people not only interact but evaluate and judge themselves and each other. Self-conscious emotions are built on reciprocal evaluation and judgment. For example, people are ashamed or guilty because they assume that someone (self and/or other) is making a negative judgment about some activity or characteristic of theirs.

This book arises directly from the affect revolution, but it is intended to move the revolution several steps further forward. Ironically, even with the major changes of recent years, the self-conscious emotions have received only sporadic empirical study. Historically, the neglect was even greater, despite the popular hypotheses of Freud (1923/1961), Erikson (1963), and others that shame and guilt play central roles in development and pathology. The emotion revolution did not produce an immediate increase in research on self-conscious emotions, perhaps because some of the roots of the revolution were in an individualistic psychology that de-emphasized the social foundations of human behavior. In the early years of the turn toward emotion, the social aspects of emotion were neglected (see Campos, Barrett, Lamb, Goldsmith, & Stenberg, 1983), and the self-conscious emotions were mostly omitted from consideration.

With this book, we aim to establish a firm foundation for the role of self-conscious emotions in human behavior, and to promote strong research on these social emotions by bringing together in one place most of the best research and theory. The self-conscious emotions are important in their own right; in addition, giving them their proper place also highlights the necessity of treating human behavior as fundamentally social at its foundation. The mind starts with the self-in-relationships (Bronfenbrenner, 1993; Fischer, Hand, Watson, Van Parys, & Tucker, 1984; Gilligan, 1982; Sullivan, 1953). To provide a way of framing the study of self-conscious emotions (and emotions more generally), we briefly review the general status of emotion research in the social sciences today, and outline a framework for the analysis of emotions in general and self-conscious emotions in particular.

FROM PERIPHERAL TO FOCAL: THE GROUNDING OF HUMAN EMOTIONS

In the classic history of the social sciences, emotion has not been so peripheral as in the mid-20th century. In the ideas of Darwin (1872/1965), Anna Freud (1936/1966), James (1890), Hebb (Hebb & Thompson, 1968), and most other major theories in the history of the social sciences, emotion has been a significant part of the foundation of explanation. The primary exceptions are the cognition- or logic-dominated theories of the mid-20th century, such as those of Chomsky (1965) and Piaget (1983).

In the behaviorist and cognitive paradigms of the mid-20th century, emotion was virtually banned from the empirical study of mind and behavior. Emotions were typically cast as vague experiences, epiphenomena that merely accompany action and thought. Many behaviorists treated emotion as nothing but activation or arousal, with some sort of categorizing label attached (Duffy, 1962; Schachter & Singer, 1962). With the cognitive revolution of the 1960s and 1970s, the model of the mind became the affectless computer or some broader machine founded in logic and mathematics, eternally consistent and without contradiction (not a characteristic of any human mind that we know!). Chomsky and his followers posited innate modules for language or other cognitive faculties, which were thought to function as domain-specific logics without affect (Chomsky, 1965; Fodor, 1983). Piaget (1957) argued that with development the mind moves toward logical structures, and that when logic is finally constructed, it catalyzes pervasive change of the entire mind into a new stage of thinking.[1] Affect was mostly ignored.

One of the seeds for the downfall of this trivialization of emotion was the powerful findings generated by behaviorist and biological researchers on the facial, vocal, and neurological underpinnings of emotion (Campos et al., 1983; Frijda, 1986; Lazarus, 1991; LeDoux, 1989). Research with facial expressions was especially influential in establishing a broad consensus that emotion expressions show many universal characteristics, indicating common emotion categories across cultures (Ekman, 1972, 1982; Izard, 1977). Research on vocal expressions also showed strong linkages of vocal characteristics to specific emotions (Scherer, 1984, 1986). Evidence about brain functioning uncovered important neural structures for regulating emotional functioning (Benes, 1994; Fox & Davidson, 1988; Papez, 1937). With so much empirical evidence grounding emotions in both behavior and neural structures, scientists could no longer dismiss emotions as mere introspective epiphenomena that could not be studied scientifically.

The early work on facial and vocal expressions, however, tended to treat emotions as virtually equivalent with their expressions. Emotions were characterized in terms of a fixed set of "basic emotions" shared by all human beings and directly evident in individual facial and vocal expressions. This effort to reduce emotions to a few expressions in individual people has been cogently criticized (Russell, 1994; Shaver, Schwartz, Kirson, & O'Connor, 1987; Shaver, Wu, & Schwartz, 1992), but other assumptions of this work have been sustained: Most scholars now accept the assumptions that emotions are real and that important commonalities in emotions exist across people.

Despite the neglect of emotions by many cognitive theorists, one of the main factors in moving the affect revolution beyond emotional expression was the cognitive focus of the social sciences in the 1960s and 1970s, which helped lay the foundations for reconceptualizing affect. Cognitive science brought a new legitimization of analysis of internal states and processes. Indeed, the study of emotion has become so closely tied with that of cognition that most of the theories of emotion process begin with cognition at their center. When the International Society for Research on Emotion was founded, it even named its new journal *Cognition and Emotion*. Most current theories assume that emotions are grounded in a process of cognitive appraisal of the significance of situations and experiences (Laird, 1989; Lazarus, 1991).

One of the main efforts of current research and theory, as represented in this book, is to uncover the social grounding of emotions. Basic-emotion theories have omitted other people from their analysis, so that, remarkably, social emotion expressions have not been described or analyzed. For example, no facial expression for love has been described, despite the obvious hypothesis that eye-to-eye contact between lovers is a prevalent human expression of love across cultures (see Fehr, 1988; Shaver et al., 1992). For the self-conscious emotions, actions of hiding or escaping from others' view were omitted from consideration as emotional expressions, despite their apparent prevalence in shame, guilt, and embarrassment situations (Scheff & Retzinger, 1988, 1991; Tangney, Chapter 4, this volume; Lindsay-Hartz, de Rivera, & Mascolo, Chapter 11, this volume).

Emotions in general—and self-conscious emotions in particular—are grounded in bodily expressions and actions, cognitive appraisals, and social interactions. Research and theory in recent years have been aimed at bringing together these various components into a common framework, which we outline here. We emphasize four key assumptions of this framework. A broad background assumption is that emotions are fundamentally adaptive, promoting successful human functioning more than interfering with it. This assumption has led some researchers to call this framework a "functional approach" to emotions (Barrett & Campos, 1987; Barrett, Chapter 2, this volume). Second, the processes of emotional reaction are pervaded with appraisal of the meaning of events: Particular appraisals lead to particular emotions, and appraisals continue as people monitor and regulate their emotions. Third, each emotion can be described by a prototypical social script—a patterned sequence of events and reactions to those events, including characteristic cognitions, affective experiences, motivations, and subsequent behaviors. Fourth, emotions are organized into families of related affects.

EMOTIONS: FUNCTIONAL ORGANIZERS OF HUMAN ACTION AND THOUGHT

Emotions play a basic, adaptive part in human functioning by organizing action tendencies that mold, constrain, or structure human activity and thought (Barrett, Chapter 2, this volume; Barrett & Campos, 1987; Frijda, 1986; Lazarus, 1991; Mascolo & Fischer, Chapter 3, this volume). These organizing effects are evident not only at the moment but in long-term consequences, such as developmental pathways induced by particular affective experiences. Behaviorally, emotions have been analyzed into three primary, related facets, all parts of the organizing action tendencies: physical signs; experiences; and regular sequences of situations, goals, actions, and consequences. Much traditional research focuses on emotion as feeling, the experiences that are part of an emotion. It neglects or omits the other two facets, especially the regular sequences of situations, goals, actions, and consequences.

In shame, for example, physical signs seem typically to include lowering the gaze, covering the face, and sometimes blushing and staying quiet.[2] The subjective experience of being ashamed includes feeling exposed, heavy, or small, and dwelling on the flaw that one is ashamed of. The organizing action tendency describes the whole sequence from situation to primary actions, perceptions, and reactions. With shame, a person wishes to be judged positively in a given situation but instead is judged negatively (by self or other) for some action or characteristic, especially something that signals a deep-seated flaw. The person reacts by trying to hide or escape, or, alternatively, trying to blame others for the event. Emotion refers to all three of these facets (physical signs, subjective experiences, and action tendencies), as well as the categories and labels we use for them—in this case, "shame," "humiliation," "embarrassment," or something similar. (Most chapters in this volume relate to how to describe these general characteristics of self-conscious emotions.)

The emotion processes by which these actions, perceptions, and reactions occur are portrayed schematically in Figure 1.1 (Fischer, Shaver, & Carnochan, 1990; Frijda, 1986; Lazarus, 1991). Although the boxes indicate an approximate sequence, the processes typically occur in parallel, so that the diagram does not indicate a rigid ordering. Also, the analysis into component processes can make them seem implausibly cognitive and deliberate, but most of the processes occur unconsciously and virtually automatically after initial learning and development. In the development of an emotion, they may be separate and partly controlled until they are mastered, but eventually they become automatic. At that point, emotions seem to wash over us without thought, even though the processes are complex and have a long developmental history.

An emotion starts with people relating to events in which they are

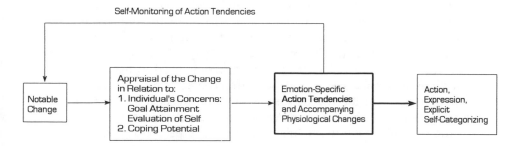

FIGURE 1.1. Functional model of emotion processes.

embedded and with which they participate. In these ongoing events, people detect a "notable change." When an event is detected as involving a change or a violation of expectations, a person continues processing the event for its affective meaning, "appraising" it. In an instance of shame, for example, people may detect that they have failed or transgressed or that someone else is frowning at them or looking at them with contempt or disgust. They then appraise the event with regard to the change.

Next, in the second box in Figure 1.1, people relate the change in the event to their "concerns"—not only their current goals and desires, but also their implicit goals. Most of this appraisal occurs quickly and unconsciously. The outcome is a general positive or negative evaluation, based on appraisal of a wide array of concerns. One large group of concerns involve whether the event interferes with or facilitates "goal attainment" or wish fulfillment. Events that interfere with concerns lead to negative emotions, such as sadness, fear, anger, and shame; events that facilitate concerns lead to positive emotions, such as joy and pride.

The self-conscious emotions involve another group of concerns that go beyond positive–negative goal attainment: how the event relates to "evaluation of self" (or the self's behavior) as worthy or unworthy. The concerns involve standards for worthy behavior or characteristics, such as performing a task well, covering the body, speaking tactfully, not harming others, and so forth. Positive evaluation with regard to these self-standards leads to emotions such as pride and respect. Negative evaluation leads to emotions such as shame, guilt, and embarrassment.

The second box also includes an appraisal of "coping potential"—how a person can cope with or modify the affect-producing event. If the event is desirable, the person may do nothing or may try to sustain or promote it. If the event jeopardizes a major concern, he or she judges whether something can be done to overcome or reverse it, alter it, or escape from it in some way. A judgment that a negative event can be overcome or undone may lead to emotions such as anger or guilt; a judgment that it cannot be overcome or undone may lead to sadness or shame; and a judgment that it can be escaped may lead to fear or shame.

For each emotion, there is a specific appraisal that produces a particular patterned reaction, called an "action tendency" (Frijda, 1986). Action tendencies are organized plans for acting in relation to the appraised events, and they are often pre-emptive, in that they take top priority in the control of action and thought. The body prepares physiologically to take the indicated actions, producing changes in expression, posture, heart rate, and so forth. Action tendencies also include effects on perception and judgment, such as biases toward detecting specific kinds of events and evaluating self or other as responsible for an outcome. With development, they come to include self-control efforts. In anger, for example, people tend to produce angry facial expressions and voice tones, increased tension and activity, increased heart rate, aggressive acts, a bias toward blaming someone or something other than the self, and often an effort to control aggression and anger by inhibition or redirection. Many of the chapters in this book provide descriptions of components of the action tendencies associated with the self-conscious emotions.

In overt behavior, the action tendencies lead to action and thought, to emotional expression, and to explicit "self-categorizing." This last component is often verbal, such as "I'm ashamed" or "I'm really mad at you!" Of course, the appraisals earlier in the emotion processes also involve categorizing, but those categories are implicit, not overtly stated or expressed.

Action tendencies not only lead to overt behavior; they also feed back through the entire sequence of emotion processes through "self-monitoring of action tendencies," such as self-control efforts and appraisals of one's own affective reactions (Fischer et al., 1990). This self-monitoring involves an additional loop through the general appraisal processes, as shown in the reverse arrow on the top of Figure 1.1. They are not separate from the general emotion processes, but instead involve reapplication of them—a second pass that appraises the action tendencies produced by the first pass. This emotion loop often produces an "emotion about an emotion." For example, when people react with shame in the first loop, their appraisal of that reaction sometimes leads to anger at being ashamed or anger at others for causing them shame. The loop can continue further, as when the anger in response to shame produces a further reaction of fear: "It scares me when I get so mad." Positive and negative emotions can also become connected through the emotion loop, as when a person feels pride at an accomplishment and then feels ashamed at being proud.

SOCIAL SCRIPTS FOR EMOTIONS

This analysis of emotions not only emphasizes their functionality; it also characterizes them as highly organizing or structuring. A useful way of depicting the organizations of emotions is through "prototypical social scripts"—patterned sequences of events and reactions that portray the prototype, gestalt, or best instance of an emotion, including its antecedents and many components. Shaver and his colleagues have studied stories that people tell about emotions and analyzed them into prototypic scripts divided into antecedents, responses, and self-control procedures (Shaver et al., 1987; see also de Rivera, 1981; Scherer, Wallbott, & Summerfield, 1986). Virtually every chapter in this volume deals in part with delineation of standard scripts for self-conscious emotions. Most of the chapters deal with North American or Western cultural depictions, but several chapters also deal with variations across cultures (see Kitayama, Markus, & Matsumoto, Chapter 18; Wallbott & Scherer, Chapter 19; and Miyake & Yamazaki, Chapter 20).

Tables 1.1 and 1.2 present proposed prototypical social scripts for the emotions of shame and pride, which seem in many ways to be parallel

TABLE 1.1. Proposed Prototypical Script for Adult Shame

Antecedents: Flaw or dishonorable or deplorable action, statement, or characteristic of a person
A person acts in a dishonorable way, says something deplorable, or evidences a characteristic that is disgraceful or flawed.
Someone (other or self) witnesses this action, statement, or characteristic and judges the person (self or other) negatively.

Responses: Hiding, escaping, sense of shrinking, feeling worthless
The person tries to hide or escape from observation or judgment; he or she feels small, exposed, worthless, powerless.
The person lowers his or her head, covers the face or eyes, or turns away from other people. Sometimes he or she strikes out at the person observing the flaw.
The person is preoccupied with the negative action, statement, or characteristic, as well as with negative evaluation of self more generally.

Self-control procedures: Undoing and redefinition
The person may try to change the negative action, statement, or characteristic; disguise it; deny its existence; or blame someone or something else for it.

emotions of opposite polarity, with shame negative and pride positive. The antecedents of shame generally involve some flaw or dishonorable action, and those of pride involve some virtue or desirable action. Shame produces responses of hiding, escaping, and feeling worthless, whereas pride produces those of displaying, engaging, and feeling worthwhile. Self-control procedures tend to predominate in negative emotions such as shame, not in positive ones such as pride. For shame, self-control procedures include trying to change the flaw or dishonorable action, denying it, or disguising it. Pride does not have self-control procedures as part of its prototype, because such efforts are not usually present, at least in North American culture. However,

TABLE 1.2. Proposed Prototypical Script for Adult Pride

Antecedents: Virtue or successful or desirable action, statement, or characteristic of a person
A person does or says something desirable or evidences some positive characteristic or virtue.
Someone witnesses this action, statement, or characteristic and judges it or the person positively.

Responses: Displaying, engaging, sense of growing large, feeling worthwhile
The person shows or displays the positive activity or characteristic for approval; he or she feels large, worthwhile, powerful.
The person is preoccupied with the positive action, statement, or characteristic, as well as with positive evaluation of self more generally.

Self-control procedures
If pride is too extreme or too public, it can become shameful, and then the shame self-control procedures come into play.

when pride is considered negative (an attribution that may be common in some cultures), it becomes a reason for shame, thus activating shame self-control procedures.

The scripts in Tables 1.1 and 1.2 are proposed as prototypes, descriptions of the best instance of shame and pride. They do not capture the range of variation of meanings in shame and pride. Much human categorization functions in terms of prototypes (Rosch, 1978), with people agreeing on the category or name of the prototype but commonly disagreeing on classifying cases that have only some of the prototype's characteristics. People agree on the core of the category but not its limits or boundaries.

A DIMENSIONAL HIERARCHY OF BASIC EMOTION FAMILIES

Besides the organizations of individual emotions into social scripts, emotions can be grouped together into broadly similar families that are structured hierarchically, as illustrated in Figure 1.2. In general, hierarchical organization by family resemblance is the normal pattern for prototypic categories. Families of emotions form clusters of "basic categories" of emotion families, such as the families of anger, sadness, fear, shame, love, and happiness in Figure 1.2. At higher degrees of generality, the families are related in terms of broad "dimensions" or superordinate categories, such as positive–negative evaluation. At lower degrees of organization, they divide into "subordinate categories" and differentiated, highly specific emotions. For example, in Figure 1.2, wrath, jealousy, and disgust constitute three subordinate categories (subfamilies) under anger, each itself containing emotion words varying from a few to more than a dozen. In general, subordinate categories seem to show wide variation across cultures, whereas basic and superordinate categories appear to show many similarities as well as some differences (The subordinate categories listed in Figure 1.2 are representative, but not exhaustive.)

The word "basic" was chosen to refer to the emotion families for two reasons. First, prototypes typically show a hierarchical classification system like that in Figure 1.2, and there the intermediate level is called "basic" because it is these categories that people most commonly use in everyday language as a common kind of starting point. Second, researchers have labeled certain emotion categories as "basic" because there is evidence that they are extremely common, both across cultures and among people within a culture. At times researchers have treated basic emotions as if they referred only to emotions tied to specific individual facial expressions, as we have noted above; within this tradition, there have been arguments about the number of basic emotions—and facial expressions of emotions (Ekman, 1982; Ekman et al., 1987; Izard, 1977; Izard & Malatesta, 1987; Russell, 1994).

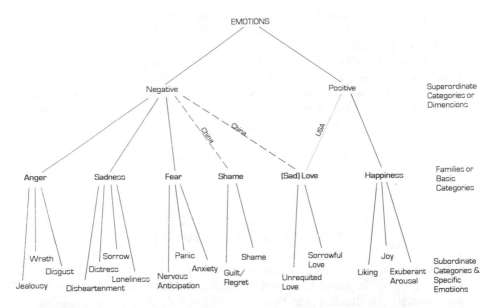

FIGURE 1.2. A hierarchy of emotion categories in Chinese. This hierarchy is based primarily on Shaver and colleagues' cluster analysis for Chinese emotion words, but U.S. and Italian findings are represented as well for basic emotion families. Shame defined a separate family only for China, not the United States or Italy. Love was positive in the United States and Italy, but negative ("Sad Love") in China. For subordinate categories and specific emotions, only the largest categories from the Chinese sample are listed here. Dashed lines indicate relations that held for the Chinese sample only, and dotted lines indicate relations that held for the U.S. and Italian samples only.

Nevertheless, many of the candidates for basic facial emotions are also present in the emotion hierarchies based on words. Anger, sadness, fear, and joy are virtually always included as facial emotions, and shame is occasionally included. We have proposed that love should also be included among the facial emotions, because in interactions among people (who interact with their faces, among other things!), there are facial expressions of love (Fischer, Shaver, & Carnochan, 1989; Fischer et al., 1990; Shaver et al., 1992). Also, research on attachment and interpersonal attraction strongly supports the argument that love is a basic emotion in the sense that it is far-reaching and foundational in human behavior (Ainsworth, Blehar, Waters, & Wall, 1978; Bowlby, 1969–1980; Bretherton & Waters, 1985; Shaver, Hazan, & Bradshaw, 1988).

The hierarchy in Figure 1.2 is based on emotion categorization in a Chinese sample studied by Phillip Shaver and his colleagues (Shaver et al., 1987; Shaver et al., 1992). They asked people in the United States, the People's Republic of China, and Italy to group emotion words (in their respective languages) according to similarities and differences. When the categorizations for each country were analyzed by hierarchical cluster analysis, the resulting emotion clusters showed a number of similar emotion families as well as important differences. Five basic families were similar across the cultures (anger, sadness, fear, love, and happiness), but in China there was a sixth family, shame. In addition, love changed its evaluation across countries, falling on the positive side in the United States and Italy and on the negative side in China. That is why it is called "(Sad) Love" in Figure 1.2. In general, then, four of the families were globally similar in the three cultures; one showed a major shift; and one was present as a basic family in only one culture.

The words used to name the emotion families were selected statistically as the most representative of the choices made within that family. Interestingly, the names for fear, anger, sadness, and joy were similar across the three languages, although there are of course issues of translation that make exact equivalence difficult to judge.

Importantly for this book, the basic emotion family that was missing in the Western nations was shame, including guilt, embarrassment, and related emotions. For the United States and Italy, shame formed a subfamily under sadness rather than constituting its own elaborated basic family. For China, shame formed its own family, with two subordinate categories of guilt/regret and shame, each containing multiple emotion words. Note that English has an impoverished set of shame words relative to Chinese; many of the differentiated Chinese words had to be translated as simply "shame" in English. That is why the same word "shame" is used in translation for both basic and subordinate categories in Figure 1.2.

The superordinate categories in Figure 1.2 are negative and positive, which form a dimension along which emotion families and specific emotions vary. The dimension of evaluation arises as dominant in virtually all studies of affective meaning (Fischer et al., 1990; Lazarus, 1991; Osgood, Suci, & Tannenbaum, 1957; Schlosberg, 1954; Wundt, 1905/1907). In addition, two other important superordinate dimensions are also commonly found: an activity or active–passive dimension, and a relatedness or engaged–disengaged dimension. These three dimensions can be thought of as organizing the basic emotion families and subordinate categories when the hierarchy is viewed from above. That is, the dimensional structure exists simultaneously with the hierarchical structure.

Although the dimensions are similar across cultures, they show important differences, just as the basic families do. Kitayama et al. (Chapter 18, this volume) argue that cultures differ powerfully on the third dimension of engagement–disengagement, and that the prevalence and form of self-conscious emotions differ substantially with variations along this dimension. For example, with a focus on independence (disengagement), pride tends to be positive; however, with a focus on interdependence (engagement), it becomes negative because it separates the self from others. Engagement is more important in Eastern, shame-oriented cultures, whereas disengagement is more important in Western, independence-oriented cultures.

In this book, with its focus on self-conscious emotions, we hope to correct some of the Western neglect of these important emotions, as well as to ground them more powerfully in their social foundations and to improve the quality and scope of research and theory on emotions.

NEW DIRECTIONS IN THE STUDY OF AFFECT: REDISCOVERING THE NEGLECTED SELF-CONSCIOUS EMOTIONS

This volume focuses on recent empirical advances in the study of the self-conscious emotions. Among the essential components of self-conscious emotions, as evident from the analysis of emotion processes in Figure 1.1, are consciousness of the self (as separate from nonself or other) and evaluation of the self against some standard (Lewis, Sullivan, Stanger, & Weiss, 1989). Key self-conscious emotions such as shame, guilt, pride, and embarrassment are each intimately related to various kinds of evaluations by self or others. For example, when good things happen, we may feel any one of a number of positive emotions—joy, happiness, satisfaction, or contentment—but feelings of pride typically arise from a recognition of our *own* positive attributes or performances, as well as a sense that important figures to whom we are close may share in recognizing these attributes or performances. In those situations where we feel pride over another person's behavior, that person is invariably someone with whom we are closely affiliated or identified (such as a family member, friend, or colleague closely associated with the self). It is because that person is part of our self-definition that we experience pride (Mascolo & Fischer, Chapter 3, this volume). By the same token, we feel ashamed of ourselves, guilty over our behavior, and embarrassed by our pratfalls. Self-conscious emotions emerge in self-relevant contexts; they draw the self into conscious awareness with evaluation by self and others; and, by their evaluative nature, they serve to sharpen and define our conception of ourselves.

Given the centrality of self-conscious emotions in human life and in classical theories of human emotions such as psychoanalysis (Freud, 1923/1961), it is puzzling that the affect revolution did not produce an immediate increase in research on them. Why have scientists so long neglected these emotions? No doubt one factor concerns problems with measurement. The self-conscious emotions are difficult to see. There has not been clear identification of facial expressions for shame, guilt, pride, and embarrassment, in contrast to joy, anger, sadness, fear, and disgust. The lack of clear expressive indices has made self-conscious emotions less amenable to direct (scientifically objective) observation. (But see Barrett, Chapter 2, Lewis, Chapter 7, and Stipek, Chapter 9, this volume, as well as

Scheff & Retzinger, 1991, for discussions of recent advances in the behavioral assessment of these emotions, including expressive indices. For example, shame seems to have clear behavioral expressions of lowering and covering the face, hiding, and trying to get away.)

Measurement problems are further compounded when one turns to self-reports as an alternative method of studying self-conscious emotions. There is a lack of clarity and precision in our language for the self-conscious emotions. For example, as indicated in various chapters of this volume (Tangney, Chapter 4; Lindsay-Hartz et al., Chapter 11; and Wallbott & Scherer, Chapter 19), psychologists and laypeople alike tend to blur the distinction between shame and guilt. More generally, the contrast between English and Chinese shows a lack of differentiation of self-conscious emotions in English. Wang and Fischer (1994) have tabulated more than 150 words for varieties of shame, guilt, and embarrassment in Chinese, in contrast to a few dozen at most in English. This problem of language poses a real challenge for both scientific conceptualization and research using self-report methods.

Empirical study of the self-conscious emotions may have been further hindered by the perception that these emotions are somehow "flaky" and unworthy of serious scientific inquiry. For many years, hard-minded social scientists tended to look askance at the study of affect in general, preferring to focus on supposedly objective observable behaviors. The self-conscious emotions—shame and guilt, in particular—may have suffered an even more dishonorable reputation, tarnished in part by their association with less rigorous psychoanalytic perspectives, and in part by their association with issues of morality at a time when psychological science strove to be an objective, value-free enterprise. But recent years have seen the study of affect come into its own as a vigorous, respectable, and productive branch of scientific psychology. With this shift has come a new interest in empirical study of the self-conscious emotions, as well as new methods for conducting such research.

TWO CONFERENCES ON EMOTIONS, AND SOME CONSENSUS ON SELF-CONSCIOUS EMOTIONS

The surging interest in emotions in general and self-conscious emotions in particular led to two conferences designed to bring together a broad range of researchers—from senior to junior, from soft and hard research traditions, from North America, Europe, and Asia. Organized by Joseph Campos and Kurt Fischer, and supported by the Sloan Foundation, the Social Science Research Council, and the MacArthur Network on Early Childhood, these conferences were designed to promote new research and theory on emotions, emphasizing how affect is linked with the rest of human action and thought.

The first conference, at Winter Park, Colorado, in the summer of 1985, focused on broad connections between cognition and emotion, especially as they relate to development. Relationships established at this conference led to a focus on self-conscious emotions as an important area that was ripe for catalyzing research and methods. This interest in the study of self-conscious emotions led to a conference on Shame and Other Self-Conscious Emotions, held at Asilomar, California, in December 1988. The 3-day conference brought together leading and emerging researchers and theoreticians from the fields of developmental psychology, clinical psychology, psychiatry, and sociology. The participants shared a focal interest in shame and related self-conscious emotions (especially embarrassment, guilt, and pride) from the perspectives of their respective fields.

The Asilomar conference was characterized by a great deal of excitement—excitement engendered by the innovative approaches and results by participants; the sense of an emerging coherence to this new research area; and the shared discovery that our interests had broad implications for many aspects of human adjustment and functioning, relating to the practical concerns of clinical practitioners, teachers, and parents. Three key themes emerged from the conference proceedings. First, there was surprising agreement on basic definitions and conceptualizations of shame, guilt, and related emotions (which most authors in this volume have sought to capture). Second, taken together, the theoretical and empirical presentations suggested that self-conscious emotions have important implications for processes at multiple levels of human behavior—individual, interpersonal, and societal. Third, participants agreed that the field was ripe for more systematic research on the nature and implications of self-conscious emotions.

Conferees noted that the rich and varied theoretical literature about these affective experiences is not matched by comparable research, in part because of problems with measurement. Many of the papers presented at the conference presented new research efforts drawing on innovative measurement methods. With these methodological advances, it seemed, the door had opened for many new avenues in research on self-conscious emotions. And in the few years since the conference, this promise has already begun to be fulfilled.

In this volume, we have attempted to capture the excitement of the Asilomar conference, highlighting and expanding on the original themes. Contributors include many of the original participants from the conference, joined by other developmental psychologists, social psychologists, sociologists, and anthropologists who have conducted research in this area. Our aim is to provide a comprehensive summary of the current theoretical and emerging empirical literature on self-conscious emotions, with a special emphasis on methodological issues.

KEY THEMES IN THE STUDY OF
SELF-CONSCIOUS EMOTIONS:
OVERVIEW OF THE CURRENT VOLUME

Although contributors to this volume represent diverse disciplines and diverse theoretical perspectives, there are several consistent issues that weave through the various chapters. One key issue concerns developmental pathways for emergence of self-conscious emotions. Do the self-conscious emotions emerge at certain ages, and what factors lead to emergence and further development of these emotions? Do they emerge because of achievement of some appraisal capacity necessary for the emotions, occurrence of some new social situation supporting the emotion, or what? At younger ages, are children's affective lives devoid of these self-conscious emotions, or are there early precursors of the more mature self-conscious emotions—appearing, say, within the first 6 months of life? How do the emotions change at later ages or stages? These questions are addressed in the following chapters: Barrett, Chapter 2; Mascolo and Fischer, Chapter 3; Zahn-Waxler and Robinson, Chapter 5; Ferguson and Stegge, Chapter 6; Lewis, Chapter 7; Griffin, Chapter 8; Stipek, Chapter 9; and Emde and Oppenheim, Chapter 17.

A second issue concerns the implications of self-conscious emotions for individual adjustment. There is a long tradition of clinical interest in the potential role of shame and guilt in psychological symptoms. Are these emotions generally maladaptive, as has sometimes been assumed, or are they an important part of normal social exchange? If self-conscious emotions are adaptive, under what circumstances do they represent functional or adaptive responses to one's failures and transgressions? There is considerable debate concerning the adaptive or maladaptive nature of guilt, as highlighted by the contrast in views between Harder (Chapter 15) on the one hand and Tangney, Burggraf, and Wagner (Chapter 14) on the other. Adaptive and maladaptive aspects of the self-conscious emotions are further explored in the following chapters: Barrett, Chapter 2; Tangney, Chapter 4; Zahn-Waxler and Robinson, Chapter 5; Baumeister, Stillwell, and Heatherton, Chapter 10; Lindsay-Hartz et al., Chapter 11; Jones, Kugler, and Adams, Chapter 12; Scheff, Chapter 16; Emde and Oppenheim, Chapter 17; and Miyake and Yamazaki, Chapter 20.

A third issue concerns the social foundations of self-conscious emotions and their place in relationships. Various theories of emotion have underscored socially defined features differentiating one type of emotion from another, as described, for example, by social scripts for emotions. How do shame, guilt, pride, and embarrassment relate to social interactions and situations? These relations involve both the ways that social situations affect the emotions and the ways that emotions affect social behavior. Regarding social effects on emotions, what sorts of social contexts set the stage for the self-conscious emotions, and can these emotions be distinguished in terms of the social structure of eliciting situations? Regarding the effects emotions have on social behavior, how do the emotions affect our interactions with others? What sorts of motivations and behaviors arise from feelings of shame, guilt, pride and embarrassment, and how do individual differences in the tendency to experience these emotions affect our long-term interpersonal adjustment? Interpersonal issues are the focus of the following chapters: Mascolo and Fischer, Chapter 3; Tangncy, Chapter 4; Baumeister et al., Chapter 10; Lindsay-Hartz et al., Chapter 11; Jones et al., Chapter 12; and Miller, Chapter 13. Related questions are examined in these chapters: Barrett, Chapter 2; Zahn-Waxler and Robinson, Chapter 5; Ferguson and Stegge, Chapter 6; Scheff, Chapter 16; and Kitayama et al., Chapter 18.

A fourth issue concerns the importance of the cultural context in understanding the nature, meaning, and functions of the self-conscious emotions. Even more than other affective experiences, the self-conscious emotions are inextricably embedded in cultural contexts. The large differences between Chinese and U.S. categorization hierarchies for self-conscious emotions are represented in the existence of a basic shame family of emotion terms in Chinese but not in U.S. English, as described earlier. Kitayama et al. (Chapter 18), Wallbott and Scherer (Chapter 19), and Miyaki and Yamazaki (Chapter 20) explore the nature and social functions of the self-conscious emotions across cultures, and show how they are both similar and different.

Finally, a unifying theme cutting across virtually all chapters is the need for innovative and diverse methodologies to systematically study the nature and functions of self-conscious emotions. This book is unique in its focus on empirical approaches to these emotions, and our hope is that it will be a useful source for the growing number of researchers interested in the study of self-conscious affect and social behavior.

The organization of this book follows these key themes closely. Part II is intended to provide general frames for conceptualization and research on the self-conscious emotions. Part III addresses developmental issues related to self-conscious emotions, including the nature of these affective experiences among children from late infancy to middle childhood, and the implications of these emotions for children's psychosocial functioning. Part IV explores the social foundations and consequences of self-conscious emotions. Part V examines the links between self-conscious emotions and various types of psychopathology. Part VI explores cross-cultural continuities and discontinuities in self-conscious affect. And, finally, the Appendix lists available measures of self-conscious emotions for research.

ACKNOWLEDGMENTS

The work in this chapter was supported by a fellowship from the Center for Advanced Study in the Behavioral Sciences and by grants from Harvard University, the

MacArthur Foundation Network on Early Childhood, the Sloan Foundation, the Social Science Research Council, and the Spencer Foundation. We thank Joseph Campos, Jane Haltiwanger, Jin Li, Michael Mascolo, Gil Noam, Phillip Shaver, Lianquin Wang, and Xiao Deng Yu for their contributions to the arguments presented here.

NOTES

1. Although Piaget neglected affect, he did acknowledge that it plays a role in motivating intelligence and its development (Piaget, 1981).
2. In another scenario, shame can turn into anger, resulting in clenched fists, bulging arteries, and so forth.

REFERENCES

Ainsworth, M. D., Blehar, M., Waters, E., & Wall, S. (1978). *Patterns of attachment: A psychological study of the Strange Situation*. Hillsdale, NJ: Erlbaum.

Barrett, K. C., & Campos, J. J. (1987). Perspectives on emotional development: II. A functionalist approach to emotions. In J. Osofsky (Ed.), *Handbook of infant development* (2nd ed., pp. 555–578). New York: Wiley.

Benes, F. (1994). Development of the corticolimbic system. In G. Dawson & K. W. Fischer (Eds.), *Human behavior and the developing brain* (pp. 176–206). New York: Guilford Press.

Bowlby, J. (1969–1980). *Attachment and loss* (3 vols.). New York: Basic Books.

Bretherton, I., & Waters, E. (Eds.). (1985). Growing points of attachment theory and research. *Monographs of the Society for Research in Child Development, 50* (1–2, Serial No. 209).

Bronfenbrenner, U. (1993). The ecology of cognitive development. In R. H. Wozniak & K. W. Fischer (Eds.), *Development in context: Acting and thinking in specific environments* (pp. 3–44). Hillsdale, NJ: Erlbaum.

Campos, J. J., Barrett, K. C., Lamb, M. E., Goldsmith, H. H., & Stenberg, C. (1983). Socioemotional development. In M. M. Haith & J. J. Campos (Vol. Eds.), *Handbook of child psychology* (4th ed.): Vol. 2. *Infancy and developmental psychobiology* (pp. 783–915). New York: Wiley.

Chomsky, N. (1965). *Aspects of the theory of syntax*. Cambridge, MA: MIT Press.

Darwin, C. (1965). *The expression of the emotions in man and animals*. Chicago: University of Chicago Press. (Original work published 1872)

de Rivera, J. (1981). The structure of anger. In J. de Rivera (Ed.), *Conceptual encounter: A method for the exploration of human experience* (pp. 35–81). Washington, DC: University Press of America.

Duffy, E. (1962). *Activation and behavior*. New York: Wiley.

Ekman, P. (1972). Universals and cultural differences in facial expression of emotion. In J. K. Cole (Ed.), *Nebraska Symposium on Motivation* (Vol. 19, pp. 207–283). Lincoln: University of Nebraska Press.

Ekman, P. (Ed.). (1982). *Emotion in the human face* (2nd ed.). Cambridge, England: Cambridge University Press.

Ekman, P., Friesen, W. V., O'Sullivan, M., Chan, A., Diacoyanni-Tarlatis, I., Heider,

K., Krause, R., LeCompte, W. A., Pitcairn, T., Ricci-Bitti, P. E., Scherer, K., Tomita, M., & Tzavaras, A. (1987). Universals and cultural differences in the judgments of facial expressions of emotion. *Journal of Personality and Social Psychology, 53, 712–717.*

Erikson, E. (1963). *Childhood and society* (2nd ed.). New York: Norton.

Fehr, B. (1988). Prototype analysis of the concepts of love and commitment. *Journal of Personality and Social Psychology, 55, 557–579.*

Fischer, K. W. (1980). A theory of cognitive development: The control and construction of hierarchies of skills. *Psychological Review, 87, 477–531.*

Fischer, K. W., Hand, H. H., Watson, M. W., Van Parys, M., & Tucker, J. (1984). Putting the child into socialization: The development of social categories in preschool children. In L. Katz (Ed.), *Current topics in early childhood education* (Vol. 5, pp. 27–72). Norwood, NJ: Ablex.

Fischer, K. W., Shaver, P., & Carnochan, P. (1989). From basic- to subordinate-category emotions: A skill approach to emotional development. In W. Damon (Ed.), *Child development today and tomorrow* (pp. 107–136). San Francisco: Jossey-Bass.

Fischer, K. W., Shaver, P., & Carnochan, P. G. (1990). How emotions develop and how they organize development. *Cognition and Emotion, 4, 81–127.*

Fodor, J. (1983). *The modularity of mind: An essay on faculty psychology.* Cambridge, MA: MIT Press.

Fox, N. A., & Davidson, R. J. (1988). Patterns of brain electrical activity during the expression of discrete emotions in ten-month-old infants. *Developmental Psychology, 24, 230–236.*

Freud, A. (1966). *The ego and the mechanisms of defense* (C. Baines, Trans.). New York: International Universities Press. (Original work published 1936)

Freud, S. (1961). The ego and the id. In J. Strachey (Ed. and Trans.), *Standard edition of the complete psychological works of Sigmund Freud* (Vol. 19, pp. 3–66). London: Hogarth Press. (Original work published 1923)

Frijda, N. H. (1986). *The emotions.* Cambridge, England: Cambridge University Press.

Gibson, J. J. (1979). *The ecological approach to visual perception.* Boston: Houghton Mifflin.

Gilligan, C. (1982). *In a different voice: Psychological theory and women's development.* Cambridge, MA: Harvard University Press.

Hebb, D. O., & Thompson, W. R. (1968). The social significance of animal studies. In G. Lindzey (Ed.), *Handbook of social psychology* (Vol. 2, pp. 729–774). Reading, MA: Addison-Wesley.

Izard, C. E. (1977). *Human emotions.* New York: Plenum.

Izard, C. E., & Malatesta, C. Z. (1987). Perspectives on emotional development: I. Differential emotions theory of early emotional development. In J. Osofsky (Ed.), *Handbook of infant development* (2nd ed., pp. 494–554). New York: Wiley.

James, W. (1890). *The principles of psychology* (2 vols.). New York: Holt.

Laird, J. D. (1989). Mood affects memory because feelings are cognitions. *Journal of Social Behavior and Personality, 4, 33–38.*

Lakoff, G. (1987). *Women, fire, and dangerous things: What categories reveal about the mind.* Chicago: University of Chicago Press.

Lazarus, R. S. (1991). *Emotion and adaptation.* New York: Oxford University Press.

LeDoux, J. E. (1989). Cognitive–emotional interactions in the brain. *Cognition and Emotion, 3, 267–289.*

Lewis, M., Sullivan, M. W., Stanger, C., & Weiss, M. (1989). Self-development and self-conscious emotions. *Child Development, 60,* 146–156.

Osgood, C. E., Suci, G. J., & Tannenbaum, P. (1957). *The measurement of meaning.* Urbana: University of Illinois Press.

Papez, J. W. (1937). A proposed mechanism of emotion. *Archives of Neurology and Psychiatry, 38,* 725–743.

Piaget, J. (1957). Logique et équilibre dans les comportements du sujet. *Études d'Épistémologie Génétique, 2,* 27–118.

Piaget, J. (1981). *Intelligence and affectivity: Their relationship during child development.* Palo Alto, CA: Annual Reviews.

Piaget, J. (1983). Piaget's theory. In W. Kessen (Ed.), *Handbook of child psychology* (4th ed.): *Vol. 1. History, theory, and methods* (pp. 103–126). New York: Wiley.

Rogoff, B. (1993). Children's guided participation and participatory appropriation in sociocultural activity. In R. Wozniak & K. W. Fischer (Eds.), *Development in context: Acting and thinking in specific environments* (pp. 121–154). Hillsdale, NJ: Erlbaum.

Rosch, E. (1978). Principles of categorization. In E. Rosch & B. B. Lloyd (Eds.), *Cognition and categorization* (pp. 27–48). Hillsdale, NJ: Erlbaum.

Russell, J. A. (1994). Is there universal recognition of emotion from facial expression? A review of the cross-cultural studies. *Psychological Bulletin, 115,* 102–141.

Schachter, S., & Singer, J. (1962). Cognitive, social, and physiological determinants of emotional state. *Psychological Review, 63,* 379–399.

Scheff, T. J., & Retzinger, S. M. (1988). *Hiding behavior: Toward resolving the shame controversy.* Paper presented at the conference on Shame and Other Self-Conscious Emotions, Asilomar, CA.

Scheff, T. J., & Retzinger, S. (1991). *Emotions and violence.* Lexington, MA: Lexington Books.

Scherer, K. R. (1984). On the nature and function of emotion: A component process approach. In K. R. Scherer & P. Ekman (Ed.), *Approaches to emotion* (pp. 293–317). Hillsdale, NJ: Erlbaum.

Scherer, K. R. (1986). Vocal affect expression: A review and a model for future research. *Psychological Bulletin, 99,* 143–165.

Scherer, K. R., Wallbott, H. G., & Summerfield, A. B. (Eds.). (1986). *Experiencing emotions: A cross-cultural study.* Cambridge, England: Cambridge University Press.

Schlosberg, H. (1954). Three dimensions of emotion. *Psychological Review, 61,* 81–88.

Shaver, P. R., Hazan, C., & Bradshaw, D. (1988). Love as attachment: The integration of three behavioral systems. In R. J. Sternberg & M. Barnes (Ed.), *The psychology of love* (pp. 68–99). New Haven, CT: Yale University Press.

Shaver, P. R., Schwartz, J., Kirson, D., & O'Connor, C. (1987). Emotion knowledge: Further exploration of a prototype approach. *Journal of Personality and Social Psychology, 52,* 1061–1086.

Shaver, P. R., Wu, S., & Schwartz, J. C. (1992). Cross-cultural similarities and differences in emotion and its representation: A prototype approach. In M. S. Clark (Ed.), *Review of personality and social psychology* (Vol. 13, pp. 175–212). Newbury Park, CA: Sage.

Sullivan, H. S. (1953). *The interpersonal theory of psychiatry.* New York: Norton.

Vygotsky, L. (1978). *Mind in society: The development of higher psychological processes* (M. Cole, V. John-Steiner, S. Scribner, & E. Souberman, Trans.). Cambridge, MA: Harvard University Press.

Wozniak, R., & Fischer, K. W. (Eds.). (1993). *Development in context: Acting and thinking in specific environments.* Hillsdale, NJ: Erlbaum.

Wundt, W. (1907). *Outlines of psychology* (C. H. Judd, Trans.). New York: Stechert. (Original work published 1905)

Wang, L., & Fischer, K. W. (1994). *The organization of shame in Chinese.* Cognitive Development Laboratory Report. Cambridge, MA: Harvard University.

II

FRAMES FOR THE STUDY OF SELF-CONSCIOUS EMOTIONS

2

A Functionalist Approach to Shame and Guilt

KAREN CAPLOVITZ BARRETT

In this chapter, I describe a model of shame and guilt development that highlights the importance of these emotions for regulation of both the individual's transactions with the environment and the individual's development of self. The model is described in terms of seven basic principles.

Principle 1: Shame and guilt are "social emotions." Shame and guilt are "social emotions." As such, they are (1) socially constructed, (2) invariably connected with (real or imagined) social interaction, (3) endowed with significance by social communication and/or relevance to desired ends (see below), and (4) associated with appreciations (appraisals) regarding others, as well as the self.

Principle 2: Shame and guilt serve important functions. The shame "family" and the guilt "family," like other emotion "families" (groups of related emotions), are defined in terms of the intrapersonal-, interpersonal-, and behavior-regulatory functions they serve for the individual. Shame reflects and organizes *different* transactions between individuals and the environment more than guilt does. Moreover, the differences in functions served by shame versus guilt are observable. For example, shame functions to distance the individual from the social environment; guilt functions to motivate reparative action.

Principle 3: Shame and guilt are associated with particular appreciations regarding self and other. Shame and guilt are associated with particular appreciations (appraisals), and these appreciations are different for shame than they are for guilt. Appreciations are intimately connected to the functions that the emotions serve for the individual in the environment.

Principle 4: Shame and guilt each are associated with particular action tendencies, which make sense given the appreciations and functions associated with these emotions. Shame is associated with withdrawal from social

25

contact. Guilt, on the other hand, is associated with outward movement, aimed at reparation for a wrongdoing.

Principle 5: Shame and guilt aid in the development of a sense of self. Shame and guilt experiences contribute in important ways to the child's development of a sense of self. Such experiences highlight the importance and consequences of a child's behavior, including successes and failures. As a result, they highlight the kind of behaviors the child can (or cannot) and does (or does not) do. In addition, such experiences highlight how others view the child and his or her behavior, which also helps the child to learn how to evaluate himself or herself.

Principle 6: Cognitive understandings do not determine the emergence of shame and guilt. Broad cognitive *understandings,* such as of "the categorical self," standards and rules for behavior, or personal responsibility for behavior are neither *necessary* nor *sufficient* for the emergence of guilt nor shame. Such understandings do, however, contribute to the nature of shame and guilt experiences as well as the conditions under which these emotions can occur.

Principle 7: Socialization is crucial to the development of shame and guilt. Socialization experiences play a major role in the development of shame and guilt. Socialization causes the child to care about the opinions of others, making the child *want* to follow social standards. It teaches the child about rules and standards for behavior, and endows particular standards with significance. All of these are central to the development of shame and guilt.

The seven principles just outlined will be elaborated below. I focus my discussion on the origins of these emotions in infancy and toddlerhood, but at times I give examples of these emotions during later periods of development. The data base regarding the origins of these emotions (especially guilt) in infancy and toddlerhood is exceedingly limited; thus, much of what is proposed here is speculative. However, evidence bearing upon the model is presented whenever possible. This model comprises an expansion and elaboration of relevant aspects of a more general model of emotional development (e.g., K. C. Barrett & Campos, 1987; J. J. Campos, R. G. Campos, & Barrett, 1989). Before I elaborate my model, I first describe a few selected theories regarding the development of shame, guilt, and embarrassment.

THEORIES OF THE DISTINCTION BETWEEN SHAME AND GUILT

The fact that this volume is devoted to the discussion of self-conscious emotions reflects a new awareness that many of these emotions have been unfairly neglected as important influences on human functioning. Now there is growing evidence of the potential importance of distinguishing shame from guilt, in terms of their implications for psychopathology and individual psychotherapy (e.g., H. B. Lewis, 1971; Nathanson, 1987b; Tangney, Wagner, & Gramzow, 1992), as well as marital and family dynamics and therapy (e.g., Bradshaw, 1988; Harper & Hoopes, 1990).

A review of the proliferating theoretical literature on shame and guilt reveals that there are both major points of convergence among the various theorists and some important points of difference. Most theories that distinguish guilt from shame agree that shame involves a sense that the entire self is bad; guilt involves a focus on particular misdeeds (see K. C. Barrett & Campos, 1987; H. B. Lewis, 1971; M. Lewis, Sullivan, Stanger, & Weiss, 1989; Nathanson, 1987; Tangney, 1990; but for a different view see Buss, 1980). Most agree that shame typically involves hiding the head or face and/or averting the gaze; guilt involves trying to make amends. On the other hand, theorists differ greatly on what is central to the definition of guilt and shame, as well as on how these emotions develop: whether guilt is "more internalized" and/or more "developmentally advanced" than is shame; when, in development, shame and guilt can be observed; what kinds of prerequisites are or are not needed to display these emotions; whether or not these are biologically based, universal emotions; what kinds of socialization backgrounds should lead to proneness to guilt and/or shame; and how guilt and shame are related to each other.

The traditional approach to the distinction between shame and guilt was that shame is a developmental precursor to guilt—an emotion that exists before one has internalized standards of good and bad behavior. Shame was viewed as the tendency to feel bad about misdeeds when caught by someone; guilt was seen as the tendency to feel bad about misdeeds because they violate one's own, internalized standards (e.g., Benedict, 1946; Erikson, 1963). In fact, this public–private distinction is still evident in some current theories (e.g., see Buss, 1980; Hogan & Cheek, 1983). Buss (1980) presents this position as follows:

> In brief, guilt involves *self-hatred;* shame involves *social anxiety.* . . . The best test of guilt is whether anyone else knows of the transgression. In true guilt, no one need know. . . . Shame is essentially public; if no one else knows, there is no basis for shame. (p. 159; italics in original)

Like many other theories, I take issue with this traditional approach to the distinction between guilt and shame, arguing that shame may be experienced even when no one else is present physically (e.g., K. C. Barrett & Campos, 1987; Creighton, 1990; H. B. Lewis, 1971, 1987; Stipek, 1983; Wurmser, 1987). In fact, most current theorists who distinguish shame from guilt do so on a different basis.

Helen Block Lewis (1971, 1987) has presented the most comprehensive position on the distinction between shame and guilt, and one that has strongly influenced the perspective to be explicated in this chapter. According to her, shame and guilt differ in several ways, including the following: (1) Shame concerns moral transgressions *or* defeats, whereas guilt only concerns moral transgressions; (2) shame involves focus on the *self's* deficiencies, whereas guilt involves focus on the negative *event* for which one is responsible; and (3) shame involves a passive or "helpless" self, whereas guilt involves an active self. This characterization of the difference between guilt and shame has been highly influential, and major ideas from it are evident in most current characterizations of the difference between shame and guilt (e.g., K. C. Barrett & Campos, 1987; M. Lewis, 1991; Nathanson, 1987a). However, it does not indicate in any detail when and how shame and guilt develop. The following section describes some major theories of shame and guilt development.

THEORIES OF SHAME AND GUILT DEVELOPMENT

There are many different theories of the development of shame and guilt; as we shall see, they propose very different mechanisms and timepoints for the development of these emotions. Most of these theories fall into one of two types—psychoanalytic theories and cognitive-prerequisite theories. I describe some important exemplars of each of these approaches here, highlighting some ways in which they are similar to and different from my own functionalist approach. Later, I elaborate my own approach.

Psychoanalytic Theories

Freud's Theory

The classic psychoanalytic view of shame and guilt was that of Freud. Freud discussed guilt at length, but wrote much less about shame. Both of these emotions were discussed in relation to conscious and unconscious conflict, and the suppression of id impulses. Guilt was viewed as the outcome of superego (conscience) conflict with id impulses and with the realization of those impulses by the ego: "The tension between the harsh super-ego and the ego that is subjected to it, is called by us the sense of guilt; it expresses itself as a need for punishment" (Freud, 1930/1961, p. 70). True guilt was thus thought to involve intrapsychic conflict, rather than real-world behavior, and was seen as connected most closely with conflict over aggressive impulses:

> Aggressiveness in introjected, internalized; it is, in point of fact . . . directed toward his own ego . . . now, in the form of "conscience," [the superego] is ready to put into action against the ego the same harsh aggressiveness that the ego would have liked to satisfy upon other, extraneous individuals. (Freud, 1930/1961, p. 70)

Thus, guilt was not believed to be possible until the superego is formed, in conjunction with the resolution of the Oedipus complex, at about 5 years of age. Freud held that before the formation of the superego, guilt-like reactions actually involve fear of loss of love (social anxiety), which Freud equated with fear of punishment:

> At the beginning, therefore, what is bad is whatever causes one to be threatened with loss of love. For fear of that loss, one must avoid it. . . . This state of mind is called a "bad conscience"; but actually it does not deserve this name. . . . A great change takes place only when the authority is internalized throught the establishment of a super-ego. . . . Actually, it is not until now that we should speak of conscience or a sense of guilt. (Freud, 1930/1961, pp. 71– 72)

Freud further noted that "guilt" from actual aggression (rather than intrapsychic conflict) should be labeled "remorse."

Shame, unlike guilt, was viewed primarily as a control on *sexual* impulses, especially exhibitionism and voyeurism. In *Three Essays on the Theory of Sexuality,* Freud (1905/1965) proposed that shame and disgust develop during the latency period (about 6 to 11 years of age), and help to suppress the inclinations of phallic/Oedipal children to exhibit themselves and to look at others' bodies. Freud submitted that shame and disgust cannot be active before the latency period, given that young children seem unconcerned about their enjoyment of these "perverse" acts. Thus, Freud seemed to place the origins of both true shame and true guilt *after* the resolution of the Oedipus complex, although he seemed to connect only guilt with the resolution of the Oedipus complex. Freud described "social anxiety" in connection with fear of loss of love as preceding true guilt, but requiring that external sanctions/authorities be present. Interestingly, other psychoanalytic theorists came to view *shame* as that social anxiety stemming from fear of loss of love, and thus came to see shame as preceding guilt developmentally (and as being "less mature" than guilt; see, e.g., Erikson, 1963).

As I elaborate later, this theory differs in almost every way from my own. I hold that guilt and shame *usually* involve real-world events and behaviors, or at least thoughts about those events and behaviors. Moreover, the point at which shame and guilt are first possible in development must be determined empirically, and should not be connected *a priori* to the development of the superego, the resolution of the Oedipus complex, or any other such constructs. Even other psychoanalytic theorists, moreover, differed from Freud in some important respects.

Piers and Singer's Theory

Piers, a psychoanalyst, and Singer, an anthropologist, collaborated on a now-classic treatise on shame and guilt (Piers & Singer, 1971). Piers proposed that both shame and guilt arise from superego functions, but that shame involves the ego ideal and guilt involves conscience.

Piers and Singer believed shame to arise when an individual fails to live up to the expectations of his or her ego ideal. Thus, it involves *shortcomings*, rather than rule violations. Guilt, on the other hand, involves *transgressions*— performing acts that violate the rules enforced by the superego. Piers noted the common belief that shame depends more on external sanctions and authority figures. He also noted that Freud postulated that the Oedipus complex needs to be resolved before the superego can be established, along with the guilt released during the operation of the superego. However, Piers in his essay disagreed with both of these notions:

> . . . it will be clear that we do not hold the formation of the superego to be contingent on the "passing of the Oedipus complex." The development of an internalized conscience with its executive arm of guilt feeling occurs prior to and in large portions independent of the oedipal situation . . . [and] shame . . . [is] a distinctly differentiated form of inner tension which as such is a normal concomitant of ego development and superego formation . . . (Piers & Singer, 1971, pp. 17– 18)

Thus, while agreeing with Freud and other psychoanalysts that guilt is a superego function, Piers disagreed on how the superego is established, and viewed shame as a different type of superego function. Like my own approach, his allowed for shame and guilt before the early childhood years, and suggested that shame can arise from many different forms of standards (all those included in the ego ideal), rather than primarily standards involving sexuality. However, Piers still accepted the superego as a psychic institution giving rise to guilt (and shame), rather than focusing on real-world behavior—a point of difference between his theory and mine, but a point of similarity with H. B. Lewis (1987), as well as with Schore (1991), whose theory is now discussed.

Schore's Theory

Schore's (1991) approach to shame and guilt is an interesting and different one, which integrates the theories of Tomkins (1987) and Mahler (1968; Mahler, Pine, & Bergman, 1975). Schore agrees with Piers that shame and guilt are different superego affects, with different developmental origins. He emphasizes the *preverbal* nature of shame, but notes that guilt emerges in the verbal child. Thus, Schore clearly distinguishes shame from guilt, and he sees shame as preceding guilt developmentally. However, he focuses on shame.

According to Schore (following Tomkins), shame functions as an inhibitor of excessive joy and/or interest/excitement. He holds that 10- to 18-month-old infants, undergoing the practicing substage of Mahler's separation–individuation, experience unbridled enthusiasm, interest, and elation while exploring the world. This excitement would become too much for a baby, were it not for the important regulating mechanism of shame.

The baby, enraptured by exploratory pursuits, returns to the mother for "refueling." The mother, although usually highly attuned to her baby, cannot always be so attuned. Thus, on some occasion she is oblivious to the baby's need for reconnection, and she mismatches the baby, triggering the emergence of shame.

According to Schore (1991), the resulting shame induces the "low-keyed" emotional state described by Mahler, and "triggers an assault on the burgeoning narcissism of the practicing infant, on the ideal ego . . . and represents the first experience of narcissistic injury and narcissistic depletion associated with all later shame experiences" (p. 206). Schore holds that the narcissism, elation, and other hyperstimulated states that characterize Mahler's practicing phase need to be attenuated to enable the resolution of the ensuing rapprochement crisis. Thus, the emergence of shame is necessary for, and makes possible, the child's movement to the next substage of separation–individuation.

Like myself, Schore allows for the early development of shame, and suggests that it aids in the development of the self. However, he does propose a particular age period for the development of shame, and connects shame and self-development to very different mechanisms from those that I propose. Moreover, his beliefs about the role of shame in self-development are much more general than those I propose, as well as those proposed by a final psychoanalytic theorist to be discussed here—Nathanson.

Nathanson's Theory

Nathanson (1987b) proposes distinctions between guilt and shame that differ somewhat from those presented by the theorists discussed so far. He submits that although both shame and guilt are unpleasant emotions that involve intrapsychic conflict, guilt involves punishment of wrongdoing, whereas, shame calls into question some quality of the self. (Theorists such as H. B. Lewis and M. Lewis would say that the entire self, rather than a particular quality, is implicated in shame.) Like myself, Nathanson argues that one should not decide a priori that shame or guilt require some particular intrapsychic event or stage, but rather should rely on observation to determine when they are possible. Unlike Freud, who placed the emergence of shame during early childhood, and Schore, who places it at around 10 or 12 months of age, Nathanson sees "primitive" shame in the younger baby. In fact, drawing on data obtained by Demos, he raises the possibility that babies as young as $2^{1}/_{2}$ months old may experience such forms of shame. However, although he opposes using a priori timetables of intrapsychic events to determine the onset of shame, he later describes an a priori cognitive prerequisite for guilt, unlike my own model.

Contrary to Freud and Schore, Nathanson holds that the baby is not "normally narcissistic," but rather is highly emotionally connected with people from birth. Nathanson believes that early shame has its origins in these interpersonal situations. Like Schore and Tomkins, Nathanson proposes that during infancy, shame acts to reduce excitement when there is a failure in social interaction. In fact, Nathanson holds that because of this, shame aids in the development of a sense of self by highlighting the distinction between self and other. That is, when the baby acts upon the other, but does not get the expected/desired response, shame is elicited, and with it the rudimentary awareness that someone beyond the self is interacting with the baby (since wish does not produce response). Later, as the child moves through different developmental stages, different situations (e.g., the toileting situation and sexuality) evoke shame.

I too believe that babies' emotionally charged interactions with others are crucial to the development of shame and guilt, and that shame and guilt contribute importantly to the development of a sense of self. However, I propose very different mechanisms for both of these developments. Finally, Nathanson, unlike myself, suggests that guilt develops out of shame—that shame is a developmental precursor of guilt, but that guilt cannot develop until a child can understand that he or she has performed an action and that the action has caused harm to another.

Cognitive-Prerequisite Theories

Nathanson's theory requires a certain cognitive understanding for the emergence of guilt. This makes his theory similar, in that way, to the theories that I now discuss, and dissimilar from my own approach. The most common nonpsychoanalytic explanation for the development of shame and guilt renders the emergence of these emotions secondary to children's cognitive development. Implicit in such approaches is the assumption that shame and guilt are *defined* by certain cognitions. Thus, what allows one to be ashamed or guilty is the ability to think in certain ways. As a result of this orientation, many theories of shame, embarrassment, and guilt preclude the possibility that infants or toddlers can experience some or all of these emotions. Some influential cognitive approaches have been proposed by Arnold Buss, Jerome Kagan, and Michael Lewis.

Arnold Buss's Self-Consciousness Theory

Arnold Buss (1980) has proposed that even embarrassment requires a rather sophisticated cognitive understanding of self. In discussing blushing as an indicator of embarrassment, he states the following:

> Infants and idiots [*sic*] surely have the psychological mechanism, but they do not blush. What do older children and adults possess—lacking in animals, infants, and the severely mentally retarded—that is required for blushing to occur? . . . Animals, infants, and the severely mentally retarded are not

aware of themselves as social objects; they lack a cognitive self and therefore do not blush. (Buss, 1980, p. 132)

Similarly, according to Buss, shame is not possible until about 5 years of age, when the cognitive self has developed. The "shame" behaviors that parents report observing in their toddlers (e.g., "shrinking and cringing after having been caught in a forbidden act"; Buss, 1980, p. 230) actually express "pseudoshame" (fear of punishment, much like Freud's "social anxiety"), according to Buss. Buss's theory differs from my own, both in requiring advanced cognition for the emergence of embarrassment and shame, and in assuming that shame is impossible until about age 5 years.

Jerome Kagan's Approach

According to Jerome Kagan (1984), it is desirable to break down unitary, broad categories of emotion such as fear or shame whenever possible, employing instead terms that explicitly acknowledge eliciting conditions (e.g., "anxiety to possible task failure"). Moreover, cognitive awareness of an emotional state is viewed as extremely significant. Although emotions may occur without such awareness, cognitive awareness leads to a different emotional state. Thus, certain terms should be used to refer to states that are detected, and other terms to those that remain unnoticed (Kagan, 1984). This is similar to my approach, in that I also note that the context is crucial in determining which emotion family is activated, and that awareness of an emotion makes the emotion different. However, I see awareness or lack of awareness as determining which *member* of an emotion family is experienced, rather than which emotion family is experienced (see below). That is, the understanding is not crucial in determining which emotion is produced, but rather which *version* of that emotion is produced.

Kagan holds that cognitive abilities determine a child's ability to respond to a particular "incentive"; since emotions are often defined in terms of incentives, then these cognitive abilities are required to experience the emotions. Thus, the ability to understand causal relations is deemed prerequisite to "anxiety regarding broken objects" (which many view as a shame-like response), because the child is concerned that someone must have caused the breakage of the object. At times, Kagan also speaks in general emotion-category terminology, however, and describes general cognitive abilities as prerequisites for these broader emotion categories. For example, he indicates that guilt is not possible until about 4 years of age:

> The appearance of guilt is delayed because its cognitive base takes time to mature. The cognitive talent in question is the ability to recognize that one has a choice. A two-year-old is not capable of recognizing that he could have

behaved in a way different from the one he has chosen. But the four-year-old has this ability and so experiences the emotion we call *guilt*. (Kagan, 1984, p. 175)

Michael Lewis's Approach

Michael Lewis's (1991) approach is elaborated elsewhere in this volume (see Chapter 7), so it is only briefly described here. He holds that embarrassment, shame, pride, empathy, guilt, and "hubris" are all "self-conscious" emotions, and that four cognitive acquisitions are relevant to the emergence of such emotions: development of self-consciousness; development of standards, rules, and goals; evaluation of one's behavior *vis-à-vis* these standards, rules, and goals; and self-focus (focus on the total self vs. a specific aspect of the self or the self's behavior).

The development of self-consciousness, which is defined as knowledge of one's knowledge of the self (metacognition about operative self-knowledge), is deemed sufficient for the development of the "exposed" emotions of embarrassment, empathy, and envy. In addition to self-consciousness, knowledge of standards, rules, and goals, and the ability to evaluate oneself *vis-à-vis* such goals and standards, are necessary for self-evaluative emotions such as shame, guilt, and pride. Guilt and shame are distinguished by cognition as well. They are distinguished by globality of attributional self-focus, with guilt involving focus on specific features or actions of the self, and shame involving focus on one's whole self.[1] Lewis (1991) describes socialization influences on the development of shame and guilt; however, these influences operate via their impact on the development of the cognitions described above.

Unlike many theorists, Lewis has conducted research aimed at supporting his perspective, and some suggestive evidence regarding the connection between these cognitive abilities and the predicted emotions has been provided. Toddlers' tendency to touch their noses when seeing rouge on them in a mirror (conceived as self-recognition) is related to their tendency to avert their gaze and smile in situations believed to elicit embarrassment (M. Lewis et al., 1989). Moreover, 3-year-olds more frequently show shame-relevant responses when failing at an easy than at a difficult task, which is interpreted as reflecting self-evaluation *vis-à-vis* standards (M. Lewis, 1991). However, another laboratory, using a larger and more diverse sample, only partially replicated the relation between self-recognition and embarrassment (see Schneider-Rosen & Cicchetti, 1991). Middle-class subjects in this study, like those in the M. Lewis et al. (1989) study, showed smile/gaze aversion more commonly if they also touched rouge on their noses while gazing in the mirror (only 2.3% of those who failed to touch their noses showed smile/gaze aversion, whereas 46% of those who touched their noses showed gaze aversion). However, subjects of lower socioeconomic status (SES) showed an opposite pattern: 35.7% of those who *failed* to touch their noses showed smile/gaze aversion, whereas only 20% of those who *did* touch their noses showed "embarrassment." Thus, further research is needed to determine whether or not self-recognition is *necessary* to the development of embarrassment.

In fact, these findings suggest a potential impact of socialization on the relationship between nose touching and smile/gaze aversion. Perhaps middle-class subjects who are prone to embarrassment are embarrassed at the "blemish" on their noses as well as at the other events, whereas lower-SES subjects who touch the rouge on their noses do so for some reason other than embarrassment. At the very least, these results suggest that, consistent with the approach that I now present, (1) the development of embarrassment may involve socialization factors other than those that lead to acquisition of self-recognition; and (2) "self-recognition," as measured by the nose-touching task, is not *necessary* for the acquisition of embarrassed responses (smile/gaze aversion).

In summary, unlike my own approach, all of these cognitive-prerequisite approaches *require* certain cognitive understandings for the development of shame and guilt. Moreover, Buss proposes that shame is impossible during infancy and toddlerhood, and Kagan suggests that guilt is impossible until about age 4, again based on the required cognitive understandings. All of these points differ from those that I now elaborate.

A FUNCTIONALIST THEORY OF SHAME AND GUILT DEVELOPMENT

The present theory of the development of shame and guilt begins with a somewhat different characterization of the role of cognition in emotion elicitation and emotional development. It is a central tenet of this position that the type of cognitive process that is emotion-relevant is not captured well by general cognitive-developmental acquisitions, such as object permanence, self-recognition, or means–ends relations. All of these general cognitive acquisitions are expected to affect emotional development, but to do so *indirectly*, via their influences upon factors such as which aspects of a situation (and which situations) are meaningful to a person (and thus capable of eliciting emotion), which types of coping responses are possible for the individual, and which types of socialization experiences influence the individual. Moreover, general cognitive acquisitions are not viewed as prerequisites for the emergence of entire emotion "families" such as shame or guilt. Before I elaborate my view of the nature of shame and guilt and their development, I briefly outline a few key concepts of the overall model of emotional development that I developed in collaboration with Joseph J. Campos (K. C. Barrett & Campos, 1987).

Appreciations

In this perspective, and similarly in many other perspectives (e.g., Frijda, 1986; Lazarus, 1991), a special type of cognition is part of the emotion process. This cognitive process, which we label an "appreciation" (see K. C. Barrett & Campos, 1987; Campos & Barrett, 1984) and others label "appraisal," brings the person into inextricable interrelationship with the environment. This cognition is not *about* the world or the self; it captures the personal *significance* of the environment for the self. An organism–environment relationship is significant to the extent that it has implications for the individual's adaptive functioning. This relationship thus may be significant if it threatens the life of the individual; however, it also may be deemed significant to the extent that it affects one's pursuit of any end state, whether that end state is comfort in a cold environment, friendship formation with a desirable person, or removing the wrapper from a chocolate chip cookie.

We call this type of cognitive process an "appreciation" to emphasize that it need not operate at a sophisticated level; incoming sensations may be processed minimally if they are significant in terms of biologically adaptive functioning. For example, sour- or bitter-tasting objects may be appreciated by a neonate as repugnant, because it is biologically adaptive to avoid unripe (sour) fruit and poisonous (bitter) foods. On the other hand, appreciations can, and often do, operate at a much more sophisticated level in more sophisticated organisms. For example, one may find the thought of a man's sexually abusing his 6-year-old daughter repugnant. In this case, the emotion is aroused by a thought rather than an overt action, and the imagined act is repugnant in relation to one's beliefs about appropriate behavior, incest, and harm to children. Fischer and his colleagues have detailed a theory that describes in greater detail the levels of understanding that can be involved in emotions (see Fischer, Shaver, & Carnochan, 1990; Fischer & Mascolo, Chapter 3, this volume).

Appreciations are typically involved in an emotion process, but, like any other aspect of the emotion process, appreciations are not viewed as *necessary* for an emotion to unfold. Brain stimulation, emotion communication from a conspecific, or other such stimuli may initiate an emotion process. The emotion process elicited without an appreciation often differs phenomenologically from that elicited by an appreciation, but it still is recognizable as a member of the same emotion "family."

Emotion Families

With the exception of Kagan's and Nathanson's theories, all of the aforementioned theories view shame, guilt, and/or embarrassment as entities or wholes that *emerge* at some point in development. That is, each emotion is absent until the point in development when criterial conditions are met (cognitive or intrapsychic developments).

In contrast, I do not believe that emotions are wholes that emerge at particular points in development. Nor do I believe it useful to characterize emotions as "true" ones versus "pseudoemotions" or "protoemotions," based upon a specific criterion. Rather, emotions are multifaceted phenomena that are well characterized by Wittgenstein's (1953) concept of "family resemblance" (see also Fischer et al., 1990; Wallbott & Scherer, Chapter 19, this volume). That is, no particular criterion is *necessary* for the presence of "the real emotion," either developmentally or concurrently. Relatives of each emotion family may be seen very early in development, given the right circumstances. Moreover, no single criterion provides sufficient information for one to infer emotionality.

There are *intrinsic* but *not invariant* links between specific emotion families and particular (1) appreciations, (2) end states with which these appreciations are concerned, (3) action tendencies, (4) vocalic patterns, (5) physiological patterns, (6) facial movement patterns, and (7) adaptive functions. That is, emotion families are typically associated with specific patterns of these characteristics; however, particular instances of an emotion (family members) may not be associated with one or more of the characteristics, and a given family member may include additional responses that are not associated with other family members (e.g., the smile of embarrassment, an emotion I view as a member of the shame family). Moreover, some *families* may not have all characteristics (e.g., no specific facial muscle movements have been documented for shame, guilt, envy, or pride; see Ekman, 1984).

Recent research suggests that people conceptualize their emotions in terms of certain shared characteristics, despite differences in the exact situations and even the cultures in which the emotions were experienced. Shaver and his colleagues apply a prototype approach to determining degree of relatedness of adults' concepts of different emotions, and then determining which categories or families are "basic-level," "superordinate-level," and "subordinate-level" (e.g., see Shaver, Schwartz, Kirson, & O'Connor, 1987). They, as well as Wallbott and Scherer, have found a great deal of consistency in the features that people use to characterize particular emotion families, across many different cultures and a variety of specific situations (see Agnoli, Kirson, Wu, & Shaver, 1989; Wallbott & Scherer, 1988 and Chapter 19, this volume).

These observed communalities suggest coherence to people's understanding of emotion families, supporting the idea that it is useful across a variety of cultures to describe these groups of emotions as families (see Fischer et al., 1990). I believe that this coherence is largely attributable to systematic covariation among different aspects of each emotion family in actual experience. Although some of this covariation may be derived from the inherent, self-organizing nature of certain physical movements (see Fogel et al., 1992), I hold that the most important reason for it is that all of the features are relevant to the important functions that each emotion serves.

Before I elaborate on these functions, however, another basic concept should be introduced.

Classes of Emotions

Many theorists distinguish "basic" or "fundamental" emotions from other emotions (or affective–cognitive structures). The term "basic emotion" is used to connote many different ideas, with theories varying as to which connotation is assumed. "Basic" is often used to mean biologically basic—the emotions that are universal and fundamental to the species (e.g., see Ekman, 1984; Izard & Malatesta, 1987). In some theories, universality of response, especially facial response, is necessary for emotions to be considered "basic" (e.g., see Izard & Malatesta, 1987). In other theories, "basic" indicates the level of category, with "basic" being the most commonly used level, and usually the one associated with the clearest imagery (e.g., see Shaver et al., 1987). And, finally, some theorists view "basic" emotions as the fundamental units out of which more sophisticated emotions are built (e.g., see Izard & Malatesta, 1987).

I have avoided the surplus meaning of "basic" emotion by introducing new terminology. Thus, in the model that I proposed in collaboration with Campos, no emotions were categorized as "basic" (K. C. Barrett & Campos, 1987). Instead, three classes of emotions were distinguished, the first two of which included most emotions viewed by others as fundamental or basic. We devised three groups, rather than the typical two (basic and complex), because we believe that there are some important and meaningful differences among the emotions often classified as "basic" by others.

Some emotions (our "primordial" emotions, such as fear and disgust) seem to be elicited in almost reflex fashion by particular stimuli. This is not to say that *only* these specific stimuli elicit primordial emotions, but rather that when these stimuli or stimulus parameters are present, the relevant emotion family is evoked, despite wide variability in the person's ongoing goals and activities. For example, certain tastants (e.g., bitter) seem to elicit disgust, and certain stimulus parameters (e.g., rapid rise time plus large amplitude) seem to elicit fear. On the other hand, other emotion families that often are considered "basic" (our "concurrent-goal" or "concurrent-desire" emotions, such as sadness and anger) seem intimately connected with the person's ongoing desires or goals and with whether these are being realized. Our third category involves emotions often considered complex (or subordinate; cf. Shaver et al., 1987). These "social" emotions, such as guilt, shame/embarrassment, pride, and envy/jealousy, are the focus of this chapter.

Classification of emotion families into primordial, concurrent-goal, or social is based on several criteria. The first criterion involves the typical processes of attaining significance associated with an emotion family—innately determined appreciation of survival value of stimuli, socially communicated significance, or relevance to desired ends. The second criterion involves the extent to which appreciations concern other organisms, as well as the organism itself. The third criterion involves the extent to which the goals with which the emotion family is concerned have been developed through socialization. Finally, the fourth criterion involves the extent to which the emotion family may be communicated socially via discrete facial signals as opposed to posture and demeanor (see K. C. Barrett & Campos, 1987). For example, primordial emotions typically attain significance innately and/or via social communication, whereas concurrent-goal and social emotions attain significance primarily through the relevance of ongoing events to the person's desired ends and/or social communication. The other criteria all distinguish social emotions from the other two classes of emotions, and are discussed shortly.

Thus, in the present model emotions belong to one of three classes, with no emotions assumed to be more basic than the others. Other theorist have argued against the idea that some emotions are more basic than others (e.g., see Ortony & Turner, 1990). Moreover, data from studies using Shaver et al.'s (1987) prototype approach suggest that although there is wide agreement on characteristics of and similarities among emotions, there is some disagreement across cultures on exactly which emotions are considered "basic." For Americans, Italians, and Chinese, the superordinate level is the same, consisting of two categories—positive and negative. However, although across these three cultures the basic level includes *most* of the same emotion families that most theorists consider "basic," shame and guilt are viewed differently in the two Western cultures, as contrasted with the one Asian culture. Adults in the United States and Italy seem to see shame and guilt as subtypes of one subordinate-level emotion family, whereas adults in China seem to see shame as an additional basic-level family (see Agnoli et al., 1989). This is particularly interesting, given the common put poorly studied notion that China and many other Asian countries are "shame" cultures (see Benedict, 1946; Creighton, 1990; Piers & Singer, 1971).

Seven Basic Principles

For the remainder of this chapter, I focus only on the class of emotion families that includes shame and guilt—the social emotions. First, I summarize why shame and guilt, as well as other emotions, are considered "social."

Principle 1: Shame and Guilt Are "Social" Emotions

The "social" emotions (such as shame, guilt, pride, and envy), which include families traditionally characterized as complex, are labeled as such because socialization both centrally influences the development of these emotions and is crucially influenced by these emotions, and another person (or perceived other) is centrally involved in each of these emotions. First, socialization centrally influences the development of these emotions. In fact, it seems accurate to characterize social emotions as social *constructions*. If humans did not live in social groups, there would be no need for the social emotions. The very goals that the social emotions help realize would not be goals, were it not for socialization. Societies must devise standards in order to facilitate human interaction (relevant to a goal for guilt). Social living and interdependence fosters the need to maintain others' respect and/or affection (relevant to a goal for shame). Social interaction amidst limited resources inspires a desire to obtain valued objects (relevant to a goal for envy/jealousy). Societies and socialization instill certain goals in people, and as Table 2.1 (see below) shows, these are the goals around which social emotions revolve. Moreover, social emotions centrally affect socialization, underscoring society's rules and standards, and motivating people to follow society's guidelines.

Finally, whereas it is quite possible to think of asocial elicitors of emotions such as anger, sadness, and fear, all instances of the social emotions involve a real or imagined other (which at times may be the "observing ego"). Relatedly, each of these emotions seems associated not only with an appreciation regarding the organism itself, but also an appreciation regarding others (see below).

There are some other important features of social emotions. First, elicitors of social emotions achieve significance via the second and third processes of achieving significance—social communication and relevance to desired ends (goals). I discuss later in this chapter how parent–infant and parent–child interactions endow shame- and guilt-relevant situations with significance via social (especially emotional) communication, and how the goals of society become the goals of the individual—capable of motivating emotion processes and associated actions.

In addition, these emotions seem to be communicated socially by voice, posture, demeanor, overt actions, and (sometimes) communicative physiological responses such as blushing, but not by discrete facial patterns that are specific to those emotions. Some coding systems (see Geppert, 1986) do propose specific facial movements for shame (downturned mouth, lip biting) and/or embarrassment (smile/gaze aversion; see M. Lewis et al., 1989). However, the smile and the downturned mouth are components of facial patterns associated with other emotions; lip biting (as well as touching and other manipulative behaviors) is used in other arousing situations, and may function (like gaze aversion) to reduce arousal and/or help one control facial responses (see Ekman & Friesen, 1975). This point is elaborated later.

Table 2.1 summarizes characteristics of the guilt and shame families, as well as some other social emotions, as suggested by current research and theory. It lists the types of goals with which each family is typically concerned, despite our realization that emotions induced via social communication may not concern these goals. Some important features of the model are outlined in this table. All of these major features, moreover, are related to the central functions that each of these emotions serve. The way to determine kinship between two emotions is by ascertaining the similarity between the functions they serve. Although sometimes emotions will not fulfill their functions—for example, because the organism is unable to act so as to fulfill the function, or because the emotion is so intense that it becomes stressful and disorganizing—emotions are organized around specific, adaptive functions. Principle 2 follows from this basic concept.

Principle 2: Shame and Guilt Serve Important Functions

As Table 2.1 indicates, shame and guilt serve important behavior-regulatory, intrapersonal (internal regulatory), and interpersonal (social regulatory) functions. Shame serves to distance the experiencing individual from important others, especially others who can evaluate or are evaluating the individual. In particular, in shame, activated behaviors are aimed at removing the face from exposure to others' evaluation. The shameful person avoids looking at others, hides the face, slumps the body, lowers the head, and/or withdraws from contact with others. These same behaviors regulate other people's reactions to the shameful individual. The gaze aversion, slumping, hiding, and social withdrawal behaviors communicate deference and submission to others, and indicate that the person feels "small," "low," or unworthy, in comparison to those others. Finally, shame makes it painful to "do wrong" (in both senses of "wrong"—moral and/or achievement standards), highlighting the importance of meeting standards, and shame behaviors act to reduce this painful arousal. In addition, as will be elaborated later, shame helps the individual in acquiring knowledge of the self as an object, by highlighting how the individual appears to others (or to the internalized other).

Guilt, on the other hand, serves different functions. Guilt-relevant behaviors act to repair the damage caused by the person's wrongdoing. Moreover, rather than removing the person from social contact, guilt often moves the individual to tell others about the wrongdoing, and thus to show them that he or she understands the standards and wishes to follow them. Finally, like shame, guilt highlights the importance of moral/behavior standards, but it helps teach the individidual about himself or herself as an agent rather than as an object. The guilty person sees that she is able/unable to cause harm (and/or repair harms), thus learning about his or her capabilities (and/or deficiencies).

It is important to note that any of these functions may be served by somewhat different behaviors, given different environmental demands; what are important are not the particular behaviors, but the implications of those behaviors for the person–environment relationship. For example, if one experiences shame at one's inability to work a puzzle while sitting at a table with one's mother, one would be expected to avert one's gaze from the mother, lower one's head, and slouch in one's seat. On the other hand, if

TABLE 2.1. Characteristics of Some Social Emotion Families

Family	Behavioral regulatory functions	Social regulatory functions	Internal regulatory functions	Goal for self	Appreciation re: self
Shame	Distance oneself from evaluating agent; reduce "exposure"	Communicate deference/submission; communicate self as "small" or inadequate	Highlight standards and importance of standards; aid in acquisition of knowledge of self as object; reduce arousal	Maintenance of others' respect and/or affection, preservation of positive self-regard	"I am bad." (Self-regard is perceived to be impaired.)
Guilt	Repair damage	Communicate awareness of proper behavior; communicate contrition/good intentions	Highlight standards and importance of standards; aid in acquisition of knowledge of self as agent	Meeting known standards	"I have done something contrary to my standards."
Envy	Protect or obtain possession or access to loved one	Inform others re: whom/what one cares about; prevent others from taking one's possessions	Highlight what one cares about/values	Obtaining an object/person that someone else possesses	"I cannot obtain the object."
Pride	Decrease distance from evaluating agents	Show others one has achieved standard; show dominance/superiority	Highlight standards and importance of standards; aid in acquisition of knowledge of self as object and agent	Maintenance of good feelings about oneself	"I am good."

*These vocalic patterns are based on the work of Scherer (1986).
*These psychological reactions are based on the work of Ekman, Levenson, and Friesen (1983).

one experiences shame in response to reading one's poor grade (posted by one's name on a professor's door) as one is standing alongside one's classmates, one would probably avert one's gaze from the classmates and/or the professor and leave the scene. In both cases, the inclination is to avoid social contact, but for the seated individual this is realized through posture and eye contact withdrawal; for the erect individual it is accomplished through gross motor withdrawal.

It seems likely, similarly, that particular components of facial patterns, vocalic patterns, and/or physiological patterns will be absent in particular family members that are elicited in contexts for which these components are dysfunctional. Moreover, other components will be present only in family members for which they are functional (see K. C. Barrett, 1993), Ortony & Turner, 1990; Scherer, 1986). For example, embarrassment, which is elicited by problems with one's appearance or self-presentation, is associated with a smile; shame, which is associated with more serious problems with the self, is not. A smile in an embarrassment context conveys to conspecifics that "it's no big deal" or "even I know what a silly thing I just did." Such

Appreciation re: other	Action tendency	Focus of attention	Vocalic pattern[a]	Physiological reaction[b]
"Someone thinks I am bad. Everyone is looking at me."	Withdrawal; avoidance of others; hiding of self	Self as object	"Narrow," moderately lax, thin voice	Low heart rate; blushing
"Someone has been injured by my act."	Outward movement; inclination to make reparation, tell others, and punish oneself	The wrongdoing; consequences of one's act; self as agent and experiencer	"Narrow," tense, moderately full voice	High heart rate and skin conductance; irregular respiration
"Someone has what I want."	Withdrawal and outward movement; inclination to avoid and/or hurt the one who possesses the desired object/person/quality	The possession; the possessor	"Narrow," moderately lax, thin voice	Irregular respiration; slightly elevated heart rate
"Someone/everyone thinks (or will think) I am good."	Outward movement; inclination to show/tell others	Self as agent and as object	"Wide," moderately tense, full voice	Flushed face; high heart rate

an attitude, however, would be deemed inappropriate for more serious failures.

It is important to recognize, however, that sometimes components are present even when their only concurrent function is their signal value for conspecifics; certain functions that are important to the more primitive members of the emotion family are not applicable to a more socialized or cognitively sophisticated context (e.g., nose wrinkling at a crass remark does not serve the function of blocking out a noxious smell).

Principle 3: Shame and Guilt Are Associated with Particular Appreciations Regarding Self and Other

The functions are the central organizing basis for each emotion family. Moreover, appreciations are closely tied to those functions. Note that each emotion has an "appreciation regarding self" and an "appreciation regarding other." Shame involves appreciations that one is bad, that someone thinks one is bad, and that everyone is looking at one. Guilt involves appreciations that one has *done* something contrary to one's standards, and that someone has been injured by this act. Like H. B. Lewis (1971), I hold that shame involves focus on a sense that one is bad, whereas guilt involves apprehension that one has committed some wrongful act. Like many theorists, I believe that shame involves the sense that another is looking at one and/or viewing one as a bad person. However, it is important to note that no other person need be physically present.

Note that appreciations are expressed in very general terms. Many particular organism–environment encounters may be appreciated in each of the ways described in Table 2.1. Moreover, organism–environment relations may be appreciated at any level of cognitive sophistication. The "I" that is bad or that has done something contrary to standards may not understand himself or herself as agent or as object; the person may have just a dim (perhaps inaccurate) notion of what he or she causes, and may not well distinguish self-evaluation from other-evaluation of self.

Principle 4: Shame and Guilt Are Each Associated with Particular Action Tendencies, Which Make Sense in Terms of Appreciations and Functions Associated with These Emotions

The action tendencies associated with shame and guilt are sensible and functional, given the different appreciations associated with these emotions. If one focuses on the self as a bad person who is evaluated as such by others, then the only recourse is to die, disappear, or at least withdraw from evaluating others. One cannot remake the self then and there. On the other hand, if the problem is that one has harmed another through one's actions, one can easily remedy the situation by confessing and/or repairing the wrong. In this model, the difference in action tendencies, and their associated functions, is central to distinguishing shame from guilt.

DEFINING ACTION TENDENCIES. Several other comments are needed regarding action tendencies. First, notice that approach tendencies accompany certain "negative" as well as certain "positive" emotions. Some researchers have attempted to distinguish between "positive" approach and "negative" approach. For example, in the questionnaire that Wallbott and Scherer (1988) devised to ask college students about emotions, they distinguished "movement against" from "movement toward." However, their college-aged informants (from a wide variety of cultures) distinguished guilt from shame on the basis of both "movement toward" and "movement against," and were slightly more likely to characterize guilt as involving "movement toward" than as involving "movement against." Negative or positive emotions can be approach emotions (see Fox & Davidson, 1988, for a discussion of this idea). In fact, inclination to inform others is predicted to accompany both guilt and pride—two emotions that some would consider "opposites." The negative–positive dichotomy does not fully capture the concept of action tendencies.

Second, because action tendencies are defined functionally, and are functional with respect to the relevant person–environment relationship, no particular movements are considered isomorphic with shame, guilt, or pride. If a particular shame-relevant movement is observed in a context in which it cannot serve shame-relevant functions, it is not viewed as indicating shame. Gaze aversion, for example, with or without a smile, is observed in a variety of contexts, including mother–infant interaction and stranger approach. In such contexts, it may serve to reduce negative arousal (cf. Cohn & Tronick, 1983; Fogel, Diamond, Langhorst, & Demos, 1981; Waters, Matas, & Sroufe, 1975), but does not function to reinforce standards for appropriate behavior or to highlight or communicate that one is bad/inadequate. For these reasons, it would not be viewed as signaling a member of the shame family. In the present model, *the meaning of a behavior pattern cannot be judged completely independently of context.* Only when the context is known can one judge what functions the behavior(s) serve for the individual.

STUDYING SHAME AND GUILT FROM A FUNCTIONAL PERSPECTIVE. If no particular behavior is a direct indicator of an emotion, then emotions are difficult to study. One may be tempted to assume that any behaviors that occur in a "shame-evoking" context must be shame. However, this assumption is clearly not warranted. Contexts are complex; many emotions can arise in most contexts. So how does one study shame and guilt? In order to study these or any other emotions, one must use converging operations and determine how behaviors function for an individual in a context. Inferences regarding the meaning of behavior patterns are strengthened when (1) the behaviors occur in a context in which the relelvant appreciations are plausible; (2) several behaviors serving a relevant function are present; and (3) internal regulatory, behavior-regulatory, and social regulatory functions of that behavior pattern are consistent with that interpretation of the behavior pattern. To the extent that more of these criteria are achieved, one can more confidently say that those behaviors are indicative that a member of a particular emotion family is being observed.

In most studies, data bearing on only one adaptive function are available (e.g., only social regulatory functions or only behavior-regulatory functions). Still, when (1) more than one indicator of a central function is present, (2) these indicators covary appropriately, (3) this function is specific to a particular emotion family, and (4) the indicators occur in a context in which the relevant appreciations are plausible, it seems reasonable to consider the reaction to be a member of the relevant emotion family.

In a recent study, my colleagues and I took this approach to distinguishing a shame-family pattern from a guilt-family pattern of response in 2-year-olds (K. C. Barrett, Zahn-Waxler, & Cole, 1993). Each child was given the experimenter's (E's) "favorite doll" (a colorful, gender-neutral clown rag doll named Pat) to play with while E left the room. The mother remained present, but was occupied with completing a questionnaire (with her back to the child) and was asked not to become involved. While the child was playing with the doll, its leg fell off. Such an event is relevant to both shame and guilt, in that it involves violating a standard of harm to another by harming the other's prized property.

After the child's spontaneous responses were videotaped, E returned to the room, at first just looking at the disembodied leg. After 1 minute, E matter-of-factly mentioned the disembodied leg. Then, with a mildly concerned tone of voice, E reminded the child that the doll was her favorite. After 30 seconds, E assured the child that he or she had not broken the doll, and brought other toys with which to play. The child's responses throughout were videotaped.

The results of this study indicated that children tended to show either a shame-relevant pattern of response ("avoiders") or a guilt-relevant pattern ("amenders"). Children prone to shame-like behavior (avoiders) averted their gaze from E when she returned after the toy was "broken," and/or physically avoided E following this incident. They were very slow to tell or show E about the incident, and waited a long time before attempting to repair the doll if they attempted to repair it at all. Moreover, they were more likely than amenders to smile following the mishap, and in particular to smile while averting their gaze from E.

Amenders, on the other hand, quickly tried to repair the doll after it "broke," very quickly told or showed E about the incident when she returned, and did not avoid E more than once via gaze nor action following her return. All of the 20 amenders attempted to repair the leg *before* E commented that it was broken; only 11 of 24 avoiders did so. Only 1 of 24 avoiders attempted repair and "confessed" (pointed out the "broken" leg to E) before E pointed out the mishap; 15 of 20 amenders did so. Moreover, according to maternal report, amenders showed more guilt relative to shame at home than did avoiders. We did not define shame or guilt for parents, so that our definitions of those emotions would not bias parental perceptions. Nevertheless, amenders' behavior at home communicated more guilt relative to shame to their mothers than did avoiders' behavior. It would be interesting in future studies to determine whether the social regulatory functions in Table 2.1 were fulfilled—whether deference and/or smallness/inadequacy are communicated by shame-relevant behaviors, and whether awareness of proper behavior and good intentions are communicated by guilt-relevant behaviors.

Principle 5: Shame and Guilt Aid in the Development of Self

One type of adaptive function of social emotions that has been virtually unstudied is the internal regulatory function. As Table 2.1 indicates, an important internal regulatory function of shame and guilt involves the impact of these emotions on the development of the self. As has been mentioned, many theorists believe that shame and guilt become possible only after the child has meta-awareness of self. It is my position that shame and guilt are highly important influences on the *development* of such awareness.

The shame experience highlights the "looking-glass self" (Cooley, 1902)—the self as others see one (or as one must appear to others). It causes one to step back from the self as agent and to evaluate that self, and thus helps one elaborate and/or modify one's view of self. Moreover, as an affective experience, it draws the person's attention to the significance of the experience.

It seems likely that most or all of a child's earliest experiences of shame occur in the presence of another person. Moreover, this person is likely to be a caregiver, with whom the child has a history of interactions. I find Bowlby's (1980) notion of a "working model" of self and other quite useful in conceptualizing the sense of self during infancy and toddlerhood, and the way in which shame may influence its development. According to Bowlby (1980), a child's interactions with a caregiver help shape "working models" of self and other. To the extent that the parent is responsive to the baby, the baby develops a view of that parent as responsive *and* a reciprocal view of the self as worthy of being responded to. To the extent that caregivers show that they love the baby, the baby develops a notion of the caregivers as loving and the self as lovable. Such working models need not be cognitively elaborate, and may at first involve simple expectancies that a child's actions will bring desired outcomes via a parent and that the parent will provide what is needed. Later, as the child's cognitive sophistication and interaction history become richer, the working models should become more elaborate and sophisticated.

When the expectations of the working model are not fulfilled, updating of the model may result. To the extent that the child views himself or herself as competent in obtaining satisfaction from the caregiver, and, in the shame-inducing situation, finds himself or herself incompetent to obtain satisfaction (e.g., the caregiver actually may attempt to *prevent* the child from obtaining a desired end, such as a china figurine), updating is needed. Moreover, the painful nature of the shame experience motivates such updating by bringing the discrepancy into vivid awareness.

The child's initial update may be that the caregiver is not so wonderful after all, or that the child is not so wonderful after all, or both. To the extent that shame is infrequent, however, and the caregiver–child relationship is good in general, the shame may serve to highlight the contexts in which child or caregiver is not wonderful, underscoring the standards being conveyed and/or the child's specific deficits. Moreover, the pain of shame should help discourage future violations of those standards. This, in turn, should result in the child's viewing himself or herself as a "good child" who does not often engage in behaviors that the parent deems undesirable, even when they would seem to bring him or her satisfaction. On the other hand, to the extent that shame experiences are very frequent, the child may come to view himself or herself as incompetent and/or bad, and to become a shame-prone (and potentially, a depression-prone) individual. As further development of a sense of self occurs, the shame experience may induce the child to compare the other's beliefs about him or her to his or her own beliefs. This may further elaborate the child's beliefs and feelings about self.

Guilt is likely to influence the development of self as agent, even more than self as object. To the extent that guilt rather than shame is more frequently experienced in the context of standard violations, the focus should be on the harmful act (and the child's responsibility for that act), rather than on a globally bad self. Thus, the child's power to harm others should be highlighted, and, to the extent that reparation occurs and leads to positive outcomes, the power of the child to help others should be highlighted as well. Therefore, whereas frequent shame experiences should cause the child to view himself or herself as bad, frequent guilt experiences should increase the child's awareness of his or her power to control his or her behavior, and of the pleasure derived from helping others, and of the discomfort derived from hurting others.[2] In fact, more frequent experience with engaging in harmful behavior, especially when such experience includes instruction and/or exposure to ways of remediating the situation rather than harsh reactions by socializing agents, may increase the child's knowledge of ways to make reparation and thus may increase the likelihood of guilt-proneness rather than shame-proneness.

One relevant finding with toddlers was obtained in the "avoider–amender" study just described: Children who, according to maternal report, had more frequently broken other children's toys in the past were more likely to be classified as amenders (K. C. Barrett et al., 1993). It seems possible that these children's more frequent experience with breaking toys taught them that they could do something to remedy the situation, and that children in our culture are more likely to be rewarded for trying to fix a broken toy than for hiding. This would also explain why many studies have revealed *positive* correlations between aggression and prosocial behavior (see D. E. Barrett & Yarrow, 1977; Friedrich & Stein, 1973; Murphy, 1937; Muste & Sharpe, 1947; Yarrow & Waxler, 1976; but for opposite findings see D. E. Barrett, 1979; Harris & Siebel, 1975; Rutherford & Mussen, 1968). Unfortunately, in the avoider–amender study, we did not inquire as to whether or not children were asked to repair and/or tried to repair the toys they broke previously, so it is not possible to know whether or not the relation between toy-breaking experience and guilt-relevant behavior was attributable to experience with reparation or to some other factor. Much more research is needed regarding the potential impact of guilt and shame on the development of self in children.

An important aspect of the current model that is not outlined in Table 2.1 is how shame and guilt develop during infancy and early childhood. For the remainder of this chapter, I discuss this topic, highlighting my belief that cognitive development contributes to but does not determine shame and guilt development, as well as that socialization is a crucial influence on shame and guilt development.

Principle 6: Cognitive Understandings Do Not Determine the Emergence of Shame and Guilt

Although cognitive development is viewed as important to the development of shame and guilt, general cognitive abilities such as object permanence or self-recognition are not deemed necessary for the emergence of shame or guilt. This is because full, accurate understanding is not necessary to the appreciation process.

As alluded to earlier, many theorists analyze elicitors of emotions in an attempt to determine what cognitions are involved. Then, upon determining requisite cognitions for a particular emotion, they use existing paradigms to determine at what point in development the cognitive prerequisite is possible. Then, they conclude, logically, that because the cognition is required for the emotion and the cognition is not possible until age X, then the emotion is not possible until age X. However, such an approach assumes that one must pass the cognitive ability test in order to be able to have the emotion (i.e., one must have complete, accurate understanding in order to have the emotion), and that the task used to measure the ability accurately captures the ability (i.e., if a baby can't pass the task, the baby does not yet have the ability).

However, many years of research on Piagetian abilities suggests that one can usually construct easier tasks for measuring cognitive abilities if only some degree of understanding is required (see Case, 1991; Fischer et al., 1990; Gelman & Baillargeon, 1983). Applying this approach to the cognitive abilities deemed necessary for shame and/or guilt, one can propose paradigms for indexing some degree of functional "understanding" of personal causation, "ought" standards, and one form of personal goodness–badness (efficacy) during the first 3 months of life.

Even a neonate is capable of some operant conditioning; thus even a young infant must have *some* sense of which behaviors produce desired results (DeCasper & Fifer, 1980; Rovee-Collier & Lipsitt, 1982). Moreover, there is evidence that even in the first 3 months of life infants form rudimentary expectations regarding their mothers' interactions with them, such that they react to a discrepancy from expected behavior—a violation of expectancies regarding how their mothers "ought" to behave (Tronick, Krafchuk, Ricks, Cohn, & Winn, 1980, cited in Tronick, Rick, & Cohn, 1982).

It is harder to operationalize functional knowledge of self as good versus bad. As mentioned earlier, Bowlby's concept of "working models" is relevant. Unfortunately, working models of self are not directly observable. Similarly, many object relations theorists propose that infants construct representations of self and other as "bad" and "good," but they do not provide empirical data to substantiate their claims (e.g., see Klein, 1975; Mahler et al., 1975).

As Stipek (1983) has pointed out, however, mastery pleasure may be a relevant, observable phenomenon. Mastery pleasure, which has been observed in the first 2 months of life (M. Lewis, Alessandri, & Sullivan, 1990; Watson, 1972), implies operative knowledge that one is "good" (efficacious). Moreover, the mastery smile seems directly associated with causal efficacy rather than just stimulation, even among 2-month-olds (M. Lewis et al., 1990). Furthermore, even 2-month-old infants who are inefficacious are likely to become distressed (M. Lewis et al., 1990), suggesting distress associated with awareness of *lack* of efficacy.

In summary, the operant conditioning results suggest some rudimentary ability to make use of information about the effects of one's behavior on other events and people; the expectancy literature implies rudimentary operational knowledge about the way things "ought" to be; and the contingency pleasure–distress findings suggest some awareness of one's efficacy–inefficacy during the first 3 months of life. My point is not that we should use these other paradigms to assess prerequisites for shame and guilt, nor that 3-month-olds are likely to experience shame and guilt. I also do not wish to suggest that 3-month-old infants *understand* personal responsibility and behavior standards, nor that they have a well-developed self-concept. My point is that, depending upon which criteria are accepted, one can grant children the requisite abiities at virtually any desired age. However, what is lacking in such an analysis is how such abilities may (or may not) create new emotions. Whether high or low levels of these abilities to "understand" are necessary for shame and guilt to be elicited, how do we get from such "understanding" to the elicitation of shame and guilt? One important vehicle, according to the present model, is socialization.

Principle 7: Socialization Is Crucial to the Development of Shame and Guilt

I have mentioned earlier that a major contributor to the development of the social emotions is socialization. Socialization is important to the development of shame and guilt not only because it is an important source of information about rules, standards, self, and so on; more importantly, it is primarily responsible for endowing those standards with significance, and making adherence to those standards an important goal for the individual. Significance is the crucial feature distinguishing appreciations from ordinary cognitive processes. A person can be aware that the speed limit is 55 miles per hour and that he or she is driving 65 miles per hour, for example, but unless abiding by the speed limit is a significant goal for the person, he or she should not experience guilt (or shame). In this section, I describe some potentially important socialization influences on the establishment of socialized goals for behavior, and the endowment of these socially valued goals with significance.

SOCIALIZATION AS A MEANS OF ESTABLISHING NEW AND SIGNIFICANT GOALS. As mentioned earlier, one attribute that distinguishes the social emotions from other classes of emotions is that their ovararching goals are socialized. It is theoretically possible that some universal moral principles exist (see Kohlberg, 1981; Turiel, 1983), leaving open the possibility that some moral principles could be "prewired" goals for humans. However, evidence for such universals is by no means clear. Moreover, cultures differ greatly with respect to whether or not many particular behaviors are pre- or proscribed, as well as which standards are held to be crucially important (Shweder, Mahapatra, & Miller, 1987). This suggests that standards are largely arbitrary and socialized by the culture. Moreover, theoretical distinctions between moral (basic, crucial, "universal") and conventional (arbitrary) standards (see Turiel, 1983) may break down when applied to particular examples. For example, Hindu Brahmans believe that it is extremely immoral for the eldest son of a man who died to have a haircut and eat chicken on the day after his death. Americans, by contrast, believe that it is immoral to *prevent* the eldest son from having a haircut and eating chicken on the day after his father's death if he wants to do so (see Shweder et al., 1987). Each of these cultures views this as a moral issue, despite its having to do with a seemingly conventional issue (what one does and eats), but the cultures have opposite views as to the "morally correct" way to behave.

We are faced with the task, therefore, of determining how such socially determined "moral" and/or "conventional" standards become goals for the individual, and, relatedly, how such goals gain significance to the individual—how the individual comes to see them as important to the self and to personal well-being. I believe that both the establishment of standards as goals and the endowment of such goals with significance begin in conjunction with the baby's interactions with parents and other loved ones.

The Importance of Relationships with Socializing Agents.   The infant's dependence places him or her in close, extended contact with a caregiver, enabling that caregiver (usually the parent) to be the first, and arguably the most important, socializing agent for the infant. In actuality, all of the many types of interactions of a parent with a baby are relevant to the development of guilt and shame. The most basic way in which parent–infant interactions help establish societal standards as goals and endow those goals with significance is through the effect of such interactions on the nature of the important parent–infant relationship. The nature of the relationship that forms should affect the child's desire to accept and heed the parents' standards—the child's belief that if the parent deems them significant, they probably are significant. In addition, the parent–child relationship should affect the child's tendency to care about hurting others, both because the child has learned to care about someone (the parent) and because a nurturant parent, with whom thc baby would be most likely to form a positive relationship, would model caring behavior. Consistent with these notions are data showing that children classified as "securely attached" as babies are more likely to comply with their parents' requests when they become toddlers (Matas, Arend, & Sroufe, 1978); that parents who are sensitive to their babies' signals have babies who both are more obedient and show greater evidence of "internalized controls" during the fourth quarter of the first year of life (Stayton, Hogan, & Ainsworth, 1971); and that children of more nurturant parents show greater empathy (e.g., Barnett, 1987).

In most discussions of socialization influences on the development of guilt, reparation, or self-regulation, emphasis is not placed on the overall relationship between parent and child, but rather on discipline strategies (e.g., Hoffman, 1984; Power & Chapieski, 1986; Schneider & Larzelere, 1988; Zahn-Waxler, Radke-Yarrow, & King, 1979). The assumption in much of this literature seems to be that discipline is important because it teaches a child to obey standards, even in the face of other desires, by teaching socially valued behavior and/or punishing socially undesirable behavior. Hoffman (1984), for example, states: "Only in discipline encounters . . . are connections often made among the norm, the child's egoistic desires, and his behavior." (p. 120).

Interestingly, however, those discipline strategies that are associated with long-term manifestation of appropriate behavior tend to be those that *highlight the significance* of appropriate behavior, and do so in a way *that does not impair the parent–child relationship*. Research with infants and toddlers has suggested that high usage of techniques that threaten the parent–child relationship are ineffective in promoting self-regulation according to social standards on a long-term basis. High usage of physical punishment is associated with lower impulse control and shorter latency to recurrence of misbehavior (Power & Chapieski, 1986; Schneider & Larzelere, 1988), and high usage of unexplained prohibitions is associated with lower levels of reparation for misdeeds (Zahn-Waxler et al., 1979). Moreover, although high usage of love withdrawal is associated with greater reparation, it is not associated with later reparation (Zahn-Waxler et al., 1979) and is associated with *shorter* latency to recurrence of misbehavior (Schneider & Larzelere, 1988).

On the other hand, when some of the same techniques are used at lower levels and in a manner that is less threatening to the parent–child relationship, they may be more effective. Use of corporal punishment at low (but nonzero) levels is not associated with poorer impulse control, and actually is associated with *longer* delay in recurrence of misbehavior when combined with inductive explanations (Power & Chapieski, 1986; Schneider & Larzelere, 1988; see also Hoffman, 1970a, in regard to older children). It seems quite possible that when such punishment does not occur sufficiently frequently and/or intensely that it impairs the parent–child bond, and it is accompanied by clear indication of which behaviors are unacceptable, it serves to highlight the significance of those particular acts.

The technique that has been associated with the greatest tendency for toddlers to make reparation for wrongdoings, both concurrently and on a long-term basis, is high usage of emotion-laden explanations—particularly those that include statements about general standards for behavior (Zahn-Waxler et al., 1979). This set of techniques highlights the significance of the misbehavior and/or the standards, while also making clear just what the standards are. Moreover, it does so in a way that is not likely to threaten the parent–child relationship; it is not excessively harsh and authoritarian. A particular version of this technique, induction (noting the consequences of misbehavior for others), has been associated with internalization and "guilt" in older children (however, the latter was not clearly distinguished from shame; see Hoffman, 1970b). This type of discipline also has been studied as part of a general style of parenting (authoritative/reciprocal) in which the child is listened to, valued, and reasoned with, and yet standards that parents believe in are highlighted and adhered to. This style, in turn, has been associated with long-term manifestation of socially valued behaviors in older children (see Baumrind, 1967, 1971; Maccoby & Martin, 1983).

The Role of Nonverbal Emotional Communication. Somewhat less attention has been given to the role of nonverbal emotional communication in the socialization of self-regulation, socially desirable behavior, or shame and guilt. There is a plethora of research indicating that during the fourth quarter of the first year of life and beyond, infants use the emotional signals of others to guide their reactions to ambiguous events, such as a short apparent dropoff on a modified visual cliff or a novel toy (e.g., Klinnert, Campos, Sorce, Emde, & Svejda, 1983; Walden, 1991). Moreover, there is some evidence that these effects may be found even when children have shown some initial reaction toward the event or stimulus (Hornik, Risenhoover, & Gunnar, 1987). Such emotional communication from adults to babies (and, later, from peers to children as well) endows those events with significance: It is dangerous/undesirable to crawl over this dropoff, or it would be fun to play with this toy. This same kind of emotional communication could highlight the significance of avoiding electrical outlets, medicine cabinets, or breakable objects, and could do so beginning at an early age. It is my position that the affectivity of the communication makes it do more than simply impart information about the objects or events; it causes the message to be appreciated as relevant to the person.

DISCIPLINE PRACTICES ASSOCIATED WITH SHAME VERSUS GUILT.   In the discussion above of socialization influences on the development of shame and guilt, I have not clearly indicated which processes should be associated with greater guilt than shame and vice versa. At this point, hypotheses regarding such differential socialization effects are extremely speculative, since most existing data regarding infants and toddlers are from studies that do not clearly distinguish guilt from shame. Moreover, data that do exist regarding disciplinary practices associated with guilt- and/or shame-relevant behavior are in some ways contrary to expectation.

It would be sensible for love withdrawal to be more closely associated with shame than with guilt, since it implies that a loved authority figure finds one wanting. In fact, love withdrawal even may involve direct suggestions that a child distance himself or herself from the authority figure. However, as described above, in the one study of the relation between socialization and reparation in toddlers, love withdrawal was (concurrently) associated with greater tendency toward reparation. At the very least, this result suggests that love withdrawal does not foster shame *rather than* guilt, although it is possible that it fosters both. Recall also, however, that love withdrawal was not associated with future likelihood of making reparation (Zahn-Waxler et al., 1979).

Another discipline type that might differentially influence guilt and shame is induction. It seems reasonable to divide the category "induction" into two subtypes, with differential relationships to guilt and shame. Induction that focuses on the harmful effects of one's action on a victim should increase guilt-relevant behavior, because it highlights the fact that another is being harmed by one's actions. However, induction focusing on the negative feeling of the parent should increase shame (and possibly also guilt, given the finding above), since it functions as love withdrawal. Unfortunately, I know of no studies that have distinguished these types of induction and tested these hypotheses.

NONDISCIPLINARY PRACTICES ASSOCIATED WITH SHAME VERSUS GUILT. Finally, it seems possible that disciplinary practices are less important in influencing propensity to shame *versus* guilt than are nondisciplinary socialization practices. One nondisciplinary socialization factor that seems likely to influence the tendency of children to become shame-prone but not guilt-prone is the degree to which parents communicate their high versus low emphasis on achievement, especially as such communication interfaces with the positivity of the parent–child relationship. M. Lewis (1991) has suggested that parents who adopt inappropriately high achievement standards for their children will make their children more likely to believe they have failed, and to experience the shame of failure. Moreover, there is reason to believe that even if standards are not inappropriately high, strong parental emphasis on the importance of achievement, especially in conjunction with a strong bond between parent and child (such that parental values matter to the child), may increase the likelihood of shame (and pride) by increasing the significance of such situations.

Some relevant data have been obtained from cross-national studies. There has long been a belief that certain Eastern cultures emphasize shame in their socialization, and that most Western cultures emphasize guilt (see Benedict, 1946; Creighton, 1990). It is important to emphasize that such a position does not imply that Eastern cultures do not induce guilt or that Western cultures do not induce shame; it merely suggests a difference in relative emphasis of the two emotions. If such cultures do differentially emphasize shame and guilt, however, one might generate hypotheses about socialization practices that are more associated with shame versus guilt by contrasting practices in "shame" and "guilt" cultures.

First, however, it it important to determine whether the distinction between "guilt" and "shame" cultures is valid. Despite the belief in a differentiation of shame and guilt cultures, there are very scant data testing the validity of this distinction; more data are urgently needed. However, as mentioned earlier, Shaver et al. (1987) found shame to be a basic emotion in China, but not in the United States or Italy. Moreover, a recent large-scale, cross-national study of college students' views of their own emotions provided some evidence supporting the distinction between "shame" and "guilt" cultures (Wallbott & Scherer, Chapter 19, this volume). Results of this study revealed that shame was "more shame-like" and more different from guilt in cultures that were high in collectivism (vs. individualism), acceptance of status differentials, and uncertainty avoidance.

Another recent study of Taiwanese and American toddlers found some support for the inference that Taiwan is more of a shame culture and the United States is more of a guilt culture (Chiang & Barrett, 1989). In this study, the "avoider–amender" paradigm described earlier was utilized with Taiwanese toddlers. Taiwanese toddlers initially were classified as avoiders versus amenders on the basis of the same criterion as were American toddlers (avoidance of E). However, this classification system did not well capture the nature of the Taiwanese toddlers' reactions to "breaking" the clown's leg, because Taiwanese amenders showed greater avoidance of E (longer latency to look at E following the "transgression") and less marked guilt-relevant behavior (longer latency to show E the "broken" leg) than did American amenders. Thus, the "guilt-relevant" Taiwanese group looked less guilty and more ashamed than did the "guilt-relevant" American group. We then examined whether or not disciplinary practices were related to these differences.

Parents from each culture were asked to report the frequency with which they used a variety of discipline techniques. However, contrary to expectation, Taiwanese parents did not report greater usage of any particular *types* of disciplinary practices than did Americans. Instead, Americans reported using virtually all discipline techniques more *frequently* than did Taiwanese.

These reports were consistent with observational data of Japanese parents and their babies, which indicated that Japanese mothers use less discipline with their babies than do Americans (Campos, Bradshaw, Usui, Miyake, & Campos, 1987).

These data have been interpreted as reflecting the difference in child-rearing emphasis in these Asian countries in comparison to the United States. The primary goal of Japanese and Taiwanese child-rearing during the child's first few years of life is reportedly to establish a harmonious relationship between parent and child; only later are behavior standards emphasized. During the first few years of life, appropriate behavior is ensured primarily by arranging the environment so that misbehavior is virtually impossible (thoroughly babyproofing) (Campos et al., 1987).

Interestingly, Taiwanese and Japanese parents reportedly constrain the environment not only by removing objects that are dangerous or breakable, but also by providing a few "desirable" toys for the babies to play with. According to observers from those cultures and self-reports by Taiwanese mothers, the toys selected are achievement-oriented (Campos et al., 1987; Chiang, 1994). Data regarding first- and fifth-graders in Taiwan, the United States, and Japan indicate that Japanese and especially Taiwanese children engage in, and appear to enjoy, more academic activities after school than do Americans. Moreover, Japanese and Taiwanese families are more likely to provide their children with their own desks at which to study than are Americans, despite typically smaller living spaces (Stevenson & Lee, 1990). These observations and data suggest that parents in the "shame" cultures of Taiwan and Japan emphasize the parent–child relationship and achievement during the early years of life. It will be recalled that shame-family emotions can be elicited in nonmoral, achievement situations as well as in moral, impulse control contexts, whereas guilt is expectable only in the latter contexts (including hurting others). Moreover, recall that shame-family emotions involve appreciation that *another* views one with disparagement. It seems possible that emphasis on the parent–child bond and upon the importance of achievement to the parent (which, in turn, would make achievement significant for the child) would foster greater shame.

Stipek, Reccia, and McClintic (1992) recently found that toddlers whose mothers more frequently praised them showed more frequent pride-like behaviors. It seems possible that greater emphasis on performance (via praise for accomplishments and scolding, love withdrawal, or negative affective responses to failures) might be associated with greater significance being placed not only on *achieving,* but on not *failing* to achieve standards (which might be associated with greater propensity to shame as well as pride). Unfortunately, although Stipek et al. (1992) examined shame-family reactions to failure, they did not relate these reactions to frequency of maternal praise.

One thing that is clear is that much more research is needed regarding the socialization of shame and guilt—particularly the socialization that occurs during infancy, before these emotions have been clearly established. It is important to study how infants learn about standards for behavior. But, in addition to studying the growth of such understanding, it is important to study how such standards become significant for the children, such that they feel good when they "do good" and feel bad when they "do bad." And it is important to determine whether there are some socialization practices that promote shame-proneness, some that promote guilt-proneness, and some that promote both. As the sparse data base for the current model suggests, data are only beginning to be gathered regarding these important issues.

SUMMARY AND CONCLUSIONS

In this chapter, I have presented seven principles that form the foundation for a functionalist approach to shame and guilt development. According to this perspective, shame and guilt are not intrinsically *bad* emotions; they are "social" emotions, and when experienced at appropriate levels, they serve important functions for the individual and society. Shame functions to highlight social standards and to maintain social hierarchies. In addition, shame draws attention to the self as object, aiding in the acquisition of knowledge about the self. Shame is associated with gaze aversion and social withdrawal, and these shame behaviors reduce the arousal experienced in shame-relevant contexts.

Like shame, guilt acts to highlight standards, and to aid in the development of self-knowledge. However, guilt aids in the development of understanding self as agent, rather than as object. Moreover, guilt brings one closer to other people rather than distancing one from others, and motivates the person to repair the harm that he or she has perpetrated.

According to the functionalist perspective espoused in this chapter, cognitive understandings do not determine the emergence of shame and guilt. Understanding is not necessary to the generation of emotion; often only very low-level sensing is involved in emotion induction. Moreover, even full understanding is not sufficient for the induction of shame, guilt, or other emotions. In order for emotion to be generated, events must be significant to the individual.

Finally, socialization is crucial to the development of shame and guilt. I have speculated about the kinds of socialization factors involved in the development of shame and guilt, as well as those differentially associated with shame versus guilt. While doing so, I have emphasized the importance of early parent–child interactions in the development of social standards as goals, and in the endowment of those goals with significance.

Throughout this chapter, I have highlighted the paucity of data bearing on the principles being espoused. More data are now being collected, but the proposed principles should be considered speculative at present, given the scant available data base for them. I hope that the theoretical model described in this chapter will help foster more research, so that what are now speculations can be carefully examined, yielding a richer and better understanding of the development of shame and guilt.

NOTES

1. At first blush, this position seems at odds with that of H. B. Lewis (1971), in that the self is a focus in both shame and guilt. However, this contradiction is more apparent than real. Focus on specific features or actions of the self is quite similar, in practice, to focusing on events for which one is responsible. For example, if one broke one's mother's favorite vase, according to both theories shame would involve thoughts such as "I'm a bad person," and guilt would involve thoughts such as "What a clumsy thing to do; I can't believe I dropped that vase; I should be more careful!" H. B. Lewis has noted also that people's thoughts often move back and forth from shame-like to guilt-like ideation.

2. This assumes that these guilt responses typically occur in relevant contexts, rather than when the experiencing person is not responsible for any harm. Moreover, it acknowledges that guilt experiences that are *extremely* frequent (especially if reparations are often ineffective) should lead to a sense of self as "evil"— as responsible primarily for bad events. In addition, to the extent that guilt is painful, it should lead to decreased likelihood of future misbehavior, such that although guilt may continue to be *proportionately* more frequently experienced than is shame, the absolute frequency of guilt (and shame) should decrease with development.

REFERENCES

Agnoli, F., Kirson, D., Wu, S., & Shaver, P. (1989). *Hierarchical analysis of the emotion lexicon in English, Italian, and Chinese*. Paper presented at the annual conference of the International Society for Research on Emotion, Paris.

Barnett, M. A. (1987). Empathy and related responses in children. In N. Eisenberg & J. Strayer (Eds.), *Empathy and its development* (pp. 146–162). Cambridge, England: Cambridge University Press.

Barrett, D. E. (1979). A naturalistic study of sex differences in children's aggression. *Merrill–Palmer Quarterly, 25,* 193–203.

Barrett, D. E., & Yarrow, M. R. (1977). Prosocial behavior, social inferential ability, and assertiveness in children. *Child Development, 48,* 475–481.

Barrett, K. C. (1993). The development of nonverbal communication of emotion: A functionalist perspective. *Journal of Nonverbal Behavior, 17,* 145–169.

Barrett, K. C., & Campos, J. J. (1987). Perspectives on emotional development: II. A functionalist approach to emotions. In J. Osofsky (Ed.), *Handbook of infant development* (2nd ed., pp. 555–578). New York: Wiley.

Barrett, K. C., Zahn-Waxler, C., & Cole, P. M. (1993). Avoiders versus amenders: Implications for the investigation of guilt and shame during toddlerhood? *Cognition and Emotion, 7,* 481–505.

Baumrind, D. (1967). Child care practices anteceding three patterns of preschool behavior. *Genetic Psychology Monographs, 75,* 43–88.

Baumrind, D. (1971). Current patterns of parental authority. *Developmental Psychology Monographs, 4*(1, Pt. 2).

Benedict, R. (1946). *The chrysanthemum and the sword: Patterns of Japanese culture.* Boston: Houghton Mifflin.

Bowlby, J. (1980). *Attachment and loss: Vol. 3. Loss, sadness and depression.* New York: Basic Books.

Bradshaw, J. (1988). *Healing the shame that binds you.* Deerfield Beach, FL: Health Communications.

Buss, A. (1980). *Self-consciousness and social anxiety.* San Francisco: W. H. Freeman.

Campos, J. J., & Barrett, K. C. (1984). Toward a new understanding of emotions and their development. In C. Izard, J. Kagan, & R. Zajonc (Eds.), *Emotions, cognition, and behavior* (pp. 229–263). New York: Cambridge University Press.

Campos, J. J., Bradshaw, D., Usui, H., Miyake, K., & Campos, R. G. (1987, April). Emotional communication and compliance: A cross-national perspective. In C. Kopp (Chair), *Moving toward intention, control, and self-regulation: Developmental trends and influences.* Symposium conducted at the meeting of the Society for Research in Child Development, Baltimore.

Campos, J. J., Campos, R. G., & Barrett, K. C. (1989). Emergent themes in the study of emotional development and emotion regulation. *Developmental Psychology, 25,* 394–402.

Case, R. (1991). Stages in the development of the young child's first sense of self. *Developmental Review, 11,* 210–230.

Chiang, T. (1994). [A cross-cultural study of childrearing and social emotions]. Unpublished raw data.

Chiang, T., & Barrett, K. C. (1989, April). *A cross-cultural comparison of toddlers' reactions to the infraction of a standard: A guilt culture vs. a shame culture.* Paper presented at the meeting of the Society for Research in Child Development, Kansas City, MO.

Cohn, J., & Tronick, E. (1983). Three-month-old infants' reaction to simulated maternal depression. *Child Development, 54,* 185–193.

Cooley, C. H. (1902). *Human nature and the social order.* New York: Scribner's.

Creighton M. (1990). Revisiting shame and guilt cultures: A forty-year pilgrimage. *Ethos, 18,* 279–307.

DeCasper, A. J., & Fifer, W. (1980). Of human bonding: Newborns prefer their mothers' voices. *Science, 208,* 1174–1176.

Ekman, P. (1984). Expression and the nature of emotion. In K. Scherer & P. Ekman (Eds.), *Approaches to emotion* (pp. 319–344). Hillsdale, NJ: Erlbaum.

Ekman, P., & Friesen, W. (1975). *Unmasking the face.* Englewood Cliffs, NJ: Prentice-Hall.

Ekman, P., Levenson, R., & Friesen, W. (1983). Autonomic nervous system activity distinguishes between emotions. *Science, 221,* 1208–1210.

Erikson, E. (1963). *Childhood and society* (2nd ed.). New York: Norton.

Fischer, K. W., Shaver, P. R., & Carnochan, P. (1990). How emotions develop and how they organise development. *Cognition and Emotion, 4,* 81–127.

Fogel, A., Diamond, G. R., Langhorst, B. H., & Demos, V. (1981). Affective and cognitive aspects of the two-month-old's participation in face-to-face interaction with its mother. In E. Tronick (Ed.), *Joint regulation of behavior* (pp. 37–57). Baltimore: University Park Press.

Fogel, A., Nwokah, E., Dedo, J., Messinger, D., Dickson, K. L., Matusov, E., & Holt, S. (1992). Social process theory of emotion: A dynamic systems approach. *Social Development, 1,* 122–142.

Fox, N. A., & Davidson, R. J. (1988). Patterns of brain electrical activity during facial signs of emotion in 10-month-old infants. *Developmental Psychology, 24,* 230–236.

Freud, S. (1961). Civilization and its discontents. In J. Strachey (Ed. and Trans.), *The standard edition of the complete psychological works of Sigmund Freud* (Vol. 21, pp. 59–145). London: Hogarth Press. (Original work published 1930)

Freud, S. (1965). *Three essays on the theory of sexuality.* New York: Avon Books. (Original work published 1905)

Friedrich, L. K., & Stein, A. H. (1973). Aggressive and prosocial television programs and the natural behavior of preschool children. *Monographs of the Society for Research in Child Development, 38*(4, Serial No. 151).

Frijda, N. (1986). *The emotions.* New York: Cambridge University Press.

Gelman, R., & Baillargeon, R. (1983). A review of some Piagetian concepts. In J. H. Flavell & E. M. Markman (Vol. Eds.), *Handbook of child psychology* (4th ed.): *Vol. 3. Cognitive development* (pp. 167–230). New York: Wiley.

Geppert, U. (1986). *A coding-system for analyzing behavioral expressions of self-evaluated emotions (technical manual).* Munich: Max-Planck-Institute for Psychological Research.

Harper, J., & Hoopes, M. (1990). *Uncovering shame.* New York: Norton.

Harris, M. B., & Siebel, C. E. (1975). Affect, aggression, and altruism. *Developmental Psychology, 11,* 623–627.

Hoffman, M. L. (1970a). Conscience, personality, and socialization techniques. *Human Development, 13,* 90–126.

Hoffman, M. L. (1970b). Moral development. In P. H. Mussen (Ed.), *Carmichael's manual of child psychology* (3rd ed., Vol. 2, pp. 261–360). New York: Wiley.

Hoffman, M. L. (1984). Parent discipline, moral internalization, and development of prosocial motivation. In E. Staub, D. Bar-Tal, J. Karylowski, & J. Reykowski (Eds.), *Development and maintenance of prosocial behavior* (pp. 117–137). New York: Plenum.

Hogan, R., & Cheek, J. (1983). Self-concepts, self-presentations, and moral judgments. In J. Suls & A. G. Greenwald (Eds.), *Psychological perspectives on the self* (Vol. 2, pp. 249–273). Hillsdale, NJ: Erlbaum.

Hornik, R., Risenhoover, N., & Gunnar, M. (1987). The effects of maternal positive, neutral, and negative affective communications on infant responses to new toys. *Child Development, 58,* 937–944.

Izard, C., & Malatesta, C. (1987). Perspectives on emotional development I: Differential emotions theory of early emotional development. In J. Osofsky (Ed.), *Handbook of infant development* (pp. 494–554). New York: Wiley.

Kagan, J. (1984). *The nature of the child.* New York: Basic Books.

Klein, M. (1975). *Love, guilt, and reparation and other works, 1921–1945.* New York: Dell.

Klinnert, M., Campos, J., Sorce, J., Emde, R., & Svejda, M. (1983). Emotions as behavior regulators: Social referencing in infancy. In R. Plutchik & H. Kellerman (Eds.), *Emotion: Theory, research, and experience* (Vol. 2, pp. 57–86). New York: Academic Press.

Kohlberg, L. (1981). *Essays on moral development: Vol. 1. The philosophy of moral development: Moral stages and the idea of justice.* San Francisco: Harper & Row.

Lazarus, R. (1991). *Emotion and adaptation.* New York: Oxford University Press.

Lewis, H. B. (1971). *Shame and guilt in neurosis.* New York: International Universities Press.

Lewis, H. B. (1987). Shame and the narcissistic personality. In D. L. Nathanson (Ed.). *The many faces of shame* (pp. 93–132). New York: Guilford Press.

Lewis, M. (1991). Self-conscious emotions and the development of self. In T. Shapiro & R. Emde (Eds.), New perspectives on affect and emotion in psychoanalysis. *Journal of the American Psychoanalytic Association (Suppl.), 39,* 45–73.

Lewis, M., Alessandri, S., & Sullivan, M. (1990). Expectancy, loss of control and anger in young infants. *Developmental Psychology, 25,* 745–751.

Lewis, M., Sullivan, M., Stanger, C., & Weiss, M. (1989). Self development and self-conscious emotions. *Child Development, 60,* 146–156.

Maccoby, E., & Martin, J. (1983). Socialization in the context of the family: Parent–child interaction. In E. M. Hetherington (Vol. Ed.), *Handbook of child psychology* (4th ed.): *Vol. 4. Socialization, personality, and social development* (pp. 1–102). New York: Wiley.

Mahler, M. S. (1968). *On human symbiosis and the vicissitudes of individuation.* New York: International Universities Press.

Mahler, M. S., Pine, F., & Bergman, A. (1975). *The psychological birth of the human infant.* New York: Basic Books.

Matas, L., Arend, R., & Sroufe, L. A., (1978). Continuity and adaptation in the second year: The relationship between quality of attachment and later competence. *Child Development, 49,* 547–556.

Murphy, L. B. (1937). *Social behavior and child personality.* New York: Columbia University Press.

Muste, M. J., & Sharpe, D. F. (1947). Some influential factors in the determination of aggressive behavior in preschool children. *Child Development, 18,* 11–28.

Nathanson, D. (1987a). The shame–pride axis. In H. B. Lewis (Ed.), *The role of shame in symptom formation* (pp. 183–205). Hillsdale, NJ: Analytic Press.

Nathanson, D. (1987b). A timetable for shame. In D. L. Nathanson (Ed.), *The many faces of shame* (pp. 1–63). New York: Guilford Press.

Ortony, A., & Turner, T. (1990). What's so basic about basic emotions? *Psychological Review, 97,* 315–331.

Piers, G., & Singer, M. B. (1971). *Shame and guilt.* New York: Norton.

Power, T., & Chapieski, M. L. (1986). Childrearing and impulse control in toddlers: A naturalistic investigation. *Developmental Psychology, 22,* 271–275.

Rovee-Collier, C., & Lipsitt, L. (1982). Learning, adaptation, and memory. In P. Stratton (Ed.), *Psychobiology of the human newborn.* Chichester, England: Wiley.

Rutherford, E., & Mussen, P. (1968). Generosity in nursery school boys. *Child Development, 39,* 755– 765.

Scherer, K. R. (1986). Vocal affect expression: A review and a model for future research. *Psychological Bulletin, 99,* 143–165.

Schneider, W., & Larzelere, R. (1988, August). *Effects of discipline strategies on delays of reoccurrences of misbehavior in toddlers.* Paper presented at the meeting of the American Psychological Association, Atlanta.

Schneider-Rosen, K., & Cicchetti, D. (1991). Early self-knowledge and emotional development: Visual self-recognition and affective reactions to mirror self-images in maltreated and non-maltreated toddlers. *Developmental Psychology, 27,* 471–478.

Schore, A. N. (1991). Early superego development: The emergence of shame and narcissistic affect regulation in the practicing period. *Psychoanalysis and Contemporary Thought, 14,* 187–250.

Shweder, R., Mahapatra, M., & Miller, J. (1987). Culture and moral development. In J. Kagan & S. Lamb (Eds.), *The emergence of morality in young children* (pp. 1–82). Chicago: University of Chicago Press.

Shaver, P., Schwartz, J., Kirson, D., & O'Connor, C. (1987). Emotion knowledge: Further exploration of a prototype approach. *Journal of Personality and Social Psychology, 52,* 1061–1086.

Stayton, D., Hogan, R., & Ainsworth, M. D. S. (1971). Infant obediance and maternal behavior: The origins of socialization reconsidered. *Child Development, 42,* 1057–1069.

Stevenson, H., & Lee, S. (1990). Contexts of achievement. *Monographs of the Society for Research in Child Development, 55*(1–2, Serial No. 221).

Stipek, D. (1983). A developmental analysis of pride and shame. *Human Development, 26,* 42–54.

Stipek, D., Recchia, S., & McClintic, S. (1992). Self-evaluation in young children. *Monographs of the Society for Research in Child Development, 57*(1, Serial No. 226).

Tangney, J. P. (1990). Assessing individual differences in proneness to shame and guilt: Development of the Self-Conscious Affect and Attribution Inventory. *Journal of Personality and Social Psychology, 59,* 102–111.

Tangney, J. P., Wagner, P., & Gramzow, R. (1992). Proneness to shame, proneness to guilt, and psychopathology. *Journal of Abnormal Psychology, 101,* 469–478.

Tomkins, S. S. (1987). Shame. In D. L. Nathanson (Ed.), *The many faces of shame* (pp. 133–161). New York: Guilford Press.

Tronick, E., Ricks, M., & Cohn, J. (1982). Maternal and infant affective exchange: Patterns of adaptation. In T. Field & A. Fogel (Eds.), *Emotion and early interaction* (pp. 83–100). Hillsdale, NJ: Erlbaum.

Turiel, E. (1983). *The development of social knowledge: Morality and convention.* Cambridge, England: Cambridge University Press.

Walden, T. A. (1991). Infant social referencing. In J. Garber & K. Dodge (Eds.), *The development of emotion regulation and dysregulation* (pp. 69–88). New York: Cambridge University Press.

Wallbott, H. G., & Scherer, K. R. (1988). How universal and specific is emotional experience? Evidence from 27 countries and five continents. In K. R. Scherer (Ed.), *Facets of emotion* (pp. 31–56). Hillsdale, NJ: Erlbaum.

Waters, E., Matas, L., & Sroufe, L. A. (1975). Infants' reactions to an approaching stranger: Description, validation, and functional significance of wariness. *Child Development, 46,* 348–356.

Watson, J. S. (1972). Smiling, cooing, and "the game." *Merrill–Palmer Quarterly, 18,* 341–347.

Wittgenstein, L. (1953). *Philosophical investigations.* New York: Macmillan.

Wurmser, L. (1987). Shame: The veiled companion of narcissism. In D. Nathanson (Ed.), *The many faces of shame* (pp. 64–92). New York: Guilford Press.

Yarrow, M. R., & Waxler, C. Z. (1976). Dimensions and correlates of prosocial behavior in young children. *Child Development, 47,* 118–125.

Zahn-Waxler, C., Radke-Yarrow, M., & King, R. (1979). Child rearing and children's prosocial initiations toward victims of distress. *Child Development, 50,* 319–330.

3

Developmental Transformations in Appraisals for Pride, Shame, and Guilt

MICHAEL F. MASCOLO
KURT W. FISCHER

> Well, my feelings were so deep that I have never forgotten it,
> and I don't think that until I leave this earth I will ever
> forget. It was the same feeling I had in "I Have a
> Dream"—when we heard that "I Have a Dream" speech. It
> was the same feeling. Number one, I never have been so
> proud to be an American. Number two, I've never been so
> proud to be an American Negro. Number three, I've never
> had such pride in seeing this Negro woman stand up there
> with this great royal dignity and sing.
> —TODD DUNCAN (speaking in James, 1991)

Psychologists and laypersons have often viewed emotions as primitive psychological entities that remain mostly invariant throughout development. Although certain aspects of emotional experiences probably remain stable throughout the lifespan, emotions in adolescents and adults differ from emotions in infants and young children in important ways. For example, one 18-month-old boy spontaneously took some tissues and dusted the room (Emde, Johnson, & Easterbrooks, 1987); his parents praised him and he beamed. Compare this child's reaction to the pride communicated by Todd Duncan, quoted above, who recalled his feelings about attending a concert at the Lincoln Memorial performed by African-American soprano Marian Anderson in 1939 after she was denied a performance at Constitution Hall

(James, 1991). Whereas the toddler exhibited a pride-like reaction to an act that earned his parents' approval, Duncan's pride flowed from his identification with another's act that implied the dignity of his race and country. Although these experiences bear some family resemblance, Duncan's pride was much more textured and complex than the child's, and was based in an appraisal or interpretation that the child could not begin to fathom.

This chapter examines developmental changes in self-evaluative emotions from infancy to adolescence and adulthood, focusing on appraisal patterns producing the emotions of guilt, shame, and pride. We focus on appraisals in this chapter because of their centrality in emotions. Emotions begin with appraisals of a person's situation; a specific emotion arises from an appraisal of how the situation relates to the person's goals, values, and concerns, including self-evaluation. Appraisals then lead to particular emotional organizations (action tendencies), determining both the person's reactions and his or her judgments (what a particular pride, shame, or guilt experience is about).

We suggest that developmental transformations in the appraisals that generate guilt, shame, and pride produce increasingly complex *forms* of these emotions. In what follows, we use dynamic skills theory to propose developmental trajectories in the appraisals that mediate pride, shame, and guilt experiences (Fischer, 1980; Fischer, Shaver, & Carnochan, 1990). This analysis includes both a functional model for unpacking each emotion and a set of sequencing tools for predicting developmental pathways.

A FUNCTIONAL MODEL OF SELF-EVALUATIVE EMOTIONS

As their name implies, self-evaluative emotions involve self-evaluation as part of the appraisal process. In pride, a person appraises the self as having responsibility for accomplishing a socially valued outcome or being a socially valued person. In shame, a person appraises the self as having failed to live up to standards of the social group. In guilt, a person appraises the self as having responsibility for a wrongdoing. These appraisals are part of the functional processes by which self-conscious emotions—the emotions more generally—play a central role in human adaptation.

According to functional approaches, emotions are much more than feelings. They are adaptive patterns of behavior arising from a person's appraised relation to ongoing events (Barrett & Campos, 1987; Fischer et al., 1990; Frijda, 1986; Lazarus, 1991; Mascolo & Mancuso, 1990, 1992; Scherer, 1984), as described in this volume by Fischer and Tangney (Chapter 1) and Barrett (Chapter 2). For each emotion, there is a prototypic script defining the sequence of events in an emotion: from precipitating events to appraisals, action tendencies, and self-monitoring procedures (Fehr & Russell, 1985; Shaver, Schwartz, Kirson, & O'Connor, 1987).

Emotions consist of felt, multicomponent evaluative reactions to appraised changes in a person's relations to events, as discussed in Chapter 1 of this volume and depicted there in the prototypic process model in Figure 1.1 (Fischer et al., 1990; Frijda, 1986, 1988; Lazarus, 1991). Emotional episodes begin with "appraisals" of notable changes in an individual's environs—assessments of the relation between perceived events and an individual's goals, motives, or concerns. "Concerns" subsume a broad range of motive-relevant phenomena, including immediate goals and wishes as well as long-term desires, values, and motives. Positive emotions arise from appraisals indicating that events meet or exceed a person's wishes or concerns, whereas negative emotions involve appraisals that events violate salient concerns.

Each appraisal prompts both internal reactions and "action tendencies" that are typical of a specific emotion (Barrett & Campos, 1987; Ekman, Levenson, & Friesen, 1983). Action tendencies are organized, motivated reactions that enable individuals to adapt to changes in appraised events. By modifying self, other, or environment in ways that help promote one's concerns, action tendencies serve important functions for individuals (Barrett & Campos, 1987; de Rivera, 1981; Fischer et al., 1990) and communities (Armon-Jones, 1986). Action tendencies amplify the importance of certain appraised events (Mandler, 1984; Tomkins, 1984) and motivate adaptive activity relative to those events. People also monitor and control their emotional reactions through the "self-monitoring of action tendencies," which through feedback direct the regulation and social display of emotions (Kopp, 1989; Hochschild, 1979; Saarni, 1990; Thompson, 1990).

Table 3.1 contains prototypic summary descriptions of major components of pride, shame, and guilt, based primarily on research with adults in North America and Europe. Research on prototypes will probably turn out to show differences as well as commonalities across cultures. In development, we predict that infants will show only parts of the prototype for their cultural group, and that they will develop gradually toward the cultural prototype.

On the basis of a growing literature, we suggest that pride is generated by appraisals that one is responsible for a socially valued outcome or for being a socially valued person (Barrett & Campos, 1987; Davitz, 1969; H. Heckhausen, 1984; Stipek, 1983; Stipek, Recchia, & McClintic, 1992). Pride comprises action tendencies to present one's worthy self or action to others, such as a broad smile, beaming face, erect posture, celebratory gestures or comments (such as hands raised in the air, applause, and cheers), and comments that call attention to the self's accomplishment. Internal reactions include increased heart rate and skin conductance, as well as erratic respiration. The subjective experience of pride involves an experience of one's body or self as taller, stronger, or bigger. Pride functions to bolster one's sense of self-worth and to direct one's actions toward behaviors that conform to social standards of worth or merit.

TABLE 3.1. Scripts for Pride, Shame, and Guilt

Emotion	Appraisal	Internal reaction and bodily experience	Motive-action tendency
Pride	Self is responsible for a socially valued outcome or for being a socially valued person.	Increase in heart rate and skin conductance, erratic respiration. Body experience as taller, stronger, or bigger.	Show worthy self to others, smile broadly, stand erect, make celebratory gestures, call attention to accomplishments.
Shame	Self has fallen short of standards of worth in the eyes of others.	Blushing, diminished heart rate. Body experienced as heavy or small.	Hide the self, avert gaze, bury face in hands.
Guilt	Self is responsible for a wrongdoing.	Increased heart rate. Body experienced as heavy.	Correct wrongdoing, apologize, confess, make reparations, fix situation, seek forgiveness.

67

In contrast to pride, shame is generated by appraisals that one has failed to live up to standards of worth in the eyes of others (Barrett & Campos, 1987; Davitz, 1969; Emde et al., 1987; H. B. Lewis, 1971; Lindsay-Hartz, 1984; Piers & Singer, 1953; Weiner & Graham, 1984). Shame involves a motive–action tendency to hide the self, which is often manifested in gaze aversion, the collapse of the body, and an attempt to cover the face with the hands. Physiological reactions often include blushing and low heart rate. Persons may experience their bodily states or selves as heavy or small. Shame functions to promote adherence to norms of esteemed behavior and to highlight behaviors that threaten honor or self-worth.

Guilt is generated by appraisals that one is responsible for committing a wrongdoing. Action tendencies for guilt include the propensities to make reparations, fix the situation, apologize, confess, or seek forgiveness (Hoffman, 1983; Lindsay-Hartz, 1984; Zahn-Waxler & Kochanska, 1990). Internal reactions seem to involve increased heart rate (Barrett & Campos, 1987) and a bodily state that is experienced as heavy (Davitz, 1969). Guilt functions to promote moral, prosocial, and allocentric behavior, a sense of moral worth, and respect for the rights and feelings of others.

Guilt and shame are similar and closely related, both involving personal responsibility for something negative; however, the appraisals for guilt and shame differ in subtle yet important ways (Barrett, Zahn-Waxler, & Cole, 1993; Lindsay-Hartz, 1984; Tangney, 1992). First, the standards that mediate guilt and shame reactions differ. Guilt follows as a reaction to self-caused wrongdoings and is mediated by standards of what is considered right or wrong (such as respect for others' feelings or rights), but shame involves failures to live up to standards of honor or worth in the eyes of others. In addition, in guilt one is concerned with a wrongful act, whereas in shame one's entire self seems to be experienced as unworthy. In guilt, one has done something wrong even though one is not really a bad person; in shame, one is an unworthy person. Although both guilt and shame can be generated by the same event, shame in these situations involves a focus on one's unworthy self in the eyes of others, whereas guilt involves a focus on one's wrongful act. This differential focus likely underlies differences in guilt and shame action tendencies, either to hide one's unworthy self in shame or to correct a wrongdoing in guilt.

Self-evaluative emotions develop as the components that comprise them undergo transformation. Emotions show large qualitative changes with development, in the same way as other behaviors in other complex domains, such as problem solving and communication. Most of the emotion components undergo development, including appraisal, action tendency, expression, and self-monitoring components. It is possible that some aspects of emotion (such as emotion-typical feeling tone) may remain stable throughout ontogenesis (Emde, 1983; Izard & Malatesta, 1987), although we expect that even feeling tone can change. For example, some aspects of feeling tone (such as intensity and detectability) may change as persons develop ways to regulate physiological arousal and other processes involved in emotional reactivity (Dienstbier, 1990). In this chapter, our focus is on changes in appraisal; we demonstrate how this component of self-conscious emotions develops, according to our analysis. This type of analysis is intended, however, to be applicable to all the components of emotions.

DYNAMIC SKILLS THEORY AS A TOOL KIT FOR MAPPING SELF-EVALUATIVE EMOTIONAL DEVELOPMENT

According to dynamic skills theory, psychological development arises from a series of transformations in skills (Fischer, 1980; Fischer et al., 1990). "Skills" are control systems for organizing or controlling one's behavior (actions, perceptions, thoughts, and feelings) for a specific context, goal, and affective state. Skills are properties not of individuals but of persons-in-context.

The focus on actions, perceptions, and control systems is compatible with a functional approach to emotion. From a functionalist view, the component emotion processes—appraisal, motivation, cognition, affect, and behavior (or some such list)—are seen not as separate but instead as inseparable aspects of organized scripts, including powerful action tendencies (Fischer & Elmendorf, 1986; Frijda, 1986). Skills theory begins with a similar framework for predicting developmental changes in the organization of behavior, no matter what the content, domain, or affective quality.

Tools for Predicting Sequences and Correspondences

A major part of skill theory is a tool kit for predicting developmental sequences and correspondences, taking into account complexity, context, domain, social support, and affect. A set of transformation rules is used to predict detailed steps in development for a given context and affective state—how simpler skills are combined and differentiated to produce more advanced skills. These rules and related tools are described in detail in Fischer (1980), Fischer and Farrar (1987), and Fischer et al. (1990). In general, skills move through a series of 13 levels divided into four tiers, with variable, multiple steps occurring at each level. Levels are defined by upper limits on the complexity of skills that a person can control, especially under optimal conditions. When we attribute specific ages to emergence of a step in development of self-evaluative emotions, we are referring to the first age at which most children can build a skill of that type under optimal conditions. There are extensive data on both behavioral and brain development that support the general ages for optimal levels (Fischer, Bullock, Rotenberg, & Raya, 1993; Fischer & Rose, 1994). However, most behavior occurs at lower levels, not at the optimal level, and so most emotions will occur at later ages than those we describe.

Skills develop through four basic tiers, which first emerge at different age periods. Each tier is defined in terms of a different skill unit: "reflexes" (beginning at birth), "sensorimotor actions" (beginning at about 3–4 months), "representations" (beginning at about 18–24 months), and "abstractions" (beginning at about 10–12 years). Each tier builds upon the preceding one in the sense that skills at a later tier emerge from hierarchical reorganizations of skills at the prior tier, with complex systems at one tier producing a new unit of behavior at the next tier. Thus, sensorimotor actions are built upon systems of reflexes, representations are built upon systems of sensorimotor actions, and abstractions are built upon systems of representations.

Skills also develop according to a series of four levels within each broad tier. For example, within the representational tier, beginning at about 18–24 months of age, the initial skills are "single representations." At this level children construct representations of self, others, or objects as independent agents, but cannot yet hold in mind or coordinate relations between two or more such representations. For example, at approximately 18–24 months children begin to show strong evidence of representing the self in this way, including recognizing the self's physical characteristics (even those visible only in a mirror) and identifying the self explicitly as an agent of action (Bertenthal & Fischer, 1978; M. Lewis & Brooks-Gunn, 1979; Pipp, Fischer, & Jennings, 1987). Beginning at about 3½–5 years, in contexts that provide high support for skill use, children coordinate representations in relations such as causality or similarity to form a "representational mapping." Thus, at this level a child should be able to construct a self-related understanding, such as "I did a good drawing, but Daphne did a poor one." At about 5½–7 years of age, under conditions of high support, children coordinate two representational mappings into a "representational system," which allows them to understand relations between at least two mappings. At this level children can understand a system such as this: "I am as good at kicking as José, and I am as good a goalie as Diane." In preadolescence (10–12 years), children gain the capacity to coordinate two representational systems into a "single abstraction." For example, in high-support contexts young adolescents construct self-evaluative abstractions, such as "I am a competent person." For this to qualify as an abstraction, the adolescent must be able to explain his or her general competence by relating two separate concrete systems of competent behavior (such as specific instances of running and jumping better than a friend, and performing better in math and science than another friend). Skills within the reflex, sensorimotor, and abstract tiers develop through an analogous sequence of levels.

Strategies for Predicting Emotional Pathways:
A Framework for Interpretation

Our general strategy for predicting changes in self-evaluative emotional appraisals consists of specifying and ordering the complexity of various appraisals involved in forms of guilt, shame, and pride relevant to Western culture as we know it. It is important to note that these developmental sequences can be predicted only within specific emotional domains, contexts, and cultures. Years of research on cognitive and emotional development have demonstrated that developmental sequences often differ with variations in domain, context, and culture. Children show a high degree of variability on structurally equivalent tasks across domains and from one context to another (Bidell & Fischer, 1992; Fischer, 1980). For example, researchers have found low correlations in level of performance across such content domains as classification, seriation, and conservation (Gelman & Baillargeon, 1983). In addition, level of cognitive performance varies drastically, depending upon the degree of available contextual support (Fischer, Bullock, et al., 1993; Rogoff, 1990). Likewise, differences in cultural meaning can produce large differences in developmental sequences, especially for self-evaluative emotions, which seem to differ greatly in importance and interpretation across cultures (see Fischer & Tangney, Chapter 1; Kitayama, Marcus, & Matsumoto, Chapter 18; Wallbott & Scherer, Chapter 19; and Miyake & Yamazaki, Chapter 20, this volume).

To begin our analysis, we have first specified meaningful domains and contexts in which pride, shame, and guilt are commonly experienced by middle-class white North American children. Then, within each developmental domain and within specified contexts, we have described a series of forms of appraisal for pride, shame, and guilt—ordered in terms of their developmental complexity. Each step of appraisal consists of our prediction of the minimum motive-relevant judgment that must be made in order for the emotion to be experienced in the context specified and at the approximate age described for optimal performance at that step.

Several points are important for interpretation of the sequences, because they are not the same kinds of sequences that are often assumed for developmental analyses, such as that specified by Kohlberg (1969). First, each sequence is meant only to illustrate the types of emotional transformations that can occur for the respective emotion, not to define one universal sequence. Each sequence is only one of many sequences that occur, even in middle-class white North American culture. Different sequences would be expected for different emotional domains, contexts, and cultures (Fajans, 1983; Kitayama et al., Chapter 18, this volume; Lutz, 1988). To illustrate this diversity in pathways, we have specified alternative skills for one step in each of the predicted sequences (steps P5a and P5b for pride, steps S5a and S5b for shame, and steps G3a, G3b, and G3c for guilt in Tables 3.2, 3.3, and 3.4, respectively). Also, within each sequence additional steps can be specified, since there is no one fixed series of steps for any sequence, but a number that varies with domain, context, culture, and affective state.

The proposed sequences are not universal or necessary in the sense that all children should pass through all the steps. To experience any given form of self-evaluative emotion, a child must not only (1) be able to make the requisite judgment or appraisal for that step, based on a given cultural and contextual interpretation; he or she must also (2) be placed in a context like the one specified, and (3) be concerned with the self-evaluative issue in question (Frijda, 1986; Roseman, 1984). Absence of any of these conditions would mean that the specific form of guilt, shame, or pride would not appear. Thus, the sequences reflect developmental orderings of forms of emotion appraisals that we believe occur in Western culture for some children some of the time.

The orderings, therefore, do not form universal stages or structured wholes in Piaget's (1957) and Kohlberg's (1969) sense. Even though there are parallels in formal structures for skill levels across the pride, shame, and guilt sequences, there are no general stages. One cannot generally predict the emergence of shame steps from steps of pride or guilt, or vice versa. Unevenness in the emergence of structurally similar forms of activity in different domains at different times is the rule rather than the exception in cognitive development. Development is uneven, not consistent. This set of limitations is not specific to the sequences we propose, but is characteristic of all sequences of emotional development that go beyond global, diffuse description.

Still, there can be degrees of relation between domains (Fischer & Farrar, 1987), and we expect the specified pride and shame sequences to be more closely related to each other than to the guilt sequence. To highlight this fact, we have made the number and spacing of some steps for the guilt sequence different from those for shame and pride.

From this interpretation of development as a variable web, not a uniform ladder of steps (Bidell & Fischer, 1992), it follows that a specific emotion such as pride, shame, or guilt does not emerge at a single point in development. It is not fruitful to debate about the point at which an emotion first "really" emerges in a child. Psychological skills and functions are not either present or absent; they develop through various forms and occur in various degrees. Treatment of emotions as developing at one point or age will lead to unproductive debates pushing the emergence of an emotion back to ever-younger ages, just as such questionable debates have occurred about knowledge of objects and other cognitive categories (Fischer & Bidell, 1991). Emotions do not emerge fully formed at one age; instead, they develop gradually over extended periods of time, taking increasingly complex forms. One can always identify some form of a given emotion or ability at multiple points in development.

SEQUENCES IN DEVELOPMENT OF
SELF-EVALUATIVE EMOTIONS

Rather than asking, "At what point does pride [shame, guilt] emerge in development?", we prefer to ask, "What *forms* do pride [shame, guilt] take at different steps in development?" In Tables 3.2, 3.3, and 3.4, we propose such sequences for pride, shame, and guilt. The boldface labels for steps in the left-hand column reflect the gradual transition in development of each emotion, such as movement from "joy" to "joy/pride" to "pride." Guilt, shame, and pride are not properties of any one particular stage or point in development, but emotions that take shape gradually along complex developmental pathways (Fischer, 1980; Fischer & Bidell, 1991; Sroufe, 1979). We begin with a detailed discussion of pride as a paradigm case, and then proceed with briefer analyses of shame and guilt.

Development of Pride

In the context we are analyzing, pride involves the appraisal that one is responsible for a socially valued outcome; therefore, changes in pride appraisals involve transformations in children's ability to represent and evaluate their own role in producing valued outcomes. Table 3.2 describes one predicted sequence for development of pride in the domain of performing physical and athletic acts in the presence of a parent or other evaluating authority.

The capacity to experience joy over actions and their outcomes develops through many forms during the first year of life, within the reflex and sensorimotor tiers of development (Fischer & Hogan, 1989). At 4 months of age and earlier, children respond with smiles to the detection of contingencies between their actions and salient outcomes. For example, Watson and Ramey (1972) provided 8-week-old infants with mobiles that moved in reaction to subtle head movements detected by a pressure-sensitive pillow. Within days of exposure to the apparatus, infants not only detected the contingency but also reacted with smiles and other positive social–emotional reactions. According to dynamic skills theory, such reactions already appear at the early level of reflex mappings, where infants of about 8 weeks control simple relations between two or more rudimentary action components (such as slight movement of the head to produce seeing a mobile move in the Watson & Ramey study). Thus, infants react with pleasure to detected action–outcome contingencies very early in development.

Our focus in Table 3.2 begins with the sensorimotor tier, where babies build actions that approach the complexity of many adult actions and express pleasure in reaction to increasingly complex action–outcome contingencies. Beginning at about 4 months, children are capable of single flexible sensorimotor actions, which arise from relations of two or more reflex

TABLE 3.2. Development of Appraisal Skills for Pride

Step	Appraisal skill	Skill structure[a]			Example context	Age of emergence[b]
		Sensorimotor actions	Representations	Abstractions		
		Level SM2: Sensorimotor mappings				
P1	Joy about simple action–outcome contingency: Child connects simple act with goal-related positive outcome.	$\begin{bmatrix} \text{ACT—} & \text{ACT—} & \text{GOAL+} \\ \text{GRASP} & \text{LET GO} & \text{SEE DROP} \end{bmatrix}$			An infant grasps a block and then drops it, coordinating hand movements with looking to achieve and enjoy the goal of seeing the block drop to the floor.	7–8 months
		Level SM3: Sensorimotor systems				
P2	Joy about complex action–outcome contingency including other's evaluation: Child connects action(s) with several goal-related positive outcomes, including other's reactions.	$\begin{bmatrix} \text{GRASP} & \text{LET GO} & \text{SEEN} \\ \text{ACT} & \leftrightarrow \text{GOAL+} & \leftrightarrow \text{PARENT+} \\ \text{MOVE ARM} & \text{SEE BLOCK FLY} & \text{HEARD} \end{bmatrix}$			An infant throws a block, coordinating arm/hand movements to achieve and enjoy the goals of seeing the block fly through the air and seeing and hearing Dad's positive reaction.	11–13 months

Level SM4/RP1: Systems of sensorimotor systems, which are single representations

P3	**Joy/pride about result caused by self:** Child carries out an action with goal-related positive results and attributes the result to the self.	$$\begin{bmatrix} \text{GRASP} & \text{LET GO} & \text{SEEN} \\ \text{ACT} & \leftrightarrow \text{GOAL}+ & \leftrightarrow \text{PARENT}+ & \text{HEARD} \\ \text{MOVE ARM} & \text{SEE BALL FLY} \\ & \Longleftrightarrow \\ \text{OWN BODY} & \text{"I"} \\ \text{SEE} & \leftrightarrow \text{SAY} \leftrightarrow \text{HEAR} \\ & \text{"ACT"} & \text{"ACT"} \end{bmatrix} \equiv \begin{bmatrix} SELF \\ RESULT+ \end{bmatrix}$$	A child throws a ball and says joyfully or pridefully to his or her pleased Mom something indicating that he or she did the throwing, such as "I throw," "Me throw," or "Robin [child's name] throw."[c]	18–24 months
P4	**Pride about result caused by self performing well:** Child carries out an action with goal-related positive results that are evaluated as special, attributes the result to the self, and labels it as good.	$$\begin{bmatrix} \text{GRASP} & \text{LET GO} & \text{SEEN} \\ \text{ACT} & \leftrightarrow \text{GOAL}+ & \leftrightarrow \text{PARENT}+ & \text{HEARD} \\ \text{MOVE ARM} & \text{SEE BALL FLY} \\ & \Longleftrightarrow \\ \text{OWN BODY} & \text{"I"} \\ \text{SEE ACT} \leftrightarrow \text{SAY "ACT"} \leftrightarrow \text{HEAR "ACT"} \\ \text{OUTCOME} & \text{"GOOD"} & \text{"GOOD"} \end{bmatrix} \equiv \begin{bmatrix} SELF \\ GOOD \end{bmatrix}$$	A child throws a ball, sees and hears it go far (or bounce high, or some other valued outcome), and says proudly to his or her pleased parent something indicating that he or she has thrown it well, such as "Throw ball far" or "I throw good."[c]	2–3 years

(continued)

TABLE 3.2. *cont.*

		Skill structure[a]				Age of emergence[b]
Step	Appraisal skill	Sensorimotor actions	Representations	Abstractions	Example context	
		Level RP2: Representational mappings				
P5a	**Pride about comparative performance:** Child judges his or her performance in some valued area as better than another person's.		$\left[\begin{array}{c} SELF \ - \ OTHER \\ \scriptstyle RESULT + \quad RESULT - \end{array}\right]$		A child throws a softball farther than another child and indicates proudly, "I can throw far and [the other child] can't," "I can throw farther than [the other child]," or something similar.	4–5 years
P5b	**Pride about valued trait:** Child compares his or her performance across several situations A and B, and judges them to show that he or she has a valued trait.		$\left[\begin{array}{c} \scriptstyle TRAIT + \\ SELF \ - \ SELF \\ \scriptstyle GOOD \ AT \ A \quad GOOD \ AT \ B \end{array}\right]$		A child throws well playing softball with big brother, and also throws well playing beachball with Mom. The child concludes with pride that he or she has a characteristic of being good at throwing balls.	4–5 years

76

RP3: Representational systems

P6 Pride about comparative concrete trait: Child judges his or her performance in several areas to be better than someone else's, and generalizes to conclude that he or she has more of a valued concrete trait.

$$\begin{bmatrix} \text{GENERAL TRAIT} \\ \textit{GOOD at A} \quad \textit{NOT GOOD at A} \\ \textit{SELF} \leftrightarrow \textit{OTHER} \\ \textit{GOOD at B} \quad \textit{NOT GOOD at B} \end{bmatrix}$$

A child performs better than some other children in both throwing and running. He or she generalizes over these acts to infer a general concrete trait (concrete generalization) that he or she is proud of: "I am good at sports, but my friend is not," or something similar.

6–8 years

Level RP4/AB1: Systems of representational systems, which are single abstractions

P7 Pride about general personality characteristic: Young person judges himself or herself to have more of two or more valued concrete traits than someone else, and generalizes these differences to characterize his or her personality as having a valued general characteristic that subsumes the traits.

$$\begin{bmatrix} \text{TRAIT X} \\ \textit{GOOD at A} \quad \textit{NOT GOOD at A} \\ \textit{SELF} \leftrightarrow \textit{OTHER} \\ \textit{GOOD at B} \quad \textit{NOT GOOD at B} \\ \Longleftrightarrow \\ \text{TRAIT Y} \\ \textit{GOOD at C} \quad \textit{NOT GOOD at C} \\ \textit{SELF} \leftrightarrow \textit{OTHER} \\ \textit{GOOD at D} \quad \textit{NOT GOOD at D} \end{bmatrix} \equiv \begin{bmatrix} \text{SELF-} \\ \text{IDENTITY} \\ \text{COMPETENT} \end{bmatrix}$$

A youth judges himself or herself to be not only good at sports (as in the preceding step), but also smart (based on good grades in school). He or she generalizes across these two traits to attribute a general personality characteristic he or she is proud of, such as "I am a competent person," "I am more competent than my friend," or something similar.

10–12 years

(continued)

77

TABLE 3.2. cont.

		Skill structure[a]				Age of emergence[b]
Step	Appraisal skill	Sensorimotor actions	Representations	Abstractions	Example context	

Level AB2: Abstract mappings

P8	**Pride about general characteristic of other person with an identity related to one's own:** Person judges other person of an identity similar to his or her own to have much of a desirable general characteristic, and relates own identity to the person's characteristic.			⎡ OTHER-IDENTITY — COMPETENT ⎤ ⎣ SELF-IDENTITY — RACIAL ⎦	A person judges someone else to be especially competent at something important, such as singing at a national event, and because of a similarity in racial/ethnic identity with that singer, the person is proud. He or she says something like, "I've never had such pride in seeing this [name of my race] woman stand up there with this great royal dignity and sing," linking her performance to his or her own identity as a person of that race, an American, or the like.	14–17 years

Note. In skill structures, each word or phrase denotes a skill component, with each large word or phrase designating a main component (set) and each adjacent smaller word or phrase designating a further specification or subset of the main component. Words in boldface designate sensorimotor actions; words in italics designate representations; and words in plain letters designate abstractions. Lines connecting sets designate relations forming a mapping; single-line arrows designate relations forming a system; and double-line arrows designate relations forming a system of systems. Step numbers indicate the developmental sequence when skills at each step are in the same domain. Steps with the same number and a letter following (such as 5a and 5b) are approximately parallel in skill structure.

[a]Sensorimotor components are specific actions and perceptions, and in most skill analyses the diagrams indicate those specific actions and perceptions. Here we have modified the diagrams so that the component names specify general categories, such as **act**, **goal**, and **parent**. Our purpose is to highlight a type of component that children often control in skills involving pride. The actual skills involve not broad categorical competences, but particular acts, goals, and people. For example, acts can include throwing a block, stacking a block, drinking from a cup, or saying "Hi." Goals can involve other actions that a child seeks to achieve, such as seeing a stack of blocks, swallowing milk, or getting a parent to greet the child. Parent can be father, mother, or some other caregiver.

Representational skill components are typically more general than sensorimotor, representing a class of activities/perceptions. Nevertheless, words such as *self, other, result,* and *good* were chosen to specify general categories for types of skills, not particular skills. There is no single general skill structure for self, other, result, or good that is the same across all relevant skills; instead, there are diverse skills that change with context, goal, and affective state (Fischer, 1980).

Representational skills eventually combine to form abstractions, which in this table are involved in the last two steps. Here the skill components are more general and intangible than actions or representations, but still they are closely tied to specific contexts, goals, and affective states.

[b]Ages of emergence specify modal times at which a level first appears, based on research with middle-class North American or European children. They may differ across cultures and other social groups.

[c]According to the skill analysis of speech, the development of simple sentences describing situations or actions involves coordination of vocalization and listening to produce words, and then coordination of words to produce a multiword utterance, as described by Fischer and Corrigan (1981).

systems (e.g., opening the hand and extending the arm toward a seen ball). At this level, children respond with pleasure to controlled actions that result in an effect on their physical or social environs. Illustrations include Piaget's (1936/1952) descriptions of circular reactions, in which his infant children reacted with pleasure when their actions produced novel or interesting effects. Sensorimotor mappings, which begin to occur at about 7–8 months, involve the coordination of two or more sensorimotor actions. Step P1 (joy about simple action–outcome contingency in Table 3.2) involves a sensori-motor mapping—the coordination of grasping an object, dropping it by letting go, and watching it drop. At about 7 months of age, infants begin to acquire the capacity to smile at being a cause of a response in another person, such as pulling a cloth out of the mother's mouth (Sroufe, 1979). Such smiles are made possible by sensorimotor mappings, which involve coordinations between sensorimotor acts such as pulling a cloth and seeing it pop out of Mom's mouth.

Beginning at about 11–13 months of age, children construct sensorimotor systems, which involve the coordination of two or more sensorimotor mappings. Children respond with pleasure to these integrations of mappings. In step P2 (joy about complex action–outcome contingency including other's evaluation), infants throw a block by coordinating a series of actions: They grasp an object, move their arm with the object, let go as they move the arm, see the block fly through the air, and look up to see Mom smile and to hear her make an exclamation ("Wow!"). The parent's reaction is an important part of this precursor of pride.

For his first birthday, Seth Kanner-Mascolo received a fire truck equipped with a siren-producing button, and he developed a joy/pride skill similar to step P2. After Seth learned to push the button, his parents praised him with smiles and excited vocalizations. Soon thereafter, he developed a routine in which he would press the button to hear the siren and then smile as he looked up and saw Mom's or Dad's positive reaction. This routine involved a sensorimotor system coordinating pressing the button and hearing the siren with looking and hearing his parents' excited reactions. We refer to children's reactions at this level as "joy" rather than "pride," but they are early positive reactions to self-caused effects and may be seen as early steps in the genesis of pride.

Step P3 (joy/pride about result caused by self) marks the transition from the sensorimotor to the representational tier of development at the end of the second year of life. Although at steps P1 and P2 a child detects contingencies between actions and their effects, he or she does not attribute those actions to himself or herself. At step P3, a child forms a representation of the self as the agent who has produced an outcome. This advance is made possible by the development of self-representation, as reflected, for example, in evidence of advanced self-recognition in a mirror (Bertenthal & Fischer, 1978; M. Lewis & Brooks-Gunn, 1979). Several findings support this proposition. In block play, beginning at about 18 months of age, children have been reported to stop and notice or "respect" their structures (Hetzer, 1931, cited in H. Heckhausen, 1981). Such reactions seem to imply that at about 18 months, toddlers begin to focus on the result per se rather than on the action–outcome contingency (H. Heckhausen, 1987). In a longitudinal study of block play and shape sorting, children stopped and noticed the outcome of their efforts from as early as 14 months of age, and occasionally they smiled at producing the outcome (J. Heckhausen, 1988). Mastery smiles (smiles in the context of successful goal-directed activity) also seem to increase in frequency between 20 and 24 months; this is also the time period when children show distress at being unable to imitate a model's action, which Kagan (1981) interprets as evidence of self-awareness and we interpret as an early step in development of the self-evaluative emotion of shame.

Step P4 (pride about result caused by self performing well) involves an early version of something akin to pride about competence. At step P3, a child attributes an outcome to the self according to simple standards, such as throwing a block or finishing a tower, but does not relate the outcome to his or her competence (Bullock & Lutkenhaus, 1988; H. Heckhausen, 1984, 1987). At step P4, beginning at about the middle of the third year of life, children attribute an outcome to their own competence. They understand not only that they have caused an outcome, but also that the outcome is socially valued and thus enhances their sense of self as worthy or good. Thus, at step P3 children make an appraisal such as "I threw the ball" or "I finished the tower," but at step P4 they make an appraisal such as "I threw the ball far" or "I built a good tower."

There is little evidence relevant to distinguishing steps P3 and P4. Children exhibit self-awareness and isolated components of pride in achievement situations by 20–24 months, the approximate age of emergence of step P3 (Stipek et al., 1992; J. Heckhausen, 1988). They often show one of the following expressive behaviors for pride: show erect posture, smile, direct eyes at parents, point at outcome, applaud, or give positive verbal self-evaluations. More full-blown pride, involving three or more of these pride components, has not been observed until 2½ to 3 years of age, when step P4 appears (Halish & Halish, 1980, cited in H. Heckhausen, 1984; M. Lewis, Alessandri, & Sullivan, 1992; Stipek et al., 1992).

Indirect evidence supporting a distinction between steps P3 and P4 comes from a small study on the development of "wanting to do it oneself" (Geppert & Kuster, 1983), which can be taken as indicating a concern with the self's competence. The investigators attempted to elicit "wanting to do it oneself" by giving unsolicited help to 9- to 78-month-olds as they attempted various tasks. They also measured self-representations through both the traditional rouge test of face recognition (Bertenthal & Fischer, 1978; M. Lewis & Brooks-Gunn, 1979) and a blanket task, in which each child was placed on a blanket and asked to give it to the mother. To show self-representation in the blanket task, children had to get off the blanket before yielding it. Results indicated that children who failed the self-assessments accepted adult interventions without protest. Those who passed the self-assessments were more likely to resist adult intervention, especially if they passed both tasks. Older, more verbal children (beyond 30 months) made explicit statements such as "I can do it alone" and attempted to stop adults from completing the task.

Steps P5a and P5b mark the onset of children's ability to construct representational mappings, which begin to emerge at about $3^{1}/_{2}$ to 4 years of age in supportive contexts. At step P5a (pride about comparative performance), children compare their performance in a simple physical task such as throwing, jumping, or tower building with that of another child. For example, after winning at a competitive task, a child makes an appraisal such as "I can throw far but Jaime can't." This skill requires that children represent the relationship between their performance on a given act and another child's performance, which involves a mapping, as shown in Table 3.2.

Research evidence shows the emergence of strong pride (and shame) reactions by $3^{1}/_{2}$ to 4 years in competitive situations of this sort. In one series of studies, children competed with an experimenter in a ring-stacking task, in which the experimenter controlled who won by modifying the speed with which she performed in competition with each child (H. Heckhausen, 1981, 1984, 1987). A minority of $2^{1}/_{2}$-year-olds, but almost all $3^{1}/_{2}$-year-olds, responded with pride after winning and shame after losing. Pride and shame reactions were a function of whether children understood who won (who finished first) (Halish and Halish, 1980, cited in H. Heckhausen, 1984). In another study, children performed a competitive ball-stacking task (Stipek et al., 1992). By $2^{1}/_{2}$ to 3 years, children smiled more when they won, but not until $3^{1}/_{2}$ years did they show appreciation of the competitive aspect of the task by pausing, slowing down, or stopping after the winner finished his or her tower. H. Heckhausen (1984) asserts that children begin to exhibit pride about competition between 3 and $3^{1}/_{2}$ years (see also Lutkenhaus, Grossmann, & Grossmann, 1985).

In addition to pride about competitive success, children can use mappings to feel proud about good performance independent of competition, as in step P5b (pride about valued trait), which develops approximately parallel to step P5a. For example, children can compare how well they throw balls in several different games and conclude that they are good at throwing balls. The mapping for this appraisal involves relating the quality of ball throwing in two or more games. Note that the skills in steps P5a and P5b are in separate domains and probably develop mostly independently. Because skills are constructed in context, two skills that involve representational mappings in different contexts are typically independent, even though they use the same general type of skill structure. To develop in synchrony, they must be coordinated together and generalized (Fischer & Farrar, 1987).

At step P6 (pride about comparative concrete trait), children move to a more complex comparison of competences, using a representational system to compare their performance with those of their friends in several areas; thus they combine steps P5a and P5b and generalize beyond them (regarding social comparison, see Butler, 1989; Ruble, 1983; Veroff, 1969). At 6 to 8 years, a child begins to relate several ways that he or she performs better than another child, and so constructs a generalization in terms of a broad comparative concrete trait: He or she not only can throw better than the friend, but also can run better in several situations, and so he or she is good at sports while the friend is not. Comparisons are also possible in which a child sees himself or herself as similar to a number of other children who are good at sports, so that the skill is based more in identification and similarity than in competition and difference.

Step P7 (pride about general personality characteristic) marks development of a more abstract, intangible kind of personality characteristic through construction of single abstractions by coordination of two or more representational systems. For example, in a competitive framework, a female student 10 to 12 years of age or older concludes that she is better at sports than her friends (as in step P6). In addition, she gets better grades than her friends in mathematics and English, and she concludes that she is more competent or intelligent than others. To integrate these two concrete traits, she constructs an identity-related abstraction, such as "I am a competent person." General abstractions can also be constructed from identifying with the admired traits of others, as a person integrates identificatory comparisons based on similarity to produce a different sense of competence to be proud of. A person is competent because he or she is like other competent people.

With step P8 (pride about general characteristic of other person with an identity related to one's own), adolescents and adults develop the sort of affective skill shown by Todd Duncan as quoted at the beginning of this chapter, describing how proud he was of singer Marian Anderson performing at the Lincoln Memorial after having been denied a performance at Constitution Hall. Through an abstract mapping connecting two general identity characteristics, they relate strongly to a stranger's special achievement, experiencing strong pride almost as if the achievement were their own. For Duncan, the mapping related Anderson's competence as a singer to their joint African-American racial identity. Of course, children at a young age can experience pride in someone else's achievement, as when a 4-year-old boy is proud of his mother's singing. But in Todd Duncan's case, the appraisal leading to the emotion involved a much more distant connection between self and other that was mediated by an identity linked to a sense of history, race, U.S. society, and personal meaning. Of course, comparisons based on competition between identities are also possible.

Step P8 is not the end of development of appraisals for pride. Development goes on beyond abstract mappings to more complex relations of abstractions. Todd Duncan may in fact have been using an appraisal more complex than the mapping of competence and racial identities in Table 3.2, since he seemed to be relating multiple aspects of his identity—including not only competence and race, but also being an American and dealing with issues of discrimination and equality. For the purposes of this chapter, however, we will not describe these later developments. See Fischer (1980) and Fischer et al. (1990) for descriptions of them.

Analyses of high-level abstract appraisals sometimes sound as if the appraisals involve long, effortful cognitive processing. Indeed, the construction of the ways of thinking and feeling at the foundation of the appraisals does take long and effortful development, but in emotional experiences like Todd Duncan's the appraisals have become automatic and nearly instantaneous. Appraisals at high steps of development integrate multiple sources of information, but the skills are used in the normal, fast-paced flow of human experience. An abstract judgment such as "I am a competent person" occurs quickly and generates immediate emotional experiences, even though the skills behind the judgment are complex and have required many years to develop.

Development of Shame

The developmental sequence that we have postulated for shame is parallel to the sequence for pride, as can be seen in Tables 3.2 and 3.3. Just as pride develops from general positive emotions such as joy, shame develops from general negative ones such as distress. Crying at lack of success of basic actions such as sucking seems to be present soon after birth. By 2 to 4 months of age, children exhibit angry facial or vocal expressions and other signs of distress to failure to achieve goals, and these reactions increase in intensity throughout infancy (H. Heckhausen, 1984, 1987; M. Lewis, Alessandri, & Sullivan, 1990; Sroufe, 1979; Stenberg & Campos, 1991). Infants who do not successfully obtain a goal often change to a more obtainable goal, and a few studies have found no postural signs of shame in early development (J. Heckhausen, 1988; Stipek et al., 1992).

Besides negative emotions, social referencing is also related to shame (and pride): Babies show distress to caregivers' negative reactions to the babies' behavior, as eventually they will show shame to some negative reactions of caregivers. Social referencing is strong and clear by 8 months of age, and may well be present in simple forms much earlier (Campos, Barrett, Lamb, Goldsmith, & Stenberg, 1983; Stern, 1985). Shame has a strong social referencing component (as do all self-evaluative emotions).

In Table 3.3, the first two steps of shame are approximately parallel to the first two steps of pride in Table 3.2. They are early developments or precursors of shame, in which children show distress about failures of outcomes that they have tried to produce through sensorimotor actions. Step S1 (distress over simple action–outcome failure) involves simple distress over failure, and step S2 (distress over complex action–outcome failure including other's evaluation) involves a more complex contingency including a caregiver as an important part of the skill. The caregiver reacts with disappointment or some other negative reaction to the child's failure.

With step S3 (distress/shame about result caused by self), a distinction between distress and shame begins to become detectable. In the context of an evaluating caregiver such as a parent, a child represents himself or herself as having failed to achieve an outcome, with the result of disappointment in the caregiver. Construction of this kind of skill relates closely to development of representation of self toward the end of the second year (Pipp et al., 1987), but added to the representation of self as ineffective agent is an interpersonal shame component of anticipation of negative evaluation from a caregiver.

At step S4 (shame about result caused by self performing poorly), the development of shame takes another significant step as children move beyond attribution of failure to attribution of lack of competence in the self. In this way, beginning at approximately 2½ to 3 years of age, failure at a task (such as throwing a ball) sometimes leads not only to a conclusion that "Mommy doesn't like what I did," but also to the further conclusion that "To Mommy (and to myself) I'm bad at throwing."

Evidence supporting the distinction between steps S3 and S4 is sparse and similar to that described for pride. Even though beginning at about 24 months children exhibit isolated shame components upon failure, a clear constellation of shame indicators has not been reported until later in development. In a study on emotional reactions to success and failure in 2- to 5-year-olds, 2-year-olds often showed one shame-like expressive behavior in reaction to failures in cup stacking or puzzle solving in the presence of an experimenter (Stipek et al., 1992). Expressive behaviors for shame included the following: avert gaze, show avoidant posture (look down, turn away), and show closed posture (body collapses, shoulders are hunched, hands under table, arms/hands in front of face or body). On the other hand, children have not been found to show a cluster of three or more of these shame behaviors until 2½ to 3 years of age, the same approximate age at which a cluster of pride reactions first appears consistently (H. Heckhausen, 1984; M. Lewis et al., 1992).

Shame based on comparisons begins to appear in high-support contexts with the onset of representational mappings at about 3½ to 4 years of age. At step S5a (shame about comparative performance), a child in a competitive context compares his or her performance on a task with that of another child, and concludes that he or she is less able to perform the task than the other child. In the studies of ring-stacking competition, shame reactions occurred in 3- to 3½-year-olds who lost the game (Halish & Halish, 1980, cited in H. Heckhausen, 1984; Lutkenhaus et al., 1985). In ball-stacking competition, only at 3½ to 4 years did losing children exhibit shame components, cease to ignore the competitor, and slow their work pace after losing (Stipek et al., 1992). Our skill analysis also predicts that shame about a valued trait (poor performance across several situations)

TABLE 3.3. Development of Appraisal Skills for Shame

Step	Appraisal skill	Skill structure[a]			Example context	Age of emergence[b]
		Sensorimotor actions	Representations	Abstractions		

Level SM2: Sensorimotor mappings

Step	Appraisal skill	Skill structure[a]	Example context	Age of emergence[b]
S1	**Distress about simple action–outcome failure:** Child connects simple act with goal-related outcome but fails to attain the outcome.	$\begin{bmatrix} \text{ACT–} & \text{ACT–} & \text{GOAL–} \\ \text{GRASP} & \text{LET GO} & \text{SEE NOT DROP} \end{bmatrix}$	An infant grasps a block and then tries to drop it, coordinating hand movements with looking, but he or she fails and becomes distressed in his or her attempts to grasp and let go of the block to make it drop.	7–8 months

Level SM3: Sensorimotor systems

| S2 | **Distress about complex action–outcome failure including other's evaluation:** Child connects action(s) with several goal-related negative outcomes, including other's reactions. | $\begin{bmatrix} \text{GRASP} & \text{LET GO} & \text{SEEN} \\ \text{ACT} \leftrightarrow & \text{GOAL–} \leftrightarrow & \text{PARENT–} \\ \text{MOVE ARM} & \text{SEE NOT FLY} & \text{HEARD} \end{bmatrix}$ | An infant tries to throw a block, coordinating arm/hand movements with looking, but he or she fails and becomes distressed in trying to get the block to fly through the air, and also in seeing and hearing Dad's disappointed reaction. | 11–13 months |

Level SM4/RP1: Systems of sensorimotor systems, which are single representations

S3	**Distress/shame about result caused by self:** Child carries out an action with goal-related negative results involving both the action and another's reaction, and he or she attributes the result to the self.	$$\left[\begin{array}{c}\text{GRASP} \quad\quad \text{LET GO} \quad\quad\quad \text{SEEN} \\ \text{ACT} \leftrightarrow \text{GOAL–} \leftrightarrow \text{PARENT–} \\ \text{MOVE ARM} \quad \text{SEE NOT FLY} \quad \text{HEARD} \\ \Longleftrightarrow \\ \text{OWN BODY} \quad\quad\quad \text{"I"} \\ \text{SEE} \leftrightarrow \text{SAY} \leftrightarrow \text{HEAR} \\ \text{ACT} \quad\quad \text{"ACT"} \quad\quad \text{"ACT"}\end{array}\right] \equiv \left[\begin{array}{c}\text{SELF} \\ \text{RESULT–}\end{array}\right]$$	A child tries to throw a ball but fails and becomes distressed or ashamed, indicating to his or her disappointed Mom that he or she failed, such as "No throw," "Me oops," or "Robin [child's name] no throw."[c]	18–24 months
S4	**Shame about result caused by self performing poorly:** Child carries out an action with goal-related negative results that are evaluated as faulty, attributes the result to the self, and labels it as bad or poor.	$$\left[\begin{array}{c}\text{GRASP} \quad\quad \text{LET GO} \quad\quad\quad \text{SEEN} \\ \text{ACT} \leftrightarrow \text{GOAL–} \leftrightarrow \text{PARENT–} \\ \text{MOVE ARM} \quad \text{SEE NOT FLY} \quad \text{HEARD} \\ \Longleftrightarrow \\ \text{OWN BODY} \quad\quad\quad\quad \text{"I"} \\ \text{SEE ACT} \leftrightarrow \text{SAY "ACT"} \leftrightarrow \text{HEAR "ACT"} \\ \text{OUTCOME} \quad\quad \text{"BAD"} \quad\quad\quad\quad \text{"BAD"}\end{array}\right] \equiv \left[\begin{array}{c}\text{SELF} \\ \text{BAD}\end{array}\right]$$	A child throws a ball, sees and hears it not go far (or not bounce, or fail to show some other valued outcome), and says shamefully to his or her disappointed parent something indicating that he or she has thrown it poorly, such as "Throw ball bad" or "I throw poor."[c]	2–3 years

(continued)

87

TABLE 3.3. *cont.*

Step	Appraisal skill	Skill structure[a]			Example context	Age of emergence[b]
		Sensorimotor actions	Representations	Abstractions		
			Level RP2: Representational mappings			
S5a	**Shame about comparative performance:** Child judges his or her performance in some valued area as poorer than another person's.		$\left[\begin{array}{c} SELF - OTHER \\ \scriptstyle RESULT- \quad RESULT+ \end{array}\right]$		A child throws a softball less far than another child and indicates with shame, "I can't throw far but [the other child] can," "[The other child] can throw farther than me," or something similar.	4–5 years
S5b	**Shame about valued trait:** Child compares his or her performance across several situations *A* and *B*, and judges them to show that he or she lacks a valued trait.		$\left[\begin{array}{c} \scriptstyle TRAIT- \\ SELF - SELF \\ \scriptstyle POOR \; at \; A \quad POOR \; at \; B \end{array}\right]$		A child throws a softball poorly with big brother, and also throws a beach-ball poorly with Mom. The child concludes with shame that he or she has a characteristic of being bad at throwing balls.	4–5 years

Level RP3: Representational systems

S6

Shame about comparative concrete trait: Child judges his or her performance in several areas to be poorer than someone else's, and generalizes to conclude that he or she has less of a valued concrete trait.

$$\begin{bmatrix} & \text{GENERAL TRAIT} & \\ POOR\ at\ A & & GOOD\ at\ A \\ SELF & \leftrightarrow & OTHER \\ POOR\ at\ B & & GOOD\ at\ B \end{bmatrix}$$

A child performs worse than some other children in both throwing and running. He or she generalizes over these acts to infer a general concrete trait (concrete generalization) that he or she is ashamed of: "I am bad at sports, but my friend is good," or something similar.

6–8 years

Level RP4/AB1: Systems of representational systems, which are single abstractions

S7

Shame about general personality characteristic: Young person judges himself or herself to have less of two or more valued concrete traits than someone else, and generalizes these differences to characterize his or her personality as having a de-valued general characteristic that subsumes the traits.

$$\begin{bmatrix} & \text{TRAIT X} & \\ POOR\ at\ A & & GOOD\ at\ A \\ SELF & \leftrightarrow & OTHER \\ POOR\ at\ B & & GOOD\ at\ B \\ & \Downarrow & \\ & \text{TRAIT Y} & \\ POOR\ at\ C & & GOOD\ at\ C \\ SELF & \leftrightarrow & OTHER \\ POOR\ at\ D & & GOOD\ at\ D \end{bmatrix} \equiv \begin{bmatrix} \text{SELF-} \\ \text{IDENTITY} \\ \text{INCOMPETENT} \end{bmatrix}$$

A youth judges himself or herself to be not only poor at sports (as in the preceding step), but also stupid (based on poor grades in school). He or she generalizes across these two traits to attribute a general personality characteristic that he or she is ashamed of, such as "I am an incompetent person," "I am less competent than my friend," or something similar.

10–12 years

(continued)

TABLE 3.3. cont.

		Skill structure[a]			
Step	Appraisal skill	Sensorimotor actions	Representations	Abstractions	Example context	Age of emergence[b]

Level A2: Abstract mappings

Step	Appraisal skill	Abstractions	Example context	Age of emergence[b]
S8	**Shame about general characteristic of other person with an identity related to one's own:** Person judges other person of an identity similar to his or her own to have an undesirable general characteristic and relates own identity to that person's characteristic.	$\begin{bmatrix} \text{OTHER-} \\ \text{IDENTITY} \\ [\text{INCOMPETENT}] \end{bmatrix} — \begin{bmatrix} \text{SELF-} \\ \text{IDENTITY} \\ [\text{RACIAL}] \end{bmatrix}$	A person judges someone else to be especially incompetent at something important, such as singing at a national event, and because of a similarity in racial/ethnic identity with that singer, the person is ashamed. He or she says something like, "I've never felt such shame at seeing this [name of my race] woman stand up there and put on such a disgusting performance," linking her performance to his or her own identity as a person of that race, an American, or the like.	14–17 years

90

Note. In skill structures, each word or phrase denotes a skill component, with each large word or phrase designating a main component (set) and each adjacent smaller word or phrase designating a further specification or subset of the main component. Words in boldface designate sensorimotor actions; words in italics designate representations; and words in plain letters designate abstractions. Lines connecting sets designate relations forming a mapping; single-line arrows designate relations forming a system; and double-line arrows designate relations forming a system of systems. Step numbers indicate the developmental sequence when skills at each step are in the same domain.

[a] Sensorimotor components are specific actions and perceptions, and in most skill analyses the diagrams indicate those specific actions and perceptions. Here we have modified the diagrams so that the component names specify general categories, such as **act, goal,** and **parent.** Our purpose is to highlight a type of component that children often control in skills involving shame. The actual skills involve not broad categorical competences, but particular acts, goals, and people. For example, acts can include throwing a block, stacking a block, drinking from a cup, or saying "Hi." Goals can involve other actions that a child seeks to achieve, such as seeing a stack of blocks, swallowing milk, or getting a parent to greet the child. Parent can be father, mother, or some other caregiver.

Representational skill components are typically more general than sensorimotor, representing a class of activities/perceptions. Nevertheless, words such as *self, other, result,* and *good* have been chosen to specify general categories for types of skills, not particular skills. There is no single general skill structure for self, other, result, or good that is the same across all relevant skills; instead, there are diverse skills that change with context, goal, and affective state (Fischer, 1980).

Representational skills eventually combine to form abstractions, which in this table are involved in the last two steps. Here the skill components are more general and intangible than actions or representations, but still they are closely tied to specific contexts, goals, and affective states.

[b] Ages of emergence specify modal times at which a level first appears, based on research with middle-class North American or European children. They may differ across cultures and other social groups.

[c] According to the skill analysis of speech, the development of simple sentences describing situations or actions involves coordination of vocalization and listening to produce words, and then coordination of words to produce a multiword utterance, as described by Fischer and Corrigan (1981).

will appear at approximately the same age, as shown for step S5b in Table 3.3.

Steps S6 through S8 are similar to the parallel steps for pride, with increasingly differentiated and integrated representations of the self's skills and traits relative to others. At step S6 (shame about comparative concrete trait), children as young as 6 to 8 years use representational systems in the context of an evaluating other, comparing their inferior performance to another child's in two athletic domains and concluding that they are poor at sports while the other child is good at sports. At step S7 (shame about general personality characteristic), using single abstractions, a youth 10 to 12 years of age or older coordinates step S6 concrete traits from two domains (such as sports and school) to construct an abstraction of an inferior general personality characteristic. This characteristic is a cause for shame: "I am an incompetent person." Step 8 (shame about general characteristic of other person with an identity related to one's own) involves abstract mappings relating someone else's incompetent identity to one's own identity because of some racial, ethnic, or cultural similarity. One experiences powerful shame even though the other person has shown the shameful behavior. This step is similar to Todd Duncan's pride reaction, but it involves shame instead. (Note that the qualifications about interpreting specific steps of pride apply to shame and guilt as well. For example, several different kinds of appraisals can produce emotions for each step in developmental complexity.)

Development of Interpersonal Guilt

Guilt experiences involve the appraisal that one is responsible for a wrongdoing. The focus in our analysis is on interpersonal guilt, which involves feelings of concern or remorse about hurting others. The steps in the sequence describe increasingly complex ways of being responsible for distress in others. Interpersonal guilt seems to have its origins in empathy or feelings of concern about distress in others. From very early in infancy, children are responsive to emotions in others; and by the second year of life, it is common for children to become obviously concerned at others' distress and to respond prosocially (Hoffman, 1983; Stern, 1985; Zahn-Waxler & Radke-Yarrow, 1982).

The analysis in Table 3.4, which describes a sample pathway of guilt about hurting a playmate, draws heavily upon Martin Hoffman's (1982, 1983) ground-breaking work on the developmental course of empathy and interpersonal guilt. Step G1 in the guilt sequence (distress about other's upset produced by simple action–outcome contingency) occurs within the sensorimotor tier of development, as infants as young as 7 to 8 months of age connect their own aggressive actions to upset in the person whom they hurt. At step G2 (distress about other's upset produced by complex action–outcome contingency), babies as young as 11 to 13 months make the same kind of connection of their own aggression with another child's distress, but the interactions and contingencies are more complex.

Separation of guilt from distress begins to become detectable with steps G3a, G3b, and G3c, which are alternative forms of attributing another's upset to one's own action. For all three forms at this step, the 2-year-old's distress/guilt reaction of "I hurt you" is mediated by the physical presence of an overtly distressed other. At step G3a (distress/guilt about other's upset caused by self's aggressive action), a child represents himself or herself as responsible for hurting another through an aggressive act such as hitting. Step G3b (distress/guilt about other's upset caused by self's negative statement) involves hurting another through a negative statement, such as "Your tower is ugly." Step G3c (distress/guilt about other's upset caused by self's refusal to act positively) involves hurting another through a refusal to react positively to a request. In many tasks that fit these general descriptions, step G3a will develop earliest, step G3b a little later, and step G3c the latest, because the response to other becomes potentially more complex in the successive steps—from hitting to criticizing to denying a request. However, very simple versions of each category are possible, with resulting early development late in the second year, as illustrated in the examples in Table 3.4.

The emergence of guilt-like behavior at the end of the second year is supported by a growing literature (Barrett et al., 1993; P. Cole, Barrett, & Zahn-Waxler, 1992; Emde et al., 1987; Zahn-Waxler & Radke-Yarrow, 1982). For example, when children themselves were the cause of another's distress in natural situations in the family, the number of prosocial reparative behaviors increased sharply between 19 and 24 months of age (Zahn-Waxler, Radke-Yarrow, Wagner, & Chapman, 1992). At 24 months, the children's reparative behavior was also correlated with various other self-related aspects of their behavior: empathic concern ($r = .58$), self-ref-erential behavior ($r = .43$), and level of self recognition ($r = .41$). Some young children even apologized after they hurt others (Zahn-Waxler & Kochanska, 1990): After accidentally hitting the babysitter, a precocious $1^1/2$-year-old said, "Sorry, Sally," kissed the babysitter, and patted her forehead. A 2-year-old who pulled her cousin's hair and was reprimanded by her mother kissed the cousin and said, "I hurt your hair. Please don't cry." These data suggest that as early as 2 years of age, reparative behavior following self-caused distress in others often has an empathic and self-ref-erential quality indicative of a guilt-like state.

At step G4 (guilt about failure to reciprocate), children begin to construct a more elaborate representation of the other, including the demands of social reciprocity. Representational mappings, which begin to appear at $3^1/2$ to 4 years, give children the potential to control relations between what another child does and what this implies that the self should do, and so a child may experience guilt about failure to reciprocate. For example, a playmate shares some of his or her wooden blocks with the child

TABLE 3.4. Development of Appraisal Skills for Guilt about Hurting Others[a]

Step	Appraisal skill	Skill structure[a]			Example context	Age of emergence[b]
		Sensorimotor actions	Representations	Abstractions		
		Level SM2: Sensorimotor mappings				
G1	**Distress about other's upset produced by simple action–outcome contingency:** Child connects simple aggressive act with goal-related outcome, and connects that with other's resulting upset.	$$\begin{bmatrix} \text{ACT} - \text{GOAL} - \text{OTHER–} \\ \text{FLING HAND} \quad \text{SEE HIT} \quad \text{HEAR CRY} \end{bmatrix}$$			One child hits a second child on purpose, and then connects that child's crying to his or her own hitting. As a result, the first child becomes distressed.	7–8 months
		Level SM3: Sensorimotor systems				
G2	**Distress about other's upset produced by complex action–outcome contingency:** Child connects own aggressive actions with goal-related outcomes, and connects those outcomes with other's resulting upset.	$$\begin{bmatrix} \text{FLING HAND} & \text{SEE HIT} & \text{SEE WINCE} \\ \text{ACT} \leftrightarrow & \text{GOAL} \leftrightarrow & \text{OTHER–} \\ \text{HIT FACE} & \text{OTHER STOP} & \text{HEAR CRY} \end{bmatrix}$$			One child hits a second child in the face on purpose to make that child stop doing something, and then connects the second child's wincing and crying to his or her own hitting. As a result, the first child becomes distressed.	11–13 months

Level SM4/RP1: Systems of sensorimotor systems, which are single representations

G3a **Distress/guilt about other's upset caused by self's aggressive action:**
Child carries out aggressive actions with goal-related outcomes that produce upset in another, and he or she attributes the cause of the upset to the self.

$$\begin{bmatrix} \text{FLING HAND} & & \text{SEE HIT} & & \text{SEE WINCE} \\ \text{ACT} & \leftrightarrow & \text{GOAL} & \leftrightarrow & \text{OTHER}- \\ \text{HIT FACE} & & \text{OTHER STOP} & & \text{HEAR CRY} \\ & & \Updownarrow & & \\ \text{OWN BODY} & & \text{``I''} & & \\ \text{SEE} & \leftrightarrow & \text{SAY} & \leftrightarrow & \text{HEAR} \\ \text{DO HARM} & & \text{``HURT''} & & \text{``HURT''} \end{bmatrix} = \begin{bmatrix} SELF \\ MEAN_1 \end{bmatrix}$$

Events like those in the prior step occur, and the first child reacts with distress or guilt and indicates that he or she has caused the upset in the other child (Jason), such as "I hurt," "Hurt Jason," or "Oops Jason."[c]

18–24 months

G3b **Distress/guilt about other's upset caused by self's negative statement:**
Child makes a negative statement about other or other's things, which produces upset in the other, and child attributes the cause of the upset to the self.

$$\begin{bmatrix} & \text{SEE} & & \text{``TOWER''} & & \text{``TOWER''} \\ & \text{TOWER} & \leftrightarrow & \text{SAY} & \leftrightarrow & \text{HEAR} \\ & \text{DISLIKE} & & \text{``UGLY''} & & \text{``UGLY''} \\ & & & \Updownarrow & & \\ \text{SEE FROWN} & & & \text{``MAKE''} & & \\ \text{OTHER}- & \leftrightarrow & & \text{SAY} & \leftrightarrow & \text{HEAR} \\ \text{HEAR CRY} & & & \text{``SAD''} & & \end{bmatrix} = \begin{bmatrix} SELF \\ MEAN_2 \end{bmatrix}$$

With two children playing blocks, one child looks at the other's block tower and says "Tower ugly," which upsets the other child. The child who spoke indicates with regret or guilt that he or she hurt the other child's feelings: "Make sad," "Hurt Jason," or "Make Jason sad."[c]

18–24 months

(continued)

TABLE 3.4. *cont.*

Step	Appraisal skill	Skill structure[a]			Example context	Age of emergence[b]
		Sensorimotor actions	Representations	Abstractions		
G3c	**Distress/guilt about other's upset caused by self's refusal to act positively:** Child refuses to act positively upon other's request, which produces upset in the other, and child attributes the cause of the upset to the self.	$\begin{bmatrix} \text{REJECT} & \text{"NO"} \\ \text{OTHER} \leftrightarrow \text{SAY} \leftrightarrow \text{HEAR} & \text{"HEAR"} \\ \text{HEAR ASK} & \text{"SHARE"} \\ \Downarrow \\ \text{SEE FROWN} & \text{"MAKE"} \\ \text{OTHER–} \leftrightarrow \text{SAY} \leftrightarrow \text{HEAR} & \text{"HEAR"} \\ \text{HEAR CRY} & \text{"SAD"} \end{bmatrix}$ "NO" "SHARE" "MAKE" "SAD"	$\equiv \begin{bmatrix} SELF \\ MEAN_3 \end{bmatrix}$	With two children playing blocks, one child has many blocks, and the other requests a few to finish his or her tower. The first child refuses: "No share," which upsets the second child. The first child indicates with distress or guilt that he or she hurt the other child's feelings: "Make sad," "Hurt Jason," or "Make Jason sad."[c]	18–24 months

Level RP2: Representational mappings

G4 **Guilt about failure to reciprocate:**
Child refuses to act positively in response to another child's positive act toward him or her. The refusal upsets the other child, and the first child attributes the upset to the self's failure to reciprocate.

$$\left[\begin{array}{c} OTHER - SELF \\ \scriptstyle NICE \quad NOT\ DO\ BACK \end{array} \right]$$

Two children are playing, one with wooden blocks, one with Legos. When the first child asks the second for some Legos, the second shares them. But when the second asks the first for some wooden blocks, the first child refuses to share, and the second one becomes upset. The first child indicates guilt for hurting the other child's feelings by not reciprocating: "I didn't share my blocks with you when you shared yours with me."

(continued)

TABLE 3.4. *cont.*

Step	Appraisal skill	Skill structure[a]			Example context	Age of emergence[b]
		Sensorimotor actions	Representations	Abstractions		
		Level RP3: Representational systems				
G5	**Guilt about violation of obligation to friend:** Child breaks an agreement with a friend who relied on him or her. The failure upsets the other child, and the first child attributes the upset to the self's failure to honor the agreement.		$\begin{bmatrix} PROMISE & NEED \\ SELF \leftrightarrow OTHER \\ FAIL\ TO\ DO & UPSET \end{bmatrix}$		To build a Lego block structure for a school project, two children agree that the first child will bring Legos to the second child's home after school and help build the structure. However, the first child goes to play with a third child instead, and the second one becomes upset. The first child indicates guilt for hurting the other child by not honoring their agreement: "I didn't do what I said I would to help with the project."	6–8 years

Level RP4/AB1: Systems of representational systems, which are single abstractions

G6	**Guilt about violation of general moral rule:** Young person judges himself or herself to have violated an abstract moral rule about how to treat other people, such as being untrustworthy by failing to honor several agreements with friends.	$$\begin{bmatrix} PROMISE\ A \\ SELF \leftrightarrow \quad \substack{NEED\ A \\ OTHER\ 1} \\ FAIL\ TO\ DO\ A \quad UPSET\ A \end{bmatrix} \Longleftrightarrow \\ \begin{bmatrix} PROMISE\ B \\ SELF \leftrightarrow \quad \substack{NEED\ B \\ OTHER\ 2} \\ FAIL\ TO\ DO\ B \quad UPSET\ B \end{bmatrix}$$ $\equiv \begin{bmatrix} SELF\text{-} \\ IDENTITY \\ IMMORAL \end{bmatrix}$	A youth agrees to help a friend with a school project and then fails to do so. He or she also agrees to speak to a teacher about a friend's crisis and fails to do so. He or she generalizes across these incidents to attribute a moral flaw and feel guilty—violating the general rule of honoring agreements with friends. He or she says, "I neglect my agreements with my friends," "I let may friends down by not doing what I say I will do," or something similar.	10–12 years

99

TABLE 3.4. *cont.*

Step	Appraisal skill	Skill structure[a]			Example context	Age of emergence[b]
		Sensorimotor actions	Representations	Abstractions		
				Level AB2: Abstract mappings		
G7	**Guilt about upholding moral rule less well than someone else does:** Person judges himself or herself to have upheld an abstract moral rule less well than others, such as fulfilling obligations to friends less well than they fulfill them to him or her.			$\begin{bmatrix} \text{OTHER-} & \text{SELF-} \\ \text{IDENTITY} - \text{IDENTITY} \\ \text{MORAL} & \text{LESS MORAL} \end{bmatrix}$	A person compares his or her own honoring of agreements with how friends honor their agreements, and concludes with guilt that in general the friends honor them more faithfully than he or she does, saying something like this: "My friends are more trustworthy than I am when we make agreements. They hold up their sides of our agreements in lots of situations, but I often don't hold up my side."	14–17 years

100

Note. In skill structures, each word or phrase denotes a skill component, with each large word or phrase designating a further specification or subset of the main component. Words in boldface designate sensorimotor actions; words in italics designate representations; and words in plain letters designate abstractions. Lines connecting sets designate sensorimotor actions forming a mapping; single-line arrows designate relations forming a system; and double-line arrows designate relations forming a system of systems.

[a]Sensorimotor components are specific actions and perceptions, and in most skill analyses the diagrams indicate those specific actions and perceptions. Here we have modified the diagrams so that the component names specify general categories, such as **act**, **goal**, and **other**. Our purpose is to highlight a type of component that children often control in skills involving guilt. The actual skills involve not broad categorical competences, but particular acts, goals, and people. For example, acts can include stacking a block, hitting someone, hearing crying, or saying "Hurt." Goals can involve other actions that a child seeks to achieve, such as seeing a stack of blocks, seeing a child being hit, or getting someone to stop crying. Others can be another child, a parent, or someone else.

Representational skill components are typically more general than sensorimotor, representing a class of activities/perceptions. Nevertheless, words such as *self*, *other*, *mean*, and *fail* were chosen to specify general categories for types of skills, not particular skills. There is not a single general skill structure for self, other, mean, or fail that is the same across all relevant skills; instead, there are diverse skills that change with context, goal, and affective state (Fischer, 1980).

Representational skills eventually combine to form abstractions, which in this table are involved in the last two steps. Here the skill components are more general and intangible than actions or representations, but still they are closely tied to specific contexts, goals, and affective states.

[b]Ages of emergence specify modal times at which a level first appears, based on research with middle-class North American or European children. They may differ across cultures and other social groups.

[c]According to the skill analysis of speech, the development of simple sentences describing situations or actions involves coordination of vocalization and listening to produce words, and then coordination of words to produce a multiword utterance, as described by Fischer and Corrigan (1981).

but the child does not share his or her Lego blocks in return, and the playmate then cries. The child can form a mapping such as "I didn't share my blocks with you even though you shared yours with me," and feel guilt about this failure of concrete reciprocity.

Step G5 (guilt about violation of obligation to friend) involves understanding the obligation that comes from agreements between friends, which becomes generally possible with the emergence of representational systems at 6 to 8 years. A child promises to help a friend with something the friend needs, such as completing a school project, and then fails to provide the help and so upsets the friend. To recognize the obligation requires coordinating the promise, the friend's need, the failure to help, and the friend's upset all together in a single skill, as shown in Table 3.4.

Step G6 (guilt about violation of general moral rule) involves the use of single abstractions to generalize about how a child honors or violates agreements with friends. At this step, youths 10 to 12 years of age and older construct abstractions with conclusions such as "I have failed to live up to my agreements with several friends," which generates guilt. At step G7 (guilt about upholding a moral rule less well than someone else does), a person compares the way he or she honors agreements with the way his or her friends do, and concludes that the friends fulfill obligations more faithfully or consistently than the self. Guilt arises from the appraisal of being less trustworthy than the friends, not necessarily from any blatant neglect of agreements. Beyond step G7, development continues to more complex forms of appraisal about interpersonal obligations.

AN ECOLOGICAL APPROACH TO CONTEXTUAL SUPPORT AND THE ISSUES OF INTERNALIZATION AND APPROPRIATION

In all three of these developmental sequences, skills move gradually toward more and more complexity as children come to control a greater number of components. This fact is often described as a process of "internalization," in which the person gains "internal" control over components (Piaget, 1936/1952; Vygotsky, 1978). Our framework is based on the ecological assumption that in the real world people do not act internally; they act in specific contexts. The context in which a person is participating comprises a fundamental part of his or her acting, thinking, and feeling. When I sit on a table, the table is part of my sitting; when I am proud of my essay, the essay is likewise part of my pride. The objects, events, and people in contexts are a part of people's skills, even a part of their perceptions (Gibson, 1979). That is one of the points of the concept of "skill:" Skills are characteristics not just of a person but of a person-in-a-context (Fischer, 1980; Fischer, Bullock, et al., 1993). More generally, skill theory is part of the radical reconceptualization of the nature of mind and understanding that is taking place in the 20th century. Within this framework, action, thought, and feeling are all grounded in human practices in context (Rotman, 1993; Wittgenstein, 1953; Wozniak & Fischer, 1993).

Within this conception of cognition and emotion as grounded in context, there is no internalized skill, no skill without context. A skill is never completely internal to a person. There is no child in a perfect vacuum.

There is still some sense to a revised concept of internalization, however. Its usefulness is most evident in the phenomena of optimal and functional levels that we have described earlier. High support in the form of social priming has a strong effect on the skill level that a person can sustain. When an adult provides priming for a particular step, such as step P6 in Table 3.2, most 6- to 8-year-olds can show that kind of pride (in this case, pride about a comparative concrete trait). That is, their optimal level is step P6. But without the priming these same children will function at a much lower level, such as step P2 or P3, which is their functional level. Their functioning at step P6 is real, and it is important to their development, but they can function there only with priming. On their own without priming, they function at a much lower level. Within a developmental sequence, children generally function several steps higher in the presence of contextual support than in its absence. With age, children become increasingly able to perform without support at levels where they previously could only perform with support. In addition, the levels that children can attain with support also increase with age, of course.

Both optimal and functional levels occur in context, and the skills for each contain the context as part of them. Nevertheless, to produce an optimal-level action, a child does require directed external support through social priming. There is some sense, therefore, to saying that the functional-level skill is more internalized than the optimal-level one, because the child exerts relatively more internal control over the functional skill, and thus needs relatively less "external" support from the context.

Analyses of self-evaluative emotions have dealt extensively with what has been called the "internalization" of moral and normative standards (Freud, 1940/1949). Unfortunately, this meaning of internalization seems to treat standards as something simply inside the person, instead of something grounded in context; simultaneously, it confuses two different meanings of internalization. In the literature on self-evaluative emotions, internalization is typically used to mean that people take a standard for their own, as opposed to having it imposed by someone else. Then the meaning of taking for one's own is confounded with the concept of internalization—that the standard moves inside people, and then they can sustain it on their own independently of the social world.

Taking a standard as one's own, as something that one is committed to, is not the same as being able to use it without strong contextual support to sustain it. These two meanings are different and really should be distinguished. A better term for the former meaning, making something one's own, is "appropriation" (Rogoff, 1990): We appropriate a standard to our own uses, committing ourselves to it. In turn, "internalization" can be reserved for the process whereby a person develops increasing self-directed control, sustaining complex skills in appropriate contexts without aid from other people's priming.

Appropriation—taking a standard as one's own—does require that a person be able to sustain the standard cognitively, but people can also cognitively sustain ("internalize") standards that they do not appropriate. Indeed, people frequently use standards that they have not taken as their own, as when they morally reject a societal standard such as racial discrimination while still taking it into account as they live in a society that practices discrimination. In less blatant ways, we all follow standards that we do not appropriate or even approve of. People can cognitively sustain standards that they take as their own, as well as ones that they do not take as their own. Appropriation is different from internalization.

In the pride, shame, and guilt sequences that we have described, each step can be performed either with or without high contextual support. Pride, shame, and guilt are social emotions, and so they naturally build on high support within the social context, especially at early developmental steps. For example, many of the guilt-like reactions found in toddlers occur after social events that can support guilt reactions, such as reprimands, parental prohibitions, or feedback from an overtly distressed child (Zahn-Waxler & Kochanska, 1990; Emde et al., 1987). The presence of a parent or other evaluator in virtually all steps of the pride, shame, and guilt sequences reflects the importance of this social support for self-evaluative emotions. Without the priming of these social events, toddlers are unlikely to experience guilt or other self-evaluative emotions.

The distinction between optimal and functional levels is powerful throughout development. Indeed, the difference between optimal and functional levels typically becomes larger at later developmental levels (Kitchener, Lynch, Fischer, & Wood, 1993). Internalization is not a phenomenon that occurs or is completed at a single point in development, as in the internalization of a "conscience" at age 5 in Freud's (1940/1949) analysis. Instead, the ability to function independently at levels where one previously required contextual support occurs over and over throughout ontogenesis, since all skills grow in contexts.

TESTING SEQUENCES OF SELF-EVALUATIVE EMOTIONAL DEVELOPMENT

The assessment of sequences of development of self-evaluative emotions poses challenges beyond those encountered in the assessment of cognitive development. The fundamental problem, in our opinion, is that because the study of emotional development has a much shorter history, fewer methods have been devised for effective research. Among the specific methodological problems that need to be addressed are how to assess emotional expressions, appraisals, and action tendencies.

The assessment of emotional expressions can be problematic, especially for the self-evaluative emotions, where there are no established facial or vocal expressions for each emotion. Methods need to be devised for assessing the appraisals and the action tendencies as well. In addition, there is the possibility that even though appraisals that generate emotions may change, overt emotional expressions may not change in ways directly related to changes in appraisals (Sroufe, 1979). The ethical problems that arise with the study of emotions, especially negative ones, must also be considered. To address these concerns, we advocate a variety of methods to assess possible developmental sequences, each with their associated strengths and weaknesses. Space limitations compel us to review these methods in very broad strokes.

Some important techniques are available for investigating development of emotions based on innovations devised originally to study cognitive and social-cognitive development. One of the most useful tools for eliciting emotional reactions without deception or stress is storytelling, especially in young children, who become engaged in stories easily and readily show emotional reactions to stories (Buchsbaum & Emde, 1991; Fischer et al., 1990). The content, complexity, and context of stories can be partly controlled and manipulated, so that, for example, the effects of different appraisals and contexts on emotions can be studied. Stories about interactions among family members or friends can be constructed to typically evoke strong emotions in children, and even negative emotions can be evoked without significant risks to the children (Fischer & Ayoub, 1993).

Modeling-and-imitation techniques have proven effective in the assessment of developmental sequences in a variety of domains and with a variety of types of tasks, including stories (Fischer & Elmendorf, 1986; Fischer, Bullock, et al., 1993; Pipp et al., 1987). In modeling and imitation, an investigator models a series of tasks such as stories, each designed to reflect a step in a developmental sequence, and asks children to act out or explain each modeled task. Modeling provides contextual support and thus usually assesses children's optimal levels; in addition, the children can be asked to make up stories of their own, so that their functional levels in the same domain can be assessed.

Methods are available to test developmental sequences like those in Tables 3.2, 3.3, and 3.4 in either cross-sectional or longitudinal research designs. With scalogram or partially ordered scaling statistics, sequences can be tested by the pattern of performances on a series of tasks. If a separate story is used to assess each step in Table 3.2, for example, and each story is scored pass or fail, then the sequence is supported if performance conforms to a Guttman (1944) scalogram or a partially ordered scale (Fischer, Knight, & Van Parys, 1993). In the simplest Guttman sequence, children pass all steps up to some point and fail all steps thereafter. Branches in pathways can be analyzed through partially ordered scaling, and more complex coding systems than pass–fail can also be used, including assessments of emotions, distortions, and many other aspects of behavior (C. F. Cole, 1993; Elmendorf, 1992).

With these techniques, one can test the sequences of emotional appraisal described in Tables 3.2, 3.3, and 3.4 by devising separate tasks to assess each step of appraisal proposed. When the tasks are administered to children of different ages (cross-sectional design) or to the same children at different ages (longitudinal design), this method enables assessment of development of appraisals in a way that allows control over variables often confounded with developmental complexity (such as content domain and context). Also, one can simultaneously assess the emotions that accompany the different appraisals in the tasks. A disadvantage to this method is that it does not ensure the occurrence of the emotional reactions themselves, although we have had good success in a number of studies at evoking emotional reactions. In addition, it is possible to supplement the assessment of appraisals mediating emotion with projective methods, such as asking children to complete incomplete stories, to evoke a wider range of emotional reactions (Buchsbaum & Emde, 1991; Zahn-Waxler, Kochanska, Krupnick, & McKnew, 1990).

Another way to assess changes in emotion is direct observation of emotional reactions either longitudinally or cross-sectionally in naturalistic contexts. Because of the relatively low incidence of specific emotional reactions such as pride, shame, or guilt, and because of the difficulties of observing them, Zahn-Waxler and her colleagues have trained parents to observe and record their children's emotional reactions across a wide range of naturalistic situations. They have achieved considerable success in collecting useful data about self-evaluative emotions with this method (Zahn-Waxler & Radke-Yarrow, 1982; Zahn-Waxler, Radke-Yarrow, Wagner, & Chapman, 1992; Zahn-Waxler, Radke-Yarrow, & King, 1979; Zahn-Waxler & Robinson, Chapter 5, this volume). With these parent report data, it has been possible to assess development and other change in the behavioral signs of emotions, as well as the situations in which emotions occur.

In recent years, investigators have also enjoyed some success in inducing and observing emotions in the laboratory or home (Barrett et al., 1993; Emde et al., 1987; H. Heckhausen, 1984; M. Lewis, Sullivan, Stanger, & Weiss, 1989). Although the induction of emotion in the laboratory enables one to exert some control over precipitating events, there are difficulties in laboratory assessment of many emotional situations that occur naturally in children's lives. For example, in laboratory settings, the development of shame has often been assessed by inducing failure in simple tasks (tower building). At home or school, many failure tasks are more complex and are embedded in natural social interactions that are not easily recreated in the laboratory. Also, it would be ideal if a series of tasks could be used, so that developmental sequences could be assessed.

In general, research on development of self-evaluative emotions has made good progress in recent years, but the research techniques still tend to be overly simple. Techniques are needed that can be used to assess developmental pathways in the multiple components of self-evaluative emotions (appraisals, action tendencies, expressive behaviors, control strategies, etc.). Investigating developmental pathways requires going beyond examining emotional expressions in one task or situation. Investigators need to use multiple tasks, to measure multiple aspects of behavior, and to focus specifically on assessing developmental changes. By combining the techniques we have described here, and using both structured and naturalistic assessments, researchers should be able to map out the shapes of self-evaluative emotional development.

CONCLUSION

Analysis of the development of self-evaluative emotions is facilitated by using a dynamic skills framework that combines the insights of functionalist approaches to emotions with the tools of analysis of skill development, and that places the developing, acting, feeling person firmly in the real world—in a body in specific contexts with concrete objects, events, and people. Within this framework, self-evaluative emotions can be seen to develop from simple positive and negative affects such as joy and distress to complex, multifaceted action tendencies that organize action, thought, and feeling. They are not simply feelings, but much more. They cannot be reduced to any one aspect of behavior, but involve many connected components. And they do not remain invariant throughout the lifespan, but show enormous qualitative changes with development.

Emotions begin with appraisals, with which the meanings of events are constructed and from which the action tendencies of emotions flow. Starting with appraisals, we have provided detailed portraits of several developmental sequences for appraisals that produce the self-evaluative emotions of pride, shame, and guilt. Table 3.1 provides an outline of the action tendencies that organize these emotions. Tables 3.2, 3.3, and 3.4 summarize the developmental sequences and illustrate how dynamic skills tools can be used to analyze self-evaluative emotional development.

The sequences proposed for pride, shame, and guilt are illustrations of the types of qualitative changes that occur in development of self-evaluative emotions, but they focus primarily on emotional appraisals. Despite the importance of appraisals in the generation of emotion, they are but one facet of emotional development. Many other components of emotions are open to developmental analysis, and the dynamic skills framework is designed to facilitate analysis across all these components, as we have tried to demonstrate by sketching how various findings and methods about other aspects of self-evaluative emotions relate to the appraisal sequences.

Research is needed not only to test and elaborate our analyses of emotion appraisals, but also to explicate changes in action tendencies and self-monitoring for self-evaluative emotions, as well as the ways in which organismic and contextual factors interact to affect emotional development. Pursuing such research will require further elaboration of methods that enable assessment of both appraisal and behavioral components of emotional reactions as they co-occur in actual emotional episodes.

ACKNOWLEDGMENTS

The work in this chapter was supported by a postdoctoral fellowship from the National Institute of Mental Health; a fellowship from the Center for Advanced Study in the Behavioral Sciences; and grants from Harvard University and the MacArthur Foundation Network on Early Childhood. We thank Joseph Campos, Johanna Fischer, Jane Haltiwanger, Jerome Kagan, Jin Li, Phillip Shaver, June Tangney, Lianquin Wang, and Chao-deng Yu for their contributions to the arguments presented here.

REFERENCES

Armon-Jones, C. (1986). The social functions of emotions. In R. Harré (Ed.), *The social construction of emotions* (pp. 32–56). Oxford: Blackwell.

Barrett, K. C., & Campos, J. J. (1987). Perspectives on emotional development: II. A functional approach to emotions. In J. D. Osofsky (Ed.), *Handbook of infant development* (2nd ed., pp. 555–578). New York: Wiley.

Barrett, K. C., Zahn-Waxler, C., & Cole, P. (1993). Avoiders versus amenders: Implications for the investigation of guilt and shame during toddlerhood? *Cognition and Emotion, 7,* 481–505.

Bertenthal, B. L., & Fischer, K. W. (1978). Development of self-recognition in the infant. *Developmental Psychology, 14,* 44–50.

Bidell, T. R., & Fischer, K. W. (1992). Beyond the stage debate: Action, structure, and variability in Piagetian theory and research. In C. Berg & R. S. Sternberg (Eds.), *Intellectual development* (pp. 100–140). New York: Cambridge University Press.

Buchsbaum, H. K., & Emde, R. N. (1991). Play narratives in 36-month-old children. *Psychoanalytic Study of the Child, 45,* 129–155.

Bullock, M., & Lutkenhaus, P. (1988). The development of volitional behavior in the toddler years. *Child Development, 59,* 664–674.

Butler, R. (1989). Mastery versus ability appraisal: A developmental study of children's observations of peers' work. *Child Development, 60,* 1350–1361.

Campos, J. J., Barrett, K. C., Lamb, M. E., Goldsmith, H. H., & Stenberg, C. (1983). Socioemotional development. In M. M. Haith & J. J. Campos (Vol. Eds.),

Handbook of child psychology (4th ed.): *Vol. 2. Infancy and developmental psychobiology* (pp. 783–915). New York: Wiley.

Cole, C. F. (1993). *Preschool children's interpretations of the intentions behind physically harmful actions: The link between behavioral characteristics and perception.* Unpublished doctoral dissertation, Harvard University.

Cole, P., Barrett, K. C., & Zahn-Waxler, C. (1992). Emotion displays in 2-year-olds during mishaps. *Child Development, 63,* 314–324.

Davitz, J. R. (1969). *The language of emotion.* New York: Academic Press.

de Rivera, J. (1981). The structure of anger. In J. de Rivera (Ed.), *Conceptual encounter* (pp. 35–81). Washington, DC: University Press of America.

Dienstbier, R. A. (1989). Arousal and physiological toughness: Implications for mental and physical health. *Psychological Review, 96,* 84–100.

Ekman, P., Levenson, R. W., & Friesen, W. V. (1983). Autonomic nervous system activity distinguishes between emotions. *Science, 221,* 1208–1210.

Elmendorf, D. (1992). *Preschool children's interpretations of the intentions behind physically harmful acts: Developmental changes in understanding, misunderstanding, and distortion.* Unpublished doctoral dissertation, University of Denver.

Emde, R. N. (1983). The prerepresentational self and its affective core. *Psychoanalytic Study of the Child, 38,* 165–192.

Emde, R. N., Johnson, W., & Easterbrooks, M. (1987). The dos and don'ts of early moral development: Psychoanalytic tradition and current research. In J. Kagan & S. Lamb (Eds.), *The emergence of morality in young children* (pp. 245–276). Chicago: University of Chicago Press.

Fajans, J. (1983). Shame, social action, and the person in the Baining. *Ethos, 11,* 166–180.

Fehr, B., & Russell, J. A. (1985). Concept of emotion viewed from a prototype perspective. *Journal of Experimental Psychology: General, 113,* 464–486.

Fischer, K. W. (1980). A theory of cognitive development: The control and construction of hierarchies of skills. *Psychological Review, 87,* 447–531.

Fischer, K. W., & Ayoub, C. (1993). Affective splitting and dissociation in normal and maltreated children: Developmental pathways for self in relationships. In D. Cicchetti & S. Toth (Eds.), *Rochester Symposium on Developmental Psychopathology: Vol. 5. The self and its disorders* (pp. 149–222). Rochester, NY: University of Rochester Press.

Fischer, K. W., & Bidell, T. (1991). Constraining nativist inferences about cognitive capacities. In S. Carey & R. Gelman (Eds.), *The epigenesis of mind: Essays on biology and knowledge* (pp. 199–235). Hillsdale, NJ: Erlbaum.

Fischer, K. W., Bullock, D. H., Rotenberg, E. J., & Raya, P. (1993). The dynamics of competence: How context contributes directly to skill. In R. Wozniak & K. Fischer (Eds.), *Development in context: Acting and thinking in specific environments* (pp. 93–117). Hillsdale, NJ: Erlbaum.

Fischer, K. W., & Corrigan, R. (1981). A skill approach to language development. In R. Stark (Ed.), *Language behavior in infancy and early childhood* (pp. 245–273). Amsterdam: Elsevier.

Fischer, K. W., & Elmendorf, D. (1986). Becoming a different person: Transformations in personality and social behavior. In M. Perlmutter (Ed.), *Minnesota Symposium on Child Psychology* (Vol. 18, pp. 137–178). Hillsdale, NJ: Erlbaum.

Fischer, K. W., & Farrar, J. (1987). Generalizations about generalization: How a theory of skill development explains both generality and specificity. *International Journal of Psychology, 22,* 643–677.

Fischer, K. W., & Hogan, A. E. (1989). The big picture for infant development: Levels and variations. In J. Lockman & N. Hazan (Eds.), *Action in social context: Perspectives on early development* (pp. 275–305). New York: Plenum.

Fischer, K. W., Knight, C. C., & Van Parys, M. (1993). Analyzing diversity in developmental pathways: Methods and concepts. In R. Case & W. Edelstein (Eds.), *Contributions to human development: Vol. 23. The new structuralism in cognitive development: Theory and research on individual pathways* (pp. 33–56). Basel: S. Karger.

Fischer, K. W., & Rose, S. P. (1994). Dynamic development of coordination of components in brain and behavior: A framework for theory and research. In G. Dawson & K. W. Fischer (Eds.), *Human behavior and the developing brain* (pp. 3–66). New York: Guilford Press.

Fischer, K. W., Shaver, P. R., & Carnochan, P. (1990). How emotions develop and how they organize development. *Cognition and Emotion, 4*, 81–128.

Freud, S. (1949). *An outline of psycho-analysis* (J. Strachey, Trans.). New York: Norton. (Original work published 1940)

Frijda, N. H. (1986). *The emotions*. New York: Cambridge University Press.

Frijda, N. H. (1988). The laws of emotion. *American Psychologist, 43*, 349–358.

Gelman, R., & Baillargeon, R. (1983). A review of some Piagetian concepts. In J. H. Flavell & E. M. Markman (Vol. Eds.), *Handbook of child psychology* (4th ed.): *Vol. 3. Cognitive development* (pp. 167–230). New York: Wiley.

Gibson, J. J. (1979). *The ecological approach to visual perception*. Boston: Houghton Mifflin.

Geppert, U., & Kuster, U. (1983). The emergence of "wanting to do it oneself": A precursor to achievement motivation. *International Journal of Behavioral Development, 3*, 355–369.

Guttman, L. (1944). A basis for scaling qualitative data. *American Sociological Review, 9*, 139–150.

Heckhausen, H. (1981). Developmental precursors of success and failure experience. In G. d'Ydewalle & W. Lens (Eds.), *Cognition in human motivation and learning* (pp. 15–32). Hillsdale, NJ: Erlbaum.

Heckhausen, H. (1984). Emergent achievement behavior: Some early developments. In J. Nicholls (Ed.), *Advances in motivation and achievement: Vol. 3. The development of achievement motivation* (pp. 1–32). Greenwich, CT: JAI Press.

Heckhausen, H. (1987). Emotional components of action: Their ontogeny as reflected in achievement behavior. In D. Gorlitz & J. F. Wohlwill (Eds.), *Curiosity, imagination, and play: On the development of spontaneous cognitive and motivational processes* (pp. 326–348). Hillsdale, NJ: Erlbaum.

Heckhausen, J. (1988). Becoming aware of one's competence in the second year: Developmental progression within the mother–child dyad. *International Journal of Behavioral Development, 3*, 305–326.

Hochschild, A. R. (1979). Emotion work, feeling rules, and social structure. *American Journal of Sociology, 85*, 551–575.

Hoffman, M. L. (1982). Development of prosocial motivation: Empathy and guilt. In N. Eisenberg (Ed.), *The development of prosocial behavior* (pp. 281–313). New York: Academic Press.

Hoffman, M. L. (1983). Affective and cognitive processes in moral internalization: An information processing approach. In E. T. Higgins, D. Ruble, & S. W. Hartup (Eds.), *Developmental social cognition* (pp. 236–274). New York: Cambridge University Press.

Izard, C. E., & Malatesta, C. Z. (1987). Perspectives on emotional development I: Differential emotions theory of early emotional development. In J. D. Osofsky (Ed.), *Handbook of infant development* (2nd ed., pp. 494–554). New York: John Wiley.

James, D. (Producer). (1991). *Marian Anderson* [Film]. Washington, DC: WETA Public Television.

Kagan, J. (1981). *The second year: The emergence of self-awareness.* Cambridge, MA: Harvard University Press.

Kitchener, K. S., Lynch, C. L., Fischer, K. W., & Wood, P. K. (1993). Developmental range of reflective judgment: The effect of contextual support and practice on developmental stage. *Developmental Psychology, 29,* 893–906.

Kohlberg, L. (1969). Stage and sequence: The cognitive developmental approach to socialization. In D. A. Goslin (Ed.), *Handbook of socialization theory and research* (pp. 347–480). Chicago: Rand, McNally.

Kopp, C. (1989). Regulation of distress and negative emotions: A developmental view. *Developmental Psychology, 25,* 343–354.

Lazarus, R. (1991). *Emotion and adaptation.* New York: Oxford University Press.

Lewis, H. B. (1971). *Shame and guilt in neurosis.* New York: International Universities Press.

Lewis, M., Alessandri, S. M., & Sullivan, M. W. (1990). Violation of expectancy, loss of control, and anger in young infants. *Developmental Psychology, 26,* 745–751.

Lewis, M., Alessandri, S. M., & Sullivan, M. W. (1992). Differences in shame and pride as a function of children's gender and task difficulty. *Child Development, 63,* 630–638.

Lewis, M., & Brooks-Gunn, J. (1979). *Social cognition and the acquisition of self.* New York: Plenum.

Lewis, M., Sullivan, M. W., Stanger, C., & Weiss, M. (1989). Self development and self-conscious emotions. *Child Development, 60,* 146–156.

Lindsay-Hartz, J. (1984). Contrasting experiences of shame and guilt. *American Behavioral Scientist, 27,* 689–704.

Lutkenhaus, P., Grossmann, K. E., & Grossmann, K. (1985). Transactional influences of infants' orienting ability and maternal cooperation on competition in 3-year-old children. *International Journal of Behavioral Development, 8,* 257–272.

Lutz, C. A. (1988). *Unnatural emotions.* Chicago: University of Chicago Press.

Mandler, G. (1984). *Mind and body.* New York: Norton.

Mascolo, M. F., & Mancuso, J. C. (1990). The functioning of epigenetically-evolved emotion systems: A constructive analysis. *International Journal of Personal Construct Theory, 3,* 205–222.

Mascolo, M. F., & Mancuso, J. C. (1992). Constructive processes in self-evaluative emotional development. In G. J. Neimeyer & R. A. Neimeyer (Eds.), *Advances in personal construct psychology* (Vol. 2, pp. 27–54). Greenwich, CT: JAI Press.

Piaget, J. (1952). *The origins of intelligence in children* (M. Cook, Trans.). New York: International Universities Press. (Original work published 1936)

Piaget, J. (1957). Logique et équilibre dans les comportements du sujet. *Études d'Épistémologie Génétique, 2,* 27–118.

Piers, G., & Singer, M. (1953). *Shame and guilt.* Springfield, IL: Charles C Thomas.

Pipp, S., Fischer, K. W., & Jennings, S. (1987). Acquisition of self- and mother knowledge in infancy. *Developmental Psychology, 23,* 86–96.

Rogoff, B. (1990). *Apprenticeship in thinking.* New York: Oxford University Press.

Roseman, I. J. (1984). Cognitive determinants of emotions: A structural theory. In P. Shaver (Ed.), *Review of personality and social psychology* (Vol. 5, pp. 11–36). Beverly Hills, CA: Sage.

Rotman, B. (1993). *Ad infinitum— The ghost in Turing's machine: Taking God out of mathematics and putting the body back in.* Stanford, CA: Stanford University Press.

Ruble, D. N. (1983). The development of social comparison processes and their role in achievement-related self-socialization. In E. T. Higgins, D. N. Ruble, & W. W. Hartup (Eds.), *Social cognition and social development: A socio-cultural perspective* (pp. 134–157). New York: Cambridge University Press.

Saarni, C. (1990). Emotional competence: How emotions and relationships become integrated. In R. Thompson (Ed.), *Nebraska Symposium on Motivation: Vol. 36. Socio-emotional development* (pp. 115–182). Lincoln: University of Nebraska Press.

Scherer, K. R. (1984). Emotion as a multicomponent process: A model and some cross-cultural data. In P. Shaver (Ed.), *Review of personality and social psychology* (Vol. 5, pp. 37–63). Beverly Hills, CA: Sage.

Shaver, P., Schwartz, J., Kirson, D., & O'Connor, C. (1987). Emotion knowledge: Further exploration of a prototype approach. *Journal of Personality and Social Psychology, 52,* 1061–1086.

Sroufe, L. A. (1979). Socio-emotional development. In J. D. Osofsky (Ed.), *Handbook of infant development* (pp. 462–516). New York: Wiley.

Stenberg, C. R., & Campos, J. J. (1990). The development of anger expressions in infancy. In N. L. Stein, B. Leventhal, & T. Trabasso (Eds.), *Psychological and biological approaches to emotion* (pp. 247–282). Hillsdale, NJ: Erlbaum.

Stern, D. N. (1985). *The interpersonal world of the infant: A view from psychoanalysis and developmental psychology.* New York: Basic Books.

Stipek, D. J. (1983). A developmental analysis of pride and shame. *Human Development, 26,* 42–54.

Stipek, D. J., Recchia, S., & McClintic, S. (1992). Self-evaluation in young children. *Monographs of the Society for Research in Child Development, 57*(1, Serial No. 226).

Tangney, J. (1992). Situational determinants of shame and guilt in young adulthood. *Personality and Social Psychology Bulletin, 18,* 199–206.

Thompson, R. A. (1990). Emotion and self-regulation. In R. Thompson (Ed.), *Nebraska Symposium on Motivation: Vol. 36. Socio-emotional development* (pp. 367–467). Lincoln: University of Nebraska Press.

Tomkins, S. S. (1984). Affect theory. In K. R. Scherer & P. Ekman (Eds.), *Approaches to emotion* (pp. 163–196). Hillsdale, NJ: Erlbaum.

Veroff, J. (1969). Social comparison and the development of achievement motivation. In C. P. Smith (Ed.), *Achievement related motives in children* (pp. 46–101). New York: Russell Sage Foundation.

Vygotsky, L. (1978). *Mind in society: The development of higher psychological processes* (M. Cole, V. John-Steiner, S. Scribner, & E. Souberman, Trans.). Cambridge, MA: Harvard University Press.

Watson, J. S., & Ramey, C. T. (1972). Reactions to response-contingent stimulation in early infancy. *Merrill–Palmer Quarterly, 18,* 219–227.

Weiner, B., & Graham, S. (1984). An attributional approach to emotional development. In C. Izard, J. Kagan, & R. Zajonc (Eds.), *Emotions, cognition, and behavior* (pp. 167–191). New York: Cambridge University Press.

Wittgenstein, L. (1953). *Philosophical investigations* (G. E. M. Anscombe, Trans.). Oxford: Oxford University Press.

Wozniak, R., & Fischer, K. W. (1993). Development in context: An introduction. In R. Wozniak & K. W. Fischer (Eds.), *Development in context: Acting and thinking in specific environments* (pp. xi–xvi). Hillsdale, NJ: Erlbaum.

Zahn-Waxler, C., & Kochanska, G. (1990). The origins of guilt. In R. Thompson (Ed.), *Nebraska Symposium on Motivation: Vol. 36. Socio-emotional development* (pp. 183–258). Lincoln: University of Nebraska Press.

Zahn-Waxler, C., Kochanska, G., Krupnick, J., & McKnew, D. (1990). Patterns of guilt and children of depressed and well mothers. *Developmental Psychology, 26,* 51–59.

Zahn-Waxler, C., & Radke-Yarrow, M. (1982). The development of altruism: Alternative research strategies. In N. Eisenberg (Ed.), *The development of prosocial behavior* (pp. 109–137). New York: Academic Press.

Zahn-Waxler, C., Radke-Yarrow, M., & King, R. (1979). Childrearing and children's prosocial initiations towards victims of distress. *Child Development, 50,* 319–330.

Zahn-Waxler, C., Radke-Yarrow, M., Wagner, E., & Chapman, M. (1992). Development of concern for others. *Developmental Psychology, 28,* 126–136.

4

Shame and Guilt in Interpersonal Relationships

JUNE PRICE TANGNEY

We often think of shame and guilt as private emotional experiences intimately related to the self. Shame and guilt derive from a sense that our behavior or some aspect of ourselves is at odds with our moral standards or ideals. Thus, shame and guilt are each highly self-relevant emotions. Yet these emotions are also clearly linked to interpersonal relationships in a number of important respects.

First, our personal moral standards and ideals for the self develop early, as a function of key socialization experiences with parents, teachers, and significant others. We learn to feel shame and guilt over failures and transgressions, and these failures and transgressions are themselves defined as such by significant people in our social milieu.

Second, empirical studies (e.g., Tangney, 1992; Tangney, Marschall, Rosenberg, Barlow, & Wagner, 1993) indicate that across the lifespan, shame and guilt are most likely to be experienced in interpersonal contexts. The nature of the interpersonal focus seems to vary somewhat, depending on which emotion is involved. But it is clear that shame and guilt are interpersonal emotions, in the sense that they are most likely to arise in relationship to others. Moreover, Baumeister, Stillwell, and Heatherton's (Chapter 10, this volume) studies of guilt indicate that guilt is most likely to occur in the context of close, intimate relationships, as opposed to casual, peripheral relationships.

Third, there is converging theoretical and empirical evidence that shame and guilt have important and very different implications for subsequent motivation and interpersonal functioning. This seems to be true both when the *states* of shame and guilt are considered, and also when

114

the *traits* or dispositions—proneness to shame and proneness to guilt—are considered.

This chapter focuses on this third set of interpersonal issues related to shame and guilt. I first provide an overview of the nature of shame and guilt experiences, highlighting key similarities and key differences between these two frequently confused emotions. I then review recent phenomenological and personality studies, which indicate that shame and guilt are differentially related to a range of motivational and interpersonal features; these include a tendency toward reparative behavior versus avoidance, interpersonal empathy, and people's characteristic anger management strategies in everyday contexts. Taken together with our examination of "Shame-Proneness, Guilt-Proneness, and Psychological Symptoms" (Tangney, Burggraf, & Wagner, Chapter 14, this volume), these findings suggest that shame and guilt are not equally "moral" or adaptive emotions. With respect to both intrapersonal and interpersonal adjustment, guilt appears to be the more adaptive response to the inevitable transgressions of everyday life.

PROTOTYPICAL SHAME AND GUILT EXPERIENCES: KEY SIMILARITIES AND DIFFERENCES

Historically, the clinical, social, and developmental literatures have often not made a clear distinction between shame and guilt. Most often, the term "guilt" is used as a catch-all phrase to refer to phenomenological aspects of both emotions. And indeed, shame and guilt share a number of important features (see Table 4.1). First, shame and guilt are generally grouped together in the class of "moral emotions" because of their presumed role in fostering moral behavior and in inhibiting all manner of moral transgressions. They are also members of the family of "self-conscious" emotions (M. Lewis, 1990), in that they each involve self-referential processes with respect to some standard for self or behavior.

In addition, both shame and guilt are negatively valanced emotions that typically arise in response to some personal failure or transgression. As such, they each involve internal attributions of one sort or another for negative self-relevant events.[1] Both emotions are typically also experienced in interpersonal contexts (Baumeister et al., Chapter 10, this volume; Tangney et al., 1993). Moreover, the specific types of situations that give rise to shame and guilt, respectively, are remarkably similar. Recent analyses of narrative accounts of personal shame and guilt experiences provided by both children and adults indicate that there are very few "classic" shame-inducing or guilt-inducing situations (Tangney, 1992; Tangney et al., 1993). Most types of events (e.g., lying, cheating, stealing, failing to help another, disobeying parents, etc.) were cited by some participants in connection with feelings of shame and by other participants in connection with guilt. Although events generally regarded as moral transgressions were about equally likely to elicit

TABLE 4.1. Key Similarities and Differences between Shame and Guilt

Features shared by shame and guilt
- Both fall into the class of "moral" emotions
- Both are "self-conscious," self-referential emotions
- Both are negatively valanced emotions
- Both involve internal attributions of one sort or another
- Both are typically experienced in interpersonal contexts
- The negative events that give rise to shame and guilt are highly similar (frequently involving moral failures or transgressions)

Key dimensions on which shame and guilt differ

Dimension	Shame	Guilt
Focus of evaluation	Global self ("*I* did that horrible thing")	Specific behavior ("I *did* that horrible *thing*")
Degree of distress	Generally more painful than guilt	Generally less painful than shame
Phenomenological experience	Shrinking, feeling small, feeling worthless, powerless	Tension, remorse, regret
Operation of self	Self "split" into observing and observed "selves"	Unified self intact
Impact on self	Self impaired by global devaluation	Self unimpaired by global devaluation
Concern *vis-à-vis* others	Concern with others' evaluation of self	Concern with one's effect on others
Counterfactual processes	Mentally undoing some aspect of the self	Mentally undoing some aspect of behavior
Motivational features	Desire to hide or escape, or desire to strike back	Desire to confess, apologize, or repair

shame and guilt, there was some evidence that nonmoral failures and shortcomings (e.g., socially inappropriate behavior or dress) were more likely to elicit shame. Even so, failures in work, school, or sports settings and violations of social conventions were cited by a significant number of children and adults in connection with guilt.

How do shame and guilt differ, if not in terms of the types of situations that give rise to these experiences? In my own work, I have drawn very heavily on Helen Block Lewis's (1971) influential distinction between these two moral emotions. In her landmark book *Shame and Guilt in Neurosis,* Lewis (1971) proposed that a fundamental difference between shame and guilt centers on the role of the self in these experiences:[2]

> The experience of shame is directly about the *self,* which is the focus of evaluation. In guilt, the self is not the central object of negative evaluation, but rather the *thing* done or undone is the focus. In guilt, the self is

negatively evaluated in connection with something but is not itself the focus of the experience. (p. 30)

According to Lewis (1971), this differential emphasis on self ("*I* did that horrible thing") versus behavior ("I *did* that horrible *thing*") gives rise to very different phenomenological experiences—termed "shame" and "guilt," respectively. Guided by recent empirical studies (Lindsay-Hartz, 1984; Lindsay-Hartz, de Rivera, & Mascolo, Chapter 11, this volume; Tangney, 1989, 1992, 1993; Tangney et al., 1993; Tangney, Miller, & Flicker, 1992; Wicker, Payne, & Morgan, 1983), I have elaborated and extended H. B. Lewis's (1971) description of the cognitive, affective, and motivational differences between shame and guilt. These key differences are summarized in Table 4.1.

In a prototypical shame experience, our primary concern is with our self as a person. Feelings of shame involve a painful negative scrutiny of the self—a feeling that "*I* am unworthy, incompetent, or bad." People in the midst of a shame experience often report a sense of shrinking or of "being small"—of feeling diminished in some significant way. They feel, for the moment, worthless and powerless. And they feel exposed. Although shame does not necessarily involve an actual observing audience, present to witness one's shortcomings, there is often the imagery of how one's defective self would appear to others. H. B. Lewis (1971) has described a split in self-functioning, which is unique to shame. An observing self witnesses and denigrates the focal self as unworthy and reprehensible. Shame, a relatively transient emotional experience, is distinct from more global and enduring cognitive conceptions of self, such as low self-esteem; that is, feelings of shame arise from specific failures or transgressions. However, the processes involved in shame extend beyond those involved in guilt. The "bad behavior" is taken not simply as a local transgression, requiring reparation or apology; instead, the offending or objectionable behavior is seen as a reflection more generally of a defective, objectionable self. There is thus a shift in focus from the behavior to the self. Because of this focus on the self, shame experiences are likely to set into motion counterfactual thinking involving the self (e.g., "If only I weren't a such-and-such kind of person"). And, as discussed at greater length later in this chapter, shame is likely to motivate either avoidance (e.g., a desire to hide or "to sink into the floor and disappear") or a tendency to lash out defensively at others involved in the shame-eliciting situation.

In contrast, the prototypical guilt experience is generally less painful and devastating than shame, because in guilt the primary concern is with a particular behavior. Feelings of guilt involve a negative evaluation of some specific behavior (or specific failure to act), somewhat apart from the self. So guilt does not affect one's core identity; the self remains unified and intact. Feelings of guilt can be painful, nonetheless. Guilt involves a sense of tension, remorse, and regret over the "bad thing done." People in the midst of a guilt experience often report a nagging focus or preoccupation with the specific transgression—thinking of it over and over, wishing they had behaved differently or could somehow undo the bad deed that was done. Counterfactual processes typically center on a mental undoing of the specific behavior (e.g., "If only I had [or had not] done such-and-such") rather than of the self. And because the behavior (not the self) is the issue, people experiencing guilt are less self-focused, and more likely to examine the effect of their behavior on others. Not surprisingly, the tension, remorse, and regret of guilt, coupled with this other-oriented focus, often motivates reparative action—confessing, apologizing, or somehow repairing the bad thing that was done.

There is now considerable empirical support for this distinction between shame and guilt (Ferguson, Stegge, & Damhuis, 1990, 1991; Ferguson & Stegge, Chapter 6, this volume; Lindsay-Hartz, 1984; Lindsay-Hartz et al., Chapter 11, this volume; Tangney, 1989, 1992, 1993; Tangney et al., 1993; Tangney, Miller, & Flicker, 1992; Wicker et al., 1983). For example, in two independent studies, we asked young adults to describe a personal shame experience and a personal guilt experience, and then to rate these experiences along a number of phenomenological dimensions (Tangney, 1993; Tangney, Miller, & Flicker, 1992). The results across the two studies were remarkably consistent. Compared to guilt, shame experiences were rated as significantly more painful and more difficult to describe. When experiencing shame, people felt physically smaller and more inferior to others; they felt they had less control over the situation (were powerless). Shame experiences were more likely to involve a sense of exposure (feeling observed by others) and a concern with others' opinions of the event. And people reported that they were more likely to want to hide, and less likely to want to confess, when feeling shame than when feeling guilt.

In these analyses of phenomenological ratings of personal shame and guilt experiences, we also attempted to directly assess the self versus behavior distinction proposed by H. B. Lewis (1971). We asked people to rate, on a single continuum, whether they viewed their *actions* or *themselves* as "bad." No significant differences emerged. Secondary analyses and anecdotal reports indicated that these lay participants (college undergraduates with little background in psychology) did not really understand the dimension we were attempting to assess. The item itself was apparently too abstract and obtuse. Subsequently, we adopted an entirely different approach that did not require the participants themselves to rate and evaluate this rather abstract concept. Instead, we coded participants' counterfactual thinking associated with shame and guilt to explore the self versus behavior distinction (Niedenthal, Tangney, & Gavanski, in press). Four independent studies provided very strong support for H. B. Lewis's (1971) notion that shame and guilt differ in focus on self versus behavior. For example, participants in one study were asked to describe a personal shame or guilt experience and then to list four things that might have been different so that the situation would not have ended the way it did, completing the stem "If only. . . ." Counterfactual responses were then coded according to whether aspects of the self, behavior, or situation were "undone." Shame descriptions were more often followed by statements undoing aspects of the self; guilt descriptions were more often followed by statements undoing aspects of behavior. Parallel results were obtained in the three other counterfactual studies, each employing a somewhat different paradigm.

In sum, there is now an impressive body of research—including qualitative case study analyses (H. B. Lewis, 1971; Lindsay-Hartz, 1984; Lindsay-Hartz et al., Chapter 11, this volume), content analyses of shame and guilt narratives (Ferguson et al., 1990; Tangney, 1992; Tangney et al., 1993), participants' quantitative ratings of personal shame and guilt experiences (e.g., Ferguson et al., 1991; Tangney, 1989; Tangney, Miller, & Flicker, 1992; Wicker et al., 1983; see also Wallbott & Scherer, Chapter 19, this volume, for pertinent cross-cultural data), and analyses of participants' counterfactual thinking (Niedenthal et al., in press)—whose results converge to support the idea that shame and guilt are distinct emotional experiences that differ substantially along cognitive, affective, and motivational dimensions.

In the remainder of this chapter, I focus on the implications of shame and guilt for interpersonal relationships. I further examine relevant empirical studies of *states* of shame and guilt, and also consider an emerging body of personality research addressing people's *dispositional* tendencies to experience shame and guilt across a range of situations.

CONTRASTING MOTIVATIONS THAT ARISE FROM SHAME AND GUILT EXPERIENCES: HIDING VERSUS AMENDING

One consistent theme emerging from the qualitative analyses (H. B. Lewis, 1971; Lindsay-Hartz, 1984; Lindsay-Hartz et al., Chapter 11, this volume) and quantitative studies of shame and guilt experiences (e.g., Ferguson et al., 1991; Tangney, 1989; Tangney, Miller, & Flicker, 1992; Wicker et al., 1983) is that these emotions lead to very different motivations for subsequent action in interpersonal contexts. A consistent finding is that shame often motivates an avoidance response. Perhaps because shame is generally a more painful experience than guilt, and because shame involves a sense of exposure before a real or imagined audience, people feeling shame often report a desire to flee from the shame-inducing situation, or to "sink into the floor and disappear." In this way, the shamed individual seeks to hide the self from others, and to escape from the overwhelming pain of the situation. Thus, shame motivates behaviors that are likely to sever interpersonal contact.

In sharp contrast, guilt is more likely to keep people constructively engaged in the interpersonal situation at hand. Both qualitative and quantitative studies indicate that, rather than motivating an avoidance response, guilt motivates corrective action. That is, the tension and regret of guilt are more likely to lead to a desire to confess or apologize for the offending behavior, and to repair the damage that was done. This motivation for reparation may stem from the fact that guilt involves a fairly persistent focus on the offending behavior—and therefore, presumably, on its harmful consequences to others. In addition, in guilt the self remains relatively intact; it is not impaired as it is in the shame experience. Thus, the self remains mobile and ready to take reparative action.

These differences between shame and guilt in terms of subsequent interpersonal behavior or motivation were highlighted in our studies of young adults' narrative accounts of their personal shame and guilt experiences (Tangney, 1989; Tangney et al., 1993; Tangney, Miller, & Flicker, 1992). For example, an 18-year-old college student shared this shame experience: "I'm not allowed to date. One day my mom found me kissing this guy. I felt ashamed of myself. *I couldn't face my mom for months*" (emphasis added). This is a graphic account of the tendency to hide that is so often associated with the experience of shame. This young woman, feeling shame, also felt moved to avoid subsequent interpersonal contact—here with her mother, someone to whom she was presumably quite close.

Contrast this with the guilt experience related by another college student: "Well, there's this girl I really like. The other day at the hotel, I kind of messed around with another girl. . . . Now I feel sort of guilty and *maybe I should tell her* . . ." (emphasis added). This young man did not want to hide. In fact, he was actively debating whether to confess to the first girl—a very different motivational picture from that observed in shame.

In sum, across a range of studies, analyses of narrative accounts of shame and guilt, as well as participant ratings of these experiences, indicate that shame and guilt lead to contrasting motives relevant to interpersonal relationships. Whereas guilt tends to motivate reparative action, shame tends to motivate escapist responses. In fact, Barrett and colleagues (Barrett, Chapter 2, this volume; Barrett, Zahn-Waxler, & Cole, 1993) use avoidant versus reparative patterns of behavior as early markers of shame-prone versus guilt-prone styles among toddlers; they have found these behavior patterns to be significantly related to independent parental reports of children's displays of shame and guilt in the home.

SHAMED INTO ANGER: SOME FURTHER MOTIVATIONAL FEATURES OF SHAME

There is now considerable theoretical and empirical evidence to indicate that shame may not only motivate avoidant behavior. Shame can also motivate a defensive, retaliative anger. Both H. B. Lewis (1971) and Scheff (1987) have suggested that the acute pain of shame can lead to a sense of "humiliated fury" directed toward the self *and* toward the real or imagined disapproving other. Because shame involves the sense of exposure and disapproval from sources outside of the self, self-directed hostility is easily redirected toward others involved in the shame-eliciting situation. Observing others may be held in part responsible for the ugly feeling of shame. In addition, H. B. Lewis (1971) has suggested that such other-directed hostility may serve a second defensive function: In redirecting anger outside the self, shamed individuals may be attempting to regain a sense of agency and control, which is so often impaired in the shame experience.

In this regard, it is interesting to note that in Wicker et al.'s (1983) study, respondents were more likely to report a desire to punish *others,* as well as a desire to hide, when rating personal shame versus guilt experiences. Similarly, we (Tangney, Miller, & Flicker, 1992) found that college students reported more feelings of anger in connection with narrative accounts of shame versus guilt experiences.

This link between shame and anger is evident at a dispositional level as well. Much of our research has concerned the personality and adjustment correlates of individual differences in proneness to shame and proneness to guilt. Although most people have a capacity to experience both emotions at various points in their lives, it appears that across a range of negative situations some people are more likely to respond with shame, while others are more likely to respond with guilt. To assess individual differences in shame-proneness and guilt-proneness, we have developed a series of scenario-based paper-and-pencil measures: the Self-Conscious Affect and Attribution Inventory (SCAAI) for adults (Tangney, Burggraf, Hamme, & Domingos, 1988); the Test of Self-Conscious Affect (TOSCA) for adults (Tangney, Wagner, & Gramzow, 1989); the TOSCA-A for adolescents (Tangney, Wagner, Gavlas, and Gramzow, 1991); and the TOSCA-C for children (Tangney, Wagner, Burggraf, Gramzow, & Fletcher, 1990). In these measures, respondents are presented with a range of situations that they are likely to encounter in day-to-day life. Each scenario is followed by a number of associated responses, two of which capture phenomenological aspects of shame and guilt. Respondents are asked to imagine themselves in each situation, and then to rate their likelihood of reacting in each of the manners indicated. Items are summed across scenarios to yield indices of proneness to shame and proneness to guilt.

In addition to shame and guilt responses, the SCAAI and TOSCA include items assessing externalization of blame. "Externalization" involves attributing cause or blame to external factors—aspects of the situation or of another person involved in the event. From an attributional perspective, one might predict that both shame-proneness and guilt-proneness would be inversely related to externalization, since shame and guilt each involve internal attributions of one sort or another, while externalization clearly involves external attributions. Our findings across a large number of studies of children, adolescents, and adults, however, indicate that proneness to the very painful experience of shame is *positively* correlated with a tendency to externalize blame (see Table 4.2). In contrast, the bivariate correlations show that proneness to guilt (about specific behaviors) is negatively or negligibly correlated with externalization of blame.

We have also conducted part correlations, in which we factored out

TABLE 4.2. Relationship of Externalization to Shame-Proneness and Guilt-Proneness in Studies of Adults, Adolescents, and Children

Externalization	Bivariate correlations		Part correlations	
	Shame	Guilt	Shame residuals	Guilt residuals
Adult Study 1 (SCAAI) (n = 101)	.55***	.13	.55***	−.12
Adult Study 2 (SCAAI) (n = 98)	.39***	−.08	.49***	−.31**
Adult Study 3 (SCAAI) (n = 63)	.23†	−.21	.36**	−.35**
Adult Study 4 (SCAAI) (n = 77)	.32**	−.05	.38***	−.20†
Adult Study 5 (SCAAI) (n = 243)	.21***	−.06	.27***	−.18**
Adult Study 6 (TOSCA) (n = 251)	.32***	.02	.40***	−.24**
	.40***	.07	.41***	−.12*
Adult Study 7 (TOSCA) (n = 198)	.44***	.11	.43***	−.04
Adult Study 8 (TOSCA) (n = 194)	.36***	−.05	.42***	−.22**
Adolescent Study 1 (TOSCA-A) (n = 244)	.28***	−.27***	.43***	−.42***
Adolescent Study 2 (TOSCA-A) (n = 444)	.23***	−.34***	.40***	−.48***
Child Study 1 (SCAAI-C) (n = 20)	.06	−.36	.38*	−.52**
Child Study 2 (SCAAI-C) (n = 108)	.17†	−.12	.35***	−.33***
Child Study 3 (TOSCA-C) (n = 364)	.19***	−.22***	.32***	−.34***
Child Study 4 (TOSCA-C) (n = 324)	.28***	−.06	.36***	−.23***

†$p < .10$. *$p < .05$. **$p < .01$. ***$p < .001$.

shame from guilt and vice versa, to more directly examine the unique variance in shame and guilt, respectively. Across studies of children, adolescents, and adults, our measures of shame-proneness and guilt-proneness are themselves substantially correlated (about .45), no doubt reflecting the fact that these are both negative emotions that can co-occur with respect to the same situation. The part-correlational analyses in Table 4.2 show clearly that a tendency to experience "shame-free" guilt is negatively associated with externalization of blame, as predicted by attribution theory. Individuals who tend to experience guilt uncomplicated by shame are less likely to externalize blame, and more likely to accept responsibility for the negative situation at hand. Shame residuals, however, remain substantially positively correlated with externalization.

This link between shame and externalization of blame is consistent with H. B. Lewis's (1971) and Scheff's (1987) descriptions of the externally directed humiliated fury that often accompanies shame. As noted above, shame typically involves a very painful condemnation of the global self, coupled with an awareness of how the self may appear to others. Externalization of blame may well represent a defensive attempt to "turn the tables" and re-empower the self by placing blame outside the self. For example, a participant from one of our noncollege studies of adult travelers passing through an urban airport shared this shame experience: "I did something I knew was wrong and a friend confronted me. *I wanted to blame him* for the awkwardness of the situation . . . even though I knew I was at fault" (emphasis added). Although this 42-year-old executive knew at heart that he was wrong, he wanted to blame his friend "for the awkwardness of the situation" (which I read as "the painfulness of the situation").

What is notable in this account, and in other similar accounts from our studies, is that this sort of shame-induced defensive externalization is fairly irrational, even from the perspective of the shamed individual. No doubt the recipient of such shame-induced externalization reactions would also experience such exchanges as unjustified and irrational. Thus, although defensive externalization may represent a short-term gain in lessening the pain of shame in the moment, on balance this sort of shame–blame sequence is likely to be destructive for long-term interpersonal relationships. Moreover, from the standpoint of the shamed person, such defensive externalization may subsequently lead either to withdrawal from the blamed person, or to the full-blown, hostile, humiliated fury described by H. B. Lewis (1971) and Scheff (1987). In either case, the ultimate result is likely to be some rift in the interpersonal relationship.

The results involving externalization of blame are consistent with the notion of a link between shame and anger, but the SCAAI and TOSCA Externalization scales assess a cognitive attributional dimension (externalization of blame), not affective anger per se. In a series of subsequent studies, we examined the link between anger and shame more directly by including measures of anger arousal and hostility (Tangney, Wagner, Fletcher, &

Gramzow, 1992). To summarize briefly, in two independent samples ($n =$ 243 and $n = 252$, respectively), college students completed the Trait Anger Scale (TAS; Spielberger, Jacobs, Russell, & Crane, 1983), the Symptom Checklist 90 (SCL-90; Derogatis, Lipman, & Covi, 1973), and the SCAAI and/or TOSCA. Across both studies, proneness to shame was significantly positively correlated with TAS Trait Anger and with the SCL-90 Hostility–Anger and Paranoid Ideation subscales. In contrast, proneness to "shame-free" guilt (i.e., independent of the variance shared with shame) was negatively or negligibly correlated with these indices of anger and hostility. In the second sample, participants also completed the Buss–Durkee Hostility Inventory (Buss & Durkee, 1957). Here, too, indices of indirect hostility, irritability, negativism, resentment, and suspicion were positively correlated with proneness to shame, and negatively or negligibly correlated with proneness to guilt uncomplicated by shame. Only the measures of more direct aggression—the Buss–Durkee Assault scale (measuring direct physical aggression) and the Verbal Hostility scale—failed to show this differential relationship to shame and guilt. These indices of direct aggression were largely unrelated to proneness to shame.

A similar pattern of results was observed in a sample of 363 fifth-grade children (Tangney, Wagner, Burggraf, Gramzow, & Fletcher, 1991) who completed the Children's Inventory of Anger (CIA; Finch, Saylor, & Nelson, 1987) and the TOSCA-C. In addition, the children's teachers completed the teacher version of the Child Behavior Checklist (CBCL; Achenbach & Edelbrock, 1986). Among the fifth-grade males, shame-proneness was positively correlated with both self-reports of anger and teacher reports of aggression, whereas guilt-proneness was negatively correlated with self-reports of anger. Among the fifth-grade females, shame-proneness was also positively correlated with self-reports of anger, but unrelated to teacher reports of aggression. No reliable links were observed between females' guilt-proneness and indices of anger and aggression.

In sum, empirical evidence from diverse methods and sources suggests that shame may often result in (or at least co-occur with) feelings of anger and hostility, and a tendency to project blame outward. In contrast, guilt has been associated with a tendency to accept responsibility, and, if anything, with a somewhat decreased tendency toward interpersonal anger and hostility.

Some question remains, however, concerning how shame-prone individuals handle their anger once they become angry. Among males in the study of fifth-grade children, shame was linked to teachers' reports of aggressive behavior as well as self-reports of anger (Tangney, Wagner, Burggraf, Gramzow, & Fletcher, 1991). But in the study of college students, shame was related to measures of anger, hostility, resentment, and indirect aggression, but not to measures of more direct aggression (Tangney, Wagner, Fletcher, & Gramzow, 1992). This raises the possibility that shame-prone adults are prone to a seething, bitter, resentful kind of anger that they find difficult to express directly. Alternately, the negligible links between shame and direct aggression may be an artifact of problems with the Buss–Durkee aggression scales. This warrants careful consideration because the Buss–Durkee measure was primarily designed to assess cognitive and affective aspects of anger and hostility, rather than actual behavioral aggression.

SHAME, GUILT, AND CONSTRUCTIVE VERSUS DESTRUCTIVE RESPONSES TO ANGER

We recently extended our investigation of the differential role of shame and guilt in anger by taking a much more in-depth look at how these individual differences in moral affective style are related to the ways in which people characteristically manage their anger across the lifespan. That is, once people become angry, what do they do? One problem we encountered is that there currently exists no measure that assesses the broad range of possible responses to anger. The literature offers many measures of anger arousal, and quite a number of measures of behavioral aggression. But in his studies of everyday episodes of anger, Averill (1982) found that aggression is by no means the dominant response to anger. Instead, adults' narrative accounts included reference to a range of nonaggressive behaviors and "cognitive reappraisals" of the situation, in addition to verbal and physical aggression. Thus, our first task was to develop a series of parallel child, adolescent, and adult measures that would assess the range of possible cognitive and behavioral responses people might select when angered.

The resulting versions of the Anger Response Inventory (the ARI for adults, Tangney, Wagner, Marschall, & Gramzow, 1991; the ARI-A for adolescents, Tangney, Wagner, Gavlas, & Gramzow, 1991; and the ARI-C for children, Tangney, Wagner, Hansbarger, & Gramzow, 1991) consist of a series of developmentally appropriate situations that are likely to elicit anger in everyday contexts. The various ARIs are similar in structure to the SCAAI and TOSCA. Respondents are asked to imagine themselves in each situation, and then to rate a number of associated responses. The ARI scales (see Table 4.3) represent four broad categories of anger-related dimensions: (1) Anger Arousal; (2) Intentions (e.g., malevolent, constructive); (3) Cognitive and Behavioral Responses to Anger (including maladaptive behaviors such as aggression, adaptive behaviors such as nonhostile discussion, escapist/diffusing responses, and cognitive reappraisals); and (4) Long-Term Consequences of the anger episode as assessed or predicted by the participants.

In a cross-sectional developmental study of 302 children (grades 4–6), 427 adolescents (grades 7–11), 176 college students, and 194 adult travelers passing through a large urban airport, participants completed the appropriate versions of the ARI and TOSCA (Tangney, Wagner, Gavlas, Barlow, & Marschall, 1992). Results indicated that across all ages, proneness to shame

TABLE 4.3. Assessment of Anger-Related Processes (ARI)

I. Anger Arousal
II. Intentions
    A. Constructive (desire to fix the situation)
    B. Malevolent (desire to hurt or get back at target)
    C. Fractious (desire to "let off steam")
III. Cognitive and Behavioral Responses to Anger
    A. Maladaptive Behaviors and Cognitions
        1. Direct Aggression toward the Target (physical, verbal, symbolic)
        2. Indirect Aggression (harming something important to target, malediction)
        3. Displaced Aggression (aggressing toward someone other than target)
        4. Self-Directed Aggression (anger at self for situation)
        5. Anger Held In (ruminating over incident without expressing)
    B. Adaptive Behaviors
        1. Discussion with Target of Anger
        2. Direct Corrective Action
    C. Escapist/Diffusing Responses
        1. Attempts to Diffuse Anger (e.g., distracting activities)
        2. Minimizing Importance of Incident
        3. Removal (leaving situation)
        4. Doing Nothing
    D. Cognitive Reappraisals
        1. Reappraising Role of Self
        2. Reappraising Role of Target
IV. Long-Term Consequences (for self, target, and relationship)

was substantially correlated with anger arousal; thus our earlier findings with more traditional measures of anger were replicated. Perhaps more importantly, the findings indicate that shame-prone individuals are not only more prone to anger in general; they are also more likely to do unconstructive things with their anger, compared to their less shame-prone peers. Across individuals of all ages (8 years through adulthood), shame-proneness was clearly related to maladaptive and nonconstructive responses to anger—including malevolent intentions; direct, indirect, and displaced aggression; self-directed hostility; and negative long-term consequences. In contrast, guilt-proneness was generally associated with constructive means of handling anger—including constructive intentions; attempts to take direct corrective action and attempts to discuss the matter with the target of the anger in a nonhostile fashion; cognitive reappraisals of the target's role in the anger situation; and positive long-term consequences.

One cluster of scales—the Escapist/Diffusing Responses—showed some interesting developmental trends. Escapist/diffusing responses are not clearly constructive or destructive. They include attempts to diffuse the anger (e.g., taking a walk, engaging in some distracting activity), minimizing the importance of the event (e.g., "It wasn't that important anyway"), removing oneself from the situation (e.g., leaving the room), and simply doing nothing. The findings involving these responses were more mixed. Among children and adolescents, these dimensions were positively correlated with guilt and largely unrelated to shame. Among older participants, however, the shame and guilt correlates were much less clear-cut. This pattern of findings is consistent with our analyses of the interrelationship of ARI scales, which indicated a developmental shift in the long-term consequences of these escapist/diffusing responses. For children, such attempts to escape or diffuse the anger-eliciting situation appear to have fairly positive outcomes. In other words, it appears that anything children can do to "keep a lid" on their anger is an adaptive strategy. This strategy, however, seems to become less adaptive with age. Among college students and adults, more direct constructive responses (e.g., corrective action and attempts to discuss the matter with the target of the anger) were most strongly linked to positive long-term consequences.

In our most recent study of 256 college students, my students and I replicated the findings concerning the relation of shame and guilt to these anger-related dimensions among young adults. Table 4.4 shows that in this sample of undergraduates, both shame-proneness and guilt-proneness were associated with anger arousal. Once respondents were angered, however, their subsequent motivations, cognitions, and behaviors differed considerably, depending on whether they were shame-prone or guilt-prone. Focusing on the part-correlational analyses, shame-proneness was associated with malevolent and fractious intentions (e.g., a desire to "let off steam"), and with a likelihood of engaging in direct verbal and symbolic aggression, indirect aggression (e.g., harming something important to the target, talking behind the target's back), all types of displaced aggression, self-directed aggression, and anger held in (a ruminative, unexpressed anger). Furthermore, shame-prone college students reported that they were less likely to discuss the matter with the target of their anger in a nonhostile, constructive fashion, and more likely simply to leave the situation, compared to their non-shame-prone peers. Finally, shame-proneness was associated with respondents' assessments of negative long-term consequences as a result of the entire episode of anger.

The patterns of findings involving guilt were strikingly different from those involving shame. Focusing again on the part correlations, proneness to "shame-free" guilt was positively correlated with constructive intentions, and negatively correlated with all indices of direct, indirect, and displaced aggression. Instead, compared to their non-guilt-prone peers, guilt-prone individuals were much more likely to report that they would engage in constructive behaviors, such as nonhostile discussion with the target of their anger and direct corrective action. Guilt-proneness was also associated with reported attempts to diffuse the feeling of anger (e.g., by engaging in some distracting activity) and with cognitive reappraisals of the target's role in the situation (e.g., "Maybe he didn't mean to do it") and of the self's role in the situation (e.g., "Maybe I had something to do with the situation").[3] Finally, proneness to shame-free guilt was associated with respondents'

TABLE 4.4. Relation of Shame-Proneness and Guilt-Proneness to Anger-Related Processes

	Bivariate correlations		Part correlations	
ARI scale	Shame	Guilt	Shame residuals	Guilt residuals
Anger arousal	.39***	.31***	.27***	.16**
Intentions				
Constructive	.11	.37***	−.07	.36***
Malevolent	.34***	.08	.33***	−.07
Fractious	.34***	.20**	.27***	.06
Cognitive and Behavioral Responses to Anger				
Maladaptive Behaviors and Cognitions				
Direct Physical Agg.	−.03	−.30***	.11	−.31***
Direct Verbal Agg.	.12	−.17**	.22***	−.25***
Direct Symbolic Agg.	.08	−.25***	.22***	−.32***
Indirect Harm Agg.	.22***	−.05	.27***	−.16*
Indirect Malediction Agg.	.18**	−.17**	.29***	−.28***
Displaced Physical Agg.	.06	−.25***	.19**	−.30***
Displaced Verbal Agg.	.38***	−.02	.43***	−.21**
Displaced to Object Agg.	.16**	−.14*	.25***	−.23***
Self-Directed Aggression	.45***	.28***	.36***	.09
Anger Held In	.49***	.19**	.45***	−.03
Adaptive Behaviors				
Discussion w/Target	.04	.42***	−.16**	.45***
Direct Corrective Action	.14*	.45***	−.07	.43***
Escapist/Diffusing Responses				
Diffusion	.13*	.23***	.02	.20**
Minimization	−.05	−.07	−.02	−.06
Removal	.32***	.21**	.25***	.07
Doing Nothing	.12	.06	.10	.01
Cognitive Reappraisals				
Target's Role	.07	.32***	−.08	.32***
Self's Role	.40***	.37***	.26***	.22***
Long-Term Consequences	−.23***	.11	−.31***	.23***

Note. n's range from 251 to 256.
*$p < .05$. **$p < .01$. ***$p < .001$.

assessments of positive long-term consequences as a result of the entire episode of anger.

Taken together, our findings from several studies indicate that across individuals of all ages, shame-proneness is associated with maladaptive and nonconstructive responses to anger, whereas guilt-proneness is associated with constructive means of handling anger—strategies that are likely to strengthen and enhance interpersonal relationships.

SHAME, GUILT, AND INTERPERSONAL EMPATHY

The observed links between shame and externalization of blame, anger, and maladaptive responses to anger raise some more general questions about the interpersonal sensitivity of the shame-prone person. Are shame-prone individuals less empathic than their peers? Over the past several years, my colleagues and I have conducted a series of studies to examine the implications of shame and guilt for interpersonal empathy.

Empathy is generally regarded as the "good" moral affective capacity. There is a vast empirical literature indicating that empathy facilitates altruistic, helping, and/or social behavior; that it fosters warm, close interpersonal relationships; and that it inhibits interpersonal aggression (e.g., Feshbach, 1987; Eisenberg & Miller, 1987; Miller & Eisenberg, 1988).

Empathy is, in essence, the vicarious sharing of another person's emotional experience, and it requires a number of interrelated skills or capacities (Feshbach, 1975). First, empathy requires the ability to take another person's perspective—a role taking capacity. Second, empathy requires the ability to discriminate or to read accurately another person's particular emotional experience. Feshbach (1975) terms this "affective cue discrimination." Third, empathy requires the ability to freely experience a range of emotions oneself, since empathy involves the sharing of the other's affective experience in one form or another.

In recent years, a number of researchers have made an important distinction between "other-oriented" empathy and a more "self-oriented" personal distress response (Batson, 1990; Batson & Coke, 1981; Davis, 1983). In "other-oriented" empathic responses, the empathic individual takes another person's perspective, imagining how a situation might seem from his or her standpoint, and is thus able to vicariously experience feelings or emotions similar to those experienced by the other. Such other-oriented empathic responses need not involve an exact "affective match" (e.g., the empathic individual does not necessarily experience the same level of grief, anger, sadness, or joy as the other), but in other-oriented empathy there is the sense that "Yes, I feel some of your pain" (or joy, or whatever). In cases of negative emotions, other-oriented empathic reactions are typically accompanied by feelings of sympathy and concern for the other. What is critical here is that the empathic individual remains focused on the experiences and needs of the other, not on his or her own empathic response. "Other-oriented" empathy heightens one's understanding of another person's experience, enhances other-directed feelings of sympathy and concern, and leads one to extend aid or comfort in the best interests of the other.

In contrast, "self-oriented" personal distress responses involve a primary focus on the needs and experiences of the *empathizer*. There may be an initial focus on the distressed other person. But as the empathic process unfolds, there is a shift in focus to the experience of the self: "*I* feel so much (of your) pain!" "It hurts *me* so much to see this happen (to you)." Such personal distress reactions may be viewed as empathy gone awry; they often represent a sense of being overwhelmed by the empathic connection.

The distinction between other-oriented empathy and self-oriented personal distress has been supported by a number of empirical studies. For example, Batson et al. (1988) found that other-oriented empathic concern, not personal distress, was related to altruistic helping behavior. And in a study of romantic couples, Davis and Oathout (1987) reported that personal distress was generally associated with negative interpersonal behaviors.

A number of features and correlates of shame and guilt suggest that these emotions should be differentially related to other-oriented empathy versus self-oriented personal distress reactions. In several respects, the ugly feeling of shame seems incompatible with an other-oriented empathic response. Shame is a very painful emotion that involves a marked self-focus. Thus, in situations involving interpersonal transgression or harm, shame serves to draw one's focus away from the distressed other and back to the self. The focal concern is no longer with the hurt that was caused, or with the pain that is experienced by the harmed other. Instead, the focal concern is with the negative characteristics of the self—"*I* am such a horrible person (for having hurt this other person)." It seems likely that instead of promoting other-oriented empathic concern, the acute self-focus of shame would foster self-oriented personal distress responses. Hoffman (1984), for example, has described a phenomenon he terms "egoistic drift," in which a self-focused person may initially feel empathy for another, but the focus on the other is lost and the empathic connection severed as the empathic affect resonates with the observer's own needs. This "egoistic drift" bears many similarities to the personal distress response described by Batson (1990) and Davis (1983). In focusing on the self, the shamed individual is one step closer to a personal distress reaction, and several steps further from true other-oriented empathy.

In addition, because shame is such a painful emotion, it is likely to motivate subsequent defensive maneuvers that would clearly hinder feelings of empathic concern. The tendency to withdraw or hide from shame-related interpersonal situations moves the shamed individual even further from an other-oriented empathic connection. And efforts to defensively externalize blame—to blame the victim of the transgression—are clearly incompatible with other-oriented empathic concern.

In contrast, the structure of guilt would appear to lead naturally to an other-oriented empathic response. In focusing on the offending behavior, not the global self, the person experiencing guilt is relatively free of the self-involved processes involved in shame. Instead, the focus on the specific behavior is likely to highlight the consequences of that behavior for the distressed other. The behavior and its effects on another are in the forefront, rather than the behavior and its reflection on the self. In this way, feelings of guilt (as opposed to shame) may foster a continued other-oriented empathic connection. In this regard, it is interesting to note the strong link observed between guilt and reparative action (e.g., H. B. Lewis, 1971; Lindsay-Hartz, 1984; Lindsay-Hartz et al., Chapter 11, this volume; Baumeister et al., Chapter 10, this volume; Tangney, 1989, 1993; Wicker et al., 1983). Guilt may lead to reparative action not only because guilt often entails a sense of personal responsibility, but also because of guilt's special link with empathic concern. As noted earlier, there is considerable empirical evidence indicating that empathy facilitates prosocial, helping behavior.

Finally, the notion of a special link between guilt and empathy is supported by several other theoretical analyses. For example, both Hoffman (1982) and Zahn-Waxler and Robinson (Chapter 5, this volume) have noted that guilt and empathy follow a common developmental pathway. These authors have gone so far as to suggest that guilt is a special case of empathy, involving feelings of concern for a distressed other coupled with a sense of personal responsibility for having caused that distress. Although the analysis by Baumeister et al. (Chapter 10, this volume) challenges the notion that guilt *necessarily* involves a sense of personal responsibility, a number of studies indicate that guilt is most likely to arise in interpersonal contexts involving harm to another (Baumeister et al., Chapter 10, this volume; Tangney, 1992; Tangney et al., 1993); and, as shown in Table 4.2, guilt is inversely associated with a tendency to externalize blame.

In recent years, we have conducted a series of studies to examine the implications of proneness to shame and proneness to guilt for a dispositional capacity for interpersonal empathy. These studies have included substantial samples of children, college students, and adults ranging in age from early to late adulthood. To assess shame and guilt, participants have completed appropriate versions of the SCAAI or TOSCA. To assess interpersonal empathy, we have used both Davis's (1983) Interpersonal Reactivity Index (IRI), which provides indices of other-oriented empathy and personal distress, and Feshbach's paper-and-pencil measures (the Empathy Scale for Children, Lipian & Feshbach, 1987; the Empathy Scale for Adults, Feshbach & Lipian, 1987; and the Parent/Partner Empathy Scale, Feshbach & Caskey, 1987), which focus primarily on a capacity for other-oriented empathy.

Taken together, our findings strongly support the hypothesized link between guilt and other-oriented empathy. In contrast, shame-proneness has been negatively or negligibly related to other-oriented empathy and positively related to personal distress. The inverse relationship between shame and empathy is most evident in studies employing Feshbach's measures. For example, in three independent samples of college students who completed the Feshbach and Lipian (1987) Empathy Scale for Adults, empathy was positively correlated with proneness to guilt and inversely related to proneness to shame (Tangney, 1991). Similarly, in a study of 229 mothers, 186 fathers, 274 grandmothers, and 170 grandfathers of fifth-grade children (Tangney, Wagner, Fletcher, & Barlow, 1994), indices of other-oriented empathy were again consistently positively correlated with guilt and negatively correlated with shame across these various subsamples. (Parents and grandparents in this study completed Feshbach & Caskey's [1987] Parent/Partner Empathy Scale.) We have also examined the relationship of shame and guilt to empathy in the sample of 363 fifth-grade children (Tangney, Wagner, Burggraf, Gramzow, & Fletcher, 1991). As in the college and adult samples, proneness to guilt was clearly related to a capacity for empathy, especially when "affective" (as opposed to "cognitive") empathy was considered. Shame-proneness, independent of guilt, was essentially unrelated to children's empathy.

As noted above, the distinction between other-oriented empathy and self-oriented personal distress is of special interest when shame and guilt are being considered. We predicted that guilt should be related to other-oriented empathy, whereas shame should be much more closely associated with self-oriented personal distress responses. The Davis (1983) IRI measure of empathy is unique in providing an explicit means of differentiating between components of other-oriented empathy and those of personal distress. Table 4.5 shows the relationship between the IRI scales and measures of shame-proneness and guilt-proneness in two independent samples of undergraduates, and a third study of noncollege adults at a large urban airport. Participants in Study 1 completed the SCAAI measure of shame and guilt.[4] Participants in Studies 2 and 3 completed the TOSCA measure of shame and guilt, drawing on an entirely different set of scenarios and associated responses. Focusing on the part-correlational results, in which shame was factored out from guilt and vice versa, results show a clear and consistent link between proneness to guilt and the scales assessing "other-oriented" empathy (i.e., Perspective Taking and Empathic Concern). In Studies 1 and 2, guilt was also related to the Fantasy scale, assessing perspective taking in the fictional realm (e.g., identifying with the feelings of a character in a book or movie). In contrast, proneness to shame-free guilt was unrelated to personal distress responses in all three samples.

The correlations involving proneness to shame showed a very different pattern of results. The inverse correlation between shame and other-oriented empathy, observed with the Feshbach measures, was replicated in Studies 1

TABLE 4.5. Relation of Shame-Proneness and Guilt-Proneness to Indices of Interpersonal Empathy

| Davis IRI Scale | Bivariate correlations | | Part correlations | |
	Shame	Guilt	Shame residuals	Guilt residuals
Perspective Taking				
Study 1 (SCAAI)	−.04	.25***	−.18**	.31***
Study 2 (TOSCA)	.07	.26***	−.05	.26***
Study 3 (TOSCA)	−.05	.29***	−.19**	.34***
Empathic Concern				
Study 1 (SCAAI)	.21***	.41***	−.07	.28***
Study 2 (TOSCA)	.19**	.39***	.02	.35***
Study 3 (TOSCA)	.11	.33***	−.04	.32***
Fantasy				
Study 1 (SCAAI)	.12	.30***	−.02	.27***
Study 2 (TOSCA)	.17**	.26***	.06	.20**
Study 3 (TOSCA)	.33***	.18**	.28***	.05
Personal Distress				
Study 1 (SCAAI)	.38***	.16*	.34***	−.01
Study 2 (TOSCA)	.41***	.17**	.38***	−.02
Study 3 (TOSCA)	.42***	.14	.40***	−.05

Note. n's were 241 for Study 1, 265 for Study 2, and 192–193 for Study 3. The Study 1 data are from Tangney (1991).
*$p < .05$. **$p < .01$. ***$p < .001$.

and 3 when Perspective Taking and the unique variance in shame were considered. The other part correlations involving shame and measures of other-oriented empathy were negligible, but in sharp contrast to the strong positive part correlations with guilt. Most interestingly, there was a strong positive link between proneness to shame and self-oriented personal distress responses in all three studies.

The empathy studies summarized thus far have considered the relation of shame and guilt to empathy at a *dispositional* level. That is, the results indicate that people who are prone to experience guilt in response to negative situations are also individuals who are likely to experience other-oriented empathy when faced with a distressed other. Similarly, the results generally indicate that shame-prone individuals are not empathic individuals. We also examined the relations of shame and guilt to empathy at the *situational* level in a recent study of children's and adults' narrative accounts of personal shame and guilt experience (Tangney et al., 1993). Among both children and adults, respondents were more likely to express other-oriented empathy when describing personal guilt experiences than when describing personal shame experiences. Thus, it appears that shame and guilt show a differential link to empathy, regardless of whether the traits or dispositions (proneness to shame and proneness to guilt) or the situational states (actual shame and guilt) are being considered.

DIRECTIONS FOR FUTURE RESEARCH

The converging empirical findings summarized in this chapter suggest strongly that shame and guilt have very different implications for motivation and behavior in interpersonal contexts. These studies have employed a range of methods, including content analyses of autobiographical accounts of real-life shame and guilt experiences, participants' retrospective ratings of these experiences, analyses of counterfactual thinking associated with shame and guilt, and self-reported behavior patterns and personality correlates of dispositional tendencies to experience shame and guilt. It should be noted, however, that most of these studies have centered on self-reports of various kinds. In light of this focus on self-reports, the results from the study of 363 fifth-grade children (Tangney, Wagner, Burggraf, & Gramzow 1991) are especially noteworthy. Teacher ratings, as well as self-reports, of children's interpersonal behavior were significantly associated with these students' affective styles.

An important direction for future research will be to extend this literature with additional studies of shame- and guilt-related behaviors, drawing on observational methods and reports of significant others. In addition, it will be useful to investigate shame and guilt experiences occurring in "real time," rather than relying solely on retrospective accounts of these experiences. To this end, we are currently embarking on a series of studies to examine interpersonal behaviors following moderate shame inductions. And we are in the midst of two large-scale investigations of shame, guilt, and anger—one among young adult couples, and the other involving parents and their adolescents. These latter studies include independent reports of real-life interactions and behaviors from the perspectives of both participants in connection with recent episodes of anger.

SUMMARY AND CONCLUSIONS

In the course of day-to-day life, we inevitably do things that hurt those around us. The opportunities for transgression are many—ranging from relatively mundane unintended slights, thoughtless remarks, or forgotten appointments to more serious betrayals of confidence, bald-faced lies, and crushing infidelities. In spite of these transgressions, most of our relationships endure; many flourish. One important factor in maintaining these relationships is our ability to recognize and care enough to take appropriate corrective action when we have caused someone harm.

Shame and guilt are generally regarded as two key "moral" emotions that prompt us to stop and take notice when we have hurt or transgressed against another. The findings presented here, however, strongly suggest that shame and guilt are not equally "moral" emotions, nor are they equally effective in the interpersonal realm. In fact, shame and guilt appear to lead us down very different paths of interpersonal behavior.

The ugly feeling of shame is related to a constellation of factors that do not augur well for interpersonal relationships. First, the self-focused experience of shame is likely to "short-circuit" feelings of other-oriented empathy. The person who feels shame upon harming another is more likely to react with self-focused personal distress, and less likely to experience other-oriented empathic concern. Second, shamed individuals are likely to engage in behaviors that impede subsequent constructive action in interpersonal contexts. Rather than promoting reparative action, shame appears to motivate either active avoidance or a tendency to blame others involved in the shame-eliciting situation. Third, there appears to be a special link between shame and anger—and shamed individuals are at a particular disadvantage in this regard. When feelings of anger ensue (either as a rational response to real provocation or as a defensive response to feelings of shame), shamed individuals are likely to manage their anger in an unconstructive fashion. Their intentions are biased toward the malicious; their behaviors are likely to be directly or indirectly aggressive or self-serving. Not surprisingly, they anticipate that the outcomes of such anger episodes will be, on balance, more harmful than beneficial—to themselves, their partners, and their relationships. And in this assessment, they are probably quite accurate.

The interpersonal picture emerging in connection with guilt is strikingly different. Guilt is associated with a range of features that are likely to strengthen and enhance interpersonal relationships. Having transgressed, the person experiencing guilt remains focused on the offending behavior, and presumably on its consequences for the other person. Rather than directing one's focus on the self, guilt fosters an other-oriented focus that promotes feelings of empathic concern. And such empathic concern, in turn, probably contributes to the press toward reparative action that is so characteristic of the guilt experience. The motivation to confess, apologize, or repair is also enhanced by the tendency for guilty people to own the offending behavior. Rather than blaming others, people in the midst of a guilt experience take responsibility for their actions; they feel remorse and regret; and they feel moved to make amends accordingly. Given these characteristics, it is not surprising that guilt-prone individuals are most likely to make constructive use of everyday episodes of anger when conflicts do arise in their relationships. Once guilt-prone individuals are angered, their intentions are likely to be constructive. Although angry, they are likely to feel a press to fix the situation. Not surprisingly, their behaviors tend to be oriented in a constructive, communicative direction. And they anticipate generally beneficial outcomes of the entire anger episode.

Taken together, these findings from a series of empirical studies provide further support for Baumeister et al.'s (Chapter 10, this volume) notion that guilt serves a number of important relationship-enhancing functions. Both shame and guilt may serve to curb a range of individually and socially detrimental behaviors. But shame brings with it a heavy burden to our relationships with friends, colleagues, and loved ones. And, as described in our subsequent chapter (Tangney et al., Chapter 14, this volume), the tendency to experience shame also brings with it a heavy price in terms of individual psychological adjustment.

ACKNOWLEDGMENTS

Preparation of this chapter was supported by Grant No. R01HD27171 from the National Institute for Child Health and Human Development. I wish to thank Deborah Hill Barlow, Tim Mohr, Donna Marschall, and Jennifer Sanftner for their assistance in preparing materials for this chapter. My thanks also to Carey Fletcher, Jim Gordon, and Sam Howell; many of the data presented in Tables 4.4 and 4.5 were drawn from a larger investigation conducted by these three students in connection with their dissertations.

NOTES

1.   Most often, these self-relevant internal attributions associated with shame and guilt relate directly to one's own actions or inactions (e.g., one may feel shame or guilt for one's role in causing harm to another), but there are also situations where self-relevant attributions are somewhat more indirect (e.g., one may feel shame or guilt when one's child, or some other closely related group member, causes harm to another). In the latter case, it seems that the notion of "self" is extended to include those with whom one is closely identified.

2.   H. B. Lewis's (1971) distinction between shame and guilt departs from the earlier anthropological view, which emphasized public versus private and internal versus external dimensions. Benedict (1946), for example, conceptualized shame as a reaction to public exposure of some personal shortcoming, whereas she saw guilt as more of a private affair between one's self and one's internalized conscience. As it turns out, this public–private distinction has not fared particularly well in recent empirical studies of shame and guilt. For example, in our study of narrative accounts of personal shame and guilt experiences provided by several hundred children and adults (Tangney et al., 1993), we found that although both shame and guilt were most often experienced in interpersonal contexts, a substantial number of these events occurred when the person was alone. More importantly, solitary shame experiences were just as common as solitary guilt experiences. In other words, there was no evidence that shame is a more "public" emotion than guilt in terms of the structure of the eliciting situation.

3.   It is interesting to note here that the unique variance in shame was also associated with these "self-reappraisals." Our guess is that such self-reapprais-als can take two very different forms, depending on whether the individual is prone to shame or prone to guilt. In the case of the guilt-prone individual, such self-reappraisals may lead to a re-examination of the role of the self in causing

a particular behavior—and ultimately to reparative action. In the case of the shame-prone individual, such self-reappraisals may lead to a re-examination of the self per se, and subsequent global self-devaluation. The ARI Reappraising Role of Self scale, unfortunately, was not designed to make such a subtle distinction.

4. Study 1 results originally appeared in a more detailed report of the relationship of shame and guilt to empathy (Tangney, 1991).

REFERENCES

Achenbach, T. M., & Edelbrock, C. (1986). *Manual for the Teacher Report Form of the Child Behavior Checklist and teacher version of the Child Behavior Profile.* Burlington: University of Vermont, Department of Psychiatry.

Averill, J. R. (1982). *Anger and aggression: An essay on emotion.* New York: Springer-Verlag.

Barrett, K. C., Zahn-Waxler, C., & Cole, P. M. (1993). Avoiders versus amenders: Implications for the investigation of guilt and shame during toddlerhood? *Cognition and Emotion, 7,* 481–505.

Batson, C. D. (1990). How social an animal? The human capacity for caring. *American Psychologist, 45,* 336–346.

Batson, C. D., & Coke, J. S. (1981). Empathy: A source of altruistic motivation for helping? In J. P. Rushton & R. M. Sorrentino (Eds.), *Altruism and helping behavior: Social, personality, and developmental perspectives* (pp. 167–187). Hillsdale, NJ: Erlbaum.

Batson, C. D., Dyck, J. L., Brandt, J. R., Batson, J. G., Powell, A. L., McMaster, M. R., & Griffitt, C. (1988). Five studies testing two new egoistic alternatives to the empathy–altruism hypothesis. *Journal of Personality and Social Psychology, 55, 52–77.*

Benedict, R. (1946). *The chrysanthemum and the sword: Patterns of Japanese culture.* Boston: Houghton Mifflin.

Buss, A. H., & Durkee, A. (1957). An inventory for assessing different kinds of hostility in clinical situations. *Journal of Consulting Psychology, 21,* 343–348.

Davis, M. H. (1983). Measuring individual differences in empathy: Evidence for a multidimensional approach. *Journal of Personality and Social Psychology, 44,* 113–126.

Davis, M. H., & Oathout, H. A. (1987). Maintenance of satisfaction in romantic relationships: Empathy and relational competence. *Journal of Personality and Social Psychology, 53,* 397–410.

Derogatis, L. R., Lipman, R. S., & Covi, L. (1973). SCL-90: An outpatient psychiatric rating scale—preliminary report. *Psychopharmacology Bulletin, 9,* 13–28.

Eisenberg, N., & Miller, P. A. (1987). Empathy, sympathy and altruism: Empirical and conceptual links. In N. Eisenberg & J. Strayer (Eds.), *Empathy and its development* (pp. 292–316). New York: Cambridge University Press.

Ferguson, T. J., Stegge, H., & Damhuis, I. (1990, March). *Spontaneous and elicited guilt and shame experiences in elementary school-age children.* Poster presented at the meeting of the Southwestern Society for Research in Human Development, Dallas, TX.

Ferguson, T. J., Stegge, H., & Damhuis, I. (1991). Children's understanding of guilt and shame. *Child Development, 62,* 827–839.

Feshbach, N. D. (1975). Empathy in children: Some theoretical and empirical considerations. *Counseling Psychologist, 5,* 25–30.

Feshbach, N. D. (1987). Parental empathy and child adjustment/maladjustment. In N. Eisenberg & J. Strayer (Eds.), *Empathy and its development* (pp. 271–291). New York: Cambridge University Press.

Feshbach, N. D., & Caskey, N. (1987). *Feshbach Parent/Partner Empathy Scale.* University of California at Los Angeles.

Feshbach, N. D., & Lipian, M. (1987). *The Empathy Scale for Adults.* Los Angeles: University of California at Los Angeles.

Finch, A. J., Jr., Saylor, C. F., & Nelson, W. M., III. (1987). Assessment of anger in children. *Advances in Behavioral Assessment of Children and Families, 3,* 235–265.

Hoffman, M. L. (1982). Development of prosocial motivation: Empathy and guilt. In N. Eisenberg (Ed.), *Development of prosocial behavior* (pp. 281–313). New York: Academic Press.

Hoffman, M. L. (1984). Interaction of affect and cognition in empathy. In C. E. Izard, J. Kagan, & R. Zajonc (Eds.), *Emotions, cognition, and behavior* (pp. 103–131). Cambridge, England: Cambridge University Press.

Lewis, H. B. (1971). *Shame and guilt in neurosis.* New York: International Universities Press.

Lewis, M. (1990). Thinking and feeling—The elephant's tail. In C. A. Maher, M. Schwebel, & N. S. Fagley (Eds.), *Thinking and problem-solving in the developmental process: International Perspectives (The WORK)* (pp. 89–110). Hillsdale, NJ: Erlbaum.

Lindsay-Hartz, J. (1984). Contrasting experiences of shame and guilt. *American Behavioral Scientist, 27,* 689–704.

Lipian, M., & Feshbach, N. D. (1987). *Empathy Scale for Children.* Los Angeles: University of California at Los Angeles.

Miller, P. A., & Eisenberg, N. (1988). The relation of empathy to aggressive and externalizing/antisocial behavior. *Psychological Bulletin, 103,* 324–344.

Niedenthal, P., Tangney, J. P., & Gavanski, I. (in press). "If only I weren't" vs. "If only I hadn't": Distinguishing shame and guilt in counterfactual thinking. *Journal of Personality and Social Psychology.*

Scheff, T. J. (1987). The shame–rage spiral: A case study of an interminable quarrel. In H. B. Lewis (Ed.), *The role of shame in symptom formation* (pp. 109–149). Hillsdale, NJ: Erlbaum.

Spielberger, C. D., Jacobs, G., Russell, S., & Crane, R. S. (1983). Assessment of anger: The State–Trait Anger Scale. In J. N. Butcher & C. D. Spielberger (Eds.), *Advances in personality assessment.* Hillsdale, NJ: Erlbaum.

Tangney, J. P. (1989, August). *A quantitative assessment of phenomenological differences between shame and guilt.* Poster presented at the meeting of the American Psychological Association, New Orleans.

Tangney, J. P. (1991). Moral affect: The good, the bad, and the ugly. *Journal of Personality and Social Psychology, 61,* 598–607.

Tangney, J. P. (1992). Situational determinants of shame and guilt in young adulthood. *Personality and Social Psychology Bulletin, 18,* 199–206.

Tangney, J. P. (1993). Shame and guilt. In C. G. Costello (Ed.), *Symptoms of depression* (pp. 161–180). New York: Wiley.

Tangney, J. P., Burggraf, S. A., Hamme, H., & Domingos, B. (1988, March). *Assessing individual differences in proneness to shame and guilt: The Self-Conscious Affect and Attribution Inventory.* Poster presented at the meeting of the Eastern Psychological Association, Buffalo, NY.

Tangney, J. P., Marschall, D. E., Rosenberg, K., Barlow, D. H., & Wagner, P. E. (1993). *Children's and adults' autobiographical accounts of shame, guilt, and pride experiences: A qualitative analysis of situational determinants and interpersonal concerns.* Manuscript submitted for publication.

Tangney, J. P., Miller, R. S., & Flicker, L. (1992, August). *A quantitative analysis of shame and embarrassment.* Poster presented at the meeting of the American Psychological Association, Washington, DC.

Tangney, J. P., Wagner, P. E., Burggraf, S. A., Gramzow, R., & Fletcher, C. (1990). *The Test of Self-Conscious Affect for Children (TOSCA-C).* Fairfax, VA: George Mason University.

Tangney, J. P., Wagner, P. E., Burggraf, S. A., Gramzow, R., & Fletcher, C. (1991, June). *Children's shame-proneness, but not guilt-proneness, is related to emotional and behavioral maladjustment.* Poster presented at the meeting of the American Psychological Society, Washington, DC.

Tangney, J. P., Wagner, P. E., Fletcher, C., & Barlow, D. H. (1994). *The relation of shame and guilt to empathy: An intergenerational study.* Manuscript in preparation.

Tangney, J. P., Wagner, P. E., Fletcher, C., & Gramzow, R. (1992). Shamed into anger? The relation of shame and guilt to anger and self-reported aggression. *Journal of Personality and Social Psychology, 62,* 669–675.

Tangney, J. P., Wagner, P. E., Gavlas, J., & Gramzow, R. (1991). *The Anger Response Inventory for Adolescents (ARI-A).* Fairfax, VA: George Mason University.

Tangney, J. P., Wagner, P. E., Gavlas, J., & Gramzow, R. (1991). *The Test of Self-Conscious Affect for Adolescents* (TOSCA-A). Fairfax, VA: George Mason University.

Tangney, J. P., Wagner, P. E., Gavlas, J., Barlow, D. H., & Marschall, D. E. (1992, August). *Shame, guilt, and constructive vs. destructive anger.* Poster presented at the meeting of the American Psychological Association, Washington, DC.

Tangney, J. P., Wagner, P. E., & Gramzow, R. (1989). *The Test of Self-Conscious Affect.* Fairfax, VA: George Mason University.

Tangney, J. P., Wagner, P. E., Hansbarger, A., & Gramzow, R. (1991). *The Anger Response Inventory for Children (ARI-C).* Fairfax, VA: George Mason University.

Tangney, J. P., Wagner, P. E., Marschall, D., & Gramzow, R. (1991). *The Anger Response Inventory (ARI).* Fairfax, VA: George Mason University.

Wicker, F. W., Payne, G. C., & Morgan, R. D. (1983). Participant descriptions of guilt and shame. *Motivation and Emotion, 7,* 25–39.

III

DEVELOPMENT OF SELF-CONSCIOUS EMOTIONS

5

Empathy and Guilt: Early Origins of Feelings of Responsibility

CAROLYN ZAHN-WAXLER
JOANN ROBINSON

Some of the self-conscious, self-evaluative emotions, such as guilt, shame, and empathy, have also been construed as "moral emotions." The purpose of this chapter is to examine the early development of two of these emotions, guilt and empathy, as reflections of more broadly based feelings of responsibility for others. We consider both commonalities and differences in empathy and guilt, focusing on theories and research pertaining to children in the early years of life. When feelings of responsibility occur in contexts where children are bystanders to others in distress, relevant constructs include altruism, prosocial behavior, and empathy. When feelings of responsibility occur in more tumultuous contexts of real or perceived wrongdoing (e.g., when a child has caused harm to another), constructs of conscience, reparation, and guilt are invoked. Early theories and research on these two different domains of moral internalization proceeded largely along separate lines.

Research of the 1950s and 1960s more generally emphasized the "thou shalt nots," or how children internalized rules and values of society with regard to acts of wrongdoing (see review by Hoffman, 1970). This work included studies of conscience, guilt, resistance to temptation, and response to prohibition. By the late 1960s and the 1970s, interest in positive aspects of morality (prosocial behaviors, empathy, and altruism) became more prevalent (see review by Radke-Yarrow, Zahn-Waxler, & Chapman, 1983). Social-cognitive dimensions (e.g., moral reasoning, perspective taking, role taking) also assumed prominence during the 1970s (e.g., Kohlberg, 1969).

Integrative efforts across research domains were not common: Older children were primarily studied, and measurement focused more on cognitive and behavioral expressions than on affective dimensions of morality.

Hoffman's theoretical work of the 1970s (Hoffman, 1975) was revolutionary in providing a conceptual framework that would integrate different approaches toward understanding internalization of responsibility. The interactive functions of affect, behavior, and cognition in prosocial and moral development were emphasized. Stages of moral development were proposed that featured the significance of early childhood, as well as middle childhood. Previous conceptualizations had not viewed children as capable of moral actions and caring behaviors until they reached school age. Psychoanalytic theory proposed resolution of Oedipal conflicts as necessary preconditions for superego development. Social-cognitive theories and stage theories of moral reasoning held highly honed capacities for symbolism and representational thought as prerequisites for moral, ethical behavior. Learning theorists also tended to study older children, perhaps more for methodological reasons. Historically, then, with few exceptions, Western approaches to moral development have led to theories and data de-emphasizing early childhood.

Hoffman's theory assumes early, common developmental origins for the "thou shalts" and the "thou shalt nots." That is, concerned, prosocial actions and reparative behaviors share a common motivational core in which empathy guides caring actions. A biologically based preparedness for empathy, first evidenced in the contagious crying of infants, was proposed (Sagi & Hoffman, 1976). As children begin to differentiate self and other during the second year of life, and hence to develop an understanding of others as separate beings, their emotional involvement in others' distress is hypothesized to evolve from personal, self-oriented distress to more other-oriented action patterns of sympathetic concern. Both empathy and guilt are hypothesized to emerge during this period and to show similar developmental trajectories (Hoffman, 1982). Empathy occurs in response to distress in a victim, whether this distress is caused or witnessed by the child. Interpersonal guilt results from the conjunction of an empathic response to someone's interpersonal distress and awareness of having caused that distress.

Hoffman's early focus on the affective dimensions of morality, as well as on the early social-cognitive underpinnings of responsible behavior patterns, anticipated a major thrust of research of the 1980s that is reflected in the focus of this volume—that is, the integration of affect, cognition, and self-development in the study of higher-order, self-evaluative, self-conscious emotions. It also provides a strong rationale not only for including the construct of empathy in the "list" of these higher-order emotions, but for viewing it as central from a developmental perspective.

"Empathy" refers to the experience of others' emotional, physical, or psychological states. It has both cognitive and affective components, reflecting the capacity to understand, imagine, and affectively share the others' states. It may also be manifested in prosocial behaviors (help, sharing, comforting) indicative of concern for others. Empathy that becomes manifested in outward expressions of sympathetic concern can be distinguished from personal distress (Eisenberg et al., 1989, 1990). Yet it is believed to evolve from the personal distress reflected in the reflexive or contagious crying of infants seen in the first days of life. The transition, however, from contagion of personal distress to empathic concern for the other rests in part on the ability to distinguish oneself from another and to feel and act on behalf of another, who is perceived to have separate needs, wishes, desires, and so forth. The orientation of this chapter reflects Hoffman's premise that one major form of guilt is a special case of empathy—namely, the case in which feelings of concern and personal responsibility for a distressed other are conjoined with awareness of having caused the problem.

According to Kagan, a "moral sense" emerges at about the age of 2: Adherence to standards (or preoccupation with correct behavior) becomes important to children; empathy with another's distress is manifested; and anxiety following the violation of adult prohibitions is seen (Kagan & Lamb, 1987). During children's second year of life, parents begin to distinguish in their acts of caregiving and discipline between the children's interpersonal transgressions (e.g., hurting others) that reflect the breaking of a (universal) moral code, and those that reflect the breaking of more arbitrarily determined conventions or rules (Grusec & Kuczynski, 1980; Zahn-Waxler & Chapman, 1982). By age 2, children are beginning to use evaluative words to judge actions of doing harm to others as wrongful or bad (Bretherton, Fritz, Zahn-Waxler, & Ridgeway, 1986). Preschool children are able to make distinctions between moral rules and social conventions as well (Tisak & Block, 1990; Smetana & Braeges, 1990; Turiel, 1983). When asked to generate things children do that are "bad," preschoolers (as young as 3) predominantly generated events entailing negative consequences to others—that is, moral transgressions. These included physical harm, property violations, and violations of interpersonal trust (physical harm being the most common).

Young children's behaviors, as well as language, reflect considerable moral understanding in the early years (Dunn, 1987). Increasingly, there is evidence to support Kagan's claim regarding the appearance of a moral sense at about age 2. There is now a large body of research on early prosocial development (see review by Radke-Yarrow et al., 1983). There is also research on signs of conscience in toddlers (e.g., Lytton, 1977; Emde, Johnson, & Easterbrooks, 1987). Naturalistic observations of 2-year-olds engaged in peer play provide evidence of reparative efforts following aggressive acts (Cummings, Hollenbeck, Iannotti, Radke-Yarrow, & Zahn-Waxler, 1986). Experimental research with 2- to 3-year-olds (Cole, Barrett, & Zahn-Waxler, 1992) confirms the fact that reparative behaviors in response to mishaps are already common at this age.

A principal social-cognitive achievement relevant to moral development during the second year of life involves the ability to recognize the separate existences of self and other. Salient socioemotional achievements during this same period include (1) regulation of affect, and (2) maintenance of effective attachments to the caregiver while beginning to establish autonomy through involvement with others. In particular, increasing modulation of the primary negative emotions (i.e., anger, fear, distress), which have emerged by the beginning of the second year, may facilitate their integration with these other social and cognitive developments to form the higher-order, self-conscious, self-evaluative emotions. Guilt and empathy (both reflecting feelings of discomfort and responsibility in relation to others) thus emerge during a period that is important both for relationship formation and for separation–individuation.

PATTERNS OF RESPONSIBILITY: EARLY DEVELOPMENT OF A MORAL SENSE

We review further evidence that very young children experience emotions of empathy and guilt that may underlie internalization of responsibility. We view these emotions as part of a complex constellation that also includes varied action patterns, social cognitions, and perceptions. We argue that the origins of these emotions can best be examined within this broader definitional framework. We first review, in some detail, research on moral development of children during the second year of life, just prior to that period when more full-blown expressions of responsibility for others appear. We begin with an examination of early prosocial and reparative behaviors, and then consider some of the affective accompaniments that may reflect empathy and guilt. Three longitudinal studies of the emergence of emotions, behaviors, and cognitions in the second year of life that appear to reflect patterns of responsibility are emphasized (Radke-Yarrow & Zahn-Waxler, 1984; Zahn-Waxler & Radke-Yarrow, 1982; Zahn-Waxler, Radke-Yarrow, Wagner & Chapman, 1992; Zahn-Waxler, Robinson, & Emde, 1992).

In these studies, a moral sense is construed in terms of two of the three dimensions used by Kagan: (1) empathy, or concern for the well-being of others; and (2) anxiety over wrongdoing, especially with regard to harm wrought in the interpersonal domain. Several questions have guided this set of studies. What are the very early signs of a moral sense? What forms do these dimensions of a moral sense take, and how do they change over the second year of life? What are the interconnections of cognitive, affective, and behavioral dimensions of morality? What are the biological and social underpinnings—that is, what are the roles of nature and nurture in shaping patterns of individual differences? What conditions determine adaptive and maladaptive forms of expression? In considering these latter questions, we review other relevant research on early moral development and socialization.

Emergence of Prosocial and Reparative Behaviors

In two longitudinal studies (Zahn-Waxler & Radke-Yarrow, 1982; Zahn-Waxler, Radke-Yarrow, Wagner, & Chapman, 1992), mothers were trained to observe their 1- to 2-year-old children's responses to (1) naturally occurring distresses that they caused or witnessed as bystanders, and (2) distresses simulated by mothers and examiners.[1] Children showed patterns of responsibility both for problems they had caused and for problems they had witnessed in others. By 1 year of age, most children provided physical comfort to another in distress (e.g., by hugging, patting, or tender touching), whether or not they had caused the distress. Such early actions may comfort the helper, as well as the recipient, in keeping with the idea that empathic concern evolves from personal distress. Between the ages of 1 and 2, most children began to show other forms of prosocial and reparative behaviors (e.g., helping, sharing, sympathizing, and comforting victims).

Children's actions on behalf of others in distress increased with age in both studies, under naturally occurring (caused and witnessed) and simulated distress conditions, especially between 1¹/₂ and 2 years (see Figures 5.1 and 5.2 for age increases in the original and replication studies). The increases in prosocial and reparative behaviors occurred in conjunction with corresponding decreases in strong emotional arousal, particularly personal distress (Zahn-Waxler & Radke-Yarrow, 1982). More modulated emotional expressions of concern increased in frequency over time, as did cognitive explorations of distress (Zahn-Waxler, Radke-Yarrow, Wagner, & Chapman, 1992). The more modulated manifestations of concern included sad

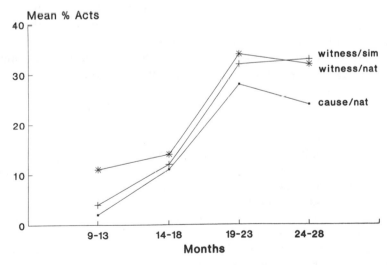

FIGURE 5.1. Age changes in prosocial and reparative behaviors in original study (Zahn-Waxler & Radke-Yarrow, 1982).

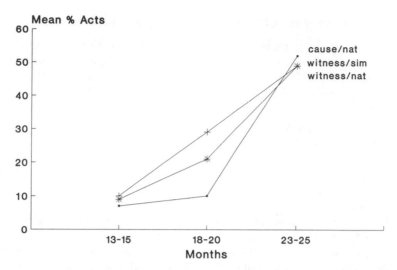

FIGURE 5.2.   Age changes in prosocial and reparative behaviors in replication study (Zahn-Waxler, Radke-Yarrow, Wagner, & Chapman, 1992).

or sympathetic facial expressions, tender statements, or cooing and vocalizing that had a soothing tone. The cognitive explorations of distress appeared as reflections of hypothesis testing, and included complex visual search patterns as well as verbal queries and statements (e.g., "Bumped head," "Hurt foot?" "What's wrong?"). Emotional concern and cognitive explorations frequently accompanied the prosocial and reparative behavior patterns, but also occurred in the absence of caring actions. The expressions of emotional concern may reflect early signs of empathy and guilt. Hypothesis testing may reflect children's earliest efforts to comprehend the circumstances of others and to take their perspectives.

This early capacity to care for others and to care about the consequences of one's actions is an important developmental milestone. In itself, it is of major adaptive significance. In addition to the developmental patterns, there is evidence for stable individual differences in prosocial orientations over time (Cummings et al., 1986). The parallel developmental trajectories for prosocial and reparative behaviors provide initial support for Hoffman's hypothesis regarding similar origins of children's feelings of personal responsibility for others' problems, regardless of whether the children cause these problems or are simply bystanders. At the same time, there were also some indications of differences (see Zahn-Waxler, Radke-Yarrow, Wagner, & Chapman, 1992, for details). Briefly, when children caused physical or psychological harm, they showed more enjoyment, more aggression, more personal distress, and less concern for the other, and were less likely to explore the reasons for distress, than when they witnessed distress as bystanders. Although prosocial *behaviors* reflecting efforts to resolve the problem increased with age, whether or not the child had caused the problem, empathic emotional expressions showed a less strong increase with age when the child had caused the problem (Zahn-Waxler, Radke-Yarrow, Wagner, & Chapman, 1992). Thus, reparative behaviors, or early signs of conscience, may more often develop within contexts of turbulence, ambivalence and conflict.

Development of Prosocial Orientations in Twins

The developmental trajectories for prosocial and reparative orientations in these longitudinal studies were partially replicated in another longitudinal study of monozygotic (MZ) and dizygotic (DZ) twins (Zahn-Waxler, Robinson, & Emde, 1992) seen at 14, 20, and 24 months.[2] Children's responses to simulations of distress were observed. At 14 and 20 months, prosocial behaviors were low in frequency and did not increase over this time period. However, affective expressions of empathic concern and cognitive explorations of the distress (hypothesis testing) did increase with age. (Observational data for 24 months have not yet been analyzed.) Differences in prosocial behaviors may reflect methodological variations across studies or developmental lags for twins (see Zahn-Waxler, Robinson, & Emde, 1992, for expanded discussion of this issue).

Mothers also completed the Differential Emotions Scale (DES; Izard, 1977), rating their children on guilt as well as other discrete emotions. The DES is a list of 30 adjectives describing affective states (3 each for 10 discrete emotions), each rated in terms of prevalence over a week's time. Figure 5.3 indicates developmental patterns for guilt as well as other negative emotions

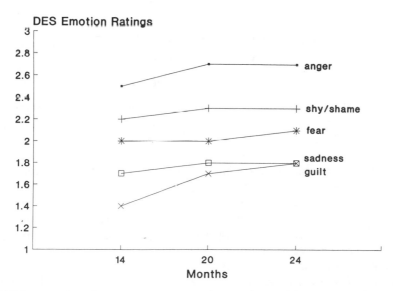

FIGURE 5.3.   Age changes in emotion (Zahn-Waxler, Robinson, & Emde, 1992).

(sadness, anger, fear, and shame), comparing children at 14, 20, and 24 months. Analyses of variance for each of the five emotions included age as a within-subjects variable and gender and zygosity as between-subjects variables. Guilt and sadness were less common than the other negative emotions. Fear was intermediate, and shame and anger were relatively high. All of the negative emotions increased with age: F (2, 364) = 65.02, $p <$ .001, for guilt; F (2, 364) = 9.06, $p <$ .001, for sadness; F (2, 364) = 3.44, $p <$ .05, for fear; F (2, 364) = 4.05, $p <$ .05, for shame/shyness; and F (2, 364) = 7.75, $p <$ .001, for anger. The graph and the F values indicate that the age increase for guilt was stronger than those for the other negative emotions, where increments were modest. There were no main effects of gender or zygosity, nor were there significant interactions present.

The three longitudinal studies, in concert, demonstrate developmental progressions in prosocial and reparative behaviors, and in the emotions and social cognitions presumably linked to moral orientations. The findings are consistent as well with the work of Stipek, Gralinski, and Kopp (1990). In their study, mothers completed questionnaires that provided descriptions of behaviors hypothesized (1) to reflect emotional responses to wrongdoing, and (2) to indicate beginnings of moral understanding. The descriptors included inhibiting behavior when watched, hiding evidence of wrongdoing, being upset by disapproval (i.e., showing shame, remorse), and calling attention to misbehavior. Mothers reported that this cluster of behaviors increased with age during their children's second and third years of life. These behaviors are viewed by Stipek et al. (1990) as precursors to moral emotions, or, in psychoanalytic terms (Sandler, 1960), as reflecting a preautonomous superego schema that precedes conscience.

INDIVIDUAL DIFFERENCES IN PATTERNS OF RESPONSIBILITY

Social-Cognitive Dimensions

A number of theorists have proposed that moral internalization rests in part on the social-cognitive ability to recognize the self and clearly differentiate the self from others. Stipek et al. (1990) have hypothesized in addition, that toddlers who have not achieved an understanding of themselves as entities with distinct characteristics that can be evaluated will not recognize themselves as the targets of caregivers' emotions, and hence will not experience negative emotions such as remorse, shame, and guilt. They used Guttman scale analyses to examine whether physical self-recognition and self-evaluation *preceded* the emergence of emotional responses to wrongdoing. Physical self-recognition preceded emotional responses to wrongdoing, but the evidence for self-evaluation was less clear-cut. Although this study emphasized self-recognition and self-evaluation as developmental phenomena that emerge during the second year, it is also important to ask whether *early* individual differences in these capacities predict differences in emotions and behaviors.

We have examined patterns of association between self-recognition and empathic orientations during the second year of life (Zahn-Waxler, Radke-Yarrow, Wagner, & Chapman, 1992), to explore whether empathic concern for others is based in part on the capacity to differentiate self and other, and hence to "know" the other's needs. With age controlled for, children who were more advanced in self-recognition also scored higher on prosocial orientations, but only near the end of the second year of life. Asendorpf and Baudonniere (1993) have recently provided evidence for synchrony between self-awareness (i.e., self-recognition) and other-oriented social interaction patterns with peers in 19-month-olds. Bischof-Kohler (1988, 1991) also reports associations between mirror self-recognition and empathic reactions to a victim of distress in 16- to 24-month-old children.

These studies demonstrate connections between self-recognition and moral emotions and behaviors, and affirm the significance of social-cognitive developments in the second year of life that may underlie moral patterns. They do not demonstrate unidirectional causal influence of self-recognition on empathic development, however. Both may develop in gradual incremental fashion to influence the further development of the other. That is, the ability to distinguish self from other may make it easier to know the other's unique circumstances. But primitively guided, affectively charged, undifferentiated caring actions toward others may also help the child to make further, more cognitively based distinctions between self and other. If self–other differentiation is a slowly developing process across the second year of life, boundary confusions may occur. Young children often will not be fully cognizant of their causal role in creating distress, or will mistakenly believe they have harmed others, because they lack a clear, separate sense of self.

Some forms of undifferentiation may reflect psychodynamic issues as well as social-cognitive deficits. That is, some young children may have the cognitive capacity to make the distinction between self and other, but by virtue of temperament or inept parenting, they may become emotionally drawn into others' problems at an early age. Finally, self-recognition is far from inevitably linked to empathic development. Self-awareness or self-consciousness also predicts noncompliance during the second and third years of life, particularly in evaluative contexts (Brownell & Gifford-Smith, 1992). Thus, self-consciousness and noncompliance also may be both functionally and developmentally related. A fruitful area of future research will concern the complex conditions early in development that determine individual differences in whether growing self-awareness is more likely to culminate in empathic or noncompliant (oppositional) orientations.

The Role of Emotion

In our earliest work on the development of a moral sense, mothers' observational reports indicated subtle expressions of emotion, potentially indicative of empathy or guilt in situations of another's distress. For example, a mother would note that "his lips quivered as he patted the crying baby" or "she looked sad as she hugged and consoled me" (Zahn-Waxler, Radke-Yarrow, & King, 1979). Frequently these emotions accompanied prosocial and reparative behaviors. As technologies for more accurate recording and assessment of emotion have developed, it has become increasingly feasible to explore potential affective mediators of dimensions of conscience and altruism.

Empathy, Personal Distress, and Prosocial/Reparative Behaviors

One issue in the literature concerns the distinction between personal distress and sympathetic concern, and whether they relate differently to prosocial behaviors. From a developmental perspective, personal distress (contagion of negative affect) diminishes over time as it evolves into empathic concern. Hence there is an initial overlay or possible fusion of the two dimensions, and both may continue to be present in varying degrees throughout development. Once sympathetic concern is present, it would be expected to facilitate expression of prosocial behaviors, whereas personal distress (if intense) may sometimes play an interfering role (Eisenberg et al., 1989, 1990). Eisenberg and her colleagues have attempted to distinguish between personal distress and sympathetic concern by means of psychophysiological measures (heart rate acceleration vs. deceleration), as well as detailed assessments of facial musculature and vocalic expressions. They report reliable associations between sympathetic concern (which has a component of sadness) and prosocial behaviors, but not between personal distress and prosocial acts. High self-focused emotional arousal is likely, then, to interfere with an outward orientation on behalf of others. This work has been done mainly with school-age and older preschool-age children.

Our own work with younger children in the second year of life has not included psychophysiological assessments. But we have examined associations between affect and behavior, based both on maternal observations and on videotapes from which empathic concern and personal distress were coded. Empathic concern was manifested in facial or vocal expressions (e.g., sad looks, sympathetic statements given in a sweet tone of voice) or gestures. In the first study in which these emotional expressions were measured (Zahn-Waxler, Radke-Yarrow, Wagner, & Chapman, 1992), they were correlated with prosocial behaviors and hypothesis testing, both when children caused distress in others and when they witnessed it. The associations became stronger as children reached the end of the second year of life.

Thus, we found a constellation of affective, cognitive, and behavioral dimensions to cohere. This pattern was replicated in the study of twins (Zahn-Waxler, Robinson, & Emde, 1992). In each study, personal distress showed more inconsistent and weak linkages to prosocial orientations. Our work with young children thus coheres with that of Eisenberg et al., indicating more consistent linkages between empathic concern and prosocial acts than between personal distress and prosocial acts.

Discrete Emotions and Reparative Behaviors

It is difficult to say what the emotion of guilt "looks like." It does not appear to have a specific facial configuration or a clear expressive component, as do other emotions. Descriptions of guilt make reference mainly to negative aspects of self (negative cognitions and attributions) and specific behavior patterns. Darwin (1872/1965) pointed out that gaze aversion and stealthy looks are sometimes indicative of guilt. He described a guilty expression following a misdeed of his $2^{1}/_{2}$-year-old as "an unnatural brightness in the eyes and an odd affected manner, impossible to describe" (p. 262). These descriptions, however, focus more on fear of detection than on remorse. Izard (1977) has noted that the other negative emotions have more distinct facial expressions than guilt, though in guilt the face sometimes takes on a heavy look. This could be interpreted as sadness or depressive affect.

It is methodologically challenging to explore questions regarding how the emotion of guilt is expressed in children. To code guilt reflective of remorse, it would be necessary to "capture" acts of transgression that children regretted, and to videotape the interaction for later microanalytic coding of affect. Although it is not possible to approximate these conditions fully in an experimental setting, we "arranged" in one study for children to be involved in mishaps (e.g., accidentally hurting mother, breaking a valued object, etc.) and videotaped these. We then coded from videotapes, toddlers' reactions, as measured by facial and vocal affect displays as well as by behavioral reparative attempts (Cole et al., 1992). Emotions coded included joy, anger, sadness, tension/worry, and tension/worry blends. Frequent reparations were linked to higher levels of sadness and little joy. Anger, tension/worry, and blends of these emotions were unrelated to reparative efforts, but related to one another. Factor analysis confirmed the presence of two separate dimensions: (1) tension/frustration (tension/worry, tension blends, and anger) and (2) concerned reparation (sadness, reparation, and low joy). The two dimensions of concerned reparation and tension/frustration show some correspondence to Eisenberg's distinction between "sympathetic" and "personal" distress (Eisenberg et al., 1989). Both sympathetic distress and concerned reparation are other-oriented reactions that involve less autonomic arousal than personal distress. The patterns are consistent as well with our other studies just described, linking empathic concern (which often contains an element of sadness) with reparative efforts when children have caused distress.

There are unlikely to be one-to-one patterns of association between particular affects and behaviors that reflect a moral sense. Empathic concern does not always translate into prosocial action, and positive actions may not always be guided by specific underlying emotions. Empathic concern may or may not also reflect guilt. And reparative efforts may be linked to anxiety as well as sadness. For example, we found in one study that reparative behaviors were associated with expressions of anxiety in toddlers (for girls only) (Zahn-Waxler, Cole, & Barrett, 1991). Correlational analyses obviously do not provide strong bases for insights into causal patterns or the meaning of the emotions that accompany behavior patterns. They do suggest, however, the importance of further inquiry into different affective mediators that may signal different meanings for prosocial and reparative behavior patterns.

Guilt and Other Negative Emotions

The longitudinal twin study provided an opportunity to examine connections between guilt and other negative emotions in young children. Affect research with adults has had two flourishing traditions: one that emphasizes specific, discrete emotions, and another that focuses on a few broad, nonspecific factors that reflect more general patterns of emotion tone. Efforts have been made to integrate these two traditions by constructing a hierarchical model in which two broad higher-order factors (negative affect and positive affect) are each composed of several correlated, yet ultimately distinct, emotional states (e.g., fear, anger, sadness, joy, guilt). In this model, the lower level reflects the specific *content* of mood descriptors, whereas the upper level reflects their valence. There is some evidence of a hierarchical structure in work with adults. One aspect of demonstrating (convergent and discriminant) validity includes assessment of level of association *between* discrete emotions. In research by Watson and Clark (1992), guilt in adults was significantly associated with other negative emotions of sadness, hostility, and fear. Correlations were mainly in the .50s and .60s.

Previous work with the twin sample (Plomin et al., 1993), using mothers' DES reports of frequency of discrete emotions, identified two broad-based factors—one for positive affect and one for negative affect. Here we explore, with this same sample, the interrelations of the individual components that contributed to the negative factor. Our particular interest is in whether and how guilt overlapped with other emotions. Because there were no zygosity differences, MZ and DZ twins were considered in the same analyses. The correlations between the negative emotions for the entire sample at 14, 20, and 24 months are presented in Table 5.1. These correlations were not so high in magnitude as those in the studies of adults (Watson & Clark, 1992); this difference may reflect, in part, greater reliability and validity of the adult measures. However, most of the correlations were significant, reflecting some interdependency and overlap between negative emotions early in development (see Table 5.1). It suggests that guilt should not be considered as a separate entity, even early in development, but rather as an emotion linked to other negative emotions.

The negative emotion most consistently correlated with guilt in this sample was sadness. This again fits with the earlier reported findings. The two "moral" emotions, guilt and shame, were significantly correlated at only one of the three age points. (It should be noted, however, that the definition of shame for this measure contains a strong component of shyness.) Nor was guilt strongly linked to fear. Because gender differences are common in research on guilt and empathy, analyses were also conducted separately for boys and girls. More often than not, boys and girls contributed similarly to the patterns in Table 5.1. There were some interesting exceptions, usually involving the "moral" emotions. Anger in girls was more clearly linked to shame ($r_g = .25$, $p < .01$; $r_b = .07$; z test of differences = 1.66, $p < .10$), to guilt ($r_g = .18$, $p < .05$; $r_b = -.05$; $z = -2.07, p < .05$), and to sadness ($r_g = .44$, $p < .001$; $r_b = .19$, $p < .05$; $z = -2.52, p < .05$) at time 1 than was anger in boys. At time 2, anger was again more strongly linked to guilt ($r_g = .22$, $p < .01$; $r_b = .09$; $z =$ n.s.) and shame ($r_g = .26$,

TABLE 5.1. Intercorrelations of DES Negative Emotions

	Guilt	Shame	Fear	Sadness	Anger
			14 months		
Guilt		.10	.05	.22***	.05
Shame			.40**	.26***	.15*
Fear				.29***	.19***
Sadness					.30***
Anger					
			20 months		
Guilt		.22***	.11*	.30***	.16**
Shame			.40***	.31***	.17**
Fear				.27***	.35***
Sadness					.35***
Anger					
			24 months		
Guilt		.06	.18***	.25***	.15**
Shame			.44***	.35***	.12*
Fear				.38***	.35***
Sadness					.42***
Anger					

Note. $n = 329$.
*$p < .05$. **$p < .01$. ***$p < .001$.

$p < .001$; $r_b = .18$, $p < .05$; $z =$ n.s.) in girls than in boys. Fear was linked to guilt in boys but not in girls at time 2 ($r_g = .05$; $r_b = .18$, $p < .05$; $z =$ n.s.) and at time 3 ($r_g = .01$; $r_b = .31$, $p < .001$; $z = 2.78$, $p < .01$). In interpreting these data, it is important to bear in mind that the emotions were based on mothers' *reports* of children's experiences; in other words, the mothers imposed their own (adult) understanding of the nature of emotions.

Genetic Influence

Biological or genetic bases for ethical norms and a sense of personal responsibility have long been proposed (e.g., Eibl-Eibesfelt, 1971), but this has been little studied, particularly in children. Evidence for genetic influence on altruism and empathy, based on self-reports of adult MZ and DZ twins, has been reported (Matthews, Batson, Horn, & Rosenman, 1981; Rushton, Fulker, Neale, Nias, & Eysenck, 1986). In our recent work with twins, we found modest evidence for heritability of empathy, based on both observational and maternal report data (Zahn-Waxler, Robinson, & Emde, 1992). Genetic influence was stronger at 14 months than at 20 months, and was most robust for the affective component relative to cognitive and behavioral expressions of concern.

Here we examine heritability of guilt and other negative emotions based on the DES data from that same sample. Previously reported heritability estimates for the two composite DES scores (one for negative emotions and one for positive emotions) indicated no genetic influence for the factor representing positive emotions, but strong evidence for heritability for the factor representing negative emotions (Plomin et al., 1993). Our interest here is in whether some negative emotions contributed more than others to the strong genetic pattern. Would the "moral" emotions (which also appear later in development and are perhaps more subject to socializing influences) show less genetic influence than other negative emotions? We report here on 82 MZ and 78 DZ pairs of twins for whom maternal report data at 14, 20, and 24 months of age are available.

A significantly greater concordance between MZ twins (who are genetically identical) than between DZ twins (who share only half their genes on the average) would suggest genetic influence on behavior. High concordance for both MZ and DZ twins would suggest that environmental influences (including mothers' perceptions of twins' similarity) are salient. Intraclass correlations, comparing concordance patterns for MZ and DZ twins, were used as a first descriptive approach to examine the heritability of guilt, shame, sadness, fear, and anger. The intraclass correlations for MZ and DZ twins' discrete negative emotions at each of the three ages are presented in Table 5.2. Genetic influence can be demonstrated when the magnitude of MZ correlations significantly exceeds DZ correlations. The

TABLE 5.2. Twin Correlations for DES Negative Emotions

Measure	14 months MZ	DZ	20 months MZ	DZ	24 months MZ	DZ
Guilt	.74**	.54**	.57**	.68**	.64**	.63**
Shame	.38**	-.07	.46**	.06	.38**	.16*
Fear	.70**	.25**	.81**	.34**	.81**	.41**
Sadness	.68**	.47**	.61**	.44**	.60**	.49**
Anger	.70**	.25**	.74**	.33**	.76**	.55**

*$p < .05$. **$p < .01$.

table indicates significant patterns of concordance for MZ and DZ twins for all emotions, with the exception of shame/shyness.

The regression model formulated by DeFries and Fulker (1985) provides more precise estimates of heritability (h^2) and shared environment (c^2). (Also see Emde et al., 1992, for details regarding genetic analyses.) Table 5.3 lists parameter estimates from these standard model-fitting procedures. In addi-

TABLE 5.3. Genetic and Environmental Parameter Estimates for DES Negative Emotions

	Model-fitting estimates				Modified (where h^2 and c^2 estimates are constrained)			
	h^2	$(\pm SE)$	c^2	$(\pm SE)$	h^2	$(\pm SE)$	c^2	$(\pm SE)$
				14 months				
Guilt	.40**	(.26)	.34*	(.18)				
Shame	.89**	(.31)	-.51**	(.24)	.26**	(.10)		
Fear	.90**	(.28)	-.20	(.21)	.65**	(.09)		
Sadness	.43*	(.27)	.26	(.20)				
Anger	.90**	(.28)	-.20	(.21)	.65**	(.09)		
				20 months				
Guilt	-.22	(.26)	.79**	(.24)			.62**	(.06)
Shame	.81**	(.30)	-.34	(.24)	.40**	(.09)		
Fear	.93**	(.24)	-.12	(.20)	.79**	(.07)		
Sadness	.35	(.27)	.26	(.21)				
Anger	.81**	(.26)	-.07	(.21)	.72**	(.08)		
				24 months				
Guilt	.03	(.24)	.62**	(.20)				
Shame	.44	(.31)	-.06	(.24)	.37**	(.09)		
Fear	.80**	(.24)	.01	(.20)				
Sadness	.21	(.27)	.39**	(.21)				
Anger	.43*	(.24)	.33*	(.20)				

*$p < .05$. **$p < .01$.

tion, it lists modified (or "constrained") estimates of those parameters that differ from the model-fitting estimates when the classic twin method is violated (e.g., when c^2 is negative). At 14 months, all five negative emotions showed genetic influence; only guilt showed an effect of shared environment as well. For guilt, the influence of shared environment became stronger with age and the evidence for genetic influence disappeared, supporting the increasing role of socialization of moral emotions. Sadness also showed a decrease in genetic influence over time, and an effect of shared environment emerged. The effect of shared environment, however, was not so strong or early for sadness as for guilt. Shame, anger, and fear, in contrast to guilt and sadness, showed mainly genetic influence. Thus, one of the moral emotions (namely guilt) and the emotion most closely associated with it in other studies (namely sadness) showed modest early genetic influence as well as some shared environmental influence, when compared to the other negative emotions.

Stronger evidence for inherent individual differences that result in different moral patterns might be detectable through other measurement strategies or conceptual approaches. For example, there has been a long-standing interest in the role of temperament in conscience. Conscience deficits are considered by some to have biological and physiological underpinnings involving the autonomic nervous system and septo-hippo-campal functioning (see review of Kochanska, 1993). Adults with extreme impairments of conscience (psychopaths) are often described as impulsive and sensation-seeking, as hyperactive, and as having low fear and low frustration tolerance. These are qualities commonly described as character-izing particular temperament types. It leads to the more general question of how temperament relates to moral patterns.

The Role of Temperament

Dienstbier (1984) has suggested that individuals with different temperaments may develop different attributional styles and levels of guilt. According to Dienstbier, a child who is temperamentally prone to high levels of emotion is also likely to feel intense discomfort and distress following a transgression. This tension is likely to be experienced as coming from inside, and therefore an attribution linking the tension with the transgression is likely (i.e., an internalizing of the responsibility). A child who is unlikely to experience negative emotion tension is likely to "condition" poorly. Recent research provides some evidence of relations between children's fearfulness in new situations and more internalized conscience. Asendorpf and Nunner-Winkler (1992) demonstrated that inhibited preschool children were less likely to cheat. Kochanska (1991) reported that children who were fearful as toddlers showed more signs of internalized conscience 5 and 6 years later, but only under certain parenting conditions.

Many associations between different temperament types and different aspects of moral development remain to be investigated. Although there is evidence for commonalities between "positive" and "negative" as dimensions of morality (i.e., connections between empathy and guilt, between prosocial and reparative behaviors, and between conscience and altruism), they are far from synonymous constructs. Qualities of temperament, such as fearfulness and tension, may be good predictors/mediators of conscience or internalization of prohibitions regarding interpersonal transgressions. They may be less predictive of positive, active, outward orientations, in which high levels of personal distress could interfere with attending to the needs of others. Sociability may be a temperament dimension more strongly implicated in expression of positive moral behaviors (Stanhope, Bell, & Parker-Cohen, 1987).

Socialization Experiences

A number of early studies identified dimensions of child rearing that were more (or less) conducive to the development of moral and prosocial behavior patterns in children (e.g., see reviews by Hoffman, 1970; Radke-Yarrow et al., 1983). Much of this work focused on disciplinary techniques that traditionally were divided into categories of power assertion, reasoning, and love withdrawal. Predictable differences were found in the effectiveness of these techniques, though effect sizes were small. Later research emphasized the co-occurrence of different techniques (e.g., Grusec & Kuczynski, 1980; Zahn-Waxler & Chapman, 1982) that influenced the outcomes. We found, for example, that mothers who used affectively charged explanations/reasoning (e.g., "You really hurt Mary and made her feel sad when you pushed her down and took her dolly," said with conviction and emotion) had toddlers who were more reparative and prosocial in their behaviors toward others in distress. Moreover, it was not unusual for these mothers to use power-assertive methods in these contexts as well (Zahn-Waxler et al., 1979).

Early studies focused mainly on proximal parental "causes" of moral and prosocial patterns. More recent work emphasizes the need to consider these more specific practices of discipline and teaching within the context of (the quality of) the parent–child relationship, child temperament, parental personality and psychopathology, and family dynamics. Moral learning occurs within a broader affective climate that includes (1) emotions directed toward the child, both during and outside disciplinary encounters; and (2) emotions the parent directs toward others in the environment, especially the spouse. Caregivers also function as models, not only of appropriate behavior patterns, but of what to do following transgressions. How do adult models repair, or fail to repair, in their own interactions when they have hurt another person? What kinds of "metamessages" do they provide more generally in their relationships, regarding how significant others are experienced and treated (e.g., valued vs. disrespected)? Cultural differences in terms of the values and expectations conveyed to children also merit consideration. In some cultures and subcultures, for example, children are viewed as responsible beings at a very young age, and this is reflected in their caregiving and prosocial behaviors (Rehberg & Richman, 1989; Edwards & Whiting, in press).

Kochanska (1993) has reviewed research on socialization and temperament, and has provided an integrative conceptual framework for understanding the *interaction* of environmental influences and more constitutionally based child characteristics that may contribute to different patterns of moral internalization. Much of this work emphasizes the interaction of parental socialization and child inhibition. Kochanska (1991), for example, found that mothers' early use of psychologically oriented practices de-emphasizing the use of power predicted the development of internalized conscience 5–6 years later, but *only* for children who had been relatively more fearful as toddlers. This is consistent with Dienstbier's (1984) hypothesis about the socialization–temperament interaction, with anxious children being more readily socialized. That is, exposure to parental techniques that de-emphasize power should foster the development of internalization.

Children who are by nature disinhibited and/or hyperactive may be less responsive to psychologically oriented child rearing that de-emphasizes the use of power, (i.e., the message may be less clear to children who are less attentive). At the same time, more firmness or forcefulness may be "heard" as anger by such children, resulting in other negative repercussions. In our work with toddler-age children, mothers' affectively arousing, forceful messages to children about the consequences of their harmful actions (Zahn-Waxler et al., 1979) were linked to prosocial and reparative behaviors. Campbell (1990) has suggested that these same techniques may not be so effective with young hyperactive children, who are more likely to respond negatively to the anger conveyed in the message. Children with difficult temperaments challenge our assumptions about "good" procedures for inculcating internalized patterns of concern and responsibility.

A recent trend in socialization research has been toward empirical consideration of parental emotions as part of the socialization "package." This is illustrated in the research of Eisenberg et al. (1992) on associations between maternal practices and characteristics, and children's empathy. They found connections between mothers' and children's heart rate, facial expressions, and self-reported reactions to a sympathy-inducing film. Maternal sympathy/perspective taking and reinforcement of sympathy/prosocial behavior, as well as negative subordinate emotion (sadness) in the home, were associated with markers of girls' sympathy. Mothers' personal distress (for girls), restrictiveness regarding displays of hurtful emotions (particularly for young girls), and negative dominant emotion in the home (for both sexes) were associated with markers of personal distress in children. Mothers' linking of others' experience to children's own experience was associated with children's responsiveness to distress, and mothers' verbalizations concerning their own emotional state and role taking were associated with boys' self-reported empathy. A study by Fabes, Eisenberg, and Miller (1990) confirms positive connections between maternal empathy and child empathy, mainly for mother–girl dyads. In research with toddlers, Crockenberg (1985) reported that maternal anger directed toward the child is associated with greater personal distress and less concern for others. The role of parental emotion as a socializing influence suggests complex linkage patterns and raises questions regarding mediating mechanisms. Although parental emotion is *experienced* by the child and hence may reflect socialization, commonalities between parents and children may also reflect the similarities in their nervous systems. Intergenerational transmission of moral emotions thus may indicate biologically based as well as environmental processes.

Gender Differences in a Moral Sense

There is a large body of research on gender differences in moral emotions and behaviors. Girls are reported to experience empathy, guilt, and prosocial and reparative behavior more often than boys in many studies (see reviews by Brody, 1985; Eisenberg & Lennon, 1983; Hoffman, 1977; Zahn-Waxler et al., 1991). Females are also underrepresented in the psychiatric disorders that reflect low levels of conscience (e.g., antisocial disorders and conduct problems). In most of our studies of children in the first years of life, prosocial behavior and empathic concern have been more prevalent for girls than for boys. Girls sometimes score higher on personal distress in the face of another's distress. When associations between aggression and guilt/reparation are examined, linkages are consistently stronger for girls than for boys. In two different studies, we found that young girls who were relatively aggressive were also more likely to make reparation (Cummings et al., 1986). This fits with results reported from the twin study, in which positive associations between anger, guilt, and shame were more strongly in evidence for girls during the second year of life. The patterns persist across studies, despite methodological differences (e.g., direct observation vs. maternal report). There seems to be a well-established gender difference by the end of the second year of life, whereby girls are more sensitized to the distress of others (whether or not they have caused it). This sensitivity occurs in conjunction with a steep decrement in their overt anger expressions, relative to those of boys, at this same time period (Goodenough, 1931).

Biologically based causes for gender differences in empathy, guilt, and anger have been proposed that are linked to the childbearing and child-rearing roles of women. Adequate caregiving requires empathy, tolerance of distress in the young, and control over one's anger. Subtle features of socialization experiences and parent–child interaction patterns may also prepare young girls for these roles from a very early age (Chodorow, 1978). In a study of individual differences in emotion regulation during the second year of life, daughters of more sensitive mothers were more empathically attuned (i.e., they matched their mothers' affective displays more closely) than daughters of less sensitive mothers (Robinson, Little, & Biringen, 1993). In early disciplinary encounters, other-oriented approaches (i.e., pointing out the harmful consequences of a child's behavior for others) are used more often with females than with males. Smetana's (1989) observational research indicated that although 2-year-old boys and girls showed similar levels of aggression, mothers used more other-oriented reasoning with girls than with boys.

In considering the role of socialization and discipline on differences in moral orientations in girls and boys, it is necessary to examine both (1) group differences in how parents rear boys and girls; and (2) different patterns of associations, for boys and girls, between parental socialization and child outcomes. Although power-assertive methods are used more commonly with boys than with girls, there are also signs that aggression is more readily tolerated in boys than in girls (e.g., Condrey & Ross, 1985). Moreover, early aggression in boys may emerge in a broader context of a sense of entitlement, in which boys are more often allowed to have what they want, without thinking about what it means for others. In observational studies of sharing in toddlers (Ross, Tesla, Kenyon, & Lollis, 1990), mothers were observed to require daughters to relinquish toys to playmates more often than sons. This sense of entitlement may develop in the context of mother–son interaction during the second year of life. In a study examining the role of maternal style on the balance of control (Biringen, Robinson, & Emde, 1994), more sensitive mothers allowed their sons to take the lead in initiating and elaborating joint play themes. More sensitive mothers of daughters, however, took the leading role during such interactions.

Research also indicates that females are judged more harshly than males for failure to engage in the same altruistic act (Barnett, McMinimy, Flouer, & Masbad, 1987). In longitudinal research, parental efforts to inhibit aggression at age 5 are linked with heightened empathy levels in adulthood, but only for girls (Koestner, Franz, & Weinberger, 1990). Malatesta and Haviland (1982) conducted microanalytic assessments of emotion expressions in 3- to 6-month-old infants and their caregivers. Anger expressions in females were likely to be followed by negative responses from mothers (frowning), whereas anger in males received more empathic responses. There appear to be deeply ingrained cultural expectations for mature interpersonal behavior in young girls. Girls seem to internalize earlier and more completely the message that it is wrong to hurt others, and more generally that it matters how people feel.

Adaptive and Maladaptive Patterns

From a functionalist perspective, each emotion has specific adaptive purposes (e.g., Izard, 1977). For the moral emotions, empathy maintains emotional attachments, guilt may restore severed bonds, and shame protects against improprieties. However, in cases of excess, deficiency, or poor regulation, any emotion can become problematic. Malatesta and Wilson (1988) argue that disturbances in different (discrete) emotion systems can lead over time to specific disturbances in mood and personality patterns that become reflected in specific forms of psychopathology. Excessive empathy is linked to boundary confusions, unhealthy dependencies, and failure to develop a sturdy sense of self; excessive guilt is integral to internalizing disorders such as depression. Deficits in empathy and guilt are implicated in externalizing disorders.

In research with children, moral emotions and behaviors are typically construed in terms of their adaptive functions: Empathy is linked to positive behaviors reflecting social competence, guilt inhibits transgression and motivates reparative behaviors, and so on. Both empathy and guilt help to rectify interpersonal problems and are part of a broader pattern of personal responsibility. Civilization requires that individuals care for the welfare of others and refrain from harming others, their possessions, and their accomplishments. Developmentalists are interested in the processes by which this internalization is achieved over time. Regardless of the theoretical framework, the overarching belief is that individuals develop "more" of these qualities as they grow older, and research repeatedly confirms and reinforces these scientific beliefs. Numerous studies demonstrate increases in moral reasoning, restraint from transgression, and helpful actions. Yet another view of human nature requires us to acknowledge the brutality, indifference, violence, and failures in taking others' needs into account that characterize a significant portion of human behavior, in both children and adults. It is worth asking how the developmental changes (presumed to reflect increases in morality) observed by scientists interface with a reality in which exploitation and abuse are so prevalent. Obviously, human beings are multifaceted in this regard. But this still begs the question of whether it can be assumed that adults are more moral beings than children, or that the capacity for personal responsibility is impoverished in young children.

The notion of increased morality with age may reflect as much developmental myth as fact. Adaptive and maladaptive expressions may occur in children of different ages, as well as adults. How does one proceed from a conception of guilt as a valued social norm that parents work hard to inculcate in their children, to a construct that is commonly construed in adult development as pathological? Descriptors that cohere as a cluster to define guilt in adults include the following: "ashamed," "blameworthy," "disgusted with self," "angry at self," and "dissatisfied with self" (Watson & Clark, 1992). These seem far removed from the earliest positive signs of concern and responsibility for the welfare of others. But perhaps not.

Pathogenic beliefs about the self may be developing as soon as the self begins to develop. From a recent review of literature of the development of social competence and adaptation in the first years of life, Shilkret (1992) has concluded that the capacity to form pathogenic beliefs is present, at least in rudimentary form. We review his position here. On the basis of their experiences with others, children develop expectations or beliefs about the realities experienced. Many of these beliefs are adaptive and nonpathogenic, but some are pathogenic and may lead to later difficulties. The early development of representational thought allows thinking to be freed from the immediate. However, it also allows for certain kinds of inferences and overgeneralizations that come to characterize pathogenic beliefs. Children also begin to develop a "theory of the mind" in the first years of life (Stern, 1985; Trevarthen, 1989); that is, they begin to realize that people have both beliefs and knowledge as well as desires and goals, and that all of these influence their behavior. Once children have a theory of mind, they can also conclude that their actions can influence others, sometimes to the detriment of those others. This allows for the development of pathogenic forms of guilt. If young children's actions are repeatedly linked to the distress of others, they come to feel they have brought harm to the others. Such beliefs about the role of the self in misfortunes befalling a loved one may become the basis for more enduring pathogenic beliefs and orientations.

We have observed patterns of "misplaced responsibility" (Zahn-Waxler et al., 1979) in children in the second year of life. Some children responded apologetically, as if they had caused distress, when in fact they had not. These same children also commonly used apology as a form of reparation for early transgressions. And they also expressed more guilt in follow-up assessments 5 years later (Cummings et al., 1986). Such overgeneralized expressions of responsibility, where guilt and empathy become merged, may reflect the early development of pathogenic beliefs. Early boundary confusions and a lack of a clear sense of self during a critical learning period may have implications for developing psychopathology as well as moral internalization.

The type of guilt being discussed here involves the inference of harm to another, as well as fear of punishment or the "superego anxiety" of Freud's structural model. Revisions of psychodynamic theory (Bush, 1989; Friedman, 1985; Modell, 1965; Shilkret, 1992) now assume that guilt is common as early as 2 or 3 years of age; that superego development begins then; that this is a continuous developmental process, rather than appearing quickly as an Oedipal solution; and that such early guilt can become the basis for symptoms. This is described by Bush (1989) in the following terms: Children typically develop unrealistic theories about how they are to blame for the traumatic experiences that befall them or other family members. These may become repressed in the course of development, and may give rise to distorted conceptions of their power to hurt others; an inner sense of wrongdoing, badness, and undeservedness; and a need to institute pathological symptoms, inhibitions, identifications, and character traits for purposes of self-punishment and making restitution.

On the basis of our research, we would emphasize in addition that some forms of empathy and guilt may become conjoined early in development under conditions that encourage the development of pathogenic beliefs. There may be gender differences regarding one's sense of responsibility for harms caused (Zahn-Waxler et al., 1991). The heightened levels of empathy and guilt that we have observed in young girls may make them particularly vulnerable to establishing beliefs about their overresponsibility, unworthiness, and blameworthiness for the problems of others. It is also possible that there are not strong gender differences in pathological guilt, but that it may take different forms in males and females. Females may have greater "access" to such feelings. Females are often characterized as having distorted conceptions of their powers to hurt others; thus, they may try harder to keep even their anger in check, as it is perceived as having the capacity to destroy. Ironically, physical aggression and destruction are primarily male activities. How are these differences between perception and action to be reconciled, and how do they evolve? Guilt may more commonly translate into reparative behaviors in females than in males; this would be consonant with their demonstrated stronger needs for maintaining relationships.

The fact that some young children were observed to show generalized and pervasive guilt expressions led us to explore family conditions and socialization experiences that might contribute to these individual differences. We focused on maternal depression as a condition in which a child is likely to be exposed to chronic and pervasive distress. We have reviewed elsewhere our own and others' research suggesting that young children of depressed mothers show higher levels of guilt and empathy. And we have developed arguments for how these may be reflections of long-term pathogenic beliefs that place children at later risk for psychopathology (Zahn-Waxler et al., 1991; Zahn-Waxler & Kochanska, 1990). More recent work conveys a similar theme. In one study (Radke-Yarrow, Zahn-Waxler, Richardson, Susman, & Martinez, in press), preschoolers of depressed mothers were found to show more empathic behaviors toward them, mainly when maternal depression was severe and when the children were already known (based on independent assessments) to have emotional problems.

Early enmeshment does not augur well for children's developing autonomy, self-sufficiency, and social relations with peers. These children, compared with agemates, often may begin to regulate emotions more strongly and precociously, and hence may be more likely to display "good" behavior. In our study of guilt-related patterns in toddlers (Cole et al., 1992), symptoms of depression and anxiety in mothers were related to a suppression of tension and frustration in their offspring. Overregulated, overcontrolled, polite behavior patterns in toddlers of depressed mothers have been found in our other work (e.g., Denham, Zahn-Waxler, Cummings, & Iannotti, 1991), with corresponding adverse implications for children's developing peer relations (see Zahn-Waxler, Denham, Iannotti, & Cummings, 1992, for a review). In the Denham et al. (1991) study, 2- and 5-year-old children of depressed mothers also were observed to be *less* prosocial toward their peers than children of well mothers. This reinforces the idea that high levels of early prosocial involvement with an affectively ill parent may actively inhibit socioemotional maturation.

Parental depression is just one of many conditions that may interfere with the development of adaptive forms of empathy and guilt. Parental abuse would also be expected to contribute to maladaptive outcomes. Children aged 2 and 3 who have experienced parental abuse show unempathic behavior and other inappropriate responses to the distress of their peers (Howes & Eldridge, 1985; Klimes-Dougan & Kistner, 1990; Main & George, 1985). We have selected parental depression as one example of a complex set of circumstances that can alter developmental trajectories of the moral emotions. Depression is comorbid with other psychiatric disorders and with other conditions of "family psychopathology" (e.g., marital discord) that may well impinge upon children's patterns of moral development, social competence, and emotional problems.

It would be misleading to imply that parental depression is associated primarily with excessive guilt and empathy in offspring, whereas abuse is linked to deficits in these domains. Parents obviously can be depressed and abusive, and these are likely to be cumulative risk factors. Similarly, offspring of depressed parents are at known risk for externalizing as well as internalizing problems. Moreover, children who show overinvolvement with "needy" caregivers early in development may turn away and show more avoidant, distancing patterns in later years of childhood (Zahn-Waxler, Kochanska, Krupnick, & McKnew, 1990). It has not been our purpose here to provide an exhaustive review of risk conditions that may produce atypicalities in empathy and guilt. We have listed a few and hope that other investigators will focus on other conditions. We have attempted to use data to illustrate the assertions of psychodynamic theorists that pathogenic beliefs leading to maladaptive feelings of responsibility can be established almost as soon as a sense of self is established. It is for these reasons, among others, that the study of self-development in relation to moral development takes on special importance. Self-awareness and self–other differentiation reflect much more than children's knowledge of their own existence. It concerns variations in how the children feel about themselves, in their competencies and capabilities, and in their general sense of worth. This broader concept of self is very difficult to measure, but is necessary to study in young children. More generally, we have bypassed in this chapter the methodological problems inherent in this line of inquiry. It is our belief that knowledge of young children's capabilities has been constrained as much by procedural challenges as by unfriendly theories.

SUMMARY AND CONCLUSIONS

We have begun this chapter with the assertion that both empathy and guilt are moral emotions, and part of the family of self-conscious emotions. We have taken the point of view that the etiology of these emotions can best be examined by considering their origins within the broader context of research on moral internalization and prosocial development. Our assumption is that these moral emotions cannot be well understood independently of the behaviors and cognitions that also underlie the development of ethical norms and personal responsibility. We have used Hoffman's conceptual framework, which is based on the premise that empathy and guilt are present in the first years of life and share a common developmental core.

We have reviewed research evidence that, to a large degree, has corroborated the theoretical work of Hoffman. Feelings and behaviors reflecting concern for others and personal responsibility emerge and increase in frequency during the second year of life. Affective, behavioral, and cognitive reflections of concern and responsibility cohere to form a moral pattern. In addition to developmental change, there are also individual variations. Some children show more concern and guilt than others, and these can take maladaptive as well as adaptive forms. Relatively little is still known about what contributes to these variations. Some genetic influence can be shown, but it appears to be very modest compared with that involved in other, more "basic" emotions. Temperament may be related to moral patterns, but it is unlikely to account for a large portion of the individual variations observed. Given that these moral emotions are also "social" emotions, making their appearance in the context of interaction or the self-in-relationship, variations in socialization experiences may assume special salience. It will be difficult, and perhaps not feasible or desirable, to parse out the precise effects of nature and nurture. For example, the anxious mother who provides many negative, guilt-inducing socialization messages, and also models a particular affective style, may be influencing her child through socialization. But the child may also have inherited a body chemistry that predisposes him or her toward high affective arousal.

Kagan has proposed that we consider families of emotions (e.g., angers rather than anger). This is equally true for empathy and guilt, neither of which can be construed as a unidimensional concept. Guilt correlates with several other negative emotions. There is some suggestion that it does so differentially for different types of children (e.g., boys vs. girls). To take this one step further, if guilt is more closely connected to anger in some children, to sadness and empathy in others, and to fear in still others, the meanings of feelings of guilt or responsibility become very different. The investigation of these different meanings and linkage patterns may shed light on differing etiologies for moral emotions in different children. Similarly, the differing etiologies of moral emotions that do or do not show close associations with moral behavior will be important to investigate.

Although there are many commonalities between empathy and guilt, the data reveal more differences than might be anticipated by Hoffman's theory. We have begun with the premise that guilt is a special case of empathy (one in which feelings of concern are linked to awareness of having caused distress). Our research has demonstrated that this is true only in part, once the different sequences and contexts that lead to these feelings are considered. That is, once a child has caused distress to another, there is the potential for *many* other feelings besides empathy to be evoked. This may be less true if the child has unintentionally caused a problem. In any case, both parents and victims prototypically respond differently when the child has caused, rather than witnessed, a problem (Zahn-Waxler et al., 1979). Often when the child has caused distress in the other, it represents an act of aggression. In such situations the child may also have hostile feelings, derive pleasure from hurting the other, be more emotionally aroused, and so on. The "empathy" that occurs in this context is likely to be less pure in form. At the same time, it is important not to lose sight of the theoretical utility of bringing the constructs of empathy and guilt together, and to consider their joint contribution to both adaptive and maladaptive patterns of moral development. It is remarkable to observe these potentials in children in the first years of life. These accomplishments reflect a view of human nature that serves as a continued reminder of our initial positive potentials.

NOTES

1. Twenty-four families participated in the first study, and 27 participated in the second study.
2. This research is part of a larger longitudinal investigation designed to examine possible genetic influences on the early origins of individual differences in the domains of temperament, emotion, and cognition/language (Emde et al., 1992; Plomin et al., 1990). Here we present a summary of our own "in press" study of empathic development. We also provide more detailed analyses of recently available data on the development and heritability of guilt, as well as the linkages between guilt and other negative emotions.

REFERENCES

Asendorpf, J. B., & Baudonniere, P. M. (1993). Self-awareness and other-awareness: Mirror self-recognition and synchronic imitation among unfamiliar peers. *Developmental Psychology, 29*(1), 88–95.

Asendorpf, J. B., & Nunner-Winkler, E. (1992). Children's moral motive strength and temperamental inhibition reduce their egoistic behavior in real moral conflicts. *Child Development, 63*(5), 1223–1235.

Barnett, M. A., McMinimy, V., Flouer, G., & Masbad, I. (1987). Adolescents' evaluations of peers' motives for helping. *Journal of Youth and Adolescence, 16,* 579–586.

Biringen, Z., Robinson, J., & Emde, R. N. (1994). Stylistic differences and maternal sensitivity during the second year of life: Gender-based relations in the dyadic balance of control. *Journal of Orthopsychiatry, 64,* 78–90.

Bischof-Kohler, D. (1988). Uber den Zusammenhang von Empathie und der Fahigbeit, sich im Spiegel zu erkennen [The relationship between empathy and mirror self-recognition]. *Schweizerische Zeitschrift für Psychologie*, 47, 147–159.

Bischof-Kohler, D. (1991). The development of empathy in infants. In M. E. Lamb & H. Keller (Eds.), *Infant development: Perspectives from German-speaking countries* (pp. 1–33). Hillsdale, NJ: Erlbaum.

Bretherton, I., Fritz, J., Zahn-Waxler, C., & Ridgeway, D. (1986). Learning to talk about emotions: A functionalist perspective. *Child Development*, 57, 529–548.

Brody, L. R. (1985). Gender differences in emotional development: A review of theories and research. *Journal of Personality*, 53(2), 102–149.

Brownell, C. A., & Gifford-Smith, M. (1992, May). *Relations between self-consciousness and non-compliance in toddlers.* Paper presented at the 8th International Conference on Infant Studies, Miami Beach, FL.

Bush, M. (1989). The role of unconscious guilt in psychopathology and psychotherapy. *Bulletin of the Menninger Clinic*, 53, 97–107.

Campbell, S. B. (1990). The socialization and social development of hyperactive children. In M. Lewis & S. M. Miller (Eds.), *Handbook of developmental psychopathology* (pp. 77–89). New York: Plenum Press.

Chodorow, N. (1978). *The reproduction of mothering.* Berkeley: University of California Press.

Cole, P. M., Barrett, K. C., & Zahn-Waxler, C. (1992). Emotion displays in two-year-olds during mishaps. *Child Development*, 63, 314–324.

Condrey, J. C., & Ross, D. F. (1985). Sex and aggression: The influence of gender label on the perception of aggression in children. *Child Development*, 51, 943–967.

Crockenburg, S. (1985). Toddlers' reactions to maternal anger. *Merrill–Palmer Quarterly*, 31(4), 361–373.

Cummings, E. M., Hollenbeck, B., Iannotti, R. J., Radke-Yarrow, M., & Zahn-Waxler, C. (1986). Early organization of altruism and aggression: Developmental patterns and individual differences. In C. Zahn-Waxler, E. M. Cummings, & R. J. Iannotti (Eds.), *Altruism and aggression: Biological and social origins* (pp. 165–188). New York: Cambridge University Press.

Darwin, C. (1965). *The expression of the emotions in man and animals.* Chicago: University of Chicago Press. (Original work published 1872)

De Fries, J. C., and Fulker, D. W. (1985). Multiple regression of twin data. *Behavioral Genetics*, 16, 1–10.

Denham, S. A., Zahn-Waxler, C., Cummings, E. M., & Iannotti, R. J. (1991). Social competence in young children's peer relations: Patterns of development and change. *Child Psychiatry and Human Development*, 22(1), 29–44.

Dienstbier, R. A. (1984). The role of emotion in moral socialization. In C. Izard, J. Kagan, & R. B. Zajonc (Eds.), *Emotions, cognition, and behavior* (pp. 484–513). New York: Cambridge University Press.

Dunn, J. (1987). The beginnings of moral understanding: Development in the second year. In J. Kagan & S. Lamb (Eds.), *The emergence of morality in young children* (pp. 91–111). Chicago: University of Chicago Press.

Edwards, C. P., & Whiting, P. B. (in press). The inadequacy of current study of differential socialization of girls and boys, in light of cross-cultural research. In C. Super (Ed.), *Anthropological contributions to theories of child development.* San Francisco: Jossey-Bass.

Eibl-Eibesfeldt, I. (1971). *Love and hate: The natural history of behavior patterns.* New York: Holt, Rinehart & Winston.

Eisenberg, N., Fabes, R. A., Carlo, G., Troyer, D., Speer, A. L., Karbon, M., &

Switzer, G. (1992). The relations of maternal practices and characteristics to children's vicarious emotional responsiveness. *Child Development*, 63(3), 583–602.

Eisenberg, N., Fabes, R. A., Miller, P. A., Fultz, J., Shell, R., Mathy, R. M., & Reno, R. R. (1989). Relation of sympathy and personal distress to prosocial behavior: A multi-method study. *Journal of Personality and Social Psychology*, 58, 55–66.

Eisenberg, N., Fabes, R. A., Miller, P. A., Shell, R., Shea, C., & May-Plumlee, T. (1990). Preschoolers' vicarious emotional responding and their situational and dispositional prosocial behavior. *Merrill–Palmer Quarterly*, 36(4), 507–529.

Eisenberg, N., & Lennon, R. (1983). Sex differences in empathy and related capacities. *Psychological Bulletin*, 94, 100–131.

Emde, R. N., Johnson, W. F., & Easterbrooks, M. A. (1987). The dos and don'ts of early moral development: Psychoanalytic tradition and current research. In J. Kagan & S. Lamb (Eds.), *The emergence of morality in young children* (pp. 245–276). Chicago: University of Chicago Press.

Emde, R. N., Plomin, R., Robinson, J., Reznick, J. S., Campos, J., Corley, R., DeFries, J., Fulker, D. W., Kagan, J., & Zahn-Waxler, C. (1992). Temperament, emotion, and cognition at 14 months: The MacArthur Longitudinal Twin Study. *Child Development*, 1437–1455.

Fabes, R. A., Eisenberg, N., & Miller, P. A. (1990). Maternal correlates of children's vicarious emotional responsiveness. *Developmental Psychology*, 26(4), 639–648.

Friedman, M. (1985). Toward a reconceptualization of guilt. *Contemporary Psychoanalysis*, 21, 501–547.

Goodenough, F. (1931). *Anger in young children*. Minneapolis: University of Minnesota Press.

Grusec, J. E., & Kuczynski, L. (1980). Direction of effect in socialization: A comparison of the parent vs. the child's behavior as determinants of disciplinary techniques. *Developmental Psychology*, 6, 1–9.

Hoffman, M. L. (1970). Moral development. In P. H. Mussen (Ed.), *Carmichael's manual of child psychology* (3rd ed., Vol. 2, pp. 261–360). New York: Wiley.

Hoffman, M. L. (1975). Developmental synthesis of affect and cognition and its implications for altruistic motivation. *Developmental Psychology*, 11, 605–622.

Hoffman, M. L. (1977). Sex differences in empathy and related behaviors. *Psychological Bulletin*, 84, 712–722.

Hoffman, M. L. (1982). Development of prosocial motivation: Empathy and guilt. In N. Eisenberg (Ed.), *Development of prosocial behavior* (pp. 281–313). New York: Academic Press.

Howes, C., & Eldridge, R. (1985). Responses of abused, neglected, and non-maltreated children to the behaviors of their peers. *Journal of Applied Developmental Psychology*, 6, 261–270.

Izard, C. E. (1977). *Human emotions*. New York: Plenum Press.

Kagan, J., & Lamb, S. (Eds.). (1987). *The emergence of morality in young children*. Chicago: University of Chicago Press.

Klimes-Dougan, B., & Kistner, J. (1990). Physically abused preschoolers' responses to peers' distress. *Developmental Psychology*, 26(4), 599–602.

Kochanska, G. (1991). Socialization and temperament in the development of guilt and conscience. *Child Development*, 62, 1379–1392.

Kochanska, G. (1993). Toward a synthesis of parental socialization and child temperament in early development of conscience. *Child Development*, 64, 325–347.

Koestner, R., Franz, C., & Weinberger, J. (1990). The family origins of empathic concern: A 26-year longitudinal study. *Journal of Personality and Social Psychology, 58,* 709–717.

Kohlberg, L. (1969). Stage and sequence: The cognitive-developmental approach to socialization. In D. A. Goslin (Ed.), *Handbook of socialization theory and research* (pp. 347–480). New York: Rand McNally.

Lytton, H. (1977). Correlates of compliance and the rudiments of conscience in two-year-old boys. *Canadian J ournal of Behavioural Science, 9,* 242–251.

Main, M., & George, C. (1985). Response of abused and disadvantaged toddlers to distress in playmates: A study in the day care setting. *Developmental Psychology, 21,* 407–412.

Malatesta, C. Z., & Haviland, J. (1982). Learning display rules: The socialization of emotion expression in infancy. *Child Development, 53,* 991–1003.

Malatesta, C. Z., & Wilson, A. (1988). Emotion/cognition interaction in personality development: A discrete emotions functionalist analysis. *British Journal of Social Psychology, 27,* 91–112.

Matthews, K. A., Batson, C. D., Horn, J., & Rosenman, R. H. (1981). "Principles in his nature which interest him in the fortune of others . . .": The heritability of empathic concern for others. *Journal of Personality, 49,* 237–247.

Modell, A. H. (1965). On having the right to a life: An aspect of the superego's development. *International Journal of Psycho-Analysis, 46,* 323–331.

Plomin, R., Campos, J., Corley, R., Emde, R. N., Fulker, D. W., Kagan, J., Reznick, J. S., Robinson, J., Zahn-Waxler, C., & DeFries, J. C. (1990). Individual differences during the second year of life: The MacArthur Longitudinal Twin Study. In J. Colombo & J. W. Fagan (Eds.), *Individual differences in infancy*: *Reliability, stability, prediction* (pp. 431–455). Hillsdale, NJ: Erlbaum.

Plomin, R., Emde, R. N., Braungart, J. M., Campos, J., Corley, R., Fulker, D. W., Kagan, J., Reznick, S., Robinson, J., Zahn-Waxler, C., & DeFries, J. C. (1993). Genetic change and continuity from 14 to 20 months: The MacArthur Longitudinal Twin Study. *Child Development, 64*(5), 1354–1376.

Radke Yarrow, M., & Zahn-Waxler, C. (1984). Roots, motives and patterning in children's prosocial behavior. In E. Staub, D. Bar-Tal, J. Karylowski, & J. Reykowski (Eds.), *The development and maintenance of prosocial behavior*: *International perspectives on positive morality* (pp. 155– 176). New York: Plenum Press.

Radke-Yarrow, M., Zahn-Waxler, C., & Chapman, M. (1983). Children's prosocial dispositions and behavior. In E. M. Hetherington (Vol. Ed.), *Handbook of child psychology* (4th ed.): *Vol. 4. Socialization, personality, and social development* (pp. 469–545). New York: Wiley.

Radke-Yarrow, M., Zahn-Waxler, C., Richardson, D. T., Susman, A., & Martinez, P. (in press). *Empathic behavior in children of clinically depressed and well mothers. Child Development.*

Rehberg, H. R., & Richman, C. L. (1989). Prosocial behavior in preschool children: A look at the interaction of race, gender, and family composition. *International Journal of Behavioral Development, 12,* 385–401.

Robinson, J., Little, C., & Biringen, Z. (1992). *Emotional communication in mother–toddler relationships: Evidence for early gender differentiation.* Manuscript submitted for publication.

Ross, H., Tesla, C., Kenyon, B., & Lollis, S. (1990). Maternal intervention in toddler peer conflict: The socialization of principles of justice. *Developmental Psychology*, 26(6), 994–1003.

Rushton, J. P., Fulker, D. W., Neale, M. C., Nias, D. K. B., & Eysenck, H. J. (1986). Altruism and aggression: The heritability of individual differences. *Journal of Personality and Social Psychology*, 50, 1192–1198.

Sagi, A., & Hoffman, M. L. (1976). Empathic distress in the newborn. *Developmental Psychology*, 12, 175–176.

Sandler, J. (1960). On the concept of the superego. *Psychoanalytic Study of the Child*, 15, 128–162.

Shilkret, R. (1992, March). *The origins of pathogenic beliefs: Comments on the developmental aspects of control mastery theory.* Paper presented at the conference of the San Francisco Psychotherapy Research Group, San Francisco.

Smetana, J. G. (1989). Toddlers' social interactions in the context of moral and conventional transgressions in the home. *Developmental Psychology*, 25(4), 499–509.

Smetana, J. G., & Braeges, J. L. (1990). The development of toddlers' moral and conventional judgments. *Merrill–Palmer Quarterly*, 36(3), 329–346.

Stanhope, L., Bell, R. Q., & Parker-Cohen, N. Y. (1987). Temperament and helping behavior in preschool children. *Developmental Psychology*, 23, 347–353.

Stern, D. (1985). *The interpersonal world of the infant.* New York: Basic Books.

Stipek, D. J., Gralinski, J. H., & Kopp, C. B. (1990). Self-concept development in the toddler years. *Developmental Psychology*, 26(6), 972–977.

Tisak, M. D., & Block, J. H. (1990). Preschool children's evolving conceptions of badness: A longitudinal study. *Early Education and Development*, 1(4), 300–307.

Trevarthen, C. (1989, Autumn). Origins and directions for the concept of intersubjectivity. *Society for Research in Child Development Newsletter*, pp. 1–4.

Turiel, E. (1983). *The development of social knowledge: Morality and convention.* Cambridge, England: Cambridge University Press.

Watson, D., & Clark, L. A. (1992). Affects separable and inseparable: On the hierarchical arrangement of the negative affects. *Journal of Personality and Social Psychology*, 62(3), 489–505.

Zahn-Waxler, C., & Chapman, M. (1982). Immediate antecedents of caretakers' methods of discipline. *Child Psychiatry and Human Development*, 12(3), 179–192.

Zahn-Waxler, C., Cole, P., & Barrett, K. C. (1991). Guilt and empathy: Sex differences and implications for the development of depression. In K. Dodge & J. Garber (Eds.), *Emotional regulation and dysregulation* (pp. 243–272). New York: Cambridge University Press.

Zahn-Waxler, C., Denham, S. A., Iannotti, R. J., & Cummings, E. M. (1992). Peer relations in children with a depressed caregiver. In R. D. Parke & G. W. Ladd (Eds.), *Family–peer relationships: Modes of linkage* (pp. 317–344). Hillsdale, NJ: Erlbaum.

Zahn-Waxler, C., & Kochanska, G. (1990). The origins of guilt. In R. Thompson (Ed.), *Nebraska Symposium on Motivation: Vol. 36. Socioemotional development* (pp. 183–258). Lincoln: University of Nebraska Press.

Zahn-Waxler, C., Kochanska, G., Krupnick, J., & McKnew, D. (1990). Patterns of guilt in children of depressed and well mothers. *Developmental Psychology*, 26(1), 51–59.

Zahn-Waxler, C., and Radke-Yarrow, M. (1982). The development of altruism:

Alternative research strategies. In N. Eisenberg-Berg (Ed.), *The development of prosocial behavior* (pp. 109–137). New York: Academic Press.

Zahn-Waxler, C., Radke-Yarrow, M., & King, R. A. (1979). Childrearing and children's prosocial initiations toward victims of distress. *Child Development,* 50, 319–330.

Zahn-Waxler, C., Radke-Yarrow, M., Wagner, E., & Chapman, M. (1992). Development of concern for others. *Developmental Psychology,* 28(1), 126–136.

Zahn-Waxler, C., Robinson, J., & Emde, R. (1992). The development of empathy in twins. *Developmental Psychology,* 28(6), 1038–1047.

6

Emotional States and Traits in Children: The Case of Guilt and Shame

TAMARA J. FERGUSON
HEDY STEGGE

During the height of behaviorism, slippery concepts fell out of favor in mainstream empirical psychology. Two emotion concepts considered particularly inane during this period were "guilt" and "shame." Interest has recently been revived in these emotions—not only in clinical psychology, but in developmental and social psychology as well. Since this renewal of interest, particular attention has been paid to developing measures of guilt and shame in both children and adults, with relatively less attention being given to the developmental course of either emotion (e.g., Harder, 1990; Harder & Lewis, 1987; Harder & Zalma, 1990; Hoblitzelle, 1987; Tangney, 1990). The overall purpose of this chapter is to provide more attention to the development of guilt and shame in the 5- to 12-year-old age range by summarizing what is known about several issues and presenting some preliminary research results from our own laboratories.

We begin the chapter by summarizing how adults perceive the states of guilt and shame; we then discuss developmental contributors to children's understanding of the two emotions. In a third section, we summarize what little is known about children's actual understanding of the two emotions. This is followed by two sections in which we discuss guilt and shame as emotion states and traits, and summarize evidence concerning possible socialization antecedents of the two emotions. We

174

close the chapter by outlining issues to be considered for future research in this area.

ADULTS' REPORTS OF DIFFERENCES BETWEEN GUILT AND SHAME

Although the terms "guilt" and "shame" are often used interchangeably, a growing body of literature reveals that the two emotion concepts refer to phenomenologically different experiences in adults (Ferguson, Stegge, & Damhuis, 1991; H. B. Lewis, 1971; Potter-Efron, 1989; Tangney, 1990, 1993; Wicker, Payne, & Morgan, 1983). Differences between guilt and shame as perceived by adult respondents can best be summarized in terms of a functionalist perspective on emotion. From this perspective, emotions are described as a constellation of five interrelated components: (1) the situational antecedents that initially give rise to the experience; (2) the reasons why the emotion is elicited by the situation; (3) expressional and experiential aspects of the emotion; (4) the meaning or significance of the emotional experience for the person; and, finally, (5) the resultant action tendencies that are associated with the emotion (e.g., Barrett & Campos, 1987; Frijda, 1986; Malatesta & Wilson, 1988).

People react with guilt when they perceive that they have failed to live up to internalized standards of conduct (Aronfreed, 1968; Ausubel, 1955; Ferguson, Mortensen, & Warner, 1990; Frijda, 1986; Higgins, 1987; Lindsay-Hartz, 1984). In terms of situational-antecedents, guilt seems to be aroused when a person (1) has directly or indirectly perpetrated a wrong-doing, by an act of either omission or commission; (2) perceives the wrongdoing as immoral; and—although this is more controversial (Baumeister, Stillwell, & Heatherton, Chapter 10, this volume)—(3) feels responsible for the resulting consequences. Shame can also be aroused by moral transgressions (cf. Ausubel's [1955] concept of "moral shame"). But, unlike guilt, shame is also experienced in what would be considered "nonmoral" situations, such as those involving a breach of propriety, a "loss of face," or other exposures of one's defectiveness and/or incompetence (Thrane, 1979; Wurmser, 1981).

Regarding the reasons why a person feels guilty or ashamed, the attribution that is made for the event is a critical factor. According to certain authors, guilt and shame are the results of an internal attribution for an aversive consequence (e.g., Weiner, 1986). However, whereas shame is mainly associated with situations perceived as uncontrollable, guilt is more frequently reported in situations perceived as controllable or avoidable in nature (Weiner, 1986). For instance, failure attributed to the internal but controllable factor of low effort presumably promotes guilt, whereas shame is fostered by failure attributed to an internal but uncontrollable cause, such as low ability.

Unlike other aversive emotions (such as anger or sadness), neither guilt nor shame has a unique facial or bodily expression (Izard, 1977); experientially, hypoactivation is associated with both emotions (Davitz, 1969). There are, however, a number of experiential differences between the two emotions (Tangney, 1992, 1993; Tangney, Marschall, Rosenberg, Barlow, & Wagner, 1993; Tangney, Wagner, & Gramzow, 1992). Guilt is characterized as an agitation-related experience involving feelings of worry, anxiety, restlessness, and tension (Higgins, 1987; Wurmser, 1981). Shame is more of a dejection-based emotion encompassing feelings of helplessness, sadness, and depression, but at times also anger (Higgins, 1987; Tangney, 1990, 1993; Tangney et al., 1993; Tangney, Wagner, Fletcher, & Gramzow, 1992; Tangney, Wagner, & Gramzow, 1992). In shame, there is a greater focus on other people's opinions of the self, accompanied by a sense of being exposed and observed (Ferguson & Mortensen, 1990; Harder, 1990; Harder & Lewis, 1987; Harder & Zalma, 1990).

An emotional event can be meaningful or significant to a person both intrapersonally (as it affects self-esteem) and interpersonally (in terms of others' reactions to the event). In guilt, strong emphasis is placed on a specific behavior ("How could I do *that*?"). The guilty person ruminates about what he or she has done, thinks self-critical thoughts, and feels regret (Aronfreed, 1968; Ausubel, 1955; Taylor, 1985; Thrane, 1979). Importantly, the sense of self as competent remains intact in guilt experiences, since the focus here is on behavior and the potential for repair is acknowledged (H. B. Lewis, 1971). Shame, in contrast, is a much more devastating experience: It involves a negative evaluation of the entire self, which conveys a sense of fundamental defectiveness ("How could *I* do that?").

Finally, guilt and shame are associated with different action tendencies, or ways in which the person deals with the emotion. In guilt, the person actively seeks control over consequences of the action. Self-criticism, rationalization of the deed, confession, and reparation are ways of exerting this control. The person who feels ashamed, in comparison, seems to react in one of two distinct ways. Shame, at times, is characterized by passivity and an extreme dependence (H. B. Lewis, 1971). When others fail to show compassion, the ashamed person may engage in "facework" (Edelman, 1985; Modigliani, 1971), withdraw from the situation, or attempt to distract the self and others from attending to the painful event (Thrane, 1979; Wurmser, 1981). At the other end of the spectrum, shame has been shown to reflect much more activity, including anger and defensive externalization (see H. B. Lewis's [1971] discussion of humiliated fury and Scheff's [1988] discussion of the shame–rage cycle; see also Potter-Efron, 1989; Tangney, Wagner, Fletcher, & Gramzow, 1992). Exactly when each pattern emerges is still being investigated, but emergence seems to depend upon factors such as gender role orientation, field (in)dependence, temperament, and the like (e.g., H. B. Lewis, 1971; Kaufman, 1989).

CONTRIBUTORS TO CHILDREN'S UNDERSTANDING OF GUILT AND SHAME

Both lay adults' and psychologists' descriptions of guilt and shame attest to the complexity of these two emotions. Understanding them presupposes several abilities, including awareness of standards of conduct, a felt obligation to regulate behavior with respect to these standards, and an ability to recognize discrepancies between one's actual behavior and these internalized values (Ausubel, 1955). The ability to form complex mental representations should thus play a critical role in the experience and understanding of these emotions (Fischer, Shaver, & Carnochan, 1988, 1990; Moretti & Higgins, 1990).

At about 18 months to 2 years of age, children begin to realize that there are associations between how they behave and how others respond to their behavior. Still lacking, however, is an understanding that people's behaviors and reactions are governed by internal representations of appropriate conduct, which exist outside of specific behavioral exchanges. Children in this age range nevertheless do behave as though they recognize that others' reactions affect their own feeling states, which may be one factor contributing to the rudimentary forms of self-regulation observed in this age period. At a behavioral level, this is illustrated by observations of reparative acts. For instance, a 2-year-old girl who has pulled her cousin's hair is told by her mother not to do so. The child crawls to her cousin, says, "I hurt your hair. Please don't cry," and gives her a kiss (Zahn-Waxler & Kochanska, 1989).

Between 4 and 6 years of age, children's ability to infer another's perspective becomes apparent. As a consequence of this perspective-taking capacity, standards are not simply tied to concrete behavioral exchanges, but become associated with the inferred perspectives of other people. A child now realizes that it is the discrepancy between his or her behavior and the other person's normative standard (i.e., the way the child should behave) that influences the person's reaction to the child. For instance, if a 6-year-old boy hurts a playmate and his mother becomes angry, the child knows that this is because his mother wants him to be nice to other children.

At an even later age (9–11 years), children also become aware of how standards regarding personal attributes affect others' reactions to them. Consequently, they are more likely to make generalized self-evaluations and to describe themselves with reference to the personality characteristics that they perceive their parents would like them to possess (e.g., "My father ideally would like me to be smart, but unfortunately I'm not"). Such perceptions contribute to children's self-evaluations and have long-lasting ramifications for their future expectations and motivation.

Thus, partly as a result of their cognitive maturation, children exhibit major changes in their conceptualization of moral issues throughout the elementary school years. Children in this age range are also increasingly able and willing to analyze the causes of social situations in greater depth. For example, from Weiner's (1986) attributional perspective, a two-step process is involved in triggering emotional reactions (see also Graham & Weiner, 1986). The first step involves a simple evaluation of the nature of the outcome: "Was I successful or did I fail?" This so-called "primary appraisal" results in an outcome-dependent emotion (e.g., happiness or sadness). A more complex process of "secondary appraisal" can then take place, which involves an evaluation of the causes of the event: "Was my success or failure due to internal or to external factors, to controllable or uncontrollable aspects of the situation, and to stable or unstable causes?" As a result of secondary appraisal, attribution-dependent emotions such as shame, guilt, pride, or gratitude may be elicited (Ferguson & Rule, 1983).

Research on attribution processes reveals that children younger than approximately 8 years focus mainly on the outcome of their actions, and therefore react primarily with outcome-dependent emotions (Harris, 1989; Meerum Terwogt & Stegge, in press). In the course of development, children's emotions come to depend more on their causal analysis of why an event occurred. At first, their usage of dimensions of causality is nondiscriminating; for example, they will profess to feel guilty not only in controllable situations (which adults claim as well), but also in uncontrollable situations (Graham, Doubleday, & Guarino, 1984; Stipek & DeCotis, 1988). It is only later in development that children's reports of emotion reflect a complex attribution-dependent structure (see Ferguson, Olthof, Luiten, & Role, 1984; Ferguson, Olthof, & Roomans, 1991; Ferguson & Rule, 1988; Thompson, 1989).

CHILDREN'S UNDERSTANDING OF GUILT AND SHAME EXPERIENCES

Although observational studies suggest that young children experience rudimentary forms of guilt and shame (Barrett & Zahn-Waxler, 1987; Bretherton, Fritz, Zahn-Waxler, & Ridgeway, 1986; Kagan, 1984; Kochanska, 1991; M. Lewis, Alessandri, & Sullivan, 1992; Zahn-Waxler & Kochanska, 1989), this certainly does not mean that they have a distinct understanding of the two emotion concepts. In addition, differences between guilt and shame are difficult to assess on the basis of observations alone. As noted earlier, neither of the two emotions has a unique facial or bodily expression, so the quality of the emotional experience must be inferred from situational cues and self-reports.[1] Using observational procedures is especially problematic in the case of guilt and shame, since both of these emotions can be experienced in the same situation (Ferguson, Stegge, & Damhuis, 1991; Tangney, 1990). Moreover, which emotion is experienced depends on a child's appraisal of the situation, including the social standards that arc applied, the attribution of responsibility made, and the importance imputed by the child to other people's reactions. Therefore, information on what children say about their subjective experience of guilt and shame is essential to mapping the developmental course of the two emotions.

Different research paradigms have been used to study children's understanding of their guilt and shame experiences. When simply asked to describe a situation in which the target emotion of guilt or shame was experienced, 5- and 6-year-old children cannot unambiguously generate appropriate events (Harris, Olthof, Meerum Terwogt, & Hardman, 1987), although they know that guilt and shame are negatively valenced emotions (Harter, 1983). In fact, before the age of 7 years, shame is viewed as an emotion that someone else feels when the child has done something wrong (Harter & Whitesell, 1989)—for example, "Mom would be ashamed of me if I did something bad or got into trouble" (p. 95). By the age of 8 years, children can give examples of situations in which they feel ashamed of themselves. However, an audience continues to play an important role in shame experiences, as becomes clear from the following statement made by a 9-year-old child: "Well, I *might* be able to be ashamed of myself if my parents didn't know, but it would sure help me to be ashamed if they were there!" (p. 96).

In our research, we (Ferguson, Stegge, & Damhuis, 1990b) asked 8- and 11-year-old Dutch children to describe situations in which they felt guilty or ashamed, with the interviewer posing questions that ascertained whether children understood the different components of these emotions (e.g., situational antecedents, concerns, action tendencies). All of the 11-year-old children, as well as a large majority of the 8-year-old children, could generate appropriate examples of shame- versus guilt-eliciting situations (see Ferguson, Stegge, & Damhuis, 1990a). In addition, they understood other components of the two emotions, such as the role that confession plays in reducing guilt or that denial plays in reducing shame.

In a second study (Ferguson, Stegge, & Damhuis, 1991), children of both age groups sorted a number of features according to whether they were characteristic of their experience of guilt, shame, both emotions, or neither. A large number of younger as well as older children associated guilt with having done something naughty, a sense of regret, a desire to make reparation, and anger at the self. Only the older age group saw the desire to confess as applicable to guilt feelings.

According to both age groups, fear of ridicule, embarrassment, and blushing were characteristic of shame; this finding points again to the significance of the audience in the shame experience. For older children, shame also seemed to influence their self-concept, since thoughts about incompetence ("Then I feel stupid" or "Then I think I do everything wrong") were sorted as being associated with this emotion.

Unlike the older children, the 8-year-olds were strongly concerned with other people's reactions in their characterizations of both guilt and shame.

They did not want the deed to be detected by others, did not want to confess, were inclined to avoid others, and did not feel in control of their feelings. This external orientation is consistent with other research on children's reactions to moral transgressions. For example, Barden, Zelko, Duncan, and Masters (1980) showed that young children experienced guilt only if their misdeed was detected. Likewise, in a slightly different area, Bussey (1992) showed that young children's moral evaluations of lying were harsher when the perpetrator was punished for doing so. Thompson and Hoffman (1980) interviewed children about hypothetical situations and found that third- and fifth-graders used principles of internal justice in explaining why they felt guilty, whereas first-graders' justifications mainly reflected a fear of being detected and punished. Harter and Whitesell (1989) also reported that the willingness to confess after having transgressed increased with the age of the child. Younger children would not confess what had happened out of a fear of punishment ("I'd be afraid, I'd get in trouble," p. 101), but older children claimed they would confess because it would make them feel better ("If you tell, then you wouldn't have a guilty conscience and that feeling would go away," p. 102).

The shift from an external to a more internal moral orientation is accompanied by a developmental change in the relevance of social norms to children's feelings after having transgressed.[2] Several studies show that children younger than approximately 8 years of age base their attributions of emotion on the valence of the outcome. Older children, in contrast, apply moral evaluative standards—independent of the outcome—to assessing emotional reactions. For example, Nunner-Winkler and Sodian (1988) presented 4- to 8-year-old children with a story character who secretly took another child's sweets, and then asked them how the story character would feel and why. Even when moral aspects were made very salient to the younger children, they actually ascribed positive feelings to the perpetrator, since the outcome was a positive one (obtaining the sweets). The older children claimed that the perpetrator would feel bad or sad because a moral rule had been violated (see also Arsenio & Kramer, 1992; Ferguson, Olthof, & Roomans, 1991, Study 2).[3]

With increasing age, children gain a deeper understanding of the psychological dimensions of emotional experiences (Thompson, 1989), including the dependence of certain emotions on the attribution made. Graham et al. (1984) showed that 6- and 7-year-old children reported feeling guilty in situations that were largely uncontrollable, whereas older children reported that guilt would be experienced in situations that involved personal control (see also Thompson, 1989). Stipek and DeCotis (1988, Study 1) found that 9- to 13-year-old children, but not 6- to 7-year-old children, acknowledged that guilt was elicited primarily by failure because of low effort. It appears, then, that younger children globally associate guilt with failure, whereas older children reserve guilt for failure that they could have avoided.

In summary, during the elementary school years, children's reports about guilt and shame start to approximate those provided by adults. With age, social norms and issues of personal responsibility become increasingly significant elicitors of the two emotions in children. Children also gain a better understanding of the critical features of guilt- versus shame-eliciting situations during this time. However, being able to understand and report on differences between guilt and shame does not validate the phenomenological significance of the two emotions in children. What purpose do the two emotions serve in children? We attempt to answer this question in the next section.

GUILT AND SHAME AS STATES AND TRAITS

From a functionalist perspective, emotional states are adaptively significant for the individual in the immediate situation, governing whether and how available information is perceived, interpreted, stored, and used to guide behavior. As a state, feelings of shame are a signal to the person that rejection by the surrounding environment is imminent. As such, shame regulates daily interaction by inhibiting arrogance, promoting humility, and fostering conformity or deference to standards of conduct valued by the group (H. B. Lewis, 1971; Scheff, 1988; Wurmser, 1981). Shame also signifies the presence of a discrepancy between a person's actual behavior and the ideals set by the person and/or significant others for the self. As a result, the person becomes motivated to change and improve himself or herself (Higgins, 1987; Potter-Efron, 1989).

The state of guilt likewise serves unique adaptive functions—in this case, by promoting prosocial behaviors, inhibiting aggressive behaviors, and (at moderate levels) indicating an empathic concern for others and a tendency to accept rather than externalize responsibility for negative events (Hoffman, 1982, 1983; H. B. Lewis, 1971). As such, guilt can be seen as a guide for moral action (Potter-Efron, 1989).

Malatesta and Wilson (1988) have also adopted a functionalist perspective in an analysis of emotions as traits. According to them, emotions can be conceptualized as affective styles that influence information processing, self-evaluation, and self-regulatory behavior across time and situations. Thus, depending on accumulated experience, individuals can develop predispositions toward particular affective styles that influence their perceptions, interpretations, and behavior in diverse ways.

From the perspective of Malatesta and Wilson (1988), repeated exposure to certain emotions can lead to mild, idiosyncratic distortions that are the foundation for individual differences or "quirks" in personality. More importantly, chronic exposure to specific emotions can lead to two major types of pathology. First, there is "surfeit pathology" (too much of an emotion), in which the person persistently organizes and interprets experience in terms of a specific affective style. This is contrasted with two subtypes of "deficiency pathology" (too little of an emotion). An "underdeveloped" deficiency pathology means that the person has simply never developed the capacity to organize experience around a particular emotion. In a "defended" deficiency pathology, the person has actually developed the capacity to experience the emotion, but it remains inaccessible in daily experience because of the operation of defense mechanisms.

In our work, we have applied the perspective of Malatesta and Wilson (1988) to the study of the development of guilt and shame as surfeit emotion traits. From this perspective, guilt and shame become maladaptive surfeit affective styles when the defining features of each emotion continually and indiscriminately manifest themselves across time and situations. Clinicians have repeatedly alluded to individuals who chronically and inappropriately accept personal responsibility for negative events, repeatedly try to make amends but fail, and are plagued by agitation-related feelings (H. B. Lewis, 1971; Potter-Efron, 1989; Zahn-Waxler & Kochanska, 1989). This is what we label a "guilt-prone" style. Conversely, a person whose daily existence is pervaded by feelings of worthlessness, incompetence, and helplessness manifests what we label a "shame-prone" style (Kaufman, 1985; H. B. Lewis, 1971). Because development of either style can be seen as an early marker variable for later symptoms, such as anxiety and depression, it is important to understand their antecedents. The question to which we now turn is how processes of socialization contribute to the development of guilt and shame, both as states and as traits.

SOCIALIZATION ANTECEDENTS OF GUILT AND SHAME REACTIONS

Since guilt and shame are self-*evaluative* emotions, socialization experiences provided by significant others should be primary contributors to the development of these emotions as both states and dispositions. In fact, the important role played by caregivers in socializing emotion is repeatedly emphasized in the clinical and empirical literature (H. B. Lewis, 1971; Moretti & Higgins, 1990; Potter-Efron, 1989; Zahn-Waxler & Kochanska, 1989; Zahn-Waxler, Kochanska, Krupnick, & McKnew, 1990). Socialization agents influence children in at least four major ways: (1) direct parental modeling of affective styles, which can be traced to a parent's own family history and contemporaneous stressors in the parent–child environment; (2) parental feedback to the child in emotion-eliciting situations that involve the child directly or indirectly, including directives about how he or she should feel in specific situations and delineations of outcome–emotion contingencies; (3) parental communication to the child about how the parent perceives the child as actually being or behaving, when compared to the parent's expectations for the child as he or she ought to be or is ideally hoped to be; and (4) parental attributional, emotional, and behavioral reactions to the child when the parent perceives that an "ideal" or "ought" has been violated.

In our earlier discussion, both guilt and shame have been proposed to have adaptive consequences. Curiously, much attention has been given to the socialization antecedents of adaptive forms of guilt, and relatively little to those of shame. Emphasizing the adaptive functions of guilt, Hoffman (1982, 1983) describes the relation between the use of different parental disciplinary techniques and the child's development of an internal versus external moral orientation. Hoffman defines the technique of "induction" as providing information or explanations that promote insight and understanding of the behavioral changes expected by the parent; in part, this involves pointing out the consequences that the child's behavior has for others. After the parent has gotten the child's attention in a disciplinary encounter, the frequent use of induction presumably facilitates high levels of moral internalization. Induction provided after a transgression therefore fosters feelings of empathy-based guilt, since it directs the child's attention to the harmful consequences that his or her behavior has had for another. Several studies provide empirical support for the relation between the use of induction and children's prosocial and moral behavior (Dienstbier, Hillman, Lehnhoff, Hillman, & Valkenaar, 1975; Hoffman, 1970a, 1982, 1983; Rollins & Thomas, 1979; Zahn-Waxler, Radke-Yarrow, & King, 1979).

In contrast, the parent who frequently wields influence through power assertion or love withdrawal is likely to encourage an external moral orientation in the child (see also Dienstbier, 1984). Both of these techniques emotionally arouse the child and actually interfere with the child's ability to attend to the consequences that his or her behavior has for another. The child is instead more concerned with his or her own interests (being punished or abandoned) than with those of the victim, and experiences a form of guilt that can be described as fear- or anxiety-based (Hoffman, 1970b; see also Zahn-Waxler & Kochanska, 1989; Zahn-Waxler et al., 1990).

There is consensus in the empirical and clinical literature regarding how power assertion and induction affect the development of moral internalization and empathy- or fear-based guilt. Less agreement exists regarding the effects that love withdrawal should have on children's feelings of guilt or moral internalization (Ferguson & Denissen, 1982). Hoffman (1970a) reported weak, inconsistent relations between the use of this disciplinary technique and children's moral orientation. In contrast, other studies have shown a relation between love withdrawal and the compliant nature of children's moral functioning (Zahn-Waxler et al., 1979), their inhibition of anger (described in Hoffman, 1970a), their poor self-esteem (Coopersmith, 1967), their compliance in disciplinary situations, and their tendency to actively avoid disciplinary encounters (Chapman & Zahn-Waxler, 1982). According to Zahn-Waxler and Kochanska (1989), love withdrawal is associated with fear- or anxiety-based *guilt*. However, certain reactions of children to love withdrawal—such as avoidance, anger inhibition, and low self-esteem—may reflect what many psychologists today would term expressions of *shame*.

Several authors have proposed models to account for the development of maladaptive guilt- and shame-prone styles. A division can be seen in this literature between authors who describe the socialization of both shame-prone and guilt-prone affective styles (of the fear- or anxiety-based variety) and authors who are primarily concerned with one of the two emotion dispositions only (historically, the development of guilt-proneness, but more recently the development of shame-proneness; e.g., M. Lewis, 1992). Among the former are Moretti and Higgins (1990), who argue that parents can focus on either matches or mismatches between standards and behavior when evaluating their children's behavior. A child whose appropriate behavior is emphasized will supposedly feel happy and confident, whereas a child whose discrepant behavior is repeatedly stressed is presumed to experience at least one of an entire range of negative emotions on a regular basis. Specifically, a child who falls short of parental hopes and wishes ("ideals") exists in an environment characterized by an absence of positive outcomes (such as praise). This type of environment is thought to promote dejection-related feelings (such as shame) in the child. In contrast, a mismatch between the child's behavior and parental "oughts" causes a parent to present negative outcomes to the child (such as punishment). The continual presence of negative outcomes supposedly facilitates the child's experience of agitation-based feelings, which would include guilt.

The view of Moretti and Higgins (1990) is consistent with Potter-Efron's (1989) clinically based description of guilt- versus shame-generating messages and behaviors in the family. According to Potter-Efron, excessive guilt is promoted by strong parental concerns with responsibility and personal control; a view of the child as always fully responsible for his or her behavior; expectations that the child should always be in control; and the parent's actually "waiting for" the child to violate moral rules. At the behavioral level, a parent who promotes extreme guilt makes frequent use of punishment (or the threat of punishment) as a means of controlling the child, even when only minor transgressions have occurred or when the parent suspects the child of merely thinking about transgressing. In Potter-Efron's view, then, guilt and the use of power are closely related. Parents who induce a maladaptive guilt-prone style are those who demand absolute obedience, blame a child without explaining what has been done wrong, and believe they are entitled to punish because of their status as parents.

Shame-proneness, in Potter-Efron's (1989) view, has less to do with the emphasis placed on the child's duties and obligations, and revolves more around the child's perceived failure to live up to parental ideals. Shame is fostered by deficiency messages communicated to the child, who learns that he or she is not, and never will be, good (enough) or lovable. At a behavioral level, the parent exerts control through refusal to communicate, threats of separation, blatant "shaming," or love withdrawal (i.e., the direct but nonphysical expression of anger or disapproval; Hoffman, 1970a). These parental reactions arouse the fear of abandonment that is so central to the experience of shame, since they involve rejecting the child's entire self and threatening the child with a loss of parental approval and affection (see also Erikson, 1963; H. B. Lewis, 1971; Piers & Singer, 1953). In this type of environment, the child is forced to search for ways to be acceptable to the parent—a task that is made almost impossible because the demand is for core features of the self to be changed, and/or because little information is provided about how desired changes can be achieved.

PARENTAL CORRELATES OF CHILDREN'S GUILT AND SHAME REACTIONS: AN EMPIRICAL STUDY

Guided by the work reviewed above we have conducted preliminary research designed to assess parental correlates of what we view as adaptive guilt responses but maladaptive shame responses by children (Ferguson, Bailey, & Palmer-Krebs, 1991, 1992; Stegge, Ferguson, & Meerum Terwogt, 1991). Two specific aims of this research were (1) to ascertain the extent to which guilt and shame responses could be predicted by parents' responses to their children in disciplinary encounters and in situations where the children actually fulfilled prescriptions regarding appropriate behavior; and (2) to ascertain the extent to which guilt and shame responses could be predicted by parental beliefs regarding appropriate standards for behavior. To achieve these aims, instruments needed to be developed that adequately measured children's guilt and shame responses, various parental socialization or disciplinary practices, and different parental standards for behavior. Since the instruments used are new to the field, brief descriptions of their content and internal-consistency reports for various scales are provided here.

Measures

Child Measure

To measure guilt and shame responses, the Child–Child Attribution and Reaction Survey (C-CARS; Stegge & Ferguson, 1990) was developed. The C-CARS is an interview measure designed for use with 5- to 12-year-old children, modeled after Burggraf and Tangney's (1989) Self-Conscious Affect and Attribution Inventory for Children (SCAAI-C). The C-CARS consists of written and pictorial representations of a child involved in four moral transgressions and four failure situations (see Stegge & Ferguson, 1990). To reduce response bias, each of the eight situations is presented on three *different* trials, and on each trial children rate the extent to which they would respond in a particular manner. Specifically, for each trial, children are asked to rate an answer precoded as reflecting one of these reactions: guilt, shame, or defensive externalization.

Abbreviated examples of shame reactions are "I am a mean kid for not helping," or "I would feel stupid." Guilt reactions include "I would feel naughty, "I would feel really sorry," or "I would feel I deserve punishment." Externalizing answers involve the child blaming the other for the negative outcome (e.g., "My teammate didn't pass me the ball right"). Across the eight stories, three subscale scores are derived for children reflecting the degree to which they react with shame, guilt, or externalization. Cronbach's alpha coefficients for these three subscales, based on a sample of 39 children, reveal satisfactory reliabilities (alphas = .67, .71, and .73, respectively).

Parent Measures

The Parent–Child Attribution and Reaction Survey—Negative Version (P-CARS-N; Ferguson & Stegge, 1990) is a paper-and-pencil instrument developed for parents of 5- to 12-year-old children. It assesses parents' attributions, emotional reactions, and disciplinary reactions to the same situations as presented in the C-CARS. In the P-CARS-N, a parent is thus asked to imagine that his or her child has been involved in failure (e.g., athletic or academic) or a moral transgression (e.g., aggression or not helping). After each incident, the parent then rates attributions made for the incident (e.g., how controllable it was), the parent's own emotional reactions to the incident (consisting of anger-related, disappointment-related, or more empathic emotions), and a series of disciplinary reactions that have been precoded as representing power assertion, induction, or love withdrawal. The alpha coefficients for subscales of this instrument are excellent, ranging from .82 (power assertion) to .95 (anger-related emotion).

A positive variant of the parent instrument has also been developed (P-CARS-P; Ferguson & Stegge, 1990), in which a parent imagines that his or her child has achieved a certain success (e.g., scoring a goal in soccer) or upheld a certain moral norm (e.g., helping a younger child in distress). As in the negative variant, parents provide attribution ratings, ratings of their emotional responses (which primarily represent pride), and ratings of the extent to which they would react in ways precoded as reflecting induction, tangibly rewarding the child, or extending affection and love to the child. Reliability coefficients for subscales on this instrument are also excellent in the current sample of 39 parents (alphas range from .93 to .98).

Higgins's (1987) self-discrepancy theory has been used as a guide in developing the Expectation Sort for Parents (ESP; Ferguson, 1990). The ESP is a measure of parents' expectations of how their children ideally would be or behave ("ideals"), expectations of how their children ought to be or behave ("oughts"), and perceptions of how their children actually are or behave ("actuals"). A parent is presented with 70 negatively worded statements, chosen from the literature to reflect child behaviors and attributes most likely to represent parental ideals and/or oughts. The four domains represented by the 70 statements are (1) morally appropriate behavior (e.g., not lying, not stealing); (2) showing respect for others' rights and requests (e.g., not disrupting conversations, not staring at strangers, not disobeying parents); (3) age-appropriate self-regulation (e.g., not demanding constant attention, not being easily distracted); and (4) possessing desirable personal attributes (e.g., not being too heavy or thin, not having just an average face, not being clumsy at sports).

Using a stepwise Q-sort procedure, the parent ipsatively rates all 70 statements in terms of how much they describe the child's actual behavior (the "actual sort"). For two other sorts, the parent discards 10 of the items and then ipsatively rates 30 self-selected statements in terms of the extent to which they represent ideals that the parent has for the child (the "ideal sort"), and 30 different self-selected statements in terms of the extent to which they describe the parent's oughts for the child (the "ought sort"). Based on comparisons of the three sorts, scores can be created for each parent reflecting the magnitude of discrepancy perceived between "actuals versus ideals" and "actuals versus oughts" (alphas across the four domains = .80 and .77, respectively; $n = 39$).

Predictors of Children's Guilt and Shame Reactions

Results of our research with 5- to 12-year-old children, and of the research of others with older children and adults (Harder & Lewis, 1987; Tangney, 1990, 1993; Tangney, Wagner, Fletcher, & Gramzow, 1992), consistently reveal a substantial correlation between scores for guilt and shame reactions (e.g., the correlation in our current sample of 39 children is .62). The most adequate explanation for these sizable relationships is subject to debate. The tendency to react with guilt *and* shame may simply reflect the many commonalities between the two emotions. After all, the two emotions fit a prototype of negative, depressed emotions, and they share critical defining features (e.g., self-consciousness, self-evaluation, internal attribution, moral overtones, and interpersonal jeopardy concerns). Nevertheless, as research with adults shows (Harder & Zalma, 1990; Smith, 1972; Tangney, Wagner, Fletcher, & Gramzow, 1992), there are reliable individual differences in the degree to which individuals respond with guilt versus shame in the same situation. Reactions of guilt and shame are also differentially related to other states and orientations, such as empathy and depression (Tangney, 1991; Tangney, Wagner, & Gramzow, 1992). Thus, their co-occurrence does not necessarily mean that the two emotions are indistinguishable in their consequences for the individual.

In fact, a goal in our research has been to relate the two emotion reactions to several predictor variables, while taking their shared variance into account. To this end, canonical correlation analyses rather than univariate correlational analyses were always conducted. Specifically, children's guilt and shame scores were always entered into one variate set, and scores for various parental reactions or standards were treated as a second variate set. In this way, patterns emerged that revealed the relative weight that needed to be assigned to guilt and/or shame to best maximize the correlation of the emotion variate set with the other variate set (and vice versa).

Parental Socialization Practices

Separate canonical correlation analyses were conducted for parental reactions in the negative versus positive child situations discussed earlier. The two functions calculated for the negative situations revealed a strong first function, with substantial loadings for *both* guilt and shame reactions in the emotion variate set. This pattern might best reflect a child's tendency to express negative self-conscious emotions generally. The corresponding discipline set revealed high loadings for negative emotional responses by parents (both anger-related and disappointment-related) and all parental practices (especially induction, but also love withdrawal and, to a lesser extent, power assertion). The first function for negative disciplinary situations was thus a broad one for both the children's emotional reactions and their parents' responses. Similar results were observed for the first function derived for the positive socialization encounters. In this case, the emotion variate set again contained high loadings for both guilt and shame, which were best predicted in the socialization set by high loadings for induction and parental pride.

The second function derived for the negative displinary encounters indicated a substantial loading for shame but a negligible loading for guilt in the emotion variate set. Shame responses were best predicted in this case by the *absence* of induction, love withdrawal, and power assertion, but by the strong presence of anger-related emotions. The second function calculated for the positive socialization encounters was also dominated by shame in the emotion variate set. Children's shame reactions, in this case, were largely predicted by the *absence* of tangible rewards for appropriate behavior.

Two points are noteworthy about these results. First, guilt did not emerge as a separate emotion category, whereas shame strongly emerged as such. This is interesting in light of recent literature, in which shame is frequently touted as the more clinically relevant trait (e.g., Kaufman, 1989; Potter-Efron, 1989). Second, shame was predicted more by the absence of high degrees of parental discipline as described by Hoffman (1970a, 1982, 1983) than by their presence. The fact that the traditional discipline triad did not do a satisfactory job of predicting either emotion separately led us to additionally consider Moretti and Higgins's (1990) analysis of socialization antecedents of various emotions.

Recall that Moretti and Higgins (1990) associate the absence of positive outcomes with the experience of shame, but the presence of negative outcomes with the experience of guilt. Measures of these tendencies were culled from the negative and positive versions of the P-CARS. Results of partial correlation analyses, which controlled each emotion for the other, revealed that guilt was best predicted by induction and by the presence of anger-related reactions by parents in the negative situations, as well as by the presence of pride reactions in the positive encounters. These results converge nicely with those reported by others (e.g., Hoffman, 1983). Shame, on the other hand, was best predicted simply by the absence of positive outcomes involving induction, tangible rewards, or parental affection. We thus again see that shame in children is associated with their parents' *not* responding positively to appropriate behavior.

Parental Standards for Behavior

A variety of claims can be found in the literature suggesting, in effect, that high degrees of guilt and shame are fostered when a child regularly violates standards that are important to a parent. The child's involvement in moral transgressions is thought to promote disciplinary reactions that would support strong shame and guilt responses by the child. On the other hand, failure by the child to meet nonmoral standards (e.g., physical attractiveness and physical or academic prowess) is thought to primarily induce high degrees of shame. Moretti and Higgins (1990) are quite outspoken regarding the differential antecedents of these two emotions in children. They claim specifically that a high discrepancy between a parent's actual and ideal perceptions of a child will promote shame, whereas a high actual–ought discrepancy should facilitate guilt.

Availability of the ESP sort data permitted at least a preliminary examination of the validity of these hypotheses. Guilt and shame reactions were related, through canonical correlation analyses, to actual–ideal discrepancies in the domains of morally appropriate behavior, respect for others, self-regulation, and possession of desirable personal attributes. The same analysis was then repeated for actual–ought discrepancies in these four domains. Results of the two analyses each revealed a function on which both guilt and shame loaded highly, suggesting to us that the dimension reflects negative self-conscious emotions generally. Interestingly, the children who behaved in accordance with parental ideals concerning respect for others and self-regulation were the ones who scored highest on indices of self-conscious emotion. In addition, when we examined the results for actual–ought discrepancies, children whose personal attributes deviated most from parental oughts also scored highly on the self-conscious emotion variate.

The two canonical correlation analyses also revealed two additional functions. One of these represented shame in relation to discrepancies between parental actuals and ideals. In this case, children providing high shame responses were perceived by parents as meeting the parents' standards in the domains of morally appropriate behavior and respect for others, but falling short of parental standards concerning personal attributes and the ability to exert self-control. The second function, as would be expected, involved guilt's loading highly in relationship to parental actual–ought discrepancy scores. In this case, a high actual–ought discrepancy for morally appropriate behavior but a low actual–ought discrepancy for self-regulation best predicted guilt reactions.

Summary of Results

All things considered, two distinct emotional orientations were detected in this set of preliminary analyses involving 5- to 12-year-old children and their parents. In some cases, guilt and shame answers surfaced simultaneously. Tangney (personal communication, December 1992) suggests that the shared variance here could reflect the maladaptive components of both emotions. However, considering the parental data, we suspect that the two embody a constructive (albeit negative) emotion orientation, in which the child critically accepts responsibility for untoward behavior but nonetheless maintains a sense of self-value and control.

Children's reactions here strongly resembled the adaptive moral orientation described by Hoffman (1982, 1983), and were in fact systematically related to the very parental variables emphasized by Hoffman as being predictive of moral internalization. That is, the correlated pattern of parental variables was directed on the whole toward stimulating a child's internalization of moral norms and emphasizing the child's responsibility for (in)appropriate behavior. In the case of negative discipline, these reactions were most strongly represented by power assertion, love withdrawal, and especially induction combined with anger-related emotion (Hoffman, 1970a, 1982, 1983). Also contributing to negative self-conscious emotion were parents' perceptions of their children as both respectful and high in self-control, but as falling short of standards concerning personal attributes. Parental reactions in positive socialization encounters further reinforced the interpretation, since they reflected primarily induction and pride.

Shame emerged as a separate emotion dimension that was best predicted by the *absence* of discipline, the strong presence of hostile emotion, little recognition of good behavior, and (more generally speaking) the absence of positive outcomes. In short, the parents of children who exhibited shame were hostile and provided little in the way of concrete feedback regarding what the children had done that was right or wrong. Importantly, too, the children responding with shame were the greatest disappointment to parents in domains involving attributes that are fairly difficult to change (e.g., temperamental characteristics, athletic prowess, and academic ability). This pattern is reminiscent of the shame-generating messages described by

Potter-Efron (1989) and Moretti and Higgins (1990). When the obtained high loadings for shame are viewed in light of the best predictive parental reactions, shame would thus seem to reflect a more maladaptive reaction consisting of passive self-criticism and a fear of ridicule.

CONCLUSIONS

We close our contribution by outlining a few of the methodological lessons gleaned from the current data set. First, the use of canonical techniques proved to be extremely revealing and should be considered in others' attempts to tease apart the measurement of guilt from that of shame. Specifically, by using canonical analysis we uncovered the multiple ways in which shame, guilt, and parenting variables all simultaneously interact and influence one another. Important in this respect was the finding that guilt and shame do share a large degree of variance, which is systematically predicted by some but not all parenting variables. Removing their shared variance then served to reveal shame as a second dimension, predicted not by the presence of negative but by the absence of positive discipline and parent perceptions.

Second, it is important to sample parental behaviors widely across a variety of domains. For example, an important predictor of shame-proneness was parents' reactions in nondisciplinary situations; such reactions are rarely discussed in the literature on the socialization of emotion (cf. Moretti & Higgins, 1990).

A third, more perplexing conceptual and methodological issue remains to be resolved. It is clear from the discussion above that questions still remain regarding the criteria that should be used to distinguish maladaptive from adaptive forms of guilt and shame. From the present results, we conclude that a frequent tendency to react with shame responses that emphasize deficiencies in the self does serve the individual maladaptively. However, an equally frequent tendency to respond with criticism of one's behavior reflects an adaptive orientation of guilt. Thus, maladaptiveness of the two emotion orientations cannot be determined by using measures that simply assess how *often* a particular response is provided. Much more attention needs to be given at a measurement level to the specific content that needs to be targeted in providing operational definitions for maladaptive forms of guilt and adaptive forms of shame. In this respect, we may need closer analyses of the reasons people provide for feeling guilty or ashamed, rather than their descriptions of their experiences as such.

ACKNOWLEDGMENTS

The two of us contributed equally to the conceptual and empirical components of this work, and the order of authorship was determined alphabetically. Over the past

4 years, many undergraduate and graduate students in psychology at Utah State University (USU) have completed research course requirements by contributing to the seemingly endless iterative task of instrument development and testing phases of the research. We would particularly like to thank Laurel Agee, Julie Anderson, Bob Bailey, Todd Baird, Kim Carstensen, Tom Englund, Ute Holmgren, Cynthia Palmer-Kerbs, Paul Maestas, Lance Mortenson, Teresa Thompson, and Tom Warner for their interest and help. Nelleke den Besten, Renate Koomen, and Sandra Schverdfeger at the Free University of Amsterdam also deserve special mention.

Portions of the research reported in this chapter were supported by a seed monies grant awarded to Tamara Ferguson by the Office of the Vice President for Research at USU, and by the Bureau of Research Services of the College of Education at USU.

NOTES

1. Therefore, it is not surprising that only one of these emotions is studied in most observational research. For instance, M. Lewis et al. (1992) studied 3-year-old children's shame reactions in achievement situations. According to these authors, shame is characterized by "a collapse of the body, a cessation of activity, often accompanied by a reduction of vocal activity and/or negative, self-depreciating statements" (p. 635). Whether the toddlers were experiencing shame rather than sadness was nonetheless inferred from finding a stronger emotional reaction to easy when compared to difficult tasks. Similarly, Zahn-Waxler and Kochanska (1989) have relied on other behavioral reactions by the child in coding guilt—namely, the emotional distress and reparative behavior following acts of wrongdoing.

2. Note that children can be aware of rules, and yet these rules do not necessarily guide their behavior. For example, although very young children already know a lot about "good" and "bad" behaviors (Turiel, 1983), this is not reflected in their behavior. Because it is the latter development in which we are interested, we only summarize research concerning children's emotional and/or behavioral reactions to transgressions, rather than their knowledge of what is good or bad.

3. At first glance, the results of these studies seem inconsistent with the results of observational research. However, it may be that young children only show negative reactions to another person's distress if the social norm matches their personal prosocial goals of the moment. In case of a conflict between social norms (not stealing) and personal motives (wanting the sweets), a young child focuses on the personal motives of the perpetrator rather than the victim's distress. Besides, observational studies also show an increase in reparative behavior with increasing age (Chapman, Zahn-Waxler, Iannotti, & Cooperman, 1987).

REFERENCES

Aronfreed, J. (1968). *Conduct and conscience: The socialization of internalized control over behavior.* New York: Academic Press.

Arsenio, W. F., & Kramer, R. (1992). Victimizers and their victims: Children's conceptions of the mixed emotional consequences of moral transgressions. *Child Development, 63*, 915–927.

Ausubel, D. P. (1955). Relationships between shame and guilt in the socialization process. *Psychological Review, 62*, 378–390.

Barden, R. C., Zelko, F. A., Duncan, S. W., & Masters, J. C. (1980). Children's knowledge about the experiential determinants of emotion. *Journal of Personality and Social Psychology, 39*, 968–976.

Barrett, K. C., & Campos, J. J. (1987). Perspectives on emotional development: II. A functionalist approach to emotions. In J. D. Osofsky (Ed.), *Handbook of infant development* (2nd ed., pp. 555–578). New York: Wiley.

Barrett, K. C., & Zahn-Waxler, C. (1987, April). *Do toddlers express guilt?* Poster presented at the meeting of the Society for Research in Child Development, Baltimore, MD.

Bretherton, J., Fritz, J., Zahn-Waxler, C., & Ridgeway, D. (1986). Learning to talk about emotions: A functionalist perspective. *Child Development, 57*, 529–548.

Burggraf, S. A., & Tangney, J. P. (1989). *The Self-Conscious Affect and Attribution Inventory for Children (SCAAI-C)*. Bryn Mawr, PA: Bryn Mawr College.

Bussey, K. (1992). Lying and truthfulness: Children's definitions, standards, and evaluative reactions. *Child Development, 63*, 129–137.

Chapman, M., & Zahn-Waxler, C. (1982). Young children's compliance and noncompliance to parental discipline in a natural setting. *International Journal of Behavioral Development, 5*, 81–94.

Chapman, M., Zahn-Waxler, C., Iannotti, R., & Cooperman, G. (1987). Empathy and Responsibility in the Motivation of Children's Helping. *Developmental Psychology, 23*, 140–145.

Coopersmith, S. (1967). *The antecedents of self-esteem*. San Francisco: W. H. Freeman.

Davitz, J. R. (1969). *The language of emotion*. New York: Academic Press.

Dienstbier, R. A. (1984). The role of emotion in moral socialization. In C. Izard, J. Kagan, & R. Zajonc (Eds.), *Emotions, cognition, and behavior* (pp. 484–513). New York: Cambridge University Press.

Dienstbier, R. A., Hillman, D., Lehnhoff, J., Hillman, J., & Valkenaar, M C. (1975). An emotion–attribution approach to moral behavior: Interfacing cognitive and avoidance theories of moral development. *Psychological Review, 82*, 299–315.

Edelman, R. J. (1985). Social embarrassment: An analysis of the process. *Journal of Social and Personal Relationships, 2*, 195–213.

Erikson, E. H. (1963). *Childhood and society* (2nd ed.). New York: Norton.

Ferguson, T. J. (1990). *The Expectation Sort for Parents (ESP)*. Unpublished manuscript, Utah State University.

Ferguson, T. J., Bailey, R., & Palmer-Kerbs, C. (1991, April). *When high effort becomes low ability: The process of guilt and shame in children of alcoholics*. Paper presented at the meeting of the Society for Research in Child Development, Seattle.

Ferguson, T. J., Bailey, R., & Palmer-Kerbs, C. (1992, March). *Socialization antecedents of guilt and shame in young children*. Poster presented at the biennial meeting of the Southwestern Society for Research in Human Development, Tempe, AZ.

Ferguson, T. J., & Denissen, K. (1982). De samenhang tussen de reacties van moeders en hun kinderen op overtredingen: Disciplinair gedrag en morele internalisatie [The relationship between mothers' and children's reactions to transgressions: Disciplinary behavior and moral internalization]. In M. Boekaerts & C. F. M.

van Lieshout (Eds.), *Sociale en motivationele aspecten van het leren [Social and motivational aspects of learning]* (pp. 137–149). Lisse, The Netherlands: Swets & Zeitlinger.

Ferguson, T. J., & Mortensen, L. (1990, April). *Self-consciousness as a predictor of guilt- versus shame-proneness.* Paper presented at the meeting of the Rocky Mountain Psychological Association, Tucson, AZ.

Ferguson, T. J., Mortensen, L., & Warner, T. (1990, March). *The role of self-guide discrepancies in adolescents' and adults' subjective experiences of guilt and shame.* Poster presented at the biennial meeting of the Southwestern Society for Research in Human Development, Dallas, TX.

Ferguson, T. J., Olthof, T., Luiten, A., & Rule, B. G. (1984). Children's use of observed behavioral frequency vs. behavioral covariation in ascribing dispositions to others. *Child Development, 55,* 2094–2105.

Ferguson, T. J., Olthof, T., & Roomans, S. (1991, July). *Developmental transformation in the relationship between conceptions of responsibility and guilt.* Poster presented at the meeting of the International Society for the Study of Behavioral Development, Minneapolis.

Ferguson, T. J., & Rule, B. G. (1983). An attributional perspective on anger and aggression. In R. Geen & E. Donnerstein (Eds.), *Aggression: Theoretical and empirical reviews* (Vol. 1, pp. 41–74). New York: Academic Press.

Ferguson, T. J., & Rule, B. G. (1988). Children's evaluations of retaliatory aggression. *Child Development, 59,* 961–968.

Ferguson, T. J., & Stegge, H. (1990). *Parent–Child Attribution and Reaction Survey (P-CARS).* Unpublished manuscript, Utah State University.

Ferguson, T. J., Stegge, H., & Damhuis, I. (1990a). Guilt and shame experiences in elementary school-age children. In R. J. Takens (Ed.), *European perspectives in psychology* (Vol. 1, pp. 195–218). New York: Wiley.

Ferguson, T. J., Stegge, H., & Damhuis, I. (1990b, March). *Spontaneous and elicited guilt and shame experiences in elementary school-age children.* Poster presented at the biennial meeting of the Southwestern Society for Research in Human Development, Dallas, TX.

Ferguson, T. J., Stegge, H., & Damhuis, I. (1991). Children's understanding of guilt and shame. *Child Development, 62,* 827–839.

Fischer, K. W., Shaver, P., & Carnochan, P. (1988). A skill approach to emotional development: From basic- to subordinate-category emotions. In W. Damon (Ed.), *Child-development today and tomorrow* (pp. 107–136). San Francisco: Jossey-Bass.

Fischer, K. W., Shaver, P. R., & Carnochan, P. (1990). How emotions develop and how they organize development. *Cognition and Emotion, 4*(2), 81–127.

Frijda, N. H. (1986). *The emotions.* Cambridge, England: Cambridge University Press.

Graham, S., Doubleday, C., & Guarino, P. A. (1984). The development of relations between perceived controllability and the emotions pity, anger, and guilt. *Child Development, 55,* 561–565.

Graham, S., & Weiner, G. (1986). From an attributional theory of emotion to developmental psychology: A roundtrip ticket? *Social Cognition, 4,* 152–179.

Harder, D. W. (1990). Additional construct validity evidence for the Harder Personal Feelings Questionnaire measure of shame and guilt proneness. *Psychological Reports, 67,* 288–290.

Harder, D. W., & Lewis, S. J. (1987). The assessment of shame and guilt. In J. N.

Butcher & C. D. Spielberger (Eds.), *Advances in personality assessment* (Vol. 6, pp. 89–114). Hillsdale, NJ: Erlbaum.

Harder, D. W., & Zalma, A. (1990). Two promising shame and guilt scales: A construct validity comparison. *Journal of Personality Assessment, 55,* 729–745.

Harris, P. L. (1989). *Children and emotion: The development of psychological understanding.* Oxford: Blackwell.

Harris, P. L., Olthof, T., Meerum Terwogt, M., & Hardman, C. E. (1987). Children's knowledge of the situations that provoke emotion. *International Journal of Behavioral Development, 10,* 319–343.

Harter, S. (1983). Children's understanding of multiple emotions: A cognitive-developmental approach. In W. F. Overton (Ed.), *The relationship between social and cognitive development* (pp. 147–194). Hillsdale, NJ: Erlbaum.

Harter, S., & Whitesell, N. (1989). Developmental changes in children's emotion concepts. In C. Saarni & P. L. Harris (Eds.), *Children's understanding of emotions* (pp. 81–116). New York: Cambridge University Press.

Higgins, E. T. (1987). Self-discrepancy: A theory relating self and affect. *Psychological Review, 94,* 319–340.

Hoblitzelle, W. (1987). Attempts to measure and differentiate shame and guilt: The relation between shame and depression. In H. B. Lewis (Ed.), *The role of shame in symptom formation* (pp. 207–235). New York: International Universities Press.

Hoffman, M. L. (1970a). Moral development. In P. H. Mussen (Ed.), *Carmichael's manual of child psychology* (3rd ed., Vol. 2, pp. 261–359). New York: Wiley.

Hoffman, M. L. (1970b). Conscience, personality, and socialization techniques. *Human Development, 13,* 90–126.

Hoffman, M. L. (1982). Development of prosocial motivation: Empathy and guilt. In N. Eisenberg (Ed.), *Development of prosocial behavior* (pp. 281–313). New York: Academic Press.

Hoffman, M. L. (1983). Empathy, guilt, and social cognition. In W. F. Overton (Ed.), *The relationship between social and cognitive development* (pp. 1–51). Hillsdale, NJ: Erlbaum.

Izard, C. E. (1977). *Human emotions.* New York: Plenum Press.

Kagan, J. (1984). *The nature of the child.* New York: Basic Books.

Kaufman, G. (1985). *Shame: The power of caring.* Cambridge, MA: Schenkman.

Kaufman, G. (1989). *The psychology of shame: Theory and treatment of shame-based syndromes.* New York: Springer.

Kochanska, G. (1989). Socialization and temperament in the development of guilt and conscience. *Child Development, 62,* 1379–1392.

Lewis, H. B. (1971). *Shame and guilt in neurosis.* New York: International Universities Press.

Lewis, M. (1992). *Shame: The exposed self.* New York: Free Press.

Lewis, M., Alessandri, S. M., & Sullivan, M. W. (1992). Differences in shame and pride as a function of children's gender and task difficulty. *Child Development, 63,* 630–638.

Lindsay-Hartz, J. (1984). Contrasting experiences of shame and guilt. *American Behavioral Scientist, 27,* 689–704.

Malatesta, C. Z., & Wilson, A. (1988). Emotion cognition interaction in personality development: A discrete emotions, functionalist analysis. *British Journal of Social Psychology, 27,* 91–112.

Meerum Terwogt, M. & Stegge, H. (in press). Emotional behavior and emotional understanding: A developmental fugue. In M. Goodyer (Ed.), *Mood disorders in childhood and adolescence*. Cambridge, England: Cambridge University Press.

Modigliani, A. (1971). Embarrassment, facework, and eye contact: Testing a theory of embarrassment. *Journal of Personality and Social Psychology, 17,* 15–24.

Moretti, M. M., & Higgins, E. T. (1990). The development of self-esteem vulner-abilities: Social and cognitive factors in developmental psychopathology. In R. J. Sternberg & J. Kolligian, Jr. (Eds.), *Competence considered* (pp. 286–314). New Haven, CT: Yale University Press.

Nunner-Winkler, G., & Sodian, B. (1988). Children's understanding of moral emotions. *Child Development, 59,* 1323–1338.

Piers, G., & Singer, M. (1953). *Shame and guilt*. New York: Norton.

Potter-Efron, R. T. (1989). *Shame, guilt and alcoholism: Treatment issues in clinical practice*. New York: Haworth Press.

Rollins, B. C., & Thomas, D. L. (1979). Parental support, power and control techniques in the socialization of children. In W. R. Burr, R. Hill, F. I. Nye, & I. L. Reiss (Eds.), *Contemporary theories about the family: Vol. 1. Research based theories*. New York: Free Press.

Scheff, F. J. (1988). Shame and conformity: The deference emotion system. *American Sociological Review, 53,* 395–406.

Smith, R. L. (1972). *The relative proneness to shame or guilt as an indicator of defensive style*. Unpublished doctoral dissertation, Northwestern University.

Stegge, H., & Ferguson, T. J., (1990). *Child–Child Attribution and Reaction Survey (C-CARS)*. Unpublished manuscript, Utah State University.

Stegge, H., Ferguson, T. J., & Meerum Terwogt, M. (1991, July). *Parental disciplinary reactions and children's proneness to guilt and shame*. Paper presented at the meeting of the International Society for Research on Emotion, Saarbrücken, Germany.

Stipek, D. J., & DeCotis, K. M. (1988). Children's understanding of the implications of causal attributions for emotional experiences. *Child Development, 59,* 1601–1616.

Tangney, J. P. (1990). Assessing individual differences in proneness to shame and guilt: Development of the Self-Conscious Affect and Attribution Inventory. *Journal of Personality and Social Psychology, 59,* 102–111.

Tangney, J. P. (1991). Moral affect: The good, the bad, and the ugly. *Journal of Personality and Social Psychology, 61,* 598–607.

Tangney, J. P. (1992). Situational determinants of shame and guilt in young childhood. *Personality and Social Psychology Bulletin, 18,* 199–206.

Tangney, J. P. (1993). Shame and guilt. In C. G. Costello (Ed.), *Symptoms of depression* (pp. 161–180). New York: Wiley.

Tangney, J. P., Marschall, D., Rosenberg, K., Barlow, D. H., & Wagner, P. (1993). *Children's and adults' autobiographical accounts of shame, guilt, and pride experiences: A qualitative analysis of situational determinants and interpersonal concerns*. Manuscript submitted for publication.

Tangney, J. P., Wagner, P., Fletcher, C., & Gramzow, R. (1992). Shamed into anger? The relation of shame and guilt to anger and self-reported aggression. *Journal of Personality and Social Psychology, 62,* 669–675.

Tangney, J. P., Wagner, P., & Gramzow, R. (1992). Proneness to shame, proneness to guilt, and psychopathology. *Journal of Abnormal Psychology, 101,* 1–10.

Taylor, G. (1985). *Pride, shame and guilt: Emotions of self-assessment*. Oxford: Clarendon Press.

Thompson, R. A. (1989). Causal attributions and children's emotional understanding. In C. Saarni & P. L. Harris (Eds.), *Children's understanding of emotions* (pp. 117–150). New York: Cambridge University Press.

Thompson, R. A., & Hoffman, M. L. (1980). Empathy and the development of guilt in children. *Developmental Psychology, 16,* 155–156.

Thrane, G. (1979). Shame. *Journal for the Theory of Social Behavior, 9,* 139–166.

Turiel, E. (1983). *The development of social knowledge: Morality and convention.* Cambridge, England: Cambridge University Press.

Weiner, B. (1986). *An attributional theory of motivation and emotion.* New York: Springer-Verlag.

Wicker, F. W., Payne, G. C., & Morgan, R. D. (1983). Participant descriptions of guilt and shame. *Motivation and Emotion, 7,* 25–39.

Wurmser, L. (1981). *The mask of shame.* Baltimore: Johns Hopkins University Press.

Zahn-Waxler, C., & Kochanska, G. (1989). The origins of guilt. In R. A. Thompson (Ed.), *Nebraska Symposium on Motivation: Vol. 36. Socioemotional development* (pp. 183–258). Lincoln: University of Nebraska Press.

Zahn-Waxler, C., Kochanska, G., Krupnick, J., & McKnew, D. (1990). Patterns of guilt in children of depressed and well mothers. *Developmental Psychology, 26,* 51–59.

Zahn-Waxler, C., Radke-Yarrow, M., & King, R. (1979). Child rearing and children's prosocial initiations toward victims of distress. *Child Development, 50,* 319–330.

7

Embarrassment:
The Emotion of
Self-Exposure and Evaluation

MICHAEL LEWIS

DIFFICULTIES IN THE STUDY OF
EMBARRASSMENT AND OTHER EMOTIONS

This chapter focuses on the emotion of embarrassment. There are many ways in which to study emotion, and before embarrassment itself can be considered, it is necessary to address the question of how to study it. Adults or children can be asked what they think embarrassment is or what kinds of situations lead to embarrassment. Alternatively, people's behavior in situations that may be related to embarrassment can be studied. Although there may be a preference for one method or the other, both are important.

When people are asked about their ideas or thoughts concerning an emotion, the data that are gathered can be used for a theory of emotion. Much like a theory of mind, these data address the topic of what and how people think about their emotional lives. The advantages of such data are many, since what people think about is often highly influential in determining what they actually do. For example, when we think about the funeral of a friend's mother that will take place tomorrow, we know many things. We know how people, especially the friend, will feel (presumably sadness and maybe other emotions); we know how people will dress (in mainstream U.S. culture, in dark somber clothes); how they will move their bodies (they will walk quietly and not run); and what their facial expressions will be like (they will look sad and concerned rather than happy and carefree). Even though we may not be sad ourselves over this loss, we may be sad for our

198

friend. Even if we are not sad, we know what others may feel, and we can adjust our behavior accordingly. Individuals' knowledge of situations, context, facial expression, and general demeanor are important features in regulating emotional life (Lewis & Saarni, 1985). Our implicit and explicit theories of emotional life inform us how to behave and may, in fact, affect the way we feel. They also allow us to behave in ways that are counter to how we feel. Deceptive emotional behavior, a phenomenon that occurs with great frequency, is predicated on our knowledge of what others believe and how they behave. We alter or adjust our behavior so as to conform to the beliefs of others (Lewis & Saarni, 1993).

Although studies of what people think about are important, there are potentially serious consequences if information about an emotion is predicated solely on people's theories. The obvious pitfalls are cultural relativism, as well as temporal or cohort effects. For example, in the case of the funeral, it is not universally true that somber dress is required in all cultures (or even in all subcultures within U.S. culture), or is in some way biologically connected to sadness. In many cultures, the wearing of white rather than black is associated with death. Situations that are likely to elicit embarrassment may also differ by culture; what is considered physical exposure in U.S. culture may be far more than what is considered exposure in Saudi Arabian Muslim culture. The effects of time differ as well: What behaviors and what situations are thought necessary at one point in time may not be thought so at another. Such criticism, either about a theory of mind or, in this case, a theory of emotion, cannot be taken lightly.

Perhaps a more serious problem in discussing emotional life has to do with the problem of language meaning. Since emotional life is shared by everyone, and since there already exists a common vocabulary, people's beliefs rest on the study of this "common language." For example, we all seem to know, and accept that we know, what we mean when we say "anger." However, there is ample evidence to indicate that even such a simple, well-understood emotion such as anger is more confusing than appears at first. The terms "anger," "aggression," "hostility," "will," and "assertiveness" are often used interchangeably, yet they imply different phenomena (Lewis, 1993). For example, Darwin (1872/1965) talked about anger as a coherent response, both facial and bodily, whose function is to help the organism overcome an obstacle. This use of "anger" is very similar to Amsel's (1958) use of the term "frustration" in describing a rat's attempt to overcome a barrier. Under this description, the affective state of a young child who hits another child in order to get a toy that is wanted can also be called "anger." But there is some trouble in accepting that anger in a rat trying to get to food has the same meaning as anger in a young child.

Recently, I (Lewis, 1990a) raised the issue of the difference between anger and instrumentality in very young infants whose learned response to a desirable goal was blocked. In the studies described, infants learned to pull a string to turn on a slide projector. After they learned this task, the conditions were changed, and pulling the string no longer resulted in the projection of a slide. Observation of the infants' facial patterns revealed a marked increase in an "anger face" (see Izard, 1979); there was also a significant increase in the rate and intensity of their pulling response. Is this type of angry response the same as the response of a child who hits another child to get a toy? In the former case, the response appears to have been an adaptive one, since it could have enabled the infants to achieve a learned, desirable goal. Instead of "anger," we might call it "efficacy" (White, 1959), "will" (Rank, 1945), or "instrumentality." The response of hitting to get the toy may not have the same meaning, yet the use of the common-language term "anger" tends to produce this type of confusion.

This language problem is made even worse when theories of what people think about involves the self-conscious emotions, such as shame, pride, guilt, and embarrassment. In a recent review of the literature on shame (Lewis, 1992), I have reported a wide and often contradictory use of the term. The varying uses of the term are found in both the clinical (Greenberg & Mitchell, 1983) as well as the developmental literature (Zahn-Waxler & Kochanska, 1990). The use of the common language remains a problem both for individuals in their daily lives and for scholars in their pursuit of understanding. Considerable progress in understanding emotional life could be made if we were prepared to reject the common language and use symbolic terms to represent specific situation–behavior coherences instead. For example, we could say A_1 for "string-pulling anger" and A_2 for "hit-someone-to-get-a-toy anger." It would be an empirical question whether A_1 and A_2 are the same, but until this could be proven, they would remain different terms.

The study of emotional life through questioning people about their beliefs, though important, is not by itself sufficient. The alternative, the study of behavior itself, must be considered. This requires experimental manipulation as well as observation. The observation of behavior across particular situations and in particular contexts allows us to study what actually happens rather than what people think. Darwin (1872/1965), in discussing emotional life, focused in part on contexts and on the behaviors exhibited. In discussing the more complex emotions, such as embarrassment, shame, and guilt, he used the blushing response. The use of behavioral observation has additional features. From a cross-cultural perspective, it permits the observation of situations and behaviors without the use of a common language. Perhaps its most important use is in studying the development of emotional life, especially in infants and young children. Here the problem of language and language meaning is particularly critical. In infants and young children, the technique of asking for ideas about emotional life is not possible. Given that blushing cannot be observed much before the age of 3 (Darwin, 1872/1965), the exploration of the origin of self-conscious emotions requires the use of experimental manipulation and observation of behavior (Lewis, Sullivan, Stanger, & Weiss, 1989).

However, there are dangers as well in the use of observation. Is the child who cries, shows a fear face, and avoids a particular situation really feeling fear? If by "feeling" we mean "experiencing the fear," we will have difficulty inferring this without language. Language readily allows for the inference of experience. For example, when people say, "I am fearful," they mean by that statement that (1) they are in a state of fear, and (2) they are experiencing that state. As we (Lewis & Michalson, 1983) have indicated, the experiencing of an emotional state and an emotional state itself do not necessarily have any one-to-one correspondence. Thus, for example, a person may be in a fearful state but may not experience it. Imagine a man driving a car and having a blowout while on a highway. During the time it takes to bring the car to a safe stop by the side of the road, the man may not be experiencing his state of fear because his attention is focused elsewhere—on the feel of the road and on visual and auditory information that will allow him to bring the car safely to a stop. He may be in a state of fear but may not experience the fear. He may only experience the fear once he turns his attention toward his state. This dissociation between state and experience occurs in many clinical examples as well (the reader is referred to Lewis & Michalson, 1983, 1985, for a complete discussion of the state–experience relation). In the same way, one can have an experience without necessarily being in a particular emotional state. Thus, a woman may experience herself as tired when, in fact, her state is one of sadness. The problem of whether or not the behavior represents "true" emotional life remains when only behavior is studied. Nevertheless, in some circumstances, it is not possible to study emotional life without studying the behavior of the organism. This is especially true when developmental functions—in particular, the origins of these emotions—are the focus of study.

The present chapter focuses on the origins of embarrassment and, because of this, it focuses on how children behave rather than on what they believe. Since there are so few studies of embarrassed behavior (see Edelmann, 1987, for a review), even for adults, it is difficult to integrate what children do with those adult studies that explore what adults think. The following topics are covered: (1) theories of embarrassment; (2) measurement issues; (3) a model of self-conscious emotions, including their developmental course; (4) embarrassment as a unique emotion; and (5) its functional significance and differentiation.

THEORIES OF EMBARRASSMENT

The literature on embarrassment can be traced from Goffman's work (see Goffman, 1956, 1959, 1967). More recent attempts at understanding embarrassment have been made by Edelmann (1987) and Parrott (Parrott & Smith, 1991; Silver, Sabini, & Parrott, 1991). Almost all theories speak of embarrassment as an unpleasant feeling having to do with some form of the discrediting of one's own image, either through the loss of self-esteem, the esteem of others, or both.

One of the critical issues in the study of embarrassment has been the terminology issue, discussed above. The particular problem here has to do with the difference between "embarrassment" and "shame" on the one hand, and between "embarrassment" and "shyness" on the other. In regard to the former difference, Edelmann (1987) has reviewed four theoretical perspectives: the psychoanalytic, existential, behavioral, and interpersonal approaches. The psychoanalytic approach makes no distinction between embarrassment and shame. Moreover, most consideration of this family of emotions is reserved for guilt rather than shame (for exceptions, see Broucek, 1991; H. B. Lewis, 1971; Morrison, 1989). In general, the literature tends to confuse "embarrassment" with "shame"; Freud wrote only of shame and did not employ another word that might be translated as "embarrassment" (Dann, 1977, p. 454; Edelmann, 1987, p. 7). If shame is discussed, it is usually discussed in terms of nakedness or in terms of impulses (either sexual or exhibitional) that need to be held in check.

Of more interest is the existential approach. Goffman (1956), for example, discusses the act of blushing as occurring when one becomes aware of one's own body. This is very similar to Darwin's (1872/1965) discussion of embarrassment; for Darwin, embarrassment occurs when one's own body becomes the focus of the attention of others. The discussion of embarrassment as an *alienation* of one's own body is the central theme of the existential position. Unfortunately, the term "alienation" suggests some negative attribution, as in being separate from one's own body. Alienation can also be viewed as self-awareness—that is, as the self's becoming the focus of the self. We are not always aware of our selves, but on some occasions we are. To be always aware would probably be pathological. Elsewhere (Lewis, 1990b, 1991, 1992), I have discussed the problems and advantages of self-awareness (see also Mandler, 1975). This theme is considered in more detail below. What is clear is that there are occasions when we become self-aware, almost as if we are suddenly unmasked. These occasions may be those in which embarrassment is the likely emotion.

It is to the interpersonal approach that Edelmann (1987) devotes most of his attention. This approach suggests that individuals feel embarrassed when they project an image of themselves incompatible with their own view *in the presence of others*: "Embarrassment . . . reflects a failure to present oneself in the way one would have wished" (Edelmann, 1987, p. 14). Such theories assume the need for three features: (1) the presence of another person, (2) the person's becoming aware that he or she is the center of attention, and (3) the person's feeling that he or she is being judged. Modigliani (1968, 1971) also argues for three basic features: (1) The incidents that cause embarrassment involve a failure on the part of the individual to fulfill certain social expectations, (2) the failure leads to diminution in the person's public esteem, and (3) this diminution in public esteem leads to a diminution in the individual's self-esteem. (Notice that in these definitions of embarrassment, both the failure of some standard and public observation of that failure need to occur.) The distinction between embarrassment and shame is not well articulated here. One could argue that the same three conditions in either set of definitions are necessary for the production of shame (see H. B. Lewis, 1971). Such a view of embarrassment is quite common (see Semin & Manstead, 1981, and, earlier, Izard, 1977, and Tomkins, 1963).

Embarrassment is often considered to be similar to shyness, especially to the extent to which embarrassment can be viewed as having a fear component (Buss, 1980). When we think of a shy child, the tendency is to think of a child who is reluctant to engage in interpersonal interactions. This factor of sociability may have less to do with evaluation and more to do with dispositional factors (see Eysenck, 1956). Kagan, Reznick, and Snedman (1988) have argued for what they call "inhibition," which bears a striking similarity to shyness (see also Zimbardo, 1977, and Jones, Cheek, & Briggs, 1986). Even when embarrassment is viewed as a form of shyness, it has a negative evaluation component. For example, Zimbardo (1977) argues that people feel most shy at being the center of attention of a large group of people. For him, a person's being watched implies a need to be seen in the *best* light. Being seen as such, in turn, implies an evaluation of the self against some kind of ideal self. Shyness has also been related to aspects of social anxiety (Buss, 1980; Cheek & Buss, 1981; Fenigstein, Scheier, & Buss, 1975), which likewise implies an evaluative component.

The discussion to follow makes use of the distinction between embarrassment as related to shyness or social anxiety, and embarrassment as related to failure of one's self-image. For now, the literature on embarrassment does not allow us to decide whether either of these definitions is correct. Starting with Darwin's analysis presented over a century ago, and continuing into the current literature, embarrassment stands as a good example of a common-language problem. Although we can all respond to the question "What embarrasses you?", and although we can all claim to have felt embarrassed at some point, we remain uncertain as to its precise meaning.

MEASUREMENT ISSUES

Darwin (1872/1965) described embarrassment as including the phenomenon of blushing; however, he also used blushing to describe the broad category of self-conscious emotions, which includes shame and guilt as well as embarrassment. The use of this measure of blushing to index a group of other self-conscious emotions renders blushing as a measurement index for embarrassment less effective than one would wish. In addition, silly smile and/or laughter, particularly giggling, has been used to index embarrassment (Buss, 1980). Hand gestures and body movement have also been suggested as components of embarrassment and have been used to distinguish it from amusement (Edelmann & Hampson, 1981; Geppert, 1986). By utilizing a combination of the criteria suggested by others, my colleagues and I (Lewis et al., 1989) have come up with an overall measure of embarrassment that is useful in studying young children. Our scoring system for embarrassment agrees with those of others who have attempted to find behavioral manifestations of this emotion (see Geppert, 1986).

In general, the behaviors believed to reflect embarrassment are a smiling facial expression followed by gaze aversion and movements of the hands to touch hair, clothing, face, or other body parts. These hand gestures appear to capture the category of nervous movements, which previous investigators believed to be characteristic of embarrassment. Such body touching can accompany smiling and gaze aversion or can immediately follow them. All three classes of behavior appear to be associated with embarrassment.

Embarrassment differs from shame or anxiety/fear in a number of critical ways. First, embarrassment seems to be marked by a "sheepish" grin or a "silly" smile, as described by others. In both shame and fear, the smiling behavior is often absent. Moreover, the smiling in embarrassment does not appear to be a frozen type of smile; rather, it is an active engagement with the other people present. Perhaps most important in differentiating embarrassment from other emotions are the gaze behavior and bodily action. In embarrassment, people are more apt to tilt their heads and to engage in gaze-avert/look-up behavior. This is not gaze aversion with the head bowed, as in an avoidance response; nor is it the immobility of action, as in removing oneself from the situation. Instead, it is a gaze-avert, gaze-return motion toward the other person (people) present. This on–off sequence is typical of embarrassment, whereas in shame, shyness, or fear the sequence seen is turning away and remaining away. Finally, nervous touching of the body, including hair, clothing, and face, seems to reflect the subject's engagement in self-directive behavior, reflecting an active focus on the self. In shame, shyness, or fear, the person is likely to be immobile, not exploratory in terms of movement toward the self. The use of such behavioral criteria is in keeping with the idea that embarrassment appears to be related to the self and requires a social object. The active nature of bodily action in embarrassment, unlike that seen in shame, suggests that embarrassment and shame are distinguishable (Lewis, 1992).

Blushing, which received so much attention in Darwin's analysis, would be a likely candidate for indexing embarrassment. However, blushing does not always occur, there being large individual differences in the likelihood of this response. Differences may be attributable in part to different physiology; it is certainly related to skin coloration, with light-skinned people blushing more visibly than dark-skinned people. In our research on self-conscious emotions, blushing in children is a relatively infrequent event. Even when children above the age of 3 show embarrassment in terms of other behaviors, it is rare to observe blushing in those children. This should not be surprising, since it is relatively unusual to see blushing in adults (Leary & Meadows, 1991). Given self-reports indicating the high incidence of embarrassment, it is interesting to note that the occasions of blushing seem to be disproportionately low.

It thus appears that in order to measure embarrassment, we need to observe facial behavior and bodily action. The particular responses described above represent the best behavioral manifestations of embarrassment, independent of self-report. They are the ones that have been used in the few studies of children's embarrassment (see Dickson, 1957; Lewis et al., 1989; Lewis & Brooks-Gunn, 1979).

It has been suggested that one way to study embarrassment is through the observation of behavior in context. If we could specify those conditions under which embarrassment is likely to occur, it would make the job of studying embarrassment easier. Given the existing theoretical arguments, we would tend to expect embarrassment to occur under conditions of social anxiety, social interaction, or evaluation of failure. Although this may be correct, such situations are not readily defined and articulated (see Miller, Chapter 13, this volume). What is surprising is the observation that embarrassment can be elicited in children when they look at their image in the mirror if the children are 18 months of age or older (see Amsterdam, 1972; Dickson, 1957; Schulman & Kaplowitz, 1977). That embarrassment occurs in such a situation has to cause difficulties for any theory based on failure vis-à-vis some ideal self or standard. Seeing oneself in the mirror has no evaluative component. Moreover, embarrassment in young children can be seen in situations where children are asked to perform some public act. Parents report that their young children show embarrassment when they are asked to "show Grandma or Grandpa how well you draw" or "show Aunt Barbara your missing tooth." Performance- or social-anxiety-related concern for presenting the self in the right light can be used as an interpretation of this behavior. Alternatively, however, these situations may not represent evaluative processes, but instances where the child focuses on the self.

A DEVELOPMENTAL MODEL OF SELF-CONSCIOUS EMOTIONS

The model to be presented here rests on the proposition that embarrassment belongs to the general class of self-conscious emotions, and that these self-conscious emotions require specific cognitions for their emergence. Most of the literature on emotional development focuses on the appearance of what have been called the "primary" or "basic" emotions. These emotions are characterized both by their early appearance and by the universal facial expressions associated with them. Beyond the appearance of these early emotions, the emergence of the other emotions remains relatively uncharted. Although some empirical work on pride, guilt, and shame, especially within an achievement situation, has recently appeared (Geppert & Kuster, 1983; Heckhausen, 1984; Stipek, Recchia, & McClintic, 1992), theories regarding the origin of the later-appearing emotions—often called "secondary" or "self-conscious" emotions—are largely unexplored. The lack of operational definitions and the need for a good measurement system are part of the problem.

The appearance of these emotions after the emergence of the earlier ones has led to their classification as secondary or derived emotions (see Plutchik, 1980). Another model considers that these emotions follow the primary ones but are not constructed from them (Izard, 1977). The model I present here proposes that emotions are tied to cognitive processes. Those needing less cognitive support emerge first, and those needing more emerge later (Lewis, 1992; Lewis & Michalson, 1983). Although the sequence of the emergence of the earlier emotions has yet to be fully articulated, it seems that by 6 to 8 months of age they have all appeared (Lewis, 1993). Even so, it is not until the middle of the second year that the secondary or self-conscious emotions are observed (Borke, 1971; Lewis & Brook-Gunn, 1979; Stipek, 1983).

The model articulated elsewhere (Lewis, 1992; Lewis et al., 1989) is illustrated in Figure 7.1. In the first months, the primary emotions appear. The time of emergence of these emotions is variable and depends upon situation and context. Again, however, it is reasonably safe to say that they either appear shortly after birth or are seen within the first 6 to 8 months of life. In the second stage, self-referential behavior emerges; this ability to recognize the self or to make reference to the self is indicative of self-consciousness. "Self-consciousness" is the capacity to attend to the self and has been called "objective self-awareness" by Duval and Wicklund (1972). This capacity emerges between 15 and 18 months, and all children appear to have it by 24 months. The emergence of self-consciousness has been discussed in great detail elsewhere and is not the focus of discussion here (see instead Lewis, 1990b, 1991, 1992; Lewis & Brooks-Gunn, 1979).

The technique used to index self-consciousness or objective self-awareness was originally developed with chimpanzees (see Gallup, 1970). It involves marking a child's nose with rouge and then placing the child in front of a mirror. When infants are placed in front of the mirror, they show a variety of behaviors. Before 15–18 months, infants do not use the mirror to find and touch the spot on their nose. They look behind the mirror, or they look and touch the image in the mirror as if they were interacting with another child. From 15–24 months of age on, they touch their faces (the mark on their noses) when placed in front of a mirror. The results from our studies were surprisingly consistent: Mark-directed behavior was never exhibited in infants younger than 15 months, and between 18 and 24 months a dramatic increase in mark-directed behavior occurred. Approximately 75% of the 18-month-olds and all of the 24-month-olds exhibited self-mark recognition (Lewis & Brooks-Gunn, 1979). This collection of findings

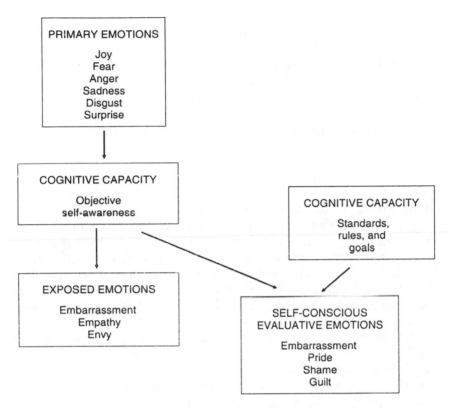

FIGURE 7.1. The development of self-conscious emotions.

appears to indicate that in the last half of the second year of life, children develop self referential behavior, which my colleagues and I believe reflects self-consciousness. Observation of Figure 7.1 indicates that the consolidation of a set of cognitive skills, centering around self-awareness or consciousness, what we call self-referential capacities, leads to the elicitation of the self-conscious *exposed* emotions. Self-expressed embarrassment, in particular, seems to be related to the emergence of self-referential behavior. Amsterdam (1972), Dickson (1957), and Shulman and Kaplowitz (1977) report instances of self-conscious behavior in children older than 15 months when viewing themselves in mirrors.

In our studies (Lewis & Brooks-Gunn, 1979), 20% of the children over 15 months of age who observed themselves in a mirror *without* rouge on their noses showed coy or silly behavior, which could be taken to reflect embarrassment. Thus, there was reason to believe that the emergence of self-referential behavior is somehow related to embarrassment. This was tested in a later series of studies (Lewis et al., 1989). We were able to demonstrate that embarrassment did not occur in children who did not show self-recognition in the mirror. In these studies, the mark-directed self-recognition mirror task was first used, and embarrassment was then observed under four different conditions. In the first of these, the "mirror conditions," the children looked at themselves in the mirror with other people observing them looking at themselves. A "complimenting condition" involved an experimenter's initiating interactions with a child, during which the child was given four to five compliments. For example, children were told that they were smart, had beautiful hair, and had lovely clothes. Two other conditions included a request for the child to perform a dance. In one, the experimenter handed the mother a small tambourine and asked the mother to coax the child to dance; in the other, the experimenter herself coaxed the child to dance. Either the mother or the experimenter said, "Let's see you dance. Dance for me. I'll sing 'Old MacDonald' [or a song familiar to the child]." The dance situation was utilized because conspicuousness is thought to be an elicitor of embarrassment (Buss, 1980). The results of these studies (reported in Lewis et al., 1989) showed a direct relation between embarrassment in these situations and self-referential behavior as measured in the previous rouge-and-mirror situation. Embarrassment was seen only for children who showed self-consciousness (touched their noses). Such findings indicate that embarrassment is related to the emergence of this feature of self.

Observation of Figure 7.1 also indicates that self-conscious *evaluative* emotions do not emerge at this time, but appear somewhat later, toward the third year of life. Although the early form of embarrassment requires only self-consciousness, a later form (to be discussed in more detail below) as well as pride, shame, and guilt, appears to require additional cognitive capacities. These include the acquisition of standards and the ability to evaluate one's behavior *vis-à-vis* these standards. Present work indicates that the emergence of self-conscious evaluative emotions occurs at about 3 years of age (see Heckhausen, 1984; Kagan, 1981; Lewis, Alessandri, & Sullivan, 1992; Stipek et al., 1992).

The emergence of shame, pride, and guilt almost $1^1/_2$ to 2 years after that of early embarrassment suggests several important points. (1) The emergence of embarrassment and that of shame are not coincidental, thus supporting the premise that early embarrassment is not the same as shame. (2) The emergence of embarrassment prior to that of a self-evaluative capacity suggests that embarrassment (at least in its initial form) does not require evaluation of the self, either in terms of potential failure or in terms of failure itself. Although such embarrassment may require a social audience, it does not appear to need a self-evaluative component. (3) Embarrassment can occur under situations in which failure is not likely to be a sufficient explanatory device. For example, in the Lewis et al. (1989) study, embarrassment was most often elicited in the complimenting and mirror conditions. Some have argued that compliments to an adult may have a negative component, since children are taught to be modest. It is possible to argue this for older children and adults; however, to argue that children 15–24 months of age have been taught and have learned the issue of modesty is hard to accept. Rather, embarrassment seen in this situation is related more to exposure or attention being paid to the self than to social mores and values.

The model presented here and the data used to test it suggest that embarrassment may be a uniquely different and powerful emotion—one that has meaning and functional significance in relationship to the self.

EMBARRASSMENT AS A UNIQUE EMOTION

This section explores three issues related to embarrassment. In the first two, embarrassment as related to other emotions is considered; in the third, two types of embarrassment are discussed.

Embarrassment and Shyness

Embarrassment has been related to shyness, so we need a working definition for the latter term. Izard and Tyson (1986) consider "shyness" to be sheepishness, bashfulness, or a feeling of uneasiness or psychological discomfort in social situations. They suggest that shyness results from a vacillation between fear and interest or between avoidance and approach. They relate shyness to fear, not to evaluation. Individuals who are considered shy are not as much concerned with the evaluation of their performance *vis-à-vis* their standards as they are with being observed. Buss's (1980) idea about shyness as an emotional response that is elicited by experiences of novelty or conspicuousness fits this definition. As already suggested, Buss believes that shyness and fear are closely related and represent a general fearfulness toward others. Shyness appears much earlier than shame, and this early emergence may prove an important clue to its distinct identity.

In a series of studies, we observed 3-month-old children interacting with their mothers (Lewis & Feiring, 1989). Two different types of children were distinguished. The first group of children appeared to be socially oriented even by 12 weeks of age. These children looked at, smiled at, and vocalized in interactive sequences with their mothers, and preferred to play with their mothers rather than by themselves. We characterized these children as "sociable." Unlike the first group, about 20% of the children preferred not to look at, smile at, or vocalize toward their mothers, and they also preferred to play by themselves and with toys more than with their mothers. These children were called "asocial." The children were observed again at 1 year of age, and these differences in sociability were maintained. These differences in sociability appear to be similar to what have been described as differences between normal and shy or inhibited children.

These findings suggest that shyness may be different from embarrassment (especially the later, evaluative form), since it appears very early—certainly before 18 months—and does not need an evaluative component. Shyness, like fearfulness, is more likely to be a biological than a psychological variable. Such an approach to shyness seems reasonable, in that it fits with a social self-view (Buss, 1980). For example, Kagan et al. (1988) have pointed out that children whom they called "inhibited" also appeared shy, withdrawn, uncomfortable in social situations, and fearful. Thus, our own observations and those of others indicate that shyness is linked to a constellation of factors not related to self-evaluation. Moreover, there is some reason to believe that these individual differences have a dispositional or constitutional basis (Eysenck, 1956; Kagan et al., 1988).

Embarrassment and Shame

In order to define embarrassment, it is important that we define shame; in this way, the distinction between the two will become clear. "Shame" is the product of a complex set of cognitive activities (for the complete definition, see Lewis, 1992). These cognitive activities involve the evaluation of an individual or his or her actions in regard to the individual's standards, rules, and goals. Moreover, it involves the global evaluation of the self as no good. The phenomenological experience of wishing to hide, disappear, or die is associated with shame. Shame is a highly negative and painful state that results in the disruption of ongoing behavior, confusion of thought, and inability to speak (H. B. Lewis, 1971). The physical actions accompanying shame include a shrinking of the body, as though to disappear from the eye of the self or the other. This emotional state is so intense and has such a devastating effect on the self that individuals in such a state attempt to rid themselves of it. However, since shame represents a global attack on the self ("I am no good"), people have great difficulty in dissipating it.

Shame is not produced by any specific situation; rather, it is produced by an individual's interpretation of a situation. Moreover, shame is not necessarily related to the public or private nature of the situation. Failure attributed to the global self can be either public or private. Shame is often public, but it is just as likely to be private. Each of us can think of private occasions when we have said to ourselves, "I am ashamed for having done that." Shame can occur in regard to moral action as well. A student reported to me that she was ashamed because she had not given enough money for a charity she thought particularly important. When I asked her why she felt shame, she replied, "I should have known better," which I took to mean that she had made a global attribution about the failure of herself. As I will discuss in detail, there is reason to believe that embarrassment may not be the same as shame.

For some, embarrassment is closely linked to shame (Izard, 1979; Tomkins, 1963). In these theories, the most noticeable difference between shame and embarrassment is in their intensity level. Whereas shame appears to be an intense and destructive emotion, embarrassment is less intense and does not involve the disruption of thought and language. In terms of body posture, people who are embarrassed do not assume the shame posture of body collapse. The bodies of the embarrassed reflect an ambivalent approach–avoidance posture characterized by multiple-gaze behavior and smiling (see Edelmann, 1987; Geppert, 1986). In shame situations, one rarely sees gaze aversion accompanied by smiling behavior. Thus, from a behavioral point of view, these two emotions appear to be different. Phenomenologically, embarrassment is less clearly differentiated from shame. People often report that "embarrassment" is a less intense experience of "shame." Situations similar to those that invoke shame are found to invoke embarrassment. Even so, the intensity and duration of the disruptive quality of shame are not matched in embarrassment. Moreover, embarrassment occurs developmentally much earlier than shame and occurs in situations that appear to be nonevaluative in nature. Because of its complex nature, there may be two types of embarrassment: embarrassment elicited by exposure, and embarrassment as mild shame.

The Two Types of Embarrassment

Embarrassment elicited by exposure appears to be more similar to shyness than to shame. In certain situations of exposure, people become embarrassed. This type of embarrassment is not related to negative evaluation, as in shame. Perhaps the best example is that of being complimented. The phenomenological experience of embarrassment when complimented is well known. For example, a speaker introduced with praise may be embarrassed. Buss (1980) has suggested that complimenting elicits social rules for modesty. Although this may be the case for adults, it is hard to argue that infants as young as 15–18 months of age have learned the rules of modesty, as noted earlier.

Another example of this type of embarrassment can be seen in people's reaction to their public display (Goffman, 1956). When people observe someone looking at them, they are apt to become self-conscious, to look away, and to touch or adjust their bodies. When the observed person is a woman, she will often adjust or touch her hair. An observed man is less likely to touch his hair, but may adjust his clothes or change his body posture. Observed people look either pleased or frightened, rarely sad.

Still another example of embarrassment resulting from exposure has to do with a series of experiments I have recently been conducting. In lecturing both to students in my classes and to other audiences, I often wish to demonstrate that embarrassment can be elicited just by exposure. To demonstrate this point, I inform the audience that I am going to point randomly to someone. I further inform the audience that my pointing will have no evaluative component, that it will be random, and that it will not be related to anything about the person. Moreover, I inform them that I will close my eyes when pointing. Following these instructions, I point to someone in the room. From the reports of those who are the targets, the pointing invariably elicits embarrassment.

The final example comes from an observation that I recently made. I have gone to a dental hygienist to have my teeth cleaned for the last several years. Once, I sat there with my mouth open, it occurred to me that if I were a dental hygienist I would have a favorite tooth, one that gave me particular pleasure to clean—in part, perhaps because it was easy to clean. With this idea in mind, I asked the hygienist, "Which is your favorite tooth?" She stopped her work, looked embarrassed, blushed, and finally said, "How did you know?" Quite by accident, I had uncovered her secret. She told me she was not ashamed at having a favorite tooth—just at being "uncovered." This example of embarrassment at being exposed or uncovered has made me realize that the exposure does not have to pertain to the physical presence; it can extend to the secret part of the self (Meares, 1992).

How, then, can embarrassment be like shame? The experience of shame is produced by the negative evaluation of the self in regard to its standards. It seems clear that situations exist in which embarrassment can be elicited by exposure, quite independently of any negative evaluation. The examples presented—the experiences of being observed, of being complimented, of being pointed to, and of having one's secret thoughts revealed—all suggest that embarrassment can be elicited by exposure.

There are many examples of embarrassment in which there is an evaluative component, yet it may be that self-exposure is in reality the elicitor. Take the simple act of walking into a lecture hall a few minutes *before* the speaker is scheduled to talk. A person who arrives on time or even early may attract attention. On such an occasion, the person is likely to experience embarrassment. This situation can promote a negative self-evaluation: "I should have been here even earlier; I should have stayed at the back of the hall." I believe, however, that the experience of embarrassment may not be caused by negative self-evaluation, but by simple public exposure. However, instead of believing that the exposure produces the embarrassment, people often choose to look for a negative evaluation. In other words, the negative evaluation follows embarrassment resulting from exposure, as people attempt to explain why they are embarrassed.

The second type of embarrassment is related to negative self-evaluation and to shame. The difference in intensity between embarrassment and shame may be attributable to the nature of the failed standard. People have different standards, some of which are more important to their identity than are others. Violations of these less important standards are likely to elicit a less intense form of shame. For example, failure at driving a car may be embarrassing rather than shaming, if driving is less closely related to the core self. On the other hand, failure at driving a car may be shaming, if it is a core capacity. In these examples, there appears to be some association between embarrassment and shame.

FUNCTIONAL SIGNIFICANCE
AND DIFFERENTIATION

Embarrassment must emerge when children develop self-consciousness. This cognitive capacity is probably maturational in nature (see Lewis & Brooks-Gunn, 1979). Self-consciousness is a cognitive capacity; it reflects the ability of the child to refer to itself. The self becomes an object to itself (Lewis, 1991, 1992). The advent of self-consciousness allows for the development of the pronouns "me" and "mine." Moreover, this cognitive capacity means that the child can put himself or herself in the place of another. This gives rise to empathy and social regulation. As the model in Figure 7.1 indicates, there is an emotional component to this cognitive milestone. This component is embarrassment related to exposure.

The question arises as to the functional significance of both the cognitive milestone and its associated affective component. The emergence of this cognitive capacity carries both advantages and disadvantages. This emerging capacity allows the child to reflect on the self, to use the self to make comparisons to others, and ultimately to develop evaluative behaviors and processes that guide his or her actions and lead to moral behavior. At the same time, this capacity to reflect on the self can be dangerous. The dangers reside in an entrapment in circular reactions. It is possible to think about the self thinking about the self thinking about the self. Such circularity would lead the child into a hopeless cycle of thought, preventing him or her from acting. To prevent such circular reactions, it would seem reasonable to imagine that self-consciousness should be accompanied by arousal containing a slight negative tone. If self-consciousness is a little uncomfortable, engaging in it becomes emotionally costly.

It is possible to be too self-conscious. Under such conditions, people have difficulty focusing on action. From a clinical perspective, we have reason to believe that much self-consciousness is related to a variety of illnesses. Sex therapy often focuses on this problem. When individuals focus too much on themselves during sexual behavior, they are likely to become sexually dysfunctional. The task of the therapist is to teach such adults how to defocus—that is, to become less self-conscious.

In this regard, Csikszenthmihalyi and Csikszenthmihalyi's (1988) analysis of "flow" is highly relevant. "Flow" is a state of mind that is achieved when an adult's capacity matches the environmental challenge. Under such conditions, adults stop making reference to themselves; that is, self-consciousness stops. For example, when people are deeply engaged in work, they often lose track of the time and do not realize how hungry they are. This phenomenological experience indicates that it is possible to lose self-consciousness, at least some of the time. The dangers of self-consciousness (as well as its advantages) suggest that embarrassment elicited by exposure reflects the emotional component of this complex cognitive capacity. At the emergence of this capacity, there emerges also embarrassment. Embarrassment, in its initial form, is functionally tied to self-consciousness and has as its primary purpose the prevention of undue self-reflection.

Although this analysis explains exposure-related embarrassment, it does not explain embarrassment associated with failure. The existence of two different types of embarrassment gives rise to the idea of a developmental sequence in which embarrassment associated with exposure is transformed into embarrassment associated with evaluation. How this transformation occurs remains unclear; however, one possibility comes from Rozin, Haidt, and McCauley's (1993) analysis of disgust. The early manifestation of disgust is an adaptive response that helps the child to get rid of an unpleasant taste. In fact, the disgust face is a prototype for expelling things from the mouth. Disgust can be observed in very young infants as they rid themselves of distasteful objects. Its functional use is rooted in a biological necessity. Disgust, as a biological event, is transformed into a social event. The disgust over an unpleasant taste becomes the disgust at seeing something gory, and this, in turn, becomes the moral disgust at seeing how someone behaves toward another person. Rozin et al. (1993) suggest that the transformation of this body-related emotion into its more complex forms is attributable to maturational processes, cognitive elaboration, and socialization.

In a similar way, it is reasonable to hypothesize that embarrassment is initially tied to the emerging cognitive milestone of self-consciousness, but is subsequently captured as part of the affective response associated with evaluation. For adults, embarrassment is more often associated with violation of standards and less often with exposure, since evaluation is a very important aspect of adult goal structure (Pervin, 1989).

The present model proposes a sequence that starts with embarrassment related to exposure and then is captured, in yet unexplained ways, and utilized in the evaluative processes centering around standards, rules, and goals. By the second half of the second year of life, children show embarrassment as self-consciousness or exposure; by the age of 3, embarrassment both for exposure and for violating a standard can be seen. Both types of embarrassment are available as a consequence of the developmental process. Thus, adults have the capacity to be embarrassed as a result of exposure, as well as to be embarrassed over violations of their own standards, rules, and goals.

Because adults utilize evaluation in all of their actions, the belief that embarrassment has to be related to some failure of the self is widespread. People and scientists alike tend to assume that embarrassment *must* be associated with evaluation. Although the developmental processes give rise to both forms of embarrassment in adult emotional life, adults are more apt to focus on embarrassment resulting from evaluation. Such an analysis suggests that embarrassment may play an important role in the emergence of all self-conscious emotions—those of evaluation and those of exposure.

SUMMARY

Embarrassment is a most interesting emotion and may play a central role in the development of all self-conscious emotions. It appears reasonable to conclude with some broad propositions that grow out of the present analysis:

1. Embarrassment is the affective component of the cognitive process of self-awareness.
2. It emerges developmentally at some time during the middle of the second year of life.
3. Individual differences in embarrassment appear at the point of its emergence, and these differences may be constitutionally based.
4. The early form of embarrrassment is not associated with the self's negative evaluation of the self's action.
5. Embarrassment's functional significance is its inhibiting effect on self-reflection.
6. At some time between the second and third years of life, embarrassment becomes associated with self-evaluation. This form of embarrassment is related to other negative self-conscious evaluative emotions, such as shame and guilt.
7. Evaluative embarrassment is a less intense form of shame.
8. The exposure-related and evaluation-related forms of embarrassment coexist in children over 3 years of age and in adults, although we often confuse embarrassment over exposure with evaluative embarrassment.

REFERENCES

Amsel, A. (1958). The role of frustrative nonreward in noncontinuous reward situations. *Psychosomatic Bulletin, 48,* 102–119.

Amsterdam, B. K. (1972). Mirror self-image reactions before age two. *Developmental Psychology, 5,* 297–305.

Borke, H. (1971). Interpersonal perception of young children: Egocentrism or empathy. *Developmental Psychology, 7,* 207–217.

Broucek, F. J. (1991). *Shame and the self.* New York: Guilford Press.

Buss, A. H. (1980). *Self-consciousness and social anxiety.* San Francisco: W. H. Freeman.

Cheek, J. M., & Buss, A. H. (1981). Shyness and sociability. *Journal of Personality and Social Psychology, 41,* 330–339.

Csikszenthmihalyi, M., & Csikszenthmihalyi, I. S. (1988). *Optimal experience: Psychological studies of flow in consciousness.* New York: Cambridge University Press.

Dann, O. T. (1977). A case study of embarrassment. *Journal of the American Psychoanalytic Association, 25,* 453–470.

Darwin, C. (1965). *The expression of the emotions in man and animals.* Chicago: University of Chicago Press. (Original work published 1872)

Dickson, J. C. (1957). The development of self-recognition. *Journal of Genetic Psychology, 91,* 251–256.

Duval, S., & Wicklund, R. A. (1972). *A theory of objective self-awareness.* New York: Academic Press.

Edelmann, R. J. (1987). *The psychology of embarrassment.* Chichester, England: Wiley.

Edelmann, R. J., & Hampson, S. E. (1981). The recognition of embarrassment. *Personality and Social Psychology Bulletin, 7,* 109–116.

Eysenck, H. J. (1956). The questionnaire measurement of neuroticism and extraversion. *Revista Psicologia, 50,* 113–140.

Fenigstein, A., Scheier, M. F., & Buss, A. H. (1975). Public and private self-consciousness: Assessment and theory. *Journal of Consulting and Clinical Psychology, 43,* 522–527.

Gallup, G. G., Jr. (1970). Chimpanzees: Self-recognition. *Science, 167,* 86–87.

Geppert, U. (1986). *A coding system for analyzing behavioral expressions of self-evaluative emotions (technical manual).* Munich: Max-Planck-Institute for Psychological Research.

Geppert, U., & Kuster, U. (1983). The emergence of "wanting to do it oneself": A precursor of achievement motivation. *International Journal of Behavioral Development, 6,* 355–370.

Goffman, E. (1956). Embarrassment and social organization. *American Journal of Sociology, 62,* 264–271.

Goffman, E. (1959). *Presentation of self in everyday life.* Garden City, NY: Doubleday.

Goffman, E. (1967). *Interaction ritual.* Garden City, NY: Doubleday.

Greenberg, J. R., & Mitchell, S. A. (1983). *Object relations in psychoanalytic theory.* Cambridge, MA: Harvard University Press.

Heckhausen, H. (1984). Emergent achievement behavior: Some early developments. In J. Nicholls (Ed.), *The development of achievement motivation* (pp. 1–32). Greenwich, CT: JAI Press.

Izard, C. E. (1977). *Human emotions.* New York: Plenum Press.

Izard, C. E. (1979). *The Maximally Discriminative Facial Movement Coding System (MAX).* Newark: University of Delaware, Instructional Resources Center.

Izard, C. E., & Tyson, M. C. (1986). Shyness as a discrete emotion. In W. H. Jones, J. M. Cheek, & S. R. Briggs (Eds.), *Shyness: Perspectives on research and treatment* (pp. 147–160). New York: Plenum Press.

Jones, W. H., Cheek, J. M., & Briggs, S.R. (Eds.). (1986). *Shyness: Perspectives on research and treatment.* New York: Plenum Press.

Kagan, J. (1981). *The second year.* Cambridge, MA: Harvard University Press.

Kagan, J., Reznick, J. S., & Snedman, N. (1988). Biological bases of childhood shyness. *Science, 240,* 167–171.

Leary, M. R., & Meadows, S. (1991). Predictors, elicitors and concomitants of social blushing. *Journal of Personality and Social Psychology, 60*(2), 254–262.

Lewis, H. B. (1971). *Shame and guilt in neurosis.* New York: International Universities Press.

Lewis, M. (1990a). The development of intentionality and the role of consciousness. *Psychological Inquiry, 1*(3), 231–248.

Lewis, M. (1990b). Social knowledge and social development. *Merrill–Palmer Quarterly, 36*(1), 93–116.

Lewis, M. (1991). Ways of knowing: Objective self awareness or consciousness. *Developmental Review, 11,* 231–243.

Lewis, M. (1992). *Shame: The exposed self.* New York: Free Press.

Lewis, M. (1993). The emergence of emotions. In M. Lewis & J. Haviland (Eds.), *Handbook of emotions* (pp. 223–235). New York: Guilford Press.

Lewis, M., Alessandri, S., & Sullivan, M. W. (1992). Differences in shame and pride as a function of children's gender and task difficulty. *Child Development, 63,* 630–638.

Lewis, M., & Brooks-Gunn, J. (1979). *Social cognition and the acquisition of self.* New York: Plenum Press.

Lewis, M., & Feiring, C. (1989). Infant, mother and mother–infant interaction behavior and subsequent attachment. *Child Development, 60,* 831–837.

Lewis, M., & Michalson, L. (1983). From emotional state to emotional expression: Emotional development from a person–environment interaction perspective. In D. Magnusson & V. L. Allen (Eds.), *Human development: An interactional perspective* (pp. 261–275). New York: Academic Press.

Lewis, M., & Michalson, L. (1985). Faces as signs and symbols. In G. Zivin (Ed.), *Development of expressive behavior: Biology–environmental interaction* (pp. 153–182). New York: Academic Press.

Lewis, M., & Saarni, C. (Eds.). (1985). *The socialization of emotion.* New York: Plenum Press.

Lewis, M., & Saarni, C. (Eds.). (1993). *Lying and deception in everyday life.* New York: Guilford Press.

Lewis, M., Sullivan, M. W., Stanger, C., & Weiss, M. (1989). Self-development and self-conscious emotions. *Child Development, 60,* 146–156.

Mandler, G. (1975). *Mind and emotion.* New York: Wiley.

Meares, R. (1992). *The metaphor of play on self: The secret and borderline experience.* Melbourne: Hill of Content Publishing Co.

Modigliani, A. (1968). Embarrassment and embarrassability. *Sociometry, 31,* 313–326.

Modigliani, A. (1971). Embarrassment, facework, and eye contact: Testing a theory of embarrassment. *Journal of Personality and Social Psychology, 17,* 15–24.

Morrison, A. P. (1989). *Shame: The underside of narcissism.* Hillsdale, NJ: Analytic Press.

Parrott, G., & Smith, R. (1991). *Distinguishing the experiences of envy and jealousy.* Unpublished manuscript.

Pervin, L. A. (Ed.). (1989). *Goals and concepts in personality and social psychology.* Hillsdale, NJ: Erlbaum.

Plutchik, R. (1980). A general psychoevolutionary theory of emotion. In R. Plutchik & H. Kellerman (Eds.), *Emotion: Theory, research, and experience* (Vol. 1, pp. 3–33). New York: Academic Press.

Rank, O. (1945). *Will therapy and truth and reality.* New York: Knopf.

Rozin, P., Haidt, J., & McCauley, C. (1993). Disgust. In M. Lewis & J. Haviland (Eds.), *Handbook of emotions* (pp. 575–594). New York: Guilford Press.

Schulman, A. H., & Kaplowitz, C. (1977). Mirror-image response during the first two years of life. *Developmental Psychology, 10,* 133–142.

Semin, G. R., & Manstead, A. S. R. (1981). The beholder beheld: A study in social emotionality. *European Journal of Social Psychology, 11,* 253–265.

Silver, M., Sabini, J., & Parrott, G. (1991). Embarrassment: A dramaturgic account. *Journal of the Theory of Social Behavior, 17*(1), 170–175.

Stipek, D. J. (1983). A developmental analysis of pride and shame. *Human Development, 26,* 42–54.

Stipek, D., Recchia, S., & McClintic, S. (1992). Self-evaluation in young children. *Monographs of the Society for Research in Child Development, 57*(1, Serial No. 226).

Tomkins, S. S. (1963). *Affect, imagery, and consciousness: Vol. 2. The negative affects.* New York: Sprunger.

White, R. W. (1959). Motivation reconsidered: The concept of competence. *Psychological Review, 66,* 297–323.

Zahn-Waxler, C., & Kochanska, G. (1990). The origins of guilt. In R. Thompson (Ed.), *Nebraska Symposium on Motivation: Vol. 36. Socioemotional development* (pp. 183–258). Lincoln: University of Nebraska Press.

Zimbardo, P. G. (1977). *Shyness.* Reading, MA: Addison-Wesley.

8

A Cognitive-Developmental Analysis of Pride, Shame, and Embarrassment in Middle Childhood

SHARON GRIFFIN

In recent years, a number of investigators have documented age-related changes in children's social–emotional understanding across the middle childhood years, using a variety of tasks and a variety of cognitive-developmental interpretive frameworks. As the following review of this literature illustrates, the aspects of social and/or emotional experience that were targeted for investigation also varied widely across these studies. Collectively, this body of evidence provides multiple perspectives on children's social–emotional understanding across this age range, as well as an opportunity to examine the degree of consistency that may be present across these findings as a function of age. In the present chapter I argue that an age-related pattern is apparent in these findings, that a central conceptual structure underlies it, and that this structure is relevant to children's experience and/or understanding of pride, shame, and embarrassment in middle childhood.

AGE-LEVEL VARIATIONS IN CHILDREN'S SOCIAL–EMOTIONAL UNDERSTANDING

To examine children's understanding of a mother's role, Goldberg-Reitman (1992) presented 4-, 6-, and 10-year-old girls with a series of illustrated story events depicting a child in neutral or hazardous situations (e.g., falling off a roof), and asked children to predict what a mother would do. She

219

found that all age groups offered a similar prediction (e.g., "A mother will catch her child"). However, in the rationale provided for this prediction, age-level differences were found. Four-year-olds explained this action by exclusive reference to the antecedent event (e.g., "Because the child is falling"); 6-year-olds referred to the mother's internal state (e.g., "Because the mother doesn't want her child to get hurt"); and 10-year-olds referred to two internal states (e.g., "Because the mother loves her child and doesn't want her to get hurt") in the explanations they provided.

Similarly, when Bruchkowsky (1992) showed children at the same age levels videotaped vignettes of a child who was in one mood at the start and a different mood at the end as a function of an intervening event, all age groups were able to identify the character's feeling at the end (i.e., happy, angry, sad). In this study as well, age-level differences were found in the explanations provided. Four-year-olds explained the feeling (e.g., happy) by exclusive reference to the antecedent event (e.g., "Because her friend came over"); 6-year-olds referred additionally to one internal state (e.g., "Because her friend came over and she really wanted her to"); and 10-year-olds typically included two internal states (e.g., "Because she was bored and she really wanted her friend to come over") in the explanations they provided.

In a series of studies that asked children to focus on their *own* happy and sad experiences and explain these to an alien child, I (Griffin, 1992) found a similar developmental progression. Four-year-olds typically described these emotions by exclusive reference to behavioral events (e.g., "Happy is a birthday party"); 6-year-olds included one internal state in their descriptions (e.g., "Happy means I get something that I want"); and 8-year-olds typically included two internal states (e.g., "Happy means I get something I like that I've been wanting for a long time"). Moreover, when asked to describe where the happiness or sadness comes from, 4-year-olds claimed that it came from the action or event; by contrast, 6- and 8-year-olds claimed that it came from within themselves (e.g., "From my heart," "From my brain"). Fitzpatrick (1985) found a similar pattern when she asked 4- and 6-year-old children where happiness and fear begin and where they are located.

When children's understanding of moral values was the subject of the inquiry, and children were asked to resolve hypothetical moral dilemmas and to provide a rationale for their prediction, Kohlberg (1976) documented a similar developmental progression. Summarizing a body of evidence, he proposed that moral value for the 4-year-old resides in external, quasi-physical happenings; that for the 6-year-old, it resides in performing good or right roles (i.e., in maintaining a social standard); and that for the 8-year-old, it resides not only in conformity to shared standards but also in avoidance of violation of the will or rights of others (i.e., in maintaining two social standards).

There appears to be a high degree of consistency in the manner in which children interpret a broad range of social–emotional situations at three age periods, which can be described as follows: In the open-ended task format that was used for each of the studies reported above, 4-year-olds focused on the action sequence (i.e., the relations between events) to make sense of the social–emotional situation; 6-year-olds focused, in addition, on one internal state dimension (i.e., a feeling or a social judgment variable); and 8- to 10-year-olds focused on two internal state dimensions (i.e., feelings and/or social value judgments) to make sense of the same social–emotional situation. Evidence that these forms of social interpretation characterize age-level performance across a broader range of task formats is provided in the studies described below.

When two social judgment variables were explicitly provided to children, they appeared unable to use them in a coordinated fashion until the age of 7–8 years. Fischer and Elmendorf (1986) found that children were unable to combine both "nice" and "mean" behaviors in one social role interaction, even when this was explicitly modeled, until the age of 7.4 years. In the period before this age, children were able to utilize only one social category, nice *or* mean behavior, in their social role interactions. Ruble (1983) reports a failure of children under the age of 7–9 years to make inferences about their own competence on the basis of social comparison information, although the ability to make social comparisons (e.g., to compare possessions) is known to be present before this age. Research from the theory of mind tradition also indicates that it is not until the age of 7–8 years that children can differentiate and coordinate two mental states in order to distinguish social interactions (e.g., the difference between jokes and deception) that require this form of thought (Perner, 1988; Astington, 1985).

When emotions rather than social judgments were the subject of the inquiry, and children were asked whether they could experience two emotions (e.g., happiness and sadness) at the same time, Harter and Whitesell (1989) found that 4-year-olds denied the possibility. Six-year-olds admitted the possibility, but claimed that these feelings could be experienced only in a temporal sequence; 8-year-olds claimed that these feelings could co-occur and coexist simultaneously. Gnepp (1985) also found that 4-year-olds denied that one event (e.g., a small dog approaching) could have more than one emotional implication; by contrast, 6-year-olds acknowledged that this event could elicit happiness or fear.

In the findings that have just been described, there is some variation in the age level at which particular forms of social interpretation were documented (i.e., at the 8-year-old level in some studies and at the 10-year-old level in others). Nevertheless, there is also a high degree of consistency across these studies in the forms of social interpretation that were used at three age periods, suggesting the presence of a general pattern. On the basis of a different but overlapping data base, we (Case & Griffin, 1990) have suggested that a general pattern exists and that a central conceptual structure underlies it. This theoretical postulate appears capable

of explaining a broad range of social–emotional experience and/or understanding across the middle childhood years. It is described in the following
section and is used in subsequent sections as a basis for an empirical
investigation of pride, shame, and embarrassment in middle childhood.

THEORETICAL FRAMEWORK

To account for age-level consistencies in children's performance across a
broad range of quantitative tasks and, as illustrated above, across a broad
range of social–emotional tasks, we (Case & Griffin, 1990) have proposed
that children construct a limited set of powerful organizing schemata (i.e.,
central conceptual structures) that shape the way physical and social reality
are construed. A central dimensional structure is proposed for the former
domain of experience, and a central intentional structure for the latter. In
contrast to Piaget's more general stage postulate, each of these structures is
seen to have a broad but delimited range of application and a unique
semantic content. Consistent with Piaget's formulations, these structures are
also seen to conform to a common developmental progression and, for the
average child in developed societies, to be similar in form at the age levels
of 4, 6, 8, and 10 years.

More specifically, we have suggested that these structures assume a
predimensional and preintentional form at the 4-year-old level, with the
implication that children do not see the world in a dimensional or intentional
fashion at this age period. Rather, the aspects of reality that are typically
attended to and represented in the preschool years are the temporal, spatial,
or referential relations between objects or events. At the 6-year-old level,
children are seen to be capable of dimensional and intentional thought, but
to be limited by their working memory capacity to the representation of
only one dimension of physical reality (with a unidimensional structure) and
one variable of social reality (with a uni-intentional structure) at any one
time. At the 8-year-old level, with an increase in working memory capacity,
children are seen to be capable of bidimensional and bi-intentional thought;
this permits them to attend to, represent, and coordinate two dimensions of
physical reality and two variables of social reality (i.e., feeling states and/or
social value judgments) in any given situation.

Implicit in these labels is the suggestion, consistent with Case's (1985)
cognitive-developmental theory, that children's central conceptual structures
undergo a major transformation at about the age of 5 years and a minor
transformation at about the age of 7 years. These two transformations not
only shape the sense children make of physical and social reality, but also
determine those aspects of reality that are attended to at any one time. In
addition, the labels imply that the changes in children's thought are
system-wide in terms of form, but differ in content depending on the domain
of experience (i.e., physical or social reality) that is being represented.

Given the generality of these structures and the empirical support these theoretical formulations have received (see Case, 1992, 1993; Griffin, 1992; Griffin, Case, & Siegler, 1994), it seems reasonable to hypothesize that the central intentional structure is relevant to children's experience and/or understanding of pride, shame, and embarrassment in middle childhood. This is what I argue in the remainder of this chapter. To investigate this hypothesis, the first step that was taken was to conduct a logical analysis of embarrassment in order to identify the core components of this emotion experience, and the manner in which these components may be related.

A LOGICAL ANALYSIS OF EMBARRASSMENT

Consider the classic "egg on your face" scenario, with all the meanings this phrase has come to imply in the English language. As a metaphor for embarrassment, this phrase is typically used by the average layperson to convey three central and interrelated meanings. First, it conveys a sense of being caught with egg on your face, in the literal sense of being found to be physically or socially inappropriate for the occasion, or in the metaphorical sense of being found to be incompetent in a particular situation. Second, it implies that there is someone out there who is doing the "catching" and thereby making the actor aware of his or her failure to meet normative standards in that situation. Finally, it communicates a particular emotion experience (i.e., embarrassment) that is presumed to occur when the first two conditions have been met. These same three components—(1) an acknowledgment of a failure to meet standards, (2) an audience that recognizes and witnesses this failure, and (3) a particular emotion experience—have also been identified in the emotion literature as being central to an adult embarrassment experience (see Faulkner, 1986, for a review of this literature).

Consider next what happens to the emotion experience when the first or second component mentioned above is missing or is systematically altered in a thought experiment. When the actor does *not* acknowledge a failure to meet standards, and an audience judges him or her negatively nonetheless, it seems unlikely that embarrassment will be experienced. Rather, depending on the particular situation that is conjured up to satisfy this condition, it seems more likely that sadness will be experienced ("Others don't like me"), or annoyance ("They don't understand me"), or anger ("They are judging me unfairly"). Similarly, when the actor acknowledges a failure to meet standards, and the audience is a 3-year-old child (not old enough to recognize the failure), it seems unlikely that embarrassment will be experienced. Rather, depending once again on the particulars of the situation that is imagined, it seems more likely that sadness will be experienced ("I have let myself down"), or annoyance ("I have done something dumb"), or fear ("I may fail again in front of a different audience").

This analysis suggests that two cognitions—a self-judgment and an audience judgment—are central to an adult's embarrassment experience. If this is indeed the case, it seems reasonable to propose that embarrassment (and other self-conscious emotions that require the same forms of social interpretation) will not be experienced in an adult-like form until a child is able to interpret social reality along two social judgment variables. Informed by the logical analysis, it also seems reasonable to propose that before this capability is present, children will experience other emotions, or earlier forms of the self-conscious emotions, in the same social situations.

The age-level postulates of the theory can be used to suggest that embarrassment and other emotions that are hypothesized to require a bi-intentional form of social interpretation will not be experienced in an adult-like form until the age of 7–8 years. Since pride and shame appear to require the same form of social interpretation, on the basis of the same sort of logical analysis that has been conducted for embarrassment, these emotions can be included in this hypothesis as well. Convergent support for this analysis is provided in findings reported by Ferguson, Stegge, and Damhuis (1991) and Harter and Whitesell (1989) (the latter are described in a later section).

It can also be suggested that emotions that can be experienced with an exclusive focus on the relations between events (i.e., with a preintentional structure), and that do not require attention to social value variables, will be experienced at earlier ages (i.e., in the preschool years). Happiness, sadness, and anger are proposed for this category, since they appear to require only that relations between events be represented as a global gain, loss, or obstruction of an action sequence, respectively. This analysis is consistent with Weiner's (1985) proposal that some emotions (e.g., happiness, sadness) are "outcome-dependent," and that others (e.g., pride, shame) are "attribution-dependent" and hence conceptually more complex.

EMPIRICAL INVESTIGATION

These hypotheses were examined empirically, in the most direct fashion possible, in the series of studies described below. The studies were not designed to provide a rigorous test of the hypotheses (which seemed premature), but rather to provide answers to the following question: Are the age-level predictions advanced in the foregoing analysis reflected in children's descriptions of their own social and emotional experience, in a variety of emotion-inducing situations? To answer this question, measures were designed to yield indices of (1) children's representations of emotions ("emotion understanding"); (2) children's feelings in hypothetical emotion-inducing situations ("emotion experience"); and (3) the manner in which children interpret the emotion-inducing situation ("social interpretation") at several age levels. Note that previous studies have typically assessed only one of these variables in any given study, which has precluded an examination of their interaction. Verbal report was the primary or exclusive response for each measure.

Study 1: Embarrassment

In the first study, two tasks were constructed to yield the three indices described above, and these were administered individually to 60 children at the ages of 4, 6, and 8 years. Emotion understanding was assessed by asking children to describe the feeling of embarrassment to an alien child by telling him or her "what it means to be embarrassed" and "what is happening when you are embarrassed." Although 4-year-olds were expected to have little understanding of this emotion, it was of interest to discover what, if any, knowledge they had. Children's responses were coded at three levels (i.e., preintentional, uni-intentional, bi-intentional), using the age-level postulates of the theory (see Griffin, 1989, for further details). Note that a bi-intentional response (e.g., mention of a social standard violation *and* a judgmental audience) was predicted for the 8-year-old level and was seen to reflect an adult-like awareness of embarrassment.

The second task presented children with a dramatic scenario in which a child forgot his or her lines in a school play. Each child was asked to pretend that he or she was the actor in the scenario, and this was facilitated by giving the actor the child's name. At the climax of the story, emotion experience was assessed by asking each child, "How are you feeling?" This was followed by "What are the other kids thinking when they watch you standing there with your mouth open, saying nothing?", which yielded an index of social interpretation. Informal observations of facial expression and body posture were noted on the emotion experience task, and thoughts attributed to the audience on the social interpretation measure were coded for presence or absence of negative judgments.

The results indicated that the majority of 8-year-olds defined embarrassment in terms of a social standard violation that was witnessed or judged by an audience (e.g., "You do something silly and other people laugh at you and you don't want them to know"). In addition, the majority of 8-year-olds reported feeling embarrassed on the emotion experience task, and many of these children also displayed prototypic embarrassment behaviors (e.g., averted head, eyes). Finally, on the social interpretation measure, the majority of this age group attributed negative judgments to the audience that had witnessed their failure (e.g., "They would think I'm stupid"; "They'd be thinking, 'Oh, she forgot her lines—what a twerp!' "). These results are consistent with the hypotheses for this age level, and they reflect the adult-like pattern.

Strong cross-task consistency was found for the younger age groups as well, although the response pattern differed considerably. Only a small percentage of 6-year-olds (15%) and no 4-year-olds produced the adult-like pattern (see Figure 8.1). Many of these younger children (approximately

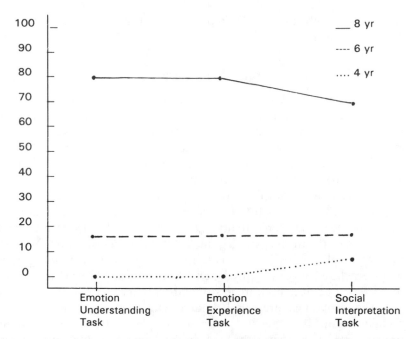

FIGURE 8.1. Percentage of children at three age levels passing three embarrassment tasks.

50%) were unable to assign a meaning to "embarrassment," although most indicated that they had heard this word before. When a meaning was assigned, it reflected the forms of social interpretation predicted by the theory, with many 6-year-olds mentioning one social judgment variable (e.g., "Doing something you shouldn't have done" or "Being teased"), and most 4-year-olds referring exclusively to behavioral actions/events (e.g., "It means going like this [frowning]") or primary emotions (e.g., "Embarrassed means you're angry").

On the emotion experience task, the majority of children at both of the younger age levels said that they were feeling sad, although a few children in the youngest age group responded with "scared," "mad," or "happy" instead. In contrast to the older children, the facial expressions of this age group did not reveal any head or eye aversion; rather, prototypic expressions of sadness (e.g., downturned mouth, slumped posture) were frequently observed. Finally, on the social interpretation task, the dominant response for both younger age groups was to suggest that the audience would be thinking about the action (e.g., "They'd be thinking, 'Let's start the play all over again'") or themselves (e.g., "They'd be happy they didn't forget their lines").

The pattern that is apparent in these findings can be summarized as follows: When children produce bi-intentional meanings for the emotion term that reflect an awareness of two social standards (on the meaning task), they attribute negative judgments to the audience, report feeling embarrassed, and tend to display hiding behaviors (on the scenario task). Conversely, when children produce uni-intentional, preintentional, or no meanings for the emotion term (on the meaning task), they attribute no judgments to the audience, report feeling sad, and tend to display dejected behaviors (on the scenario task). As predicted, this pattern was strongly related to age.

Since it was possible that some unspecified factor related to age might have influenced children's performance on these tasks, a second analysis of the data was conducted. The relationship among reported emotion experience, form of social interpretation, and level of emotion understanding was examined across the age ranges included in this study. No 4-year-old reported feeling embarrassed on the emotion experience task, and this analysis was therefore necessarily confined to data derived from the 6- and 8-year-old samples. For this age range, the results (presented in Table 8.1) indicate a strong relationship across these measures that is independent of age and that is consistent with the general hypothesis framing this investigation.

A second factor that could possibly account for the findings is exposure to the emotion word. Many of the younger children were unable to assign a meaning to "embarrassment"; although this could be accounted for by suggesting that they were not yet capable of representing the aspects of reality the word refers to, it could also be explained by inadequate exposure to the emotion word. If children have not heard this word with sufficient frequency, they obviously cannot be expected to use it to describe their emotion experience. In the next study, therefore, an emotion was examined that is talked about with much greater frequency in the preschool years, in the middle-income homes from which this sample was drawn.

Study 2: Pride

The same children who participated in the embarrassment study also participated in the pride study, and the same methods were used. The scenario that was constructed to induce pride told a story about a group of

TABLE 8.1. Cross-Task Performance for Children Reporting Embarrassment and Sadness on the Emotion Experience Task

Emotion experience	Emotion understanding (self-judgment and audience)	Social interpretation (audience judgment)
Embarrassment ($n = 19$)	89%	79%
Sadness (n = 29)	7%	7%

children who participated in a snowman-building contest at school, with each child working very hard to make the best snowman. At the climax of the story, when the first prize was awarded to the actor in the story (named after each subject), the task questions were posed.

In the results, the same pattern that was found for embarrassment was also found for pride, although the differences across the age levels were not as strong. The majority of 8-year-olds defined pride in terms of a social standard that was met or exceeded and that was witnessed or judged by an audience (e.g., "Proud means you do something really good, like helping someone, and you feel happy and proud of yourself that you did it"). The majority of 8-year-olds also reported feeling proud on the scenario task and attributed positive judgments to the audience (e.g., "They would think I'm really good at making snowmen"). By contrast, only a minority of the younger children produced this pattern, as depicted in Figure 8.2.

The definitions the younger children provided for pride were very similar to the definitions 4- and 6-year-olds provided for happiness in an earlier study (Griffin, 1992), described in a previous section. Many 6-year-olds defined pride as "getting something or doing something you really like," or as "feeling happy when special things happen"; 4-year-olds who were able to provide a meaning (55% of the sample) typically made exclusive reference to actions or events (e.g., "Pride means you have a party"; "Pride means when I put my clothes away"). The majority of both younger age

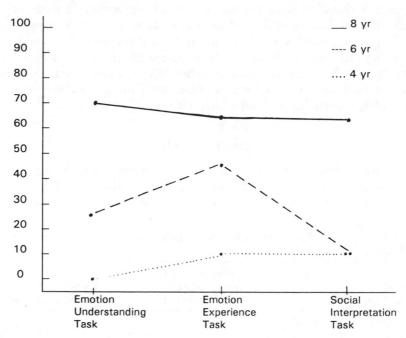

FIGURE 8.2.   Percentage of children at three age levels passing three pride tasks.

groups reported feeling happy on the scenario task, and they did not attribute self-directed judgments to the audience.

The results of this study, as well as those of the first study, suggest that there is a relationship between the manner in which the social situation is interpreted and the emotion that is reported. Although pride was reported with greater frequency than embarrassment by both of the younger age groups, it was still the case that these emotions were not reported by the majority of children until the age of 8 years and the stage of bi-intentional thought. Thus, the documented patterns appear to be relatively independent of the frequency with which these emotion words are used with preschool children. However, it should be noted that self-conscious emotion words are much less common in the general culture than are "happy" and "sad"; for this reason, the experience factor cannot be ruled out as an explanation. In addition, children's experience with the social situations depicted in the scenario tasks might have made these tasks more familiar to the older age groups and influenced the results. In the study described below, a fortuitous situation made it possible to examine both of these counterinterpretations.

Study 3: Shame

Although the word "shame" appears to be used with much less frequency than "embarrassment" in modern U.S. society, I stumbled upon a kindergarten classroom where the word was commonly used by the classroom teacher to correct children who were cutting incorrectly or coloring outside the lines. At the end of the school year, this population of children had ample exposure to this emotion word, in situations that were highly familiar (e.g., "Shame on you. You colored outside the lines. You should be ashamed of yourself"). Children from other classrooms in the same school, where the word was not heard once in several days' observations, comprised the normative kindergarten and second-grade samples. These groups were younger than the children included in the previous studies (i.e. 5 and 7 years), but were still within the age ranges predicted for uni-intentional and bi-intentional thought.

The task that was constructed to assess shame was a line drawing that illustrated a typical scene in the "shame" classroom. It showed a group of children around a table with their completed assignments in front of them; a target child with a downcast appearance; half-smirks on the faces of two observing children; and a teacher speaking to the target child. In a bubble over the teacher's head were the words: "Look at your picture. You know how to color better than that. All the others got it right." As a shame-inducing task, this picture was ambiguous. It made a social standard violation and a judgmental audience highly salient. On the other hand, the line drawing could not capture the subtleties of an emotion response, and the posture of the target child depicted global dejection (e.g., sadness) rather than embarrassment.

The picture was handed to each subject, and the teacher's words were read aloud. When a minute had elapsed, the child was asked to describe how the target child was feeling and what the other kids were thinking. Finally, three emotion words were drawn from an envelope in a counter-balanced order and read to the child, and the child was asked to choose the best word to place on the picture to tell how the target child was feeling. The words presented were "ashamed," "embarrassed," and the emotion word the child had spontaneously reported.

In the results (shown in Table 8.2), the majority of children at both age levels reported "sad" (or "bad," "mad") when asked how the target child was feeling. However, on the remaining two measures, age-related and experience-related differences were apparent. The majority of 7-year-olds attributed negative judgments to the audience that were specifically directed at the target child himself (e.g., "They're thinking he's dumb"; "They're thinking he doesn't know anything"). By contrast, the majority of both younger age groups suggested that the audience would be thinking about the work products on the table (e.g., "They're thinking his picture is messy"; "They're thinking their picture is nice"). Although more children in the linguistically experienced group attributed child-directed judgments to the audience, the percentage producing this form of response did not reach the majority criterion (i.e., 60%).

Similarly, on the forced-choice measure, the majority of 7-year-olds abandoned the emotion word they had originally reported and selected "ashamed" or "embarrassed" instead, with equal frequency. By contrast, although many 5-year-olds also selected these words, and more children in the experienced group did so, the percentage abandoning their original choice (e.g., "sad") did not reach the majority criterion for either group. In addition, the percentage choosing "ashamed" rather than "embarrassed" did not differ across these groups (see Griffin, 1991, for a more detailed description of these findings).

TABLE 8.2. Percentage of Normative and Linguistically Experienced Children Responding in Selected Coding Categories on the Shame Picture Task

Tasks	Normative 5-year-olds (n = 21)	Experienced 5-year-olds (n = 18)	Normative 7-year-olds (n = 20)
Emotion reported			
Embarrassed/ashamed	5	0	0
Sad (bad, mad)	95	100	70
Others' thoughts			
Judging target child	24	39	70
Judging/describing product	76	61	30
Emotion word chosen			
Embarrassed/ashamed	43	56	70
Sad (bad, mad)	57	44	30

On the basis of these findings, three conclusions seem warranted. First, exposure to the emotion word "shame" appeared to make little difference in the frequency with which this emotion word ("ashamed" vs. "embarrassed") was reported on the open-ended task or selected on the forced-choice measure. Second, exposure to shaming situations (e.g., a judgmental teacher) appeared to make some difference in the frequency with which self-conscious emotion words (i.e., "ashamed" and "embarrassed" vs. "sad") were selected on the forced-choice measure. Third, neither of these factors was sufficient to override the age and/or form-of-social-interpretation factor which appeared to influence the emotion that was selected to a greater extent than experience did. Note that these findings were obtained on a task that provided substantial environmental facilitation (i.e., salience of a social standard violation *and* a smirking audience; availability of the emotion words) for a self-conscious emotion choice.

The fact that almost no child in any group initially assigned a self-conscious emotion to the target child can be explained by suggesting that children picked an emotion word that matched the target child's dejected appearance. When subjects were then led to consider other aspects of the social situation (i.e., what the audience might be thinking) and were then told, "You're the same age as this child; you must know how he is feeling. . . . Pick the very best word . . .", the majority of 7-year-olds switched from their initial emotion choice and selected a self-conscious emotion. By contrast, a substantial proportion of the younger children claimed that their initial emotion choice (i.e., "sad," "bad," or "mad") was the best.

SUMMARY OF THE FINDINGS

In three separate studies and for three separate emotions, the findings indicated a relationship between the manner in which the social situation was interpreted and the emotion that was reported. Specifically, when children were placed in hypothetical situations where a social standard was exceeded or violated, and they attributed self-directed positive or negative judgments to the audience in the situation, they reported feeling proud, embarrassed, or ashamed. By contrast, in the same social situations, when children did not attribute self-directed judgments to the audience, they reported feeling other emotions (i.e., happy, sad) that are hypothesized to be precursors of pride, embarrassment, and shame.

As predicted, this relationship was found to be related to cognitive transformations predicted by the theory (see Case & Griffin, 1990), in that the majority of children did not report self-conscious emotion experiences until they reached the age of 7–8 years and the stage of bi-intentional thought. In the first study, this relationship was found to be independent of age, and in the second and third studies, it was found to be independent of exposure to self-conscious emotion words. Although experience with judgmental situations appeared to make some difference in the emotions children reported, its influence was less than the dominant explanatory factor: age and/or form of social interpretation.

DISCUSSION

At least two possible interpretations can be offered for these findings. The first is to suggest that the findings reflect age-level variations in children's cognitive structures (i.e., their emotion understanding) and/or their linguistic structures (i.e., their ability to talk about emotions), but they say little about emotion experience itself. This interpretation would be consistent with the view that emotions are primary in the human organism and that, although they are increasingly linked with cognitions as the organism matures, the core experience remains invariant over the lifespan (see Izard, 1984). This interpretation is also consistent with a commonly held belief that verbal report is not a reliable index of internal experience, at least across the childhood years.

The second possible interpretation is to suggest that the findings reflect age-level variations in children's emotion experience and, in doing so, provide some support for the hypothesis that core emotion experiences (e.g., pride, shame, embarrassment) change systematically over the childhood years in a manner that is consistent with the way an individual construes social reality. This interpretation is consistent with Kagan's (1984) suggestion that emotions are mediated by cognition, and it is broadly consistent (or at least not inconsistent) with the newer componential theories of emotion (see Case et al., 1988; Fischer, Shaver, & Carnochan, 1990; Scherer, 1988). This interpretation is also consistent with a belief that is widely held by adult emotion researchers—namely, that emotion talk is a reasonably reliable index of emotion experience (see Ortony, Clore, & Collins, 1988).

In the absence of a direct measure of emotion experience, there is no straightforward and compelling evidence to adjudicate between these competing interpretations. However, in the present findings and in the emotion research literature, there are several pieces of evidence that provide convergent support for the second interpretation; these are described briefly below.

1. Those who hold that verbal report is not a reliable index of children's internal experience typically cite age, linguistic experience, and inadequate self-reflective capacities as factors that can confound the findings. In the present studies, this concern seems to be justified for the youngest age group included, in that many 4-year-olds did not demonstrate a familiarity with the terms "pride" and "embarrassment" or a level of self-reflective capacity that was commensurate with that demonstrated by the older children. However, for the majority of children in the older age groups, there was

evidence that this familiarity and this capacity were present. Therefore, it can be suggested that the concerns that are typically raised to question verbal report in research with children are not relevant to the findings documented for these age groups. Moreover, when age and exposure to emotion words were systematically examined in the present investigation, the emotions that were reported by the older age groups were found to be influenced by form of social interpretation to a much greater extent than by age or exposure to emotion words.

2. Studies that have reduced reliance on verbal report, by asking children to match emotion labels and/or expressions (and presumably the experiences they symbolize) to appropriate emotion-inducing scenarios, have yielded age-level progressions that are consistent with the one documented in the present investigation. Weiner, Kun, and Benesh-Weiner (1980) found that young children were more likely than older children to choose outcome-dependent emotions (e.g., happiness, sadness) and less likely to mention attribution-dependent emotions (e.g., pride, shame), regardless of the reported cause of the outcome. Tiller (1986) found that 8-year-olds were significantly better than 5-year-olds at linking happiness-inducing and pride-inducing situations to the appropriate emotion word, leading him to conclude that pride is not sufficiently differentiated from happiness until the age of 8 years.

Similarly, Harter and Whitesell (1989) found that 8-year-olds were consistently better than younger children at assigning pride and shame to a child in a scenario, leading them to conclude that pride and shame do not function as self-affects until this age. Children in the 6–7 age group assigned pride and shame to the child in the scenario only when a parental audience was included and only after these emotions had first been attributed to the parent. Younger children selected other emotion words (e.g., "happy," "bad," "scared") for the same scenario, with no acknowledgment of pride or shame.

3. Studies that have examined the relationship between form of social interpretation and reported emotion experience for a range of emotions (i.e., "happy," "sad," "bad") known to be present in the preschool years and very familiar to children (see Bretherton, Fritz, Zahn-Waxler, & Ridgeway, 1986, for a review of children's emotion talk) have found age-level variations consistent with the general hypotheses documented in the present chapter. Nunner-Winkler and Sodian (1988) found that when children were presented with stories in which the main character deliberately stole, lied, or attacked another child, 4-year-olds claimed that the character would be happy about the misdeed, and backed up their judgment by referring to the outcome of the story (e.g., the protagonist acquired the stolen goods). By contrast, 8-year-olds claimed that the character would feel sad or bad, and explained this by reference to moral values (e.g., a bad conscience). A similar finding is reported by Barden, Zelko, Duncan, and Masters (1980). In both studies, the emotions that were reported varied with the forms of social

interpretation (i.e., preintentional vs. intentional) that were apparent in children's explanations.

4. Finally, in the first study reported in this chapter (i.e., the embarrassment study), there was evidence to suggest that bodily expressions of emotion (e.g., eye contact, head aversion, body posture) varied systematically with age in a manner that was consistent with the emotion that was reported and the manner in which the social situation was interpreted.

Taken as a whole, the findings that have just been described lend weight to the credibility of verbal report as an index of emotion experience. In doing so, they provide convergent support for the second interpretation. If verbal report *can* be considered a reasonably reliable index of emotion experience over the middle childhood years, the findings provide strong grounds to suggest that the general hypothesis guiding the present investigation—namely, that emotion experience is shaped by the manner in which social reality is construed—warrants further consideration. A useful approach for future research may be to obtain multiple measures of emotion experience (e.g., more detailed indices of emotion expression and action tendencies than were obtained in the present studies), which will yield a more comprehensive and detailed portrait of this experience at various age levels.

With this information in hand, it may be possible to resolve discrepancies that are apparent in the literature in the ages at which various self-conscious emotions have been reported. For example, Lewis, Sullivan, Stanger, and Weiss (1989) have suggested that embarrassment and shame are present as early as 18 months. The framework adopted in the present paper can be used to suggest that the evidence cited to support this claim (i.e., increased touching of the body when an audience witnesses self gazing into a mirror) indicates only that children are aware of an audience at this age (without judgmental implications) and experience some emotion (possibly discomfort), which may very well be a precursor to an adult-like embarrassment experience.

Similarly, Stipek and McClintic's (1989) findings that toddlers exhibit gleeful, smiling behaviors upon completion of a task, and direct these behaviors toward their mothers, may indicate only that they have extended the range of situations in which happiness can occur to ones where a change in events (i.e., a gain) is produced by their own agency. As Stipek and McClintic suggest, these are pride-like behaviors; however, they may reflect an emotion experience that is closer to happiness than to pride in an adult-like form. As with the larger issue raised in the opening paragraphs of this section, a resolution to the counterinterpretations that have just been offered awaits further research with more refined and/or comprehensive assessments of emotion experience. On the basis of the findings reported in this chapter, it can be suggested that the framework guiding the present investigation may continue to provide a productive approach for this endeavor.

REFERENCES

Astington, J. W. (1985). *Children's understanding of promising.* Unpublished doctoral dissertation, University of Toronto.

Barden, R. C., Zelko, F. A., Duncan, F. W., & Masters, J. C. (1980). Children's consensual knowledge about the experiential determinants of emotion. *Journal of Personality and Social Psychology, 39,* 968–976.

Bretherton, I., Fritz, J., Zahn-Waxler, C., & Ridgeway, D. (1986). Learning to talk about emotion: A functional perspective. *Child Development, 57,* 529–548.

Bruchkowsky, M. (1992). The development of empathic cognition in middle and early childhood. In R. Case (Ed.), *The mind's staircase: Exploring the conceptual underpinnings of children's thought and knowledge.* Hillsdale, NJ: Erlbaum.

Case, R. (1985). *Intellectual development: Birth to adulthood.* New York: Academic Press.

Case, R. (Ed.). (1992). *The mind's staircase: Exploring the conceptual underpinnings of children's thought and knowledge.* Hillsdale, NJ: Erlbaum.

Case, R. (1993, April). *The role of central conceptual structures in the development of children's numerical, literary, and spatial thought.* Final report submitted to the Spencer Foundation.

Case, R., & Griffin, S. (1990). Child cognitive development: The role of central conceptual structures in the development of scientific and social thought. In C. A. Hauert (Ed.), *Developmental psychology: Cognitive, perceptuo-motor and psychological perspectives.* Amsterdam: Elsevier/North-Holland.

Case, R., Hayward, S., Lewis, M., Hurst, P. (1988). Toward a neo-Piagetian theory of cognitive and emotional development. *Developmental Review 8,* 1–51.

Faulkner, D. (1986). *Children's understanding of emotion.* Unpublished doctoral dissertation, University of Michigan.

Ferguson, T. J., Stegge, H., & Damhuis, I. (1991). Children's understanding of guilt and shame. *Child Development, 62,* 827–839.

Fischer, K. W., & Elmendorf, D. M. (1986). Becoming a different person: Transformations in personality and social behavior. In M. Perlmutter (Ed.), *Minnesota Symposia on Child Psychology: Cognitive perspectives on children's social development.* Hillsdale, NJ: Erlbaum.

Fischer, K. W., Shaver, P. R., & Carnochan, P. (1990). How emotions develop and how they organize development. *Cognition and Emotion, 4,* 81–128.

Fitzpatrick, C. J. (1985). Children's development out of event-bound conceptions of their emotions. In I. Fast (Ed.), *Event theory: An integration of Piaget and Freud.* Hillsdale, NJ: Erlbaum.

Gnepp, J. (1989). Children's use of personal information in predicting and explaining emotions. In C. Saarni & P. L. Harris (Eds.), *Children's understanding of emotion.* New York: Cambridge University Press.

Goldberg-Reitman, J. (1992). Young girls' conception of their mothers' role: A neo-structural analysis. In R. Case (Ed.), *The mind's staircase: Exploring the conceptual underpinnings of children's thought and knowledge.* Hillsdale, NJ: Erlbaum.

Griffin, S. (1989, May). *Children's understanding of pride and embarrassment.* Paper presented at the meeting of the Society for Research in Child Development, Kansas City, MO.

Griffin, S. (1991). *The construction and reconstruction of emotion experience.* Paper presented at the XXI Annual Symposium of the Jean Piaget Society, Philadelphia, PA.

Griffin, S. (1992). Young children's awareness of their inner world: A neo-structural analysis of the development of intrapersonal intelligence. In R. Case (Ed.), *The mind's staircase: Exploring the conceptual underpinnings of children's thought and knowledge*. Hillsdale, NJ: Erlbaum.

Griffin, S., Case, R., & Siegler, R. (1994). Rightstart: Providing the central conceptual prerequisites for first formal learning of arithmetic to students at risk for school failure. In K. McGilly (Ed.), *Classroom lessons: Integrating cognitive theory and classroom practice*. Cambridge, MA: Branford Books/MIT Press.

Harter, S., & Whitesell, N. R. (1989). Developmental changes in children's understanding of single, multiple, and blended emotion concepts. In C. Saarni & P. L. Harris (Eds.), *Children's understanding of emotion*. New York: Cambridge University Press.

Izard, C. E. (1984). Emotion–cognition relationships and human development. In C. E. Izard, J. Kagan, & R. B. Zajonc (Eds.), *Emotions, cognition, and behavior*. Cambridge, England: Cambridge University Press.

Kagan, J. (1984). The idea of emotion in human development. In C. E. Izard, J. Kagan, & R. B. Zajonc (Eds.), *Emotions, cognition, and behavior*. Cambridge, England: Cambridge University Press.

Kohlberg, L. (1976). Moral stages and moralization: The cognitive-developmental approach. In T. Lickona (Ed.), *Moral development and behavior*. New York: Holt, Rinehart & Winston.

Lewis, M., Sullivan, M. W., Stanger, C., & Weiss, M. (1989). Self development and self-conscious emotions. *Child Development, 60*, 146–156.

Nunner-Winkler, G., & Sodian, B. (1988). Children's understanding of moral emotions. *Child Development, 59*, 1323–1238.

Ortony, A., Clore, G., & Collins, A. (1988). *The cognitive structure of emotions*. Cambridge, England: Cambridge University Press.

Perner, J. (1988). Higher-order beliefs and intentions in children's understanding and social interaction. In J. W. Astington, P. L. Harris, & D. R. Olson (Eds.), *Developing theories of mind*. New York: Cambridge University Press.

Ruble, D. N. (1983). The development of social-comparison processes and their role in achievement-related self-socialization. In E. T. Higgins, D. N. Ruble, & W. W. Hartup (Eds.), *Social cognition and social development*. Cambridge, England: Cambridge University Press.

Scherer, K. R. (1988). *Facets of emotion: Recent research*. Hillsdale, NJ: Erlbaum.

Stipek, D. J., & McClintic, S. (1989). *Socializing pride: A study of mother–toddler interactions*. Paper presented at the meeting of the Society for Research in Child Development, Kansas City, MO.

Tiller, D. K. (1986). *What children know about pride and jealousy*. Paper presented at the meeting of the Canadian Psychological Association, Toronto.

Weiner, B. (1985). An attributional theory of achievement motivation and emotion. *Psychological Review, 92*, 548–573.

Weiner, B., Kun, A., & Benesh-Weiner, M. (1980). The development of mastery, emotions, and morality from an attributional perspective. In W. Collins (Ed.), *Minnesota Symposia on Child Psychology* (Vol. 13). Hillsdale, NJ: Erlbaum.

9

The Development of Pride and Shame in Toddlers

DEBORAH STIPEK

Emotions that are associated with self-evaluation (e.g., pride and shame) are believed to play an important role in the development of self-regulation and conscience (Emde, Johnson, & Easterbrooks, 1987). Self-evaluative emotions are also central to most theories of achievement motivation (e.g., Atkinson, 1964; Weiner, 1986), and they may have profound implications for mental health, especially in cultures in which personal achievements and competencies are highly valued.

This chapter discusses what is known (or believed) about the early development of pride and shame. It also describes research that my colleagues and I have conducted, and proposes systematic, age-related changes in young children's experience of pride and shame. Because there has been little research on the development of emotions associated with self-evaluation, the analysis is based as much on theory and conjecture as on empirical evidence. My goal is to promote further investigation rather than to present a definitive picture of development in this domain.

The focus is on self-evaluation in "achievement contexts"—that is, in situations in which a child produces some outcome that can be compared to a standard, and a judgment of the child's performance or competence can be made. Self-evaluative emotions that occur when children meet or fail to meet standards for behavior (e.g., toileting) are not discussed, although it is likely that young children do not distinguish between these two domains and that experiences related to one domain affect emotional reactions in the other.

THE DEVELOPMENT OF SELF-EVALUATIVE EMOTIONS

The joy or pleasure that infants express as the result of having some effect on the environment or of exercising some newly developing skill looks similar to older children's expressions of pride (Piaget, 1962; White, 1959). But most theorists assume that there are significant differences in infants' experience of pleasure in causality and older children's experience of pride in accomplishments. Heckhausen (1984) has argued that infants' pleasure arises from their experience of agency, and that older children's is the result of reflecting on the outcome they have produced. Thus, infants take pleasure in producing noise by banging on an object or in producing a colorful display by pushing a button on a toy. The pleasure is presumed to be in the immediate experience of causality and the effect produced.

Infants are assumed not to engage in the kind of self-reflection that Heckhausen claims is necessary for pride to be experienced. His view is consistent with Piaget's (1954, discussed in Mischel, 1971) claim that because infants do not have a concept of the self as a separate, stable entity, their pleasure in their achievements is "momentary," and not "esteem-enhancing" as it is for older children. Lewis and colleagues (see Lewis, 1990) add that self-reflective pride, in contrast to pleasure in having an effect on the environment, requires a concept of the self as a distinct entity with identifiable features that can be evaluated.

Thus theorists have posited particular cognitive prerequisites for pride and other emotions associated with self-evaluation, but not for pleasure in causality. There is little dispute concerning the timing of two prerequisites. It is now widely accepted that normally developing children develop a concept of self as a distinct physical entity—referred to as a "categorical self-concept"—sometime in the second half of the second year. Evidence for this ability comes, for example, from toddlers' ability to recognize themselves in mirrors (Lewis & Brooks-Gunn, 1979) and their use of personal pronouns (Baldwin, 1897; Kagan, 1981).

The ability to judge whether a behavior or outcome meets or fails to meet some standard is also assumed to be required for a child to experience pride or shame, and most researchers agree that children have symbolic-representational skills and can represent standards of behavior and performance by age 2 years. Kagan (1981) describes three kinds of evidence for this ability. First, he reports that between 18 and 24 months of age, the children in his longitudinal study began to comment and show concern about objects that had flaws (e.g., a shirt with a hole) and behaviors that violated social norms, suggesting an ability to recognize deviations from standards or norms. (See also Dunn, 1987.) Second, he reports that by the age of 2 years many of his subjects began to cry, cling to their mothers, and manifest other evidence of distress when an experimenter modeled a set of acts (e.g., fed a bottle to a zebra, put a doll in a bed). He claims that these behaviors suggest that children were aware of their lack of competence to achieve the implicit performance standard; they interpreted the adult's behavior as an invitation to repeat the same act, and they experienced "anxiety to possible task failure" (Kagan, 1984, p. 60). Third, Kagan found that "mastery smiles"— smiles directly contingent upon completion of some goal-directed activity—

emerged at about 18 months and peaked between 20 and 26 months of age. He argues that such smiles are evidence for an ability to represent a goal and to evaluate whether it has been achieved.

Heckhausen (1984) also emphasizes the ability to compare one's own performance to a standard as a prerequisite to pride, but he has proposed that self-evaluative emotions also require a concept of personal competence, which he claims does not develop until after the age of 3 years. Although he too has observed children aged between $1^{1}/_{2}$ and $2^{1}/_{2}$ years to show joy or delight in producing certain outcomes (i.e., Kagan's "mastery smiles"), he argues that their lack of a concept of personal competence precludes them from experiencing genuine, self-reflective pride. In Heckhausen's view, evidence for the latter comes from children's looking in "an approval-seeking manner" at the experimenter and reacting negatively to failure—behaviors that he and his colleagues did not observe on a competitive task (e.g., a race between a child and an experimenter to stack a set of rings on a spoke) until as late as $3^{1}/_{2}$ years.

In summary, there is some dispute about whether self-evaluative emotions are experienced by the age of 2 or not until after the age of 3. It is difficult to reconcile Kagan's (1981) observations of stress reactions to the *anticipation* of being unable to execute a modeled behavior with Heckhausen's (1984) failure to see negative reaction to losing a race in 2-year-olds. Together, these sets of findings suggest that different task situations may give different developmental pictures of children's ability to compare their performance to a standard and their emotional reactions to outcomes.

THE ROOTS OF SELF EVALUATIVE EMOTIONS

Although the emergence of the cognitive prerequisites discussed above may explain why children—but not infants—*can* engage in self-evaluation, it does not explain why they *do* so or why such evaluation engenders emotional reactions. Two sets of factors no doubt play a role. First, self-evaluation and self-evaluative emotions related to achievement may in part be natural consequences of the development of cognitive processing abilities. Some developmental theorists have proposed that as children develop the ability to symbolically represent a standard of behavior, they are concurrently naturally disposed to evaluate discrepancies and to try to reduce differences between their own behavior or performance and the symbolically represented standard (Hunt, 1963, 1965; Kagan, 1981). Kagan (1981), for example, suggests that interest in standards—both social norms for behavior and mastery standards—may be "an inevitable event in ontogeny" (p. 125), and that once a child "is mature enough to generate a goal she is able to meet . . . she feels obliged to meet it" (p. 127). Positive judgments of achieving the standard naturally result in positive affective reactions, and negative judgments result in negative affective reactions.

Socialization is the second factor that can be assumed to give rise to self-evaluation and self-evaluative emotions. Caretakers' approval or disapproval, for example, calls children's attention to the social value of certain kinds of outcomes. Thus, the achievement in infancy that resulted in spontaneous feelings of efficacy or mastery takes on new significance when children learn that their mastery efforts also engender parental approval. The recognition that some outcomes cause positive reactions in adults probably explains why children often call their caretakers' attention to the products they have created. Their behavior in such instances may be motivated by a desire to receive the approval they anticipate as the result of having been praised in the past for similar efforts.

Young children's interest in caretakers' responses to their accomplishments may be related to Campos and Stenberg's (1981) notion of "social referencing" (see also Barrett & Campos, 1987; Campos, Campos, & Barrett, 1989). They argue that caretakers are sources of affective information and that children use caretakers' emotional signals to "disambiguate" uncertain events. Because toddlers and preschoolers have limited knowledge regarding both what activities and outcomes are valued in their social environment and what standards are being applied to them, they should be fairly dependent on adults to identify socially valued achievements. If the nature of adult reactions to particular classes of activities or outcomes remains repetitive over time, children may develop "dispositions"—that is, generalized responses that they will manifest independently of adult reactions (Campos et al., 1989). As they internalize cultural values and standards for mastery, children should become increasingly less dependent on others' approval or disapproval in evaluating their behavior and products.

My colleagues' and my work, discussed below, has been guided by the supposition that both pride and shame have a strong social component and may not be experienced by children until they appreciate others' reactions to their behavior. This assumption has prompted us to attend carefully to children's behaviors that suggest concern or interest in others' reactions to their achievement outcomes.

MEASUREMENT ISSUES

Measurement problems no doubt contribute to researchers' reluctance to study self-evaluative emotions in young children. Although Izard and others agree that there is evidence for a characteristic neuromuscular–expressive pattern for joy, no universal pattern has been observed for pride or any positive affect specifically associated with reflective self-evaluation (Izard & Malatesta, 1987). The absence of a unique facial expression associated with pride, and the similarity between behavioral responses to joy in having an effect on the environment and self-reflective pride, conspire to make it difficult to study the development of pride in young children.

One of the few attempts to identify behaviors associated with self-evaluation was made by Geppert and Gartmann (1983), who assessed, in toddlers aged 18–42 months, the presence of a variety of facial expressions and postural reactions to experimentally manipulated success and failure. Behaviors that were found to be more likely to occur following success than following failure included an open smile, a closed smile while looking at the experimenter, head up and chin out, trunk erect, and trunk leaned back. Those more likely to occur following failure included mouth corners lowered, looking around, looking down, head down and chin in, and trunk forward and down. Heckhausen (1984) reports that for children over the age of about $3^{1}/_{2}$ years, success resulted in an open posture (body stretched, hands open or high), whereas failure resulted in a closed posture (the body "collapses, is bent down, the head tilted to the side," p. 2).

These behaviors found to differentiate children's reactions to success and failure provide some guidance for the study of pride as well as shame, but none of the behaviors are uniquely associated with pride. Moreover, it is not clear which expressions reflect genuine pride and which are manifestations of the kind of joy in causality that theorists believe infants experience.

In contrast to pride in achievement, shame in failure may not have an earlier-developing, analogous emotion, and it appears to pose fewer measurement problems. Shame is considered to be a "fundamental emotion," and is characterized in the literature by blushing (Darwin, 1872; Tomkins, 1963) and universal facial expressions consisting of eyes lowered, lips rolled inward, mouth corners depressed, and lower lip tucked between the teeth (Izard & Dougherty, 1980). Postural cues that appear to reflect a desire to avoid social contact, such as lowering the head and turning the face away, have also been associated with shame (Izard, 1977). Looking away or avoiding eye contact with others following failure suggests, furthermore, an understanding that failure to complete a task has implications for the value of the self in another's eyes, or at least an understanding that the outcome is not socially valued and therefore may provoke disapproval. Although it is not always easy to differentiate shame from a related negative self-evaluative emotion, guilt, the facial and postural cues associated with shame suggest self-reflection more than reactions to failure (such as anger or frustration), which might be expected in children who have not developed the cognitive-representational abilities needed to reflect on the self.

Shame may be easier to differentiate from other emotions than pride, but it is not easy to study. Children's reactions to failure in achievement situations are, like their reactions to success, highly variable. Failure itself is difficult to identify in young children, who do not necessarily accept an adult's definition of the goal as their own in an achievement situation. Thus, for example, a child initially having difficulty completing a puzzle may begin stacking the puzzle pieces into a tower or placing them in a line like a train—expressing great pleasure in an outcome that, according to the adult's definition of the task, is unsuccessful.

My colleagues and I have dealt with the measurement problems primarily by being as comprehensive as we could in our observations. But as will become clear in the next section, empirical work on self-evaluative emotions in young children involves a considerable degree of guesswork and tolerance for data that are open to interpretation.

PRIDE AND SHAME IN ACHIEVEMENT CONTEXTS

The studies summarized here were designed, first, to describe children's emotional reactions to success and failure at different ages and in different contexts. (These studies are described in detail in Stipek, Recchia, & McClintic, 1992.) One specific goal was to assess the effect of the nature of the standard for success on children's reactions to task outcomes. Thus, we compared reactions to tasks in which success feedback was built into the task, with salient visual cues clearly indicating successful completion (a puzzle and nesting cups), to reactions to a task in which success was defined competitively (a race between agemates to stack balls over a series of prongs).

Second, we hoped to identify behavioral and emotional displays that might differentiate self-evaluation (in the self-reflective sense) from the feelings of efficacy or joy in causality that are presumed to be manifested earlier. We were also interested in identifying reactions to failure that clearly reflected negative *self*-evaluation, as opposed to frustration or anger directed toward the task.

Our third goal was to assess the effect of praise on children's reactions to success. We reasoned that if others' evaluations—expressed, for example, in praise—play a role in shaping children's emotional reactions in achievement contexts, then praise for particular achievements should elicit pride-like emotional reactions in children. Thus, the effect of mothers' praise on toddlers' affective reactions was assessed in a naturalistic situation in one study, and the effect of an unfamiliar adult's praise on preschoolers' affective reactions in an experimental situation was assessed in another study.

Toddlers' Reactions to Success

In our first study, we observed toddlers' reactions to having produced an outcome in two contexts. In one of them, we compared the reactions of 59 toddlers (aged 13 to 39 months) to having produced an outcome themselves versus observing an outcome produced by an experimenter. For each child, the experimenter demonstrated a toy that had an unambiguous, visually salient purpose (e.g., rolling a ball to knock down a plastic bowling pin, pounding a wooden ball with a hammer to make it go through a hole on a bench and roll out onto a platform). She then gave it to the child, saying,

"Now you do it. See if you can do it." Children's emotional reactions to the goal's being achieved by the experimenter were compared to their reactions to achieving the goal themselves. We assumed that the difference in children's reactions in these two situations would provide information on expressions and behaviors uniquely associated with *personal* accomplishments.

Two behaviors occurred frequently enough to be analyzed statistically— smiling and looking up at the experimenter. The results indicated that children in all age groups were no more likely to smile when they produced the outcome than when it was produced by the experimenter. This result suggests that smiles, at least in this situation, were just as likely to have reflected joy or pleasure in the outcome itself as positive self-evaluation.

In contrast to smiling, strong age effects were found in the likelihood of a child's looking up at the experimenter. Toddlers aged 22 to 39 months were more likely to look up at the experimenter after they had produced the outcome themselves than after the experimenter had produced it. The difference was especially strong for children over the age of $2^1/2$ years: Whereas only 10% of the 30- to 39-month-old children looked up at the experimenter after the experimenter completed the task, 65% did so after they completed the task on their own. (The difference was 15% vs. 45% for the 22- to 29-month-olds, which was statistically significant, and 22% vs. 30% of the 13- to 21-month-olds, which was not significant.) It seems unlikely that children looked up at the experimenter simply to make social contact, because there is no reason why social contact would be more desirable after they had completed a task on their own than after they had watched the experimenter complete a task. It is also unlikely that children were seeking information about whether they had completed the task, since the goal was visually salient and clear-cut, and the experimenter had just demonstrated the task. We interpreted the social referencing behavior as indicating that the older children either desired confirmation that they had achieved the goal, or anticipated and desired praise for their achievement.

Taken together, the findings suggest that smiling cannot be assumed to reflect positive self-evaluation or feelings of mastery or pride. In contrast to smiling, behaviors suggesting an interest in others' reactions to their behavior, which appeared when the children in this study approached 2 years of age, may be a precursor to or the first evidence of a propensity to evaluate the self. This interpretation—consistent with some theorists' claims that self-evaluation has its roots in others' evaluation (Cooley, 1902; Harter & Whitesell, 1989)—was pursued further in our analyses of attention-seeking behavior in a more naturalistic context.

Toddlers' reactions to their achievements were also observed in a free-play situation with their mothers. Eighty-six mother–toddler pairs were videotaped for 10 mintues while they played with a set of age-appropriate toys, most of which provided opportunities for achievements (e.g., puzzles, blocks, a shape-sorting cube, a drawing board). Mothers were instructed to play with their children as they would at home. (This session was presented as a "warm-up" session for the experimental study, described above.)

Each child's emotional reactions were coded when they occurred within 3 seconds of the child's producing some identifiable outcome. Each mother's praise, and whether the mother or the child defined the goal, were also coded. The study produced several findings related to the questions posed above.

First, there were no age differences in the proportion of toddlers who spontaneously expressed positive emotions, including smiling, exclaiming, or clapping their hands. The age effect found in this naturalistic situation, like the age difference found in the experiment discussed above, involved social referencing. Nearly half of the 22- to 39-month-old children called their mothers' attention to at least one achievement (e.g., a child held a toy up in front of the mother's face and said, "Look"), whereas only 14% of the younger children did. Thus, again, we found that as children approached the age of 2, they began to manifest an interest in others' reactions to their achievements.

A second important finding is that children in all age groups were more likely to express positive emotion (e.g., smiling, exclaiming, clapping) about, and were more likely to call attention to, achieving goals that they had determined for themselves than achieving goals that their mothers had proposed. And children whose mothers were relatively intrusive (i.e., they defined a relatively high proportion of goals for their children) were less likely to display positive emotional expressions, less likely to call attention to their accomplishments, and more likely to look up at their mothers when they produced some outcome.

In contrast to mothers' proposing goals, which appeared to undermine children's spontaneous pleasure in their accomplishments, the results suggested that mothers' praise enhanced positive emotional expressions associated with achievements. Although children often spontaneously expressed pride-like behaviors when they achieved some outcome—indicating that praise was not required for them to experience a positive emotion related to their accomplishments—children whose mothers praised them frequently during the 10-minute play period exhibited relatively more positive emotional reactions and called attention to more of their achievements.

Taken together, these data suggest a picture of intrinsically motivated children who spontaneously took pleasure in the outcomes they produced, especially the ones they initiated themselves. Social approval was not necessary for them to experience pleasure in their accomplishments (although it appeared to add to their value), and they usually did not seek adult reactions.

As children approached the age of 2 years in both the experimental and the naturalistic situations, they appeared to have developed some desire for social recognition. Of all of the behaviors coded in these two sets of observations, only the social orienting behaviors showed consistent increases with age. Attention-seeking behavior does not necessarily indicate that children are able to reflect on the implications achievements have for their competence. The apparent anticipation of a positive adult response does suggest, however, that by the age of 2 years toddlers are able to reflect on the implications that their achievements have on *others'* reactions.

Although praise was not at all necessary for children to express positive emotional reactions to their achievements, it did appear to have a general positive effect on their emotional experience. There are several ways in which maternal praise may have enhanced children's positive emotional experiences in this setting. First, frequent praise may have contributed to a positive atmosphere that made the situation more pleasant and the children happier. Although this might explain why relatively highly praised children expressed more positive emotion when they produced outcomes, it is an unlikely explanation of the finding that highly praised children called attention to their achievements more often than children who were praised less frequently. A more likely explanation is that more frequently praised children learned that their activities in this setting were socially valued (or prideworthy). This knowledge may have prompted more pride in the outcomes they produced, or it may have generated positive affect associated with the anticipation of praise. It is, however, also possible that the more expressive children elicited their mothers' praise by their own emotional reactions. A longitudinal study is needed to assess the direction of these correlations. The possibility suggested by our data—that praise may have a general affect on children's emotional experiences in achievement settings—is certainly worth pursuing in future research.

Reactions to Success and Failure

A second set of studies examined 2- to 5-year-olds' reactions to success and failure in an experimental context. Originally we had planned to include subjects as young as 18 months, but it proved impossible to create a failure experience for most children below the age of 2 years. When younger children had difficulty performing a task the experimenter had proposed, they simply changed the task. In many respects this observation itself is important, in that it suggests that young toddlers do not feel bound by adult-imposed goals, and thus can easily avoid failure. Nevertheless, it also created a methodological problem that we failed to overcome; as a consequence, children under 2 years were not included in the study.

The 214 children who served as subjects were given two tasks, a puzzle and a set of nested cups. Half of the children were given tasks (adjusted in difficulty level to be age-appropriate) that could be completed within a few minutes. The other half were given a puzzle in which one piece was a little too large, making it impossible to fit all of the pieces in the border, and a set of cups that included two of the same size.[1] The entire session was videotaped, and children's emotional reactions to success or failure were coded from the videotapes.

Analyses of the videotapes revealed that children at all ages responded very differently to success and failure. Children who succeeded were more likely than children who failed to smile, have an open posture (head up, arms apart, shoulders back), make a comment regarding their successful performance (e.g., "I did it"), pause and regard their outcome, call attention to their outcome, look up at the experimenter, and look up at the camera. Children's positive reactions to success are not surprising, because all children were above the age of 2—and thus, according to developmental research, cognitively capable of experiencing pride in their achievements. The absence of observable differences in the reactions of 2-year-olds and children over 3 years of age is contrary to Heckhausen's (1984) claim that true self-reflective pride does not appear until about the age of 3 1/2 years.

Behaviors manifested by children at all ages after failure more than after success included sighing, expressing frustration, seeking help, reducing attention to the task, changing the goals of the task, and giving up. These behaviors do not necessarily suggest negative *self*-evaluation, and casual observations suggest that even young toddlers manifest these behaviors when they are unable to achieve a goal.

What was surprising was that behaviors presumed to be associated with negative self-evaluation were also observed in children as young as 2 years. Children at all ages in this study were more likely to avoid eye contact with the experimenter after failing, both by looking away and by turning their bodies away. They also had, on average, a more closed posture (e.g., shoulders hunched, arms close to or across the body) immediately after they ceased working on the task. These social avoidance behaviors strongly suggest negative self-evaluation, or at least the recognition that an adult might evaluate them negatively for their performance.

Significant age differences were found only for one expression that might be associated with negative self-evaluation. Almost none of the children who succeeded frowned (e.g., mouth corners down, lips rolled inward), and among those who failed, fewer than 10% of the 24- to 32-month-olds frowned. The proportion of children who frowned when they failed increased substantially, however, with over 20% of the 33- to 41-month-old children and nearly half of the 42- to 60-month-old children frowning.

We speculated that looking away would suggest a desire to avoid the anticipated disapproving regard of the experimenter, whereas frowning was more autonomous. It is conceivable that the frowns observed in the older children in this study reflected a more independent or internalized self-evaluation and expression of shame, whereas the turning away shown by the younger children reflected the anticipation of another's disapproving reaction.

Whatever the meaning of the frowning, the social avoidance behavior suggests that under certain circumstances, children as young as age 2 years experience negative reactions to achievement failures. These results are inconsistent with Heckhausen's (1984) observations of children in a competitive achievement situation. We did a third study, therefore, to examine age differences in children's reactions to success and failure defined by a competitive standard.

Emotional Reactions of Winning versus Losing a Competition

In this third study, 112 children aged 2 to 5 years were paired with agemates to compete in a ball-stacking task. The experimenter focused the pairs' attention on winning by finishing first as the criterion for success; "losers" of the race were allowed, but not explicitly encouraged, to complete their towers. This made it possible to compare reactions related to two different criteria for success—a competitive criterion (winning), and a task-intrinsic criterion (finishing the tower). We also assessed reactions to failure, as defined by the competitive standard (i.e., losing) at the point at which the loser was informed that the winner had completed his or her tower. Because all children were allowed to complete the task, failure defined in terms of a task-intrinsic criterion could not be examined in this study.

In the study discussed above, children as young as 2 years reacted very differently to success and failure, as defined by visually salient, task-intrinsic criteria. Two-year-olds did not, however, react differently to success and failure in this subsequent study, in which a competitive standard was used to determine the outcome. Children under 33 months who completed their task first did not even report above a chance level that they had won, and those who lost the race were just as likely to smile when they eventually completed the task as were their agemates who won the race. For children over the age of 33 months, either winning added some value or losing diminished the value of task completion; in all three of the older groups, children who finished first were more likely to smile than those who completed the task after losing the competition.

Additional evidence for age increases in attention to the competitive criterion is seen in children's reactions to seeing the winners complete their towers. Very few children under 42 months paused, slowed their pace, or stopped working on their towers when the winners finished, whereas about a fourth of the 42- to 50-month-old children and about half of the 51- to 60-month-old children exhibited one of these behaviors, thus indicating an understanding of the competitive quality of the task.

Taken together, the results suggest that these children understood success versus failure in terms of our task-intrinsic criterion before they understood it in terms of the competitive (win–lose) criterion. Consistent with Heckhausen's (1984) observations, it was not until the age of $3^{1}/_{2}$ years that children appeared to care much about the competitive aspect of the task, since only children above this age paused, slowed down, or stopped working when the winners finished.

Our research suggests that developmental changes in children's self-evaluative emotions are contingent to some degree on the criteria for success and failure, and that developmental findings in studies of self-evaluative emotions will vary considerably as a function of those criteria. Our studies therefore explain the discrepancy between Kagan's (1981) observation that 2-year-olds were distressed when an adult modeled a simple activity (a situation in which "success" was visually salient and intrinsic to the task), and Heckhausen's (1984) failure to see negative reactions to failure (defined competitively) in 2-year-olds.

DEVELOPMENTAL CHANGES IN SELF-EVALUATIVE EMOTIONS

My colleagues and I have proposed, on the basis of previous theoretical work and of our own and others' empirical evidence (taking considerable inferential license), three stages in the early development of self-evaluative emotions (see Stipek et al., 1992).

First, our data are consistent with the position taken by most other theorists. That is, infants and young toddlers, who lack the cognitive-representational skills required for self-conscious emotions (e.g., a categorical self-concept, the ability to represent standards of behavior and performance), experience joy in causality or feelings of effectance, but they do not experience self-evaluative emotions in a self-reflective or self-conscious sense. For example, although even the youngest toddlers in the first study described above smiled when they produced some outcome, toddlers under 22 months showed no evidence of having reflected upon the effect that their achievement might have on another individual's reactions toward them; in contrast to the older children, they did not look up at the experimenter when they achieved a goal that the experimenter had proposed, and they rarely called their mothers' attention to an achievement. Young toddlers' failure to seek adult praise or reactions for their achievements does not, by itself, demonstrate that they do not experience self-evaluative emotions. It is nevertheless consistent with such a view, which has been held by most theorists, and is also supported by research on the presumed cognitive prerequisites of self-evaluative emotions.

We propose that children begin to anticipate adult reactions to their achievements and failures sometime in the second half of their second year, and that this anticipation constitutes an important milestone in the development of self-evaluative emotions. Nearly half of the children over age 21 months called their mothers' attention to some achievement during the 10-minute free-play period in one of our studies, and in the experimental situation many toddlers over this age looked up at the experimenter after they completed a task. The attention-seeking behavior suggests that the children knew (or suspected) that they had achieved some socially valued outcome that was likely to earn approval, and that they desired this approval.

Children's reactions to failure in the success–failure study also suggest concerns about adult reactions. The social avoidance behavior (turning the head or body away or contracting posture) suggests that children antici- pated, and desired to avoid, a negative evaluation. This evidence for the anticipation of others' reactions to outcomes suggests that children have begun to reflect upon the implications of performance outcomes, at least for others' reactions.

The results of these studies suggest that significant others play an important role in the early development of self-evaluative emotions. But the data do not allow us to draw conclusions about whether others are *essential* to this process. We do not know, for example, whether 2-year-olds experience pride and shame only inasmuch as they anticipate a positive or negative reaction from another, or whether they engage in *self*-evaluation— and would experience pride or shame even in the absence of another individual. A comparison of children's reactions to failure with and without an adult present would help answer this question.

Negative facial expressions (a frown) following failure were not observed until sometime between the ages of 3 and 3½ years—long after children manifested attention-seeking and avoidant reactions. It is possible that the older children's frowns marked a second milestone in the development of self-evaluative emotions: a shift toward more auton- omous self-evaluation—evaluation that is not mediated by expectations or concerns about an adult's reaction. Thus, we have proposed that children move from self-evaluative emotions based primarily on the anticipation of others' reactions to self-evaluative emotions based on personal judgments about whether internalized standards of achievement have been met.

In a sense, we are suggesting a curvilinear pattern in the development of self-evaluative emotions. Initially, children experience immediate and autonomous pleasure from having some effect on their environment; they are not particularly interested in or concerned about others' reactions to their behaviors or outcomes. Before they reach the age of 2 years they become concerned about others' reactions, and their own emotional expe- riences are, to a considerable degree, linked to the anticipation of others' reactions. As they internalize standards and increase in their ability to judge their own performance according to these standards, self-evaluative emo- tions again become independent of the anticipation of others' approval or disapproval.

Thus, children in the first and third stages are relatively more autono- mous in their emotional reactions to their performance. The difference is that only the older children make a judgment about the value of their performance relative to a standard, and about its implications for their competence. For older children, but not infants, self-evaluative emotions really involve *self*-evaluation and may have long-term effects on self-esteem.

Because in everyday contexts most caretakers do not impose unobtainable goals on young children, as we did in our experiments, the negative reactions to failure that we observed may be uncommon in the lives of most young children. Our data suggest, however, that the predominance of positive emotional expressions in achievement contexts is not inevitable. The reactions to failure that we observed indicates that failure takes a greater toll on very young children than is suggested by the current literature on achievement motivation, which portrays young children as little affected by failure (e.g., Rholes, Blackwell, Jordan, & Walters, 1980; Stipek, 1984a, 1984b). Toddlers and preschoolers may be more resilient than older children, but they clearly can be affected emotionally by failure. If the circumstances we imposed occurred frequently in children's daily lives, or if disapproval for violating behavioral norms were frequent, children might typically express as much negative as positive affect in achievement settings.

NOTE

1. To alleviate any negative effects of failure in this condition, the experimenter immediately "noticed" that she had given a child the wrong tasks. She looked in her bag and exclaimed, "Oh, no, I gave you one of the puzzles that doesn't work. Nobody can do that puzzle; one of the pieces is too big." Children were then given a solvable puzzle and praised for their performance.

REFERENCES

Atkinson, J. (1964). *An introduction to motivation*. Princeton, NJ: Van Nostrand.
Baldwin, J. (1897). *Social and ethical interpretations in mental development*. New York: Macmillan.
Barrett, K., & Campos, J. (1987). Perspectives on emotional development: II. A functionalist approach to emotions. In J. Osofsky (Ed.), *Handbook of infant development* (2nd ed., pp. 555–578). New York: Wiley.
Campos, J., Campos, R., & Barrett, K. (1989). Emergent themes in the study of emotional development and emotion regulation. *Developmental Psychology, 25*, 394–402.
Campos, J., & Stenberg, C. (1981). Perception, appraisal and emotion: The onset of social referencing. In M. Lamb & L. Sherrod (Eds.), *Infant social cognition* (pp. 273–314). Hillsdale, NJ: Erlbaum.
Cooley, C. (1902). *Human nature and the social order*. New York: Scribner's.
Darwin, C. (1872). *The expression of the emotions in man and animals*. London: Murray.
Dunn, J. (1987). The beginnings of moral understanding: Development in the second year. In J. Kagan & S. Lamb (Eds.), *The emergence of morality in young children* (pp. 91–112). Chicago: University of Chicago Press.

Emde, R., Johnson, W., & Easterbrooks, M. (1987). The dos and don'ts of early moral development: Psychoanalytic tradition and current research. In J. Kagan & S. Lamb (Eds.), *The emergence of morality in young children* (pp. 245–276). Chicago: University of Chicago Press.

Geppert, U., & Gartmann, D. (1983, August). *The emergence of self-evaluative emotions as consequences of achievement actions.* Paper presented at the biennial meeting of the International Society for the Study of Behavioral Development, Munich.

Harter, S., & Whitesell, N. (1989). Developmental changes in children's understanding of simple, multiple, and blended emotion concepts. In C. Saarni & P. Harris (Eds.), *Children's understanding of emotion* (pp. 81–116). Cambridge, England: Cambridge University Press.

Heckhausen, H. (1984). Emergent achievement behavior: Some early developments. In J. Nicholls (Ed.), *Advances in motivation and achievement: Vol. 3. The development of achievement motivation* (pp. 1–32). Greenwich, CT: JAI Press.

Hunt, J. M. (1963). Piaget's observations as a source of hypotheses concerning motivation. *Merrill–Palmer Quarterly, 9,* 263–275.

Hunt, J. M. (1965). Intrinsic motivation and its role in psychological development. In D. Levine (Ed.), *Nebraska Symposium on Motivation* (Vol. 13, pp. 189–282). Lincoln: University of Nebraska Press.

Izard, C. (1977). *Human emotions.* New York: Plenum Press.

Izard, C., & Dougherty, L. (1980). *A system for identifying affect expressions by holistic judgments (AFFEX).* Newark: University of Delaware, Instructional Resources Center.

Izard, C., & Malatesta, C. (1987). Perspectives on emotional development: I. Different emotions theory of early emotional development. In J. Osofsky (Ed.), *Handbook of infant development* (2nd ed., pp. 494–553). New York: Wiley.

Kagan, J. (1981). *The second year: The emergence of self-awareness.* Cambridge, MA: Harvard University Press.

Kagan, J. (1984). The idea of emotion in human development. In C. Izard, J. Kagan, & R. Zajonc (Eds.), *Emotions, cognition, and behavior* (pp. 38–72). Cambridge, England: Cambridge University Press.

Lewis, M. (1990). Thinking and feeling: The elephant's tail. In C. Maher, M. Schwebel, & N. Fagley (Eds.), *Thinking and problem solving in the developmental process: International perspectives* (pp. 89–110). Hillsdale, NJ: Erlbaum.

Lewis, M., & Brooks-Gunn, J. (1979). *Social cognition and the acquisition of self.* New York: Plenum Press.

Mischel, T. (1971). *Cognitive development and epistemology.* New York: Academic Press.

Piaget, J. (1954). *Les relations entre l'affectivité et l'intelligence dans le développement mental de l'enfant.* Paris: Centre Documentation Universitaire.

Piaget, J. (1962). *Play, dreams and imitation in childhood.* New York: Norton.

Rholes, W., Blackwell, J., Jordan, C., & Walters, C. (1980). A developmental study of learned helplessness. *Developmental Psychology, 16,* 616–624.

Stipek, D. (1984a). Developmental aspects of motivation in children. In R. Ames & C. Ames (Eds.), *Research on motivation in education: Vol. 1. Student motivation* (pp. 145–174). New York: Academic Press.

Stipek, D. (1984b). Young children's performance expectations: Logical analysis or wishful thinking? In J. Nicholls (Ed.), *The development of achievement motivation* (pp. 33–56). Greenwich, CT: JAI Press.

Stipek, D., Recchia, S., & McClintic, S. (1992). Self-evaluation in young children. *Monographs of the Society for Research in Child Development, 57*(1, Serial No. 226).

Tomkins, S. (1963). *Affect, imagery, consciousness: Vol. 2. The negative affects.* New York: Springer.

Weiner, B. (1986). *An attributional theory of motivation and emotion.* New York: Springer-Verlag.

White, R. (1959). Motivation reconsidered: The concept of competence. *Psychological Review, 66,* 297–323.

IV

SELF-CONSCIOUS EMOTIONS AND SOCIAL BEHAVIOR

10

Interpersonal Aspects of Guilt: Evidence from Narrative Studies

ROY F. BAUMEISTER
ARLENE M. STILLWELL
TODD F. HEATHERTON

Psychologists have discussed guilt for decades, but solid and reliable conclusions have not emerged. Theoretical difficulties and methodological obstacles have plagued empirical work, resulting in a scarcity of data. The *Journal of Personality and Social Psychology* contained only three titles that referred to guilt in the entire decade of the 1980s (plus a couple more on sex guilt). In that same decade, the *Annual Review of Psychology* volume indices listed only three pages on which the word "guilt" appeared. Many textbooks on emotion and motivation do not cover guilt at all.

The 1990s have begun with a renewed or reborn interest in guilt. Tangney (1990, 1991; see also Tangney, Wagner, Fletcher, & Gramzow, 1992) has shown that it is possible to distinguish guilt from shame and to study the behavioral consequences of each. Zahn-Waxler and Kochanska (1990) have demonstrated that developmental psychologists have slowly built up an enlightening collection of guilt-related empirical findings, and they have called for new theories to integrate these findings and shape further research.

Responding to that call, we have outlined a theory of the interpersonal aspects of guilt (Baumeister, Stillwell, & Heatherton, 1994). Our argument may be summarized briefly as follows. Whereas traditional theories have depicted guilt as a largely intrapsychic phenomenon based on self-judgment, we regard guilt as an interpersonal phenomenon based in close relationships, especially in certain interactions with intimate partners. To some extent, this is merely a shift in emphasis—a shift toward considering self-judgment the derivative phenomenon and interpersonal dynamics the main foundation. Still, we do reject the strongest assertions of intrapsychic theories, such as that of Lewis (1971), who asserted that "guilt is evoked only from within the self" (p. 85) and "the imagery of the self vis-a-vis the 'other' is absent in guilt" (p. 251).

INTERPERSONAL FUNCTIONS OF GUILT

Our contention is that guilt serves to protect and strengthen interpersonal relationships. The prototype cause of guilt is hurting a relationship partner. (We use the term "relationship partner" in a broad sense, referring to the other person involved in any type of relationship, and thus not just a romantic partner.) Generally, people will feel guilty when they benefit inequitably at a partner's expense or inflict harm, loss, distress, disappointment, or other misfortune on a significant other person. Subjectively, guilt is an unpleasant emotional state, and we suggest two affective bases for it—namely, empathic distress over the suffering of one's partner and victim (e.g., Hoffman, 1982), and separation or exclusion anxiety over the possible loss or damage to the relationship that may be caused by one's transgression (see Baumeister & Tice, 1990; Bowlby, 1969, 1973). Three main specific functions of guilt can be identified.

The first is that guilt directly contributes to good relationships by promoting behaviors that benefit relationships and by serving as a symbolic affirmation of the relationship. Guilt causes people to act in ways that will be beneficial to relationships, such as expressing affection, paying attention, and refraining from transgressions. Furthermore, relationships may be threatened by even seemingly mild transgressions, because such actions symbolically convey that the transgressor does not care enough about the partner or the relationship to behave as the other wishes. By feeling guilty (and showing it), the transgressor can then erase the symbolic damage to the relationship, because the presence of guilt indicates that the transgressor really does care.

The second function of guilt is as an influence technique. One person may get his or her way by making the other feel guilty. To use guilt as an influence technique, the influencer communicates to the partner that some action or inaction will hurt the influencer in some fashion (including disappointing, distressing, or harming him or her). That action or inaction will therefore make the partner feel guilty because it entails hurting the influencer. To avoid the aversive state of guilt, the partner avoids that action or inaction. In this case, merely the threat of impending guilt is enough to keep the potentially offending partner from acting in the undesirable fashion. Guilt may thus operate either as a deterrent (before the fact) or as an impetus for desired behavior change (after the fact).

Guilt is an influence technique that operates in the absence of formal, objective, status-based, or physical power; indeed, it may be especially useful to the less powerful partners in relationships. As such, guilt serves to equalize the balance of power. It also emphasizes the relationship bond and should therefore be far more effective for influencing intimate partners than for influencing casual acquaintances or strangers. Although guilt may be an effective influence technique, its use may involve significant costs, one of which is a partner's resentment (despite compliance). Another potential cost is "metaguilt"—that is, guilt over inducing guilt. Guilt results from hurting a partner, and making the partner feel guilty is a form of hurting, so some people could conceivably feel guilty over making intimate partners feel guilty.

The third function of guilt is to redistribute emotional distress. Transgressions may create affective inequities, because one person did what he or she wanted and therefore may feel good, while the victim suffers the negative consequences. Such affective inequities are bad for relationships and hamper effective communication and interaction (e.g., Locke & Horowitz, 1990). Guilt, however, reduces the benefits of the transgressor. Moreover, the transgressor's guilt may make the victim feel better. The net effect of guilt is therefore to reduce the negative affect of the victim and increase that of the transgressor, as if transferring the negative affect from the victim to the transgressor—who, after all, is its rightful owner in the sense of being the person who has caused it.

Why might victims feel better when they see that transgressors feel guilty? At least two sets of reasons can be offered. First, a transgressor's guilt already helps rectify the inequity, because the transgressor can be seen as suffering for his or her misdeed rather than enjoying his or her ill-gotten gains, so to speak. Second, as noted earlier, the guilt feelings may serve as evidence that the transgressor cares about the relationship and about the victim, and this affirmation of the social bond may be reassuring to the victim. In other words, feeling guilty may be an effective way of communicating the existence of affectional ties.

AUTOBIOGRAPHICAL NARRATIVES

The research we conducted (Baumeisterf, Stillwell, & Heatherton, in press; see also Baumeister, Reis, & Delespaul, in press) was not explicitly designed to test these assertions about guilt. Rather, it was designed to explore in a broad way the interpersonal transactions and contexts of guilt. Both studies used autobiographical-narrative methodology, which in recent years has been particularly useful in shedding light on guilt (e.g., McGraw, 1987; Tangney, 1992).

As suggested earlier, methodological and ethical difficulties have plagued and retarded the empirical study of guilt. Experimental studies have mainly relied on accidental transgressions, because it is nearly impossible to induce subjects systematically or reliably to commit intentional transgressions in the laboratory. Even if it were possible to induce subjects to act in highly immoral ways, it would not be ethical to do so. McGraw (1987) has noted that accidental transgressions do not necessarily produce the same effects as intentional transgressions, and it is very difficult to elicit the latter in the laboratory. Moreover, our emphasis on the interpersonal context suggests that empirical studies of guilt should focus on transgressions within intimate relationships, but it seems highly unethical to use laboratory procedures to induce serious intentional transgressions (or indeed guilt of any sort) within important relationships.

Our empirical approach has thus made use of autobiographical narratives, a methodology that has become increasingly available to personality and social psychologists in recent years (Gergen & Gergen, 1988; Harvey, Weber, & Orbuch, 1990; McAdams, 1985; Ross & Holmberg, 1990). It has proven particularly useful in exploring topics that resist conventional laboratory methods, such as the termination of intimate relationships (Harvey, Flanary, & Morgan, 1988; Harvey, Weber, Galvin, Huszti, & Garnick, 1986; Vaughan, 1986), unrequited love (Baumeister & Wotman, 1992), criminal and antisocial activity (J. Katz, 1988), the interpersonal genesis of anger (Baumeister, Stillwell, & Wotman, 1990), lay understanding of emotion (Shaver, Schwartz, Kirson, & O'Connor, 1987), and sexual masochism (Baumeister, 1988a, 1988b, 1989). Guilt falls into this category of theoretically important but empirically elusive phenomena, and so it seems a prime candidate for this methodology (Brooke, 1985; McGraw, 1987; Tangney, 1992).

In essence, the method relies on having people relate significant stories from their own lives pertaining to a particular theme (which is defined by the topic of study). The stories are then coded for content on dimensions relevant to the hypotheses. Our approach has generally relied on comparisons between two sets of stories. Thus, in previous research we have compared male against female accounts of masochistic experiences (Baumeister, 1988b), and compared perpetrators' and victims' accounts of interpersonal transgressions (Baumeister et al., 1990). In our first study on guilt, we compared interpersonal transgressions that led to guilt with transgressions that did not lead to guilt. In a second one, we compared accounts of being made to feel guilty with accounts of making someone else feel guilty (Baumeister, Stillwell, & Heatherton, in press).

The methodological implications and limitations of autobiographical narratives are discussed elsewhere (see, e.g., Baumeister et al., 1990; Baumeister & Stillwell, 1992). Briefly, autobiographical narratives sacrifice some of the precision, control, and homogeneity that are obtainable with laboratory experimentation. The benefits include an increase in external validity (because of using real stories from actual lives rather than laboratory simulations) and, most important, the capacity to study topics that resist laboratory methods. As noted elsewhere, we regard laboratory experimentation as the best methodology when viable, but the inability of laboratory experimentation to provide a thorough understanding of guilt has encouraged us to pursue this alternative method (see also Brooke, 1985; McGraw, 1987).

GUILT OR NO GUILT?

Our first investigation in this line of research (Baumeister, Stillwell, & Heatherton, in press, Study 1) was an attempt to explore the factors related to feeling guilty over a transgression. We collected first-person accounts of transgressions, specifying that these had to be things about which the person later felt guilty. To furnish a basis for comparison, we also collected accounts of transgressions that did not lead to guilt. In order to define the transgression in a comparable way, the instructions for all stories requested each subject to relate an incident in which he or she had done something that made someone else angry. Using anger as a criterion is an effective way of eliciting stories about interpersonal transgressions (cf. Baumeister et al., 1990), but of course it may not cover the full range of guilt-inducing episodes. Thus, every subject wrote two stories about transgressions that he or she had committed—one chosen so that the transgressor did not feel guilty, and the other so that the transgressor did feel guilty. In other respects the instructions for the two stories were identical; thus the two sets of stories were comparable in terms of another person's condemnation and disapproval of the subject's actions, and they differed as to whether the subject felt guilty afterwards.

The stories were provided by upper-level college students. We randomly varied the order in which each subject wrote the two stories, but there did not seem to be any effect of which one the person wrote first. Subjects were assured of confidentiality and asked not to identify themselves or anyone else in the stories. A secretary then typed the stories, and a judge coded them along a series of dimensions. We used a dichotomous coding system, in which the coder simply made a series of binary judgments as to whether the story contained a given feature or not (e.g., "Did the transgressor apologize in the story?"). Table 10.1 summarizes the main results.

The first issue that concerned us was whether guilt is linked to close or otherwise special relationships. To examine this, we looked for differences in the relationship between transgressor and victim in the guilty stories as opposed to the not-guilty stories. Consistent with the interpersonal view of guilt, people were significantly more likely to express high esteem for the other (angry) person in the guilty stories than in the not-guilty stories. More specifically, 85% of the guilty stories expressed some high or positive regard for the partner, as compared to only 37% of the not-guilty stories. This pattern fits the view that guilt is characteristic of offenses within the context

TABLE 10.1. Comparison of Stories in Which the Author Did versus Did Not Feel Guilty

	Percentage coded yes	
Coding dimension	Guilty	Not guilty
Lesson learned	40.4	0.0
Mitigating circumstances	46.8	80.4
Perpetrator regards victim highly	85.1	36.9
Apology given	36.1	6.5
Author still feels bad	21.3	2.1
Perpetrator was selfish	42.5	8.7
Perpetrator's actions were justified	27.6	97.8
Victim helped provoke incident	44.6	82.6
Perpetrator confessed misdeed	8.5	0.0
Perpetrator happy with outcome	8.5	56.5
Perpetrator's behavior changed	21.3	2.1
Things now back to normal	44.6	69.5
Perpetrator foresaw outcome	29.7	78.2

Note. n = 86–93 stories.

of valued relationships. People apparently feel less guilty about their transgressions against people whom they dislike or disrespect.

As examples, many episodes referred to partners in intimate relationships. Others described close friends and emphasized that the guilt was linked to remorse over potential damage to the relationship. In one subject's words, "We had been really good friends during the year. . . . I felt bad that our friendship had gone bad." One woman's story indicated that her rising esteem for the partner produced the guilt. She had been dating several men innocently, but when she fell in love with one of them she felt guilty over having dated the others, even though she stopped seeing them. Another wrote of leaving for the summer without saying goodbye to a close friend.

It must be kept in mind that these results are correlational. There is no way of assessing whether the disrespect eliminated the guilt or whether the lack of guilt led to disrespect, although the former seems far more plausible. Our results do suggest, however, that derogating a victim would be an effective way of minimizing guilt. Previous studies have shown tendency for people to derogate their victims (Lerner & Matthews, 1967). Such derogation may accomplish the result of making one's relationship to the victim trivial, expendable, or undesirable. By thus severing the social bond, one removes an important basis for guilt. It is also noteworthy that Noel (1973) failed to replicate the standard finding that people become more helpful and compliant after committing a (usually accidental) transgression. In Noel's study, the transgression involved derogating another person; possibly the derogation of the victim removed the guilt that often mediates subsequent altruistic behavior.

An experimental study by I. Katz, Glass, and Cohen (1973) is also relevant to the implication that derogation may reduce guilt. In that study, white subjects derogated black victims more than white victims, which seems to suggest that severing the tie of fellow-feeling is easier when one's victim is from another race. This suggestion seems to fit several observational studies, which have proposed that perpetrators of crimes and atrocities tend to derogate their victims to remove any sense of fellow-feeling; perpetrators even sometimes regard their victims as subhuman, especially when the victims belong to some ethnic or social group that can be clearly separated from their own (Conquest, 1986; Lifton, 1986).

Taken together with these past conclusions, our work thus seems to suggest that a positive relationship context is an important foundation for guilt. People feel guilty about offenses against esteemed others. Such transgressions may pose a risk to a valued relationship, and so the resultant guilt may well be regarded as an adaptive reaction if guilt is indeed (as we have suggested) a relationship-enhancing pattern born out of positive concern over a desired relationship.

Our theory has suggested further that guilt has relationship-enhancing functions. Because the interpersonal relationships varied systematically between the two sets of stories (as our first finding indicated), it was not feasible to code the stories for comparative relationship outcomes. One dimension that could be effectively coded, however, was whether the narrator indicated having learned a lesson or changed subsequent behavior patterns as a result of this. To be sure, anger may be understood generally as an objection to another's actions (e.g., Averill, 1982), so one might expect all incidents to lead to behavior change. But we found that guilt feelings were apparently a powerful mediator of such changes. Only one not-guilty story referred to behavior change, whereas 21.3% of the guilty stories did, and the difference was significant. An even stronger finding was obtained by coding whether subjects indicated that they had learned a lesson or changed in any positive fashion. Forty percent of the guilty stories contained some indication of having learned or changed, whereas none of the not-guilty stories contained such an indication.

Several examples are useful to illustrate these lessons. One subject described an argument and looked back with regret: "If I had to do it over again, I would have tried to be more tactful. As a matter of fact, if I ever see that guy and his truck, I do plan to apologize to him." Insight into self was often mentioned, as in this example: "I regretted treating my friend badly and I decided to apologize to her. I explained to her why I did what I did, and it really helped me understand my feelings." Other lessons pertained to relationship partners, as in the case of the woman who had a summer romantic fling while away from her boyfriend, who was quite upset by the affair: "I never realized how fragile he was, and I wish to God I had thought things through first." Yet other lessons referred to improvements in interpersonal relationships, as in the following example: "Some good came out of this, however. We agreed from then on that if we ever got into a dumb argument on the phone, we won't let it escalate; instead, we will wait until we see each other and can talk it over in a civilized manner."

These results are nicely consistent with suggestions that guilt is an effective internal mechanism for adaptation and self-control (e.g., Freud, 1930; Wertheim & Schwarz, 1983). Although some studies have suggested that people who feel guilty are better socialized and more responsible than people like sociopaths, who are relatively immune to guilt feelings (e.g., Zahn-Waxler & Kochanska, 1990), our results extend that argument by replicating the effect within subjects. All our subjects (except one) wrote both a guilty story and a not-guilty story, and as a general pattern they learned and changed more when they had felt guilty. In other words, guilt is linked with learning and changing in socially desirable ways, and this link obtains both in comparisons of guilty versus not-guilty people and in comparisons of guilty versus not-guilty episodes within the same individual's experience.

The fact that guilt leads to behavior change is of course particularly important in laying the foundation for the influence function we have proposed. That is, guilt will only serve as an effective influence technique if it does cause people to alter their behavior. Study 2 has examined the interpersonal manipulation of guilt feelings directly.

Several findings of lesser importance can be briefly mentioned. As compared with the not-guilty stories, guilty stories were more likely to suggest that the author still felt bad about the incident, more likely to include having apologized, less likely to cite mitigating circumstances, less likely to place some causal blame or responsibility on the other person, less likely to contain self-justifications, more likely to portray the author's action as selfish, less likely to portray the author as happy with the outcome, less likely to indicate that things had gotten back to normal, and less likely to suggest that the author had foreseen the outcome. The last point corroborates McGraw's (1987) ironic finding that people tend to report more guilt about unintended actions or unforeseen consequences.

MAKING SOMEONE FEEL GUILTY

Our second study (Baumeister, Stillwell, & Heatherton, in press, Study 2) was directly concerned with the interpersonal manipulation of guilt. Specifically, we asked people to describe incidents in which they caused someone to feel guilty or in which someone made them feel guilty. The sample for this study was comprised of adults of all ages, as most of them were drawn from among visitors to the Ontario Science Centre. (Others came from an upper-level psychology course.) Most of our results involved comparing the two sets of accounts based on the two situational roles: guilt inducers and their targets. Comparing accounts based on different situational roles has been a standard way of using this methodology (e.g., Baumeister et al., 1990;

Baumeister, Wotman, & Stillwell, 1993). Table 10.2 presents the main comparisons.

A set of hypotheses about the interpersonal manipulation of guilt follows directly from our theoretical exposition. When one person harms, frustrates, upsets, or disappoints another, the latter may be motivated to make the former feel guilty, especially because of the relationship-enhancing effects of guilt. Making the other feel guilty should involve displaying one's suffering or misfortune and emphasizing the other's responsibility for it. Simple disclosure may be enough, but people may understandably be tempted to facilitate the induction of guilt by exaggerating their suffering. Thus, one person portrays a vivid or enhanced image of one's suffering to the other and then relies on the other's concern to induce guilt. The attempted induction of guilt should ostensibly serve some relationship-enhancing function, particularly getting the other to affirm his or her commitment to the relationship.

Successful guilt induction should have several consequences. It should lead to behavior change on the part of the guilty person. It should make the victim/manipulator feel better in some way, thereby redistributing the negative affect (i.e., transferring it from victim to transgressor). In some cases, however, the affective improvement may be tempered by "metaguilt"—that is, guilt over inducing guilt. Also, in some cases guilt may succeed in eliciting behavioral compliance but may generate resentment or other

TABLE 10.2. Comparison of Guilt Induction Stories Written by Reproachers and Targets

Category	Percentage coded yes	
	Target	Reproacher
Reference to other's standards	55.1	13.0
Metaguilt	0.0	21.2
Target did something wrong	22.7	52.9
Target failed to act (sin of omission)	70.2	53.1
Target resents	37.2	1.9
Interpersonal neglect as offense	58.7	32.7
Self-justifying statements	62.5	60.4
Self-blame	34.8	19.2
Reproacher was frankly manipulative	14.6	32.7
Differing expectations as cause	49.0	29.1
Target apologizes, regrets	20.8	46.3
Reproacher used past	18.4	37.0
Reproacher lied or falsified	0.0	16.4
Reproacher felt better afterward	4.7	44.0
Target felt bad	49.0	67.3
Target overreacted	4.1	5.6
Reproacher overreacted	44.9	16.7

Note. n = 93–104 stories.

negative reactions, which should be more apparent to the person who is made to feel guilty than to the manipulator.

Before we proceed to described how the accounts by inducers differed from those of their targets, we want to emphasize a basic issue that was already raised in our previous study—namely, the relationship context of guilt. We wanted to see whether guilt induction would be linked to close relationships as clearly as simple accounts of feeling guilty (in Study 1) were. And they were. Although subjects were free to describe episodes of guilt induction between themselves and strangers, they overwhelmingly chose instead to describe incidents between themselves and intimate partners such as family members, lovers, and close friends. We coded whether the other person in the guilt story was (1) an intimate, such as a relative, lover, or close friend; (2) a casual acquaintance or work/business associate; (3) a stranger to whom the author had some role relationship; or (4) a stranger with whom the author had no relationship. The fourth category was completely empty. Only one incident fell into the third category, and that incident involved a lifeguard making a child feel guilty for heedless behavior that might have hurt someone. Six incidents fell into the second category; these involved four teacher–student relationships, one coach–athlete relationship, and one relationship of a businessman to a long-term client. The remaining 95 (not counting two ambiguous ones, which also seemed to suggest long-term relationships) fell into the first category because of overt references to close relationships. Apparently those whom people deliberately cause to feel guilty are mainly friends, relatives, and lovers.

Guilt may therefore be considered an influence technique that is particularly suited to close relationships. There are several possible reasons for this. First of all, many influence techniques are exploitative or coercive, or may rely on deceptive manipulations that cannot be repeated or sustained indefinitely (see Cialdini, 1984), and so these may not be suitable for long-term relationships. Indeed, explicit coercion may be sustained in a relationship if one person is clearly more powerful, but the greater the assumptions of equity and equality, the more costly direct coercion becomes. Guilt may seem preferable to coercion because the other person seemingly complies freely rather than under duress, although, as we have suggested, this is probably an illusion; guilt has its costs, but they are simply hidden. Guilt is also available to the person with less power in the relationship. Perhaps most importantly, guilt depends on empathy and on the mutual commitment to the relationship, and so it is really most viable in the context of a long-term, emotionally intense relationship.

The first function of guilt we have described is to motivate people to affirm their social bonds by expressing commitment or affection, or at least paying attention to relationship partners. Consistent with the hypothesis that guilt serves this function, the single biggest category of causes of interpersonal guilt induction was neglecting one's partner. Although this was substantial in both samples, it was more common in the accounts of the targets than in those of the reproachers. Targets may have preferred to describe such incidents because there was little moral wrongdoing on their part and because many of them were able to justify having neglected others because of devoting themselves to their work or other preoccupations. Still, it is apparent that people are quite aware of being made to feel guilty for not paying enough attention to others.

Neglecting to attend to someone is a sin of omission rather than a sin of commission, which is of particular interest, insofar as previous studies have largely focused on sins of commission (as noted by Zahn-Waxler & Kochanska, 1990). Indeed, Tangney (1992) has suggested that guilt is overwhelmingly associated with sins of commission rather than omission. Our results differed from that view, however: Over half the reproachers' accounts and two-thirds of the targets' accounts referred to sins of omission. It appears that the interpersonal manipulation of guilt is often associated with failure to act rather than with actions. Possibly when people are asked to recall an incident that evoked guilt, they recall a sin of commission, but when they are asked to recall an interpersonal induction of guilt, the sins of omission come more readily to mind.

Our model suggests that people may sometimes be tempted to exaggerate their suffering in order to generate guilt in others, and these accounts confirmed that pattern. A significant minority of reproachers referred to bare-faced attempts to make others feel guilty, and some even acknowledged having dissembled, distorted, misled, or used falsehoods in order to generate guilt. In this sample, none of the targets' accounts referred to such bare-faced or hypocritical tactics in the attempt to generate guilt, although many targets did feel that the reproachers had overreacted (which could have a similar meaning). These findings suggest that people sometimes do successfully deceive others, such as by exaggerating or misrepresenting their suffering, to make others feel guilty.

Negative reactions by the target have been proposed as one potential cost of the use of guilt as an influence technique. The most important among these reactions may be resentment, which was apparent in our sample. Target resentment was significantly more common in the targets' own accounts than in the reproachers' accounts. This suggests that many targets may keep their resentment more or less to themselves, indeed often complying overtly with the wishes of the reproachers. The lack of references to resentment among the reproachers' accounts suggests that they may often be unaware of (or choose to ignore) this negative reaction among the people they manipulate with guilt. This important cost of guilt as an influence technique may not be immediately apparent to guilt inducers.

A second possible cost of using guilt as an influence technique is metaguilt—that is, feeling guilty over making others feel guilty. This cost was also apparent in our sample, although, like resentment, it was only apparent in one of the two sets of accounts. Although the targets' accounts made no reference to the notion that reproachers might feel guilty, a significant minority of reproachers did indicate that they felt guilty about their manipulation.

The fact that some reproachers felt guilty about inducing guilt helps to explain one surprising result, which was that both groups of authors included self-justificatory statements at approximately the same rate. One might assume that people who feel guilty would be moved to justify themselves, and thus that statements of self-justification would be more common in the targets' accounts, but many reproachers felt it necessary to justify their actions too. Apparently, deliberately making someone feel guilty violates some norms (especially norms of not making others feel bad), and so inducers had to justify what they did.

Our third hypothesized interpersonal function of guilt is the redistribution of negative affect, and this too was apparent in our sample. Not surprisingly, targets generally were made to feel bad and feel guilty as a result of the reproachers' efforts. Of greater interest is the finding of significant affect improvements by the reproachers: Almost half the reproachers' accounts indicated that they felt better after the incident. These affective improvements suggest that a transfer model describes guilt induction better than a contagion model, because the contagion model would entail that one person would feel worse and the other would continue feeling bad. Instead, we found that one's feeling worse was linked to the other's feeling better, as if some of the negative affect had been transferred out of one person and into the other.

Furthermore, we have reasoned that one cause of a reproacher's affective improvement would be the positive expressions of guilt and remorse by the partner, whose visible remorse should presumably operate as a symbolic indication of his or her commitment to the relationship and caring about the other. Consistent with this finding, a significant number of accounts included references to the targets' remorse or overt apologies. What was especially striking was that these references were more common in the reproachers' accounts than in the targets' own accounts. In a recent study of accounts involving anger, offenders were far more likely than their victims to mention apologies (Baumeister et al., 1990). That pattern also conforms to a more general property of autobiographical narratives, which is that people refer to their own feelings and actions more than to those of other people. Yet in the present study the opposite pattern emerged: Reproachers' accounts featured the apologies of their targets more than the targets' own accounts did.

One plausible explanation for this remarkable salience of the apology to its recipient is, again, the relationship-enhancing message that it conveyed. If a reproacher were indeed to feel better as a result of the guilt induction and the other's guilty affirmation of the relationship, then that would explain why the apology would be sufficiently important as to be included in many reproachers' accounts. A related reason was that reproachers were describing their efforts to make someone feel guilty, and so the targets' apologies were a form of proof that their efforts had been successful.

It is also worth mentioning that targets' accounts had a relatively high number of references to differing expectations and to the other persons' (i.e., the reproachers') standards. Such discrepancies between one's own standards or expectations and the other person's may be especially salient to a target, for they form the basis for the guilt induction. Furthermore, appealing to such discrepancies may allow the target to feel justified and decent while still acknowledging that another made him or her feel guilty, as if the target were to say that his or her behavior was objectionable in another's view but nonetheless correct in his or her own estimation. This finding underscores our argument that guilt is not necessarily or even primarily a result of a self-evaluation process. Contrary to Mosher's (1965) exclusive focus on one's own internalized standards, it is quite apparent that people do feel guilty in response to the standards of others, and even feel guilty despite discrepancies between their standards and others' standards. Indeed, Mosher's hypothesis that guilt is an expectancy of self-mediated punishment (1965, p. 162) received no support in either of these two studies, for no subject referred to an expectancy of self-mediated punishment.

Following Locke and Horowitz (1990), we have suggested (Baumeister et al., 1994) that part of the value of redistributing negative affect is that it brings the partners into similar emotional states, which facilitates communication between them; and of course the improved communication may be beneficial for the relationship. Our data cannot assess relationship outcomes in any systematic fashion, but there were some indications that guilt inductions did have that effect. Here is a good example stating explicitly that guilt induction helped the two people communicate better:

> When I was about 18–19 years old, I was still living at home with my parents and I stayed out all night at a party—got home 8–9 A.M. the next day. I didn't call—it didn't even cross my mind to call home. When I did get home, kind of hung-over, tired—my mother was waiting for me with the biggest guilt trip known to man. She started the "you don't love me—you make me worry so much—I though you were dead" routine. She told me—worst of all—that she was disappointed in me! This is my mother, who fawned over every little achievement I had from kindergarten to getting my driver's license. The way she made me feel stuck with me. We made up, of course, after lots of crying and explaining. But, to this day, I can still picture the look of disappointment on her face and the tone of her voice. I hope to God I never make her feel like that again.

Thus, this story about guilt testifies to redistribution of negative affect, to improved communication, and to positive and lasting behavior change.

GUILT, OTHER EMOTIONS, AND INTERPERSONAL RELATIONS

The studies we have described shed light on the likely interpersonal dynamics of guilt, but they were not designed to address the basic question of how interpersonal a phenomenon guilt is. The instructions in the preceding studies specifically asked people to describe interpersonal incidents, and so episodes of solitary guilt would be left out. To be sure, there was no pressure to describe incidents involving close relationships, and the high frequency of such relationships in these samples of stories does suggest that guilt is mainly linked to them, but there remains the possibility that guilt is often felt in connection with solitary transgressions and reflections.

One of us participated in some research that was directly concerned with examining the solitary versus interpersonal nature of guilt (Baumeister, Reis, & Delespaul, in press). In one of the studies in that project, subjects were asked to provide the most recent incident in which they had felt guilty. They were also asked to describe their most recent experiences of anxiety, sadness, frustration, fear, and anger or irritation (the sequence was varied). These were then coded for whether the episode was solitary versus interpersonal. In this way, guilt could be compared with other emotions with regard to its "interpersonalness"; after all, even if most incidents of guilt were found to be interpersonal, this might be trivial if most reports of incidents involving any other emotion were equally interpersonal.

The results of that study indicated, however, that guilt seems to be one of the more interpersonal emotions. Indeed, among the six emotions included in the study, guilt ranked the highest on interpersonalness. There were fewer solitary guilt episodes than episodes of any of the other emotions, and the degree of close or intimate relatedness was higher in the guilt stories than in any of the other emotion stories. Sadness was the only emotion to score close to guilt on interpersonalness. Frustration, anxiety, and fear were often associated with being alone.

In that study, the stories were also subjected to content analysis, in order to determine what sorts of things led to guilt. Consistent with the evidence we have already reported, this study found that neglecting a relationship partner was the single largest category of incidents that caused guilt. Failing to live up to an interpersonal obligation was another large category (indeed, these two categories combined accounted for about a third of the total causes of guilt in this sample). Romantic infidelities and other betrayals also accounted for quite a few of the stories. Thus, transgressions against close relationships predominated.

To be sure, a number of solitary transgressions were reported, and so it would be excessive to claim that other people are always centrally involved in guilt. People reported guilt over neglecting their studies (especially for procrastinating on an assignment), failing to exercise, and overeating (especially breaking a diet). Although there may have been some interpersonal concerns in the background of these incidents, such as the feeling that one is letting one's parents down by not studying, these do seem to indicate that guilt can be felt on a fairly solitary basis. Still, cases of solitary guilt appear to constitute a small minority. Most guilt is interpersonal.

Further light on the interpersonal nature of guilt was shed by the other study in this investigation (Baumeister, Reis, & Delespaul, in press). This study used an experience-sampling methodology: Subjects carried a beeper that went off at random intervals, and they were instructed to stop and record their thoughts, feelings, and activities whenever they were beeped. This study found that people often happened to be alone when they felt guilty—but that the guilt usually referred to interpersonal problems or concerns.

One of the beeper study's analyses looked at the relation between the subjects' thoughts and feelings and their reporting of guilt. It was surprising how little relation there was; evidently, subjects could feel guilty when engaged in almost any activity or thinking about almost any topic. Forty-five large categories of thoughts and activities were constructed, and the frequency of guilt reports in each of them was computed. Only one of these categories departed from the overall mean (using a 1% confidence interval) frequency of guilt: People were especially likely to feel guilty when they were thinking about themselves in relation to other people. In other words, there is almost no relation between what a person is doing or thinking and the likelihood that the person may feel guilty—with one big exception: namely, that people are extra likely to feel guilty when thinking about themselves in relation to others. The fact that this exception stood out from the typical pattern seems very consistent with the hypothesis that guilt is rooted in interpersonal relatedness.

CONCLUDING REMARKS

We have suggested that guilt should be understood as something that happens between people as much as it happens inside them. Instead of studying guilt by examining how people judge their own actions, we propose studying guilt by examining the exchanges within close relationships. Inequities and transgressions can cause guilt, and if the transgressor does not seem to feel guilty enough, the partner may do or say things to stimulate and increase guilt feelings. By manipulating the target's feelings of guilt, the partner seeks and often finds confirmation of the target's continuing investment in the relationship.

The need for an interpersonal understanding of guilt is supported by recent accumulating evidence. Hoffman (1982) has argued that guilt is based in empathic distress, which is an affective response to another person's suffering. Tangney (1992) concluded that all categories of guilt-inducing incidents she examined were interpersonal except one—namely, breaking a diet. We would even question that one exception; dieting, after all, is guided and motivated by interpersonal concerns (such as being attractive to others), and we doubt that people living in extreme solitude would be dieters. Lastly, our own data attest to the importance of the relationship bond for causing guilt. In our work, transgressions that led to guilt were linked to important social bonds, whereas transgressions toward unimportant other people were less likely to cause guilt. In addition, reports of making someone else feel guilty were overwhelmingly presented in the context of close relationships.

Three interpersonal functions of guilt have been suggested. The research we have described provided some support for each of them. The first function is that guilt directly strengthens relationships by stimulating relationship-enhancing patterns of behavior. Guilt makes people learn lessons and change their behavior so as to avoid doing things that will threaten their social attachments, such as hurting, distressing, or upsetting partners in relationships. Guilt also apparently functions as a form of pressure to make people pay positive attention to their partners, which presumably will benefit a relationship. It would be foolish to contend that guilt is invariably effective, but its general function seems to be to make people know not to repeat actions that have hurt, disappointed, or distressed an intimate partner.

The second function of guilt is as an influence technique. People make use of others' capacity for guilt in order to get their way. The apparently high rate of behavior change following guilt confirms that guilt induction can be an effective way of altering a partner's behavior. It is apparent that people sometimes exaggerate their suffering or distress in order to increase a partner's guilt feelings, presumably with the goal of altering that person's future behavior.

The third function of guilt is to redistribute emotional distress within the dyad. We have described evidence that guilt makes the transgressor feel worse and the victim feel better, thus effectively transferring the negative affect from the victim to the transgressor (who was responsible for causing it in the first place). We have also provided some evidence that interpersonal guilt manipulations sometimes bring people into similar emotional states, thereby facilitating communication and enhancing the relationship (cf. Locke & Horowitz, 1990).

Further research is needed to illuminate the interpersonal implications of guilt. A particularly fruitful area may be the negotiation of guilt over long periods of time in close relationships; one may speculate that transgressions and inequities are tracked by both partners, resulting in a kind of guilt accounting. A return to the laboratory study of guilt would also be desirable, once the underlying mechanisms that result in guilt are better understood. More data on metaguilt would also be valuable.

For the present, however, it appears that guilt does serve important functions for strengthening and maintaining close relationships. The undeniable importance of maintaining close relationships in human social life may help explain why our society continues to cultivate people's capacity for feeling guilty. Psychological theory may gain a better understanding of guilt by analyzing the interpersonal context in which guilt is created, negotiated, and resolved.

REFERENCES

Averill, J. (1982). *Anger and aggression: An essay on emotion.* New York: Springer-Verlag.

Baumeister, R. F. (1988a). Masochism as escape from self. *Journal of Sex Research, 25,* 28–59.

Baumeister, R. F. (1988b). Gender differences in masochistic scripts. *Journal of Sex Research, 25,* 478–499.

Baumeister, R. F. (1989). *Masochism and the self.* Hillsdale, NJ: Erlbaum.

Baumeister, R. F., Reis, H. T., & Delespaul, P. (in press). Subjective and experiential correlates of guilt in daily life. *Personality and Social Psychology Bulletin.*

Baumeister, R. F., & Stillwell, A. M. (1992). Autobiographical accounts, situational roles, and motivated biases: When stories don't match up. In J. Harvey, T. Orbuch, & A. Weber (Eds.), *Accounts, attributions, and close relationships* (pp. 52–70). New York: Springer-Verlag.

Baumeister, R. F., Stillwell, A. M., & Heatherton, T. F. (1994). Guilt: An interpersonal approach. *Psychological Bulletin, 115,* 243–267.

Baumeister, R. F., Stillwell, A. M., & Heatherton, T. F. (in press). Personal narratives about guilt: Role in action control and interpersonal relationships. *Basic and Applied Social Psychology.*

Baumeister, R. F., Stillwell, A. M., & Wotman, S. R. (1990). Victim and perpetrator accounts of interpersonal conflict: Autobiographical narratives about anger. *Journal of Personality and Social Psychology, 59,* 994–1005.

Baumeister, R. F., & Tice, D. M. (1990). Anxiety and social exclusion. *Journal of Social and Clinical Psychology, 9,* 165–195

Baumeister, R. F., & Wotman, S. R. (1992). *Breaking hearts: The two sides of unrequited love.* New York: Guilford Press.

Baumeister, R. F., Wotman, S. R., & Stillwell, A. M. (1993). Unrequited love: On heartbreak, anger, guilt, scriptlessness, and humiliation. *Journal of Personality and Social Psychology, 64,* 377–394.

Bowlby, J. (1969). *Attachment and loss: Vol. 1. Attachment.* New York: Basic Books.

Bowlby, J. (1973). *Attachment and loss: Vol. 2. Separation: Anxiety and anger.* New York: Basic Books.

Brooke, R. J. (1985). What is guilt? *Journal of Phenomenological Psychology, 16,* 31–46.

Cialdini, R. B. (1984). *Influence: How and why people agree to things.* New York: Morrow.

Conquest, R. (1986). *The harvest of sorrow: Soviet collectivization and the terror-famine.* New York: Oxford University Press.

Freud, S. (1930). *Civilization and its discontents* (J. Riviere, Trans.). London: Hogarth Press.

Gergen, K. J., & Gergen, M. (1988). Narrative and the self as relationship. In L. Berkowitz (Ed.), *Advances in experimental social psychology* (Vol. 21, pp. 17–56). San Diego: Academic Press.

Harvey, J. H., Flanary, R., & Morgan, M. (1988). Vivid memories of vivid loves gone by. *Journal of Social and Personal Relationships, 3,* 359–373.

Harvey, J. H., Weber, A. L., Galvin, K. S., Huszti, H. C., & Garnick, N. N. (1986). Attribution in the termination of close relationships: A special focus on the account. In R. Gilmour & S. Duck (Eds.), *The emerging field of personal relationships* (pp. 189–201). Hillsdale, NJ: Erlbaum.

Harvey, J. H., Weber, A. L., & Orbuch, T. L. (1990). *Interpersonal accounts: A social psychological perspective.* Oxford: Basil Blackwell.

Hoffman, M. L. (1982). Development of prosocial motivation: Empathy and guilt. In N. Eisenberg (Ed.), *Development of prosocial behavior* (pp. 281–313). New York: Academic Press.

Katz, I., Glass, D. C., & Cohen, S. (1973). Ambivalence, guilt, and the scapegoating of minority group victims. *Journal of Experimental Social Psychology, 9,* 423–436.

Katz, J. (1988). *Seductions of crime: The moral and sensual attractions of doing evil.* New York: Basic Books.

Lerner, M. J., & Matthews, G. (1967). Reactions to suffering of others under conditions of indirect responsibility. *Journal of Personality and Social Psychology, 5,* 319–325.

Lewis, H. B. (1971). *Shame and guilt in neurosis.* New York: International Universities Press.

Lifton, R. J. (1986). *The Nazi doctors: Medical killing and the psychology of genocide.* New York: Basic Books.

Locke, K. D., & Horowitz, L. M. (1990). Satisfaction in interpersonal interactions as a function of similarity in level of dysphoria. *Journal of Personality and Social Psychology, 58,* 823–831.

McAdams, D. P. (1985). *Power, intimacy and the life story: Personological inquiries into identity.* Homewood, IL: Dorsey Press.

McGraw, K. M. (1987). Guilt following transgression: An attribution of responsibility approach. *Journal of Personality and Social Psychology, 53,* 247–256.

Mosher, D. L. (1965). Interaction of fear and guilt in inhibiting unacceptable behavior. *Journal of Consulting Psychology, 29,* 161–167.

Noel, R. C. (1973). Transgression–compliance: A failure to confirm. *Journal of Personality and Social Psychology, 27,* 151–153.

Ross, M., & Holmberg, D. (1990). Recounting the past: Gender differences in the recall of events in the history of a close relationship. In J. M. Olson & M. P. Zanna (Eds.), *The Ontario Symposium: Vol. 6. Self-inference processes* (pp. 135–152). Hillsdale, NJ: Erlbaum.

Shaver, P., Schwartz, J., Kirson, D., & O'Connor, C. (1987). Emotion knowledge: Further exploration of a prototype approach. *Journal of Personality and Social Psychology, 52,* 1061–1086.

Tangney, J. P. (1990). Assessing individual differences in proneness to shame and guilt: Development of the Self-Conscious Affect and Attribution Inventory. *Journal of Personality and Social Psychology, 59,* 102–111.

Tangney, J. P. (1991). Moral affect: The good, the bad, and the ugly. *Journal of Personality and Social Psychology, 61,* 598–607.

Tangney, J. P. (1992). Situational determinants of shame and guilt in young adulthood. *Personality and Social Psychology Bulletin, 18,* 199–206.

Tangney, J. P., Wagner, P. E., Fletcher, C., & Gramzow, R. (1992). Shamed into anger? The relation of shame and guilt to anger and self-reported aggression. *Journal of Personality and Social Psychology, 62,* 669–675.

Vaughan, D. (1986). *Uncoupling*. New York: Oxford University Press.
Wertheim, E. H., & Schwartz, J. C. (1983). Depression, guilt, and self-management of pleasant and unpleasant events. *Journal of Personality and Social Psychology, 45*, 884–889.
Zahn-Waxler, C., & Kochanska, G. (1990). The origins of guilt. In R. A. Thompson (Ed.), *Nebraska Symposium on Motivation: Vol. 36. Socioemotional development* (pp. 182–258). Lincoln: University of Nebraska Press.

11

Differentiating Guilt and Shame and Their Effects on Motivation

JANICE LINDSAY-HARTZ
JOSEPH DE RIVERA
MICHAEL F. MASCOLO

From the perspective of the structural theory of emotions (de Rivera, 1977, 1991), emotions are transformations of an individual's relationship to objects, persons, or events in the world. Any particular emotion can be described in terms of a specific dynamic structure that distinguishes it from other emotions. The structure of any emotion is a gestalt comprised of several interrelated parts. The first part is the "situation," which consists of one's interpretation of the meaning of a given emotional event. Any specific situation is one of many choices that can be made about how to interpret a given event. The situation is the result of a transaction between a person and an event, and is not simply a passive response. The second part of an emotion is the "transformation," which involves a change in one's way of being in the world, including one's experience of one's body, other people, space, and time. Emotions involve not only distinct physiological changes, but also broader transformations in the ways one's body or relation to the world is experienced (e.g., as expanding or shrinking, strengthening or collapsing). Finally, emotions involve an "instruction," or impulse to act in certain ways. These interrelated parts of the emotion always have a particular "function"—to preserve certain core personal values. The function of an emotion may be regarded as adaptive or maladaptive, depending upon the extent to which the person's perception of the situation makes sense and the extent to which the function promotes personal development.

Working from this perspective, we set out to examine, describe, and discriminate experiences of guilt and shame in terms of their different situations, transformations, instructions, and functions. Many theorists have sought to understand shame (or guilt) as a field of emotions, subsuming such emotions as humiliation, embarrassment, and shyness under the "shame-field" umbrella (e.g., Lewis, 1971; Miller, 1985). In contrast, we sought to differentiate shame and guilt from each other and from other similar emotions, such as humiliation, anxiety and depression.

We first report the results of two studies. In the first study, we developed structural descriptions of shame and guilt, using a phenomenological methodology. In the second study, we tested the validity of the resulting descriptions with a different sample of subjects. These subjects matched different parts of the resulting descriptions with their own narrative descriptions of experiences of guilt and shame. In the last section, we discuss the structures of guilt and shame, with a focus on their role in the motivation of psychological and social activity.

STUDY 1: THE STRUCTURES OF GUILT AND SHAME

The purpose of Study 1 was to produce structural descriptions of guilt and shame. We used a phenomenological method called "conceptual encounter" (de Rivera & Kreilkamp, 1981). Using this method, an investigator engages research participants in an encounter in which they compare the investigator's conceptualization of a phenomenon (in this case, guilt and shame) with their own concrete experiences of the phenomenon. During the course of the encounter, the analysis of concrete instances may change the investigator's conceptualization of the phenomenon. On the other hand, a sound conceptualization may change how a participant experiences concrete instances of the phenomenon. Thus, the emotion descriptions that are developed through this method are the results of an interactive process occurring between investigators and participants.

Research participants included 19 persons (10 males and 9 females) between the ages of 18 and 65. The conceptual encounter method involved three phases each for guilt and shame. In the first phase, in an individual interview, each participant described a specific personal experience of guilt and an experience of shame. The investigator (Lindsay-Hartz) asked the participant to be sure to describe an experience of guilt (or shame), as opposed to an experience of humiliation, embarrassment, depression, or other similar emotions. In the second phase, after encouraging each participant to describe all he or she could remember about the experience, the investigator then probed for more details, using a series of 20 questions designed to explore all aspects of the experience. These questions included such items as queries about what the person felt like doing and queries about how the person's experience of self and others was changed. (See Lindsay-Hartz, 1980, for the script of the 20 questions used.)

In the final encounter phase of each interview, possible structural descriptions of guilt and shame were tested, revised, and validated. The investigator (Lindsay-Hartz) gave participants possible descriptions of the various aspects of guilt and shame ("situations," "transformations," "instructions," and "functions"), and asked them whether the descriptions captured the essential aspects of their guilt or shame experiences. The descriptions came from three sources: (1) models of guilt and shame developed by other theorists (e.g., Freud, 1923/1961; Lewis, 1971; Lynd, 1958; Piers & Singer, 1953); (2) ideas developed from the second phase of the interview with the research participants; and (3) the results of analyses of interviews of other participants. Because of the interactive nature of the conceptual encounter process, participants were presented with different hypothetical descriptions as the various descriptions were tested and revised throughout the course of the study.

The investigator asked the participants questions such as these: "Does the description fit? Why? Why not? Does the description reveal anything new about the experience? Can you suggest any revisions of the descriptions?" Within a given interview, once a given description was seen as appropriate, it was tested further. The investigator asked the participant whether the description fit any other experiences of shame or guilt. Most importantly, the investigator challenged the participant to try to think of experiences of guilt or shame that did not fit the description in question.

We analyzed qualitatively all collected examples of guilt and shame, in order to develop descriptions of the characteristics of guilt and of shame. In contrast to an attempt to describe a "family resemblance," our goal was to develop abstract descriptions of guilt and shame that would describe *each and every example* of guilt and of shame. We neither expected nor found sets of explicit, concrete features that were common to each of the descriptions provided by subjects. Rather, we attempted to create abstract descriptions that would convey common *meanings* implicit in the various interviews.

We used a variety of procedures in our attempt to create such descriptions. First, we looked for phrases and words present in each of the examples that might provide clues to the structure of the emotion. For example, in the process of analyzing the examples of guilt, we discovered that the words "I could . . ." or "I could have . . ." were repeated several times by every participant and were not used to describe experiences of shame. In one description of guilt, a young woman said, "I could have done something—maybe I could have forced her to go to the hospital earlier and she wouldn't have died." The words "I could . . . ," no matter what the content that followed, suggested something characteristic of guilt: Participants felt that they could have prevented something bad from happening, convinced that they had some control. In our analyses, we used such key phrases and words to describe and make explicit abstract characteristics of guilt and shame that we regarded as implicit in the concrete examples collected. The various other methods of qualitative analysis used are detailed elsewhere (Lindsay-Hartz, 1980).

The process of involving the research participants in the qualitative analyses provided rebuffs of some ideas, and confirmation and development of other ideas. For example, influenced by psychodynamic theorists (Piers & Singer, 1953; Lewis, 1971), we first hypothesized that shame involved a failure to be who one wants to be or to achieve some ego ideal, and we thought that participants were describing such a phenomenon. To our surprise, most of the participants rejected this formulation. Rather, when ashamed, participants talked about being who they did *not* want to be. That is, they experienced themselves as embodying an anti-ideal, rather than simply not being who they wanted to be. The participants said things like "I am fat and ugly," not "I failed to be pretty"; or "I am bad and evil," not "I am not as good as I want to be." This difference in emphasis is not simply semantic. Participants insisted that the distinction was important; in clinical practice, moreover, Lindsay-Hartz (1987, 1992) has found this distinction to be important to patients in therapy, as it serves to differentiate feelings of shame from feelings of inferiority.

The qualitative analyses culminated in descriptions of each structural part of guilt and shame—the situation, transformation, instruction, and function—and a final summary statement. Although space does not permit our listing the entire text of the descriptions of the four parts of guilt and of shame, the summary statements are presented in Tables 11.1 and 11.2. (See Lindsay-Hartz, 1980, 1984, for the complete text of each description and for further illustration.)

Quotes from a 20-year old female research participant illustrate the components of the experience of guilt, as summarized in Table 11.1.

Situation

I felt guilty when my mother died. . . . I felt like it was all my fault. Like if I would have paid more attention to her and helped her, that she wouldn't be dead right now. . . . She was an alcoholic. And I knew it, and instead of helping her and trying to understand her, I'd fight with her. [She died] of a stroke. I also blame that on myself because we had an argument before she went to the hospital. . . . [After she died] I started thinking over and over of all the things I could have done to keep her from doing what she did. . . . At one point after she died, I thought I hated her, like, good riddance. . . . I was mad because she died before my graduation. . . . I used to fight with her every day because I didn't want to do [physical therapy for her cerebral palsy]. She used to take that as an excuse sometimes, to drink. . . . I didn't sit down and try to talk to her. . . . I should have been more open. . . . I didn't push my own problems aside . . . so I could help her. It's the heart keeps on telling me it's wrong. [There were] things I could have done. Things I did that didn't work out. I should have tried harder.

Transformation

I felt lost. . . . It's like a split personality. Like an angel and a devil. . . . I feel like a monster, and that I'm evil. That I'm an evil person, or there's

TABLE 11.1. Summary Description of Guilt

Emotion component	Content
Situation	We experience this emotion when *there is a violation of the moral order for which we take responsibility with our conviction that we could and should have done otherwise and that there then would have been no violation.* A violation of the moral order involves something bad and wrong happening or involves our doing what we should not or not doing what we should. The moral order, consisting in part of particular moral values, is implicitly upheld by the members of a community to which we belong, and we must uphold such values to belong to the community. Since we are responsible for the violation of the moral order . . .
Transformation	. . . we find ourselves *on the boundary* of our community. On the boundary, we are neither here nor there. It is as if we were a bad person; we lose certain of our rights and feel out of place and alone.
Function	Wanting *to uphold the moral order and be reconciled* with the community and be *forgiven,* and *believing that we have some control* over events . . .
Instruction	. . . we attempt *to set things right* and in some way repair the breach in the moral order.

TABLE 11.2. Summary Description of Shame

Emotion component	Content
Situation	We experience this emotion when, upon viewing ourselves *through the eyes of another, we realize that we are in fact who we do not want to be and that we cannot now be otherwise.* We usually try to avoid being who we do not want to be. Yet, we have somehow not avoided this, often because we have been unaware of the implications of our acts or have not understood something about ourselves that is now revealed to us.
Transformation	Being who we do not want to be, we *shrink* in relation to our previous image of ourselves and we are *exposed* before the other. As we shrink, a single characteristic or action seems to define the whole of who we are; we are worthless; and our view of the world may shrink to one small detail.
Function	Upholding our *ideals about who we want to be* and *maintaining our commitment to a social determination of who we are* . . .
Instruction	. . . we wish *to hide* in order *to get out* of the interpersonal realm and escape our painful exposure before the other.

something evil in me. . . . I feel that I'm evil, but yet I know I'm not evil. . . . Like you're a human being, but you're missing something. . . . I don't have the right to be happy when I feel guilty. I could have done anything [to help my mother] if I really wanted to. And that's the question, why I didn't want to . . . there's something else . . . I don't think it's [my hating her and being angry] an answer. I'm looking for something. That doesn't satisfy me. . . . I figure there's a reason, has to be a reason for everything.

Function
I think it's important if you care about people to at least give a real big effort to do it. . . . I feel like a person should feel those things. He should help. He should try to understand. If he wants to be a complete human being, if he wants people to care for him, he has to care for other people. . . . [If you don't], you're missing understanding, love, and relationship. I figure if I don't do those things, people won't like me, and I'll be a bad person. . . . I know I did what I thought had to be done, what should be done [to help my mother.] . . . I felt like I tried and it didn't work. I also felt like I didn't try. That I tried, but not hard enough . . . all the things I could have done.

Instruction
I just wanted to die when I felt guilty. . . . [If I'm] feeling guilty, I eat, I stuff my face. . . . I figure that's one sense of punishment that I'm giving myself. . . . I feel like you have to help people, you have to care for people, even if they don't care for you back.

In this example, the violation of the moral order (the situation) consisted of the wrongness of the participant's mother's untimely death and of her sense that she participated in her mother's death by hating her and by not doing all that she could have done to support her life. She took responsibility ("I felt like it was all my fault"), with the conviction that there were "things I could have done" to prevent her from dying. In terms of the transformation that accompanies guilt, we can see that the participant experienced a split in her identity ("It's like a split personality") and the loss of the "right to be happy." Furthermore, adding to her confused identity, the motive concerning why she acted as she did remained in part a mystery. The guilt functioned to maintain the participant's belief that she had some control over events ("I tried, but not hard enough . . . all the things I could have done"). Her guilt also functioned to uphold her moral values (to "care about people"). Finally, her guilt motivated her to set things right and balance out the moral order. This participant looked to accomplish this act by punishing herself, following an "eye for an eye" philosophy. She also felt motivated to make reparations ("you have to help people, you have to care for people") elsewhere in the world, as a way of setting right the moral order.

Table 11.2 gives the summary description for shame. Quotes from a 25-year-old female participant illustrate the components of shame experiences. This woman felt ashamed when she called her employer and told her that she was breaking her promise to take a job at the employer's nursing home.

Situation

Offering something [to take the job] . . . and then taking it back . . . it makes you worth nothing . . . like a liar, or really a fake. It's a feeling of being a fake, a phony. It [to be a humanitarian] was something that I may have thought I could do at one time. All of a sudden I realized that I couldn't. . . . Shame has something to do with . . . something you can't control. Even if it's [confronting something about yourself] in front of the person, of the other one, that person, you're ashamed in front of yourself also. It's like her presence brought about the real confrontation of myself with myself.

Transformation

Shame is just total. . . . [It] makes you like a worthless kind of person, like a liar, really a fake. It's a feeling of being a fake, a phony. . . . Here I am— bad. . . . I was, like, ashamed of my *being*. . . . It's like I'm being looked at, I'm being judged or examined in some way. . . . Just by your mere existence is causing you shame. . . . It was a total feeling of terribleness. . . . Time . . . seemed like an eternity, but it was like frozen. . . . Me and the phone were in the middle of this big empty space . . . as if I were in the middle of an arena and being looked at. And here I am this tiny speck all alone . . . small and inadequate . . .

Function

When I realized how it was making me feel [ashamed], then all of a sudden this whole idea of humanitarian came to my head, and—gee, it would be such a great thing to do and you don't want to do it [take the job at the nursing home]. . . . I had this vision of myself as some kind of humanitarian . . . doing good stuff for people. . . . I want to be a good person. . . . It's like her [her employer's] presence brought about the real confrontation of myself with myself. . . . It's like here this woman faces this every day. She's the kind of woman I should be. [To not be ashamed, I'd have to not] care what other people think.

Instruction

Shame is, like, give me a hole to crawl into. Let me just cover myself up and nobody can see me. . . . Shame is just total—you want to disappear. . . . [I wanted to] get out of the room so fast . . . to get out of it. I wanted a hole to open up in the ground and just suck me and cover me up. . . . I wished I wasn't born. . . . In person—phew!—I never would have been able to look into her eyes. Like on the phone, I still had the feeling, like if we were together, I would have wanted to just leave, get out of the room so fast. . . . I can't put it a better way than to say, like if there could only be a hole in the ground I could sink into and nobody would see me . . . the actual feeling is hiding everything . . . hiding every inch of myself. You want to hide yourself. You want to be where you cannot be seen. There is no way out. Just by your mere existence is causing you shame. There's nothing you can do except *get out* of the situation when you're being looked at.

Although guilt and shame are both self-evaluative emotions, they are quite different emotional experiences. To produce further evidence that the abstract descriptions in Tables 11.1 and 11.2 indeed capture the differences between guilt and shame, and to demonstrate that these descriptions differentiate guilt and shame from related emotions, we performed an additional study.

STUDY 2: TESTING THE STRUCTURAL DESCRIPTIONS OF GUILT AND SHAME

Although the abstract descriptions developed during Study 1 appear to differentiate the essential features of guilt and shame, it might be argued that the research participants were influenced by the investigator's beliefs and suggestions throughout the course of the study. In Study 2, we assessed the validity of the structural descriptions of guilt and shame, using a more objective methodology.

The purpose of Study 2 was to determine whether subjects could match the statements produced in Study 1 with their own experiences of guilt and shame, in a manner that discriminated between their guilt and shame experiences. We presented subjects with unlabeled statements describing different parts of the experiences of guilt and shame. Because guilt and shame are conceptually often confused or merged with anxiety and depression (see, e.g., Beck, 1967; Gottschalk, 1971), we gave the subjects unlabeled statements describing these emotions as well. We asked the subjects to select from all these statements the descriptive statements that best fit their own personal experiences of guilt and shame. We predicted that subjects would match the guilt descriptions with their guilt experiences and the shame descriptions with their shame experiences. We also predicted that subjects would not match the descriptions of anxiety and depression with their experiences of guilt and shame. Such results would demonstrate that the guilt and shame descriptions differentiate guilt and shame not only from each other, but also from related emotions.

In research interviews, we have found that persons presented with a structural description of an emotion often report seeing something new in their experiences that they did not see before. A reasonable explanation of this phenomenon is that the structural description captures something central or important about the experience in question. From this view, whether or not a person gains insight into his or her experience after being presented with an emotion description might be taken as an index of the validity or utility of the description in question. Thus, a second purpose of Study 2 was to determine whether our guilt and shame descriptions were valid in the sense that they could lead subjects to have insights into the nature of their experiences. We predicted that subjects would report more insight about their guilt and shame experiences after selecting our target guilt and shame statements than after selecting alternative statements.

We formulated a total of 20 statements describing characteristics of four different emotions—guilt, shame, anxiety, and depression. For each emotion, we included a statement describing (1) the situation, or central event, of the emotion; (2) the transformation, or change in experience of self, others, and surroundings; (3) the instruction, or the motivation to act in a certain way; and (4) the function of the emotion, or the values and goals of the person highlighted or created by the emotion. We also included a summary statement that contained an integrated description of the four components. The statements used for guilt and shame were developed in Study 1 (see the "Content" column of Tables 11.1 and 11.2 for the summary

TABLE 11.3. Summary Descriptions of Depression and Anxiety

Emotion component	Content
Depression	
Situation	We experience this emotion when *we are in a situation which conflicts with the assertion of our values. If we asserted our values, something important to us would be destroyed.* These values, which dictate either what we feel ought to be or how we want things to be, require us to take certain actions. However, the conflict between the situation and the assertion of our values is overwhelming.
Transformation	Consequently, we *lose our energy* and *withdraw* from the world.
Function	Wanting both *to preserve our values* and *protect* things important to us from being destroyed . . .
Instruction	. . . we convince ourselves that we *cannot* act and must give up trying to act.
Anxiety	
Situation	We experience this emotion when *we are beginning to face something that is unknown, and there is an anticipated risk. We may or may not become who we must become.* The person who we must become in facing the unknown situation relates to the vital core of our identity, and is based on our own expectations and the expectations of the community to which we want to belong.
Transformation	Facing the unknown situation, we find ourselves *impaired.* We are critical of ourselves, experience bodily impairment, and find it difficult to think, perceive, or act.
Function	Finding ourselves impaired and wanting *to take responsibility* and *to belong* to a community . . .
Instruction	. . . we desire *to hold on* to where we are at. We may seek things that are familiar, secure and comfortable and hold on to our certain membership in other communities.

Note. These statements are loosely based on descriptions by de Rivera (1977, 1991), Goodman (1981), and Kane (1976).

statements). The summary statements for anxiety and depression were loosely based on descriptions by de Rivera (1977, 1991), Goodman (1981), and Kane (1976), and appear in the "Content" column of Table 11.3 (the "emotion component" labels have been added here to provide clarity).

The situation, transformation, instruction, and function statements consisted of expanded descriptions of each of the four parts described in the summary statements and can be found in Lindsay-Hartz (1980). As examples of these statements, we present the instruction statements for guilt and shame:

Instruction (Guilt)
When we experience this emotion, we experience a desire *to set things right.* We might attempt to set things right in a number of ways. First, setting things right can involve confessing the wrong we have done, acknowledging that things have to be set right, and making reparations (or atoning) for what we have done wrong. Making reparations may involve repairing the actual wrong; or, if this cannot be done, making reparations may involve trying to make amendments for our wrong action in other ways and/or vowing never to do such a thing again. Second, although there are many wrongs which we cannot undo, we may *wish* to undo them or try magically to undo them by undoing other things which are reversible. Third, we may attempt to set things right by setting things right elsewhere in our world. For example, we may order the objects in our house, or in our thoughts we may order words or numbers. Fourth, we may find ourselves following an "eye for an eye, a tooth for a tooth" philosophy. Since we are responsible for things' not being right, we will be punished; and we may fear this punishment. In order to gain control over the punishment, some persons often punish themselves or seek out punishment. (p. 227)

Instruction (Shame)
When we experience this emotion, we experience a desire *to hide,* in order *to get out* of the interpersonal realm in which we find ourselves. Typically, we wish to "sink into the ground." We desire to bury ourselves and to be enclosed, covered, hidden, and alone. "Sinking into the ground" is a way to cut off our contact with the world, to enter a more secure space, and to escape the interpersonal realm and socially defined reality. If only we could sink into the ground, we would be all alone; and then the other's view of us and our social identity would be meaningless. (p. 228)

Thirteen persons (eight females and five males) between the ages of 18 and 36 participated. Subjects volunteered in response to announcements made in their undergraduate psychology class or to leaflets distributed in a middle-class residential neighborhood. Each subject participated in an individual interview on shame and an individual interview on guilt. In the first part of these interviews, the interviewer elicited a detailed description of a guilt (or shame) experience, and asked a series of questions designed to inquire about the meaning of the central event of the subject's experience and to gather information about all aspects of the experience. (See Lindsay-Hartz, 1980, for the complete schedule of questions.)

The next phase provided the data of immediate interest and was designed to test the validity of the abstract descriptions of guilt and shame produced in Study 1. Within each individual guilt and shame interview, the interviewer gave each subject four sets of emotion component statements (i.e., situations, transformations, functions, and instructions). Each set of emotion components contained a separate description of guilt, shame, depression, and anxiety, respectively. All statements and statement sets were unlabeled. That is, no emotion label (e.g., "guilt") or component label (e.g., "situation") was included. The order of presentation was random both within and between sets. Within each individual guilt or shame interview, for each set of statements, the subject was instructed (1) to select the statement that best described his or her guilt or shame experience; (2) to go through each selected statement and indicate what parts of his or her experience fit the description; and (3) to indicate whether any parts of the statement selected led the subject to see something new about his or her experience, or highlighted something that he or she had not thought about before. Insight was coded as present if a subject responded "yes" to this final question. The interviewer asked each subject to explain what insight he or she had gained.

The interviewer then repeated the interview for the second emotion, following the procedure described above. During the second interview, the interviewer told the subjects that they could select the same statements as they selected for the first emotion if they thought they were appropriate.

After both individual interviews were completed, the interviewer gave each subject the four summary statements for guilt, shame, anxiety, and depression, and asked each subject to select the one statement that was the best overall description of his or her guilt experience and the one statement that was the best overall description of his or her shame experience. Again, the subjects were allowed to choose the same statement twice if they so desired. As before, the interviewer asked the subjects to indicate which parts of their experiences fit the selected description and which parts of the selected description did not fit their experiences, and to recount any insight gained.

We expected that the subjects would match the guilt statements with their guilt experiences and the shame statements with their shame experiences. Table 11.4 shows the actual matches made. About half of the matches were made as expected, which was greater than the one out of four that would be expected by chance. The number of matches for the situation, instruction, and summary statements were statistically significant for both guilt and shame ($p < .05$, binomial test, one-tailed). For the transformation statements, the number of matches approached significance for shame ($p = .08$), but not for guilt. The matches with the function statements did not approach significance for either shame or guilt.

We hypothesized not only that the subjects would match their experiences with the predicted statements, but also that they would more often gain insight into their experiences when they made the expected matches

TABLE 11.4. Matches between Emotion Statements and
Emotion Experiences

Statement type	Guilt experiences		Shame experiences	
	Matches	Percentage reporting insight	Matches	Percentage reporting insight
Situations				
Guilt	11 (.85)***	45%	3 (.23)	00%
Shame	1 (.08)	00%	8 (.62)**	63%
Depression	1 (.08)	00%	1 (.08)	100%
Anxiety	0 (.00)	00%	1 (.08)	00%
Transformations				
Guilt	3 (.23)	33%	1 (.08)	00%
Shame	2 (.15)	00%	6 (.46)	67%
Depression	5 (.38)	40%	3 (.23)	00%
Anxiety	3 (.23)	00%	3 (.23)	33%
Instructions				
Guilt	7 (.46)*	86%	5 (.38)	00%
Shame	3 (.23)	33%	7 (.54)*	43%
Depression	0 (.00)	00%	0 (.00)	00%
Anxiety	3 (.23)	67%	1 (.08)	00%
Functions				
Guilt	4 (.31)	100%	4 (.31)	00%
Shame	1 (.08)	00%	4 (.31)	50%
Depression	5 (.38)	00%	3 (.23)	00%
Anxiety	3 (.23)	33%	2 (.15)	00%
Summaries				
Guilt	8 (.62)**	13%	3 (.23)	00%
Shame	0 (.00)	00%	8 (.62)**	38%
Depression	4 (.31)	25%	1 (.08)	00%
Anxiety	1 (.08)	00%	1 (.08)	00%

Note. We compared the number of expected matches to the number of unexpected matches, using the binomial test (Siegel, 1956). For the "Matches"
columns, the listed numbers are frequencies; the numbers in parentheses are
proportions.
*$p < .05$. **$p < .01$. ***$p < .001$.

than when they made unexpected matches. As a test of this latter hypothesis,
we calculated the percentage of subjects who reported insight when they
made the expected matches, and compared this percentage with the
percentage of subjects who reported insight when they made the unexpected
matches. As hypothesized, subjects reported insight 52% of the time after
matching their experiences to predicted emotion statements ($n = 34$ reports
of insight), but only 14% of the time after matching their experiences to
unpredicted statements ($n = 9$; $\chi^2 = 34.37$, $p < .01$).

We then looked at the percentage of subjects reporting insight for each
set of statements (see Table 11.4). For each set of statements (e.g., the

situation statements), we compared the percentage of subjects reporting insight when an expected match was made with the percentage reporting insight when an unexpected match was made. For 23 of the 26 possible comparisons, we found that a greater percentage of subjects reported insight with the expected than with the unexpected matches ($p < .001$, binomial test, two-tailed). Thus, the guilt and shame statements were more likely to provide subjects with insight into their respective guilt and shame experiences than were alternative statements describing other emotions.

These patterns of insight reports suggest that the ability of an emotion statement to generate insight into a subject's guilt or shame experience may provide information about the validity of that emotion statement, above and beyond that provided by an analysis of the proportion of predicted versus unpredicted matches alone. For example, although almost as many subjects matched the guilt instruction statement with guilt experiences (7) as with shame experiences (5), no subject who matched the guilt instruction statement to a shame experience reported insight. In contrast, six of the seven subjects (86%) who matched the guilt instruction statement with their guilt experiences reported insight.

Moreover, the insights that subjects gained were sometimes very powerful, as in the following instance. A young male professional described feeling guilty because he was often late for work. After matching his experience with the guilt situation statement, he suddenly recalled a core experience of guilt. When he was 8 years old, his dying and delirious father started choking him. He felt enraged and wished his father would die so that he could escape. He was rescued by an uncle, and his father then did die. He had felt guilty for wishing his father dead, right at the time his father did die. When he later matched the guilt function statement with his "late for work" guilt experience, he stated that it gave him insight about "forgiveness." He said, "I didn't really know about being forgiven. I repressed it." He became aware that seeking forgiveness was an important part of his experience of guilt.

When asked whether the value placed on being forgiven applied also to his guilt experience with his father, he said, "I also forgave my father." Then he paused and in a noticeably lighter, relieved, but excited tone said, "Would he forgive me? I never thought of that! I think that he would. . . . I know he would. That's exactly what—I mean, all what he was up to was just to get close to me [before he got sick]." His new insight that he did long for his father's forgiveness, and his conviction that his father would forgive him, came with the force of an organizing "aha" experience.

When this subject returned a few days later for the second interview on shame, he spontaneously noted that he had gotten much out of the guilt interview and had felt quite relieved and energized afterwards. Since the interview, he had not been late for work once and no longer felt guilty about such past incidents.

In this example, we can see that this subject's insights about forgiveness were particularly helpful. After obtaining this insight, he reported that his guilt was relieved and that he no longer needed to punish himself by being late for work. Nor did he have to cover over his past guilt over his father's death with guilt that he created in the present by being late to work. Prior to reading the guilt function statement, he had not been in touch with his intense longing for his father's forgiveness; this longing emerged as he read and thought about the function statement.

Overall, these results suggest that of all the statements tested in Study 2, the situation, instruction, and summary statements provided the best descriptions of subjects' shame and guilt experiences. Although the number of subjects who matched the shame transformation statement with their shame experiences approached significance, subjects did not regard the guilt transformation statement or the guilt and shame function statements as adequate descriptions of their guilt and shame experiences.

We now turn to a discussion of the results that were inconsistent with our hypotheses. We first note that although the number of expected matches with the guilt and shame instruction statements were statistically significant, there were a number of "crossover" matches—that is, guilt instruction statements matched with shame examples, and shame instruction statements matched with guilt examples. We examined the comments made by the subjects when they made these "crossover" matches. We found that the subjects who selected the guilt instruction statement to describe their shame experiences all described a desire to hide (the shame instruction) when they described their experiences of shame. However, they were attracted to the idea of "setting things right" (a part of the guilt instruction statement) as a way of resolving their experiences of shame. Those subjects who selected the shame instruction statement to describe their experiences of guilt all spontaneously noted during their interviews that they felt a bit of shame mixed in with their experiences of guilt. Thus, the presence of "crossover" matches does not appear to provide a serious challenge to the validity of the guilt and shame instruction statements.

We also examined the comments made by the subjects when they made their matches with the transformation and function statements, to try to learn why these statements were not selected as the best descriptions of shame and guilt. For the guilt transformation statement, the subjects' comments indicated that our statement did not succeed in communicating our ideas. Although subjects generally indicated that parts of the guilt transformation statement seemed appropriate, including "feeling lost and alone," "feeling as if we are bad," and "running around in circles," many subjects noted that they could not relate the metaphor of "being on the boundary" to their experiences of guilt. Thus, based on the comments of subjects and on an examination of the examples of guilt collected in the first and second studies, we revised the description of the transformation of guilt to include the following:

When we are experiencing this emotion, our way of being in the world involves a dynamic tension. We feel like a bad person, yet know that while we did a bad thing, we are not really bad. We feel out of place and feel lost and alone, unconnected with other things or persons. We feel unsettled and not at peace. We may become stuck repeatedly thinking about our past actions or past events, unable to leave such thoughts behind, yet unable to come to terms with them in the present. In terms of our past actions, our motivations are clouded. We may not be entirely certain why we did a bad thing or what we actually did that was wrong.

We shall need to conduct future studies to test the appropriateness of this revised description of the transformation of guilt.

For the shame transformation statement, some of the subjects' comments indicated that feeling "exposed" may not be essential to experiences of shame. Most of the subjects who did not select the shame transformation statement nevertheless spontaneously mentioned that they felt "small" when feeling ashamed. Thus, although the number of matches with the shame transformation statement was not significantly greater than matches with alternative transformation statements, one might argue that the major portion of the transformation statement—the experience of shrinking and feeling small and worthless—is an appropriate description of experiences of shame.

As indicated, subjects did not regard the guilt and shame function statements as suitable descriptions of their guilt and shame experiences. Many of the subjects commented that *none* of the function statements seemed applicable to their experiences. They had difficulty understanding these descriptions and relating them to their experiences. Nevertheless, subjects reported insight more frequently when they matched their experiences to predicted rather than unpredicted function statements. In addition, when subjects selected a summary statement as expected, they often commented that the function part of the summary was an accurate description of their experiences. Perhaps people have difficulty getting enough distance from the values and goals described by the function statements to see the relations between these rather abstract concepts and a particular emotional experience. It is also possible that a description of the function of an emotion becomes clear or meaningful only in the context of a broader description of the emotion. Alternatively, it is possible that the function of any given emotion is not as readily specified in one's experiences as are other components. Understanding the function may require inference and further reflection. In this case, we may need to devise a different kind of validity test, perhaps one that uses trained judges. Future research may contribute to our understanding of the functional aspects of guilt and shame.

IMPLICATIONS FOR MOTIVATION

Analysis of each aspect of guilt and shame (the situation, transformation, instruction, and function) reveals something different about these emotions and the ways in which they affect our lives. A discussion of all these aspects and their interrelationships is beyond the scope of this chapter. We focus here on the instructions of guilt and shame and their direct effects on motivation, the complicated interplay between the components of the situations and the motivation of moral and prosocial behavior, and the adaptiveness and maladaptiveness of guilt and shame as related to their functions. Finally, we explore the ways in which guilt and shame cloud or clarify our motives.

The psychological situation of guilt involves a violation of the moral order, for which we take responsibility. The primary motivational instruction of guilt is the felt desire somehow to "set things right," to restore the balance in the moral order. Various outcomes are possible, depending upon the opportunities afforded by the circumstances. If the circumstances permit confession, reparation, or a request for forgiveness, then the guilt may be ended. If such actions are not feasible, the person may seek magically to undo the wrong, to inquire repeatedly how he or she could have done something that would have prevented the wrong, to make up for the wrong by "right" action elsewhere in the world, or to punish the self.

Self-punishment, one manifestation of the instruction of guilt, often seems to carry out an "eye for an eye" philosophy. Some of our research participants reasoned that they could balance out the wrong for which they felt responsible by punishing themselves. Other participants described trying to set things right by cleaning obsessively ("cleaning the floor with a toothbrush") and trying to order objects in their environment when they felt helpless to set right the actual moral situation. The particular way in which an individual is motivated to "set things right" may depend in part on that individual's level of social and moral development. For example, Zahn-Waxler and her colleagues (Zahn-Waxler & Kochanska, 1990; Zahn-Waxler, Radke-Yarrow, Wagner, & Chapman, 1992; Zahn-Waxler, Radke-Yarrow, & King, 1979) have reported that children exhibit reparative and self-punitive behaviors after causing distress in others as early as the second year of life. A more advanced level of development may perhaps lead to spontaneous confessions or to symbolic reparation when specific reparation is impossible.

If an experience of guilt is not resolved, it may persist as an unresolved tension. Unresolved guilt may lead to continual attempts to restore the moral balance by "being good," punishing the self (as in Freud, 1923/1961), giving up rights, performing actions that appear to be symbolic substitutes for making reparations, undoing a wrong, or making order out of disorder. Unresolved guilt can also lead a person to "choose" to feel guilty in future situations that do not really warrant guilt, or even to create circumstances to match a sense of unresolved guilt (as described by Freud, 1916/1957). We can speculate that this phenomenon would contribute to a person's being very guilt-prone or susceptible to being "guilt-tripped." Additional research is needed to explore this process further.

Many might suggest that guilt motivates moral behavior primarily through guilt avoidance—the tendency to act morally in order to avoid the feelings of guilt that one knows would result if one had failed to act as such. Although people certainly do resist (or attempt to resist) temptations because they do not want to feel guilty, we suggest that there is a far richer and more complex interplay between the experience of guilt and the motivation of moral and prosocial behavior. Several conditions increase the likelihood that a person will perceive his or her situation as a moral violation and will be motivated to correct a wrongdoing either before, during, or after its occurrence. These conditions include (1) the tendency to take responsibility for preventing bad things from happening; (2) the conviction that one has some control over such bad things; (3) the propensity to empathize with others; and (4) the desire to honor personal and moral commitments. These components do not motivate moral behavior simply through guilt avoidance, but rather operate as central aspects of a person's social or moral disposition relative to others. They are often directly implicated in the situational perception of guilt and in the motivation of moral and prosocial behavior. We now take a closer look at the interplay between these components and the production of guilt and moral behavior.

First, the motivation to make reparations has its origins in the acceptance of responsibility for a moral violation. The mere existence of a moral violation is not a sufficient condition for guilt; to feel guilty, we must take responsibility for the violation, with the conviction that we could have done something to prevent it. In addition, it does not matter whether we are objectively responsible for the violation; only a subjective sense of responsibility is required. For example, perhaps the earliest guilt-like reactions occur when toddlers misattribute responsibility to themselves for acts that they did not perform (Hoffman, 1983). Zahn-Waxler et al. (1979) reported that upon seeing their mothers cry, 2-year-olds sometimes made apologetic statements such as "Did I make you sad?" or "Sorry, I be nice." Similarly, but at a more advanced level of development, survivors of traumas often feel guilty and take responsibility for an awful event with the conviction that they could have done something to prevent the trauma, no matter how irrational the conviction. For example, one of our research participants, a police sergeant, felt guilty when he simply watched two of his men standing next to him get shot by a sniper no one knew was there. He said:

> I was the one making decisions here [to lead his men down the street]. . . . It was my responsibility. . . . He got hit and I didn't. . . . I brought him to that door. . . . Maybe if I was slower or faster . . . if I had been on the right side instead of the left side. . . . Did I do something wrong? Was there any other way I could have handled it? . . . I was responsible. . . . Maybe we could have hit the door a second earlier.

The fact that guilt is not an automatic response, but only occurs when a person takes responsibility for what ought not to have happened, leads to an interesting paradox. On the one hand, people who are quite guilty in an objective sense—sociopathic criminals, or bureaucrats like Adolf Eichmann— often do not experience any guilt. They cannot, because they do not accept responsibility for the evil caused by their behavior or do not view what they have done as wrong. On the other hand, saints—whose lives are filled with loving acts—often appear to experience an immense amount of guilt, perhaps because their identification with humankind leads them to accept responsibility for all human evil (see Houselander, 1951). Most people fall somewhere between these extremes, and Fingarette (1967) has convincingly argued that people choose to accept varying degrees of responsibility for their fellow humans as their own humanity develops. The acceptance of responsibility means that one must think that an injustice or wrong could have been prevented if one had acted differently.

There seem to be many opportunities for persons to make such judgments. Montada and Schneider (1989) have suggested that "existential guilt" (the acceptance of responsibility for social ills because of one's own unjustified relative privileges) may motivate much prosocial behavior. In fact, their data suggest that existential guilt is a far better predictor of prosocial political behavior than is sympathy. Similarly, Chapman, Zahn-Waxler, Cooperman, and Iannotti (1987) showed that children's ability to experience guilt is a better predictor of personal helping behavior than is empathy. Note that this is not to say that guilt is the motivation for helping behavior. Rather, the acceptance of responsibility is a better predictor than empathy, and this acceptance also leads to feelings of guilt when a person sees the self as responsible for the wrongness of some situation. Thus, we would predict that the more a person has a tendency to take responsibility for things, the more that person will encounter opportunities to experience guilt and the accompanying impulse to set things right. Likewise, the more a person experiences guilt, the more likely the person will be to develop a tendency to take responsibility for things.

A second component of the situation of guilt is the conviction that one has some control over bad events. Because taking responsibility involves the conviction that a person could have done something to prevent the violation of the moral order, we would expect that people who are more likely to be convinced that they have or had control would have more opportunity to take responsibility, and thus to experience guilt and the accompanying motivation to set things right. Hence, we would predict that people with a higher internal locus of control, as opposed to an external locus of control, will be more likely to experience guilt. We also would predict that guilty experiences (and guilt-inducing child-rearing techniques) will reinforce and strengthen the development of an internal locus of control, as well as the attribution of having some control and having a sense of responsibility for bad events. We hope that future research will explore these predicted relations.

The third component, an ability to empathize with others, is important in one's experience of another as harmed or in pain. Experiencing guilt, which involves experiencing something as a violation of the moral order, requires some ability to notice the effects of events on others. We would expect that people who show more ability to empathize will encounter more opportunities to experience guilt than will people with more limited empathic abilities. Hoffman (1982) has suggested that guilt over harming others has its origins in empathic reactions to the distress of others, which occur early in infancy. Hoffman suggests that empathic concern becomes transformed into guilt in the second year of life, when children become aware that their actions lead to pain in others.

Several findings support this assertion. First, there are similarities in the developmental course of empathic concern and guilt-like reactions. Zahn-Waxler and her colleagues (Zahn-Waxler et al., 1979, 1992) reported that in naturalistic situations where toddlers were both witnesses and causes of the distress of others, prosocial and reparative responses increased in frequency during the second year of life. Second, young children's reparations are often accompanied by expressions of concern for others. For example, after an 18-month-old accidentally hit a babysitter, the child said, "Sorry, Sally," patted her forehead, and kissed her. A 2-year-old who pulled a cousin's hair and was told not to by the mother crawled to the cousin and said, "I hurt your hair, please don't cry," and then gave her a kiss (Zahn-Waxler & Kochanska, 1990). Working with older children, Thompson and Hoffman (1980) asked 6-, 8-, and 10-year-olds to complete stories in which a protagonist harms another person. Children who were asked to think about the victim of each story attributed more guilt to the story protagonists than children who were not asked to do so, further suggesting that being oriented toward thinking about the plight of others can enhance the experience of guilt. These findings are consistent with the view that guilt has its origins in feelings of empathic concern.

The fourth component that contributes to the situation of guilt is the desire to honor personal and moral commitments. We suggest that the more people are committed to a community of others (close relationships, family, or the larger community), the more likely they will be to experience guilt. Persons who are more committed to their community may be more likely to define the moral concerns of the community as their own and to feel an obligation to uphold them. Likewise, we predict that experiences of guilt will foster ties to others, because upholding a moral standard strengthens one's ties to the community defining that standard. It is also likely that persons who maintain strong commitments to their communities will be more likely to empathize with the plights of others in their community; thus, as discussed above, they will be more likely to experience guilt. These predictions are supported by findings indicating that persons with little or no commitment to others, such as sociopaths (persons with antisocial personality disorder), experience little if any guilt (Cleckley, 1982; American Psychiatric Association, 1987).

Thus, the components of taking responsibility, the conviction one has or had some control, the propensity to empathize with others, and the desire to honor personal and moral commitments all function as important influences on the situation of guilt, and both affect and are affected by moral and prosocial motivations in complex ways. Future research is needed to clarify further the nature of this rich interplay.

Because *both* the absence of the ability to experience guilt and the presence of excessive guilt-driven behavior appear extremely dysfunctional, it would be helpful to find some way to distinguish between adaptive and maladaptive guilt. De Rivera (1989) has proposed one way of making such a distinction. He has suggested that whether guilt (or any other emotion) is a "good" or a "poor" choice is dependent on the particular situation in which a person finds himself or herself. A "good" or adaptive choice may be defined as one that leads a person primarily to focus on caring for some person or prospect other than the self (with the ego receding to the background), while a "poor" or maladaptive choice may be defined as one that leads a person to focus on the ego (with concern for the other receding). This line of thought suggests that the experience of guilt is adpative to the extent that it is congruent with a genuine caring for others who have been injured, and maladaptive to the extent that it is motivated by a fear of rejection or is used as a defense against a realization that one cannot control certain unwanted events (leading to a denial of certain limitations).

Alternatively, the adaptiveness or maladaptiveness of an emotion may be explored by looking at the function of the emotion in the context of the individual person's life. For example, one of our subjects reported that she felt guilty when she "took $10" from her mother and "lied about it." One might suggest that her guilt served an adaptive function by highlighting her commitments to the moral value of honesty and respect for other's property, her belief that she had control over her stealing, and her wish to be reconciled with her parents. However, not all guilt experiences are so clearly adaptive. For example, persons who have experienced the traumatic death or injury of someone else while they have remained unharmed often experience a debilitating sense of survivor guilt. Survivor guilt is likely to develop in a variety of contexts, including survivors of family suicide or death, survivors of plane or car accidents, spouses of rape victims, war veterans who have witnessed the death of fellow soldiers, and Holocaust survivors. Consider the case of parents of children with fatal diseases, who often experience self-blame and guilt, and become convinced that they could have done something to prevent their children's disease (Chodoff, Friedman, & Hamburg, 1964). In these circumstances, a parent's sense that he or she could have controlled such an uncontrollable event as cancer can create a maladaptive sense of guilt that impedes the commencement of more adaptive processes, including accepting the uncontrollable and meaningless nature of the child's disease and mourning the loss.

However, in addition to its maladaptive elements, even survivor guilt may serve adaptive functions. Survival guilt can function as a defense, helping people preserve a comforting sense of control and order in the face of uncontrollable, impersonal, and meaningless horrible events, even when such order and control come at the cost of the torture of guilt. For a while, parents of dying children may need to cling to such a sense of control and order. Furthermore, in cases where individuals have survived trauma or death to others, survivor guilt may function to preserve ties of loyalty and community to those who were killed or injured. For example, after surviving torture in Argentina while other political prisoners were tortured and killed, Jacobo Timerman (Moyers, 1981) described this aspect of guilt:

> I know that going to a psychiatrist, I will lose all the world of pain, to which I am so loyal, after seeing the people who were killed in prisons. And I don't want to lose this relation with the world I was in. I don't know if this is clear to you, I feel like a kind of loyalty to the people who were killed. . . . I feel this [abandoning my guilt and putting it behind me] is disloyal. I belong to that world, and I want to belong to that world, and I don't want to belong to any other world.

Although there may be more life-sustaining ways of developing a sense of loyalty and connection to lost others, survivor guilt may sometimes function as an adaptive first step in dealing with the meaninglessness of a horrible trauma to others. Ultimately, judgments about the adaptiveness or maladaptiveness of a particular experience of guilt are embedded in the complex tapestry of people's lives.

Whether a guilt experience is adaptive or maladaptive, it always intensifies one motivation—the desire to set things right. At the same time, it often clouds the understanding of a person's specific motivation. Guilty people often search for motives for their actions, but to no avail. For example, one of our research participants felt guilty because she did not return a sketch she had promised to give back to a child. She concluded, "I just never did it." Although she considered the possibility that perhaps she broke her promise to return the sketch because she wanted it, she was uncertain of this motive. When guilty, a person may consider many motives for wrong action (or lack of action), but important motives seem to remain a mystery. Ultimately, persons fall back on the word "just": "I just did it," or "I just didn't do it," or even "It just happened."

This clouding of motives may occur for a variety of reasons. For example, persons may be unwilling to admit undesirable motives to themselves or to an interviewer, and thus may gloss over their motives by stating, "I just did it." Similarly, persons may find it difficult to integrate unacceptable motives with their beliefs that they are basically good persons. Alternatively, difficulty in gaining clarity about motives may indicate that the guilt involves some unconscious processes. Consider the example of the research participant whose remarks have been used earlier in this chapter to illustrate the structure of guilt. This participant felt guilty when her mother died. She was convinced she could have done *something* more to help prevent her mother's death, and was confused about her motivations for not doing more. This participant pondered the reasons why she did not help more. She said:

> And that's the question, why I didn't want to . . . there's something else . . . I don't think it's [my hating her and being angry] an answer. I'm looking for something. That doesn't satisfy me. . . . I figure there's a reason, has to be a reason for everything.

We can see here how guilt often involves a clouding of one's understanding of one's motivations.

Because our motives when guilty often remain a mystery, guilt is easily enlisted as a defense that protects us from exploring potentially worrisome motives (see also Gray's [1987] exploration of the defensive functions of guilt). When guilty, we feel "as if" we are bad. Because of the "as if" quality of guilt, as long as we feel guilty, the reasons why we acted as we did remain obscured. As a result, guilt enables us to avoid integrating the negative implications of our actions with our sense of identity.

Unlike experiences of guilt, experiences of shame do not obscure our motives in a cloud of mystery. Instead, when ashamed, we are quite clear, and what we are clear about is our sense of identity as a horrible, ugly, bad, or awful person. We are who we do not want to be; we embody an anti-ideal. Indeed, when guilty people become clear about their motives, then they often begin to feel ashamed instead of feeling guilty.

The primary motivational instruction of shame is the impulse to get out of the interpersonal realm, usually by hiding. Others can see the awful, ugly, or bad person we think we are; and we wish not to be this person. If only we could sink through a hole in the floor and disappear, even from ourselves, then we would not have to face what seems to be the fact of who we are. (See the statement above describing the instruction of shame.)

The instruction to get out may have several manifestations. Ashamed people frequently wish to get up and run out of the room, which they sometimes do. At other times, they simply look down, avoid eye contact, and lower their shoulders, seeming to shrink in size. One of our research participants continually had to leave the interview room to "go to the bathroom" and take other breaks, in order to cope with his urge to run out of the room. Another participant described moving and giving no one his new phone number or address, in response to feeling ashamed and wishing to hide. Therapy patients often wish to flee therapy and get out of the therapist's presence when experiences of shame first emerge. Failure to help patients with their sense of shame often means disaster for the therapy, because the patients may then quit therapy prematurely. Working as a therapist, Lindsay-Hartz has observed that intense experiences of shame and urges to get out of the interpersonal realm may also motivate suicidal actions. Some people may see suicide as the ultimate way to escape the interpersonal realm.

Shame also seems to motivate some people to react with rage. This type of rage reaction can be seen as a common defense against shame, but it is not an essential part of the experience of shame. Patterns of narcissistic injury (leading to shame), followed by rage, are well documented in the clinical literature (Kohut, 1977; Lewis, 1971; Morrison, 1989); have been supported by experimental research (Tangney, Wagner, Fletcher, & Gramzow, 1992); and were also evident in the experiences of some of the participants and subjects in these studies. As long as one remains in the interpersonal realm, then one's worthless, horrible self is exposed to oneself and to all others. If one feels helpless to hide or to get out of the interpersonal situation in which one finds oneself, then shame can motivate one to attempt to obliterate the other. Attacking the other, or symbolically putting out the eyes of the other, is another way to escape the interpersonal realm. An ashamed person may literally become physically violent, as Lansky (1987) has documented in cases of spouse abuse. An ashamed person may become verbally enraged, hurling insults and hateful attacks at others. By putting another down, one may attempt defensively to repair and in comparison raise up one's shattered sense of self-worth.

Comparing shame with guilt, we can see that the opportunity for empathy is much reduced during experiences of shame. While ashamed, one focuses on the painful experience of being a negative self. Beyond a conviction that others view one negatively, one is not likely to be thinking much about any feelings that others may be experiencing. Consequently, we would predict that shame-prone people may evidence less empathy than guilt-prone people, and that people who evidence greater ability to empathize may experience more guilt than shame. Similarly, children who are frequently shamed during their childhood, leading to a painful preoccupation with a negative self-image, may not develop as much ability to empathize with others. Further research is required to explore the connections among empathy, shame, and guilt. What is clear is that guilt and empathy are likely to be found together, and that shame, low empathy, and high self-preoccupation are likely to be found together. Indeed, Tangney (1991) has found that empathic responsiveness is positively related to the tendency to experience guilt and is inversely related to the tendency to experience shame.

As is the case with guilt, clarifying whether or not a particular shame experience is adaptive or maladaptive is furthered by reviewing the adaptiveness of the function of that shame experience in the context of a person's life. According to the findings of our first study, described earlier, shame functions to uphold our ideals about who we want to be and to maintain our commitment to a social determination of who we are. Feeling ashamed can be adaptive if the functional values supported are adaptive. For example, one of our subjects, who felt ashamed when he violently shook his girlfriend in a fit of rage, described his shame as functioning to support his ideal of being a kind, good, nonviolent person and to maintain his commitment to the socially positive value of such an identity. His shame served adaptively to help him face the destructiveness of his violent behavior, to highlight the motives for this behavior, and to motivate him to change it.

Shame may be regarded as a maladaptive "choice" of emotion when it involves supporting unattainable or unrealistic ideals (such as the ideal of having a different skin color or sexual orientation, or the ideal of having unflawed parents). Shame may also be maladaptive when a person accepts the view of others that a particular way of being is unacceptable when it need not be viewed that way (e.g., viewing a racial characteristic or "disability" as lowly or terrible). In such cases, an adaptive choice may involve the challenge of educating others about the positive value of such characteristics, or accepting that others may not always share one's perceptions. A person may also be able to join other communities whose social definitions of what is ideal and anti-ideal are more adaptive for that person. For example, a person may join with others who value something such as his or her racial characteristics or sexual orientation, even if the dominant culture does not.

Like guilt, shame can be enlisted as a defense. As a defense, shame can be either adaptive or maladaptive, depending on whether it provides needed protection or cripples personal development. For example, shame involves taking a single unworthy action or characteristic to be the whole of a person's identity. This process can defensively prevent the person from thinking clearly about his or her identity in a more integrated manner. Furthermore, the belief that the person cannot change his or her shameful identity sets up a defense of passivity and helplessness. As painful as shame is, it can be invoked to relieve a person of the task of making difficult but desirable changes in his or her life.

In the place of feeling ashamed, other, more adaptive choices sometimes exist. An adaptive choice may involve accepting that some aspect of one's self is contrary to one's ideals, but not taking this aspect to be the whole of who one is, and committing oneself to change in this area. For example, one of our subjects felt ashamed when she overheard two boys say that she was fat. She took her weight to be the whole of who she was—a fat, ugly person—and was not able to appreciate in the moment of shame the fact that she had a pretty face and a pleasant personality. She also felt helpless to do anything about her being fat. Later, she was able to confront this experience of shame, to realize that her fatness was not the whole of herself, and to decide that she could go on a diet and change how she looked, which she did. Her shame first functioned in a defensive manner, prompting her to hide, to feel helpless, and to avoid thinking about herself or the experience. However, her shame did highlight her ideal of being an attractive, thin person. Later, she became committed to changing her weight and appearance. Sometimes, facing something about which a person feels ashamed can motivate that person to commit to change and can resolve the experience of shame. Ward (1972) long ago recognized that facing experiences of shame in psychotherapy can be an adaptive and important turning point.

Guilt and shame appear, at first glance, to be similar emotions. However, our studies have shown that they are qualitatively different from each other. They differentially affect our motivations and actions, and these differences affect our lives markedly and profoundly. We hope that by studying the differences, therapists and researchers can explore and develop techniques to help individuals with patterns of making maladaptive choices begin making better choices and freeing themselves from the entanglements that these emotions can generate.

REFERENCES

American Psychiatric Association. (1987). *Diagnostic and statistical manual of mental disorders* (3rd ed., rev.). Washington, DC: Author.

Beck, A. T. (1967). *Depression: Clinical, experimental and theoretical aspects.* New York: Harper & Row.

Chapman, M., Zahn-Waxler, C., Cooperman, G., & Iannotti, R. (1987). Empathy and responsibility in the motivation of children's helping. *Developmental Psychology, 23,* 140–145.

Chodoff, P., Friedman, S., & Hamburg, D. (1964). Stress, defenses and coping behavior: Observations in parents of children with malignant disease. *American Journal of Psychiatry, 120,* 742–749.

Cleckley, H. (1982). *The mask of sanity.* New York: New American Library.

de Rivera, J. (1977). A structural theory of emotions. *Psychological Issues,* 4(Monograph No. 40).

de Rivera, J. (1989). Choice of emotion and ideal development. In L. Cirillo, B. Kaplan, & S. Wapner (Eds.), *Emotions in ideal human development* (pp. 7–31). Hillsdale, NJ: Erlbaum.

de Rivera, J. (1991). The structure and dynamics of emotion. In R. Hogan & W. Jones (Eds.), *New perspectives in personality* (Vol. 3, pp. 191–212). London: Jessica Kingsley.

de Rivera, J., & Kreilkamp, T. (1981). Conceptual encounter. In J. de Rivera (Ed.), *Conceptual encounter: A method for the exploration of human experience* (pp. 1–34). Washington, DC: University Press of America.

Fingarette, H. (1967). *On responsibility.* New York: Basic Books.

Freud, S. (1957). Some character-types met with in psycho-analytic work. In J. Strachey (Ed. and Trans.), *The standard edition of the complete psychological works of Sigmund Freud* (Vol. 14, pp. 309–336). London: Hogarth Press. (Original work published 1916)

Freud, S. (1961). The ego and the id. In J. Strachey (Ed. and Trans.), *The standard edition of the complete psychological works of Sigmund Freud* (Vol. 19, pp. 3–66). London: Hogarth Press. (Original work published 1923)

Goodman, S. (1981). The experience of anxiety as differentiated from panic. In J. de Rivera (Ed.), *Conceptual encounter: A method for the exploration of human experience* (pp. 83–162). Washington, DC: University Press of America.

Gottschalk, L. A. (1971). Some psychoanalytic research into the communication of meaning through language: The quality and magnitude of psychological states. *British Journal of Medical Psychology, 44,* 131–147.

Gray, P. (1987). On the technique of analysis of the superego: An introduction. *Psychoanalytic Quarterly, 56,* 130–154.

Hoffman, M. L. (1982). Development of prosocial motivation: Empathy and guilt. In N. Eisenberg (Ed.), *Development of prosocial behavior* (pp. 281–313). New York: Academic Press.

Hoffman, M. L. (1983). Affective and cognitive processes in moral internalization: An information processing approach. In E. T. Higgins, D. Ruble, & S. W. Hartup (Eds.), *Developmental social cognition* (pp. 236–274). New York: Cambridge University Press.

Houselander, C. (1951). *Guilt.* New York: Sheed & Ward.

Kane, R. (1976). *Two studies on the experience of depression.* Unpublished master's thesis, Clark University.

Kohut, H. (1977). *The restoration of the self.* New York: International Universities Press.

Lansky, M. (1987). Shame and domestic violence. In D. Nathanson (Ed.), *The many faces of shame* (pp. 335–362). New York: Guilford Press.

Lewis, H. B. (1971). *Shame and guilt in neurosis.* New York: International Universities Press.

Lindsay-Hartz, J. (1980). *Two studies of guilt and shame experiences.* Unpublished doctoral dissertation, Clark University.

Lindsay-Hartz, J. (1984). Contrasting experiences of shame and guilt. *American Behavioral Scientist, 27,* 689–704.

Lindsay Hartz, J. (1987). *Shame, guilt, and survivor guilt: Phenomenological and psychoanalytic theories.* Paper presented at the meeting of the American Psychological Association, New York.

Lindsay-Hartz, J. (1992). *Shame and the therapist's blind spot.* Paper presented at a Divison 39 symposium at the meeting of the American Psychological Association, Washington, DC.

Lynd, H. M. (1958). *On shame and the search for identity.* New York: Harcourt, Brace & World.

Miller, S. (1985). *The shame experience.* Hillsdale, NJ: Erlbaum.

Montada, L., & Schneider, A. (1989). Justice and emotional reactions of the disadvantaged. *Social Justice Research, 3,* 313–344.

Morrison, A. (1989). *Shame: The underside of narcissism.* Hillsdale, NJ: Analytic Press.

Moyers, B. (Executive Editor). (1981). The ordeal of Jacobo Timerman. *The Bill Moyers Show* (No. 724). New York: WNET/Thirteen.

Piers, G., & Singer, M. B. (1953). *Shame and guilt.* Springfield, IL: Charles C Thomas.

Siegel, S. (1956). *Nonparametric statistics for the behavioral sciences.* New York: McGraw-Hill.

Tangney, J. (1991). Moral affect: The good, the bad, and the ugly. *Journal of Personality and Social Psychology, 61,* 598–607.

Tangney, J., Wagner, P., Fletcher, C., & Gramzow, R. (1992). Shamed into anger? The relation of shame and guilt to anger and self-reported aggression. *Journal of Personality and Social Psychology, 62,* 669–675.

Thompson, R. A., & Hoffman, M. L. (1980). Empathy and the arousal of guilt in children. *Developmental Psychology, 15,* 155–156.

Ward, H. (1972). Shame—a necessity for growth in therapy. *American Journal of Psychotherapy, 26*, 232–243.

Zahn-Waxler, C., & Kochanska, G. (1990). The origins of guilt. In R. A. Thompson (Ed.), *Nebraska Symposium on Motivation: Vol. 36. Socioemotional development* (pp. 183–258). Lincoln: University of Nebraska Press.

Zahn-Waxler, C., Radke-Yarrow, M., & King, R. (1979). Childrearing and children's prosocial initiations towards victims of distress. *Child Development, 50*, 319–330.

Zahn-Waxler, C., Radke-Yarrow, M., Wagner, E., & Chapman, M. (1992). Development of concern for others. *Developmental Psychology, 28*, 126–136.

12

You Always Hurt the One You Love: Guilt and Transgressions against Relationship Partners

WARREN H. JONES
KAREN KUGLER
PATRICIA ADAMS

Psychology and other social sciences have recently rediscovered personal relationships. Much of what people want, think, feel, and do, beyond the tissue level of existence, is in the service of acquiring, maintaining, renegotiating, or terminating the close personal relationships in which they are involved. Furthermore, human relational behavior has an evolutionary/biological history. That is, humans evolved as group-living and highly sociable creatures, and these features promote reproductive capacity as well as individual survivial and the development of culture (Hinde, 1979; Hogan, 1983). Extensive documentation has accumulated that personal relationships are more than just ubiquitous in human experience; they are fundamental to existence. For example, it is conceivable that without the propensity for such relationships, humans would not have survived as a species (Hogan, 1983).

Although guilt is sometimes described in relation to its societal and interpersonal functions, a major controversy remains with respect to the role of guilt in the context of personal relationships. Specifically, is guilt one of the so-called "social emotions," which arise from threats to the self in the context of other people (e.g., shyness, embarrassment, audience anxiety, etc.), or is it an essentially private emotion arising from the recognition that one has violated a personal standard of moral relevance? Put another way, what is it that people feel guilty about and why? The nexus between personal relationships and guilt is the focus of our chapter. We begin with a discussion of previous research and theorizing on guilt, with a particular emphasis on the various ways in which guilt has been conceptualized and measured. Subsequently, we turn our attention to our own program of research on guilt, beginning with a brief review of the development of a new measure called the Guilt Inventory. Next, we present available evidence regarding the association between indices of guilt and variables assessing the quality and quantity of interpersonal ties, as well as exploratory data concerning the kinds of transgressions associated with guilt. We conclude with a brief discussion of the implications of the relational aspects of guilt in light of existing theory and research.

CONCEPTUALIZATION AND MEASUREMENT OF GUILT

The word "guilt" derives from an Old English root that carries the double meaning of "transgression" and "debt" (Lynd, 1958). The implication is that not only has a crime or violation of a societal standard been committed, but that something is owed—a debt, a duty, or an obligation—and thus retribution or punishment should follow. In the psychological literature, guilt is conceived of as the cognitive awareness and negative feelings associated with violation of a moral standard. It is an important element in the socialization of the individual. Indeed, according to Ausubel (1955), guilt is "one of the most important mechanisms through which an individual becomes socialized in his culture. It is also an important instrument for cultural survival since it constitutes a most efficient watchdog within each individual, serving to keep his behavior compatible with the moral values of the society in which he lives" (p. 378). In this view, then, guilt performs important societal functions—fostering responsibility, reducing aggression, and encouraging cooperation among members, and at the same time ensuring the survival of the individual as a group member. A less adaptive side of guilt has also been described, however. For example, Freud (1930/1961) believed that guilt is the most important problem in civilization. From this perspective, guilt is neurotic, destructive, largely unconscious, and irrational. The guilty individual withdraws socially, ruminating over transgressions, castigating the self for real or imagined shortcomings. Thus, although guilt is necessary, it can become a dysfunctional experience, and possibly the basis of mental illness.

Models of Guilt

Psychodynamic Views

Freud's (1930/1961) ideas about guilt were tied to his theorizing about the origin of neurosis. Although he acknowledged the necessity of social constraints, Freud observed that many of his patients developed neurotic symptoms because of the limitations their culture placed on their behavior, thoughts, and emotions. Freud believed that the conflict between the satisfaction of the individual's id impulses and the rules imposed by society (represented by the superego) is inevitable. Thus, the pursuit of happiness inherent in the pleasure principle is, to some extent, likely to be thwarted, and the individual may face an internal struggle resulting in the development of ego defenses and possibly neurosis.

Subsequent revisions of the psychoanalytic view have shifted the emphasis from the relatively impersonal societal influence described by Freud to a more direct and clearly interpersonal influence. In particular, Lewis (1971, 1981, 1984) took exception to Freud's account of the superego, arguing instead that emotions are best understood within the context of the human affectional system. According to Lewis, Freud overlooked the importance of the role of the caretaker's relationship with the infant in the development of the superego.

An important issue in the psychodynamic view of guilt has been the distinction between guilt and shame. The root meaning of "shame" is "to cover up, to envelop" (Lynd, 1958). Like guilt, shame can refer both to a subjective feeling of the person and to the objective nature of an act. However, the impulse in guilt is to atone, whereas the impetus in shame is to hide or conceal. According to Lewis, shame functions to restore the bond between self and other; guilt functions to restore the bond between one's behavior and the expectations of the social environment. Lewis (1971, 1979) argued that shame and guilt frequently co-occur and that one may mask the other. For example, a conscious experience of shame may be preferable to a feeling of guilt, depending on the individual. Thus the individual may become caught in a cycle of experiencing shame for feeling guilt and guilt for feeling shame. The net result may be that one is mistaken for the other, interfering with effective treatment. This distinction was also central to an effort among anthropologists to classify societies as either "shame cultures" or "guilt cultures," with the expectation that one or the other would predominate in social control within a culture (e.g., Malinowski, 1924). Guilt was thought to be the result of internalized sanctions, whereas shame was believed to result from external sanctions only. Guilt cultures thus were believed to provide for progressive change, whereas shame cultures were declared to be more static, backward, lacking in absolute moral standards, and dominated by "crowd psychology."

Emotion Theory

In general, emotions are seen as socially adaptive, communicating information about the individual, and therefore having an expressive feature

(Plutchik, 1980). Emotions provide information about the probability of behavior, serving to prepare the individual for appropriate action. Both positive and negative emotions may serve as motivators to action. Cognitive or evaluative factors influence the specific emotion experienced. In addition emotion theorists have devoted considerable attention to identifying emotions termed "basic" or "innate," either because all other emotions can be derived from them or because they are believed to be experienced and expressed in the same ways across all cultures.

Tomkins (1987) identified nine innate affects. Interest or excitement, enjoyment or joy, and surprise or startle are the positive affects. The negative affects are distress or anguish, fear or terror, shame or humiliation, contempt, disgust, and anger or rage. In Tomkins's view, guilt is subsumed under shame. Shame, though innate, is not a primary emotion, but an auxiliary one; that is, it operates only after the activation of either interest or joy. The innate activator of shame is the incomplete reduction of interest or joy. Tomkins noted that shame (and, by extension, guilt) can become pathological if it is magnified in frequency, duration, and strength to such an extent that it becomes a chronic, intense state.

In Izard's (1977) conceptualization, emotion is placed in a larger personality context. It is seen as one of six subsystems—homeostatic, drive, emotion, perceptual, cognitive, and motor—that interact to create personality. These subsystems produce four types of motivations: drives, emotions, affect perception, and affect cognition. Beyond the basic physiological drives, emotions motivate not only independently, but also in combination with perceptions and cognitions. Indeed, emotions are seen as the predominant motivators and organizers of behavior. Izard proposed that 10 emotions are innate and transcultural, although each culture will have different display rules and attitudes toward emotional experience. Guilt is described as one of these 10 discrete emotions. Developmentally, Izard proposed, emotions occur as a part of the maturational process, and the appearance of each will depend on the individual's learning experiences as a part of the socialization process. In this formulation, guilt occurs relatively late, after the child has developed the capacity to distinguish self from other and to recognize that self as responsible for one's own actions. Therefore, the child must have learned the rules governing social behavior within the culture in order to experience guilt.

Other emotion theorists have emphasized the cognitive aspects of guilt, such as the greater likelihood of feeling guilty for foreseeable versus unanticipated transgressions (e.g., Weiner, 1985). By contrast, some theories emphasize the social aspects of guilt. For example, de Rivera (1984) has proposed that emotions develop as a result of their adaptive function in relationships. In his view, all emotions are concerned with adjusting this relationship between self and other, and each emotion functions to maximize the values of the relationship.

Other Theories

Buss (1980) discussed guilt and shame in relation to his theory of public and private self-consciousness. Buss noted that an individual's awareness of self has two aspects. The individual may attend to the public features of the self—those that are available for observation by others, such as appearance, overt behavior, and personal history. Alternately, the focus may be on the private features of the self—those that are available only to the individual, such as bodily sensations, thoughts, feelings, and motives. Situational events can induce one or the other aspect of self-awareness, with the result that the relevant self-view is intensified. According to Buss, individuals tend to become habitually attuned to one aspect of the self or the other, which he distinguished from the immediate experience of self-awareness by using the term "self-consciousness." Buss then explained the distinction between guilt and shame in terms of public and private self-consciousness. In his view, guilt is private. The test of guilt is whether anyone knows about it or not; in true guilt, no one need know. Shame, on the other hand, is public. Without an observer, Buss argued, there is no basis for shame. As a consequence, Buss classified shame as a social emotion along with shyness, embarrassment, and audience anxiety, and defined guilt as a private emotion.

Mosher's (1961, 1966, 1968) conceptualization is based on principles of social learning theory. Mosher defined guilt as a generalized expectancy for self-mediated punishment for violating (or the anticipation of violating) internalized standards of moral behavior. As such, guilt represents a cognitive predisposition rather than an affective state. The emphasis in Mosher's conceptualization is on inhibition of behavior as evidence of guilt-proneness. Thus it represents a hypothetical "readiness" for guilt rather than a measure of one's actual response; guilt as disposition or readiness is thereby distinguished from guilt as affect. In a review of the literature on his scales (see below), Mosher (1979) acknowledged that the scales do not sample the entire domain of guilt, but represent instead specific areas within the domain. He argued, however, for even more specific measures—for example, measures of masturbation guilt or self-punishment.

Measurement

Early attempts to measure guilt did so in an indirect way, assuming that guilt would follow as the affective outcome of failures of moral behavior. Adapting the techniques of Piaget, researchers (Miller & Swanson, 1966; Allinsmith, 1966; Aronfreed, 1966; Hoffman & Saltzstein, 1967) developed projective stories illustrating presumed moral dilemmas, and allowed subjects to create their own endings to the stories. These endings were then rated independently for the intensity of guilt expressed. Behavioral observation was also utilized, with guilt assumed to be the motivator of behavior.

Sears, Maccoby, and Levin (1957), for example, interviewed mothers for evidence in their children's behavior of the capacity for guilt.

Self-report measures of guilt have tended to adopt one of a few distinct formats. One has been the use of brief scenarios reflecting situations in which guilt (and often shame) might be experienced (e.g., Evans, Jessup, & Hearn, 1975; Hogan & Cheek, 1983; Klas, 1986; Tangney, 1990). The utility of this approach derives from the standardization of stimuli and the provision of context via the situations in which guilt-relevant experiences are likely to occur. An alternative format is to generate a list of adjectives (e.g., Harder & Lewis, 1986; Otterbacher & Munz, 1973) or statements (e.g., Buss & Durkee, 1957; Hogan, 1985; Izard, 1977; Kugler & Jones, 1992; Mosher, 1961, 1966) reflecting feelings that are related to guilt. In this approach, the emphasis is on the experience of affect, regardless of setting. This format also has standardized stimuli, but shifts the focus to the time frame in which guilt is experienced. For example, if the respondent reports guilt at the time of assessment, it may be a transient state rather than a more chronic feature of the individual's personality. Yet another approach has been the development of lists of behaviors presumed to result in guilt if engaged in (London, Schulman, & Black, 1964).

Mosher (1961, 1966, 1968) was one of the first researchers to develop an objective measure of guilt as a personality dimension. The Mosher scale consists of three subscales: Sex Guilt, Hostility Guilt, and Morality–Conscience. The first two adopt the psychoanalytic model of sex and aggression as primary id impulses, whereas the latter reflects the individual's tendency toward negative self-judgment and self-punishment. The item content of the Mosher scales suggests, however, that they largely measure ascription to moral standards.

Empirical Research

Guilt has been studied as a complex construct with affective, cognitive, personality, genetic, cultural, and dynamic aspects. There is evidence that guilt is universally experienced and innate, although the specific standards triggering guilt will vary not only across cultures but from individual to individual (Izard, 1977; Tomkins, 1987). On the other hand, guilt has little expressive distinction, beyond a certain heaviness of expression and perhaps the hanging of the head. Guilt has been shown to be most closely related to distress, followed by fear, and least closely related to joy and surprise (Izard, 1977). Individual guilt responses are probably highly dependent on the situation and how it is perceived by the person (Lindsay-Hartz, 1984). It appears likely that there are gender differences in the experience of guilt, although these differences may have more to do with gender roles deemed appropriate within a culture than with innate male–female differences (Mosher, 1979).

It is generally assumed, and there is some empirical evidence to suggest, that the capacity for guilt is developed in social interaction, beginning with the very first infant–caregiver relationship (Hoffman, 1977; Moulton, Liberty, Burnstein & Altucher, 1966). As noted earlier, guilt is sometimes described as socially adaptive, inhibiting "antisocial" behaviors; at the same time, extremes of guilt experience are believed to be related to at least some forms of psychopathology. Correspondingly, evidence that guilt—conceptualized in certain ways—aids society by inhibiting immoral behavior has been reported by numerous researchers (e.g., London et al., 1964; Mosher, 1966, 1979; Okel & Mosher, 1968; Persons, 1970), but there is also evidence that it is linked to certain forms of psychopathology and dysfunctional patterns of behavior (e.g., Buss & Durkee, 1957; Fehr & Stamps, 1979; Wertheim & Schwarz, 1983). Also, the literature clearly demonstrates the relevance of various cognitive (e.g., McGraw, 1987), affective (Buss & Durkee, 1957), and personality processes (e.g., Moulton et al., 1966; Schwartz, 1973) in the experience of guilt.

Less clear is the empirical support for the distinction between guilt and shame, as well as its underlying implications for whether or not guilt is a social emotion. On the other hand, several attempts to demonstrate this distinction empirically have provided at least some support (e.g., Hogan & Cheek, 1983; Lindsay-Hartz, 1984; Tangney, 1990; Wicker, Payne, & Morgan, 1983). By contrast, several attempts to show the distinction have been unsuccessful (e.g., Harder & Lewis, 1986; Hoblitzelle, 1987; Kugler & Jones, 1992), and there is some direct evidence suggesting that interpersonal events and behaviors (e.g., harming others) are more closely linked to the experience of guilt than are violations of moral standards and failures (Evans et al., 1975; Klas, 1986). Also, a specific test of Buss's prediction that guilt should be more strongly related to private self-consciousness, whereas shame should be more strongly related to public self-consciousness, did not provide supportive evidence (Jones & Kugler, 1993).

Regarding efforts to operationalize and measure guilt, Mosher's scales have been compared to measures of delinquent and criminal behaviors (Persons, 1970), laboratory-induced transgressions (Mosher, 1979), moral judgments (D'Augelli & Cross, 1975), guilty affect (Okel & Mosher, 1968), and personality (Fehr & Stamps, 1979), with results generally supportive of the validity and reliability of this approach. Studies using alternative measures, though less numerous, have yielded results supportive of their utility as well (e.g., Janda & Magri, 1975; Kugler & Jones, 1992; Otterbacher & Munz, 1973; Tangney, 1990, 1991; Tangney, Wagner, Fletcher, & Gramzow, 1992).

Conceptual and Measurement Issues

We believe that much of the previous research and theorizing on guilt contains two types of disagreement and confusion, which restrict the understanding of its origins and implications. The first issue concerns how guilt is defined and measured. As noted above, there are several competing definitions of guilt, which vary according to the extent to which moral values as compared to the emotional experience of guilt are emphasized. In the former instance (represented by the emotion theory approach), guilt is expected to be higher among those who have engaged in violations of those standards to which they subscribe; in the latter approach (illustrated by Mosher's theory), guilt defined as subscription to moral standards is expected to inhibit or lower the probability of moral transgressions.

Furthermore, even among definitions that emphasize affective experience, there are definitions and corresponding measures that may be differentiated according to whether they point to immediate emotional experience or refer to the frequency or chronicity of emotional experience over time. The former derive from the emotion theory approach to guilt, which posits a motivational function to redress a grievance resulting from the recognition that one has violated a moral standard, whereas the latter reflect the psychodynamic conceptualization of guilt resulting either from the accumulation of past transgressions or from faulty personality development. In this distinction, the actual and immediate experience of the emotion of guilt would be expected to be related to an individual's recent behavior, thoughts, and verbalizations of relevance to his or her moral values, whereas chronic and repeated experiences of guilt could conceivably function independently of what a person actually says, thinks, or does. This distinction is also consistent with the differentiation between the social value of guilt and guilt as an underpinning to the development of psychopathology.

In our view, the solution to this diversity is to conceptualize (and measure) three separate constructs as follows: "moral standards" (i.e., what a person believes to be right or wrong with respect to various moral issues, or the strength of the individual's moral values, independent of specific content); "state guilt" (i.e., the extent to which an individual feels guilty at the moment, presumably as a result of some relatively recent moral transgression); and "trait guilt" (i.e., the extent to which a propensity toward guilt characterizes an individual's personality broadly considered, independent of any specific transgression).

Careful examination of the literature and some recent research (Kugler & Jones, 1992) shows clearly that some putative measures of guilt are better understood as measures of moral standards (e.g., Mosher's Sex Guilt scale), that some are better measures of trait guilt than of standards, and that some confound the two more or less equally. As we discuss below, our approach has been to define and attempt to measure these three separate constructs independently.

The second issue concerns the implication (contained in many statements of guilt) that because guilt presumably can be experienced without the awareness of anyone other than the experiencing individual, it is more closely related to the intricacies of ethics and religion than to direct violations of the expectations of personal relationships. The traditional view is that guilt derives from what might be called an indirect interpersonal mechanism:

Moral standards are acquired from the interaction between the individual and significant others (especially interactions in infancy and early childhood), but once such standards become the person's own (i.e., the superego), guilt will result from their violation even if no one else becomes aware of the violation. This is, of course, consistent with the Freudian view; Mosher's approach is generally consistent with it as well, and even focuses on the two main behavioral prohibitions against sex and aggression proposed by Freud. The difference is that Mosher has emphasized the inhibiting effects of the predisposition toward guilt, rather than the internal and eternal conflict between id and moral impulses. In either case, however, guilt is conceived of as being tied to the occurrence of thoughts and behaviors that the experiencing individual has come to believe are wrong, as translated via socialization to the individual by his or her caregivers. For purposes of discussion, we refer to this conceptualization of guilt as the "moral perspective."

By contrast, Lewis and other more recent writers in the psychodynamic tradition, as well as some emotion theorists, have conceived of guilt as deriving from transgressions not so much because they are wrong in the moral sense, but because they threaten the bond between the experiencing individual and his or her important relationships. We call this the "relational perspective." The relational approach to guilt is consistent with the recent emphasis on the importance of maintaining personal relationships as a fundamental motive in human experience (e.g., Baumeister & Tice, 1990; Hogan, Jones, & Cheek, 1985).

The distinction between these two perspectives is subtle but important, because it highlights the importance of the type of transgression and its connection to either morality or guilt. In the moral view, morality and moral behavior are inextricably linked, resulting in the following implications: (1) Guilt follows the violation of a moral standard; and/or (2) violations of moral standards are less likely or do not occur because of the threat of guilt. Thus, guilt either results from immoral behavior or prevents it. In the relational view, the connection between guilt and moral behavior is more complex, in that they are linked only when the violation in question threatens the bond between the experiencing individual and his or her relational partners. One implication of this approach is that serious violations of moral standards should not be expected to result in guilt if they do not harm the individual's personal relationships, whereas even minor transgressions that are not viewed by society as serious misbehaviors, but that threaten the bond between the individual and his or her relationship partners, may lead to strong feelings of guilt.

THE GUILT INVENTORY

Our program of research on guilt (Jones & Kugler, 1993; Kugler & Jones, 1992) has attempted to address the conceptual and measurement issues outlined above; has been focused on the interpersonal implications of guilt; and has paralleled the development and exploration of a self-report instrument, the Guilt Inventory (GI). The GI partitions participants' responses into three relevant domains, two pertaining to affective guilt and the third to the strength of moral values. The three scales are called Trait Guilt, State Guilt, and Moral Standards. Items for the two guilt scales are temporally anchored; thus State Guilt items refer to how one is currently feeling, whereas Trait Guilt items refer to how one generally or usually feels. Neither scale mentions any specific moral standard or transgressions. Moral Standards contains items requesting information regarding the strength of the individual's moral values and their level of importance to the individual. Again, reference is not made to specific behaviors.

Psychometric Issues

Development and Reliability

Initially, the GI contained 89 items written to reflect definitions and conceptualizations found in the extant literature assessing the three content domains listed above. Illustrative items for the Trait Guilt scale are as follows: "Guilt and remorse have been a part of my life for as long as I can recall," "I often have a strong sense of regret," and "Frequently I just hate myself for something I have done." The State Guilt scale is exemplified by these items: "At the moment, I don't feel particularly guilty about anything I have done," "Recently, I have done something that I deeply regret," and "Lately, I have felt good about myself and what I have done." Finally, our measurement of Moral Standards is illustrated by these items: "I believe in a strict interpretation of right and wrong," "If I do something that I believe is wrong, I will feel terrible whether or not anyone knows about it," and "I believe there are situations in which the end justifies the means."

These items were administered to college students, and items were retained for the subsequent version of the GI on the basis of corrected item–total correlations within each domain. In the final version, the Trait Guilt scale consists of 20 items, the State Guilt scale has 10 items, and the Moral Standards scale has 15 items. The item responses are on a 5-point, verbally anchored, Likert-type scale. Half of the items are worded in the reverse direction to reflect lack of guilt. The scales are administered as one 45-item inventory. Subsequent research (Kugler & Jones, 1992) indicated that the scales of the GI appear to be internally reliable as indicated by coefficient alpha and the mean interitem correlations, as well as stable over time. For example, in a sample of over 1,000 respondents, coefficient alpha was .89 for Trait Guilt, .83 for State Guilt, and .81 for Moral Standards, whereas the mean interitem correlations were .34, .31, and .29, respectively. Test–retest reliabilities were assessed by administrations of the GI over intervals of 10 and 36 weeks. Results indicated the greatest stability for

Moral Standards for both intervals (r's = .81, .77), followed by Trait Guilt (r's = .72, .75) and State Guilt (r's = .56, .58); all correlations were significantly different from zero.

Covariation among the GI Scales

The intercorrelations of the three scales has also been determined. The correlation between Trait Guilt and State Guilt, r (1,041) = .67, p < .001, suggested that although the two are strongly related, they still measure somewhat different aspects of the construct. Relationships between Moral Standards and both Trait Guilt, r (1,041) = .03, and State Guilt, r (1,041) = .01, were negligible.

Validity

The validity of the GI has been assessed in various ways (Jones & Kugler, 1993; Kugler & Jones, 1992). For example, convergent validity was suggested by significant correlations between State Guilt and responses to such self-descriptive adjectives as "guilty," "withdrawn," "anguished," "resentful," "alone," "helpless," and "depressed." Trait Guilt was significantly correlated with such adjectives as "guilty," "depressed," "regretful," "alone," "distressed," "insecure," "lonely," and "resentful." In contrast, scores on the Moral Standards scale were significantly related to such self-labeling items as "moral," "obedient," "predictable," and "cautious," and inversely related to "exhibitionistic," "pleasure-seeking," and "rebellious." In addition, in one study participants with higher scores on Trait Guilt were more likely to be rated by friends and family members as "detached," "disenchanted," "contemptuous," "resentful," "argumentative," and "angry," and less likely to be rated as "friendly" and "affectionate." For Moral Standards, friends and family members were significantly more likely to rate high scorers as "moral," "religious," "self-reliant," "competent," and "humble," and less likely to rate them as "arrogant" and "vindictive."

Additional evidence of concurrent validity was demonstrated by comparisons of the GI scales to measures of affective guilt (both trait and state guilt) and measures of morality. Results (see Kugler & Jones, 1992) clearly indicated a broad pattern of convergence, with the Trait Guilt and State Guilt scales most strongly related to alternative measures of trait and state guilt, and with the Moral Standards scale most strongly related to measures conceived as indices of morality or the capacity to experience guilt (e.g., Mosher's Sex Guilt scale). Furthermore, comparisons between measures suggested that the GI scales performed as well as or better than alternative measures in this regard. Also, significant correlations between both the Trait Guilt and State Guilt scales and measures of resentment, suspicion, loneliness, depression, anxiety, anger, shyness, and both public and private self-consciousness were found (Jones & Kugler, 1993). Generally, these measures were unrelated to Moral Standards, as would be expected. Finally, a comparison involving the Differential Emotions Scale (DES; Izard, 1977), which purports to assess the full range of emotional experience, may be interpreted as indicating the divergent validity of the Trait Guilt and State Guilt scales, in that the correlation of each with the DES measure of guilt was significantly stronger than the mean of the correlations with other emotions (e.g., shyness, sadness, fear, disgust, anger, surprise, joy, and contempt). By the same token, it should be mentioned that neither the Trait Guilt nor the State Guilt scale of the GI was distinguishable from measures of shame in these studies (see Kugler & Jones, 1992); this was also the case for most alternative measures of guilt.

Demographic Correlates

Evidence for divergent validity was also provided by differences among the GI scales in relation to other variables. Differences among demographic variables, for example, were apparent. Male participants scored higher on State Guilt, but there were no gender differences for Trait Guilt. Female respondents, on the other hand, reported higher levels of Moral Standards. These patterns held true for both adult and student groups (Kugler & Jones, 1992). Adults reported higher levels of Moral Standards than did college students. Although there were no differences between adults and students on Trait Guilt, students appeared to experience more State Guilt. There was some evidence that Trait Guilt and Moral Standards were inversely related to level of education or occupational prestige, although these relationships varied by gender and age of the respondents.

A final variable of interest was the religious activity of the respondents. Religion provides standards by which an individual may regulate and judge behavior. Previous studies (e.g., Moulton et al., 1966) suggested that the particular religious orientation has no relationship to guilt. However, guilt has been found to be related to measures of religious values and of religious orthodoxy (e.g., Fehr & Stamps, 1979). In one of our studies, participants were asked to report frequency of attendance of religious activities. For adults there were modest negative relationships between both State Guilt and Trait Guilt scores and religious involvement. At the same time, there was a significant positive relationship with Moral Standards scores. This is as would be expected, given the GI items assessing guilt, which are moderately to strongly negative in tone. The correlations with Moral Standards scores were even stronger for college students. However, the relationship between religious attendance and both State Guilt and Trait Guilt scores was near zero for students.

Interpersonal Correlates

As indicated earlier, we assume that guilt develops in an interpersonal context and is salient in interpersonal relationships. Indirect evidence for these assumptions has been found in our research using the GI. For example, the evidence that Trait Guilt is related to ratings by friends and family members suggests that it is an interpersonally discernible characteristic (Jones & Kugler, 1993). Also, State Guilt and Trait Guilt scores have been found to be directly correlated with measures of interpersonal problems and traits that would be expected to inhibit social interaction (e.g., loneliness, shyness, self-consciousness, suspicion), and inversely correlated with relational competence among both college students and adults (Jones & Kugler, 1993; Kugler, 1989), whereas these characteristics were unrelated to Moral Standards. In another study (Jones & Kugler, 1993), both Trait Guilt and State Guilt scores were inversely related to reported satisfaction with relationships among friends and in work or school settings.

In one study involving psychiatric outpatients and inpatients (Carver, 1990), Trait Guilt was found to be inversely related to such self-reported interpersonal and relational variables as intimacy, trust, perspective taking, satisfaction with family, and both the size and supportiveness of the social network, and directly correlated with loneliness, the betrayal of relational partners, and personality disorder dimensions linked to relational problems (e.g., borderline, avoidant, schizoid, dependent, and passive–aggressive personality). In the same study, patients scoring higher on Trait Guilt were rated by their therapists as less capable of engaging in mature, mutually satisfying relationships, and structured interviews revealed that higher scores on the Trait Guilt scale were inversely associated with the experience of fewer and less satisfying relationships in each of several relational domains (parent–child relationships, sibling relationships, marital and romantic relationships, friendships, etc.). Also, in a program of studies focused on betrayal and violations of expectations within relationships (see Jones & Burdette, 1994), we have found that betrayals are most likely to occur among one's most intimate relational partners and that guilt is a common emotional concomitant of having betrayed or having been betrayed by an intimate relational partner.

Thus, in research involving the GI, results generally indicate that guilt is associated with interpersonal problems. This is probably attributable to the conceptualization of guilt inherent in the GI scales, and is inconsistent with the few traditional approaches that portray an adaptive role for guilt in interpersonal contexts (e.g., Ausubel, 1955). It is also inconsistent with findings reported by Tangney and her associates (Tangney, Wagner, Gavlas, Barlow, & Marschall, 1992) suggesting a linkage between guilt and such adaptive characteristics as empathy and constructive anger.

GUILT AND RELATIONSHIP TRANSGRESSIONS

One of our approaches to validation for the scales of the GI was to compare its scores to ratings on a list of behaviors presumed to be guilt-inducing for college students. Initially, 99 behaviors reflecting a wide variety of transgressions from a moral or religious perspective were generated. Sixty-eight college students were asked to rate each item on 5-point rating scales twice, indicating (1) the degree to which each student believed the behavior in question to be wrong or a serious violation of his or her moral standards, and (2) the frequency with which each student had engaged in the behavior in question during the last 6 months. Examples of the behaviors listed are as follows: "Cheating on an exam," "Masturbation," "Shoplifting something worth over $100.00," "Lying to a friend," "Making a promise to a family member with no intention of keeping it," "Fantasizing having sex with a desirable stranger," "Driving while intoxicated," "Telling 'dirty' jokes," and "Taking illegal drugs." As illustrated, the behaviors ranged from relatively minor transgressions to more serious behaviors. Care was taken to include only behaviors of moral relevance in which college students might have engaged. Subsequently, both sets of ratings were compared to participants' scores on the GI.

Examination of the results for each item suggested several interesting patterns. First, for most items, ratings of wrongfulness and frequency were significantly and inversely correlated, as would be expected. In other words, the more serious a transgression in the view of a respondent, the less likely he or she was to have participated in the behavior. Second, ratings for wrongfulness were significantly and positively correlated with scores for Moral Standards for most of the items. In other words, as would be expected, respondents' subscription to Moral Standards was significantly related to their judgments regarding the wrongfulness of an act. Third, wrongfulness ratings were positively and significantly related to State Guilt and Trait Guilt scales for many items. Thus, for judgments of wrongfulness, all three scales of the GI were more or less likely to be related to specific transgressions and in the same direction.

Although this was not our original purpose in collecting the data, we also noticed an apparent difference in the correlations between frequency ratings and the GI scales, based on whether the rating item involved harming—either symbolically or in reality—a partner in a close relationship (e.g., "Lying to one's parents," "Having a serious argument with a friend," etc.), or did not involve a relational partner (e.g., "Taking illegal drugs," "Shoplifting," etc.). As a result, we sorted the 99 items into ones involving harming a relational partner ($n = 40$) and ones involving what might be called "nonrelational transgressions" ($n = 59$). Specifically, for ratings of frequency, scores on the Moral Standards scale of the GI were *inversely* correlated with more than one-third of the nonrelational items, whereas in only a few cases was a similar "inhibiting" effect of Moral Standards observed for relational items. By contrast, the proportion of significant *positive* correlations between GI scores and the frequency of the behavior was greater for relational than for nonrelational items for both State Guilt and (especially) Trait Guilt. Thus, participants scoring higher on Moral

Standards reported less frequently engaging in nonrelational transgressions. On the other hand, participants scoring higher on Trait Guilt reported more frequently engaging in relational transgressions.

In order to explore these results further, we expanded the list of 99 items to a total of 128 items in a subsequent study. To further aid in analysis, we logically grouped the items into 10 clusters that were either relational or nonrelational in content. The relational clusters were as follows: (1) Fantasy Transgressions, in which respondents merely imagined or thought about wrongdoing (e.g., imagining the death of a family member with whom a respondent was angry); (2) Coercive Transgressions, in which participants involved others in wrongdoing (e.g., forcing a friend into doing something he or she believed was wrong, such as smoking marijuana, or pressuring a reluctant girlfriend to have sex); (3) Rebellion, violations of parental wishes or standards (e.g., engaging in activities of which parents would disapprove); (4) Hostility, a general interpersonal cluster referring to situations in which anger was expressed (e.g., shouting angrily at a family member); and (5) Deceit, referring to more covert relationship transgressions (e.g., lying to a friend or cheating on a romantic partner).

The nonrelational categories of transgressions were as follows: (1) Illegalities, activities for which one could be arrested, excluding those involving drugs (e.g., shoplifting, writing bad checks, etc.); (2) Substance Use, activities involving the use of illegal drugs or the illegal use of alcohol; (3) Sexual Behavior, any sexual activity considered deviant or generally prohibited by at least some moral and religious systems; (4) Unethical Behavior, activities in which school ethics were violated, as well as more general items (e.g., use of racial slurs, swearing, cheating at cards); and (5) Passive Irresponsibility, failure to act in responsible ways toward others (e.g., missing deadlines or forgetting a promise). The Sexual Behavior cluster was classified as nonrelational because the majority of these items either did not directly involve another person (e.g., "Looking at dirty pictures") or did not involve a continuing and close personal relationship (e.g., "Sex with a casual date").

Psychometric analyses of these item clusters were based on the responses of a sample of college students ($n = 169$). Internal-consistency coefficients ranged from .65 to .89, and means of item–whole correlations ranged from .17 to .40. The clusters thus appeared to have adequate internal consistency, although the items were not redundant. Subsequently, participants ($n = 226$) who were not involved in the earlier version of this study were asked to rate the items on a 5-point scale for the frequency with which they had engaged in the behavior in question during the period of the previous 6 months.

Table 12.1 shows the correlations between scores on the behavior list summed within clusters, and scores from each of the GI scales. The pattern of correlations was generally the same for both State Guilt and Trait Guilt. Tests of significant differences in correlation for men and women, using the

TABLE 12.1. Correlations between Scores on the Behavior List Clusters and GI Scale Scores

Cluster	GI scale		
	State Guilt	Trait Guilt	Moral Standards
Nonrelational			
Illegalities	.01	.01	−.29*
Substance use	−.07	−.05	−.32*
Sexual behavior	−.04	.05	−.41**
Passive irresponsibility	.01	.13	−.06
Unethical behavior	.16*	.15*	−.17*
Relational			
Coercive transgressions	.06	.15*	−.13
Fantasy transgressions	.19*	.28**	−.17*
Deceit	.16*	.21**	−.10
Hostility	.19*	.21**	−.16*
Rebellion	.21**	.33**	−.23*

Note. $n = 226$.
*$p < .05$. **$p < .01$.

Fisher's r-to-z transformation, showed no differences. Overall, the direction of association was as expected; that is, Trait Guilt and State Guilt were positively associated with the self-reported commission of most relational transgressions. Also of interest was the fact that there were no significant correlations between these two measures and the self-reported frequency of behaviors in four of the five nonrelational clusters (Sexual Behavior, Illegalities, Substance Use, and Passive Irresponsibility). That Trait Guilt and State Guilt were significantly related to Unethical Behavior may have resulted from the fact that several of these items described behaviors that involved lying to or cheating one's college professors. In this regard, relationships with professors may have been more important to the respondents than we initially imagined.

Table 12.1 also shows the correlations between Moral Standards and the self-reported frequency of transgressing behaviors, again summed within clusters. There were significant negative correlations with 7 of the 10 clusters, suggesting that these behaviors were related to student values about conduct. Comparisons using the Fisher's r-to-z transformation showed no significant differences between men and women in correlations between Moral Standards scores and the behavioral clusters. Generally, the pattern of correlation for Moral Standards was the reverse of that for Trait Guilt and State Guilt; that is, whereas the two guilt scales were positively associated with transgression, Moral Standards was negatively associated. As before, Moral Standards scores were generally more extensively and strongly related to nonrelational than to relational transgression categories.

DISCUSSION

A number of conclusions can be drawn from the previous literature and the results presented above. First, data from several studies have demonstrated the extensive connections between guilt as an affective trait or state, and variables assessing both interpersonal abilities and the number and quality (i.e., satisfaction) of one's available personal relationships. This raises questions regarding the characterization of guilt as a nonsocial emotion. In contrast to some social emotions such as embarrassment, the actual presence of other people may not be necessary for the experience of affective guilt. On the other hand, these results suggest that guilt is decidedly social in its connection to the status of one's relationships.

Second, data from our studies using the GI (which incorporates the three major operational definitions of guilt found in the literature) suggest that whereas the strength of one's moral standards is related to judgments regarding both relational and nonrelational transgressions, this is more clearly so for violations of broad societal prohibitions against sex and aggression than it is for everyday wrongdoing directed toward one's relational partners. This conclusion is further confirmed by evidence that morality (as reflected by Moral Standards scores) is more frequently and more strongly (inversely) related to the self-reported frequency of having engaged in nonrelational as compared to relational transgressions. Thus, although the direction of causality cannot be determined from these data, guilt defined as subscription to moral standards appears to inhibit the expression of immorality, as suggested by Mosher (1979) and others. For the sake of clarity, then, it may be more useful to refer to this factor as "morality" than to refer to it as "guilt."

Third, research involving the GI also shows that although both State Guilt and Trait Guilt scores are directly correlated with judgments of wrongfulness involving both relational and nonrelational transgressions, these affective measures of guilt are more likely to be significantly (and positively) related to the commission of relational as compared to nonrelational transgressions. Although the direction of causality is again uncertain, this would imply that what people typically feel guilty about are behaviors (both symbolic and real) that harm their relational partners, and that risk undermining the emotional bond necessary for ongoing and intimate relationships.

Research using our measure of Moral Standards indicates that morality appears to function in accordance with the traditional view, with the possible exception that guilt may not be involved. Presumably, morality is interpersonal in the sense that moral standards derive from interactions with others and serve to facilitate the individual's functioning within society, which prohibits (whether by codified laws or general societal norms) certain behaviors as disruptive or harmful, and which promotes other behaviors as conducive to general well-being and survival. By contrast, guilt appears to be relational in origin and much more closely related to the status and quality of one's personal relationships (see Baumeister, Stillwell, & Heatherton, Chapter 10, this volume). Thus state guilt is apparently experienced following transgressions that harm relational partners and thereby threaten the emotional bond with significant others, whereas trait guilt may reflect a continuing and habitual lack of mutual satisfaction and intimacy between the guilty person and his or her network of intimate and social relationships. Furthermore, it may be that guilt is related to the violation of general moral prohibitions (as opposed to relational transgressions), but perhaps only when these behaviors threaten the status of one's relationships—for example, when a spouse seeks a divorce following the arrest and conviction of his or her partner for a serious crime.

In conclusion, our view is that moral standards and moral behavior are bound together. People who have higher standards do not commit crimes or violate important social norms, and people who engage in such behaviors appear to have lower or nonexistent standards. This view is consistent with that of Mosher (1966, 1968, 1979), with the exception that we would restrict the use of the term "guilt" to affective or dispositional characteristics, while referring to what Mosher calls "sex guilt" and "hostility guilt" as "moral standards." Guilt may or may not be experienced in either case, however, and thus guilt and moral standards are not necessarily linked, as our data have indicated. Instead, guilt appears to be experienced when personal relationships are harmed or in disarray, whether or not the behaviors in question are against the law or even frowned upon by society in general. It should be acknowledged that our data are preliminary and based exclusively on self-report. However, if replicable and generalizable, this pattern of results suggests the need for a new and expanded view of guilt and its connections to morality and morally relevant behavior. In particular, our approach to examining guilt emphasizes its signal importance in reflecting the status of one's close personal relationships and its divergence from morality as traditionally construed. This approach is similar to that of Baumeister and his colleagues (Baumeister et al., Chapter 10, this volume; Baumeister & Tice, 1990; Baumeister, Wotman, & Stillwell, 1993) in positing the relational functions and consequences of emotions and their concomittants. Indeed, future programs of research on emotion, in our view, would do well to consider the extent of and the circumstances attending the role of emotions in inhibiting and/or facilitating close personal relationships.

REFERENCES

Allinsmith, W. (1966). The learning of moral standards. In D. R. Miller & G. E. Swanson (Eds.), *Inner conflict and defense* (pp. 141–176). New York: Schocken Books.

Aronfreed, J. (1966). Moral behavior and sex identity. In D. R. Miller & G. E. Swanson (Eds.), *Inner conflict and defense* (pp. 177–193). New York: Schocken Books.

Ausubel, D. B. (1955). Relationships between shame and guilt in the socializing process. *Psychological Review, 62,* 378–390.

Baumeister, R. F., & Tice, D. M. (1990). Anxiety and social exclusion. *Journal of Social and Clinical Psychology, 9,* 165–195.

Baumeister, R. F., Wotman, S. R., & Stillwell, A. M. (1993). Unrequited love: On heartbreak, anger, guilt, scriptlessness, and humiliation. *Journal of Personality and Social Psychology, 64,* 377–394.

Buss, A. (1980). *Self-consciousness and social anxiety.* San Francisco: W. H. Freeman.

Buss, A., & Durkee, A. (1957). An inventory for assessing different kinds of hostility. *Journal of Consulting Psychology, 21,* 343–349.

Carver, M. D. (1990). *Personality disorder dimensions and relational functioning.* Unpublished doctoral dissertation, University of Tulsa.

D'Augelli, J. F., & Cross, H. J. (1975). Relationship of sex guilt and moral reasoning to premarital sex in college women and in couples. *Journal of Consulting and Clinical Psychology, 43,* 40–47.

de Rivera, J. (1984). The structure of emotional relationships. In P. Shaver (Ed.), *Review of personality and social psychology: Emotions, relationships, and health* (pp. 116–145). Beverly Hills, CA: Sage.

Evans, D. R., Jessup, B. A., & Hearn, M. T. (1975). Development of a reaction inventory to measure guilt. *Journal of Personality Assessment, 39,* 421–423.

Fehr, L. A., & Stamps, L. E. (1979). Guilt and shyness: A profile of social discomfort. *Journal of Personality Assessment, 43,* 481–484.

Freud, S. (1961). *Civilization and its discontents* (J. Strachey, Ed. and Trans.). New York: Norton. (Original work published 1930)

Harder, D. W., & Lewis, S. J. (1986). The assessment of shame and guilt. In J. N. Butcher & C. D. Spielberger (Eds.), *Advances in personality assessment* (Vol. 6, pp. 89–114). Hillside, NJ: Erlbaum.

Hinde, R. A. (1979). *Towards understanding relationships.* London: Academic Press.

Hoblitzelle, W. (1987). Differentiating and measuring shame and guilt: The relation between shame and depression. In H. B. Lewis (Ed.), *The role of shame in symptom formation* (pp. 207–235). Hillsdale, NJ: Erlbaum.

Hoffman, M. L. (1977). Moral internalization: Current theory and research. In L. Berkowitz (Ed.), *Advances in experimental social psychology* (Vol. 10, pp. 85–133). San Diego, CA: Academic Press.

Hoffman, M. L., & Saltzstein, H. D. (1967). Parent discipline and the child's moral development. *Journal of Personality and Social Psychology, 5,* 45–57.

Hogan, R. (1982). A socioanalytic theory of personality. In M. M. Page (Ed.), *Nebraska Symposium on Motivation* (pp. 55–89). Lincoln: University of Nebraska Press.

Hogan, R. (1985). *Manual for the Hogan Personality Inventory.* Minneapolis: National Computer Systems.

Hogan, R., & Cheek, J. (1983). Self-concepts, self-presentations, and moral judgments. In J. Suls & A. G. Greenwald (Eds.), *Psychological perspectives on the self* (Vol. 2, pp. 249–273). Hillsdale, NJ: Erlbaum.

Hogan, R., Jones, W. H., & Cheek, J. (1985). Socioanalytic theory: An alternative to armadillo psychology. In B. Schlenker (Ed.), *Self and identity: Presentation of self in social life* (pp. 175–198). New York: McGraw-Hill.

Izard, C. E. (1977). *Human emotions*. New York: Plenum Press.

Janda, L. H., & Magri, M. B. (1975). Relation between affective and dispositional guilt. *Journal of Consulting and Clinical Psychology, 43*, 116.

Jones, W. H., & Burdette, M. P. (1994). Betrayal in close personal relationships. In A. L. Weber & J. H. Harvey (Eds.), *Perspectives on close relationships* (pp. 243–262). Boston: Allyn & Bacon.

Jones, W. H., & Kugler, K. E. (1993). Interpersonal correlates of the Guilt Inventory. *Journal of Personality Assessment, 61*, 246–258.

Klas, E. T. (1986). Situational approach to assessment of guilt: Development and validation of a self-report measure. *Journal of Psychopathology and Behavioral Assessment, 9*, 35–48.

Kugler, K. E. (1989). *Guilt: Conceptualization and measurement*. Unpublished doctoral dissertation, University of Tulsa.

Kugler, K. E., & Jones, W. H. (1992). On conceptualizing and assessing guilt. *Journal of Personality and Social Psychology, 62*, 318–327.

Lewis, H. B. (1971). *Shame and guilt in neurosis*. New York: International Universities Press.

Lewis, H. B. (1979). Guilt in obsession and paranoia. In C. E. Izard (Ed.), *Emotions in personality and psychopathology* (pp. 399–414). New York: Plenum Press.

Lewis, H. B. (1981). *Freud and modern psychology: Vol. 1. The emotional basis of mental illness*. New York: Plenum Press.

Lewis, H. B. (1984). *Freud and modern psychology: Vol. 2. The emotional basis of human behavior*. New York: Plenum Press.

Lindsay-Hartz, J. (1984). Contrasting experiences of shame and guilt. *American Behavioral Scientist, 27*, 689–704.

London, R., Schulman, R. E., & Black, M. S. (1964). Religion, guilt, and ethical standards. *Journal of Social Psychology, 63*, 145–159.

Lynd, H. M. (1958). *On shame and the search for identity*. New York: Harcourt, Brace & World

Malinowski, B. (1924). Psychoanalysis and anthropology. *Psyche, 4*, 293–332.

McGraw, K. (1987). Guilt following transgression: An attribution of responsibility approach. *Journal of Personality and Social Psychology, 53*, 247–256.

Miller, D. R., & Swanson, G. E. (Eds.). (1966). *Inner conflict and defense*. New York: Schocken Books.

Mosher, D. L. (1961). *The development and validation of a sentence completion measure of guilt*. Unpublished doctoral dissertation, Ohio State University.

Mosher, D. L. (1966). The development and multitrait–multimethod matrix analysis of three measures of three aspects of guilt. *Journal of Consulting Psychology, 30*, 25–39.

Mosher, D. L. (1968). Measurement of guilt in females by self-report inventories. *Journal of Consulting and Clinical Psychology, 32*, 690–695.

Mosher, D. L. (1979). The meaning and measurement of guilt. In C. E. Izard (Ed.), *Emotions in personality and psychopathology* (pp. 105–129). New York: Plenum Press.

Moulton, R. W., Liberty, P. G., Burnstein, E., & Altucher, N. (1966). Patterning of parental affection and disciplinary dominance as a determinant of guilt and sex typing. *Journal of Personality and Social Psychology, 4*, 356–363.

Okel, E., & Mosher, D. L. (1968). Changes in affective states as a function of guilt over aggressive behavior. *Journal of Consulting and Clinical Psychology, 37*, 265–270.

Otterbacher, J. R., & Munz, D. C. (1973). State–trait measure of experiential guilt. *Journal of Consulting and Clinical Psychology, 40,* 115–121.

Persons, R. W. (1970). The Mosher Guilt Scale: Theoretical formulation, research review and normative data. *Journal of Projective Techniques and Personality Assessment, 34,* 266–270.

Plutchik, R. (1980). A general psychoevolutionary theory of emotion. In R. Plutchik & H. Kellerman (Eds.), *Emotion: Theory, research, and experience. Vol. 1. Theories of emotion* (pp. 3–34). Orlando, FL: Academic Press.

Schwartz, S. (1973). Multimethod analysis of three measures of six common personality traits. *Journal of Personality Assessment, 37,* 559–567.

Sears, R. R., Maccoby, E. E., & Levin, H. (1957). *Patterns of child rearing.* New York: Harper & Row.

Tangney, J. P. (1990). Assessing individual differences in proneness to shame and guilt: Development of the Self-Conscious Affect and Attribution Inventory. *Journal of Personality and Social Psychology, 59,* 102–111.

Tangney, J. P. (1991). Moral affect: The good, the bad, and the ugly. *Journal of Personality and Social Psychology, 61,* 598–607.

Tangney, J. P., Wagner, P. E., Fletcher, C., & Gramzow, R. (1992). Shamed into anger? The relation of shame and guilt to anger and self-reported aggression. *Journal of Personality and Social Psychology, 62,* 669–675.

Tangney, J. P., Wagner, P. E., Gavlas, J., Barlow, D. H., & Marschall, D. E. (1992, August). *Shame, guilt, and constructive vs. destructive anger.* Poster presented at the annual meeting of the American Psychological Association, Washington, DC.

Tomkins, S. S. (1987). Shame. In D. L. Nathanson (Ed.), *The many faces of shame* (pp. 133–161). New York: Guilford Press.

Weiner, B. (1985). An attributional theory of achievement motivation and emotion. *Psychological Review, 92,* 548–573.

Wertheim, E. J., & Schwarz, J. C. (1983). Depression, guilt, and self-management of pleasant and unpleasant events. *Journal of Personality and Social Psychology, 45,* 884–889.

Wicker, F. W., Payne, G. C., & Morgan, R. D. (1983). Participant descriptions of guilt and shame. *Motivation and Emotion, 7,* 25–39.

13

Embarrassment and Social Behavior

ROWLAND S. MILLER

Embarrassment is a ubiquitous human experience. When they are asked to keep track of embarrassing episodes, a sizable majority of college students report being embarrassed at least once a week (Stonehouse & Miller, 1994). Younger teenagers become embarrassed even more often (Horowitz, 1962; Shields, Mallory, & Simon, 1990). Moreover, embarrassment occurs around the world in Eastern, as well as Western, cultures (Edelmann, 1990; Sueda & Wiseman, 1992). Whenever people care what others are thinking of them, embarrassment is possible, so that total immunity to embarrassment is probably rare indeed. In fact, a capacity for embarrassment may be one marker of normality; as Crozier (1990) has colorfully suggested, "we might think that a person who is never embarrassed . . . is lacking some important human quality, is insensitive, thoughtless, or uncaring, a 'brazen hussy' or an 'arrogant son of a bitch' " (p. 7).

Still, despite its prevalence, embarrassment is not an uneventful or mundane experience. As an aversive state of mortification, abashment, and chagrin that follows public social predicaments, embarrassment can have a substantial impact on social behavior. Both an embarrassed actor and his or her audience may find themselves affected. This chapter examines the personal and interactive causes and consequences of embarrassment, describing both the sources and sequelae of this potent social emotion. As we will see, embarrassment appears to be an emotion with a distinct physiological profile that prompts a recognizable nonverbal display, which in turn often serves as an important communicative act in ongoing interactions. The first step toward documenting these points, however, is to determine whether embarrassment is really a self-conscious emotion.

THE SOCIAL NATURE OF EMBARRASSMENT

Although emerging susceptibility to embarrassment coincides with the development of mature public self-consciousness in children (Bennett, 1989), theorists disagree about the fundamental nature of embarrassment. Many believe that embarrassment is based wholly on public self-awareness and a concern for what others are thinking of us, but others hold alternative views.

Theoretical Perspectives on Embarrassment

Two major explanations of embarrassment have gained empirical support. The first holds that embarrassment occurs when unwanted public events create acute concern for how one is being evaluated by others. This "social evaluation" perspective suggests that embarrassment results when one's desired public identity is endangered; the threat of unwanted social evaluations is believed to cause the physical and psychological arousal that is recognized as embarrassment (e.g., Edelmann, 1987; Miller, 1994). This view has evolved from Goffman's (1967) basic notions of self-presentation, in that the events that cause embarrassment are thought to be primarily those in which unanticipated events communicate undesired information about oneself to others (Schlenker, 1980). However, the social evaluation perspective further holds that public self-consciousness is needed for self-presentational failures to be aversive. In order to be embarrassed, one must both understand and care about *others'* evaluations of oneself (see Schlenker & Leary, 1982). A person who is too immature to apprehend others' judgments, or who simply does not care what a particular audience thinks, should not be embarrassable.

A different spin on self-presentational failure is offered by the second model of embarrassment, the "dramaturgic" perspective. This alternative perspective holds that awkward interaction, and not a fear of unwanted social evaluation, is the primary cause of embarrassment (Parrott, Sabini, & Silver, 1988; Parrott & Smith, 1991; Silver, Sabini, & Parrott, 1987). Disruptions of interaction are thought to be intrinsically aversive, especially when unwanted events disorder one's expectations. The loss of a coherent self-presentational script, and the flustered uncertainty that follows, are believed to cause the aversive arousal of embarrassment, regardless of what others are presumed to be thinking.

Both the dramaturgic and social evaluation perspectives portray embarrassment as a uniquely social emotion that depends on the presence of other people, either as interactive partners or as evaluative observers. They differ, however, in the assumed centrality of public self-consciousness in the origins of embarrassment. The social evaluation model suggests that embarrassment would not exist without concern for others' opinions, and that embarrassment should covary with the extent of one's fear of negative social evaluation. In contrast, the dramaturgic model argues that although one must be aware of oneself as a social object to be motivated to engage in self-presentation, the severity of one's embarrassment depends on the extent of one's indecisiveness and uncertainty in interaction, rather than on one's level of public self-awareness.

Both perspectives are plausible, and each has garnered some support. For instance, both awkward uncertainty and concerns over social evaluation are components of prototypical embarrassment. When Parrott and Smith (1991) asked respondents to describe embarrassment's key elements, both flustered indecision and dread of others' judgments were typically mentioned.

Furthermore, awkward interactions can clearly cause embarrassment (Miller, 1992; Parrott et al., 1988). Parrott and his colleagues (1988) demonstrated this with a clever procedure in which subjects were asked to envision an interpersonal rejection under one of several conditions. In one scenario, subjects imagined being refused a date because their partners had a class to attend; this innocuous refusal was not expected to be embarrassing. In another condition, subjects suffered a blunt rebuff, an awkward and threatening event expected to cause consternation and embarrassment. In a third, critical condition, however, subjects were refused with an ostensibly legitimate reason that they privately knew to be a lie. This "transparent pretext" for an interpersonal rejection was also expected to threaten the subjects' self-esteem, but without disrupting the predictability of the interaction. Parrott et al. argued that an esteem-based model of embarrassment would predict substantial embarrassment in both the second and third conditions, whereas a dramaturgic approach would expect embarrassment only in the second, awkward condition (the obvious rebuff).

Subjects' reports of their expected embarrassment in each condition demonstrated that, indeed, the "transparent pretext" scenario seemed less embarrassing than the outright snub. Consistent with the dramaturgic model, the awkward rebuff was clearly believed to be highly embarrassing. However, Parrott et al. (1988) also suggested that these results were inconsistent with a social evaluation model of embarrassment—a point that was much less clear. I countered (Miller, 1994) that subjects may have considered the transparent pretext a kinder, albeit untrue, method of refusal that communicated higher regard for the person who was turned down than the blunt rejection did; in that case, a social evaluation model would also predict the results that Parrott et al. obtained.

I then tried (Miller, 1994) to disentangle the overlapping predictions of the two models with an adaptation of Parrott et al.'s technique. Subjects were asked to imagine being refused a date either with innocuous, non-threatening reasons, or with a disguised but "transparent" rejection that was more threatening. Now, however, the news of the refusal was brought to them by a messenger who also believed the rejection to be threatening or benign. The subjects thus knew that they had or had not been spurned, and independently envisioned either an awkward interaction with a messenger who considered them scorned or an innocent interchange with one who saw nothing wrong. The procedure thus orthogonally manipulated awkwardness and social evaluation, and found that each influenced subjects' reports of expected embarrassment. A clumsy current interaction was more embarrassing than one that was more mundane, just as a dramaturgic approach would suggest. However, a threatening rejection was even more embarrassing, whether or not that rejection was apparent to the current interactive partner; despite their symmetric, similar manipulations, the evaluation variable accounted for twice as much variance in expected embarrassment as awkwardness did.

Both the social evaluation and dramaturgic perspectives apparently carry some weight. Nevertheless, in a head-to-head experimental comparison of the two perspectives, concern over social evaluation was a more potent cause of embarrassment than was awkward uncertainty per se. In real predicaments, of course, the two influences can interact and exacerbate each other; a sudden loss of script can quickly create concerns about what others are thinking, and a fear of negative evaluation can rob one of poise and grace. Still, concern about social evaluation appears to be the predominant cause of embarrassment—a point that also emerges from studies of embarrassability, or dispositional susceptibility to embarrassment.

Embarrassability

Some people are more embarrassable than others. People vary in the intensity of their reactions to any given predicament, and examination of the traits that predict high embarrassability provides further insight into the social nature of embarrassment. Embarrassability itself can be assessed with Modigliani's (1968) Embarrassability Scale, a reliable, valid inventory (Leary, 1991) that briefly describes 26 different social predicaments (e.g., "Suppose you walked into a bathroom at someone else's house and discovered it was occupied by a member of the opposite sex"). Respondents are asked to judge how embarrassed they would be in each case, and the sum of their responses is their embarrassability score.

Highly embarrassable people do not appear to encounter predicaments that are different from those of other people (Miller, 1992); they simply are more affected by those they do confront. Several recent studies indicate why. Embarrassability is more highly related to public than to private self-consciousness (Edelmann, 1985); highly embarrassable people are keenly aware of others' evaluations of themselves. By itself, this public self-consciousness is not problematic, but highly embarrassable people also have stronger fears of negative evaluation (Leary & Meadows, 1991); they dread disapproval from others and are especially motivated to seek liking and acceptance. Furthermore, their desire to avoid exclusion tends to be coupled with high sensitivity to social norms and attention to the appropriateness of behavior. They worry about the propriety and correctness of social conduct, and are likely to be affected by small transgressions that others shrug off (Miller, in press).

A large survey study that compared dramaturgic and social evaluation predictors of embarrassability also showed that highly embarrassable people report lower skill at self-presentation than do those who are less embarrassable (Miller, in press). They believe that they are less adept at interaction, and are presumably less deft at repairing interactive predicaments when they occur. This finding obviously supports the dramaturgic perspective, which would predict that people with lower interactive dexterity should be more likely to experience awkward interactions and thereby should be more embarrassable.

However, deficiencies in self-confidence and social skill are more closely associated with dispositional shyness than they are with embarrassability (Miller, in press). By far the best predictors of susceptibility to embarrassment are attentiveness to social norms and fear of negative evaluation; in general, highly embarrassable people dread public violations of social norms and expect the worst when they occur (Miller, in press), a pattern that clearly fits a social evaluation model of embarrassment. Once again, although skill and awkwardness influence one's embarrassability, concern over social evaluation appears to be a more central component of embarrassment.

Embarrassment is unquestionably a self-conscious emotion rooted in social experience, but awareness of one's social self alone does not cause it to occur. Instead, mature embarrassment seems to result from the acute realization that one's social self is imperiled and that others may be judging one negatively (see Bennett, 1989, and Crozier & Burnham, 1990; cf. Lewis, Chapter 7, this volume, and Lewis, Stanger, Sullivan, & Barone, 1991). Whatever their dramaturgic abilities, it appears that if people were heedless of others' opinions, they would not be very embarrassable.

A Few Words about Measurement

It is circumspect at this juncture to note that all of the studies mentioned thus far (and most of those to follow) have measured embarrassment through self-report. This method is convenient and useful, and devices such as the Embarrassability Scale have proven their worth. Still, there are important limitations associated with asking subjects how they feel.

People can have difficulty characterizing their emotions. For that reason, researchers should beware of using single items to indicate whole emotions (simply asking, for instance, "how embarrassed were you?"). Instead, a variety of response formats and phraseology, such as Likert and bipolar scales and adjective checklists, should be employed to record any particular feeling (e.g., Apsler, 1975; Miller, 1987). Apsler (1975) assessed embarrassment with several bipolar items (e.g., "embarrassed–unembar-rassed," "flustered–calm") that worked well.

More subtly, people may be experiencing an admixture of emotions at any one time. Embarrassment is highly correlated with shyness (Miller, in press) and largely resembles shame on Izard's (1977) Differential Emotions Scale (Mosher & White, 1981). It *can* be discriminated from its neighbors; one study (Miller, in press) distinguished embarrassment from shyness by demonstrating its different relationships to a variety of predictors (e.g., low self-esteem and deficient social skill were more closely linked to shyness than to embarrassment). In another study (Miller & Tangney, 1994), embarrass-ment and shame were differentiated with a sorting procedure involving 39 specific descriptors (shame was a darker, more lasting emotion that followed different transgressions). Still, the similarities among these emotions can complicate their measurement.

Therefore, researchers should be attentive to the role that *behavioral* measures may be able to play in future studies of the self-conscious emotions. As methods improve, nonverbal and physiological measures may be able to provide less reactive and more reliable indices of the presence and extent of embarrassment. Indeed, in some cases, behavioral measures may provide the only clear indication of which of a number of emotions may be predominant. For instance, when I (Miller, 1987) asked subjects to observe other people's embarrassing activities, they reported a variety of feelings: They felt sorry for the actors, and they were embarrassed by the procedure, but they also rather enjoyed the spectacle. The subjects' self-reports of these diverse feelings were similar, and did not allow strong conclusions about their emotional responses. However, a measure of physiological arousal (in this case, skin potential) was significantly more highly correlated with their reports of embarrassment than with any other feeling, permitting the conclusion that "empathic embarrassment" was possible. In this study, the combination of self-report and physiological data provided more compelling results than did self-report alone—a point to be kept in mind as we next consider the nonverbal and physiological aspects of embarrassment.

Physiological Responses in Embarrassment

Embarrassment has long been grouped with the social anxieties, or anxieties at the prospect of real or imagined interpersonal evaluation (such as stage fright or shyness; see Schlenker & Leary, 1982). However, intriguing work by Leary, Rejeski, Britt, and Smith (1994) now suggests that embarrass-ment is quite distinct from anxiety per se. Leary et al. forewarned their subjects of an upcoming embarrassing event—a mortifying physical examina-tion of the fat on their thighs and waists—and then assessed the subjects' heart rate, blood pressure, and finger temperature as they waited for the examina-tion to begin. The subjects' responses were characteristic of anxious, sympathetic arousal: Their heart rate and blood pressure increased, while their finger temperature went down (cf. Buck & Parke, 1972). Once the embarrassing inspection actually started, however, their cardiovascular responses slowed significantly—and their fingers cooled even further—as they apparently began a parasympathetic inhibition of their earlier arousal. Leary et al. likened this pattern to the sight of an immobile deer frozen in oncoming headlights; instead of bounding away with a burst of sympathetic "fight-or-flight" activity, the trapped and embarrassed subjects passively tried to shrink away from the humiliating situation.

Interestingly, the subjects' physiological profiles were different if they were surprised by an unexpected physical exam. If the subjects were embarrassed by an unforeseen predicament (the manner in which people encounter most real-life embarrassments), they exhibited both sympathetic surprise and the parasympathetic withdrawal noted above. Leary et al. (1994) concluded that embarrassment stimulates both sympathetic and parasympathetic pathways in varying proportions, which depend on the level of personal threat an embarrassed actor perceives.

In any case, embarrassment can be clearly distinguished at the physiological level from both social anxiety (Leary et al., 1994) and fear (Buck & Parke, 1972), and may even emerge from a discrete locus in the brain. Neurological studies suggest that patients can lose their capacity for embarrassment when the medial frontal lobe is damaged (Devinsky, Hafler, & Victor, 1982).

Nonverbal Displays

Embarrassment may also be accompanied by readily recognizable nonverbal behaviors. Embarrassed people typically avert their gaze, looking away from others, and display a nervous, silly smile; their body motion and speech dysfluencies also tend to increase (Edelmann & Hampson, 1979, 1981a). Moreover, the timing and pattern of these behaviors can reliably communicate their abashment and chagrin to others. Asendorpf (1990) demonstrated that observers can distinguish embarrassed from nonembarrassed smiles by the timing of gaze aversion; people who are embarrassed typically break off eye contact 1 1/2 seconds before their smiles reach peak intensity, whereas those who are not embarrassed look away just after the broadest part of their smiles.

Of course, embarrassed people may also blush, as the capillaries in the skin of their cheeks dilate and become engorged with blood. People sometimes blush without being embarrassed (and may be embarrassed without blushing; see Leary, Britt, Cutlip, & Templeton, 1992), but a facial blush is nevertheless considered "the hallmark of embarrassment" (Buss, 1980, p. 129). It appears that people of all races (Leary et al., 1992) and nationalities (Edelmann, 1990) blush, and the mere act of blushing may induce facial feedback that exacerbates embarrassment in some people

(Edelmann, 1987). A blush not only may make one's embarrassment obvious, but may make one more abashed as well.

These involuntary nonverbal responses can have a cumulative result that produces a consequential effect of embarrassment on social behavior: A person's embarrassment may be plainly evident to any observers. Edelmann and Hampson (1981b) showed that with all these nonverbal cues available, audiences could recognize targets' embarrassment with high accuracy. Embarrassment is thus much more than a private emotional response to an untoward social situation; it can also be a vivid social *communication* that has important, widespread impact on what happens next. Documentation of this point takes us next to consideration of the influence of embarrassment on social interaction.

EMBARRASSMENT IN INTERACTION

The thesis in this section of the chapter is that embarrassment can have dramatic effects on social conduct. As a colleague and I (Miller & Leary, 1992) have suggested, "the possibility of being embarrassed seems to dictate and constrain a great deal of social behavior; much of what we do, and perhaps more importantly what we don't do, is based on our desire to avoid embarrassment" (p. 210). Furthermore, once it occurs, an embarrassing episode may entrap all the participants in an interaction. Both an embarrassed actor and all of his or her observers may find themselves involved in remediating and overcoming an embarrassing incident. The responses people select may depend on the specific circumstances they face, however, so a survey of the events that can create embarrassment is in order.

Embarrassing Circumstances

The embarrassing pitfalls of social life are remarkably diverse. I (Miller, 1992) constructed a catalog of embarrassing predicaments by asking 350 high school or college students to describe their most recent embarrassments. A varied assortment of reliable categories emerged; as one would expect, most embarrassments resulted from an *individual's* publicly behaving in clumsy, absent-minded, or hapless ways. These obvious departures from acceptable conduct, termed "normative public deficiencies," included various physical pratfalls, episodes of forgetfulness, uncontrolled flatulence, and inept invasions of others' baths and bedrooms. As one respondent simply reported, "I caught my hair on fire by leaning over a bunsen burner during lab" (Miller, 1992, p. 193).

More rarely, people were embarrassed by inadvertently inconveniencing, embarrassing, or insulting others ("abashed harmdoing"), or by merely standing out from the crowd even when they had not done anything wrong. These latter episodes of simple "conspicuousness" were interesting; they demonstrated that, even in the absence of deficient or undesirable behavior, people were often mortified to become the salient focus of others' attention.

Altogether, however, only two-thirds of the respondents' embarrassments involved such individual pitfalls. The remaining incidents were more complex, involving more participants. For instance, *interactive* predicaments emerged from a person's association with others as interaction partners or as fellow group members. Just as a dramaturgic model of embarrassment would predict, people could be embarrassed by interactions gone awry that suddenly became uncomfortable and uncertain. Such "awkward interactions" could occur either because of an unexpected loss of script or because of participants' guilty knowledge of past events that made them ill at ease. One respondent suffered a loss of script when a new male coworker arrived at her home with flowers when her steady boyfriend was already there; the coworker departed quickly but left the flowers, leaving the respondent unsure of what to say to her boyfriend. (In fact, neither of them said anything, and she finally retreated to her book and he to his television.) Another respondent was abashed to encounter a fellow with whom she had drunkenly had a "one-night stand" a few nights before; she had not seen him since, and her guilty knowledge of the private event made her unsure of how to treat him publicly now. Predicaments like these lent credence to the dramaturgic perspective, because such interactive uncertainty was clearly disconcerting.

However, some predicaments involving others did not seem to entail scripted interaction at all. Still another respondent was embarrassed when two companions made loud racist remarks in a shopping mall. Such "team transgressions," in which people were concerned that others would judge them by the inappropriate behavior of their associates, often seemed to hinge on people's desire to avoid negative evaluations from distant audiences of total strangers. (This was also true of various individual embarrassments, such as public pratfalls, in which a respondent tripped or fell within sight of other people.) In general, I (Miller, 1992) found that a social evaluation model of embarrassment was able to explain most embarrassments more parsimoniously than the dramaturgic perspective could.

Another striking result was that roughly a fifth of the respondents' recent embarrassments would not have occurred had other people not provoked them. In these cases of "audience provocation," others either publicized people's past misbehavior or (more often) teased or badgered them when they had really done nothing wrong. In such cases, people were typically made the butt of others' jokes, and in most such cases those others *intended* to make the target embarrassed (see Sharkey, 1991). In one remarkable example, a high school student was urged to participate in a "banana-eating contest" during a pep rally (Miller, 1992); while blindfolded, he gobbled a banana with the crowd cheering, only to learn (when the blindfold was removed) that he had been the only contestant. Events like these clearly indicate that people are sometimes faced with predicaments that are not of their making, and that too narrow a focus on a particular actor's ineptitude obscures the interactive origins of many embarrassments.

This is especially true of the last major category of embarrassment obtained (Miller, 1992). Simply as *bystanders* of others' predicaments, people can experience "empathic embarrassment" as they imagine how they would feel in another's position. It can be affecting to watch another person's embarrassment (Miller, 1987)—a fact that, as we will see, may influence the social consequences of embarrassment.

A second useful scheme for categorizing embarrassments has been developed by William Cupach and Sandra Metts (1990, 1992). Their scheme is entirely independent of the one described above—neither research team knew of the other's work—but the two frameworks nicely complement and cross-validate each other. In general, the first approach (Miller, 1992) is broader, delineating several specific categories of embarrassment not described by Cupach and Metts. Nevertheless, Cupach and Metts have suggested some valuable refinements of the larger model. First, they clearly differentiate predicaments for which an *actor* is personally responsible from those caused by *others* (a distinction that is only implicit in my own scheme). Furthermore, when others are responsible, Cupach and Metts have suggested that the embarrassed target may be *directly* involved, being the intended victim of the others' actions, or only *indirectly* involved, as in "team" or "empathic" embarrassments.

In addition, Cupach and Metts (1990, 1992) have subdivided the "audience provocation" category (Miller, 1992) into specific acts, such as criticism/correction, recognition/praise, and violations of privacy or trust. They have also added a new individual predicament—actions inconsistent with one's "idealized self-image." This interesting category includes embarrassments resulting from behavior that is incompatible with one's personal goals for one's behavior but is not normatively deficient.

Together, these two classification schemes provide the most comprehensive and useful guide to embarrassing circumstances yet produced. Table 13.1 sets forth a combination of the two approaches.

Avoiding Embarrassment

People will steer clear of embarrassing predicaments if they can. Embarrassment can be aversive enough that people will forego tangible rewards in order to avert it. For instance, Brown (1970; Brown & Garland, 1971) showed that subjects would sacrifice cash payments from an experimenter in order to avoid public disclosure of their embarrassing actions (such as sucking on a pacifier or singing off-key).

Thus it is not surprising that social behavior is often influenced by a desire to avoid embarrassment. In fact, fear of embarrassment is one factor that can keep bystanders from helping during public emergencies (Latané & Darley, 1970). In one commonplace example, Foss and Crenshaw (1978)

TABLE 13.1. Types of Embarrassing Circumstances

Category	Frequency of mention[a]
I. Individual behavior	
A. Normative public deficiencies	
1. Physical pratfalls and inept performances	22%
2. Cognitive errors (e.g., forgetfulness)	16%
3. Loss of control over:	11%
a. One's person (e.g., belching, flatulence)	
b. One's emotions (e.g., excessive temper)	
c. One's environment (e.g., clothes, cars)	
4. Failures of privacy regulation (e.g., nudity)	8%
B. Abashed harmdoing: Chagrin over inconvenience caused others	2%
C. Departures from idealized self-image: Behavior inconsistent with personal goals	—
D. Conspicuousness: Suffering the attention of others when one is *not* deficient	7%
II. Interactive behavior	
A. Awkward interaction	
1. Loss of script: Uncertainty from unexpected interactive events	6%
2. Guilty knowledge: Knowledge of past transgressions is currently discomforting	2%
B. Team transgressions: Others in one's group transgress	7%
III. Audience provocation	
A. Real transgressions: Others publicize one's past predicaments	5%
1. With the intent to embarrass (e.g., teasing, criticism/correction)	—
2. Without the intent to embarrass (e.g., inadvertent disclosures)	—
B. No real transgressions: Others single one out in the absence of any normative deficiency	13%
1. With the intent to embarrass (e.g., teasing)	—
2. Without the intent to embarrass (e.g., recognition/praise)	—
IV. Bystander behavior	
A. Empathic embarrassment: Discomfort felt for others whose actions do not reflect upon onself	2%

[a]These figures reflect the prevalence of each category in the self-reports of my subjects (Miller, 1992). Where no figures are provided, the category is one suggested by Cupach and Metts (1990, 1992) that I did not use.

demonstrated that men were much less likely to help a woman pick up a dropped package when it was a box of tampons than when it was a box of envelopes. Indeed, people are even less likely to seek help or to engage in self-protective behavior if they might be embarrassed by doing so. Druian and DePaulo (1977) found that adults who needed aid on a spelling test were less likely to ask for help from a competent child than from another adult, and two studies have shown that the more embarrassed people are by the prospect of obtaining contraception, the less likely they are to use contraception during sexual activity (Herold, 1981; Leary & Dobbins, 1983). People are evidently highly motivated to avoid embarrassment, even when they incur real costs by doing so.

Reactions to Embarrassment

If a predicament is unavoidable and embarrassment does occur, it is rarely ignored. Consistent with a social evaluation model, embarrassed people often engage in "facework"—coping behavior meant to regain social approval and re-establish an endangered social identity. They may justify or explain their actions, apologize, try to make amends (Gonzales, Pederson, Manning, & Wetter, 1990), or resort to humor (Fink & Walker, 1977). Furthermore, the strength of these efforts may depend upon the extent of their embarrassment; the more embarrassed people are, the harder they may try to regain lost face (Gonzales et al., 1990; Modigliani, 1971). In fact, the urge to remediate embarrassment may even persist for some time, affecting behavior in subsequent, new situations. Apsler (1975) found that embarrassed subjects were more generous than nonembarrassed people, volunteering more of their time to help someone else, even when the person making the request had no knowledge of their prior embarrassment.

Such kindly reactions do not always follow embarrassment, however. Embarrassed people occasionally just flee their predicaments without trying to repair them, or, more rarely, challenge or attack those who have provoked their chagrin. In fact, two research teams (Cupach & Metts, 1990, 1992; Sharkey & Stafford, 1990) have shown that when people are asked to recall their past embarrassments, they report a wide variety of specific responses. Cupach and Metts found that the most common response was avoidance; about a fourth of the time, people tried to continue as if nothing had happened by ignoring the predicament or quickly changing topics of conversation. On other occasions, people tried to escape predicaments by simply running away. Together, these tactics of evasion followed a third of remembered embarrassments.

More often, people chose to acknowledge their predicaments and tried to repair or explain them away. Remediation was a common strategy (Cupach & Metts, 1990); in almost a fifth of their embarrassments, people offered to correct the cause of their predicaments (by, for instance, cleaning up their spills or promising recompense for injury). Accounts and apologies also occurred; people tried to excuse their actions with explanations that minimized their blame, or, alternatively, accepted the responsibility with an expression of remorse. One or the other of these blame-based tactics occurred one-quarter of the time. A sixth of the recalled embarrassments were handled with humor, as people wryly admitted their difficulties; and, in rare instances, people reacted with aggression and hostility against those presumed to have created the predicament.

Importantly, some responses were more likely to follow certain incidents than others. Normative public deficiencies (see Table 13.1) frequently engendered accounts, as people explained that such behavior was not characteristic of them (Sharkey & Stafford, 1990); and humor and remediation were more likely after individual than after interactive or audience predicaments (Cupach & Metts, 1990, 1992). When aggression occurred, it usually followed an intentional audience provocation (Sharkey & Stafford, 1990). After a third of their embarrassments, people also reported using more than one specific response, stringing together two or more tactics into an elaborate sequence of facework (see Cupach, Metts, & Hazleton, 1986). Such sequences often started with apologies that led to offers of remediation or subsequent escape. Moreover, Edelmann (1994) has found that these responses to embarrassment are universal, differing only slightly from culture to culture (cf. Sueda & Wiseman, 1992).

Accompanying these deliberate responses are other cross-cultural, largely involuntary responses—embarrassment's characteristic nonverbal display—that may have some of the most important interactive effects. As we have seen, embarrassment is easily recognized (Edelmann & Hampson, 1981b). Thus, whether or not one chooses to acknowledge one's embarrassment verbally, it may be apparent to observers and may serve as a nonverbal apology for any misbehavior (Semin & Manstead, 1982). As Castelfranchi and Poggi (1990) have argued, by blushing, embarrassed people communicate that "they know, care about, and fear others' evaluations and that they share those values deeply; they also communicate their sorrow over any possible faults or inadequacies" (p. 240). Obvious embarrassment may serve to deflect negative social evaluation by clearly signaling one's chagrin. In particular, blushing may be a gesture of appeasement and contrition that mollifies critical audiences and reduces the threat of social rejection (Leary & Meadows, 1991).

In fact, if their blushing is obvious, people apparently feel less need to engage in facework after an embarrassing event. Landel and Leary (1992) found that embarrassed subjects did not engage in extensive facework if an experimenter mentioned that she saw them blush; in contrast, when the experimenter seemed unaware of their facial blushing, the subjects were much more ingratiating. People's strategic, verbal reactions to embarrassment may thus depend on both their nonverbal responses and their audience's reactions to their plight. How, then, do others respond to embarrassment in their midst?

Others' Responses

It can be affecting to witness another's embarrassment. Goffman (1967) argued that embarrassing predicaments often involve all those present; "when an individual finds himself in a situation which ought to make him blush, others present usually will blush with him" (p. 100), so that empathic embarrassment is possible (Miller, 1987, 1992). Even when observers do not share an actor's embarrassment, however, they may participate in the remedial interchanges through which an embarrassing disruption is overcome.

Indeed, Cupach and Metts (1990) and Sharkey and Stafford (1990) have shown that observers may respond with a variety of responses much like those available to the embarrassed actors themselves. Apologies are rare, but accounts, remediation, avoidance, humor, and even occasional aggression occur, along with two types of response unique to observers: empathy and support. Audiences are sometimes hostile to embarrassed actors (Cupach et al., 1986), but far more often they are supportive, quickly reassuring abashed actors of their continued positive regard. They are also often empathic, advising the actors that their situations are not unique or uncommon (e.g., "I know how you feel; it happens to me all the time"). Support and empathy are the most common observer reactions, with one of them occurring in about half of all recalled predicaments (Cupach & Metts, 1990).

In studies of accounts of past embarrassments, observers' choices of strategies depended somewhat on both the situation and the actor's reaction; for instance, observer aggression was most common when an actor was forgetful, and observer avoidance was likely when the actor also pretended that nothing had happened (Sharkey & Stafford, 1990). If an actor decided not to acknowledge an embarrassing incident, the audience rarely brought it up. Across the board, however, audiences were more often kindly and benign than punitive and malicious. Even laughter from an audience, although sometimes distressing, was often judged to be an effective way of reassuring an embarrassed actor that a transgression would not be taken seriously (Cupach & Metts, 1990; Edelmann, 1994).

THE OUTCOME OF EMBARRASSMENT

The importance of this typical benevolence from the witnesses of embarrassing incidents should not be overlooked. Embarrassed people usually believe that they have made more negative impressions on their audiences than they really have (Semin, 1982); as a result, their fears of negative evaluation tend to be exaggerated (Semin & Manstead, 1981). This fact, coupled with the possibility that embarrassed behavior itself can act as a nonverbal social apology, suggests that embarrassing circumstances seldom turn out as badly as people fear.

Indeed, there is evidence that embarrassment has instrumental value that may make it a *desirable* reaction to social predicaments. When, in the judgment of an audience, embarrassment seems appropriate to one's circumstances, an obvious display of embarrassment actually elicits more favorable responses from observers than do cool calm and poise. Semin and Manstead (1982) showed subjects a videotape of a shopper accidentally knocking down a large grocery store display, and found that he was liked better when he reacted with evident embarrassment than when he calmly rebuilt the display. Similarly, Levin and Arluke (1982) demonstrated that someone who became embarrassed while asking for volunteers from a large class received more help than someone who was unruffled and composed. Semin and Papadopoulou (1990) have even shown that embarrassment can forestall parental punishment; mothers are less punitive if their children seem embarrassed after some misdeed than if they seem heedless of their sins.

Thus embarrassment is more than just a painful self-conscious response to untoward social conditions; it serves useful social functions as well. The desire to avoid embarrassment guides social conduct as an important agent of social control; as Gibbons (1990) has argued, "fear of embarrassment helps bring behavior in line with certain accepted social rules. . . . Without its impact, there would be social anarchy, and social discourse, as it exists, would be virtually impossible" (p. 138). Once predicaments occur, moreover, embarrassment is often an adaptive response that signals one's chagrin and regret, and decreases the chances of social rejection. Imagine a person who cannot be embarrassed; such a person would seem brazenly heedless of others' opinions, and would leave others ill at ease when predicaments do occur. Embarrassment can be painful, but we would be less well off without it, lacking a useful mechanism that helps us overcome and repair the inevitable pitfalls of interaction and social life.

REFERENCES

Apsler, R. (1975). Effects of embarrassment on behavior toward others. *Journal of Personality and Social Psychology, 32,* 145–153.

Asendorpf, J. (1990). The expression of shyness and embarrassment. In W. R. Crozier (Ed.), *Shyness and embarrassment: Perspectives from social psychology* (pp. 87–118). Cambridge, England: Cambridge University Press.

Bennett, M. (1989). Children's self-attribution of embarrassment. *British Journal of Developmental Psychology, 7,* 207–217.

Brown, B. R. (1970). Face-saving following experimentally induced embarrassment. *Journal of Experimental Social Psychology, 6,* 255–271.

Brown, B. R., & Garland, H. (1971). The effects of incompetency, audience acquaintanceship, and anticipated evaluative feedback on face-saving behavior. *Journal of Experimental Social Psychology, 7,* 490–502.

Buck, R. W., & Parke, R. D. (1972). Behavioral and physiological response to the presence of a friendly or neutral person in two types of stressful situations. *Journal of Personality and Social Psychology, 24,* 143–153.

Buss, A. H. (1980). *Self-consciousness and social anxiety.* San Francisco: W. H. Freeman.

Castelfranchi, C., & Poggi, I. (1990). Blushing as a discourse: Was Darwin wrong? In W. R. Crozier (Ed.), *Shyness and embarrassment: Perspectives from social psychology* (pp. 230–251). Cambridge, England: Cambridge University Press.

Crozier, W. R. (1990). Introduction. In W. R. Crozier (Ed.), *Shyness and embarrassment: Perspectives from social psychology* (pp. 1–15). Cambridge, England: Cambridge University Press.

Crozier, W. R., & Burnham, M. (1990). Age-related differences in children's understanding of shyness. *British Journal of Developmental Psychology, 8,* 179–185.

Cupach, W. R., & Metts, S. (1990). Remedial processes in embarrassing predicaments. In J. Anderson (Ed.), *Communication yearbook 13* (pp. 323–352). Newbury Park, CA: Sage.

Cupach, W. R., & Metts, S. (1992). The effects of type of predicament and embarrassability on remedial responses to embarrassing situations. *Communication Quarterly, 40,* 149–161.

Cupach, W. R., Metts, S., & Hazleton, V., Jr. (1986). Coping with embarrassing predicaments: Remedial strategies and their perceived utility. *Journal of Language and Social Psychology, 5,* 181–200.

Devinsky, O., Hafler, D. A., & Victor, J. (1982). Embarrassment as the aura of a complex partial seizure. *Neurology, 32,* 1284–1285.

Druian, P. R., & DePaulo, B. M. (1977). Asking a child for help. *Social Behavior and Personality, 5,* 33–39.

Edelmann, R. J. (1985). Individual differences in embarrassment: Self-consciousness, self-monitoring, and embarrassibility. *Personality and Individual Differences, 6,* 223–230.

Edelmann, R. J. (1987). *The psychology of embarrassment.* Chichester, England: Wiley.

Edelmann, R. J. (1990). Embarrassment and blushing: A component-process model, some initial descriptive data and cross-cultural data. In W. R. Crozier (Ed.), *Shyness and embarrassment: Perspectives from social psychology* (pp. 205–229). Cambridge, England: Cambridge University Press.

Edelmann, R. J. (1994). Embarrassment and blushing: Factors influencing face-saving strategies. In S. Ting-Toomey (Ed.), *The challenge of facework* (pp. 231–267). Albany: State University of New York Press.

Edelmann, R. J., & Hampson, R. J. (1979). Changes in non-verbal behaviour during embarrassment. British Journal of Social and Clinical Psychology, 18, 385–390.

Edelmann, R. J., & Hampson, R. J. (1981a). Embarrassment in dyadic interaction. *Social Behavior and Personality, 9,* 171–177.

Edelmann, R. J., & Hampson, R. J. (1981b). The recognition of embarrassment. *Personality and Social Psychology Bulletin, 7,* 109–116.

Fink, E. L., & Walker, B. A. (1977). Humorous responses to embarrassment. *Psychological Reports, 40,* 475–485.

Foss, R. D., & Crenshaw, N. C. (1978). Risk of embarrassment and helping. *Social Behavior and Personality, 6,* 243–245.

Gibbons, F. X. (1990). The impact of focus of attention and affect on social behavior.

In W. R. Crozier (Ed.), *Shyness and embarrassment: Perspectives from social psychology* (pp. 119–143). Cambridge, England: Cambridge University Press.

Goffman, E. (1967). *Interaction ritual: Essays on face-to-face behavior.* Garden City, NY: Anchor Books.

Gonzales, M. H., Pederson, J. H., Manning, D. J., & Wetter, D. W. (1990). Pardon my gaffe: Effects of sex, status, and consequence severity on accounts. *Journal of Personality and Social Psychology, 58,* 610–621.

Herold, E. S. (1981). Contraceptive embarrassment and contraceptive behavior among young single women. *Journal of Youth and Adolescence, 10,* 233–242.

Horowitz, E. (1962). Reported embarrassment memories of elementary school, high school, and college students. *Journal of Social Psychology, 56,* 317–325.

Izard, C. E. (1977). *Human emotions.* New York: Plenum Press.

Landel, J., & Leary, M. R. (1992, March). *Social blushing as a face-saving display.* Paper presented at the meeting of the Southeastern Psychological Association, Knoxville, TN.

Latané, B., & Darley, J. (1970). *The unresponsive bystander: Why doesn't he help?* New York: Appleton-Century-Crofts.

Leary, M. R. (1991). Social anxiety, shyness, and related constructs. In J. Robinson, P. Shaver, & L. Wrightsman (Eds.), *Measures of personality and social psychological attitudes* (pp. 161–194). New York: Academic Press.

Leary, M. R., Britt, T. W., Cutlip, W. D., II, & Templeton, J. L. (1992). Social blushing. *Psychological Bulletin, 112,* 446–460.

Leary, M. R., & Dobbins, S. E. (1983). Social anxiety, sexual behavior, and contraceptive use. *Journal of Personality and Social Psychology, 45,* 1347–1354.

Leary, M. R., & Meadows, S. (1991). Predictors, elicitors, and concomitants of social blushing. *Journal of Personality and Social Psychology, 60,* 254–262.

Leary, M. R., Rejeski, W. J., Britt, T., & Smith, G. E. (1994). *Physiological differences between embarrassment and social anxiety.* Manuscript submitted for publication.

Levin, J., & Arluke, A. (1982). Embarrassment and helping behavior. *Psychological Reports, 51,* 999–1002.

Lewis, M., Stanger, C., Sullivan, M. W., & Barone, P. (1991). Changes in embarrassment as a function of age, sex, and situation. *British Journal of Developmental Psychology, 9,* 485–492.

Miller, R. S. (1987). Empathic embarrassment: Situational and personal determinants of reactions to the embarrassment of another. *Journal of Personality and Social Psychology, 53,* 1061–1069.

Miller, R. S. (1992). The nature and severity of self-reported embarrassing circumstances. *Personality and Social Psychology Bulletin, 18,* 190–198.

Miller, R. S. (1994). *Delineating the causes of embarrassment: Awkward interaction versus social evaluation.* Manuscript submitted for publication.

Miller, R. S. (in press). On the nature of embarrassability: Shyness, social evaluation, and social skill. *Journal of Personality.*

Miller, R. S., & Leary, M. R. (1992). Social sources and interactive functions of emotion: The case of embarrassment. In M. S. Clark (Ed.), *Review of personality and social psychology* (Vol. 14, pp. 202–221). Newbury Park, CA: Sage.

Miller, R. S., & Tangney, J. P. (1994). Differentiating embarrassment and shame. *Journal of Social and Clinical Psychology, 13,* 273–287.

Modigliani, A. (1968). Embarrassment and embarrassability. *Sociometry, 31,* 313–326.

Modigliani, A. (1971). Embarrassment, facework, and eye contact: Testing a theory of embarrassment. *Journal of Personality and Social Psychology, 17,* 15–24.

Mosher, D. L., & White, B. R. (1981). On differentiating shame and shyness. *Motivation and Emotion, 5,* 61–74.

Parrott, W. G., Sabini, J., & Silver, M. (1988). The roles of self-esteem and social interaction in embarrassment. *Personality and Social Psychology Bulletin, 14,* 191–202.

Parrott, W. G., & Smith, S. F. (1991). Embarrassment: Actual vs. typical cases, classical vs. prototypical representations. *Cognition and Emotion, 5,* 467–488.

Schlenker, B. R. (1980). *Impression management: The self-concept, social identity, and interpersonal relations.* Monterey, CA: Brooks/Cole.

Schlenker, B. R., & Leary, M. R. (1982). Social anxiety and self-presentation: A conceptualization and model. *Psychological Bulletin, 92,* 641–669.

Semin, G. R. (1982). The transparency of the sinner. *European Journal of Social Psychology, 12,* 173–180.

Semin, G. R., & Manstead, A. S. R. (1981). The beholder beheld: A study of social emotionality. *European Journal of Social Psychology, 11,* 253–265.

Semin, G. R., & Manstead, A. S. R. (1982). The social implications of embarrassment displays and restitution behavior. *European Journal of Social Psychology, 12,* 367–377.

Semin, G. R., & Papadopoulou, K. (1990). The acquisition of reflexive social emotions: The transmission and reproduction of social control through joint action. In G. Duveen & B. Lloyd (Eds.), *Social representations and the development of knowledge* (pp. 107–125). Cambridge, England: Cambridge University Press.

Sharkey, W. F. (1991). Intentional embarrassment: Goals, tactics, and consequences. In W. Cupach & S. Metts (Eds.), *Advances in interpersonal communication research, 1991* (pp. 105–128). Normal: Illinois State University.

Sharkey, W. F., & Stafford, L. (1990). Responses to embarrassment. *Human Communication Research, 17,* 315–342.

Shields, S. A., Mallory, M. E., & Simon, A. (1990). The experience and symptoms of blushing as a function of age and reported frequency of blushing. *Journal of Nonverbal Behavior, 14,* 171–187.

Silver, M., Sabini, J., & Parrott, W. G. (1987). Embarrassment: A dramaturgic account. *Journal for the Theory of Social Behavior, 17,* 47–61.

Stonehouse, C., & Miller, R. S. (1994, July). *Embarrassing circumstances, week by week.* Paper presented at the meeting of the American Psychological Society, Washington, DC.

Sueda, K., & Wiseman, R. L. (1992). Embarrassment remediation in Japan and the United States. *International Journal of Intercultural Relations, 16,* 159–173.

V

SELF-CONSCIOUS
EMOTIONS AND
PSYCHOPATHOLOGY

14

Shame-Proneness, Guilt-Proneness, and Psychological Symptoms

JUNE PRICE TANGNEY
SUSAN A. BURGGRAF
PATRICIA E. WAGNER

Shame and guilt have generated considerable interest among psychologists not only as moral emotions regulating interpersonal behavior, but also as potentially important components of a range of psychological disorders. An earlier chapter (Tangney, Chapter 4, this volume) has examined the differential implications of shame and guilt for interpersonal motivations and behaviors. In this chapter, we further argue that it is critical to make a clear distinction between shame and guilt when examining the role of self-conscious emotions in the formation of psychological symptoms.

DIFFERING IMPLICATIONS OF SHAME AND GUILT FOR INTERPERSONAL FUNCTIONING AND INTRAPERSONAL ADJUSTMENT

The results of Lindsay-Hartz (1984) and our own findings (Tangney, 1989) indicate that even verbal, well-educated adults have difficulty defining and distinguishing between shame and guilt in the abstract. Psychologists, too, tend to blur the distinction between these two emotions. The subject index for *Psychological Abstracts,* for example, refers readers interested in shame to the subject heading "Guilt." And this tendency to equate shame with guilt permeates much of the psychological literature.

The distinction between shame and guilt, however, is an important one.

Tangney (Chapter 4, this volume) has presented a detailed analysis of the key similarities and differences between these two frequently confused emotions. Numerous empirical studies (Ferguson, Stegge, & Damhuis, 1990, 1991; Ferguson & Stegge, Chapter 6, this volume; Lindsay-Hartz, 1984; Lindsay-Hartz, de Rivera, & Mascolo, Chapter 11, this volume; Tangney, 1989, 1992, 1993; Tangney, Marschall, Rosenberg, Barlow, & Wagner, 1993; Tangney, Miller, & Flicker, 1992; Wicker, Payne, & Morgan, 1983), underscore that shame and guilt differ importantly along affective, cognitive, and motivational dimensions.

To summarize briefly, both shame and guilt are negative affective experiences that involve self-relevant negative evaluations. The focus of these negative evaluations differs, however, leading to distinct phenomenological experiences. In shame, the focus of the negative evaluation is on the entire self. Following some transgression or failure, the entire self is painfully scrutinized and found lacking. With this painful self-scrutiny come a sense of shrinking, a feeling of being small, and a sense of worthlessness and powerlessness. Shame also involves the imagery of being exposed before a real or imagined disapproving audience. Although empirical findings indicate that shame can be experienced when a person is alone (Tangney et al., 1993), shame typically involves an awareness of how the defective self may appear to others. Not surprisingly, the shame experience is often accompanied by a desire to hide—to sink into the floor and disappear. And research also indicates that shame can engender a hostile, defensive type of anger (Tangney, Wagner, Fletcher, & Gramzow, 1992; Tangney, Wagner, Gavlas, Barlow, & Marschall, 1992), presumably aimed at a real or imagined disapproving other.

Guilt, in contrast, is a bad feeling, but it is a less global and devastating emotion than shame. Guilt arises from a negative evaluation of a specific behavior, somewhat apart from the global self; this specific behavior is found to be immoral, lacking, or otherwise defective. The global self, however, remains intact. With this focus on a behavior (rather than the self) comes a sense of tension, remorse, and regret. The person in the midst of a guilt experience often feels a press to confess, apologize, or make amends for the bad deed that was done. This is, without question, an unpleasant emotion. But because a behavior—not the self—is the object of approbation, the self remains mobilized and ready to take reparative action to the extent that circumstances allow.

Tangney (Chapter 4, this volume) has presented an in-depth examination of the interpersonal implications of these two closely related but distinct emotions. Various empirical studies suggest that guilt fosters an adaptive, constructive orientation toward others, whereas shame invokes a number of processes that are likely to be detrimental to interpersonal relationships. For example, the self-focused nature of shame appears to interfere with other-oriented empathic concern, whereas the feeling of guilt (focusing on a specific behavior and its consequences for others) appears to enhance other-oriented empathy. Perhaps more importantly, feelings of shame tend to motivate behaviors that impede subsequent constructive action in inter-personal contexts (e.g., active avoidance or a tendency to blame others). Feelings of guilt tend to motivate reparative action. Not surprisingly, there appears to be a special link between shame and anger; once angered, moreover, shamed individuals are likely to manage their anger in an unconstructive fashion. In contrast, guilt is less likely to foster feelings of anger, but when angered, guilt-prone individuals tend to handle interper-sonal conflict constructively—for example, by attempting to discuss the matter in a nonhostile fashion.

In sum, shame and guilt appear to set the stage for very different interpersonal dynamics in our day-to-day relationships with friends, col-leagues, and loved ones. When we consider our interpersonal relationships, guilt appears to be the more adaptive response to the inevitable transgres-sions of everyday life. But are there parallel implications for *intrapersonal* adjustment? Is guilt also the more adaptive response when we consider our psychological well-being as individuals?

In this chapter, we first review the theoretical literature, showing that many psychologists have failed to distinguish between shame and guilt when discussing the role of these emotions in psychological disorders. In fact, many references to the psychopathological aspects of guilt describe phenom-ena that are more akin to shame experiences. We focus on depression, in particular, to argue that proneness to shame—not guilt—is a potent and potentially maladaptive affective style with negative implications for psy-chological adjustment. We then review the relevant empirical literature to demonstrate that when shame and guilt are measured in a theoretically appropriate manner, shame-proneness is associated with depression and other psychological symptoms, whereas a tendency to experience "shame-free" guilt is essentially unrelated to maladjustment. In doing so, we highlight results from a recent study considering two different methods for assessing a dispositional tendency toward shame and guilt. We then speculate about the nature of "pathological" guilt as discussed in much of the clinical literature, suggesting that guilt experiences become maladaptive largely when they become fused with shame. Finally, we consider some of the clinical implications of these findings.

THEORETICAL PERSPECTIVES ON SHAME AND GUILT IN PSYCHOPATHOLOGY

The potential relevance of shame and guilt to psychological disorders has long been noted in the clinical and theoretical literature, dating back to the early writings of Freud (1896/1962). In fact, the most comprehensive discussion of shame and guilt in psychopathology can be found in analyti-cally oriented theories. These theories, however, vary considerably in their emphasis on shame versus guilt. Early psychoanalytic perspectives focused largely on the pathogenic implications of guilt. Freud (1909/1955, 1917/1957, 1924/1961), in delineating his conflict–defense model of psychological functioning, highlighted the role of guilt in a range of psychological problems, including melancholia, obsessional neuroses, and masochism. From his perspective, when id impulses and ego-directed actions clash with superego standards, the superego retaliates with feelings of guilt and a variety of related self-punitive maneuvers, which in turn can lead to significant psychological symptoms. In contrast, Freud was much less systematic in his treatment of shame. By 1905, he had developed a fairly circumscribed view of shame as largely a reaction formation against sexually exhibitionistic impulses (Freud, 1905/1953). Recently, a number of theorists have suggested that Freud's relative neglect of shame may have been the result of his focus on a conflict–defense model of psychological functioning, as well as of his failure to distinguish between ego and self (Lewis, 1987a; Miller, 1985; A. P. Morrison, 1989; see also Tangney, in press). A. P. Morrison (1989), for example, has suggested that Freud might have elaborated further on the nature and implications of shame, had he pursued the concepts of ego ideal, narcissism, and self-regard (so central to shame) in greater depth. Instead, Freud's work subsequent to "On Narcissim: An Introduction" (1914/1957) focused to a much greater extent on guilt-inducing Oedipal issues and on a structural theory that emphasized intrapsychic conflict among ego, id, and superego (with little regard for the more self-relevant ego ideal). Lewis (1971) argued that in developing a theory that focused almost exclusively on guilt, Freud may have mislabeled his patients' shame experiences as guilt experiences. She suggested that much of Freud's case material and theoretical formulations might be better conceptualized in terms of shame.

More recently, shame has moved to the forefront of psychodynamically oriented conceptualizations of psychopathology, in part because of the shift toward self-related issues. Shame has been highlighted as a key component of such disorders as depression, narcissism, bipolar illness, schizophrenia, and spouse abuse (Goldberg, 1991; Kohut, 1971; Lansky, 1987; A. P. Morrison, 1989; N. K. Morrison, 1987; Nathanson, 1987). These theories differ in the functional role assigned to shame. Some theories view shame as the cause of psychological symptoms, whereas others see shame as arising from a more fundamental defect in the self system. But, together, these more recent formulations share a new focus on shame and a corresponding de-emphasis of guilt. So again, in much of this literature, the distinction between shame and guilt has been lost.

It is also worth mentioning that the recent resurgence of interest in shame extends beyond the psychoanalytic literature. Shame has been cited as a significant factor in family-systems-oriented conceptualizations of substance abuse, depression, eating disorders, and child abuse (Fossum & Mason, 1986), in the codependency literature (Bradshaw, 1988; Potter-Efron, 1989), and in social-cognitive conceptualizations of eating disorders

(Rodin, Silberstein, & Striegel-Moore, 1985). Here, too, these theories differ in the functional role assigned to shame, and in the degree to which guilt is considered as a distinct and relevant affective phenomenon. But in most cases, guilt has been ignored or relegated to a very subsidiary role in the genesis of psychological and relationship dysfunctions.

Helen Block Lewis (1971) is one of the few theorists who has presented an integrated conceptualization of the differential roles of shame and guilt in psychopathology. Drawing on her earlier work with Witkin (Witkin et al., 1954; Witkin, Lewis, & Weil, 1968), Lewis (1971) hypothesized that individual differences in cognitive style (i.e., field dependence vs. field independence) lead to contrasting modes of superego functioning (i.e., shame-proneness and guilt-proneness), and that together these cognitive and affective styles set the stage for differential symptom formation. She suggested that the global, less differentiated self of the field-dependent individual is vulnerable to the global, less differentiated experience of shame—and ultimately to disorders in affect (particularly depression). In contrast, the more clearly differentiated self of the field-independent individual is vulnerable to the experience of guilt (which requires a differentiation between self and behavior)—and also to obsessive and paranoid symptoms involving vigilance directed toward the "field," separate from the self.

In sum, various psychological theories have identified shame and/or guilt as potentially important factors in the formation of psychological symptoms. The literature, however, is inconsistent regarding the relative importance of shame versus guilt in specific disorders. Much of the inconsistency can be attributed to the fact that most theoretical perspectives (with the exception of Lewis, 1971) have failed to make a clear distinction between shame and guilt.

SHOULD ONE EXPECT A LINK BETWEEN GUILT AND DEPRESSION (AND OTHER PSYCHOLOGICAL SYMPTOMS)?

Harder (Chapter 15, this volume; see also Harder, Cutler, & Rockart, 1992; Harder & Lewis, 1987) has strongly asserted that both a tendency to experience shame and a tendency to experience guilt should be related to depressive symptoms. Although shame-proneness is expected to be more strongly associated with depression, he believes that the link between guilt and depression is unquestionable, and that failure to demonstrate such a link constitutes a serious threat to the validity of any measure of guilt.

Why should one expect a link between guilt and depression? To begin with, the revised third edition of the *Diagnostic and Statistical Manual of Mental Disorders* (DSM-III-R; American Psychiatric Association, 1987) includes "excessive or inappropriate guilt" as one of the likely symptoms of a Major Depressive Episode (p. 222). In fact, until recently the theoretical and clinical literature has generally cited feelings of guilt, not shame, in connection with depression.

We would argue, however, that the theoretical links between guilt and depression are not as clear-cut as they might seem at first glance. The crux of the problem lies in psychologists' tendency to blur the distinction between shame and guilt, in many cases ignoring shame as a construct in its own right. We would argue that in doing so, many theorists have used the term "guilt" as a nonspecific, catch-all phrase to include phenomenological aspects of shame, guilt, or both. Thus, when clinicians or theorists refer to "guilt," it is not always clear whether they mean guilt or shame. Freud's (1917/1957, 1923/1961, 1933/1964) conceptualization of the role of guilt in melancholia, for example, has been recently questioned by a number of theorists cognizant of the shame–guilt distinction, who have suggested that many of Freud's discussions of the pathogenic implications of guilt are in fact discussions of shame.

The ambiguity introduced by a failure to distinguish between shame and guilt is evident in contemporary writings on depression as well. For example, in his description of introjective depression, Blatt (1974) also emphasized the role of guilt. But a closer reading of the phenomenology of introjective depression suggests that shame, not guilt, may be central to this type of depression. Blatt (1974) stated that introjective depression involves "feelings of being unworthy, unlovable . . . of having failed to live up to expectations, . . . a constant self-scrutiny and evaluation . . . and extensive demands for perfection" (p. 117). This description bears a close resemblance to many of the phenomenological aspects of shame described by Lewis (1971) and Lindsay-Hartz (1984). Even the DSM-III-R (American Psychiatric Association, 1987) is ambiguous in this regard. In citing "*feelings of worthlessness* or excessive or inappropriate guilt" (our emphasis) in connection with a Major Depressive Episode (p. 222), the manual is unclear whether feelings of worthlessness (akin to shame) and guilt are seen as essentially synonymous (as in a previous symptom, "fatigue or loss of energy") or as two distinct phenomena.

There are some rather compelling conceptual arguments to suggest that depression should be associated with a predisposition to shame, but *not* guilt, even beyond Lewis's (1971) ground-breaking work. Perhaps most compelling are the cognitive-attributional models of depression (e.g., Beck, 1983; Abramson, Seligman, & Teasdale, 1978). Lewis (1987b) and Hoblitzelle (1987) have noted conceptual parallels between Lewis's (1971) view and current cognitive perspectives on depression. To the extent that guilt involves a focus on some specific behavior, the guilt experience is likely to involve internal, specific, and fairly unstable attributions. Shame, on the other hand, involves a focus on the global self that is presumably relatively enduring. Thus, the shame experience is likely to involve internal, stable, and global attributions (or, in Janoff-Bulman's [1979] terms, "characterological self-blame"). An extensive empirical literature has demonstrated a link between depression and a tendency to make internal, stable, and global attributions for negative events (for a review, see Robins, 1988). There is little theoretical or empirical support for a link between depression and a tendency to make internal, *unstable,* and *specific* attributions for negative events. Thus, the attributional literature is consistent with Lewis's notion that there may be a special link between depression and proneness to shame, but not guilt.

From an entirely different perspective, self-discrepancy theory (Higgins, 1987) provides additional support for the notion that shame and guilt should be differentially related to depression. Higgins's theory focuses on discrepancies between an individual's current self-perception (the actual self) and four key "self-guides" to which one aspires. The "ideal/own self" is the one that an individual himself or herself wishes to ideally possess. The "ideal/other self" is the one that some significant other (typically a parent) wishes the individual would ideally possess. The "ought/own self" is the one that an individual himself or herself believes he or she *ought* to possess. And the "ought/other self" is the one that some significant other believes the individual *ought* to possess. Dejection-related emotions, including depression, are hypothesized to arise from discrepancies between the actual self and the two ideal selves; in particular, shame is thought to derive from discrepancies between the actual self and the ideal/other self. In contrast, agitation-related emotions, including anxiety, are hypothesized to arise from discrepancies between the actual self and the two ought selves; in particular, guilt is thought to derive from discrepancies between the actual self and the ought/own self. Thus, self-discrepancy theory predicts that shame and guilt are associated with discrepancies involving different self-guides.[1] Similar self-discrepancies are implicated in depression and shame, but not guilt.

In fact, we would argue that there is little reason to expect that guilt should be associated with psychological problems, once one makes the critical distinction between shame and guilt. In moving beyond the layperson's conception of guilt as a rather generalized self-directed negative affect—that is, in viewing guilt as a sense of remorse or regret in connection with some *specific behavior,* rather than as a global condemnation of the self—one might argue that, if anything, guilt should be *adaptive.* The implicit distinction between self and behavior, inherent in guilt, may serve to protect the self from unwarranted global devaluation, while at the same time keeping the door open for remedying the guilt-inducing behavior and/or for making amends for its consequences. In a very real sense, then, guilt is a hopeful, future-oriented moral affective experience. In our view, two implications arise from this conceptualization of guilt (as distinct from shame). First, a tendency toward "shame-free" guilt should be unrelated to psychological symptoms. And second, a tendency toward guilt should be differentially related to positive interpersonal factors, such as empathy (e.g., Tangney, 1991; Tangney, Chapter 4, this volume).

EMPIRICAL STUDIES OF THE RELATION OF SHAME AND GUILT TO PSYCHOLOGICAL SYMPTOMS

Empirical investigations of the links between shame and guilt and psychopathology have lagged far behind the relevant theory, in large part because of difficulties in the measurement of shame and guilt. The earliest guilt scales (e.g., the Mosher Forced-Choice Guilt Inventory, Mosher, 1966; the Guilt scale from the Buss–Durkee Hostility–Guilt Inventory, Buss & Durkee, 1957) were developed without consideration of the shame–guilt distinction. Thus, these scales are of little use in distinguishing between the psychopathological correlates of shame and guilt, because they assess aspects of both emotions.

More recently, a number of researchers have attempted to develop scales that differentiate proneness to shame and proneness to guilt. Using the Early Memories Test, Smith (1972) found that severely depressed patients reported more shame than guilt themes in their recollections. Crouppen (1977), however, failed to replicate this finding in a subsequent similar study. Using the Revised Shame–Guilt Scale, an adjective checklist yielding Shame and Guilt scales, Hoblitzelle (1987) reported a link between depression and shame-proneness in two independent studies of college students. Evidence for a link between depression and guilt-proneness, however, was less consistent across the two studies.

Most recently, Harder and his colleagues (Harder, Chapter 15, this volume; Harder & Lewis, 1987; Harder, Cutler, & Rockart, 1992) have reported several studies indicating that various psychological symptoms are associated with a dispositional tendency toward both shame and guilt. In contrast, in several independent studies of children and young adults, we have found that shame-proneness is associated with an array of psychological symptoms, whereas proneness to "shame-free" guilt is essentially unrelated to psychological maladjustment (Tangney, Wagner, & Gramzow, 1992; Gramzow & Tangney, 1992; Burggraf & Tangney, 1990; Tangney, Wagner, Burggraf, Gramzow, & Fletcher, 1991).

The difference in the relationship of guilt-proneness to psychological symptoms observed across these two most recent sets of studies would appear to center on differences in the assessment of guilt-proneness.[2] Harder and his colleagues have advocated use of the Personal Feelings Questionnaire (PFQ), and more recently a somewhat extended revision, the PFQ2. In these measures, respondents are presented with a list of shame- and guilt-related affective descriptors (e.g., for guilt, "regret," "remorse," "worry about hurting or injuring another") and asked to rate the frequency with which they experience such feelings, from never experiencing the feeling (0) to experiencing the feeling continuously or almost continuously (4).

In contrast, our studies have employed the Self-Conscious Affect and Attribution Inventory (SCAAI; Tangney, Burggraf, Hamme, & Domingos, 1988; Tangney, 1990), and the more recent revision, the Test of Self-Conscious Affect (TOSCA; Tangney, Wagner, & Gramzow, 1989).[3] The structure of the SCAAI and TOSCA is very different from that of the PFQ and PFQ2. In our SCAAI/TOSCA measures, respondents are asked to imagine themselves in a series of specific, common, day-to-day situations (e.g., "You make a big mistake on an important project at work. People were depending on you and your boss criticizes you"). Each scenario is followed by a number of alternative responses representing brief phenomenological descriptions of shame, guilt, and other related self-conscious emotions with respect to the specific context (e.g., for shame, "You would feel like you wanted to hide"; for guilt, "You would think, 'I should have recognized the problem and done a better job'"). Across the various scenarios, the responses capture affective, cognitive, and motivational features associated with shame and guilt, respectively, as described in the theoretical, phenomenological, and empirical literature.[4] The measures are not forced-choice in nature. Respondents are asked to rate, on a 5-point scale, their likelihood of responding in each manner indicated. This allows for the possibility that some respondents may experience both shame and guilt in connection with a given situation.

The PFQ/PFQ2 and the SCAAI/TOSCA thus represent very different methods for assessing proneness to shame and proneness to guilt. In the case of the PFQ/PFQ2, respondents are asked to make global ratings of the degree to which shame and guilt are pervasive aspects of their emotional experience. In the case of the SCAAI/TOSCA, respondents are asked to rate their likelihood of experiencing phenomenological aspects of shame and guilt in situation-specific contexts.

We would argue that the scenario-based approach of the SCAAI and TOSCA represents the more construct-valid method for assessing guilt. To the extent that guilt is an emotion that arises in connection with a negative evaluation of *specific* behaviors, embedded in *local contexts*, such a scenario-based approach seems uniquely well suited for assessing this affective experience. In fact, we have suggested elsewhere that global rating scales, devoid of specific contexts and behaviors, essentially pose respondents with a shame-like task—that of making global ratings about the self (or the self's general affective state) (Tangney, Wagner, & Gramzow, 1992). Perhaps equally problematic, the PFQ and PFQ2 rely heavily on respondents' ability to distinguish between the terms "shame" and "guilt" in an abstract context. In the case of the PFQ, two of the three guilt items center on the term "guilt"; similarly, two of the six PFQ2 items center on the term "guilt." Although such items certainly have good face validity, there is good reason to question whether respondents are able to rate their frequency of guilt experiences as conceptually independent of shame experiences. As noted above, empirical studies indicate that even well-educated adult laypersons are unable to provide meaningful definitions of shame and guilt in the abstract. It seems likely that in rating the PFQ/PFQ2 guilt items, respondents are reporting a generalized tendency to experience negative self-directed affect (e.g., both guilt and shame).

In two recent papers, we reported the relationship of proneness to shame and guilt (as assessed by the SCAAI and TOSCA) to a range of psychological symptoms (Tangney, Wagner, & Gramzow, 1992) and to the capacity for interpersonal empathy (Tangney, 1991). In one of the studies, 230 undergraduate participants also completed the PFQ (Harder & Lewis, 1987) and measures of a number of other theoretically relevant constructs. Thus, the data set provides an opportunity to assess the degree to which indices derived from the two different measurement methods relate differentially to aspects of psychological, self, and interpersonal adjustment. Of central interest here are differences in the correlates of the guilt measures. We assume that the scenario-based and global rating assessment methods represent different, but conceptually valid, approaches to the assessment of proneness to shame.

First, we examined the interrelations of the measures of shame and guilt themselves. Within all three measures, the indices of proneness to shame and proneness to guilt were substantially correlated. The PFQ Shame and Guilt subscales correlated .64, the SCAAI Shame and Guilt subscales correlated .63,[5] and the TOSCA Shame and Guilt subscales correlated .45. This covariation between shame and guilt is consistent with earlier studies, and probably reflects the features shared by the two emotions (e.g., both involve negative affect and internal attributions of one sort or another) and the fact that these emotions can co-occur with respect to the same situation. Of special interest is the unique variance in shame and guilt, respectively. Thus, in our discussion we focus on the part-correlational results, where Shame was partialed out of Guilt and vice versa, within each measure.

The first question is whether the PFQ, SCAAI, and TOSCA are tapping similar dimensions in their assessment of shame and guilt. Table 14.1

TABLE 14.1. Interrelationship of PFQ, SCAAI, and TOSCA Measures of Shame-Proneness and Guilt-Proneness

	Bivariate correlations		Part correlations	
	Shame	Guilt	Shame residuals	Guilt residuals
PFQ				
SCAAI				
Shame (and Shame resid.)	.47**	.45**	.25**	.10
Guilt (and Guilt resid.)	.22**	.26**	−.11	.04
TOSCA				
Shame (and Shame resid.)	.50**	.44**	.27**	.08
Guilt (and Guilt resid.)	.26**	.27**	−.03	.08
TOSCA				
SCAAI				
Shame (and Shame resid.)	.75**	.40**	.62**	−.26**
Guilt (and Guilt resid.)	.49**	.59**	−.19*	.48**

Note. n's range from 225 to 230.
*$p < .01$. **$p < .001$.

presents the relationships between PFQ, SCAAI, and TOSCA Shame and Guilt scales. The top portion of the table shows that both the PFQ Shame *and* PFQ Guilt scales were substantially correlated with the SCAAI and TOSCA *Shame* scales, while only modestly linked to SCAAI and TOSCA *Guilt*. The part-correlational analyses (factoring out the shared variance between each measure's Shame and Guilt scales) indicated some overlap between the unique variance in PFQ Shame and the unique variance in SCAAI and TOSCA Shame, respectively. In contrast, PFQ Guilt residuals (e.g., the unique portion of PFQ Guilt variance independent of PFQ Shame) were unrelated to the unique variance in SCAAI or TOSCA Guilt. In other words, there was little evidence that the PFQ Shame and Guilt scales related differentially to the scenario-based measures of shame and guilt. In particular, there is little convergence between the methods of assessing guilt.

The correlations between the SCAAI and TOSCA scales showed a quite different pattern of results, as indicated in the bottom of Table 14.1. SCAAI Shame was more highly correlated with TOSCA Shame than TOSCA Guilt, and SCAAI Guilt was more highly correlated with TOSCA Guilt than TOSCA Shame. Moreover, there was a striking convergence between the residual variables assessing the same construct. For example, SCAAI Shame residuals were highly correlated with TOSCA Shame residuals, but inversely related to TOSCA Guilt residuals. (It should be noted that although the SCAAI and TOSCA measures share the same scenario-based format, there is virtually no overlap in item content. That is, the two measures contain different sets of scenarios and associated responses.)

The results in Table 14.1 are consistent with the notion that the scenario-based SCAAI and TOSCA measures provide distinct indices of shame and guilt, whereas the PFQ does not. In particular, these findings provide some initial evidence to suggest that the PFQ Shame and Guilt scales *both* assess shame-related phenomena. A much stronger test of this notion, however, lies in the degree to which the respective Shame and Guilt scales relate differentially to measures of other constructs in a theoretically consistent manner.

In the foregoing theoretical analysis, we have challenged Harder's (Harder, Chapter 15, this volume; Harder et al., 1992) assertion that a tendency to experience "shame-free" guilt should be associated with psychological symptoms, particularly depression. To the contrary, drawing on a number of theories, we have argued that the capacity to experience guilt (uncomplicated by shame) should be adaptive. Table 14.2 shows the relationship of shame and guilt (as measured by the PFQ, SCAAI, and TOSCA) to measures of psychological maladjustment, as assessed by the Symptom Checklist 90 (SCL-90; Derogatis, Lipman, & Covi, 1973), the Beck Depression Inventory (BDI; Beck, 1972), and the State–Trait Anxiety Inventory (STAI; Spielberger, Gorsuch, & Lushene, 1970). Results of the part correlations indicated that all three measures of proneness to shame were consistently positively correlated with a range of psychological symp-

TABLE 14.2. Relationship of Indices of Psychopathology to Shame and Guilt (as Assessed by the SCAAI, TOSCA, and PFQ)

Psychopathology indices		Bivariate correlations		Part correlations	
		Shame	Guilt	Shame residuals	Guilt residuals
SCL-90					
Somaticization	(PFQ)	.43***	.33***	.28***	.07
	(SCAAI)	.26***	.18**	.18**	.03
	(TOSCA)	.27***	.11	.25***	−.02
Obsessive–	(PFQ)	.52***	.45***	.30***	.15*
Compulsive	(SCAAI)	.38***	.21***	.32***	−.03
	(TOSCA)	.38***	.22***	.31***	.05
Psychoticism	(PFQ)	.54***	.49***	.29***	.19**
	(SCAAI)	.39***	.23***	.32***	−.03
	(TOSCA)	.34***	.15*	.31***	−.01
Paranoid Ideation	(PFQ)	.50***	.42***	.30***	.13
	(SCAAI)	.40***	.17*	.38***	−.11
	(TOSCA)	.35***	.08	.35***	−.09
Hostility–Anger	(PFQ)	.37***	.36***	.18**	.16*
	(SCAAI)	.19**	.01	.23***	−.14*
	(TOSCA)	.20**	−.05	.24***	−.15*
Interpersonal	(PFQ)	.58***	.49***	.35***	.15*
Sensitivity	(SCAAI)	.56***	.29***	.49***	−.08
	(TOSCA)	.46***	.21***	.42***	−.00
Anxiety	(PFQ)	.53***	.45***	.31***	.14*
	(SCAAI)	.36***	.25***	.26***	.03
	(TOSCA)	.34***	.19**	.29***	.04
Phobic Anxiety	(PFQ)	.36***	.33***	.19**	.13*
	(SCAAI)	.32***	.18**	.26***	−.03
	(TOSCA)	.25***	.01	.27***	−.11
Depression	(PFQ)	.56***	.50***	.31***	.19**
	(SCAAI)	.41***	.22***	.36***	−.05
	(TOSCA)	.43***	.15*	.41***	−.06
Other measures					
BDI	(PFQ)	.62***	.54***	.36***	.18**
	(SCAAI)	.47***	.24***	.41***	−.07
	(TOSCA)	.51***	.19**	.47***	−.05
STAI Trait Anxiety	(PFQ)	.57***	.53***	.30***	.22***
	(SCAAI)	.52***	.22**	.50***	−.15*
	(TOSCA)	.53***	.17*	.51***	−.09
STAI State Anxiety	(PFQ)	.51***	.46***	.28***	.19**
	(SCAAI)	.36***	.09	.39***	−.17*
	(TOSCA)	.41***	.10	.41***	−.10

Note. n's range from 212 to 231 for the PFQ, from 206 to 225 for the SCAAI, and from 212 to 230 for the TOSCA. SCAAI and TOSCA correlations are from Tangney, Wagner, and Gramzow (1992).
*$p < .05$. **$p < .01$. ***$p < .001$.

toms. In contrast, the psychopathological correlates of "shame-free" guilt varied considerably as a function of measurement method. PFQ Guilt residuals were significantly positively correlated with 10 of the 12 indices of psychological maladjustment. The SCAAI and TOSCA Guilt residuals were negatively or negligibly correlated with psychological symptoms, consistent with our theoretical analysis.

To further clarify the differences in the nature of guilt, as assessed by the PFQ versus the SCAAI and TOSCA, we also considered measures of a number of self-related constructs. Participants in this study completed the Rosenberg Self-Esteem Scale (Rosenberg, 1965) which yields an index of global self-esteem and an index of stability of the self (e.g., the degree to which one's self-esteem fluctuates across time); the Janis–Field Self-Esteem Scale (Janis & Field, 1959); the Self-Consciousness Scale (Fenigstein, Scheier, & Buss, 1975); the Fear of Negative Evaluation Scale (Watson & Friend, 1969); and the Splitting Scale (Gerson, 1984).

Given the global negative self-focus of shame, we would expect shame-proneness to be associated with low self-esteem and with considerable local variability in self-esteem, since shame in effect involves transient, dramatic drops in self-evaluation. In contrast, a tendency to experience shame-free guilt about specific behaviors, somewhat apart from the self, should be unrelated to these aspects of self-esteem. Because shame also involves the imagery of a real or imagined disapproving other (Lewis, 1971), we would expect shame-proneness to be associated with self-consciousness (especially public self-consciousness), fear of negative evaluation, and social anxiety. There is no compelling theoretical reason to expect such an association with guilt. Finally, we would also expect shame, but not guilt, to be differentially related to the defense of splitting. Splitting involves a gross isolation or separation of good and bad images of the self and others. Shame-prone individuals, who engage in global negative self-evaluations in response to negative events, should be particularly likely to make use of the defense of splitting. The shame experience can be viewed as tapping into the "all-bad" aspect of the self. In contrast, the experience of guilt involves an implicit differentiation of self and behavior, and thus the capacity to simultaneously maintain images of a "good" self engaged in objectionable behavior. Such a capacity is incongruent with the psychological processes involved in splitting.

Table 14.3 shows the relationship of shame and guilt (as measured by the PFQ, SCAAI, and TOSCA) to measures of these self-related constructs. The patterns of results involving the SCAAI and TOSCA are most consistent with our hypotheses, showing that shame and guilt are differentially related to aspects of the self in a theoretically consistent manner. Shame-proneness, as assessed by the scenario-based measures, was consistently negatively correlated with the measures of self-esteem and stability of the self, and positively correlated with self-consciousness, fear of negative evaluation, social anxiety, and use of the defense of splitting. In contrast, part-correla-

TABLE 14.3. Relationship of Self-Related Variables to Shame and Guilt (as Assessed by the SCAAI, TOSCA, and PFQ)

Self-related variables		Bivariate correlations		Part correlations	
		Shame	Guilt	Shame residuals	Guilt residuals
Rosenberg self-esteem	(PFQ)	−.58***	−.51***	−.34***	−.19**
	(SCAAI)	−.53***	−.21***	−.52***	.16*
	(TOSCA)	−.55***	−.16*	−.54***	.11
Rosenberg stability of self	(PFQ)	−.41***	−.30***	−.29***	−.04
	(SCAAI)	−.31***	−.03	−.38***	.21**
	(TOSCA)	−.31***	−.10	−.31***	.06
Janis–Field self-esteem	(PFQ)	−.59***	−.47***	−.39***	−.13
	(SCAAI)	−.62***	−.34***	−.53***	.07
	(TOSCA)	−.60***	−.28***	−.53***	.00
Private self-consciousness	(PFQ)	.27***	.30***	.10	.17**
	(SCAAI)	.26***	.12	.24***	−.06
	(TOSCA)	.21**	.14*	.17*	.04
Public self-consciousness	(PFQ)	.24***	.27***	.09	.16*
	(SCAAI)	.27***	.16*	.22***	−.01
	(TOSCA)	.19**	.15*	.14*	.07
Social anxiety	(PFQ)	.45***	.29***	.35***	.00
	(SCAAI)	.42***	.15*	.42***	−.15*
	(TOSCA)	.42***	.17*	.39***	−.03
Fear of negative evaluation	(PFQ)	.46***	.39***	.28***	.13
	(SCAAI)	.54***	.27***	.48***	−.09
	(TOSCA)	.42***	.23**	.35***	.03
Splitting	(PFQ)	.45***	.41***	.24**	.17*
	(SCAAI)	.42***	.24**	.34***	−.03
	(TOSCA)	.41***	.18*	.36***	.00

Note. n's range from 167 to 220 for the PFQ, from 161 to 214 for the SCAAI, and from 167 to 219 for the TOSCA.
*$p < .05$. **$p < .01$. ***$p < .001$.

tional analyses involving the scenario-based measures indicated that a tendency to experience shame-free guilt was positively or negligibly related to self-esteem, stability of the self, and social anxiety, and unrelated to self-consciousness, fear of negative evaluation, and splitting. The findings involving the PFQ Shame scale were largely consistent with those involving the SCAAI and TOSCA Shame scales, again showing a convergence of shame derived from different measurement strategies. The findings involving the PFQ Guilt scale, however, were generally inconsistent with the theoretical predictions and with the SCAAI/TOSCA Guilt results. PFQ Guilt residuals were negatively correlated with the Rosenberg measure of self-esteem, and positively correlated with the measures of self-consciousness and splitting.

   Taken together, the results in Tables 14.1–14.3 suggest that the SCAAI and TOSCA yield distinct measures of proneness to shame and proneness to guilt that are differentially related to indices of psychopathology and aspects of self-functioning in a theoretically meaningful manner, whereas the PFQ does not. The evidence thus far, however, centers on hypothesized negligible relationships between "shame-free" guilt on the one hand, and psychological maladjustment and negative aspects of self-functioning on the other. One question that arises is whether the observed patterns of findings can simply be attributed to an artifact of measurement. That is, in factoring out Shame from Guilt, have we factored out most of the reliable and valid variance in SCAAI and TOSCA Guilt? Are the differential correlates of Shame and Guilt residuals simply due to restricted valid variance in the Guilt residuals?

To answer this question, we considered one last set of findings concerning interpersonal empathy. Elsewhere (Tangney, 1991; Tangney, Wagner, Fletcher, & Gramzow, 1992; Tangney, Wagner, Gavlas, Barlow, & Marschall, 1992; Tangney, Chapter 4, this volume), we have suggested that guilt has especially important implications in the interpersonal realm. For example, whereas the global, painful self-focus of shame is likely to interfere with an other-oriented empathic response, guilt—in its focus on a specific behavior—is likely to foster interpersonal empathy by bringing the person one step closer to a focus on the consequences of negative or harmful behavior for others. Moreover, Hoffman (1982) and Zahn-Waxler and Robinson (Chapter 5, this volume) have emphasized the common developmental roots of guilt and empathy.

Table 14.4 shows the relationship of shame and guilt (as measured by the PFQ, SCAAI, and TOSCA) to components of interpersonal empathy, as measured by the Feshbach and Lipian (1987) Empathy Scale for Adults. To focus first on the part-correlational results involving the SCAAI and TOSCA, Shame residuals were negatively or negligibly correlated with a capacity for interpersonal empathy. But as predicted, a tendency to experience shame-free guilt was clearly positively related to empathic responsiveness—*only* for the scenario-based measures. PFQ Shame and Guilt measures did not relate differentially to empathy; they were largely unrelated to subscales from the Feshbach and Lipian Empathy Scale. This last set of results offers further evidence that the SCAAI and TOSCA are unique in yielding distinct and conceptually valid indices of shame and guilt. Moreover, these results emphasize that the negligible relationship of shame-free guilt to psychological maladjustment is not simply attributable to a restriction of valid variance. A tendency to experience shame-free guilt appears to have implications for interpersonal, but not intrapersonal, aspects of functioning.

WHAT IS THE NATURE OF "PATHOLOGICAL" GUILT?

Our theoretical analyses, and the empirical findings presented above, suggest that a tendency to experience guilt uncomplicated by shame is unrelated to

TABLE 14.4. Relationship of Empathy to Shame and Guilt (as Assessed by the SCAAI, TOSCA, and PFQ)

Empathy dimensions		Bivariate correlations		Part correlations	
		Shame	Guilt	Shame residuals	Guilt residuals
Cognitive empathy	(PFQ)	−.13	−.14*	−.05	−.08
	(SCAAI)	.07	.23***	−.10	.24***
	(TOSCA)	−.01	.10	−.06	.12
Affective cue discrimination	(PFQ)	−.16*	−.09	−.13	.01
	(SCAAI)	−.10	.04	−.17*	.13
	(TOSCA)	−.09	.03	−.12	.08
Emotional arousal	(PFQ)	.00	−.06	.06	−.09
	(SCAAI)	−.04	.19**	−.20**	.28***
	(TOSCA)	.01	.22***	−.10	.25***
General empathy	(PFQ)	.20**	.17*	.12	.06
	(SCAAI)	.29***	.49***	−.02	.40***
	(TOSCA)	.29***	.43***	.11	.33***
Total empathy	(PFQ)	.00	−.02	.02	−.02
	(SCAAI)	.11	.37***	−.15*	.39***
	(TOSCA)	.10	.31***	−.04	.29***

Note. n's are 219 for the PFQ, 213 for the SCAAI, and 218 for the TOSCA. SCAAI correlations are from Tangney (1991).
*p < .05. **p < .01. ***p < .001.

psychological maladjustment. In fact, such shame-free guilt appears to be quite adaptive, especially when interpersonal issues are considered (see also Tangney, 1991; Tangney, Wagner, Fletcher, & Gramzow, 1992; Tangney, Wagner, Gavlas, Barlow, & Marschall, 1992; Tangney, Chapter 4, this volume). What then is the pathological guilt described in much of the clinical literature? We do not dispute that in some significant instances, guilt takes a turn for the worse. Clinical theory and clinical case studies make frequent reference to a maladaptive guilt characterized by chronic self-blame and an obsessive rumination over some objectionable or harmful behavior. And, in fact, a number of clinical theorists from diverse orientations have made a distinction between normal or reality-based guilt and exaggerated, spurious, or neurotic guilt (e.g., Angyal, 1965; Menninger, 1938; May & Yalom, 1984).

Our view is that guilt becomes maladaptive most typically when it becomes fused with shame, and that the component of shame sets the stage for a pathogenic sequence of affect and cognitions. A guilt experience that begins with the notion of "Oh, look at what a horrible thing I have done," but that is then magnified and generalized to the self (". . . and aren't I a horrible person"), represents a sequence leading from tension and remorse over a specific behavior to much more global feelings of self-contempt and disgust. And the shame component of this sequence, not the guilt component, is more likely to present an insoluble dilemma. In many instances, an objectionable behavior can be altered, the negative effects can be repaired, or a person can at least offer a heartfelt apology. Even in cases where direct reparation or apology is not possible, the person can make indirect reparation or amends (e.g., it may be impossible to apologize directly to a now-deceased loved one, but the person can consciously make an effort to do some special "good deeds" to other family members as an atonement). In contrast, a self that is defective at its core is much more difficult to transform or amend. Even its attempts at reparation or atonement may be deemed unworthy.[6] Thus, shame—and, in turn, shame-fused guilt—offers little opportunity for redemption. In our view, it is guilt *with an overlay of shame* that is most likely to lead to the interminable rumination and self-castigation so often described in the clinical literature.

Our empirical findings are quite consistent with this view. First, studies involving the SCAAI and TOSCA indicate considerable shared variance between the Shame and Guilt scales; that is, it appears that many individuals are prone to experience both shame and guilt in response to negative events. Furthermore, the bivariate correlations involving Guilt (e.g., correlations including the variance shared with Shame) are largely consistent in sign with correlations involving Shame (and, indeed, those involving Shame residuals). Guilt colored by shame appears to be fairly maladaptive, as indicated by the bivariate correlations with indices of psychopathology and maladaptive aspects of self-functioning. It is only when Shame is factored out from Guilt (e.g., when the Guilt residuals are considered) that we see a very different pattern of results emerging. Proneness to shame-free guilt appears to be the more adaptive affective style across many different aspects of psychological functioning.

CLINICAL IMPLICATIONS

One key implication from our theoretical analysis is that over the years, guilt has received an undeserved bad reputation. Perhaps in our rush to free ourselves from a repressive Victorian moral orientation, we have too quickly dismissed the adaptive functions of guilt. In the course of day-to-day life, we and our clients *do* occasionally transgress, offend, or otherwise cause harm to others. It may be uncomfortable, but still adaptive (for ourselves and others), to experience guilt in connection with such specific behavioral transgressions. The tension, remorse, and regret of guilt cause us to stop and rethink. Moreover, guilt generally offers a way out: In its focus on a specific behavior, guilt presses us to repair, apologize, or make amends, thereby strengthening our interpersonal ties (as suggested by Baumeister, Stillwell, & Heatherton, Chapter 10, this volume). Problems may arise, however, when a reality-based guilt is transformed into shame or some shame–guilt derivative.

The consistent links observed between shame and psychopathology suggest that a consideration of shame-related issues may be useful in the treatment of a number of psychological problems. Moreover, in working with clients, it is useful to keep in mind the subtle but critical distinction between shame and guilt.

One problem posed by shame is that clients typically have difficulty identifying and verbalizing the shame experience. Helen Block Lewis (1971) noted the primitive, nonverbal nature of shame, based on her clinical case studies. This inability to identify and articulate episodes of shame may, in part, account for the persistent nature of the shame experience. And this characteristic may also cause therapists to overlook significant shame episodes experienced by their clients.

In treating clients, it is helpful to listen with a "third ear" for shame-based experiences. Clients often provide subtle cues that signal the possibility of a shame episode. There may be an abrupt interruption in a client's account of previous events, accompanied by signs of discomfort or agitation, nervous laughter, and/or downcast eyes. The client may have difficulty articulating his or her experience of the moment. Or the client may describe a disproportionate sense of anger in connection with a negative interpersonal event. Lewis (1971) and Scheff (1987) have described the rage or humiliated fury that often accompanies episodes of shame—rage over being "made" to feel so bad for such a seemingly minor event. And in fact, in our own research, we have found a consistent link between shame-proneness and a bitter, seething, resentful kind of anger (Tangney, Wagner, Fletcher, & Gramzow, 1992; Tangney, Wagner, Gavlas, Barlow, & Marschall, 1992). Such cues can alert the therapist to explore the possibility of an underlying shame experience.

What sorts of interventions are effective in diffusing shame reactions? First, simply verbalizing the events and associated experiences often serves to ameliorate the feeling of shame. As clients translate into words their preverbal, global shame reaction, they bring to bear a more logical, differentiated thought process, which often leads them to spontaneously re-evaluate the global nature of the shame-eliciting episode. Second, in the process of exploring the shame-eliciting episode, the therapist can further assist the client in making such cognitive re-evaluations. In fact, many of the key cognitive–behavioral interventions for depression described by Beck (1983) and Ellis (1962) are likely to be an effective means of addressing *shame*-inducing cognitions. Shame, too, is associated with irrational beliefs and dysfunctional thoughts that are amenable to cognitive restructuring. Third, in sharing shame experiences within the context of a supportive relationship, clients meet with acceptance and understanding. Thus, the therapist's reaction provides the client with an alternative to the self-disgust and self-disdain inherent in the shame experience. Fourth, Retzinger (1987) has presented data suggesting that humor may be an effective antidote to shame. As clients bring dreaded shame experiences to light, a shared joke about some irony of the situation, or about the disproportionate nature of their shame reaction, can help dispel the ugly feeling of shame.

Finally, it is helpful to be alert to shame reactions not only in clients' accounts of daily life, but also within the therapeutic context itself. In the course of psychotherapy, clients frequently reveal painful and negative personal material; thus, in a very real sense, the therapy room creates many opportunities to experience shame. As noted above, the pain of shame can lead either to withdrawal from interpersonal interactions or to a hostile, humiliated fury. Thus, when the flow of the therapeutic interaction grinds to a halt, when the client responds to the therapist with apparently irrational anger, or when the client suddenly and inexplicably decides to end treatment, the possibility of an underlying sense of shame *vis-à-vis* the therapist might be considered. Lewis (1971) believed that shame plays a critical role in many negative "transference" reactions—reactions that often lead to interrupted or prematurely terminated treatment.

Empirical studies of both children and adults indicate that proneness to the ugly feeling of shame is associated with a range of psychological symptoms (Burggraf & Tangney, 1989b; Tangney, Wagner, & Gramzow, 1992; Tangney et al., 1991). Thus, many clients are likely to be predisposed to this overwhelming affective experience. In a number of respects, we may be able to enhance our treatment of depression and other psychological disorders by recognizing and developing a deeper understanding of shame in our clients, and by fostering our clients' capacity to experience appropriate (and adaptive) feelings of guilt over the inevitable transgressions that are a part of everyday life.

ACKNOWLEDGMENTS

Preparation of this chapter was supported by Grant No. R01HD27171 from the National Institute for Child Health and Human Development to June Price Tangney. We wish to thank Carey Fletcher, Elly Bordeaux, Joe Constantin, Laura Flicker, Richard Gramzow, William Harman, Donna Marschall, James Maxfield, Julie Morig, Yvette Nageotte, Gary Russell, Provie Rydstrom, Gordon Shaw, and Chris Smart for their assistance with the larger studies from which this report was drawn. Portions of this chapter were adapted from Tangney, Wagner, and Gramzow (1992) and Tangney (1991).

NOTES

1.   In contrast to Higgins's (1987) theory, our own view is that self-discrepancies involving each of these "self-guides" are more theoretically relevant to the phenomena of shame, across the board. To the extent that shame involves a

negative evaluation of the self (in contrast to guilt's negative evaluation of specific behaviors), it seems likely that discrepancies noted between an actual self and any "self-guide" deemed important by an individual should set the stage for feelings of shame. In contrast, such self-evaluations and self-discrepancies are rather remote, theoretically, from the behavioral focus of guilt. And, in fact, this is exactly what was found in a recent study of self-discrepancies and self-conscious affective style (Tangney & Niedenthal, 1994). Individual differences in proneness to shame were substantially related to discrepancies between one's actual self and all manner of self-guides (ideal and ought, own and significant other), whereas proneness to guilt was not.

2.   Harder (Chapter 15, this volume) has also noted differences in our conceptualizations of shame and guilt, some of which appear to stem from a misreading of our definitions of these two emotions. Throughout our writings (Tangney, 1990, 1991, 1992, 1993, in press, and Chapter 4, this volume; Tangney, Wagner, & Gramzow, 1992; Tangney, Wagner, Fletcher, & Gramzow, 1992) and in the development of our measures, we have explicitly defined shame and guilt as each representing a complex interplay of affective, cognitive, and motivational features, drawing heavily on Lewis (1971). We are somewhat perplexed by Harder's (Chapter 15, this volume) assertion that the distinction between global self and specific behavior has become "the *only* basis for a distinction" (p. 382; emphasis Harder's) between shame and guilt in our work. It is an important component of the distinction, but one of an array of dimensions along which shame and guilt differ (see Tangney, Chapter 4, this volume, for an extended discussion of the similarities and differences between shame and guilt). Although Harder has generally not provided explicit formal definitions of shame and guilt (Harder & Lewis, 1987; Harder, 1990; Harder & Zalma, 1990; Harder et al., 1992), his working conceptualization also seems to draw quite heavily on Lewis's (1971) framework. In contrast to Lewis, however, Harder (Chapter 15, this volume; Harder & Lewis, 1987) appears to give fairly strong emphasis to the public–private and internal–external dimensions highlighted by the much earlier anthropological view. As discussed by Tangney (Chapter 4, this volume), recent empirical findings call into question this "traditional" notion: Shame is no more likely than guilt to occur in social contexts. In any event, this emphasis on the public–private distinction is primarily evident in Harder's theoretical analyses; it is not a key component of the PFQ or PFQ2.

3.   Studies of children have employed the SCAAI-C (Burggraf & Tangney, 1989a) and the TOSCA-C (Tangney, Wagner, Burggraf, Gramzow, & Fletcher, 1990), which were modeled after the adult versions.

4.   The SCAAI scenarios and associated responses were written by Tangney and a team of graduate students familiar with the theoretical and phenomenological literature on shame and guilt. These items were written with a college-age population in mind. The TOSCA was developed for a broader population of adults of all ages. To enhance ecological validity, the TOSCA scenarios were drawn from several hundred adults' accounts of shame- and guilt-inducing situations. The TOSCA responses were selected from a much larger pool of responses generated by a second sample of several hundred adults. Like the TOSCA, the TOSCA-C was based on subject-generated scenarios and responses (in this case, provided by several hundred children ages 8–12).

5.   The correlation between SCAAI Shame and Guilt scales was unusually high in

this sample. In previous and subsequent studies, the correlation between these two scales has tended to hover between .42 and .48. An inspection of the joint distribution revealed that the correlation was inflated by a few outliers who had responded to the questionnaire in an idiosyncratic manner (e.g., mostly endorsing the extreme ends of the rating scales for individual items). Without these outliers, the observed correlation between SCAAI Shame and Guilt scales dropped to the range typical of other samples.

6. The guilt-to-shame sequence may also be evoked or further exacerbated when efforts at reparation are thwarted. When a person feeling guilt attempts to make amends, and the injured party rejects those attempts, the focus of the would-be amender may shift from the "bad behavior" to the unworthiness of the self. Consider the example of a child who breaks a window and then confesses and apologizes to a parent, who responds with rejection. The child may read into the parent's rejection (or the parent may explicitly state), "I've had it with you! You always ruin things!" This shift in focus to global, stable negative aspects of the self is likely to induce feelings of shame—shame that may be further enhanced by the apparent disruption in attachment (see Nathanson, 1987, for a discussion of link between shame and disruption of attachment).

REFERENCES

Abramson, L. Y., Seligman, M. E. P., & Teasdale, J. (1978). Learned helplessness in humans: Critique and reformulation. *Journal of Abnormal Psychology, 87,* 49–74.

American Psychiatric Association. (1987). *Diagnostic and statistical manual of mental disorders* (3rd ed., rev.). Washington, DC: Author.

Angyal, A. (1965). *Neurosis and treatment: A holistic theory.* New York: Viking Press.

Beck, A. T. (1972). Measuring depression: The Depression Inventory. In T. A. Williams, M. M. Katz, & J. A. Shields (Eds.), *Recent advances in the psychobiology of the depressive illnesses* (pp. 299–302). Washington, DC: U.S. Government Printing Office.

Beck, A. T. (1983). Cognitive therapy of depression: New perspectives. In P. Clayton & J. Barrett (Eds.), *Treatment of depression: Old controversies and new approaches* (pp. 265–290). New York: Raven Press.

Blatt, S. (1974). Levels of object representation in anaclitic and introjective depression. *Psychoanalytic Study of the Child, 29,* 107–157.

Bradshaw, J. (1988). *Healing the shame that binds you.* Deerfield Beach, FL: Health Communications.

Burggraf, S. A., & Tangney, J. P. (1989a). *The Self-Conscious Affect and Attribution Inventory for Children (SCAAI-C).* Bryn Mawr, PA: Bryn Mawr College.

Burggraf, S. A., & Tangney, J. P. (1989b, June). *Proneness to shame, proneness to guilt, and self-concept.* Poster presented at the meeting of the American Psychological Society, Alexandria, VA.

Burggraf, S. A., & Tangney, J. P. (1990, June). *Shame-proneness, guilt-proneness, and attributional style related to children's depression.* Poster presented at the meeting of the American Psychological Society, Dallas.

Buss, A. H., & Durkee, A. (1957). An inventory for assessing different kinds of hostility in clinical situations. *Journal of Consulting Psychology, 21,* 343–348.

Crouppen, G. A. (1977). Field dependence–independence in depressive and "normal" males as an indicator of relative proneness to shame or guilt and ego-functioning. *Dissertation Abstracts International, 37,* 4669B–4670B. (University Microfilms No. 77-6292)

Derogatis, L. R., Lipman, R. S., & Covi, L. (1973). SCL-90: An outpatient psychiatric rating scale—preliminary report. *Psychopharmacology Bulletin, 9,* 13–28.

Ellis, A. (1962). *Reason and emotion in psychotherapy.* New York: Lyle Stuart.

Fenigstein, A., Scheier, M. F., & Buss, A. H. (1975). Public and private self-consciousness: Assessment and theory. *Journal of Consulting and Clinical Psychology, 43,* 522–527.

Ferguson, T. J., Stegge, H., & Damhuis, I. (1990, March). *Spontaneous and elicited guilt and shame experiences in elementary school-age children.* Poster presented at the meeting of the Southwestern Society for Research in Human Development, Dallas, TX.

Ferguson, T. J., Stegge, H., & Damhuis, I. (1991). Children's understanding of guilt and shame. *Child Development, 62,* 827–839.

Feshbach, N. D., & Lipian, M. (1987). *The Empathy Scale for Adults.* Los Angeles: University of California at Los Angeles.

Fossum, M. A., & Mason, M. J. (1986). *Facing shame: Families in recovery.* New York: Norton.

Freud, S. (1953). Three essays on the theory of sexuality. In J. Strachey (Ed. and Trans.), *The standard edition of the complete psychological works of Sigmund Freud* (Vol. 7, pp. 125–243). London: Hogarth Press. (Original work published 1905)

Freud, S. (1955). Notes upon a case of obsessional neurosis. In J. Strachey (Ed. and Trans.), *The standard edition of the complete psychological works of Sigmund Freud* (Vol. 10, pp. 151–318). London: Hogarth Press. (Original work published 1909)

Freud, S. (1957). On narcissism: An introduction. In J. Strachey (Ed. and Trans.), *The standard edition of the complete psychological works of Sigmund Freud* (Vol. 14, pp. 67–102). London: Hogarth Press. (Original work published 1914)

Freud, S. (1957). Mourning and melancholia. In J. Strachey (Ed. and Trans.), *The standard edition of the complete psychological works of Sigmund Freud* (Vol. 14, pp. 237–260). London: Hogarth Press. (Original work published 1917)

Freud, S. (1961). The ego and the id. In J. Strachey (Ed. and Trans.), *The standard edition of the complete psychological works of Sigmund Freud* (Vol. 19, pp. 3–66). London: Hogarth Press. (Original work published 1923)

Freud, S. (1961). The economic problem of masochism. In J. Strachey (Ed. and Trans.), *The standard edition of the complete psychological works of Sigmund Freud* (Vol. 19, pp. 155–170). London: Hogarth Press. (Original work published 1924)

Freud, S. (1962). Further remarks on the neuro-psychoses of defence. In J. Strachey (Ed. and Trans.), *The standard edition of the complete psychological works of Sigmund Freud* (Vol. 3, pp. 157–185). London: Hogarth Press. (Original work published 1896)

Freud, S. (1964). Dissection of the personality. In J. Strachey (Ed. and Trans.), *The standard edition of the complete psychological works of Sigmund Freud* (Vol. 22, pp. 57–81). London: Hogarth Press. (Original work published 1933)

Gerson, M. J. (1984). Splitting: The development of a measure. *Journal of Clinical Psychology, 40,* 157–162.

Goldberg, C. (1991). *Understanding shame.* Northvale, NJ: Jason Aronson.

Gramzow, R., & Tangney, J. P. (1992). Proneness to shame and the narcissistic personality. *Personality and Social Psychology Bulletin, 18,* 369–376.

Harder, D. W. (1990). Additional construct validity evidence for the Harder Personal Feelings Questionnaire measure of shame and guilt proneness. *Psychological Reports, 67,* 288–290.

Harder, D. W., Cutler, L., & Rockart, L. (1992). Assessment of shame and guilt and their relationships to psychopathology. *Journal of Personality Assessment, 59,* 584–604.

Harder, D. W., & Lewis, S. J. (1987). The assessment of shame and guilt. In J. N. Butcher & C. D. Spielberger (Eds.), *Advances in personality assessment* (Vol. 6, pp. 89–114). Hillsdale, NJ: Erlbaum.

Harder, D. W., & Zalma, A. (1990). Two promising shame and guilt scales: A construct validity comparison. *Journal of Personality Assessment, 55,* 729–745.

Higgins, E. T. (1987). Self-discrepancy: A theory relating self and affect. *Psychological Review, 94,* 319–340.

Hoblitzelle, W. (1987). Attempts to measure and differentiate shame and guilt: The relation between shame and depression. In H. B. Lewis (Ed.), *The role of shame in symptom formation* (pp. 207–235). Hillsdale, NJ: Erlbaum

Hoffman, M. L. (1982). Development of prosocial motivation: Empathy and guilt. In N. Eisenberg (Ed.), *Development of prosocial behavior* (pp. 281–313). New York: Academic Press.

Janis, I. L., & Field, P. B. (1959). A behavioral assessment of persuasability: Consistency of individual differences. In C. I. Hovland & I. L. Janis (Eds.), *Personality and persuasibility* (pp. 29–54). New Haven, CT: Yale University Press.

Janoff-Bulman, R. (1979). Characterological versus behavioral self-blame: Inquiries into depression and rape. *Journal of Personality and Social Psychology, 37,* 1798–1809.

Kohut, H. (1971). *The analysis of the self.* New York: International Universities Press.

Lansky, M. (1987). Shame and domestic violence. In D. L. Nathanson (Ed.), *The many faces of shame* (pp. 335–362). New York: Guilford Press.

Lewis, H. B. (1971). *Shame and guilt in neurosis.* New York: International Universities Press.

Lewis, H. B. (1987a). Introduction: Shame—the "sleeper" in psychopathology. In H. B. Lewis (Ed.), *The role of shame in symptom formation* (pp. 1–28). Hillsdale, NJ: Erlbaum.

Lewis, H. B. (1987b). The role of shame in depression over the life span. In H. B. Lewis (Ed.), *The role of shame in symptom formation* (pp. 29–50). Hillsdale, NJ: Erlbaum.

Lindsay-Hartz, J. (1984). Contrasting experiences of shame and guilt. *American Behavioral Scientist, 27,* 689–704.

May, R., & Yalom, I. (1984). Existential psychotherapy. In R. J. Corsini (Ed.), *Current psychotherapies* (pp. 354–391). Itasca, IL: Peacock.

Menninger, K. (1938). *Man against himself.* New York: Harcourt, Brace.

Miller, S. (1985). *The shame experience.* Hillsdale, NJ: Erlbaum.

Morrison, A. P. (1989). *Shame: The underside of narcissism.* Hillsdale, NJ: Analytic Press.

Morrison, N. K. (1987). The role of shame in schizophrenia. In H. B. Lewis (Ed.), *The role of shame in symptom formation* (pp. 51–87). Hillsdale, NJ: Erlbaum.

Mosher, D. L. (1966). The development and multitrait–multimethod matrix analysis of three measures of three aspects of guilt. *Journal of Consulting and Clinical Psychology, 30, 25–29.*

Nathanson, D. L. (1987). A timetable for shame. In D. L. Nathanson (Ed.), *The many faces of shame* (pp. 1–63). New York: Guilford Press.

Potter-Efron, R. T. (1989). *Shame, guilt and alcoholism: Treatment issues in clinical practice.* New York: Haworth Press.

Retzinger, S. R. (1987). Resentment and laughter: Video studies of the shame–rage spiral. In H. B. Lewis (Ed.), *The role of shame in symptom formation* (pp. 151–181). Hillsdale, NJ: Erlbaum.

Robins, C. J. (1988). Attributions and depression: Why is the literature so inconsistent? *Journal of Personality and Social Psychology, 54, 880–889.*

Rodin, J., Silberstein, L., & Striegel-Moore, R. (1985). Women and weight: A normative discontent. In T. B. Sondregger (Ed.), *Nebraska Symposium on Motivation: Vol. 32. Psychology and gender* (pp. 267–307). Lincoln: University of Nebraska Press.

Rosenberg, M. (1965). *Society and the adolescent self-image.* Princeton, NJ: Princeton University Press.

Scheff, T. J. (1987). The shame–rage spiral: A case study of an interminable quarrel. In H. B. Lewis (Ed.), *The role of shame in symptom formation* (pp. 109–149). Hillsdale, NJ: Erlbaum.

Smith, R. L. (1972). The relative proneness to shame or guilt as an indicator of defensive style. *Dissertation Abstracts International, 33,* 2823B. (University Microfilms No. 72-3258)

Spielberger, C. D., Gorsuch, R. L., & Lushene, R. E. (1970). *Manual for the State–Trait Anxiety Inventory.* Palo Alto, CA: Consulting Psychologists Press.

Tangney, J. P. (1989, August). *A quantitative assessment of phenomenological differences between shame and guilt.* Poster presented at the meeting of the American Psychological Association, New Orleans.

Tangney, J. P. (1990). Assessing individual differences in proneness to shame and guilt: Development of the Self-Conscious Affect and Attribution Inventory. *Journal of Personality and Social Psychology, 59, 102–111.*

Tangney, J. P. (1991). Moral affect: The good, the bad, and the ugly. *Journal of Personality and Social Psychology, 61, 598–607.*

Tangney, J. P. (1992). Situational determinants of shame and guilt in young adulthood. *Personality and Social Psychology Bulletin, 18, 199–206.*

Tangney, J. P. (1993). *Shame and guilt.* In C. G. Costello (Ed.), *Symptoms of depression* (pp. 161–180). New York: Wiley.

Tangney, J. P. (in press). The mixed legacy of the superego: Adaptive and maladaptive aspects of shame and guilt. In J. M. Masling & R. R. Bornstein (Eds.), *Empirical studies of psychoanalytic theories* (Vol. 5). Washington, DC: American Psychological Association.

Tangney, J. P., Burggraf, S. A., Hamme, H., & Domingos, B. (1988). *The Self-Conscious Affect and Attribution Inventory (SCAAI).* Bryn Mawr, PA: Bryn Mawr College.

Tangney, J. P., Marschall, D. E., Rosenberg, K., Barlow, D. H., & Wagner, P. E. (1993). *Children's and adults' autobiographical accounts of shame, guilt, and pride experiences: A qualitative analysis of situational determinants and interpersonal concerns.* Manuscript submitted for publication.

14. Shame-Proneness, Guilt-Proneness, and Symptoms   367

Tangney, J. P., Miller, R. S., & Flicker, L. (1992, August). *A quantitative analysis of shame and embarrassment*. Poster presented at the meeting of the American Psychological Association, Washington, DC.

Tangney, J. P., & Niedenthal, P. (1994). *Failing to measure up to our "ideals" and "oughts": An empirical examination and reformulation of the relation of self-discrepancies to shame and guilt*. Manuscript in preparation.

Tangney, J. P., Wagner, P. E., Burggraf, S. A., Gramzow, R., & Fletcher, C. (1990). *The Test of Self-Conscious Affect for Children (TOSCA-C)*. Fairfax, VA: George Mason University.

Tangney, J. P., Wagner, P. E., Burggraf, S. A., Gramzow, R., & Fletcher, C. (1991, June). *Children's shame-proneness, but not guilt-proneness, is related to emotional and behavioral maladjustment*. Poster presented at the meeting of the American Psychological Society, Washington, DC.

Tangney, J. P., Wagner, P. E., Fletcher, C., & Gramzow, R. (1992). Shamed into anger? The relation of shame and guilt to anger and self-reported aggression. *Journal of Personality and Social Psychology, 62,* 669–675.

Tangney, J. P., Wagner, P. E., Gavlas, J., Barlow, D. H., & Marschall, D. E. (1992, August). *Shame, guilt, and constructive vs. destructive anger*. Poster presented at the meeting of the American Psychological Association, Washington, DC.

Tangney, J. P., Wagner, P. E., & Gramzow, R. (1989). *The Test of Self-Conscious Affect*. Fairfax, VA: George Mason University.

Tangney, J. P., Wagner, P. E., & Gramzow, R. (1992). Proneness to shame, proneness to guilt, and psychopathology. *Journal of Abnormal Psychology, 103,* 469–478.

Watson, D., & Friend, R. (1969). Measurement of social-evaluative anxiety. *Journal of Consulting and Clinical Psychology, 33,* 448–457.

Wicker, F. W., Payne, G. C., & Morgan, R. D. (1983). Participant descriptions of guilt and shame. *Motivation and Emotion, 7,* 25–39.

Witkin, H. A., Lewis, H. B., Hertzman, M., Machover, K., Meissner, P., & Wapner, S. (1954). *Personality through perception*. New York: Harper & Brothers.

Witkin, H. A., Lewis, H. B., & Weil, E. (1968). Affective reactions and patient–therapist interaction among more differentiated and less differentiated patients early in therapy. *Journal of Nervous and Mental Disorders, 146,* 193–208.

15

Shame and Guilt Assessment, and Relationships of Shame- and Guilt-Proneness to Psychopathology

DAVID W. HARDER

Early in the era of psychological therapies, guilt assumed the status of a pre-eminent pathogenic emotion (e.g., Freud, 1909/1955). Guilt was the central negative affect that, in theory, contributed to and maintained a panoply of psychically determined symptoms. Even in his first formulations, however, Freud (1905/1953, 1909/1955) occasionally invoked shame as an important pathological influence, chiefly when parents harshly criticized a child for open expressions of erotic longings, which were then repressed and partially re-expressed as symptoms. Freud's theory of neurosis never carefully differentiated guilt from shame, so that when guilt came permanently to the fore in his theoretical writings, shame was neglected. Once shame did reappear in psychoanalytic theories as a potentially important affect (Piers & Singer, 1953), it tended to be placed in opposition to guilt, as though personalities prone to one affect could not be liable to the other. Accounts of personality development (Erikson, 1959; Piers & Singer, 1953) placed the emergence of shame at an earlier and more primitive point in time, thus linking it, in those cases exhibiting psychopathology, with the more severe syndromes. Guilt, in contrast, was associated with the Oedipal stage, which was thought to herald the beginnings of a mature superego (conscience), suitable identity formation, and the internalization of appropriate behavioral controls. Excessive susceptibility to guilt was seen as neurotic, but much closer to psychological health than were problems of excessive shame.

With time, many clinicians (most of them psychoanalytic in orientation) gradually came to recognize shame as a second crucial dysphoric emotion, besides guilt, that was instrumental in the creation of much if not all psychopathology. At first this emphasis upon shame was muted (e.g., Levin, 1967, 1971; H. B. Lewis, 1971; Mayman, 1974). But in recent years an enormous flood of books and articles (e.g., Bradshaw, 1988; Broucek, 1991; Harper & Hoopes, 1990; Kaufman, 1989; Morrison, 1989; Nathanson, 1987a), mostly directed at clinical practitioners, has placed excessive shame in the forefront of processes leading to the formation and maintenance of symptoms at all levels of pathology. There is currently very little expectation that being prone to shame precludes proneness to guilt, or vice versa. Hence, irrespective of considerations regarding guilt, shame has of late been implicated significantly in an extremely wide range of pathologies: alcoholism and its sequelae (Cook, 1987, 1993; Evans, 1987; Gomberg, 1987; Potter-Efron, 1987), abuse of other substances (Brown, 1987; Cook, 1993; Fossum & Mason, 1986; Harper & Hoopes, 1990), antisocial personality (Wright, 1987), borderline personality (Fischer, 1985; Lansky, 1987b), conduct disorders and delinquency (Bilmes, 1967; Cassorla, 1986), depression (Cook, 1993; H. B. Lewis, 1971; Harder & Lewis, 1987; Hoblitzelle, 1982; Tangney, 1993; Wright, O'Leary, & Balkin, 1989), eating disorders (Cook, 1987; 1993; Floyd & Floyd, 1985), pathological narcissism (Kernberg, 1970; Kohut, 1971; Miller, 1988; Morrison, 1989), psychoanalytic neuroses (hysteria and obsessive–compulsiveness; H. B. Lewis, 1971; Shapiro, 1965), paranoia (Colby, 1976; Kaufman, 1989), post-traumatic stress disorders (Cook, 1993), sexual and physical abuse syndromes (Cook, 1993; Kaufman, 1989), sexual dysfunctions and paraphilias (Kaufman, 1989; Katz, 1988; Stoller, 1987), excessive shyness (Harder & Lewis, 1987; Mosher & White, 1981), suicide (Harper & Hoopes, 1990; Shreve & Kunkel, 1989), and violence (Harper & Hoopes, 1990; Katz, 1988; Lansky, 1987a).

THEORIES OF SHAME AND GUILT

Paralleling this burgeoning clinical interest in shame, increased research and theoretical attention have begun to elucidate the role of shame in psychopathology formation and in personality functioning, both normal and abnormal. Much of this work has taken place with earlier, largely Freud-influenced notions about guilt (subsuming shame) still very much in focus. Thus, most often, the study of shame and the study of guilt have proceeded side by side, with explicit efforts to distinguish the two.

Clinicians (most notably H. B. Lewis, 1971) have focused primarily upon the phenomenological differences between shame and guilt. Typically, shame is described as an experience of awkwardness, exposure, self-paralysis, ridicule, and scorn; the entire self is felt as a focus of disapproving observations (made by an "other," who is a real individual, an imagined person, or someone unconsciously identified with). The self is often sensed as childish, silly, embarrassed, and humiliated, and rageful anger is a frequent concomitant. The ashamed person feels bad, because another (or others) disapproves of an aspect or behavior of the self. In contrast, guilt is ordinarily less disruptive to the self as a whole. The focus is on some behavior or set of behaviors that has transgressed a moral standard (or, on the fantasy level, would transgress one if enacted), and that generates feelings of regret, remorse, and/or concern (sometimes extreme) for an injured party. The guilty person feels bad, because he or she internally evaluates the self's behavior as bad. This emotion can reach the level of self-hating despair, however, especially when the sense of harm done is irreparable (H. B. Lewis, 1971, p. 43).

In recent years there has also been strong interest, mostly among less clinically oriented theorists, in an alternative characterization of shame and guilt set forth by the affect theory of Tomkins (1987). This view does not center upon the phenomenological differences between the two emotions, but rather upon basic, innate emotional patterns that are presumed to be in evidence soon after birth and that underlie all of the subtleties of emotion so central to clinical discourse. The complexities of specifically experienced emotions are viewed as epiphenomena, produced by various combinations of the basic nine affects in conjunction with individually unique perceptions and cognitions. This theory, which has some impressive empirical support (e.g., Fridlund, Ekman, & Oster, 1986), holds that shame is one of the innate affect mechanisms—expressed by lowered eyes and head, resulting from a loss of muscle tonus in the face and neck—whereas guilt is only one of several variants of shame. Shame has the adaptive purpose of checking excessive excitement/interest or enjoyment/joy affects, but can become excessive if shame-inducing interruptions to normal physiological excitement or enjoyment sequences are too frequent or severe. (One might ask, however, whether shame always follows the interruption of enjoyment, as Tomkins maintains. For example, does a person feel shame if a computer game being enjoyed suddenly ceases because of power failure? Cf. Broucek, 1991, p. 21.)

A few clinicians, such as Kaufman (1989) and Nathanson (1987b), have enthusiastically followed Tomkins's lead in their own theorizing. In addition to the elegance of the affect theory and its empirical support, it also has current appeal because it helps establish the centrality of shame to emotional problems—an idea that has shown itself prominently in the numerous clinical writings cited above. In particular, Kaufman (1989, p. 26) has faulted more traditional theories, which focus on guilt–shame differences and grant guilt an important place in etiology, for maintaining an artificial distinction between the two affects. Rather, he maintains that guilt as a theoretical concept is, in actuality, merely morally concerned shame. Furthermore, he argues that the word "guilt," as used in the everyday world and by clinicians (without much concern for theoretical rigor), is a confusingly broad term for a variety of negatively toned, self-directed emotional states produced from various combinations of other, more fundamental affects (shame, distress, fear, anger, disgust, and "dissmell"; Tomkins, 1987).

Even if Kaufman's contentions about the fundamental physiological identity of shame and guilt are valid, however, most clinical theorists probably remain doubtful about the extent of their clinical—and hence their theoretical—significance. Psychotherapist theorists are often much more impressed by the phenomenological differences between shame and guilt that they encounter in practice and that seem to require different styles of intervention. Tomkins (1987, p. 143) himself has commented interestingly upon the phenomenological distinctness of shame and guilt: ". . . the core affect . . . is identical, although the coassembled perceptions, cognitions, and intentions may be vastly different." Fresh from therapy sessions focusing upon these "coassembled" epiphenomena of patients' emotions, Levin (1971), H. B. Lewis (1971), Mayman (1974), and I (Harder, 1990b) have all argued that special technical attention to shame is critical for psychotherapeutic improvement with shame-prone patients, though not as crucial with the more guilt-prone. Similarly, a clinical enthusiast of Tomkins's theory, such as Nathanson (1987b), still asserts that important treatment decisions hinge upon whether a patient is more shame- or guilt-prone. Indeed, Kaufman (1989, pp. 259–273) himself makes treatment prescriptions that emphasize the necessity of focus upon the phenomenology of an individual's specific shame *variants,* such as shameful inferiorities versus guilty sins of commission. Making a distinction, then, between underlying physiological "affect" on the one hand, and the more psychological terms "experience," "feeling," and "emotion" on the other (Basch, 1988), captures the separate emphases of Tomkins's and the clinicians' (e.g., H. B. Lewis's) theories. The latter group of writers would argue that for purposes of clinical theory and personality assessment, the qualitative distinctions between shame and guilt outlined above (H. B. Lewis, 1971; Lynd, 1958) remain important.

A third school of theoretical thought regarding shame and guilt is comprised of the academically influential theorists on cognitive attribution and appraisal (e.g., Lazarus, 1991; Schachter & Singer, 1962). Interestingly, a similar distinction to that outlined just above demarcating physiological affect from experience ("experience" here denotes cognitions more than feelings) also comprises a major, essential difference between these cognitive theories and that of Tomkins. Thus, although affect theory remains largely at the physiological level, both the cognitive and psychodynamic theories of emotion offer formulations on the more experiential levels of appraisal patterns and/or individual motivational tendencies, where shame and guilt appear to be quite distinct.

The central theoretical challenge made by Tomkins to these more "psychological" perspectives is whether differences between shame and guilt are ultimately of minor or of major importance. If affect theory accurately makes guilt and shame only variants of one basic emotion, are those variants nonetheless disparately influential enough on personality patterns, symptoms, phenomenological experience, and implications for therapy that the shame–guilt distinction should be maintained? Taken together, clinical experience, clinical theory, and cognitive-appraisal theory all suggest that the answer is yes. Certainly the theoretical formulations of the psychodynamic and cognitive-appraisal writers, as opposed to the affect theorists, lend themselves more easily to clinical phenomena and to psychotherapeutic planning. Empirical studies with children and adults (Ferguson, Stegge, & Damhuis, 1991; Tangney, 1992) convincingly verify that important phenomenological differences between the two emotions do exist. Such differences also appear in factor analyses (Harder & Zalma, 1990; Hoblitzelle, 1982) of scales constructed to assess the two affect dispositions. Theories including such differences as important constructs can, with more ease than Tomkins's affect theory, address the consciously (and perhaps even the unconsciously) experienced, complex feelings of social and clinical situations.

In the present chapter, the focus is on those conscious and unconscious emotions of shame and guilt that are of great concern to clinical investigators. The term "affect" is used interchangeably here with "emotion," with none of the physiological implications of the concept "affect" in Tomkins's theory. Of most concern are the structured personality dispositions ordinarily known as "shame-proneness" and "guilt-proneness." Although every person experiences both kinds of dysphoric feelings at one time or another, characteristic individual tendencies toward the experience of shame or guilt are assumed to exist. Such traits can be considered analogous to other elements of character style (Shapiro, 1965) that incline a person toward associated personality patterns and typical symptoms. Although shame and guilt can often be kept out of full awareness, high chronic levels of such unconscious and preconscious feelings are expected to be mirrored imperfectly by characteristic, conscious emotions or behaviors. Such an assumption implies that shame and guilt dispositions can be assessed by measures that tap subjectively perceived emotional experiences and/or their behavioral reflections.

SHAME AND GUILT ASSESSMENT

Certainly the differentiation of guilt from shame by psychological assessment techniques is not an easy matter, even if one grants the clinical and theoretical importance of keeping the two emotions distinct. Overlap of the two affects, even extensive overlap, is expected on theoretical grounds other than those advanced by Tomkins. For example, despite major differences on the prominence of unconscious versus conscious influences, both psycho-dynamic theorists (e.g., H. B. Lewis, 1971) and cognitive-appraisal theorists (e.g., Lazarus, 1991) have proposed much in common between the still distinguishable emotions of guilt and shame. Both of these viewpoints regard shame and guilt similarly as internalized, negatively toned self-evaluations that mediate socialized conduct. H. B. Lewis (1971, p. 23) states that shame and guilt are two equally advanced, although different, superego functions. Advanced psychic development or the lack of it in personality growth will thus provide a level of self-regulation (mature or immature, respectively) in an individual, whether that individual is more prone to shame, to guilt, or to neither. Lazarus (1991, pp. 240–243) indicates that both emotions involve internalized social proscriptions, even though their core relational patterns are distinct. He makes a shame–guilt differentiation between ego-ideal shortfall (shame) and moral transgression (guilt) similar to H. B. Lewis's in the third step of the general appraisal process that he describes.

Existence of overlap between the two emotions is also to be expected for other reasons. First, they share some experiential similarities, which may explain why many individuals show descriptive confusion when attempting to distinguish between the two (Binder, 1970; Shaver, Schwartz, Kirson, & O'Connor, 1987; Tangney, 1992; Wicker, Payne, & Morgan, 1983). Second, shame and guilt frequently co-occur (Ferguson et al., 1991; Levin, 1967, 1971; H. B. Lewis, 1971; Mayman, 1974; Tangney, 1992), which probably also gives rise to some of the descriptive overlap. Two short examples can illustrate the intertwined nature of much shame and guilt. A depressed soldier experiences intense discomfort for avoiding the worst of a wartime battle by separating himself from his comrades. He is humiliated by his fellows' knowing glances after the fighting, and feels guilty for leaving them to face death alone. Another individual feels great distress immediately after experiencing enjoyment, especially when it relates to sexuality, because he anticipates humiliating disapproval of others. At the same time, he experiences guilt at the prospect of enjoying himself more in the future, because he thinks it will cause him to "leave my parents behind" in their own states of depression. In both examples, shame and guilt occur side by side.

Although most scale development research in the past 20 years has made efforts to discriminate between the two states, there have been two notable exceptions (Klass, 1983; Mosher, 1966, 1968). Mosher's scale (for "guilt") antedated the emergence of interest in shame, and Klass's scale has seemed designed more to assess the overall degree of negative self-evalua-tions ("guilt") than to carefully delineate the two varieties of such feelings. Both scales may well be satisfactory in the general assessment of dysphoric self-evaluations, but close inspection of the items used shows that they could be separated into more typically shame- or guilt-oriented subscales.

Obviously, for research in shame- and guilt-proneness and for clinical screening as well, valid assessment of each disposition is required. This task necessitates careful attention to discriminant as well as convergent validity, because the expected overlap in the constructs raises questions about the permitted extent of intercorrelation between acceptable measures of the two affects. Unfortunately, much of the past assessment work (Binder, 1970; Hoblitzelle, 1982, 1987; Klass, 1983; Smith, 1972) in this area has not involved extensive attempts to establish such validation with constructs external to the measures.

With that problem in mind, a colleague and I (Harder & Lewis, 1987) tested four promising measures of each emotional disposition by examining their relationships to other personality constructs theoretically tied to each affect. Unfortunately, the Gottschalk and Gleser (1969) Shame and Guilt Anxiety Scales showed test–retest reliability inadequate to qualify them as trait measures for further validity testing. The Binder–Harder Shame Scale (Binder, 1970; Harder, 1975, 1984) and the Beall Situational Upset Scale (Smith, 1972) measures of shame and guilt exhibited only weak construct validity. Similarly, the Mosher (1966, 1968) Total Guilt Scale received only weak support, especially for women. The Personal Feelings Questionnaire (PFQ; Harder & Lewis, 1987) Shame and Guilt subscales were the sole instruments for each affect that appeared valid after construct validity testing. Even in the case of these two valid measures, though, there were some indications of difficulty in the discrimination afforded by the scales. A review by Polivy (1981) suggests that this problem may be inherent to *all* self-report affect scales; however, the clinical and personality importance of the concepts assessed makes the effort worth continuing.

Other difficulties appear in such validation work as well. Ideally, one could hypothesize clear, discriminating physiological or behavioral differences between shame and guilt that might be observed in laboratory studies. However, this ideal appears difficult to realize. If the affect theory (Tomkins, 1987) is correct, shame and guilt should show identical (or at least very similar) facial muscle configurations and other physiological properties (Ekman, Levenson, & Friesen, 1983). Indeed, Izard (1972, 1977, 1979) has not been able to distinguish shame from guilt by facial expression. The prediction of behavioral differences also seems problematic, because the intermixture of shame and guilt that often occurs in clinical settings probably occurs just as frequently in nonclinical populations (Ferguson et al., 1991; Tangney, 1992). Perhaps experimental groups could be selected for strong proneness to one emotion and not the other (though such individuals may be rare); affect induction could then be stimulated under laboratory conditions designed to trigger either shame or guilt; and differences in behavior could be observed. Polivy's (1981) review adds some discouragement to this prospect, but again, the effort is an important one.

Ethical issues regarding the induction of negative emotional states also loom over such research, but mild inductions should create no lasting harm in most cases. Whether such mild emotional inductions would constitute sufficient stimulation to engender observable shame and guilt differences remain to be seen.

Current attempts along these lines also raise interpretive difficulties. M. Lewis (1992), following the lead of Barrett and Zahn-Waxler (1987), has advocated an experimental induction paradigm that he argues adequately separates shame- from guilt-prone children. A doll designed to break after several minutes of normal play is presented to a child subject, whose response to the breakage becomes the basis of classification. Shame is indicated if averted gaze, bodily "collapse," and no attempt to fix the toy are in evidence. Guilt is presumably marked by the opposites of these characteristics, particularly attempts to repair the doll or induce the experimenter to do so. Besides the ethical concerns raised by this stressful situation, there are also questions about the adequacy of the behavioral operations. Their validity hinges upon the assumption that guilt intrinsically involves both reparative action and a "focus upon the toy and not upon the self" (M. Lewis, 1992, pp. 25–26). Conversely, shame involves helplessness and focus upon the self. Whether these disparate behavioral responses actually correspond, respectively, to inner experiences of injuring the doll's owner (guilt) versus appearing deficient in front of others (shame) has no immediately obvious answer. One could just as easily conceive of the opposite behavioral reactions as products of habitually active versus passive coping styles rather than of differentiable emotions.

One additional potential difficulty facing assessment research with all emotions is the unconscious nature of many affects, perhaps especially those that might be expected to create or maintain pathological states, such as extreme shame and guilt. Although an ideal instrument would accurately be able to indicate total conscious and unconscious motivational tendencies produced by these affects, the only way to obtain convincing measures of unconscious feelings would be through inferences made by observers intimately knowledgeable about a person's psychological dynamics. Such in-depth study of each subject would require prohibitive amounts of time and effort. Psychological testing batteries, including projectives, might offer an alternative approach, but the scoring and inference processes involved are also lengthy procedures. Furthermore, measuring emotion through test responses, themselves removed from the immediacy of a subject's feelings and personal history, may introduce additional errors. An assumption was made earlier, based on clinical work, that most individuals with high levels of unconscious or preconscious shame and guilt will also show high conscious "overflows" of the corresponding feelings. However, there is no independent way to verify this belief.

The best chance to assess as much unconscious emotion as possible, then, may well be with self-report scales that try to capture the phenomenological experience of emotions, such that the fully upsetting shame or guilt "meaning" of the feelings can be left somewhat unstated (and thus partly unconscious). In contrast, subject reports that describe behavioral responses to situations may be more vulnerable to social desirability and repression confounds. Ideally, careful in-depth, clinical study of some subjects could verify whether the measure(s) used did or did not assess unconscious emotional states. It is possible, however, that shame and guilt assessment will not be able to tap the unconscious level successfully. Still, the identification of conscious, characteristic shame- and guilt-proneness alone would itself be a valuable contribution to research on personality and psychopathology.

RECENT RESEARCH

A systematic research program (Harder & Lewis, 1987; Harder, 1990a; Harder & Zalma, 1990; Harder, Rockart, & Cutler, 1993) testing available shame- and guilt-proneness instruments with a construct validation strategy had, by 1992, established the viability of two shame measures and one guilt measure. The shame measures were the Hoblitzelle (1982, 1987) Adapted Shame and Guilt Scale (ASGS) Shame subscale, as slightly modified (Harder & Zalma, 1990), and the Shame subscale of the Personal Feelings Questionnaire 2 (PFQ2; Harder & Lewis, 1987; Harder, 1990a; Harder & Zalma, 1990; Harder, Cutler, & Rockart, 1992). The only guilt-proneness assessment measure that remained viable after validity testing was the Guilt subscale of the PFQ2.

In these studies, valid shame measures were expected on theoretical grounds to relate to self-derogation, low positive self-esteem, self-instability, inadequacy of self, social anxiety, public self-consciousness, shyness, depression, anxiety, hostility, defensive narcissism, defensively low social desirability, external locus of control, and a tendency to use denial/repression defenses. Convincing guilt measures were expected to correlate significantly with self-derogation, low positive self-esteem, self-instability, inadequacy of self, and depression, but at magnitudes lower than those shown by shame. In addition, guilt was not expected to relate to social anxiety, public self-consciousness, shyness, defensive narcissism, or defensively low social desirability. Guilt was predicted to show associations with private self-consciousness, internal locus of control, and use of intellectualization defenses, in contrast to shame. In general, the findings have been quite consistently in line with expectations for the ASGS and PFQ2 Shame subscales, but less consistently similar to predictions for the PFQ2 Guilt subscale.

Two very recent studies reported in detail elsewhere (Harder et al., 1992) that have continued this research program are summarized here, in order to accomplish three objectives. First, the overall research strategy is illustrated. Second, recommendations are made about the best shame and guilt measures available for use by assessment investigators—including consideration of one relatively new scale, the Test of Self-Conscious Affect (TOSCA; Tangney, Burggraf, & Wagner, Chapter 14, this volume; Tangney,

Wagner, & Gramzow, 1992), a revision of the Self-Conscious Affect Attribution Inventory (SCAAI; Tangney, 1990). These suggestions derive from a test of the TOSCA against the ASGS and the PFQ2. And third, tests of hypothesized relationships between shame and guilt dispositions and various types of symptomatology are described.

The first study to be summarized here (Harder et al., 1992) examined construct validity of the substantially revised version of the SCAAI (Tangney, 1990), the TOSCA (Tangney et al., 1992), in comparison to both previously validated shame measures (the ASGS and PFQ2 Shame subscales) and to the less well-established PFQ2 Guilt subscale. Following the design of previous concurrent validation studies (Harder & Lewis, 1987; Harder & Zalma, 1990), nine personality dimensions were used as external criteria against which to evaluate the validity of the shame and guilt scales. These constructs were depression, self-derogation, social anxiety, shyness, public self-consciousness, private self-consciousness, narcissism, social desirability, and locus of control. Specific predictions based on theory were made about the relationships between these constructs and valid shame and guilt measures. These predictions and their rationales are detailed in earlier reports (Harder & Lewis, 1987; Harder & Zalma, 1990; Harder et al., 1992) and summarized schematically here in Table 15.1. In general, shame was expected to relate directly and more strongly than guilt to depression, self-derogation, social anxiety, shyness, public self-consciousness, and external locus of control. Shame was expected to show stronger inverse associations with narcissism and social desirability. And guilt was expected to demonstrate a significant or near-significant positive relationship with private self-consciousness.

Fifty-eight college undergraduates (30 female and 28 male), from urban

TABLE 15.1. Predicted Construct Validity Relationships for Shame and Guilt Scales

Construct validity variable	Shame measure	Guilt measure
Depression	++	+
Self-derogation	++	+
Social anxiety	+	o
Shyness	++	o
Public self-consciousness	+	o/−
Private self-consciousness	o/−	+/o
Narcissism	−	o
Social desirability	−	o
(External) Locus of control	+/o	−/o

Note. +, positive significant correlation; ++, high positive significant correlation; −, negative significant correlation; o, no significance predicted. From "Assessment of Shame and Guilt and Their Relationships to Psychopathology" by D. W. Harder, L. Cutler, & L. Rockart, 1992, *Journal of Personality Assessment, 59,* 584–604. Copyright 1992 by Lawrence Erlbaum Associates. Reprinted by permission.

and suburban upper-middle-class backgrounds, anonymously completed randomly arranged packets of questionnaires, including the ASGS, the PFQ2, the TOSCA, and the scales assessing the other nine personality dimensions. These nine personality instruments were the following: the Beck (1967) Depression Inventory; the Kaplan (1975; Kaplan & Pokorny, 1969) Self-Derogation Scale; the Narcissistic Personality Inventory (short form; Raskin & Hall, 1979, 1981); the Zimbardo (1977; Harder & Lewis, 1987) Stanford Shyness Inventory; three Fenigstein, Scheier, and Buss (1975; Carver & Glass, 1976) scales—the Social Anxiety Scale, the Private Self-Consciousness Scale, and the Public Self-Consciousness Scale; the Marlowe–Crowne (Crowne & Marlowe, 1960, 1964) Social Desirability Scale; and the Rotter (1966) Locus of Control Scale.

The correlational results, detailed in the original article (Harder et al., 1992) and presented here in Table 15.2 in partial form, indicated that all three shame measures produced a pattern consistent with hypothesized expectations for valid measures. The ASGS and PFQ2 scales continued to demonstrate construct validity, while the new TOSCA did the same. In addition, all three shame instruments intercorrelated well, with coefficients ranging from .52 to .61.

TABLE 15.2. Construct Validity Correlations for ASGS, PFQ2, and TOSCA Shame Scales, and for PFQ2 and TOSCA Guilt Scales (Partialed, Respectively, for ASGS Shame and for ASGS Shame and Sex) ($n = 58$)

Construct validity variable	ASGS Shame	PFQ2 Shame	TOSCA Shame	PFQ2 Guilt (partialed for ASGS Shame)	TOSCA Guilt (partialed for ASGS Shame and sex)
Depression	.44***	.43***	.38**	.22†	−.16
Self-derogation	.64***	.49***	.50***	.24†	−.19
Social anxiety	.49***	.23†	.30*	.03	−.12
Shyness	.55***	.25†	.26*	.00	−.04
Public self-consciousness	.18	.35**	.26*	.23†	.31*
Private self-consciousness	.05	.20	.13	.08	.27*
Narcissism	−.37**	−.09	−.38**	.18	.12
Social desirability	−.03	−.12	.10	−.05	.15
Locus of control	.15	.15	.05	.08	−.23†
ASGS Shame	—	.61***	.54***	—	—
PFQ2 Shame	.61***	—	.42**	.28*	.10
TOSCA Shame	.54**	.42**	—	.06	.31**
PFQ2 Guilt	.52***	.52***	.33**	—	−.05
TOSCA Guilt	.24†	.17†	.47***	−.11	—

Note. Adapted from "Assessment of Shame and Guilt and Their Relationships to Psychopathology" by D. W. Harder, L. Cutler, & L. Rockart, 1992, Journal of Personality Assessment, 59, 584–604. Copyright 1992 by Lawrence Erlbaum Associates. Adapted by permission.
†$p < .10$. *$p < .05$. **$p < .01$. ***$p < .001$.

Of the three shame instruments, the ASGS Shame subscale appeared to be the best by a slight margin. It is very quickly administered, and, compared to other shame measures it has demonstrated slightly superior construct validity in both this most recent study (Harder et al., 1992) and one previous investigation (Harder & Zalma, 1990). Its one liability appears to be a reliance upon an extensive vocabulary reflecting shame-related experiences. If a research sample is less educated than the college students serving as subjects in these studies, problems in obtaining valid data might occur. Even among college students, there has been some reported confusion over ASGS item meanings (Harder & Zalma, 1990).

The PFQ2 and TOSCA Shame scales similarly showed a largely expectable pattern of correlations with the construct validity variables, though to a somewhat less impressive extent. The reliance of these scales upon experiential terms and the TOSCA's use of shame-eliciting scenarios that are described with simple vocabulary may thus make these two the more useful shame measures with less educated samples.

It should be noted that the TOSCA Shame scale demonstrated one possible problem for ease of usage—a highly significant difference between the scores of male and female subjects. Women registered the higher scores—a result consistent with the hypotheses of some theorists (H. B. Lewis, 1976; Wright et al., 1989), but not a result shown previously with the ASGS or PFQ2 scales (Harder et al., 1992; Harder & Zalma, 1990; Wright et al., 1989). The configuration of validity correlations produced by the TOSCA with the sex difference removed was still largely consistent with predictions. Hence, the validity of the new TOSCA Shame scale was supported for both sexes, though the observed sex difference on the scale raises questions about the possible necessity of separate interpretations for men and women.

Because a difference in means by gender does not, in itself, indicate a different pattern of validity correlations for each sex, the coefficients for men and women were examined separately. Independent sample z-transform t tests indicated that only one TOSCA Shame scale difference proved to be near-significant (for shyness, $t = 1.93$, $p < .06$); none of the PFQ2 or ASGS Shame scale sex differences were anywhere near significant. Because the relatively low number of subjects in the present study dictates that a group difference in r of approximately .54—rarely even seen in empirical investigations—is necessary to reach statistical significance, these data do not allow any firm conclusions regarding the sex difference question. Further examination of the signs and magnitudes of the coefficients indicated that out of nine validity relationships, the TOSCA Shame scale showed men and women having opposite signs on four of them—social anxiety, shyness, social desirability, and locus of control—with an average difference of 35 points. The ASGS showed an opposite sign for only one validity correlation, private self-consciousness (a 20-point difference), and the PFQ2 showed two relationships with opposite signs, narcissism and locus of control (a 32-point average difference). Overall, the foregoing suggests that the question of possible divergence in TOSCA validity by sex deserves further investigation, though it may prove to be no problem for usage.

In contrast to the encouraging findings for the three shame measures studied, results for the validity of the guilt measures tested in the Harder et al. (1992) study did not indicate great success. Validity correlations for both the TOSCA and PFQ2 Guilt subscales presented mixed conclusions.

The validity correlations not involving depression and self-derogation suggested that the TOSCA was superior to the PFQ2. The TOSCA Guilt subscale showed six out of seven relationships consistent with predictions, whereas the PFQ2 Guilt subscale produced only four out of seven. However, the other two validity results for the TOSCA Guilt scale were strikingly inconsistent with theoretical predictions. Unexpected, near-zero relationships with both depression and self-derogation appeared. To find no such relationships accords badly with the substantial theoretical and clinical evidence linking characteristic guilt dispositions with depressive mood and self-devaluational attitudes. Furthermore, the data revealed no significant association between the TOSCA Guilt scale and the previously more externally validated PFQ2 Guilt instrument. The TOSCA Guilt scale did, however, correlate significantly with the TOSCA Shame scale, with the PFQ2 Shame scale, and (at the $p < .10$ level) with the ASGS Shame scale.

Although this overall configuration of variable relationships is seen here as more supportive of the PFQ2 Guilt scale than of the TOSCA Guilt scale, our data (Harder et al., 1992) also indicate discriminant validity problems for the PFQ2 Guilt and Shame subscales. These difficulties were not entirely unexpected, because previous research has already provided somewhat equivocal evidence (Harder, 1990a; Harder & Zalma, 1990; Harder et al., 1993) for the discriminant validity of the two PFQ2 measures. The most recent data (Harder et al., 1992) add to these questions, because they produce a correlation pattern uncomfortably similar to what would be expected of a valid shame measure, and the relationship between the two PFQ2 scales was in the low .50s, typical of the earlier studies.

In order to further examine the TOSCA and PFQ2 Guilt scale validity correlations without confounding overlaps attributable to shame, we (Harder et al., 1992) then adopted the strategy of partialing the TOSCA and PFQ2 Guilt scores by the best available measure of shame-proneness (ASGS) and redoing the construct validity analyses. The TOSCA Guilt scale was also partialed for sex because, as with its Shame counterpart, women provided significantly higher scores. The results pointed toward a generally improved picture for the validity of the PFQ2 Guilt measure, whereas the TOSCA measure still exhibited near-zero associations with depression and self-derogation. Examination of TOSCA results separately for men and women did not change the validity picture for either gender.[1]

Thus (despite measurement problems in the discrimination of guilt from shame), for all the reasons discussed in the preceding sections of this chapter, the PFQ2 Guilt scale still appears to be the best such instrument available. Perhaps the partialing of PFQ2 Guilt scores for shame should become a routine research procedure, though it does run the risk of eliminating some valid guilt variance in the overlap of the two affect dispositions. Similarly, to test hypotheses about shame-proneness, as entirely distinct from guilt tendencies, it will also be necessary to conduct analyses only after partialing shame scores for guilt.

Given the difficulties noted here in discriminating guilt from shame with self-report instruments, one might be tempted to ask: Why continue the attempt? One might surmise either that the affect theorists (e.g., Izard, 1972; Tomkins, 1987) are correct and that there is no difference major enough to be found, or, alternatively, that the available instruments are just not sufficiently sensitive. Factor analyses of the PFQ2 and ASGS (Harder et al., 1992), largely successful at placing *a priori* shame and guilt items on orthogonal dimensions, suggests that real differentiation of fundamental constructs does exist, despite overlaps. The partialing procedure would seem to best approximate these "pure" emotions.

Tangney et al. (Chapter 14, this volume) have argued in favor of the TOSCA Guilt measure over that of the PFQ2 by contending that associations between guilt and depression or self-derogation should *not* be expected on the basis of theory. Their argument hinges upon the essential definitional distinction they make between shame and guilt (which echoes that of M. Lewis [1992], cited earlier): Shame is a global negative self-evaluation that creates helplessness; guilt is a negative assessment of a specific action that is largely divorced from overall disapproving self-evaluations and usually includes a tendency to correct the misdeed.[2] According to this view, if a person feels so terrible about doing (or not doing) something that he or she feels globally bad and/or does not attempt to (or cannot) make amends, then that person is suffering predominantly from shame, not guilt. As Tangney et al. (Chapter 14, this volume) state it,

> [G]uilt [is] a sense of remorse or regret in connection with some *specific behavior*, rather than . . . a global condemnation of the self . . . if anything, guilt should be *adaptive* (p. 349; emphasis Tangney et al.'s). . . . [G]uilt involves . . . the capacity to simultaneously maintain images of a "good" self engaged in objectionable behavior (p. 355). . . . [G]uilt becomes maladaptive most typically when it becomes fused with shame. . . . And the shame component of this sequence, not the guilt component, . . . is most likely to lead to the interminable rumination and self-castigation [of depression]. (pp. 358–359)

Thus, by this definition, when a person feels devalued that person is primarily ashamed, even if the basis for his or her feeling is a bad deed condemned by an internal standard, without reference to any condemning other. Hence, any depressive experience involving a negative self-statement automatically becomes shame-fused and, consequently, only minimally a guilt-related symptom.

This same definitional distinction leads M. Lewis (1992, p. 101) to conclude that a student who feels it is his fault that his father died (because he did not visit during a holiday) is experiencing shame, not guilt, and that a disturbed man who believes he brought on his mother's severe headaches (because of his noise) is likewise experiencing shame, not guilt. These are examples that have, in clinical circles, traditionally been considered strong guilt reactions, not shame-based phenomena. It would seem that one aspect of H. B. Lewis's (1971) shame–guilt distinction—the *relative* difference in experienced origin of negative self-evaluation, global self or specific behavior—has, for Tangney et al. (Chapter 14, this volume) and M. Lewis (1992), become the *only* basis for a distinction.

The tendency to consider almost all negative self-evaluations as shame, and to restrict guilt to specific actions unconnected with negative self-judgments, is also evident in the wording of the TOSCA scale items. Close to half (7 of 15) of the Guilt scale responses involve statements of planned actions to correct a reprehensible behavior (e.g., "You would try to make it up to him as soon as possible"), which do not allow for much in the way of experienced negative self-feeling; the majority of the Shame scale items (10 of 15) are worded in negative terms toward the self (e.g., "I'm inconsiderate"), which might actually reflect guilt feelings (as in "I'm inconsiderate" because I did an inconsiderate thing). Given this item structure, it may be that a failure to find relationships between the TOSCA Guilt Scale and depression (or self-derogation) is a consequence of the theoretical distinction between shame and guilt upon which the TOSCA is based. Because the intense guilt that plays an important part in psychopathology (according to clinical theorists, such as H. B. Lewis, 1971) involves negative self-feelings that are classified as shame by the TOSCA, the TOSCA Guilt scale may also underestimate the role of guilt in other psychological symptoms.

For purposes of conceptual clarity in the assessment of shame- and guilt-proneness, it is important to underline that the definitions of shame and (especially) guilt underlying the TOSCA and PFQ2 are different. The basis of the TOSCA consists of two conceptually differentiable elements of a person's behavior: globality of cognition and coping reaction. Shame involves a global negative self-evaluation and is associated with a sense of helplessness or passivity in correcting the perceived fault. Guilt, on the other hand, involves criticism of a specific act, not of the self, usually combined with a plan or specific intention to remedy the problem. Thus, global self-criticism is linked with a passive coping style, whereas criticism of a specific action is associated with an adaptive (nonpathological) response style. These presumed connections between cognition and coping dispositions need to be empirically demonstrated and should not be accepted only on the basis of theory. However, even if one grants their plausibility, they give rise to a differentiation of shame and guilt that is discrepant from the usual clinical distinction. The PFQ2 is based more on the experienced primary locus of self-evaluation, whether it is the view of the "other" (shame) or one's internal standards, irrespective of others' opinions (guilt). The traditional clinical definition emphasizes this internal–external dimension, rather than the global–specific distinction or the type of behavioral response.

It is perhaps noteworthy that the shame and guilt measures showing the foremost validity in previous investigations (Harder & Lewis, 1987; Harder et al., 1992)—that is, the ASGS Shame scale, the TOSCA Shame scale, and the two subscales of the PFQ—have all consisted of experiential items. It may also be the case that individuals can experience similar events as triggering shame and/or guilt (Tangney, 1990), depending upon their own emotional liabilities (H. B. Lewis, 1971) and/or their cognitive-appraisal tendencies (Lazarus, 1991). Such a likelihood makes the prospect dimmer that reliable cross-subject behavioral indices of shame- and guilt-proneness can be found for investigation in the laboratory. The best such research strategy may be, as suggested earlier, to identify high-shame/low-guilt and high-guilt/low-shame groups, and then to test hypotheses regarding differential behaviors expected from these two groups under varying laboratory conditions designed to potentiate the activation of one emotion or the other.

SHAME, GUILT, AND SYMPTOMATOLOGY

The second study to be described briefly here (Harder et al., 1992) tested hypotheses regarding the relationships between shame, guilt, and a number of symptom types. It was undertaken for two reasons. First, theoretical assertions about differences in the relative importance of shame and guilt to various symptom clusters may well have important implications for optimum treatment procedures (Harder, 1990b; Levin, 1971; H. B. Lewis, 1971; Mayman, 1974; Nathanson, 1987b). Second, one earlier investigation (Tangney et al., 1992) obtained strongly counterintuitive results suggesting that guilt plays almost no role across the spectrum of psychopathological symptoms. Because those results were based upon use of the TOSCA Guilt subscale, which we (Harder et al., 1992) found to be insufficiently valid in the research summarized above, the relative roles of shame and guilt in symptom formation clearly need much empirical clarification.

On the basis of our earlier findings, we (Harder et al., 1992) chose the most valid instruments for the assessment of shame- and guilt-proneness—the ASGS and PFQ2, respectively. We then used the resulting scale scores, after partialing each measure for the other affect, to test a series of theoretically derived hypotheses regarding emotion and symptom links (for complete details, see Harder et al., 1992).

A summary of the predictions follows. Overall indices of psychopathology severity were expected to relate with similar strength to shame- and guilt-proneness, even though some theorists (e.g., Kaufman, 1989) have predicted a much stronger relationship for shame. Shame and guilt were predicted to be equally important for phobic and paranoid symptoms. Shame was expected to show somewhat stronger relationships than guilt with depression, somatic complaints, interpersonal sensitivity, hostility–anger, psychoticism, and possibly manifest anxiety problems. These differences in association magnitude were expected to be quite small for somatic complaints, hostility, and anxiety. Guilt was expected to be more highly associated only with obsessive–compulsive symptoms. Thus, if any difference emerged between the two affect dispositions and overall pathology, it was expected to be slightly stronger for shame-proneness.

Subjects were 71 undergraduate students (42 female and 29 male), from the same university that provided the sample for the first study described. The procedure was the same as in the first study, except that the Symptom Checklist 90—Revised (SCL-90-R; Derogatis, 1983; Derogatis, Lipman, & Covi, 1973) was added to the research packet. The SCL-90-R provides several indices of general psychopathology severity, as well as subscales assessing the nine specific symptom types named in the summary of hypotheses above. The general severity measures are the Global Severity Index (GSI; a summation of distress intensity ratings across all 90 symptoms) and the Positive Symptom Total (PST; the number of reported symptoms out of 90 possible).

Pearson correlations were calculated between the ASGS Shame scale and the SCL-90-R symptom variables, and likewise between the PFQ2 Guilt scale and the SCL-90-R variables. Then, to examine the separate and distinguishably independent associations between shame and guilt and the symptom types, correlations were calculated again, this time partialing shame for guilt and guilt for shame. These results are presented in Table 15.3.

Relationships between the unpartialed Shame and Guilt subscales and the two SCL-90 summary variables were almost identical, and all were significant at the .001 level (Shame: GSI, $r = .44$; PST, $r = .47$; Guilt: GSI, $r = .45$; PST, $r = .47$). Thus, as expected, both kinds of dysphoric affect appear to be moderately to strongly, and about equally, associated with the entire range of symptomatology shown by undergraduate students.

As also indicated by Table 15.3, the ASGS Shame subscale exhibited significant first-order associations with seven of the SCL-90-R subscales assessing specific symptom types, and a trend with one other. The PFQ2 Guilt subscale correlated significantly with each and every specific SCL-90-R subscale.

The partial correlations revealed a more differentiated set of relationships between shame- and guilt-proneness and the symptom measures. ASGS Shame, after partialing, related significantly to the SCL-90-R Depression, Obsessive–Compulsive, Interpersonal Sensitivity, and Phobic Anxiety sub-

TABLE 15.3. First- and Second-Order Correlations (Partialed for Each Other) of ASGS Shame and PFQ2 Guilt Scales with SCL-90-R Symptom Variables (n = 71)

SCL-90-R variable	ASGS Shame	PFQ2 Guilt	Shame (partialed for guilt)	Guilt (partialed for shame)
GSI	.44***	.45***	.26*	.28*
PST	.47***	.47***	.24*	.30**
Depression	.38**	.34**	.24*	.17
Somaticization	.34**	.42***	.14	.30**
Obsessive–Compulsive[a]	.50***	.38**	.38**	.15
Interpersonal Sensitivity	.47***	.48***	.29*	.31**
Anxiety	.31**	.33**	.16	.21†
Hostility–Anger[b]	.02	.24*	−.12	.28*
Psychoticism	.37**	.40**	.20†	.26*
Phobic Anxiety	.35**	.29*	.24*	.12
Paranoid Ideation	.23†	.25*	.11	.16

Note. Adapted from "Assessment of Shame and Guilt and Their Relationship to Psychopathology" by D. W. Harder, L. Cutler, & L. Rockart, 1992, *Journal of Personality Assessment, 59,* 584–604. Copyright 1992 by Lawrence Erlbaum Associates. Adapted by permission.
[a]Difference between partialed coefficients is $p < .10$ ($t = 1.93$).
[b]Difference between partialed coefficients is $p < .001$ ($t = 3.49$).
†$p < .10$. *$p < .05$. **$p < .01$. ***$p < .001$.

scales, and showed a trend with Psychoticism. Shame also remained significantly associated with both SCL-90-R summary measures, the GSI (r = .26, $p < .05$) and the PST ($r = .24, p < .05$). PFQ2 Guilt, after partialing, was significantly associated with SCL-90-R Somaticization, Interpersonal Sensitivity, Hostility–Anger, and Psychoticism, and showed a trend with Anxiety. Guilt also remained significantly related to the GSI ($r = .28, p < .05$) and the PST ($r = .30, p < .05$). Examination of the number of symptom types with which each affect showed significant second-order relationships suggests that guilt may show slightly more involvement in symptom presence than does shame.

These partial-correlation results provide the clearest evaluation to date of the earlier hypotheses regarding the relative importance of shame and guilt to various symptom clusters. If the observed coefficient magnitudes are accepted at face value, guilt-free shame appears to be more highly related to depression, obsessive–compulsiveness, and phobic anxiety, whereas shame-free guilt appears to be more strongly related to somaticization, psychoticism, hostility–anger, overt anxiety, and possibly paranoia. However, it should be stressed that only two differences reported in Table 15.3 achieved or approached statistical significance (for Hostility–Anger, dependent-sample t = 3.49, $p < .001$; for Obsessive–Compulsive, $t = 1.93, p < .06$). Hence, for now any supposition of real differences must be held very tentatively, pending replications. Coefficient magnitudes ("effect sizes") were discrepant by as much as .20 only for the Obsessive–Compulsive and Hostility–Anger subscales, and even these results require confirming replication for full acceptance.

Should the findings presented in Table 15.3 eventually prove to be durable, they offer empirical support for only one of the original differentiating hypotheses—that asserting a greater relationship between shame and depression. An expected equivalent relationship for shame and guilt with phobic problems did not appear, because shame emerged as more important in such exaggerated fears. Also, a hypothesized slightly stronger association between shame and overall psychopathology (the GSI and PST) was unsupported by these data, since a somewhat stronger association emerged between guilt and the global symptom measures.

As noted in our original publication (Harder et al., 1992, pp. 600–601),

> although these partial correlations can indicate the portion of variance of each affect not attributable to the other kind of emotion, they do remove any variance which validly reflects the co-occurrence of the two dysphoric emotional tendencies. As such, the partials may be underestimations of the true associations between shame and guilt and the symptom scales . . . [A]ll nonsignificant partial correlations in this analysis, except for shame with hostility, showed positive magnitudes ("effect sizes") of .11 or greater. With large samples such relationships could prove significant—and non-trivial (Rosnow & Rosenthal, 1989).

Our findings (Harder et al., 1992) thus contradict the negligible involvement of guilt in symptomatology that has been reported by Tangney and her colleagues (Tangney et al., 1992; Tangney et al., Chapter 14, this volume), whose measure of guilt-proneness has been the promising but questionably valid TOSCA. Tangney et al., of course, would doubt the validity of the present findings (based upon the PFQ2), but one might ask in response: What exactly could the shame-partialed PFQ2 Guilt scale be representing in its significant relationships to symptoms, if not guilt? In my view, then, guilt does appear to show associations with the entire range of symptomatology observed among college undergraduates, and its influence upon such symptoms appears to be at least equal to that exerted by shame.

The numerous unsupported hypotheses regarding different relationships for shame and guilt with various symptom clusters suggest that much more research in this area is needed. The current data suggest that many of these hypotheses may require revision or eventual abandonment. Further studies with a wide range of samples, some using the SCL-90 (see Tangney et al., Chapter 14, this volume) and others using independent measures of symptoms, such as the Psychiatric Assessment Inventory (Strauss, Harder, & Chandler, 1979), would ultimately provide the answers.

The current available evidence described above argues that guilt is more important to symptomatology than the present clinical and theoretical emphasis on shame would imply. Perhaps "theoretical and research attention should once again be directed towards some of the earlier guilt hypotheses of the psychodynamicists" (Harder et al., 1992, p. 601).

CONCLUSIONS

1. In recent years, shame has received strong emphasis as a causal factor in the formation and/or maintenance of almost every conceivable type of psychopathology. This trend has eclipsed theoretical attention to guilt.

2. The physiological affect theory of Tomkins (1987) can be contrasted with the more clinically relevant theories of the psychodynamics (e.g., H. B. Lewis, 1971) and the cognitive-appraisal theorists (e.g., Lazarus, 1991).

3. Assessment of shame- and guilt-proneness involves a number of methodological difficulties, including the extensive overlap between the two emotions, the operationalization of phenomenological experiences, ethical problems in laboratory affect inductions, and the extent of correspondence between conscious and unconscious affect.

4. A series of recent construct validation studies suggests that the ASGS Shame scale is the best instrument for the measurement of shame-proneness, but that the PFQ2 Shame scale is also quite useful whenever subjects might have trouble with the extensive vocabulary of the ASGS. A newer instrument, the TOSCA Shame scale, also shows validity for the assessment of shame without the complicated wording of some ASGS items.

5. The same set of validity studies indicates that the PFQ2 Guilt scale is the sole guilt instrument that has shown reasonable concurrent validity across several investigations, although its extensive overlap with shame measures makes the separate assessment of shame and guilt problematic.

6. The TOSCA Guilt scale can be regarded as an equal or superior guilt measure if one's conceptual definition of shame includes *all* instances of negative self-evaluations and the definition of guilt does not permit any (even those generally regarded as guilt-based).

7. Conclusion 5 above suggests that in order to test hypotheses about differential influences of shame and guilt, it will probably be necessary to partial each affect variable for the other emotion. Researchers should remember, however, that such a procedure eliminates potentially valid overlapping variance from each variable.

8. Evidence available so far (from the ASGS and PFQ2) generally does not support a widely held hypothesis that women are more prone to shame than men. Nor does the evidence support the existence of a sex difference for guilt-proneness. The TOSCA, however, suggests that women show more of both emotions.

9. Data (Harder et al., 1992) summarized here on relationships between shame and guilt and a variety of symptom types indicate that both

affect dispositions are about equally important in the presence of overall psychopathology. Shame appears to be more associated than guilt with depression and obsessive–compulsiveness, whereas guilt appears more associated with hostility or anger. Other observed differences were quite small. All of these relationships, other than that of shame with depression, clearly require replication.

10. The current theoretical emphasis upon the role of shame in psychopathology has thus been supported by recent data, but the simultaneous importance of guilt should not be neglected.

NOTES

1. It should be noted that a sex difference in guilt reporting has appeared in one previous study (Harder & Zalma, 1990) with the PFQ2 Guilt scale, but not in two others (Harder et al., 1992, 1993).
2. H. B. Lewis (1971), one of the theorists cited by Tangney et al. in support of their shame–guilt distinction in Chapter 14, does not exclude guilt from the self-evaluation functions of the self (p. 29): "equally negative self-evaluations may be experienced by the self in the different modes: shame or guilt."

REFERENCES

Barrett, K. C., & Zahn-Waxler, C. (1987, April). *Do toddlers express guilt?* Poster presented at the meeting of the Society for Research in Child Development, Toronto.

Basch, F. (1988). *Understanding psychotherapy: The science behind the art.* New York: Basic Books.

Beck, A. T. (1967). *Depression: Causes and treatment.* Philadelphia: University of Pennsylvania Press.

Bilmes, M. (1967). Shame and delinquency. *Contemporary Psychoanalysis, 3,* 113–133.

Binder, J. (1970). *The relative proneness to shame or guilt as a dimension of character style.* Unpublished doctoral dissertation, University of Michigan.

Bradshaw, J. (1988). *Healing the shame that binds you.* Deerfield Beach, FL: Health Communications.

Broucek, F. J. (1991). *Shame and the self.* New York: Guilford Press.

Brown, J. A. (1987). Shame, intimacy, and sexuality. *Journal of Chemical Dependency Treatment, 1,* 61–74.

Buss, A. H. (1980). *Self-consciousness and social anxiety.* San Francisco: W. H. Freeman.

Carver, C., & Glass, D. C. (1976). The Self-Consciousness Scale: A discriminant validity study. *Journal of Personality Assessment, 40,* 169–172.

Cassorla, A. A. (1986). A preliminary investigation of the experience of shame in psychiatrically hospitalized, conduct disordered adolescents. *Dissertation Abstracts International, 47,* 1715B. (University Microfilms No. DA 8614664)

Colby, K. M. (1976). Clinical implications of a simulation model of paranoid processes. *Archives of General Psychiatry, 33,* 854–857.

Cook, D. R. (1987). Measuring shame: The Internalized Shame Scale. *Alcoholism Treatment Quarterly, 4,* 197–215.

Cook, D. R. (1993). *The Internalized Shame Scale manual.* Menomonie, WI: Channel Press. (Available from the author at Rt. 7, Box 270A, Menomonie, WI 54751)

Crowne, D., & Marlowe, D. (1960). A new scale of social desirability independent of psychopathology. *Journal of Consulting and Clinical Psychology, 24,* 349–354.

Crowne, D., & Marlowe, D. (1964). *The approval motive.* New York: Wiley.

Derogatis, L. R. (1983). *SCL-90-R manual.* St. Petersburg, FL: Clinical Psychometrics.

Derogatis, L. R., Lipman, R. S., & Covi, L. (1973). SCL-90: An outpatient psychiatric rating scale—a preliminary report. *Psychopharmacology Bulletin, 9,* 13–28.

Ekman, P., Levenson, R., & Friesen, W. (1983). Autonomic nervous system activity distinguishes between emotions. *Science, 221,* 1208–1210.

Erikson, E. H. (1959). Identity and the life cycle. *Psychological Issues Monographs, 1*(Whole No. 1).

Evans, S. (1987). Shame, boundaries and dissociation in chemically dependent, abusive and incestuous families. *Alcoholism Treatment Quarterly, 4,* 25–38.

Fenigstein, A., Scheier, M. F., & Buss, A. H. (1975). Public and private self-consciousness: Assessment and theory. *Journal of Consulting and Clinical Psychology, 43,* 522–527.

Ferguson, T. J., Stegge, H., & Damhuis, I. (1991). Children's understanding of guilt and shame. *Child Development, 62,* 827–839.

Fischer, S. F. (1985). Identity of two: The phenomenology of shame in borderline development and treatment. *Psychotherapy, 22,* 101–109.

Floyd, D. S., & Floyd, W. A. (1985). Bulimia: The secretive cycle of shame/superiority. *Journal of Human Behavior and Learning, 2,* 6–12.

Fossum, M., & Mason, M. (1986). *Facing shame: Families in recovery.* New York: Norton.

Freud, S. (1953). Three essays on the theory of sexuality. In J. Strachey (Ed. and Trans.), *The standard edition of the complete psychological works of Sigmund Freud* (Vol. 7, pp. 125–243). London: Hogarth Press. (Original work published 1905)

Freud, S. (1955). Notes upon a case of obsessional neurosis. In J. Strachey (Ed. and Trans.), *The standard edition of the complete psychological works of Sigmund Freud* (Vol. 10, pp. 151–318). London: Hogarth Press. (Original work published 1909)

Fridlund, A. J., Ekman, P., & Oster, H. (1986). Facial expressions of emotion: Review of literature, 1970–1983. In A. Seligman & S. Feldstein (Eds.), *Nonverbal behavior and communication* (pp. 143–223). Hillsdale, NJ: Erlbaum.

Gomberg, E. L. (1987). Shame and guilt issues among women alcoholics. *Alcoholism Treatment Quarterly, 4,* 139–155.

Gottschalk, L., & Gleser, G. (1969). *The measurement of psychological states through the content analysis of verbal behavior.* Berkeley: University of California Press.

Harder, D. W. (1975). *The defensively high self-esteem male.* Unpublished doctoral dissertation, University of Michigan.

Harder, D. W. (1984). Character style of the defensively high self-esteem man. *Journal of Clinical Psychology, 40,* 26–35.

Harder, D. W. (1990a). Additional construct validity evidence for the Harder Personal Feelings Questionnaire measure of shame and guilt proneness. *Psychological Reports, 67,* 288–290.

Harder, D. W. (1990b). Comment on Wright et al., "Shame, guilt, narcissism, and depression: Correlates and sex differences." *Psychoanalytic Psychology, 7,* 285–289.

Harder, D. W., Cutler, L., & Rockart, L. (1992). Assessment of shame and guilt and their relationships to psychopathology. *Journal of Personality Assessment, 59,* 584–604.

Harder, D. W., & Lewis, S. J. (1987). The assessment of shame and guilt. In C. D. Spielberger & J. N. Butcher (Eds.), *Advances in personality assessment* (Vol. 6, pp. 89–114). Hillsdale, NJ: Erlbaum.

Harder, D. W., Rockart, L., & Cutler, L. (1993). Additional validity evidence for the Harder Personal Feelings Questionnaire-2 (PFQ2): A measure of shame and guilt proneness. *Journal of Clinical Psychology, 59,* 584–604.

Harder, D. W., & Zalma, A. (1990). Two promising shame and guilt scales: A construct validity comparison. *Journal of Personality Assessment, 55,* 729–745.

Harper, J. M., & Hoopes, M. H. (1990). *Uncovering shame.* New York: Norton.

Hoblitzelle, W. (1982). *Developing a measure of shame and guilt and the role of shame in depression.* Unpublished predissertation, Yale University.

Hoblitzelle, W. (1987). Differentiating and measuring shame and guilt: The relation between shame and depression. In H. B. Lewis (Ed.), *The role of shame in symptom formation* (pp. 207–235). Hillsdale, NJ: Erlbaum.

Izard, C. E. (1972). *Patterns of emotions: A new analysis of anxiety and depression.* New York: Academic Press.

Izard, C. E. (1977). *Human emotions.* New York: Plenum Press.

Izard, C. E. (1979). *The Maximally Discriminative Facial Movement Coding System (MAX).* Newark: Instructional Resources Center, University of Delaware.

Kaplan, H. B. (1975). Increase in self-rejection as an antecedent of deviant responses. *Journal of Youth and Adolescence, 4,* 281–292.

Kaplan, H. B., & Pokorny, A. (1969). Self-derogation and psychosocial adjustment. *Journal of Nervous and Mental Disease, 149,* 421–434.

Katz, D. S. (1988). An analysis of defense mechanisms, moral reasoning, and shame–guilt proneness in pedophiles, rapists, and nonoffenders. *Dissertation Abstracts International, 49,* 544B–545B. (University Microfilms No. DA 88 01218)

Kaufman, G. (1989). *The psychology of shame.* New York: Springer.

Kernberg, O. F. (1970). Factors in the psychoanalytic treatment of narcissistic personalities. *Journal of the American Psychoanalytic Association, 18,* 51–85.

Klass, E. T. (1983). *Guide to the use of a situational self-report measure of guilt.* Unpublished manuscript, Hunter College, City University of New York.

Kohut, H. (1971). *The analysis of the self.* New York: International Universities Press.

Lansky, M. R. (1987a). Shame and domestic violence. In D. L. Nathanson (Ed.), *The many faces of shame* (pp. 335–362). New York: Guilford Press.

Lansky, M. R. (1987b). Shame in the family relationships of borderline patients. In J. S. Grotstein, M. F. Solomon, & J. A. Lang (Eds.), *The borderline patient* (pp. 187–199). Hillsdale, NJ: Analytic Press.

Lazarus, R. S. (1991). *Emotion and adaptation.* New York: Oxford University Press.

Levin, S. (1967). Some metapsychological considerations on the differentiation between shame and guilt. *International Journal of Psycho-Analysis, 48,* 267–276.

Levin, S. (1971). The psychoanalysis of shame. *International Journal of Psycho-Analysis, 52,* 355–362.

Lewis, H. B. (1971). *Shame and guilt in neurosis.* New York: International Universities Press.

Lewis, H. B. (1976). *Psychic war in men and women.* New York: New York University Press.

Lewis, M. (1992). *Shame: The exposed self.* New York: Free Press.

Lynd, H. M. (1958). *On shame and the search for identity.* New York: Harcourt, Brace & World.

Mayman, M. (1974, August). *The shame experience, the shame dynamic, and shame personalities in psychotherapy.* Paper presented at the annual meeting of the American Psychological Association, New Orleans. (Available from the author at 1027 E. Huron St., Ann Arbor, MI 48109)

Miller, S. B. (1988). Humiliation and shame: Comparing two affect states as indicators of narcissistic stress. *Bulletin of the Menninger Clinic, 52,* 40–51.

Morrison, A. (1989). *Shame: The underside of narcissism.* Hillsdale, NJ: Analytic Press.

Mosher, D. L. (1966). The development and multitrait–multimethod matrix analysis of three measures of guilt. *Journal of Consulting and Clinical Psychology, 30,* 25–29.

Mosher, D. L. (1968). Measurement of guilt in females by self-report inventories. *Journal of Consulting and Clinical Psychology, 32,* 690–695.

Mosher, D. L., & White, B. B. (1981). On differentiating shame and shyness. *Motivation and Emotion, 5,* 61–74.

Nathanson, D. L. (Ed.). (1987a). *The many faces of shame.* New York: Guilford Press.

Nathanson, D. (1987b). A timetable for shame. In D. L. Nathanson (Ed.), *The many faces of shame* (pp. 1–64). New York: Guilford Press.

Piers, G., & Singer, M. B. (1953). *Shame and guilt: A psychoanalytic and cultural study.* New York: Norton.

Polivy, J. (1981). On the induction of emotions in the laboratory: Discrete moods or multiple affect states? *Journal of Personality and Social Psychology, 41,* 803–817.

Potter-Efron, P. S. (1987). Creative approaches to shame and guilt: Helping the adult child of an alcoholic. *Alcoholism Treatment Quarterly, 4,* 39–56.

Raskin, R. N., & Hall, C. S. (1979). A narcissistic personality inventory. *Psychological Reports, 45,* 590.

Raskin, R. N., & Hall, C. S. (1981). The Narcissistic Personality Inventory: Alternate form reliability and further evidence of construct validity. *Journal of Personality Assessment, 45,* 159–162.

Rosnow, R. L., & Rosenthal, R. (1989). Statistical procedures and the justification of knowledge in psychological science. *American Psychologist, 44,* 1276–1284.

Rotter, J. B. (1966). Generalized expectancies for internal versus external control of reinforcement. *Psychological Monographs, 80*(1, Whole No. 609).

Schachter, S., & Singer, J. (1962). Cognitive, social and physiological determinants of emotional state. *Psychological Review, 69,* 379–399.

Shapiro, D. (1965). *Neurotic styles.* New York: Basic Books.

Shaver, P., Schwartz, J., Kirson, D., & O'Connor, C. (1987). Emotion knowledge: Further exploration of a prototype approach. *Journal of Personality and Social Psychology, 52,* 1061–1086.

Shreve, B. W., & Kunkel, M. A. (1989, August). *The role of shame in adolescent suicide: A self-psychological perspective.* Paper presented at the meeting of the American Psychological Association, New Orleans.

Smith, R. L. (1972). The relative proneness to shame or guilt as an indicator of defensive style. *Dissertation Abstracts International, 33B*, 2823B–2824B. (University Microfilms No. 72-32582)

Stoller, R. (1987). Pornography: Daydreams to cure humiliation. In D. L. Nathanson (Ed.), *The many faces of shame* (pp. 292–307). New York: Guilford Press.

Strauss, J. S., Harder, D. W., & Chandler, M. (1979). Egocentrism in children of parents with a history of psychotic disorders. *Archives of General Psychiatry, 35*, 191–196.

Tangney, J. P. (1990). Assessing individual differences in proneness to shame and guilt: Development of the Self-Conscious Affect and Attribution Inventory. *Journal of Personality and Social Psychology, 59*, 102–111.

Tangney, J. P. (1992). Situational determinants of shame and guilt in young adulthood. *Personality and Social Psychology Bulletin, 18*, 199–206.

Tangney, J. P. (1993). Shame and guilt. In C. G. Costello (Ed.), *Symptoms of depression* (pp. 161–180). New York: Wiley.

Tangney, J. P., Wagner, P., & Gramzow, R. (1992). Proneness to shame, proneness to guilt, and psychopathology. *Journal of Abnormal Psychology, 103*, 469–478.

Tomkins, S. S. (1987). Shame. In D. L. Nathanson (Ed.), *The many faces of shame* (pp. 133–161). New York: Guilford Press.

Wicker, F. W., Payne, G. C., & Morgan, R. D. (1983). Participant descriptions of shame and guilt. *Motivation and Emotion, 7*, 25–39.

Wright, F. (1987). Men, shame, and antisocial behavior: A psychodynamic perspective. *Group, 11*, 238–246.

Wright, F., O'Leary, J. O., & Balkin, J. (1989). Shame, guilt, narcissism, and depression: Correlates and sex differences. *Psychoanalytic Psychology, 7*, 285–289.

Zimbardo, P. (1977). *Shyness*. Reading, MA: Addison-Wesley.

16

Conflict in Family Systems: The Role of Shame

THOMAS J. SCHEFF

This chapter concerns the problem of *interminable* conflict in families. What are the origins of quarrels that are unending? Even a casual glance at current newspapers assures us that such conflicts constitute a vast human problem. Scientific and scholarly reports suggest the same conclusion. There is a specific type of escalating conflict that has proved extremely difficult to understand, not only for the participants, but for researchers as well. In this type of conflict, the initial sources of conflict may be trivial; in any case, once in conflict, the disputants may forget its origins. More important, conflict often continues even when it is clear that even the winner faces ruin if fighting does not stop. What are such fights about?

This chapter builds upon previous discussions (Scheff, 1990; Scheff & Retzinger, 1991; Retzinger, 1991) of the emotional origins of interminable conflict. I suggest that the answer may be found in emotions that are so disguised from self and others as to be almost invisible. The hypothesis proposed here derives from the work of Helen B. Lewis (1971) on unacknowledged shame. In my formulation, interminable conflicts are caused by hidden shame.

This chapter also proposes a novel methodology. In the present-day human sciences, there is a vast gap between qualitative and quantitative approaches. Here I explore a method that might help fill this void. (More comprehensive descriptions of this method can be found in Scheff, 1990, Retzinger, 1991; and Scheff, 1994.) I apply the new approach to a specific problem—sequences of shame and anger in family interaction. If shame is evoked but goes unacknowledged, the result may be a repetitive cycle of insult and revenge. Unacknowledged shame in party A can lead to A's rage or further shame, which can lead to A's hostility toward or withdrawal from party B. If A's hostility or withdrawal leads to unacknowledged shame in

393

B, then *B* may repeat the same cycle as *A*. When this is the case, the two parties become trapped in an interminable quarrel (hostility–hostility) or impasse (withdrawal–withdrawal).

In the new theory, shame is treated as both an individual and a social phenomenon. It is both a genetically determined emotion within individuals, and equally a signal of the state of a social relationship, revealing the degree of alienation (separation or engulfment) of the participants. Shame cues signal crisis in social interaction; too great or too little exposure of one's position can disrupt the relationship. (Too much exposure may feel like suffocation or violation; too little may feel like invisibility or rejection.) By treating shame as part of a transpersonal system, this chapter bridges two hitherto disparate literatures—the individual and social psychologies of shame. I articulate the components of a complex system: the degree of attunement in social relationships (the mix between solidarity and alienation); sequences of emotions; and, finally, the participants' degree of awareness of their level of alienation and of their emotions.

PREVIOUS STUDIES OF INTERMINABLE CONFLICTS

The principal literature on interminable conflicts is found in the anthropology of duels, feuds, and vendettas (for a review, see Scheff, 1994). These reports show that unending conflicts between individuals and groups is a universal feature of the human condition, to be found in virtually all historical eras and cultural contexts. This literature is particularly useful in teaching us that such conflicts can transcend individuals: they are often handed down from one generation to another.

Descriptions of never-ending conflicts can also be found in reports on family systems, although this literature is less clearly defined. The linguistic analysis of family discourse by Labov and Fanshel (1977) is a well-known example in this genre. In this study, the researchers conducted an extremely detailed analysis of both verbal and nonverbal behavior, second by second, in the discourse of a family of an anorexic woman. They were surprised to find that virtually every word and gesture used by family members was conflictual, and that the family members themselves were almost completely unaware of their own contributions to the conflict. Many clinical accounts make the same point less explicitly: Unending conflict between family members is quite common, even though in many of the cases the participants themselves seem unaware or only partially aware of their own hostility and aggression, and that of the other members.

Although the studies of group and family conflict are helpful in framing the problem of interminable quarrels, most of them provide little or no explanation of its sources, being descriptive rather than explanatory. The anthropological studies in particular limit themselves to describing the patterns of behavior, with no attempt at causal explanations. Most of the studies of family conflict are also descriptive; however, there is a tradition of studies of family communications and family systems that powerfully advances our understanding. Summarizing this tradition, Watzlawick, Beavin, and Jackson (1967) carefully define interminable conflict and review earlier studies of family conflict. These studies focus upon defective communication practices that lead to conflict. In this same tradition is the work of Bowen (1978), who calls attention to specific types of conflict-producing communication patterns.

The family systems approach has been extremely important in increasing our understanding of quarrels and impasses. The present chapter is based in part on these earlier studies. It is probably true that interminable conflict is caused by dysfunctional communication patterns, but what causes these patterns? As in most theories of human behavior, even those studies that attempt explanations content themselves with emphasizing a single link in what may be a long causal chain.

Other examples of partial approaches can be found in the literature of experimental social psychology and in marital communication studies (for a review of these studies, see Retzinger, 1991). For brevity, I comment here on only one study, since it is representative of the approach. Brockner and Rubin (1985) review a series of laboratory experiments concerning entrapment in and escalation of conflict. These experiments all involve a single causal variable (e.g., individual differences in "self-justifying commitments to past actions"). Although most of the results are statistically significant, the amount of variation explained is always extremely small, suggesting that many other variables not included in the study are much more important causes than those included.

Another limitation of the experimental literature is that it virtually excludes contextual cues of the kind that are necessary for detecting unacknowledged shame. Laboratory experiments seek to *verify* rather than *generate* theory. For this reason, they use settings and instruments that provide little biographical or interactional information. But emotion cues are embedded in this kind of information. Context plays a significant role in the kinds of interpretations that are central to my analysis of conflict systems in families.

It is significant that the adherents of the various approaches to conflict seldom cite approaches other than their own, or even seem to be aware of their existence. Experimental social psychologists, for example, do not cite family systems literature, and vice versa. It is my belief that in order to make progress, we must utilize the insights available in the various approaches, integrating them into a complete theory of conflict. In this chapter I draw upon several approaches, particularly family systems theory, sociolinguistics, and sociology of emotions, in an attempt to *generate* rather than *verify* a theory of interminable conflict (for a justification of this approach, see Gleser & Strauss, 1967).

A useful theory should do more than explain the relation between two aspects of conflict; it should clearly spell out the whole system that results in conflict. That is, it should provide both conceptual and operational definitions of the concepts that are needed to explain the conflict, and the causal links between these components. At least in the early stages of theory development, the complexity of such a system makes attempts at verification premature. The theory first needs to be stated clearly enough that it can ultimately be tested.

This approach focuses on an issue seldom broached in the human sciences literature: the huge gap between qualitative and quantitative methods. Qualitative methods are used to describe human behavior and to generate theory, but these types of studies have many limitations from a scientific point of view. Typically, there is little attention to falsifiability—the concept that lies at the heart of all science. Qualitative workers claim that their work is "more valid" than that of quantitative workers, but they provide little or no documentation to back up this claim. Furthermore, studies of this kind pay no attention whatever to reliability, the repeatability of methods and techniques. Both shortcomings limit the credibility and, more importantly, the usefulness of qualitative findings.

Most quantitative studies have strengths and limitations that are just the opposite of those of qualitative studies. Quantitative methods stress reliability, but give little attention to validity. As already indicated, most of these studies also avoid testing general, comprehensive theories, and delete from their data the kinds of evidence that would allow the assessment of context.

One way of bridging the gap between the two standard approaches is to blend the strongest elements of each, with a comprehensive metatheory. Here I combine the elements of flexibility and intuition that underlie effective qualitative methods with the explicitness and direct orientation to empirical data that underlie effective quantitative methods. Because of lack of space, this chapter must gloss over many details of the new approach. The interested reader is referred to earlier studies by myself and by Retzinger for the details. Particularly crucial for my analysis here is the explicit coding system for shame and anger described by Retzinger (1991; see Table 16.1).

TABLE 16.1. Cues for Shame and Anger

Verbal Markers

Shame:

   Alienated: rejected, dumped, deserted, rebuffed, abandoned, estranged, deserted, isolated, separate, alone, disconnected, disassociated, detached, withdrawn, inhibited, distant, remote, split, divorced, polarized.

   Confused: stunned, dazed, blank, empty, hollow, spaced out, giddy, lost, vapid, hesitant, aloof.

   Ridiculous: foolish, silly, funny, absurd, idiotic, asinine, simple-minded, stupid, curious, weird, bizarre, odd, peculiar, strange, different.

   Inadequate: helpless, powerless, defenseless, weak, insecure, uncertain, shy, deficient, worse off, small, failure, ineffectual, inferior, unworthy, worthless, flawed, trivial, meaningless, insufficient, unsure, dependent, exposed, inadequate, incapable, vulnerable, unable, inept, unfit, impotent, oppressed.

Uncomfortable: restless, fidgety, jittery, tense, anxious, nervous, uneasy, antsy, jumpy, hyperactive.

Hurt: Offended, upset, wounded, injured, tortured, ruined, sensitive, sore spot, buttons pushed, dejected, intimidated, defeated.

Anger: cranky, cross, hot-tempered, ireful, quick-tempered, short fuse, enraged, fuming, agitated, furious, irritable, incensed, indignant, irate, annoyed, mad, pissed, pissed off, teed off, upset, furious, aggravated, bothered, resentful, bitter, spiteful, grudge (the last four words imply shame–rage compounds).

Other verbal markers:

Shame: mitigation (to make appear less severe or painful); oblique, suppressed reference (e.g., "they," "it," "you"); vagueness; denial, defensiveness; verbal withdrawal (lack of response); indifference (acting "cool" in an emotionally arousing context).

Anger: interruption; challenge; sarcasm; blame.

Shame–rage: Temporal expansion/condensation or generalization ("you always . . . ," "you never . . ."); triangulation (bringing up an irrelevant third party or object).

Paralinguistic Markers

Shame (vocal withdrawal/hiding behaviors, disorganization of thought): oversoft; rhythm irregular; hesitation; self-interruption (censorship); filled pauses (-uh-); long pauses ( ); silences; stammer; fragmented speech; rapid speech; condensed words; mumble; breathiness; incoherence (lax articulation); laughed words; monotone.

Anger: staccato (distinct breaks between successive tones); loud; heavy stress on certain words; sing-song pattern (ridicule); straining; harsh voice qualifiers.

Shame–rage: whine; glottalization (rasp or buzz); choking; tempo up/down; pitch up/down.

Visual Markers

Shame: (1) Hiding behavior: (a) the hand covering all or parts of the face; (b) gaze aversion, eyes lowered or averted. (2) Blushing. (3) Control: (a) turning in, biting, or licking the lips, biting the tongue; (b) forehead wrinkled vertically or transversely; (c) false smiling (Ekman & Friesen, 1982); or other masking behaviors.

Anger: (1) Brows lowered and drawn together, vertical lines appear between them. (2) The eyelids are narrowed and tense in a hard fixed stare and may have a bulging appearance. (3) Lips pressed together, the corners straight or down, or open but tense and square. (4) Hard direct glaring. (5) Lean forward toward other in challenging stance. (6) Clenched fists, wave fists, hitting motions.

Like all human expressions (including words), the meaning of these markers is context-related; that is, their relevance depends on the relationship between self and other. Look for constellation of markers in context; the more markers from each category, the stronger the evidence.

Note. From *Violent Emotions: Shame and Rage in Marital Quarrels* by S. Retzinger, 1991, Newbury Park, CA: Sage. Copyright 1991 by Sage Publications, Inc. Reprinted by permission.

An approach to the methods I use here was earlier suggested by Campbell and Fiske (1959): the idea that concepts and theories might be validated by a multitrait, multimethod orientation. However, in my judgment, they did not carry their suggestion far enough. In particular, they did not include elements of qualitative technique; all of the methods they suggest are quantitative. The great advantage of the qualitative approach is that it allows the researcher to get quite close to the original events from which data is generated. By looking closely enough at discourse, the researcher is able to detect contexual clues to meaning, as already indicated, and also to observe unambiguous temporal relationships. This latter advantage is a powerful tool for generating causal theories. Combining the advantages of qualitative and quantitative approaches, I use concepts that are at least partly explicated, and show causal sequences of behavior in discourse.

In this chapter I develop a theory of conflict systems by closely examining discourse in families. My method follows that used by Labov and Fanshel (1977), but is more detailed and has a broader scope than theirs. In particular, I do not limit my analysis to cognition and behavior, as they did, but give equal attention to emotions and emotion cues. I outline the interrelations among thoughts, emotions, and behaviors as these components occur in social interaction.

METHOD

In my university classes, I investigated family systems by having students role-play brief exchanges with their parents. In this way I taught students to examine their own contributions to the family status quo, as well as those of the other members. Initially most students were unaware of their own part in family problems. Although other kinds of exchanges were also touched upon, the most useful place to start seems to be conflictual exchanges—brief excerpts from quarrels of the kind that are discussed below.

At first sight it might seem misleading to try to understand a whole relationship, much less a whole family, on the basis of excerpts from conversations. I propose, however, that because of the complexity of human communication, every exchange is a microcosm, representing many of the elements of the larger relationship of which it is a part. Each exchange is like the smallest functioning unit of the relationship, standing to the whole as a cell does to the living organism of which it is a part. One cannot understand everything about the host organism from the cell; on the other hand, knowledge of the cell is of considerable help in understanding the larger system of which it is a part.

I propose that human communication is so complex and ambiguous that in order to understand it, participants must constantly be shuttling back and forth between the smallest moving parts (the words and gestures) and the largest wholes—not only the whole conversation of which the exchange is a part, but the whole relationship, family, society, and civilization out of which each utterance has grown. If the excerpt is the smallest cell, the civilization is the host organism. Human communication is an open system, incredibly charged with both meaning and ambiguity. Correctly deciphering human expressions requires skill, agility, and perseverance in the participants. In particular, a skill at improvisation seems necessary in order to understand dialogue.

Researchers must be no less diligent and inventive than participants if they are to understand human behavior. In this chapter, I employ the same kind of part–whole analysis of utterances that participants seem to use (Scheff, 1990). I apply this kind of analysis to a set of verbatim texts. My interpretation of some of the dialogue also uses my own eyewitness observation, as in the case of the three students' role plays of dialogues in this chapter, and conversations with students in my office. Direct observation allows one access not only to the words but to the paralanguage, the manner of talk, as well as its verbal content. Like the thicket of gestures in which dialogue is enclosed, these facts provide a backdrop for a part–whole analysis (Scheff, 1990), in order to ground verbal texts in their larger matrix of meaning. Specifically, I rate recurring communication patterns, which are directly observable, and hidden emotions, which can only be inferred from verbal and nonverbal cues.

My approach to the analysis of meaning in discourse has two advantages over being an actual participant. First, I can make explicit my assumptions and observations, describing in great detail how I have come to make my interpretation, and the facts upon which it is based. Actual participants are usually too immersed in their activity to have the luxury of such explicitness. The second advantage is closely related to the first. Unlike the participant, the researcher is able to replay an event as many times as necessary before making a decision. These two advantages suggest a resolution to the problem of meaning in human relationships—the problem that Geertz (1973) has described as "thick description" (Scheff, 1986).

One way to make one's assumptions explicit is to use a formal theory. My theory concerns communication patterns, the emotion of shame, and the relationship between the two. Personal relationships are based on communication, on dialogue. My basic hypothesis is that interminable conflict is generated by dysfunctional communication patterns and by unacknowledged shame. I first discuss communication patterns.

Effective cooperative relationships involve more than a little "leveling," to use one of Satir's (1972) terms. That is, it is possible to voice one's immediate thoughts, feelings, and needs to others without injuring or insulting them, so long as one's *manner* is respectful. Leveling is an important idea, since we often assume that in our relationships to particular persons, some topics are automatically dangerous, others completely safe. As it turns out, this is not the case; we can get into trouble with safe topics and escape trouble with dangerous ones, depending not only on *what* we say, but *how* we say it. In close relationships, nonverbal elements like tempo, loudness, facial expression, and other bodily gestures are often as important as words.

Offense, insult, and humiliation (i.e., shame) usually arise out of manner; if one is respectful, any topic can be discussed, any criticism can be made. In interminable conflicts, I propose that the *manner* of the disputants is always disrespectful, which evokes shame. Continued escalation may be caused not by conflicts of interests, but by disrespectful words and manner, and by shame that is not acknowledged. In the absence of shame, or if shame is acknowledged, disputing parties can always find a compromise that provides maximum reward or at least minimum punishment to the parties. In other words, it is hidden shame leading to insult and retaliation that interferes with rational compromise.

Communication tactics involve not only manner, but also a wide variety of styles that are seldom noticed. Most of these styles are ways of avoiding leveling; at best they do not result in the growth of a relationship, and at worst they may actually damage it. Satir (1972) has called attention to several of these styles; "blaming," "placating," "distracting," and "computing" are some of her categories. Another maneuver for avoiding leveling has been called "triangling" (Bowen, 1978). Instead of revealing their own immediate thoughts, feelings, and needs, one or both parties can resort to talking about a third party who is not present. This device not only excludes the absent party, but also interferes with the relationship between the speakers, since it substitutes for revealing the self and learning about the other.

Given these concepts, it is possible to discern a type of alienation that usually goes unnoticed—what Bowen (1978) has called "engulfment." The style of alienation that Bowen calls "isolation" is obvious enough; one or both parties place the self over and above the relationship, resulting in distance and separation. Computing, blaming, and open conflict usually occur in this mode. Engulfment is the opposite mode of alienation, in which one or both parties place the relationship over and above self. One or both give up significant parts of the self in order to be loyal. Placating and distracting usually occur in this mode. Since the participants in engulfed relationships usually think of themselves as close and supportive, considerable self-deception is also involved. Engulfment is a pervasive mode in normal families, since it involves the appearance of solidarity and closeness.

FAMILY DISCOURSE

Becky's Family: A Father–Daughter Alliance

The dialogues reported here are taken from a larger study of family systems. A total of 41 protocols were available to me, as well as 14 role plays in either classroom or my office. I report here on several typical protocols. The student in the first set of excerpts, Becky, saw her mother as her enemy in two different ways—one direct, one indirect. She believed that her mother was hostile and critical toward her, and that she also interfered with her (Becky's) relationship with her father by nagging him about her. Becky illustrated both points with dialogue concerning her car.

1. Father–Daughter Dialogue

FATHER: Your mom's really bugging me to do something about your car, so if you don't deal with it, I'm selling it. And I mean it this time.

BECKY: Okay, Dad. I'll do something. I want my car.

2. Mother–Daughter Dialogue

MOTHER: It's the same thing with your car. You don't want to deal with it. What's it gonna take?

BECKY: Why is my car always brought up? It happened a year ago. I'm sorry. It wasn't on purpose.

I proposed that Becky's understanding of both these dialogues with her parents was faulty, as was her understanding of her relationships with her parents as a whole. The texts of the dialogues suggested that she was idealizing her father and vilifying her mother. Furthermore, they suggested that all three relationships in the triangle were alienated, and that none of the participants was aware of the depth of the alienation.

Becky's comments about her mother suggested a third dialogue between the father and mother:

3. Father–Mother Dialogue*

(Note that the asterisk is the conventional symbol for a counterfactual text—imagined dialogue.)

MOTHER: Why are you so lenient with Becky about the car? She is being completely irresponsible. You have got to come down on her.

FATHER: Yes, dear, you're right. I'll take care of it.

Although I imagined this third dialogue, Becky confirmed that it was similar to an exchange she had overheard (but on a topic other than the car).

Family systems theory points to dysfunctional communication patterns in all three of these dialogues. One of the faulty tactics can be seen in two of the conversations—what Bowen (1978) has called "triangling." In each case, one of the participants brought in an absent person rather than revealing his or her own position. For instance, In the first dialogue, Dad made a threat: If Becky didn't take care of her car, he would sell it. However, he didn't take responsibility for the threat himself; rather, he blamed it on his wife. Thus, instead of revealing something about himself (in this case, his desires about Becky's car), he invoked an absent third party.

The daughter was also implicated in Dad's maneuver, since she didn't complain: *"Never mind what Mom wants, Dad, what do you want?" Since Becky did not complain, she was colluding with Dad in blaming Mom. She allowed Dad to maintain the fiction that he was the good person and that Mom was the bad person. In this respect, he was probably deceiving not only Becky, but also himself. He was ensnared in his own communication tactics.

In Bowen's theory, as noted earlier, this type of alienation is referred to as "engulfment"—a type of false solidarity. Both parties were withholding thoughts and feelings, which gave each a false sense of security. However, both parties were giving up parts of themselves to maintain this pretence. Dad might have been quite angry at Becky, but denied his anger; at least he did not acknowledge it explicitly. The threat and the abruptness of his language suggested anger that was being denied. Just as he was probably unaware of his desire in the case of Becky's car, he was probably also unaware that he was angry at Becky, and (as suggested below) at Mom also.

Becky's evasiveness was more subtle than Dad's. First, in allowing him to blame Mom for the threat he was making, she was giving up the opportunity to come to know Dad better. What did he actually want her to do, and, more indirectly, how did he feel about Mom's nagging? Second, by colluding in blaming Mom, she was setting up obstacles to resolving her own differences with her mother.

The second dialogue, between Becky and Mom, also suggested alienation, but of a different type than that between Becky and Dad. If Becky and her father were engulfed, then she and her mother were isolated, to use Bowen's term. In this case, Mom was openly critical and disrespectful toward Becky, and there were signs of anger on both sides. Mom implied that Becky was not only irresponsible, but grossly unresponsive to her, the mother ("What's it gonna take [*to get you to respond to my request, an earthquake]?"— the language of insult).

Becky responded in kind, with a counterinsult: "Why is my car always brought up? It happened a year ago." Just as Mom implied that Becky was unresponsive, Becky in turn implied that Mom was unreasonable, that she was a nag. Immediately after insulting Mom, however, Becky retreated by apologizing in a half-hearted way, and then, again half-heartedly, attempted to justify herself ("It wasn't on purpose"). If the style of interaction between Becky and Dad was one of false (exaggerated) solidarity, the style between Becky and Mom was one of conflict.

The third exchange, the counterfactual dialogue between Mom and Dad, showed many of the same characteristics as the other two exchanges. As in the first dialogue, the two participants were triangling against a third who was not present: Mom was complaining about Becky; Dad did not object to her practice. Mom was also critical of Dad, but in a somewhat indirect way. Rather than stating her criticism of him directly (*"You are too lenient with Becky"), she asked a question—"Why are you so lenient . . ." —which implied a criticism of Dad. However, she was direct about criticizing Becky, who was not present, in the second sentence. In the third sentence, she issued a command: "You have got to come down on her."

Although Dad had indicated to Becky in the first exchange that it was not he but Mom who was critical of Becky, he did an about-face in his exchange with Mom. That is, he made no effort to defend Becky, siding instead with Mom's criticism of her with a blanket agreement ("Yes, dear, you're right"). Mom and Dad colluded in vilifying Becky.

It can be seen in this dialogue that Mom was angry at Dad, but was not expressing it directly. She was indirectly critical of Dad; she was demanding; and she used a word in describing Becky ("completely") suggesting that she might be not only angry at Becky, but in a state of anger at the time of this dialogue. Words like "completely," "never," "always," and so forth are called "extenders" in the analysis of emotions in discourse. Since they are exaggerations, they suggest hidden anger (Retzinger, 1991). Mom was in an angry, blaming mode.

Since Mom was critical and demanding toward Dad, we might expect that he might be angry in return. However, his words showed no evidence of anger; they were placating. Nonetheless, some of his comments in the first exchange suggested in an indirect way that he might be angry at Mom. He told Becky that Mom was "really bugging me" in regard to Becky's car. This phrase could have a double meaning—that Mom was pressing him, but also that she was making him angry.

The three dialogues could be used to derive a style of communication tactics and emotion management for each of the family members. There was no leveling in any of the dialogues; no one was direct in a respectful way. All three parties were indirect both about their needs and about their feelings. Mom was an angry blamer and critic with Becky, and critical and blaming in an indirect way with Dad. Dad was completely placating with Mom, but threatening and indirectly blaming with Becky. Becky, finally, was placating with Dad, and first blaming, then placating with Mom. The three exchanges illustrated a system of dysfunctional communication in this family; instead of leveling, all three dialogues were in the blaming–blaming or blaming placating mode.

The exchanges shown above supplied only verbal information; no nonverbal information was included. In the role-playing exercises with Becky, however, she provided nonverbal gestures as well—her own, and in her portrayal, those of Dad and Mom. On the basis of both the verbal and nonverbal information, a classification of the styles of emotion management could be made, with emphasis on the management of shame and anger.

Mom was the most overt with anger; she showed anger in her words and gestures directed at Becky, and in a less overt way, toward Dad. Becky was next most overt; she showed some overt anger toward Mom, but quickly took it back. She showed none at all toward Dad. Dad was the least overt; he showed no anger at all toward Mom in her presence, and only covert signs of anger toward her in her absence. In Becky's presence, his words and gestures suggested covert anger.

The indications of shame in this family were much more subtle than those of anger. One indication of shame was how indirect all three members were with each other, when in each other's presence. The indirection of anger was particularly indicative that each person was ashamed of this anger. Another indication was that all three dialogues were entirely oriented toward a topic, the car; no one commented on relationship issues. For example, no one complained directly about the other's manner toward him or her, although respect was clearly an issue in the dialogue between Becky and Mom, and indirectly between Mom and Dad. To understand the shame dynamics in this family, it would help to discuss how the three relationships might affect one another over time.

I suggested that Becky and Dad idealized themselves and each other, and colluded in vilifying Mom. Becky and Mom engaged in overt, angry conflict. Mom showed covert anger toward Dad, but he placated in return. One place to start to understand the interactions between each of the subsystems would be to visualize what would happen if Dad tried to level with Mom. Suppose that in the dialogue with Mom, instead of his blanket endorsement of her criticism of him, her criticism of Becky, and her demand that he take action against her, he had said:

*FATHER: I'd prefer that together you and I talk about this issue directly with Becky, rather than behind her back.

Although Mom might experience this line as an attack, she might also feel relieved that the issue was finally out in the open: How did Dad himself feel on this (and other) issues? Mom might have experienced the placation in his actual response as somewhat false; his four affirmations of her position in two short sentences had a monotony and flatness. She also might have a sense that Becky's defiance of her wishes might mean that Dad was covertly backing Becky and defying Mom. The combination of Dad's bland compliance toward her (Mom) and the sense of a secret alliance between Dad and Becky could generate feelings of confusion, powerlessness, rejection and anger in Mom—a situational paranoia.

The new counterfactual material was used to illustrate the abstract idea of the dynamic interaction among the three relationships. I started arbitrarily with one of the relationships, without implying that it was the cause: To the extent that Becky and Dad idealized themselves and each other, and vilified Mom because she was so critical (angry), to that extent Mom would feel excluded, rejected, and angry (critical) toward both of them. To the extent that Mom was critical and angry toward Dad, to that extent he would placate and withhold his own feelings. To the extent that he placated and withheld toward Mom and Becky, to that extent would the anger between Mom and Becky be increased—a perfect feedback loop around the three-way system.

Janie's Family: A Mother–Daughter Alliance

Another student's family system showed much the same patterns as Becky's, except that in this case the daughter and mother were allied against the father. The topic for Janie's dialogues was the father's TV habits.

1. Father–Daughter Dialogue

FATHER: Sssh! I'm watching the news!

JANIE: That's all you ever do, watch TV. TV is more important to you than your own daughter!

2. Mother–Daughter Dialogue

MOTHER: Oh! I just don't understand your father. I just don't understand why he won't help with the housework.

JANIE: I don't know, Mom. I just don't know.

3. Father–Mother Dialogue*

FATHER: The roast is overcooked again.

MOTHER: Sorry. I didn't watch it because I was so busy cleaning the house.

Although, as in Becky's case, this last dialogue was hypothetical, Janie confirmed that she had heard many such exchanges between her father and mother on various topics.

As indicated, the communication patterns in this family were quite similar to those already discussed in regard to Becky's family. To begin with the father–daughter exchange, Janie walked into the living room where her father was watching TV. Rather than go all the way around him to get his attention, she spoke to him from behind, as she was walking toward him: "Dad, I have a question—." As indicated in the exchange above, he interrupted her by shushing her before she could finish her sentence. This exchange took the form of an overt quarrel, with both father and daughter raising their voices angrily, and with no eye contact during the whole dialogue. The consequences were predictable: Janie left the room hurt and offended. Characteristically, instead of confronting the problem, she withdrew.

The father's response to Janie's request to talk was disrespectful; he commanded her to keep quiet in a loud voice, and he did not turn away from the TV to face her. Without the courtesy necessary to turn down her request without offense, his words and manner were harsh, abrupt, and rejecting.

Although Janie was unaware of it at the time, her approach to her father was also disrespectful. Although she didn't raise her voice in requesting his attention, she also was discourteous. A more respectful beginning would have been to avoid talking to the back of his head. Janie could have walked up to him from the side, seeking eye contact, but waited to speak until he turned toward her. This approach would have been a tacit admission that she was interrupting him. She might even have apologized for the interruption: *"Dad, I know you're busy, but I need to talk to you." If she had begun this way, perhaps the dialogue would have taken a different direction:

*FATHER: Can you wait 10 minutes till the news is over?
JANIE: Yes.

Like Becky, Janie was unaware of her own part in the ongoing quarrel with her father. She became aware only in re-enacting it in class.

Students often had strong emotional reactions when they became aware of some new feature of their family relationships, but not always. Becky's emotional reactions were mild; she shed a few tears when she realized her role in excluding her mother. Janie's reactions were much stronger. At first, when she became aware of her part in excluding her father, she seemed a bit stunned. She also seemed excited to have discovered something new about herself and her family. Her emotional response to new knowledge about her relation with her mother was stronger still, as I now discuss.

The exchange between Janie and her mother, like the one between Becky and her father, was an example of triangling. Instead of thrashing the issue of housekeeping duties out with the father, the mother complained about the father to Janie. Although the mother's statement was in the form of an indirect question, it was not a real question, but a complaint. (Janie indicated that her mother had asked her the same question many times.) Like Becky, Janie also colluded with one parent against the other, since she did not object. Instead of suggesting to her mother that she complain directly to the father, Janie evaded answering by stating that she didn't know.

In the role playing that took place during class, Janie became aware of the part she was playing in the ongoing quarrel with her father, but did not become aware of her role in the impasse with her mother. Awareness in this instance occurred later, in my office, when Janie and I were discussing her dialogue with her mother.

I questioned her about what she was feeling when her mother complained about her father to her. First she said that she felt proud that her mother was confiding in her. In response to my question about any other feelings, at first she said there were none. When I repeated the question, however, she began to cry and became red in the face. When I asked her what she was feeling, she said that she felt anger at her mother for coming between her and her father. She cried deeply and for a considerable length of time. At the end of our talk, however, she was alight with enthusiasm. In response to my question about how she was feeling, she said she was hopeful, because now she saw that there was something that she herself could do to improve her relationships with both her parents.

Lyn's Family: A Father–Daughter Impasse

I present one exchange from the family system of a third student, Lyn, because this system differed somewhat from the two already discussed. Both Becky and Janie were involved in an overt quarrel with one of their parents:

Becky with her mother, Janie with her father. Lyn's relationship with one of her parents (her mother) was one of idealization and pseudosolidarity, much like the relationship between Becky and her father and between Janie and her mother. However, Lyn's relationship with her father involved little or no quarreling. It involved instead a silent impasse: tension, distance, and the slow withdrawal of affection. Lyn's exchange with her father illustrated this kind of conflict:

FATHER: Do you have something in mind that you want to do tonight?

LYN: No, nothing in particular.

The impasse in this situation was carefully disguised. Both participants seemed to be hiding their thoughts and feelings not only from each other, but even from themselves. The father's question came at the end of dinner. When he asked it, Lyn was expecting her father to suggest an activity that the two of them could do together—a game, perhaps, or watching a particular TV program. She was disappointed and somewhat stunned when instead he rose to go, saying, "Well, then, I have some work to do in my room."

Apparently Lyn and her father had played out similar exchanges many, many times before. Both seemed hesitant to make the first step. Each did not want to intrude on the other's privacy. This hesitancy and mutual misunderstanding are reminiscent of Harrington's (1992) study of romantic propositions: Although both participants may want to date, each waits for the other to be the initiator. Apparently this kind of dance is not limited to romantic invitation, but can obtain in any kind of relationship, as in the case of the father–daughter situation in Lyn's exchange.

Lyn was quite surprised when she realized during role play in my office that she was as responsible for the impasse as her father; she had been assigning all the responsibility to him. Lyn had a strong emotional reaction to her realization; she wept intensely. However, when she later role-played the exchange in class, she showed little emotion. She told me afterwards that she felt she needed to swallow her feelings in front of such a large group.

There was one other case, Richard, whose family system was somewhat different from any of the others. The exchanges he presented involved his mother and his stepfather. Unlike the other students, he was combative and seemingly alienated from both parents. His exchange with his stepfather was particularly intense, each forcefully criticizing the other's actions. However, I gathered from the way he role-played the exchanges that his bonds were probably more secure than most of the other students, since the conflict in his family was largely out in the open. Conflict does not necessarily lead to alienation; the crucial issue is the manner that the participants show in quarrels. If one's manner is respectful, than quarrels can have beneficial effects. Open conflict can lead to needed adjustments in relationships, as Simmel (1955) and others have argued (Scheff & Retzinger, 1991; Retzinger, 1991).

Are Gender Issues Significant?

My experience with the students in this class caused me to change my mind about gender issues in the family. Like most of the students, I had assumed that the traditional role of the father—the hard-driving, somewhat distant breadwinner—was one of the fundamental causes of the high levels of alienation in modern families. In these students' families, the father was more often cast in the role of the distant or vilified parent, by a ratio of almost 2:1. However, after seeing the same faulty communication patterns repeated by all three of the participants described above, I concluded that gender is not a central component in the problem. In all of the family systems examined here, all three family members—father, mother, and offspring—seemed equally implicated in causing and maintaining the status quo.

When the father is the odd man out, his exclusion is more noticeable than the mother's; his isolation is more visible than the mother–child engulfment, to use Bowen's (1978) terms. In our society, the male role is correlated with the isolated style of alienation, and the female role with the engulfed style. Judging from these students' family systems, however, these differences are only superficial; the emotional and communication patterns are equally dysfunctional and disruptive, regardless of whether a relationship is isolated or engulfed. Janie's and Lyn's relationships with their mothers were as alienated as their relationships with their fathers, since they maintained them by ignoring key parts of themselves, such as their anger.

Awareness, Emotion, and Change

In the class as a whole, there were variable reactions to the family system exercises. The students could be divided into three roughly equal groups. About a third did not seem to gain any new awareness of their own family systems (even though virtually all students claimed that they understood family systems better in the abstract). Another third obviously gained awareness but had little or no emotional reaction, like Becky. The last third, finally, reacted like Janie and Lyn: They seemed to grow in awareness and had strong emotional reactions.

Judging from their later comments, I would guess that few of the students in the first group will undergo change as a result of the class. In the second group, perhaps half or fewer may change. In the last group, virtually all will probably change. In other words, I believe that new awareness is unlikely to result in personal growth unless it is accompanied by strong emotional responses.

One reason for students' resistance to awareness, emotion, and change was that they were all enmeshed, in varying degrees, with their own family systems. How can such a self-perpetuating system change? As we have described elsewhere (Scheff & Retzinger, 1991), the following are needed: changes in the communication tactics, and acknowledgment and discharge of emotions by one or more of the participants. In Becky's case, for example, if Dad leveled with Mom instead of withholding, or leveled with Becky instead of colluding with her against Mom, the whole system would have to change.

Three key dimensions of the system must be considered: solidarity–alienation, communication tactics, and emotion management. "Solidarity" as the term is used here involves attunement: Each party understands self and other, both cognitively and emotionally. "Alienation," by contrast, involves misunderstanding or lack of understanding. Solidarity promotes trust and effective cooperation; alienation promotes suspicion and conflict. The relationships among various factors that result in (and are created by) solidarity and cooperation versus alienation and conflict are depicted in Figure 16.1.

Solidarity reflects and generates effective communication tactics—some form of respectful leveling. These tactics involve both truthfulness toward others and self-knowledge. Dad was not intentionally deceptive with Mom and Becky; his deceptiveness, and the deceptiveness of the other two family members as well, arose out of self-deception. He was not aware of many of his own desires and emotions. Alienation from self and others reflects and generates dysfunctional communication tactics. Blaming flows from idealization of self and one's allies, and vilification of one's opponents. Blaming

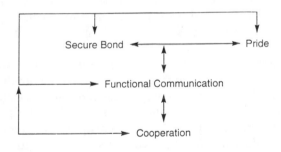

Alienation and Conflict

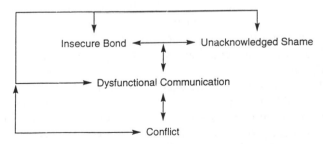

FIGURE 16.1.   The proposed relationships resulting in (and created by) solidarity and cooperation on the one hand, and alienation and conflict on the other.

the other party may generate placating, distraction, or computing, but it can also generate counterblaming, as in the exchange between Becky and Mom. This analysis suggests that because of the interactions between the relationships in a system, a blaming–placating relationship (peace) in one part or phase of a system can generate an interminable blaming–counterblaming relationship (war) in another part of the system.

Triangling would seem to be a crucial tactic leading to interminable conflicts. Two or more parties in the system communicate secretly concerning a third party; these two parties usually become engulfed in a mutual admiration society, which conspires against the third party. This engulfment may be quite ineffective in the long run, however, because the parties become zealots or yes-persons who overconform, idealizing themselves and each other, and undervaluing the opponent. Bowen (1978) defines triangling strictly in terms of two parties communicating about a third party rather than revealing themselves. However, there is another type of faulty communication tactic involving a triangle; in this case, the "third party" is an object or topic rather than another person. In dysfunctional family systems, communication is usually locked into topics (money, sex, education, ideas, etc.) in such a way that relationship issues are avoided. In such systems, parties do not reveal or even reflect on their own positions; instead, they triangle onto other persons or topics. For this reason, there is considerable misunderstanding or ignorance of one's own position and that of the other members, a state of alienation. As my students sometimes remarked, one or both of their parents were strangers, even though they had lived with them their whole lives.

It is of great interest and concern that in the large class from which this case was taken, transfer of knowledge to the students' own family systems from knowledge of other students' systems seemed to take place only very slowly. That is, students watched case after case of role playing that revealed the alienation underlying the appearance of solidarity and/or a topic-related conflict. Students could correctly apply concepts such as engulfment and isolation to others' dialogues, but most seemed to find it difficult to see the same patterns in their own. When students finally role-played their own family systems, they could become aware of the systems' dynamics. It appeared that their awareness was blocked by intense emotions, which they were unable to countenance on their own. In the safety of the class setting (or, more likely, my office), at least some of them seemed able to deal with these emotions; then they could apply what they had learned abstractly in the class to their own cases.

Since I did not role-play dialogue with all 40 of the students in this class, it is possible that there were exceptions—students who correctly understood their own family systems on their own. Even so, it seems to me that for the majority of people, abstract, dispassionate knowledge is not enough. Contact with their own painful emotions is a precondition for increased self-awareness.

SUMMARY

The family systems of my students—the three described in some detail here, as well as the others in the class that I have not included in this chapter—had several patterns in common. In the great majority of cases (all but one), communication among family members seemed to be extraordinarily indirect. The evasiveness and indirectness of communication suggested that shame was a pervasive presence in these families, even though it was usually denied. Family members seemed ashamed of the thoughts and feelings, especially shame and anger, that are inevitable in close relationships.

In the theory proposed here, shame is both a cause and an effect of protracted conflict. It is a signal of the alienation in a family (i.e., the lack of understanding and misunderstanding between the members), but a signal that is uniformly ignored and denied. It is not shame that causes interminable conflict, but its denial. Continuing shame is also a consequence of unending conflict: Family members cycle through disrespectful words and gestures, shame, and anger, which leads to further disrespectful gestures, and so on around the loop.

Whether conflict was openly expressed or bypassed, family members in most of the dialogues did not seem to understand each other, or misunderstand each other (or, in most cases, a mixture of both). Denial of shame is both cause and effect of a continuing cycle of deception and self-deception about thoughts and feelings. Judging from some of the students' comments, the system of relationships in each family was static, having existed for as long as the students could remember, and showed virtually no change or variation over time.

Most students seemed completely unaware of basic features of their family systems. Typically, students idealized one parent and vilified or misunderstood the other. In every case, students seemed unaware of their own contributions to maintaining the system. They saw their family conflicts as exterior and constraining, to use Durkheim's (1915/1965) phrase. That is, by denying their own part in producing unresolved quarrels and impasses, they experienced them as coming from others (exterior) and as controlling and limiting their own behavior (constraining). As already indicated, students were always surprised and often stunned or shocked when they discovered their own role in maintaining their family systems. This effect stood out particularly in the students who showed understanding of others' family systems; even though they had gained abstract understanding of alienation and faulty communication tactics, they had been unable to apply these ideas to their own families.

I summarize these findings in order to suggest that they may also apply not only to families, but also to societies. Durkheim (1915/1965) proposed that social facts—permanent, institutionalized patterns of collective behavior—are experienced by individuals as exterior and contraining, coming from outside themselves. By this definition, the quarrels and impasses described above were social facts. It follows from my discussion that interminable conflicts in families are social facts; they are stable patterns of behavior that are experienced by the participants as exterior and constraining. My analysis suggests that such patterns are not inevitable, as most social scientists believe, but are results of the types of relationships, communication patterns, and emotion management that obtain in our historical era. (For a brilliant analysis of the role of shame in our civilization, see Elias, 1978.) If my theory proves to be true, it may be possible to decrease the level of conflict in our civilization by changing our relationships, communication patterns, and patterns of emotion management.

ACKNOWLEDGMENT

The study reported in this chapter was developed in close collaboration with Suzanne Retzinger. It is particularly dependent on her coding scheme for shame and anger (Retzinger, 1991) for rating emotion cues in videotaped interaction.

REFERENCES

Bowen, M. (1978). *Family therapy in clinical practice*. New York: Jason Aronson.

Brockner, J., & Rubin, J. (1985). *Entrapment in escalating conflicts*. New York: Springer-Verlag.

Campbell, D. T., & Fiske, D. W. (1959). Convergent and discriminant validation by the multitrait, multimethod matrix. *Psychological Bulletin, 56*, 81–105.

Durkheim, E. (1965). *Elementary forms of the religious life*. Glencoe, IL: Free Press. (Original work published 1915)

Ekman, P., & Friesen, W. (1982). Felt, false, and miserable smiles. *Journal of Non-verbal Behavior. 6*: 238–252.

Elias, N. (1978). *The history of manners*. New York: Pantheon.

Geertz, C. (1973). *The interpretation of cultures*. New York: Basic Books.

Gleser, B., & Strauss, A. *The discovery of grounded theory*. Chicago: Aldine.

Harrington, C. L. (1992). Talk about embarrassment: Exploring the taboo–denial–repression hypothesis. *Symbolic Interaction, 15*, 203–225.

Labov, W. & Fanshel, D. (1977). *Therapeutic discourse*. New York: Academic Press.

Lewis, H. B. (1971). Shame and guilt in neurosis. New York: International Universities Press.

Retzinger, S. (1991). *Violent emotions: Shame and rage in marital quarrels*. Newbury Park, CA: Sage.

Satir, V. (1972). *Peoplemaking*. Palo Alto, CA: Science & Behavior Books.

Scheff, T. J. (1986). Toward resolving the controversy over "thick description." *Current Anthropology, 27*, 408–409.

Scheff, T. J. (1990). *Microsociology*. Chicago: University of Chicago Press.

Scheff, T. J. (1994). *Bloody revenge: Emotion, nationalism, and war*. Boulder, CO: Westview Press.

Scheff, T. J., Retzinger, S. (1991). *Emotions and violence*. Lexington, MA: Lexington Books.

Simmel, G. (1955). *Conflict and the web of group affiliations*. Glencoe, IL: Free Press.

Watzlawick, P., Beavin, J., & Jackson, D. (1967). *Pragmatics of human communication*. New York: Norton.

17

Shame, Guilt, and the Oedipal Drama: Developmental Considerations Concerning Morality and the Referencing of Critical Others

ROBERT N. EMDE
DAVID OPPENHEIM

Classic psychoanalytic theory from its beginnings has been concerned with guilt as a central moral emotion (Fenichel, 1950; Rapaport, 1967). Shame has been less central and has only intermittently received psychoanalytic attention (e.g., Abrams, 1990; Gillman, 1990; Kohut, 1977; Lewis, 1991; Piers & Singer, 1953; Yorke, 1990). This chapter focuses on shame in relation to guilt. Both shame and guilt are moral emotions that involve self-consciousness in relation to others. We focus on the individual level of experience, but find that shame and guilt involve interpersonal communications and cultural immersions. More recent psychoanalytic theory, in contrast to earlier theory, has emphasized dyadic perspectives concerning the development of social relationships in terms of object relations (e.g., Bowlby, 1988; Sandler, 1987; Winnicott, 1965) and in terms of psychoanalytic self psychology (Kohut, 1971, 1977). Such thinking has not been integrated, however, with the earlier thinking regarding triadic and more complex configurations of social relationships, as portrayed in Freud's interpretation of the classic Oedipal drama of development. In Freud's theory of moral development, guilt is considered a function of superego development, which in turn is an outcome of Oedipal resolution; shame is not prominent.

The present chapter is a working paper to bring together some of these areas. We propose a contemporary psychoanalytic perspective that makes use of developmental research. We begin with the phenomenology of shame and guilt, with a focus on shame and with suggestions for distinguishing the two moral emotions. We next discuss the Oedipal drama, because of its posited role in the development of shame and guilt, suggesting that Freud's individual-based view must be supplemented with two other views: the interpersonal and the community/cultural. Developmental considerations then lead us to propose a relationship-motivational view of the Oedipus complex, as the child moves from dyadic experiences to larger social referencing configurations and experiences involving both shame and guilt. Finally, we discuss the moral emotions and the referencing of others beyond the family. The need for research involving differences among individuals and differences among contexts is highlighted.

THE EXPERIENCE OF SHAME AND
ITS CONTRAST WITH GUILT

Before we discuss the phenomenology of shame and guilt, it seems appropriate to provide a framework for how we think about emotions. Like most contributors to this volume, we regard emotions as active, ongoing, and adaptive processes. This view is in contrast, however, to that of an earlier generation of emotion theorists (including those in the field of psychoanalysis), who previously regarded emotions as reactive, intermittent, and disruptive states. We regard shame and guilt as exemplars of a class of moral emotions that are more complex and later-developing than are the discrete Darwinian emotions (joy, surprise, anger, fear, sadness, disgust, and interest); as such, the more complex emotions do not have any simple correspondence to patterns of expression in face, voice, or posture. This view, we believe, is also in accordance with many other views expressed in this volume.

Moral emotions as a class are characterized by additional features. They are based on relationships—on a past history of experience with particular individuals in particular contexts—and they presuppose a developed sense of shared meaning with significant others. Moral emotions are also based on some sense of struggle, dilemma, or conflict. They are anticipatory, signaling, and representing in some way the consequences of an intended outcome. Moral emotions often lead to a desire to repair a problem or motivate a prosocial action. As the title of this volume suggests, the class of moral emotions of which shame and guilt are a part can be thought of as "self-conscious emotions." From our point of view, these emotions organize access to consciousness; they organize our attention to the possibility that a violation has occurred or to the possibility of hurting another. As discussed elsewhere (Emde & Clyman, in press), we believe that moral emotions have a function of making procedurally known, nonconscious moral goals conscious. The mobilization of a moral emotion is automatic and leads to an appraisal of self (who may be in control and responsible) in relation to one or more meaningful others (who may appraise one's actions as positive or negative—see Lewis, 1992 and Chapter 7, this volume). Such appraisals may be nonconscious (Lazarus, 1991), but when supplemented by moral emotions, they are likely to become conscious.

Now we turn to the phenomenology of shame and guilt from a psychoanalytic perspective. The feeling of shame, like the feeling of guilt, involves mental pain plus a desire to do something to counteract the pain. But the comparison with guilt is revealing because of its contrasts. Guilt involves either a desire to repair the situation where one feels bad about hurting someone, or a desire to atone or propitiate for a forbidden act. Guilt can also involve a desire to punish the self. With the feeling of guilt, self-criticism is experienced as an inner voice. Shame, like guilt, also involves mental pain and the desire to counteract it. But with shame, there is a contrasting experience: The desire is to "shrink out of sight," to avoid the gaze of the other, and to avoid seeing the gaze of a critical other. Shame involves a feeling of being small and powerless. With the feeling of shame, the internalized criticism is not vocal, but instead works through a visual image of the other.

A recent psychoanalytic discussion of shame summarized the experience of many clinicians and highlighted some of the points above while adding others.[1] Shame, as contrasted with guilt, involves the imaging of one or more observers who are experienced as disapproving or condemnatory. It is a powerful and painful affect, often sudden in onset and experienced as overwhelming. Shame carries with it a strong sense of exposure or fear of exposure of bodily or psychological nakedness, and it carries with it a shrinking feeling and a need to hide, with a wanting to avoid being looked at and looking.

The connection of shame with concerns about physical appearance and bodily functions is another psychoanalytic theme. Earlier psychoanalytic thinking connected shame experiences with training and mishaps centering around the child's urination and defecation, in accordance with Freud's anal stage of psychosexual development (Freud, 1905/1953; Yorke, 1990)—a theme that Erikson later broadened to include a theory about the toddler's development of autonomy that has considerable cultural variation (Erikson, 1950). Being regarded as small or incompetent is among the more common classes of shaming experiences in childhood (Yorke, 1990), and others have noted the connection of shame experiences with physical deformity—experiences that are often prevalent with war injuries and continue throughout life (A. Solnit, personal communication, 1988; L. Kohler, personal communication, 1988).

This brings us to another aspect of shame: It is a complex emotion that may contain within it the experience of helplessness and a loss of self-esteem, both of which occur as a consequence of failure. Guilt, in contrast, is often more specific and connected with having done something forbidden or with a deed of omission. Shame often has to do with awareness of a discrepancy between the ideal self and the perceived self. But shame is only one way of feeling inferior or not facing up to one's ideals (cf. feelings of disgust with oneself, helplessness, humiliation). Thus, there appears to be only a "loose coupling" of shame and loss of self-esteem.

The Early Development of Shame and Its Aspects

The complex qualities of shame experiences, as well as their contrasts with guilt experiences, are illustrated by the developmental courses of these emotions. Shame appears earlier in development than does guilt, and, paradoxically, shame seems to continue developing throughout life more than does guilt. A review of the accumulated developmental observations from the Hampstead Nurseries and Clinic (Kennedy & Yorke, 1982) was surprising and informative. Observers found it difficult to tell when shame began. Usually, shame would be indicated first by parents, caregivers, and older peers who were "shaming" a child (i.e., expressing something like "You should be ashamed"), considerably before the time when one would expect to see evidence of avoidance or shaming expressions on the part of the child. Early developmental sequences often seemed to include observations of shame's being connected with avoiding being seen and evading the look of another. Early shame thus seemed connected with the motivation of avoiding social exposure. A more complex form of shame, narcissistic humiliation, seemed connected with feeling small and helpless in the midst of the other or others. Later in development, it seemed that shame might be linked to secrets in which a child imagined that he or she would be seen or discovered so as to be put down—a fear of mental exposure somehow analogous to bodily exposure. Indeed, shame as a regulator of thinking seems often to be a part of cultural and religious socialization (e.g., "God is watching you and your thoughts").

Mastery, pleasure, and pride expressions are observed in development prior to shame expressions. The wartime Hampstead Nurseries observations indicated that toddlers typically showed little concern about wetting accidents. Instead, as noted above, observers saw parental and caregiver concern and shame in the absence of toddler shame—evidence that was often reflected in the expressions of older children as well.

A striking observation recorded by Kennedy and Yorke (1982) illustrates how a preschool child in the Hampstead Nursery setting seemed to be internalizing the disapproval and shaming of others. The child, Bridget, had difficulty in acquiring bladder control. But she "reached a turning point when she was able to announce, with a great deal of affect, 'no more wee-wee on the floor: Mummy doesn't like it; Nurse doesn't like it; Bridget doesn't like it' " (Kennedy & Yorke, 1982, p. 225).

A number of developmental hypotheses can be elaborated as a result of these considerations. First, it may be that pride or enduring feelings of mastery pleasure have to be experienced in the course of development before the acquisition of a capacity for shame. Second, in spite of the case made by Darwin (1872) and others (Izard, 1977; Tomkins, 1962) for biological preparedness, shame may have its necessary developmental origins in parental socialization experiences. It may be necessary for a parent to experience and express shame in front of a child before the child experiences shame. Shame may therefore need to be taken in through concrete experiences with parents or older peers before the child can be said to have acquired this moral emotion.

The considerations above have led us to propose two aspects to the experience of shame, both of which are vivid and either of which can be prominent, depending on the circumstances. One aspect is shame over being small or "not measuring up." This aspect of shame is based on developmental experiences when a child is smaller than others and is concerned about growing up. A maturational basis for this aspect of shame was implied by Freud when he suggested the idea of "organic repression" as a process that results when shame accompanies pleasures of earlier psychosexual stages experienced when a person is older (Freud letter to Fliess, 1950/1966; see discussion in Greenberg, 1991). Strong influences from socialization experiences—experiences with parents, siblings, and peers—undoubtedly contribute to this aspect of shame. Such experiences include the "shaming" of the child for "acting like a baby." Shameful experiences of this sort may be strongly re-experienced when they are recalled and are among the most vivid of early childhood memories, with shame induced by parents, siblings, peers, and teachers (Yorke, 1990).

Another aspect is shame over transgressions. This is based on a sense that an individual has broken rules or not lived up to socially accepted standards. This aspect of shame has developmental origins in many experiences of prohibitions with parents, teachers, siblings, and peers. Its origins are in "shaming criticisms" that occur face to face. Why do we sometimes see guilt over transgressions and sometimes shame? Are these related to differing socialization experiences? Are some children exposed to more harsh shaming in parental practices or in peer group experiences?

Both aspects of shame (over being small and over having transgressed) involve the imaging of one or more significant others who, the individual fears, "see into me." The person therefore wants to shrink out of sight and not be seen (cf. the primitive mechanisms of hiding the eyes, averting the eyes, or self-blinding, as in the Oedipal drama—see below).

Social Referencing and Internalized Dialogues
with "Dos" and "Don'ts"

As mentioned earlier, shame appears to have its origins in early interactions with significant others. In what follows, we suggest that social referencing may be one of the central mechanisms by which shame experiences are transformed in the course of early development from the interpersonal/intersubjective to the intraindividual level of experience.

We have defined "social referencing" as a process that involves three components. When an individual encounters (1) a situation of uncertainty, there is (2) a tendency to seek out an emotional signal of a significant other in order to (3) regulate behavior accordingly (Emde, 1992; Klinnert, Emde, Butterfield, & Campos, 1986; Sorce & Emde, 1981). Thus a moving 1-year-old who is exploring and encounters a surface of uncertain solidity or an unusual approaching toy will look to the mother; if the mother then expresses pleasure or interest, the infant will approach and explore further; if, on the other hand, the mother expresses fear or anger, the infant is likely to avoid or cease exploring. Parental prohibitions become an occasion for social referencing during the child's second year. Thus, when the child approaches a tempting object such as the stereo, there will tend to be repeated looks back and forth to the mother's face, and checks in the course of prohibitions from the mother. There may even be social referencing checks following the resistance of the temptation and acceptance of the prohibition, perhaps even with an acknowledgment of pride and a shared smile. Parents often refer to such sequences as "testing"; elsewhere, we have referred to them as "negotiation experiences," with social referencing having a role in the child's internalization of such experiences (Emde, Johnson, & Easterbrooks, 1987). Social referencing in infancy can therefore be thought of as mediating two features of early moral development, both involving the seeking of guidance from a significant other in order to regulate behavior when there is uncertainty or when there is conflict. One feature involves what we have referred to as the "dos" of regulation; the other involves the "don'ts."

As we have discussed, shame involves a vivid imaging of one or more significant others. As such, it involves a special form of social referencing. We believe that social referencing beyond infancy becomes more and more internalized, even as it continues to be influential as an interpersonal behavior. Internalized social referencing has two components, both involving shared meaning. One component is experienced as *proactive*, and can be thought of as relevant to the "dos" of early moral development. This component involves the seeking of guidance from internalized referents with whom an individual has a dialogue in situations of uncertainty. The dialogue results in a feeling of encouragement, of joint interest, of expansion (possibly of pride), and of "we-go"—a dyadic ego, as it were. In contrast, the other component of internalized social referencing is experienced as *reactive*, and can be thought of as relevant to the "don'ts" of early moral development. The individual experiences one or more internalized significant others who are vigilant and who see him or her as not "measuring up." The feeling is one of deflation, of shrinking, and of shame. There is a feeling of smallness and aloneness, rather than of "we-go."

Our infancy work has focused on social referencing as predominantly a visual process of emotional communication. Although it may be more difficult to investigate, it seems highly likely that a similar process involves the auditory channels of emotional communication. As the child develops beyond infancy and acquires narrative capacity, it seems highly likely that moral development increasingly involves internalized dialogues—conversations with inner voices—as well as imagined visual scenarios. Support for this idea comes from observations of toddlers' and preschoolers' monologues before bedtime and during solitary play, both of which may include "re-envoicements" of disciplinary parental actions (Dore, 1989). In more complex social referencing processes that are internalized, we would suspect that dialogues involving inner voices would be associated with guilt, whereas dialogues with imagined faces would be associated with shame or its counterpart, pride (see the previously cited example of Bridget in the Hampstead Clinic; Kennedy & Yorke, 1982). But these are areas in which we have little developmental knowledge, and considerable investigation is called for.

Thus far we have been discussing shame (and, to a lesser extent, its contrast with guilt) in the context of twosomes—of dyadic relationship experiences with a significant other who is a caregiver. Before moving beyond this, we would like to take note of some other areas needing investigation. Little is known about the developmental precursors of shame (see Lewis, Chapter 7, this volume) and of guilt (see Zahn-Waxler & Robinson, Chapter 5, this volume), or about variation in the separate experiences of shame and guilt for the young child. Little is known about the *meaning* of shame or guilt for different relationship contexts. Quite surprisingly, little is known about the developmental consequences of variations in early emotional communications of shame and guilt. Much research needs to be done. This leads us to another dimension of the moral emotions we have been discussing, which is seldom made explicit in developmental discussion: Shame and guilt also have community/cultural aspects.

Beyond the Dyad: The Broader Social Aspects of Shame and Guilt

We have thus far been focusing on the intraindividual and interpersonal aspects of shame in relation to guilt. There is also a phenomenology of shame and guilt that involves the community and is defined by one's culture. States of conflict, of choice, and of personal responsibility are recognized publicly and are a matter of regular discourse. A publicly defined state of being is shared, and is often codified in a way that sets down the consequences of actions that violate the rules and norms of one's community or society. There is considerable cross-cultural and family variation with respect to those aspects of shame and guilt that are given a community-conscious or explicit public emphasis. These represent different perspectives and aspects of experience. In Japan, for example, shame is experienced much more in public terms—that is, of being in a mental state of mortification wherein a person has "brought shame to the family or group." We believe that the broader social aspects of shame and guilt have been under-emphasized in our developmental considerations. Indeed, these moral emotions are central mediators for regulating behavior in a variety of relationship and community contexts. The developing individual experiences shame or guilt as communications from within or from others. Communities are organized according to shared moral norms, and violations of what is expectable and "right" in practice are communicated either implicitly or explicitly by moral emotions. The processes by which the moral emotions signal conflict and its consequences are remarkably dynamic ones, and these processes interpenetrate multiple levels of organization: intraindividual, interpersonal, and community.

A psychoanalytic developmental perspective for shame and guilt must now consider the "family drama" of the young child's Oedipus complex. This chapter proposes a fresh look at the theory of the Oedipus complex—one that includes our considerations of broader social aspects. Moreover, our "fresh look" is enhanced by revisiting the literary creation that inspired Freud in the first place: the classic Oedipal drama of ancient Greece.

SHAME, GUILT, AND THE OEDIPAL DRAMA

The psychoanalytic theory of the Oedipus complex deals with the typical configurations of conflicts experienced by children 3 to 6 years of age. What has been referred to as a "complex" involves a child's experiencing of emotional conflict within the family, the child's growing understanding of a uniqueness within multiple social relationships, and immersions in a context for experience that goes beyond the dyadic. The Oedipal time of development involves emotional conflict, tension, and phases of resolution. Whether from the child's point of view or from the perspective of those around the child, the Oedipus complex of development involves a family drama.

Freud's account of the development of morality was centered around his theory of the Oedipus complex and was inspired by Sophocles's 5th-century B.C. drama *Oedipus Rex*. The drama was seen to contain enduring truths about the human condition. Guilt (in the form of the superego) was seen by Freud to emerge as a consequence of resolution of the Oedipal complex. Today's psychoanalytic theory of the Oedipus complex and of its links to moral development is in need of major revision, in the light of recent developmental knowledge. Before we turn to such a revision, however, it is informative to review the drama that inspired the theory. A fresh look, as we have discovered, extends Freud's view by providing a broader social context for shame, as well as guilt.

Freud was highly selective in his view of Sophocles's drama. When it is considered as a narrative, there are two other retellings of this drama in addition to the one chosen by Freud, with each contributing broader social influences to the drama. The reader who is used to thinking of Oedipus as a protaganist/hero in Sophocles's drama, as did Freud, may be puzzled as to why other views are worth considering. First, we can remind ourselves that societies are organized functionally as "moral communities" (Shweder, 1991), and that they typically prohibit incest and put boundaries of functioning across generational lines. From time to time there are disruptions, and communities need to review their assumptions and rules about such matters. Communities do this by the enactment of rituals, including the telling of legends and the performing of dramatic tragedies. The Oedipal drama as an exemplar dramatic tragedy has quite literally been enacted throughout Western history across more than 100 generations. Second, we can remind ourselves that the Oedipal drama, in addition to being psychological, is also interpersonal. The centeredness of the Oedipal drama takes place within the family, acted on an interpersonal stage. Thus, shame and guilt both result from intergenerational conflict. Shame occurs because of a conflict about "not measuring up," and because of a feeling of powerlessness and being small in the face of others. Guilt results because of a conflict about having done wrong, having hurt another or others, and being accused (and punished) by voices of others. And it is harder to escape from voices than it is from faces.

Now we turn to the drama. In the tradition of the classic Greek tradition, let us forecast the retellings. One version has Oedipus as provocateur, another as victim, and still another as a seeker of secret knowledge. The first retelling calls for an individual/intrapsychic level of action, the second calls for an interpersonal level, and the third brings a focus to the community level. Oedipus is a tragic hero in each of these retellings, but the meaning of each story is different.

Oedipus as Provocateur

In Freud's original retelling for psychoanalysis, Oedipus is the primary agent of action, and the level of interest is *intrapsychic*. The story involves a conflict of wishes and of intentions, as well as a history of conflicted events and entanglements. Throughout, circumstances are set in motion *by the individual*; correspondingly, repression and denial happen within the individual. Let us hear about it in the voice of Freud, writing in 1900:

Oedipus, son of Laius, King of Thebes, and of Jocasta, was exposed as an infant because an oracle had warned Laius that the still unborn child would be his father's murderer. The child was rescued, and grew up as a prince in an alien court, until, in doubt as to his origin, he too questioned the oracle and was warned to avoid his home since he was destined to murder his father and take his mother in marriage. On the road leading away from what he believed was his home, he met King Laius and slew him in a sudden quarrel. He came next to Thebes and solved the riddle set him by the Sphinx who barred his way. Out of gratitude the Thebans made him their king and gave him Jocasta's hand in marriage. He reigned long in peace and honour, and she who, unknown to him, was his mother bore him two sons and two daughters. Then at last a plague broke out and the Thebans made enquiry once more of the oracle. It is at this point that Sophocles' tragedy opens. The messengers bring back the reply that the plague will cease when the murderer of Laius has been driven from the land. . . .

The action of the play consists in nothing other than the process of revealing, with cunning delays and ever-mounting excitement—a process that can be likened to the work of a psycho-analysis—that Oedipus himself is the murderer of Laius, but further that he is the son of the murdered man and of Jocasta. Appalled at the abomination which he was unwittingly perpetrated, Oedipus blinds himself and forsakes his home. . . . His destiny moves us only because it might have been ours—because the oracle laid the same curse upon us before our birth as upon him. It is the fate of all of us, perhaps, to direct our first sexual impulse towards our mother and our first hatred and our first murderous wish against our father. Our dreams convince us that that is so. King Oedipus, who slew his father Laius and married his mother Jocasta, merely shows us the fulfillment of our own childhood wishes. . . . Like Oedipus, we live in ignorance of these wishes, repugnant to morality, which have been forced upon us by Nature, and after their revelation may all of us well seek to close our eyes to the scenes of our childhood. (1900/1953, Vol. 4, pp. 261– 264)

It is hardly necessary to review the coherence of this retelling of the story for a Victorian age of repression and guilt about sexual impulses. This retelling also had special coherence for a psychoanalytic theory of neurosis and its origins in conflicted childhood wishes—one that dominated clinical thinking for the next 50 years.

Oedipus as Victim

The next retelling brings in more elements. Again, Oedipus is struggling, but he comes across in many respects as more virtuous. "Repression" is overt rather than covert, even though deceit may be involved.

The story goes as follows. Long before Oedipus's birth, his father, Laius, consults an oracle and is told that he should beware of having a son, for, according to a curse, such a son will kill him and then marry Jocasta. [2] When Oedipus is born, Laius and Jocasta abandon the young infant in order to thwart the prophecy. To make sure of the infant's demise, Laius pierces the heels of Oedipus and ties his feet together, leaving him on a hill. Oedipus, who gets his name (i.e., "swollen feet") from this form of maltreatment, is saved by a shepherd and later adopted by the King of Corinth. Later, when the grown Oedipus leaves the home where he has been reared, he encounters another traveling party at a crossroads where three roads meet. Those meeting him provocatively issue an order to give way, and although they do not identify themselves, they push Oedipus off the road. A fight ensues. Oedipus kills all except one.

In this retelling, Laius is provocative in the extreme. Intergenerational conflicts go back to before Oedipus was born, and Jocasta is complicitous. She wants a son but then participates in the newborn's abandonment. Later, she becomes a willing wife for a triumphant Oedipus who has saved the city of Thebes. When the Oedipus of the drama then begins to unravel the mystery of the past—of parricide and of incest—Jocasta makes a plea not to pursue matters further. Many men, she says, before this time have encountered ideas from dreams and from oracles about sleeping with their mothers; these ideas are best ignored.

In this version of the drama, Oedipus is the victim of child abuse, neglect, and seduction. Conflicts are interpersonal, and the self-conscious moral emotion is shame. Shame is experienced *vis-à-vis* others, and there is little guilt.[3] This version of the Oedipal drama is about struggling with intergenerational conflict and making one's way in the midst of child maltreatment. Freud began with a theory of neurosogenesis based on childhood seduction and abuse; he then abandoned it for his theory of universal, biologically based Oedipal wishes in the child, causing repressed intrapsychic conflict in the adult. Today, we are aware of the devastating realities of child maltreatment. Clinical experience has shown that there *are* naturally occurring urges of love and hate that arise toward parental figures at particular phases of development. But clinical experience has shown that child maltreatment and seduction by parents are widespread. Such experiences can generate profound influences on development, including pervasive shame and dissociations (Cicchetti & Carlson, 1989; Putnam, 1994).

Oedipus as Seeker

The third retelling adds more to the "whole story." All through the drama, there is a searching for secret knowledge. Oedipal conflicts involve exclusion in relation to others. We are reminded that the drama of Sophocles takes place in the course of a single day. It is similar to a detective story, with Oedipus trying to find out the facts that have been withheld from him. The level of action for this retelling is beyond the intrapsychic and interpersonal; it involves the community and what is shared and not shared.

The past events of the drama can be summarized in a way that enables us to understand more about the secrets. Things go along quite in ordinary fashion for Oedipus until the day he hears a provocative outburst from a drunken guest at the home of his parents in Corinth. The guest reveals that Oedipus is not the child of his Corinthian parents. Oedipus then consults an oracle, who warns him of a profound secret: He must beware of a pre-existing curse wherein he will kill his father and marry his mother. Confused, Oedipus sets out on a journey. He will leave Corinth, find out who he is, and avoid the curse with respect to his "parents" in Corinth. Oedipus then comes to the well-known crossroads, where he is provocatively ordered to give way by the travelers who do not identify themselves, and a fight ensues. Oedipus kills all except one. Unbeknownst to Oedipus, he has killed his own biological father; moreover, the one witness to the act who escapes returns to Thebes and remains silent. Oedipus next comes upon the Sphinx, who has put a curse on the people of Thebes in the form of a plague. If Oedipus can solve the riddle, the plague will cease. Oedipus solves the riddle with the answer of "man," a creature who changes the way he walks and by implication his power over the course of a life. The first Theban plague of the drama lifts. Oedipus enters Thebes and is welcomed as a hero who has ended the plague. Since the king of Thebes has recently died, Oedipus is encouraged to be the new leader; according to custom, he also takes the former king's widow as his own wife.

The play itself opens later in the city of Thebes. Oedipus has ruled successfully for 17 years, but now there is a second plague. The oracle is once again consulted, and Oedipus learns that the plague will only cease when another secret is revealed and a mystery resolved. The plague will stop when the murderer of the former king, Laius, is revealed and punished. Oedipus sets about discovering who this person is, and eventually comes to learn of his parricide at the crossroads 17 years earlier and of his incest. The major secret seems revealed.

But there are other aspects to the secret. The city is silent for 17 years, during which Oedipus rules quite successfully in Thebes. The original witness at the crossroads recounts that the king has been slain by a band of robbers, but says no more than that. Creon, the brother of the king's wife at the time, does not pursue matters further. When Oedipus first arrives in Thebes, there is no further inquiry about his origin or possible connection with the event, nor does anyone discuss the coincidences concerning the age of Oedipus and his family resemblance to Laius and Jocasta. These considerations have led Steiner (1985) to postulate a widespread, Watergate-style "cover-up."

The secrets in this tale are multiple. The ones involving parricide and incest are prominent. But Oedipus is also driven to discover secrets of his origins, secrets of his relationships with others, and secrets that undo plagues. Moreover, the audience knows of the intergenerational secrets preceding Oedipus's searching. The audience knows of the oracle's secret revealed to Laius, the abandonment, the heel piercing, and the saving of the infant by a shepherd (who later turns up in Thebes in the play), as well as of Oedipus's adoption in Corinth.

The formal property of a secret is that it consists of knowledge held by some and excluded from others. Secret knowledge often contains within it a statement of who does what in relation to whom, what is held in awe, and what is forbidden. When the secret is revealed, shame results. As Siegler (1983) points out, great myths deal with the tension between revealed and concealed knowledge—between knowing and not knowing, seeing and not seeing, hiding and finding.

This retelling is a quest tale—about significant past events involving others, about one's origins, and about the meaning of life itself. But what makes it different from other quest tales is that the sought-after knowledge is secret. It is kept secret because there is collusion among a community of others who harbor the knowledge. Thus, an additional dimension of conflict is added to the Oedipal drama. In addition to conflict because of fear of the unknown and of what will be discovered, there is conflict because of others' not wanting the hero to know. There is a secret jealously guarded by others for reasons of protection, for reasons of keeping power, and for reasons of the special privileges of intimacy. The struggle is of a different kind than in the first two retellings. The hero is motivated against the elements to discover more about his life space, about its meaning and its possibilities, about his past, and about his awareness of the present. This kind of quest and its retelling is apt to change one's perception of the world.

Shame and Guilt in the Oedipal Drama

Freud emphasized guilt in his interpretation of the Oedipal drama. But there is also shame. Both of these moral emotions are played out in the drama in terms of their psychological and public manifestations. On the psychological level, Oedipus gouges out his eyes with the brooch from Jocasta's gown, upon discovering the full horror of his circumstances as he encounters his wife/mother's having killed herself. The standard interpretation is that Oedipus punishes himself, presumably a reflection of guilt. But there is also shame. Oedipus also blinds himself to avoid mutual gaze, and he later states that he could not stand the idea of facing the tormenting looks of others. On a more public level, Oedipus's shame shows itself in community action in the form of scorn, humiliation, and banishment. He is sent away, not killed. We can also remind ourselves that there is public shame as well as guilt represented in the plague on Thebes. The plague is understood not only as a punishment but as a shaming of the community, which must face up to the fact that a public ideal and code have been violated.

In summary, we have seen how a broader interpretive view of the drama that inspired Freud directs our attention to additional aspects of the self-conscious, moral emotions. Shame, as well as guilt, is prominent in the Oedipal drama, and both shame and guilt can result from the kind of intergenerational conflict that is portrayed in the Oedipus complex. Both emotions involve self-consciousness about responsibility for transgressions.

Shame can occur because of a conflict about "not measuring up," because of feeling excluded and powerless, and because of feeling small in the face of others. Moreover, our interpretive analysis emphasizes important inter-personal and community influences in shame and shaming that supplement important psychological influences. Guilt can result because of a conflict over having done wrong, having hurt another or others, and being accused (and possibly punished) by voices of others. Guilt, on a psychological level, is different from shame: A person cannot get away from voices, and hence does not show the shrinking, avoiding the gaze of others, and wanting-to-hide tendency that are characteristic of shame. Guilt also has important interpersonal and community influences.

A review of Freud's theory of the Oedipus complex, to which we turn now, also shows an evolution to a broader view. Following our review, we focus on more recent developmental research and bring our interpretive views to bear on broader social aspects of the child's development of shame and guilt.

THE OEDIPAL DRAMA AND THE CHILD'S OEDIPUS COMPLEX

As a result of Freud's own self-analysis and his reconstructions from adults whom he analyzed, a theory of Oedipus as child was created. The theory became the centerpiece of Freud's theory of infantile sexuality, and told of natural impulses appearing in early childhood and then becoming repressed in the course of continued development. The original formulation of the child's Oedipus complex held closely to Freud's retelling of the Sophoclean drama. There were three postulates. The first was that the preschool child normally experiences sexual desires toward the parent of the opposite sex (at the extreme, a desire for sexual possession). The second postulate was that the child naturally has feelings of competitive rivalry with the parent of the same sex (at the extreme, a murderous rage). A third postulate was that the child encounters fear of retaliation from the parent of the same sex for such wishes. Fears of this kind involve fantasies of bodily harm and castration. Freud understood the latter as the psychological version of the ancient Talion Law (i.e., the rule of "an eye for an eye") experienced by the child at this age.

As Freud originally saw it, what initiates the Oedipus complex is a maturation of naturally occurring psychosexual urges. By implication, mental development, including the child's increasing curiosity, was also seen to have an influence. The usual outcome of the Oedipus complex was thought to include an identification with the parent of the same sex and the formation of the basic structure for morality, the superego. Both outcomes were expectable between 5 and 7 years of age.

Other features of Freud's basic theory of the Oedipus complex were implicit. It was considered a universal aspect of human development and important from the standpoint of the child's motivations. Oedipal urges in the young child would be manifested in behavioral enactments and interpersonal interactions; increasingly, however, the forces of repression occasioned by fear and guilt would make Oedipal wishes unconscious. Finally, by implication, the Oedipus complex was perceived as an organizational construct. According to Freud's theory of psychosexual development (Freud, 1905/1953), earlier-appearing components of libidinal instincts are organized by the Oedipus complex, with a major reorganization taking place during puberty.

Freud and the early psychoanalysts soon found it necessary to make additions. Originally modeled for boys, the Oedipus complex became elaborated for girls, with the patterns of object choice and emotions adding further complexity. Other additions resulted from the appreciation of ambivalent motivations (i.e., both love and hate) in human relationship ties, where a "negative Oedipus patterning" was seen as often generating still other conflictual emotions. Although prime emphasis was put on intrinsically generated drives, the environment was seen as increasingly influential in causing variations in the complex. Parental overstimulation then became a concern, and Freud came to think of a complemental series between drive development and the experienced environment as the child experiences Oedipal conflicts through the course of development (Freud, 1926/1959).

Post-Freudian psychoanalysis has continued to document extensive variations in the Oedipus complex. But, more importantly, clinical experience with children and research has introduced other facts that require a modification of the theory. First, a superego or conscience is not a direct outcome of the resolved Oedipus complex, as Freud thought, since clinical examples show superego formation without oedipal resolution (Sandler, 1960). Moreover, considerable moral development takes place prior to age 3 and prior to Oedipal conflict (Emde et al., 1987). Second, research has shown that gender identity is not an outcome of the Oedipus complex, since core gender identity is established earlier, usually in the child's second and third years (Stoller, 1973, 1976). Third, the father does not appear later in the child's world to interrupt an earlier affectionate relationship with the mother when the child becomes 3 or 4. Research has clearly shown that fathers under normative conditions have qualitatively separate affectionate relationships during infancy with both girls and boys, including definable attachment relationships (Fonagy, Steele, & Steele, 1991; Fonagy, Steele, Steele, Moran, & Higgitt, 1991; Lamb, Hwang, Frodi, & Frodi 1982). Fourth, variations in the family environment are the source of major influences in the child's Oedipal conflicts. Since Fenichel's (1945) review, which emphasized family variations, we have come to appreciate the widespread existence of child maltreatment by parents (Cicchetti & Carlson, 1989; Kempe, 1980; Mrazek & Mrazek, 1985) and the circumstances under which there are repetitions of maladaptive Oedipal conflict across generations (Brazelton & Cramer, 1990; Fraiberg, 1980; Stoller, 1980). Correspondingly, the British object relations school of psychoanalysis and Kohut's self psychology school (Kohut, 1971) have influenced clinicians to be more outward-oriented as contrasted with inward-drive-oriented in their views of early childhood conflicts. Bowlby (1973), following Winnicott (1965), theorized about a splitting of self-experience during early childhood, based on the harsh realities presented by many abusing families.

Where does this leave the developmental theory of the child's Oedipus complex? There is clearly a need for a fresh look. A relationship-motivational theory of the child's early development offers one such look (Emde, 1988; Emde, Biringen, Clyman, & Oppenheim, 1991). In this theory, early versions of moral emotions develop from a set of biologically prepared basic motives, and these emotions are likely to be activated within the context of interactions containing shared meaning with each parent. The emotions include positive affect sharing and pride; empathy in the context of another's distress; distress in situations that violate the child's internalized standards and expectations; and manifestations of shame and hurt feelings.

The relationship-motivational theory proposes that a new element appears during the child's Oedipus complex. This element consists of a newly acquired sense of exclusion. The child begins to understand that two other people whom he or she cares about are intimately involved with each other. Because of advances in the child's understanding, there is now a new kind of painful exclusion. The child realizes that two others are committed to each other and enjoy themselves when the child is not present. And, as the research of Watson and colleagues has emphasized, the child still has a limited understanding: He or she may not realize that there can be love between parent and child while the parents continue to love each other. In other words, the exclusion sense can be understood as an all-or-none phenomenon, since preschool children may not see how their parents can simultaneously be both parents to them and spouses to each other (Watson, 1984; Watson & Getz, 1990).

The two other levels of action that we have seen in the Oedipal drama must now be added to the individual's development. In addition to the individual/psychological level of the child's understanding, there is an interpersonal/intergenerational level. This introduces the connected idea of "triangulation," an interpersonal construct with motivational properties involving influences among three persons. Triangulation is a situation in which one person is excluded, while two others are involved in a coalition.

Clinical experience has shown us that Oedipal conflicts persist when there are failures in asymmetric parental responsibility. There is no way of understanding the child's developing Oedipal conflicts and their resolution without including an interpersonal perspective. Intergenerational boundaries of responsibility are crucial. Parents cannot substitute for intimacy in the spousal relationship by means of intense and inclusive intimacy with a child without risking disturbances in development (Sameroff & Emde, 1989). It is therefore appropriate for the child to be excluded during some times of parental intimacy, and it is necessary for the child to come to grips with clearly communicated adult boundaries.

The version of the Oedipal story with the hero as seeker of secret knowledge emphasizes a broader social view, wherein family and community influences can operate in such a way as to keep secrets and perpetuate what we might regard as a maladaptive socially shared script for interactions. Intersystemic approaches to understanding are also important in our relationship-motivational view. All too often families, after language development, can use words to overlay the child's experience in such a way that reality is portrayed in ways other than what the child feels or knows to be true (Bowlby, 1973; Stern, 1985). Similarly, beginning during the child's second year, the family typically socializes an awareness concerning what actions are "nice" versus "nasty," and what actions should be put out of mind or not made public (Emde et al., 1987; Stipek, Gralinski, & Kopp, 1990). Family secrets, reinforced by collusions among sets of individuals, can introduce a common censorship that functions to preserve triangulations. Such triangulating situations are problematic and can violate appropriate intergenerational boundaries; families can also become isolated from the community, and can thus find inadvertent support for maintaining "enmeshed" family styles (Minuchin, 1974; Reiss, 1989).

THE MORAL EMOTIONS AND THE REFERENCING OF OTHERS BEYOND THE FAMILY: THE INCREASING SIGNIFICANCE OF THE "PUBLIC EYE"

Up to this point, we have discussed the origins of shame and guilt within the context of early caregiving relationships and family interactions. We have hypothesized that the child's social referencing of critical others within this context may serve as an important mechanism in the development of shame and guilt. Our consideration of the child's family Oedipal drama has highlighted the significance of broader social aspects concerning shame and guilt. We would now like to extend this line of thinking by considering contexts beyond the family. Particularly with regard to shame, a moral emotion that continues to develop across the lifespan, we speculate that experiences in broader social contexts assume increasing regulatory importance. The preschool child becomes increasingly socialized by peers, "near-peers," and other groups outside the family (Leiderman, 1989). Social referencing of caregivers now becomes extended to social referencing of members within a group and to the group itself. The concept of a "reference group" has been a long-standing idea in sociology (see review of this point by Feinman, 1992); it seems logical to assume that group experiences outside the family may have a major role in the child's continued development with respect to shame. Group experiences are clearly among the most powerful and painful of remembered shame experiences.

The child's peer group becomes increasingly important for the preschool and school-age child. Most of us have experienced the powerful shaming processes that happen among groups of young children. These experiences seem related to a sense of not being "big" or competent—one of the two aspects of shame mentioned earlier. They are magnified in peer group settings when a significant part of the group focuses on one child as a target of teasing, ridicule, or humiliation. Given the importance of peer relations in adaptation to school and work settings, these early peer-related shaming experiences may set in motion long-lasting and important influences.

When we consider peer relations, we also need to address the powerful influence of gender. From 3 years of age and onward, developmental observers have documented a strong tendency for gender segregation, with boys gravitating toward larger-group play with other boys, and girls preferring dyadic and triadic connected play with other girls. It is in these contexts that behavioral differences between the genders become amplified (Maccoby & Jacklin, 1980). Many speculations have been offered for why gender segregation occurs. We suggest that shaming may be a strong motivator. Children may be shamed by their peers for playing with cross-sex peers, and avoiding the toxic experience of shame may be a powerful mechanism for maintaining gender segregation.

School provides another emerging context for middle childhood. Children may become a target of peer shame when they are identified as "teachers' pets" or as not fitting in with the peer group norms. Moreover, teachers may use shaming as a powerful control device. Shame, as we have described earlier, becomes amplified from an exposure to the "public eye." When a child is exposed as deserving of criticism in front of a large group of children such as a classroom, the impact is especially painful. And, as our analyses of the Oedipal drama remind us, there may be important community influences on painful feelings following transgressions. Schools, for example, have been shown to differ dramatically in their organizational cultures with respect to learning and behavioral control (Rutter, Maughan, Mortimore, Ouston, & Smith, 1979).

CONCLUSION: A CULTURAL FRAME
FOR SHAME AND GUILT

We have focused our chapter on two early-appearing self-conscious moral emotions that involve transgressions—namely, shame and guilt. We have not focused on the other early-appearing self-conscious moral emotions that do not involve transgressions—namely, pride, mastery feelings about "getting it right," pleasure in social reciprocity, and empathy. Our thinking in the chapter has moved to a recognition that shame has been relatively neglected in our developmental theories (particularly psychoanalytic ones), and to a recognition that both shame and guilt are as much interpersonal as intraindividual phenomena in terms of their origins and consequences, as well as in terms of their narrative flow. Indeed, the psychology of these self-conscious moral emotions has led us increasingly outward as we have considered family and community influences. A fresh look at the Oedipal drama has pointed up the limitations of an earlier psychoanalytic thinking that focused too sharply on the intraindividual level of desires and intentions, and the fresh look has led us to an expansion of levels of meaning that include important intergenerational and community influences.

Cultural factors interpenetrate all levels of meaning: psychological, interpersonal, intergenerational, family, and community. Cultural knowledge provides guidance for action according to what is commonly acceptable and collectively shared over time. Cultural groups are organized along moral lines (Shweder, 1991). Conflict is inevitable in the human condition, and it occurs at all levels—within the individual, between people, and among groups within communities. Guidance in the face of conflict is provided by cultural tradition, which is often accessed by a referencing of others and emotional communication. Guidance from one's culture is accessed even more profoundly during everyday activities and without self-conscious emotions. As we have noted above, there are more moral emotions than those that involve transgressions; moral emotions other than shame and guilt provide positive guidance and a sense of what "feels good" for the "dos" of everyday actions (as contrasted with the "don'ts"). The cultural embeddedness of the developing child involves continued implicit encounters with a moral environment of others, both past and present, who provide guidance for the procedures of everyday life. Transgressions and self-consciousness about them are typically interruptions in the flow of procedures that are ordinarily culturally defined and supported.

The importance of cultural embeddedness can be illustrated by some final reflections concerning variability in what shame means in Japan and in Israel as contrasted with the United States. Shame in Japan has a locus of meaning that involves the imagined specter of bringing denigration to one's family, whereas shame in the United States has a locus of meaning that involves the image of a belittled self in the face of others. We have come to appreciate that a sense of self is actively constructed under cultural support and influence; correspondingly, self-consciousness is likely to be different according to the two meaning settings in Japan and the United States. The more the locus of what is important in self is defined in terms of group experience, the more it is likely that group referencing and shame in the context of the group will be a strong developmental influence. What is needed is more research in a variety of contexts within and between cultures, as we attempt to understand emotions such as shame or guilt and their relations to self-consciousness and the consciousness of others.

Our final cross-cultural reflection concerns Israel. One of us (Oppenheim) had the experience of moving back to Israel with his family during the course of the time this chapter was written, after having lived in the United States for 7 years. The following observations about shame in his preschool-age son are poignant.

The living arrangements, cultural heritage, and social values of Israel support a high level of interconnectedness, thus making shame a powerful socializing force. Many eyes are looking at the child, and many of the same eyes appear in overlapping circles of home, neighborhood, preschool, and community. To continue the metaphor, many of the same eyes follow the child through the lifespan; thus the child's history, including potentially shameful aspects, may influence the present not only through internalized experiences but also through the continued presence of many of the same figures. An anecdote from the life of a 4-year-old boy provides illustration.

The young boy misbehaved at preschool, throwing sand at another child. To control him, the teacher said in front of the other children: "Do you want me to tell your mother about what you did today?" The child responded with hurtful crying. The teacher told the mother about the events of the day, pointing out, in a somewhat surprised manner, how "sensitive" the child was to cry in response to what seemed to her a mild threat. In her statement to the child, the teacher used a combination of implied threat (the child might be punished at home); however, perhaps more importantly and more painfully to the child, the teacher shamed the child in front of his peers and threatened to shame him in front of his mother. The Israeli context of high social embeddedness for such a situation can become more complicated, because many of a child's preschool peers, often quick to tell their parents about a peer or about teacher–child conflicts at school, are also the child's neighbors. Moreover, the peers' parents are often friends or acquaintances of the child's parents. The child is likely to become increasingly aware of the widening audiences for shameful behavior, and this adds to socializing influences.

These reflections lead us to the conclusion that more culturally sensitive research is needed to discover the processes involved in children's awareness of the wider social networks that become engaged as socializing agents. The self-conscious moral emotions, including shame and guilt, are important regulators that are likely to operate differently in different cultures—not only cross-nationally (see Wallbott & Scherer, Chapter 19, this volume), but within culturally pluralistic nations such as the United States. Understanding the variations in the self-conscious moral emotions that are introduced by variations in culturally prescribed social networks in the young child's expanding world should present exciting opportunities for research.

NOTES

1. Much of the psychoanalytic resumé in this section is based on a colloquium held at the Anna Freud Centre in 1988, in which one of us (Emde) participated.

Some of the points of the colloquium were previously summarized by Yorke (1990).

2. In a version of the legend that surrounds the play but is not in it, the audience knows that the curse is issued by King Pelops because Laius has raped and sodomized his illegitimate son, Chrysippus. The legend also has it that Laius avoids intercourse with Jocasta and that she seduces him in order to have a son. Sophocles depicts Oedipus as an old man in Colonus, defending himself bluntly to Creon, who comes to rile him with others from Thebes. Oedipus attempts to turn the shame upon Creon and others who are still shaming him. He invokes the image of the three intersecting roads where he was knocked off the pathway: "Just answer me one thing:/If someone tried to kill you here and now,/You righteous gentleman, what would you do,/Inquire first if the stranger is your father?/Or would you not first try to defend yourself?/I think that since you like to be alive/You'd treat him as the threat required . . ." (Fitzgerald trans., 1941/1954, lines 991 through 996).

3. In the account above, I have made use of a number of literary and psychoanalytic criticisms. In particular, I am grateful for the discussions in Devereux (1953), Kanzer (1950), Rascovsky and Rascovsky (1968), Ross (1982), Pollock and Ross (1988), and Weiss (1988). The role of Oedipus as victim and the interpersonal nature of the core conflicts are highlighted by the three plays of Sophocles's trilogy.

REFERENCES

Abrams, S. (1990). Orienting perspectives on shame and self-esteem. *Psychoanalytic Study of the Child, 45,* 411–416.

Bowlby, J. (1973). *Attachment and loss: Vol. 2. Separation: Anxiety and anger.* New York: Basic Books.

Bowlby, J. (1988). Developmental psychiatry comes of age. *American Journal of Psychiatry, 145*(1), 1–10.

Brazelton, T. B., & Cramer, B. G. (1990). *The earliest relationship.* Reading, MA: Addison-Wesley.

Cicchetti, D., & Carlson, V. (Eds.). (1989). *Child maltreatment: Theory and research on the causes and consequences of child abuse and neglect.* Cambridge, England: Cambridge University Press.

Darwin, C. (1872). *The expression of the emotions in man and animals.* London: John Murray.

Devereux, G. (1953). Why Oedipus killed Laius: A note on the complementary Oedipus complex in Greek drama. *International Journal of Psycho-Analysis, 34,* 132–141.

Dore, J. (1989). Monologue as reenvoicement of dialogue. In K. Nelson (Ed.), *Narratives from the crib* (pp. 231–260). Cambridge, MA: Harvard University Press.

Emde, R. N. (1988). Development terminable and interminable: I. Innate and motivational factors from infancy. *International Journal of Psycho-Analysis, 69,* 23–42.

Emde, R. N. (1992). Social referencing research: Uncertainty, self, and the search for meaning. In S. Feinman (Ed.), *Social referencing and the social construction of reality in infancy* (pp. 79–94). New York: Plenum Press.

Emde, R. N., Biringen, Z., Clyman, R. B., & Oppenheim, D. (1991). The moral self of infancy: Affective core and procedural knowledge. *Developmental Review, 11*, 251–270.

Emde, R. N., & Clyman, R. B. (in press). "We hold these truths to be self-evident": The origins of moral motives in individual activity and shared experience. In J. Noshpitz (Ed.), *The handbook of child and adolescent psychiatry*. New York: Wiley.

Emde, R. N., Johnson, W. F., & Easterbrooks, M. A. (1987). The dos and don'ts of early moral development: Psychoanalytic tradition and current research. In J. Kagan & S. Lamb (Eds.), *The emergence of morality in young children* (pp. 245–277). Chicago: University of Chicago Press.

Erikson, E. (1950). *Childhood and society*. New York: Norton.

Feinman, S. (Ed.). (1992). *Social referencing and the social construction of reality in infancy*. New York: Plenum Press.

Fenichel, O. (1945). *The psychoanalytic theory of neurosis*. New York: Norton.

Fitzgerald, R. (Trans.). (1954). Oedipus at Colonus. In D. Grene & R. Lattimore (Eds.), *Sochocles I*. Chicago: University of Chicago Press. (Fitzgerald translation originally published 1941)

Fonagy, P., Steele, M., & Steele, H. (1991). Maternal representations of attachment during pregnancy predict the organization of infant–mother attachment at one year of age. *Child Development, 62*, 880–893.

Fonagy, P., Steele, M., Steele, H., Moran, G. S., & Higgitt, A. C. (1991). The capacity for understanding mental states: The reflective self in parent and child and its significance for security of attachment. *Infant Mental Health Journal, 13*, 200–216.

Fraiberg, S. (1980). *Clinical studies in infant mental health*. New York: Basic Books.

Freud, S. (1966). Extracts from the Fliess papers, letter 75, written in 1897. In J. Strachey (Ed. and Trans.), *The standard edition of the complete psychological works of Sigmund Freud* (Vol. 1, pp. 268–271). London: Hogarth Press. (Original work published 1950)

Freud, S. (1953). The interpretation of dreams. In J. Strachey (Ed. and Trans.), *The standard edition of the complete psychological works of Sigmund Freud* (Vol. 4, pp. 1–338; Vol. 5, pp. 339–627). London: Hogarth Press. (Original work published 1900)

Freud, S. (1953). Three essays on the theory of sexuality. In J. Strachey (Ed. and Trans.), *The standard edition of the complete psychological works of Sigmund Freud* (Vol. 7, pp. 125–143). London: Hogarth Press. (Original work published 1905)

Freud, S. (1959). Inhibitions, symptoms and anxiety. In J. Strachey (Ed. and Trans.), *The standard edition of the complete psychological works of Sigmund Freud* (Vol. 20, pp. 75–175). London: Hogarth Press. (Original work published 1926)

Gillman, R. D. (1990). The Oedipal organization of shame. *Psychoanalytic Study of the Child, 45*, 357–375.

Greenberg, J. (1991). *Oedipus and beyond—A clinical theory*. Cambridge, MA: Harvard University Press.

Izard, C. (1977). *Human emotions*. New York: Plenum Press.

Kanzer, M. (1950). The Oedipus trilogy. *Psychoanalytic Quarterly, 19*, 561–572.

Kempe, C. H. (1980). Incest and other forms of sexual abuse. In C. H. Kempe &

R. E. Holfer (Eds.), *The battered child* (3rd ed. pp. 198–214). Chicago: University of Chicago Press.

Kennedy, H., & Yorke, C. (1982). Steps from outer to inner conflict viewed as superego precursors. *Psychoanalytic Study of the Child, 37,* 221–228.

Klinnert, M. D., Emde, R. N., Butterfield, P., & Campos, J. J. (1986). Social referencing: The infant's use of emotional signals from a friendly adult with mother present. *Developmental Psychology, 22,* 427–432.

Kohut, H. (1971). *The analysis of the self.* New York: International Universities Press.

Kohut, H. (1977). *The restoration of the self.* New York: International Universities Press.

Lamb, M. E., Hwang, C. P., Frodi, A., & Frodi, M. (1982). Security of mother– and father–infant attachment and its relation to sociability with strangers in traditional and non-traditional Swedish families. *Infant Behavior and Development, 5,* 355–367.

Lazarus, R. S. (1991). *Emotion and adaptation.* New York: Oxford University Press.

Leiderman, P. H. (1989). Relationship disturbances and development through the life cycle. In A. J. Sameroff & R. N. Emde (Eds.), *Relationship disturbances in early childhood: A developmental approach* (pp. 165–190). New York: Basic Books.

Lewis, M. (1991). Self-conscious emotions and the development of self. *Journal of the American Psychoanalytic Association, 39*(Suppl.), 45–73.

Lewis, M. (1992). *Shame: The exposed self.* New York: Free Press.

Maccoby, E. E., & Jacklin, C. N. (1980). Psychological sex differences. In M. Rutter (Ed.), *Scientific foundations of developmental psychiatry* (pp. 92–100). London: Heinemann Medical Books.

Minuchin, S. (1974). *Families and family therapy.* Cambridge, MA: Harvard University Press.

Mrazek, D., & Mrazek, O. (1985). Child maltreatment. In M. Rutter & L. Hersov (Eds.), *Child and adolescent psychiatry* (pp. 679–697). Oxford: Blackwell Scientific.

Piers, G., & Singer, M. D. (1953). *Shame and guilt.* Springfield, IL: Charles C Thomas.

Pollock, G. H. & Ross, J. M. (Eds.). (1988). *The Oedipus papers* (Classics in Psychoanalysis Monograph Series, No. 6). Madison, CT: International Universities Press.

Putnam, F. W. (1994). Dissociation and disturbances of self. In D. Cicchetti & S. L. Toth (Eds.), Rochester Symposium on Developmental Psychopathology: Vol. 5. Disorders and dysfunctions of the self. Rochester, NY: University of Rochester Press.

Rapaport, D. (1967). A theoretical analysis of the superego concept. In M. M. Gill (Ed.), *The collected papers of David Rapaport* (pp. 685–709). New York: Basic Books.

Rascovsky, A., & Rascovsky, M. (1968). On the genesis of acting out and psychopathic behavior in Sophocles' Oedipus: Notes on filicide. *International Journal of Psycho-Analysis, 49,* 390–394.

Reiss, D. (1989). The represented and practicing family: Contrasting visions of family continuity. In A. J. Sameroff & R. N. Emde (Eds.), *Relationship disturbances in early childhood: A developmental approach* (pp. 191–220). New York: Basic Books.

Ross, J. M. (1982). Oedipus revisited: Laius and the "Laius complex." *Psychoanalytic Study of the Child, 37*, 167–200.

Rutter, M., Maughan, B., Mortimore, P., Ouston, J., & Smith, A. (Eds.). (1979). *Fifteen thousand hours.* Cambridge, MA: Harvard University Press.

Sameroff, A. J., & Emde, R. N. (Eds.). (1989). *Relationship disturbances in early childhood: A developmental approach.* New York: Basic Books.

Sandler, J. (1960). On the concept of superego. *Psychoanalytic Study of the Child, 15*, 128–162.

Sandler, J. (1987). *From safety to superego: Selected papers of Joseph Sandler.* New York: Guilford Press.

Shweder, R. A. (1991). *Thinking through cultures.* Cambridge, MA: Harvard University Press.

Siegler, A. L. (1983). The Oedipus myth and the Oedipus complex: Intersecting realms, shared structures. *International Journal of Psycho-Analysis, 10*, 205–214.

Sorce, J., & Emde, R. N. (1981). Mother's presence is not enough: Effect of emotional availability on infant exploration. *Developmental Psychology, 17*(6), 737–745.

Steiner, J. (1985). Turning a blind eye: The cover up for Oedipus. *International Review of Psychoanalysis, 12*, 161–172.

Stern, D. N. (1985). *The interpersonal world of the infant.* New York: Basic Books.

Stipek, D. J., Gralinski, J. H., & Kopp, C. B. (1990). Self-concept development in the toddler years. *Developmental Psychology, 26*, 972–977.

Stoller, R. J. (1973). Overview: The impact of new advances in sex research on psychoanalytic theory. *American Journal of Psychiatry, 130*(3), 241–251.

Stoller, R. J. (1976). Primary femininity. *Journal of the American Psychoanalytic Association, 24*(5), 59–78.

Stoller, R. J. (1980). A different view of Oedipal conflict. In S. Greenspan & G. Pollock (Eds.), *The course of life: Vol. 1. Infancy and early childhood* (pp. 589–602). Adelphi, MD: Mental Health Study Center.

Tomkins, S. S. (1962). *Affect, imagery, consciousness: Vol. 1. The positive affects.* New York: Springer.

Watson, M. W. (1984). Development of social role understanding. *Developmental Review, 4*, 192–213.

Watson, M. W., & Getz, K. (1990). Developmental shifts in oedipal behaviors related to family role understanding. In I. Bretherton & M. W. Watson (Eds.), *New directions for child development: No. 28. Children's perspectives on the family* (pp. 29–45). San Francisco: Jossey-Bass.

Weiss, S. (1988). How culture influences the interpretation of the Oedipus myth. In G. H. Pollock & J. M. Ross (Eds.), *Classics in psychoanalysis: Monograph 6. The Oedipus papers.* Madison, CT: International Universities Press. (Original work published 1985)

Winnicott, D. W. (1965). *The maturational processes and the facilitating environment.* New York: International Universities Press.

Yorke, C. (1990). The development and functioning of the sense of shame. *Psychoanalytic Study of the Child, 45*, 377–409.

VI

CROSS-CULTURAL PERSPECTIVES ON SELF-CONSCIOUS EMOTIONS

18

Culture, Self, and Emotion: A Cultural Perspective on "Self-Conscious" Emotions

SHINOBU KITAYAMA
HAZEL ROSE MARKUS
HISAYA MATSUMOTO

Many emotions, especially those common in social life, are inherently interpersonal. Anger, for example, involves a negative attitude toward someone who unduly interferes with one's own goals, rights, or interests (Averill, 1983). Positive emotions, such as feelings of respect, love, or attachment, include as their essential element a favorable attitude or positive affect toward another person. The participation of others is critical, not only for these "other-conscious" emotions, but also for the "self-conscious" emotions of pride, shame, guilt, and embarrassment that are the focus of this volume. Thus, pride often results from a sense of accomplishment; however, because this sense is usually based on a comparison of the self's performance with those of relevant others or on direct complimentary remarks made by others, pride cannot exist in a social vacuum. The same is true for shame or guilt. These emotions involve a negative attitude toward the self, but most often these negative evaluations hinge on others' view of the self. It is impossible to understand these emotions apart from their interpersonal or social context: They are relational in their meaning and in their source, and often in their experience and expression as well.

One of the stumbling blocks to implicating the social context in the analysis of emotions is to determine what exactly is meant by the "interper-

439

sonal or social context." In the cultural perspective to be developed here, we argue that significant aspects of the social context of emotions include the meaning and practices of the self and the meaning and practices of the relationships between self and others, and that these features of the social context are in high relief for the self-conscious emotions. In particular, we focus here on variation in emotion as a consequence of whether the social context fosters and implements a view of the self as independent from others, or, in contrast, as interdependent with others.

A CULTURAL PERSPECTIVE ON EMOTION

In the emerging interdisciplinary field of cultural psychology, a central concern is with how culture and the psyche "make each other up" (Shweder, 1991). Recent studies reveal that the construction of the self and the specific implementation of social relationships are highly cross-culturally variable (e.g., Bruner, 1990; Berman, 1989; Fiske, 1991; Gergen, 1990; Markus & Kitayama, 1991a; Shweder & Bourne, 1984; Sampson, 1985, 1988; Rosenberger, 1993; Triandis, 1989). As a consequence, any phenomenon such as emotional experience that has the self as its anchor, target, or referent will vary accordingly. Emotions, then, are viewed here not as natural or biological events that are prewired and self-contained (e.g., Ekman, 1984; Davidson & Cacioppo, 1992), but rather as amalgams of component processes that reflect the functional relationship between the organism and the environment—and, in the case of the self-conscious emotions, the relationship between the self and the cultural environment (Kitayama & Markus, 1994).

This emphasis on social process does not presume that biological or physiological processes are unimportant in emotion. On the contrary, extensive research on the biological basis of emotion has amply demonstrated that these processes are pivotal and crucial in emotional processes (Derryberry & Tucker, 1991; LeDoux, 1987). From the cultural perspective, however, these biological processes and substrates are best understood as component constituents that enable but, by themselves, cannot uniquely determine the functional interdependence between the self and its surroundings. Because this interdependence is both afforded and constrained by ecological, social, and cultural conditions, the roles or functions that the internal biological processes may serve in emotional activation must be carefully analyzed in reference to a correspondingly broader ecological or cultural niche of the individual.

We suggest that the development and organization of emotional processes and experience with all their biological underpinnings may be significantly influenced (either sustained or modified) by the systems of meaning in which the self, others, and other social events or objects are made personally significant. And the extent of this cultural influence may be far greater than has previously been assumed in psychology. This view of emotion from the cultural perspective places cultural analysis at the very center of emotion research, and may highlight some aspects of emotion that have not been well captured by the universalistic and mostly biological perspective on emotion.

We expect that emotions should play powerful roles in defining and constructing the self, and, furthermore, in regulating and creating an unfolding pattern of social interaction between the self and others. The emerging social interaction pattern and the understanding of this pattern, together, may consequently transform the very nature of emotional experience. In short, there should exist a mutual and highly dynamic interaction among emotions, the self, and social relationships. Our goals in the current chapter are, first, to delineate a cultural approach to emotion by describing intimate interactions between emotions and culturally constituted processes of self and social interaction; and, second, to discuss some implications of the cultural approach for the "self-conscious" emotions.

Before we begin this cultural analysis, two possible meanings of the "self-consciousness of emotion" should be distinguished. We assume that emotional experience is a way of perceiving internal sensations as arising from, or otherwise as embedded in, an interaction between the self and its surroundings. This interaction is dynamic, in that any changes in or of the self cause corresponding changes in the surroundings (either actual or imagined), and conversely, changes in the latter also immediately lead to changes in the former; this mutual influence transforms the embodied experience of emotion. Accordingly, by their very nature, emotions implicate the self, and in this sense all emotions are "self-conscious." Nevertheless, it is also possible to use the term more narrowly to refer to a particular subset of emotions—those derived from evaluations that have the self as their primary (although not sole) focus, such as pride, shame, and guilt. These emotions can be contrasted with those that have other people as their primary (although not sole) focus, such as friendly feelings, feelings of respect, and anger. It is this second sense in which the term "self-conscious" is being used in this volume, and we follow this convention.

In our discussion, we highlight two ramifications of taking a cultural perspective in the analysis of self-conscious emotions. First, these emotions can best be understood as variants of interpersonal emotions. Different "self-conscious" emotions are simultaneously signified by, and signify, different forms of social relationships. We believe that this point can be best appreciated when these emotions are examined in conjunction with "other-conscious" emotions (friendly feelings, anger)—namely, those based relatively more on an evaluation of other persons in social relationships, and thus directed toward these others.

Another implication concerns the social functions of the "self-conscious" emotions across different cultures. Because of the interdependence between emotional experience and social relationships, emotions may be pivotal in managing relationships with other persons, defining the self, maintaining the self's worth or dignity, and organizing appropriate action in many social situations. Furthermore, social relationships take place within a set of culturally shared attitudes, practices, conventions, and implicit or explicit rules of social interaction, or what can be called the "cultural frame" (Holland & Quinn, 1987). And the social functions of many emotions may be inseparable from the very cultural frame in which the relevant social relationships are situated. Accordingly, we anticipate wide-ranging cultural differences in ways in which interpersonal emotions are experienced, expressed, recruited, and regulated in social life.

INTERPERSONAL EMOTIONS AND VIEWS OF SELF

Views of Self as Independent and as Interdependent

We (Markus & Kitayama, 1991a, 1992) have distinguished between two broad sets of tasks people need to perform in social life: independence and interdependence. "Independence" refers to a set of tasks or psychological tendencies to separate the self from social context; it encompasses goals of agency, autonomy, and disengagement from others. "Interdependence," on the other hand, refers to a set of tasks or psychological tendencies to connect the self with others; it encompasses such goals as affiliation, communion, and engagement with others.

We have suggested that these two sets of tasks are differently combined and incorporated into the definition and construction of the self, as well as into the pattern of cultural ideology, customs, and institutions. Thus people in different cultures may have very different construals of the self, of others, and of the relations between the self and others. Specifically, in many Western (particularly North American) cultures, there is a strong faith in separateness of the self, and the tasks of independence take precedence over those of interdependence. That is, the self is conceived of primarily as an autonomous entity. Its major normative task, then, is to maintain the independence of the individual as a self-contained entity—or, more specifically, to be unique, to express the self, to realize and actualize the inner self, to promote the self's own goals, and so on. Within this independent view of self, individuals tend to focus on their own internal attributes (their preferences, traits, and abilities). There is a concern with expressing and verbalizing these attributes in both public and private. Other people are crucial in maintaining the independent construal of self, but they are crucial primarily for their role in evaluating and appraising the self.

By contrast, many non-Western (particularly Asian) cultures believe in the inherent connectedness among different individuals, emphasizing the tasks of interdependence over those of independence. That is, the self is conceived of primarily as part of ongoing relationships. The major normative task of the self, then, is to maintain the interdependence among individuals—or more specifically, to adjust to and fit into important relationships, to occupy one's proper place, to engage in appropriate actions, and to promote relevant others' goals. Within this interdependent view of self, individuals tend to focus on their interdependent status with other people and strive to meet duties, obligations, and social responsibilities. Their thoughts, feelings, and actions are organized and made meaningful in reference to the thoughts, feelings, and actions of others in relationships. And others in relationships are crucially important in the very definition of the self.

It must be noted that independence and interdependence are assumed to be present in every culture, and that cultures vary in the ways in which these two sets of tasks are weighted and organized in social life. Thus, many Western cultures typically emphasize and elaborate independence in their dominant ideology (e.g., individualism, the Declaration of Independence), patterns of social customs, practices (e.g., importance and prevalence of personal choice), and institutions (e.g., merit-based pay systems). Each individual adjusts himself or herself to a segment of the society that consists of an idiosyncratic yet widely overlapping set of customs, practices, and institutions sampled from the entire societal and cultural reality. The psychological tendency of the person toward independence, therefore, is manifested as relatively habitual actions and thoughts scripted after the culturally elaborated and shared ideology, customs, and practices. In these cultures, the tendency toward *inter*dependence, also necessary and critical for effective social functioning, remains in the background; it is relatively implicit and not collectively elaborated or prescribed. Instead, these tasks are left to the intentions and initiatives of each individual member. The psychological tendency toward interdependence, therefore, is manifested as relatively intentional or voluntary actions and thoughts that are less constrained or less supported by culturally shared ideology, customs, and practices.[1]

In contrast, many Asian cultures emphasize and elaborate interdependence in their dominant ideology (e.g., collectivism), patterns of social customs, practices (e.g., reading others' minds and acting accordingly), and institutions (e.g., seniority-based pay systems). Individuals adjust themselves to idiosyncratic yet overlapping segments of this societal and cultural reality, leading to habitual action or thought patterns conditioned on or scripted after the cultural reality of interdependence. In these cultures, the tendency toward independence is also important and necessary for effective social functions, but it is neither culturally elaborated nor prescribed. Instead, the tasks of independence are relegated to intentions and initiatives of each individual member; they are largely "optional." In these cultures, therefore, the psychological tendency toward interdependence is more tightly scripted after culturally shared ideologies, customs, and practices, whereas the psychological tendency toward independence is neither strongly constrained nor widely supported by those cultural devices.

Social Engagement and Disengagement as a Dimension of Emotional Experience

If independence and interdependence as cultural tasks are central in social life, especially in defining the self's relationships with relevant others, there must be some close links between these cultural tasks on the one hand, and interpersonal emotions on the other. Indeed, there are several suggestions in the literature that emotions do vary in the degree to which they either engage and connect the self in ongoing relationships, and thereby promote the interdependence of the self with others (social engagement), or disengage and separate the self from such relationships, and thereby promote the independence of the self from others (social disengagement).

Consider, first, emotions such as pride and feelings of superiority. These emotions most typically result from the satisfaction or confirmation of internal attributes, such as goals, desires, or rights (e.g., "I met my goal," "I performed better than others"). Experiencing and expressing these emotions highlights these internal attributes, thereby affirming the identity of the self as an entity that is independent and disengaged from others. By contrast, some other positive emotions, such as communal feelings and feelings of respect, most typically result from having connected with others in relationships. When these feelings are experienced and expressed, certain features of interdependent relationships (e.g., harmony, unity) are highlighted, and the self is perceived as being embedded and assimilated within the relationships. These emotions, then, affirm the sense of the self as an entity that is connected and engaged with others.

The same dimension of social engagement–disengagement can be illustrated for negative emotions as well. Some negative emotions, such as anger and frustration, result most typically from the blocking of goals, desires, or rights (e.g., "I am treated unfairly"), thus imposing a threat to the sense of the self as an independent entity. These emotions, in turn, motivate the person to eliminate the threat and thus to restore and assert the self's independence. This motivational tendency toward independence affirms the sense of the self as an independent, socially disengaged entity. By contrast, some other negative emotions, such as guilt and feelings of indebtedness, result most typically from the failure to participate fully in an ongoing relationship (e.g., "I caused trouble for him") or otherwise to live up to the expectations of relevant others (e.g., "People expected me to do that, but I couldn't do it"), thus posing a threat to the sense of the self as a fully interdependent entity. These emotions, in turn, motivate the person to eliminate the threat by restoring the harmony or unity in the relationship. This motivational tendency toward interdependence reaffirms the sense of the self as an interdependent, socially engaged entity.

Notice that positive disengaged emotions (e.g., pride) are mostly based on a positive evaluation of the self and are thus "self-conscious," whereas positive engaged emotions (e.g., friendly feelings) are largely derived from a positive evaluation of relevant others and are thus "other-conscious." By contrast, negative disengaged emotions (e.g., anger) are based on a negative evaluation of relevant others and are thus "other-conscious," whereas negative engaged emotions (e.g., shame) are characterized by a negative evaluation of the self and thus "self-conscious." In short, quite different patterns of social relationships are inherent in the "self-conscious" and "other-conscious" emotions, depending on their dominant evaluation. Thus, the current formulation of social orientation of emotion provides an alternative analytic framework for the "self-" and "other-conscious" emotions that may prove to be useful for some research purposes. Further below, we argue and present evidence that the social orientation dimension is the key to an analysis of (1) the organization of emotional experience, (2) lay understanding of emotions, and (3) culturally divergent social functions of emotions.

Evidence from Non-Western Cultures

Although the dimension of social engagement–disengagement in emotional experience has so far been relatively neglected in the contemporary psychological literature on emotion, its importance has been suggested by some recent anthropological evidence. For example, Lutz (1988) identified *fago* as a feeling that serves a central function in daily life on the Micronesian atoll of Ifaluk. Glossed as a combination of compassion, love, and sadness, *fago* typically arises in the presence of someone else in need; once induced, it is likely to motivate helping behaviors. *Fago,* in other words, is defined in terms of a highly interdependent relationship and also promotes such a relationship. In Ifaluk, this socially engaged emotion of *fago* is contrasted against a "dangerous, socially disruptive emotion" of *ker,* glossed as a combination of happiness and excitement. A similar distinction between socially engaged emotions and socially disengaged emotions has been suggested by several other anthropological studies on non-Western, especially southern Pacific, communities (e.g., White, 1989; see Lutz & White, 1986, for a review).

The social nature of emotion is also recognized explicitly in another non-Western culture, Japan. As Doi (1973) pointed out, the Japanese language has many vocabularies of emotion that pertain directly to various subtle, yet distinct, aspects of interpersonal relationships. Some both arise from and encourage a cohesive, and often communal, relationship. These include *amae* (a hopeful expectation for another's benevolence and favor, or a sense of indulgent dependence on the other), *sugari* (a desire to lean toward another), and *tanomi* (a desire to rely on others). Also included in this category is *haji* (shame), which is seen by Benedict (1946) as constituting the Japanese "ethos." *Haji* results most typically from the failure to meet expectations of relevant others. It occurs in the presence of others whose opinion a person cares about; once induced, it further highlights the person's indebtedness or inferiority to these others and the ultimate significance of the others to the person. In addition to these socially engaged emotions, there are quite a few emotions that signify social disengagement, including *yuetsukan* (feelings of superiority), *yokkyufuman* (frustration), and *futekusare* (sulky feelings). These disengaged emotions are, in general, socially disapproved and considered undesirable.

The salience of the dimension of social engagement–disengagement in many non-Western cultures has been more directly suggested by Menon & Shweder (1994). They presented respondents from India and the United States with three emotions—anger, shame, and happiness—and asked them to choose the one that was most different from the rest. The Indian respondents chose anger, because this feeling state disrupts interpersonal relationships and is related to separation and disconnection of the self from others in these relationships. This finding is in stark contrast with that for the U.S. respondents, who tended to choose happiness because it is positive and the other two are negative. Thus, for the U.S. respondents, evaluation (positive vs. negative) was a more salient feature of emotion than social orientation. This does not preclude the possibility that the dimension of social orientation is also recognized in the United States and other Western cultures, however. Indeed, there are some suggestions to this effect in the current psychological literature on emotion.

Evidence from Western Cultures

A number of researchers have tested a multidimensional structure underlying perceived similarities among different emotional states (Russell, 1980). These studies typically find two highly robust dimensions: positive versus negative evaluation (or pleasantness) and activation. Yet another replicable dimension often emerges. This dimension has been variously interpreted by different investigators, but, interestingly, many of these interpretations seem to carry some resemblance to the notion of social engagement–disengagement. According to one prominent interpretation, this additional dimension represents the extent of aggression, dominance, or potency (as opposed to submissiveness) (e.g., Bush, 1973; Frijda, 1969; Mehrabian & Russell, 1974; Shaver, Schwartz, Kirson, & O'Connor, 1987). This dimension, however, may be more broadly and fully understood as interpersonal or social in nature. Indeed, the dominance or aggression of the self over others may be typical in the social disengagement of the self, whereas submissiveness may arise from the intention to keep engaged in an ongoing relationship. Some other researchers have explicitly acknowledged this possibility. Thus, Block (1957) identified a dimension of "interpersonal relatedness," and Dittman (1972) named his dimension "trustful versus untrustful." A similar interpersonal dimension has also been suggested more recently by Kemper (1978) and Riesenzein and Hoffman (1990), and further explored in the structure underlying interpersonal personality traits (Wiggins, 1979).

Another interpretation of the third dimension focuses on the object that has "caused" an emotion and therefore toward which the emotion is "directed" (e.g., de Rivera & Grinkis, 1986; Roseman, 1990; Smith & Ellsworth, 1985). This interpretation is similar to the distinction between "self-conscious" and "other-conscious" emotions, insofar as "self-conscious" emotions are largely caused by the self and thus directed toward the self, and "other-conscious" emotions are caused by and directed toward relevant others. As noted earlier, the causal locus or relative salience of self versus other in emotions, on the one hand, and the social orientation as engaged or disengaged, on the other, provide alternative and mutually incompatible ways to interpret the social nature of emotional experience (cf. p. 445). These two interpretations, however, may both be valid, and their theoretical utility may depend on specific analytic purposes.

Structure of Emotional Experience in Japan and the United States

In a recent study, we have obtained more direct evidence for the social orientation dimension of emotion (Kitayama, Markus, & Kurokawa, 1994). We reasoned that if interpersonal configurations defined along the dimension of engagement and disengagement are central in defining the nature of emotional experience, then emotions that share similar interpersonal configurations should co-occur across individuals. That is to say, those who frequently experience some disengaged emotions will also frequently experience other disengaged emotions. Similarly, those frequently experiencing some engaged emotions will also frequently experience some other engaged emotions. In an initial empirical test of this hypothesis, we took a confirmatory approach: We sampled emotions that varied in both dominant evaluation (positive vs. negative) and social orientation, and had respondents report how frequently they experienced those emotions. A matrix of correlations among the emotions, computed over the respondents, was then submitted to a multidimensional scale (MDS) analysis. In this type of analysis, emotions that have a high degree of co-occurrence are located in regions near one another in an n-dimensional space, and those that have a relatively low extent of co-occurrence are placed in regions far apart from one another. We sought to determine whether the two dimensions used in the sampling of the emotions could be reliably recovered in an MDS analysis. Such a result would indicate the empirical validity of the social engagement–disengagement dimension.

Japanese undergraduates at a Japanese university and U.S. undergraduates at a U.S. university reported the frequency of experiencing each of 31 different emotions on a 7-point rating scale (1 = "not at all"; 7 = "always"). A majority of emotions were chosen according to our theoretical classification of emotions on the basis of evaluation and social orientation. First, some emotions are positive and socially disengaged (pride, feelings of superiority, feeling like being at the top of the world). Some other emotions are equally positive and yet socially engaged (friendly feelings, feelings of closeness, feelings of respect). Similarly, some negative emotions are socially disengaged (anger, frustration, sulky feelings), whereas some others are socially engaged (guilt, shame, feelings of indebtedness). Notice, again, that positive disengaged emotions and negative engaged emotions are what may be called the "self-conscious" or "self-caused/directed" emotions, and positive engaged emotions and negative disengaged emotions are what may be called the "other-conscious" or "other-caused/directed" emotions. This design enabled us to compare the relative importance of social orientation versus "self-consciousness" or "other-consciousness" as an organizing dimension of emotional experience.

In both the Japanese and the U.S. data, two dimensions were consistently recovered; moreover, they were unequivocally interpretable as dimensions of evaluation (positive vs. negative) and social orientation. The two-dimensional solutions are illustrated in Figure 18.1A (the Japanese data) and 18.1B (the U.S. data). In these figures, the emotions predesignated into one of the four types are abbreviated in uppercase letters, and other emotions included in this study are abbreviated in lowercase letters. The names for these emotions are given in the list included in each figure caption. We return later to more specific results from the analysis of these latter emotions. For the moment, it is noteworthy that all the predesignated emotions were successfully recovered in the predicted regions on this two-dimensional space. That is to say, the entire space could be segregated into four nonoverlapping areas that corresponded to the four hypothesized types of emotions. Thus, for both cultures disengaged emotions were located in the upper half of the space and engaged emotions in the lower half, whereas positive emotions were located in the left half of the space and negative emotions in the right half. In other words, the vertical dimension defined the social orientation associated with the emotions, and the horizontal dimension defined their dominant evaluation.

These results indicate that emotions indeed co-occur if they are similar in social orientation and evaluation. It is noteworthy that "self-consciousness" or "other-consciousness" of emotions did not emerge as a significant dimension for the co-occurrence pattern. This means that emotions do not co-occur because they share the object of the evaluation (i.e., either the self or the other). Rather, these "self-" or "other-conscious" emotions entail diametrically opposite social orientations, depending on their dominant evaluation. And it is these interpersonal configurations that primarily determine the co-occurrence pattern of the emotions.

Lay Understanding of the Social Nature of Emotion in Japan and the United States

It is reasonable to assume that our own emotional experience becomes an important basis for our understanding about emotions, and that once this

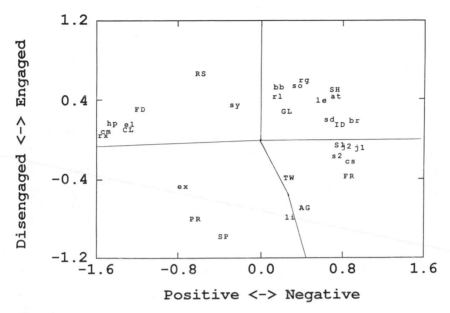

FIGURE 18.1A. The structure of emotional experience: Japanese data. The following abbreviations are used:

Socially engaged positive emotions: **CL**, Feelings of closeness; **FD**, Friendly feelings; **RS**, Feelings of respect.

Socially disengaged positive emotions: **PR**, Pride; **SP**, Feelings of superiority; **TW**, Feeling like being at the top of the world.

Socially engaged negative emotions: **GL**, Guilt; **ID**, Feelings of indebtedness; **SH**, Shame.

Socially disengaged negative emotions: **AG**, Anger; **FR**, Frustration; **S1**, Sulky feelings (strong).

Others: **at**, Afraid of causing trouble for someone; **bb**, Feeling like being babied; **br**, Boredom; **cm**, Calm feelings; **cs**, Feelings of constraint; **el**, Elated feelings; **ex**, Excitement; **hp**, Happiness; **j1**, Jealousy (Higami); **j2**, Jealousy (Shitto); **le**, Feeling like leaning toward someone; **li**, "Licking" someone; **rg**, Resigned feelings; **rl**, Feeling like relying on someone; **rx**, Relaxed feelings; **s2**, Sulky feelings (weak); **sd**, Sadness; **so**, Feeling that one is superficially optimistic; **sy**, Sleepy feelings.

understanding develops, it in turn is incorporated into the very experience of the corresponding emotional states. Accordingly, if social orientation indeed underlies the pattern of emotional experience, this same dimension may also serve as an important element of lay understanding, or folk psychology, of emotion. And once this understanding exists, it may in turn transform the nature of the experience itself.

In another recent study (reported in Markus & Kitayama, 1991b), we investigated this issue in both Japan and the United States. We prepared 20 emotion terms, about half of which were positive and the others negative.

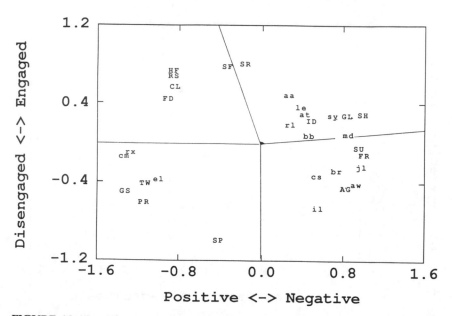

FIGURE 18.1B. The structure of emotional experience: U.S. data. The following abbreviations are used:

Socially engaged positive emotions: **CL**, Feelings of closeness; **FD**, Friendly feelings; **HF**, Feeling happy for someone; **RS**, Feelings of respect.

Socially disengaged positive emotions: **GS**, Feeling good about oneself; **PR**, Pride; **SP**, Feelings of superiority; **TW**, Feeling like being at the top of the world.

Socially engaged negative emotions: **GL**, Guilt; **ID**, Feelings of indebtedness; **SF**, Feeling sad for someone; **SH**, Shame; **SR**, Feeling sorry for someone.

Socially disengaged negative emotions: **AG**, Anger; **FR**, Frustration; **SU**, Sulky feelings.

Others: **aa**, Afraid of angering someone; **at**, Afraid of causing trouble for someone; **aw**, Awkward feelings; **bb**, Feeling like being babied by someone; **br**, Boredom; **cm**, Calm feelings; **cs**, Feelings of constraint; **el**, Elated feelings; **il**, Ill feelings for someone; **jl**, Jealousy; **le**, Feeling like leaning on someone; **md**, Moody; **rl**, Feeling like relying on someone; **rx**, Relaxed feelings; **sy**, Sleepy feelings.

Furthermore, some of the positive emotions were socially engaged (e.g., friendly feelings, feelings of respect), and some others were socially disengaged (e.g., pride, feelings of superiority). Similarly, some of the negative emotions were socially engaged (e.g., shame, guilt) and some others were socially disengaged (e.g., anger, frustration). Subjects were presented with every possible pair of the 20 emotions and asked to judge how similar emotions were for each pair. No specific criteria or standards were given in judging similarities. In this way, we sought to determine what dimensions laypeople *spontaneously* use in understanding and thinking about these emotions.

Mean similarity ratings were computed for all the pairs and submitted to an MDS analysis. Replicating previous work in this area, we found evaluation (or pleasantness) and activation as the first two dimensions. Nevertheless, in both Japan and the United States, a third dimension was recovered reliably. This dimension was defined with the socially engaged emotions (both positive and negative) at one end and the socially disengaged emotions (both positive and negative) at the other end. This is a clear indication that lay individuals, in both the United States and Japan, spontaneously recognize the social orientation of emotion. It also suggests that "self-consciousness" versus "other-consciousness"—whether evaluation is directed to the self or to others—may *not* be habitually acknowledged in lay understanding of emotion. This is another reason why the "self-conscious" emotions can best be understood in conjunction with their "other-conscious" counterparts.

Emotion and the Self

The evidence reviewed above suggests that once individuals experience any given emotion, they will spontaneously recognize the characteristic social orientation this emotion entails, and consequently will anticipate a likely state of the relationship between the self and relevant others in the next moment (viz., whether the self is likely to be more engaged in or more disengaged from the current relationship). This anticipated state of the social relationship primed by the original emotion can, by itself, be a powerful basis for transforming the current emotional state.

Specifically, we have suggested that the self's independence is immediately signified, highlighted in conscious awareness, and affirmed when individuals experience socially disengaged emotions. This will be especially the case when such an emotion is based on a success in independence (e.g., pride); even when it is derived from a threat to independence (e.g., anger), the experience may still affirm the sense of the self as independent, insofar as the emotion motivates individuals to restore their independence. By contrast, the self's interdependence with others is signified and highlighted in conscious awareness when individuals experience socially engaged emotions. Such an emotion may be especially powerful in affirming the identity of self as interdependent if it is positive (e.g., friendly feelings); even when it is negative (e.g., shame), it may still be self-affirming for those with interdependent selves, insofar as the experience prompts the person to restore the harmony in the relationship.

An affirmation of the self or a threat to the self may well induce a broad, more diffuse emotional state within which the initial emotion of social engagement or disengagement is subsumed. Thus, affirmation of the self may result in a general satisfaction or "generic happiness," which arises from the sense that the self is successfully performing the culturally sanctioned task of interdependence (in many Asian cultures) or independence (in Western cultures) and is morally adequate (cf. Steele, 1988). A threat to the self may occasion a general fear or "generic anxiety" of losing the sense of the self as independent or interdependent.

Such satisfaction and fear are "self-conscious" emotions of a special kind. The satisfaction of having affirmed the self, and the fear of having obscured the very definition of "who I am," can be reframed as "existential satisfaction" and "existential fear," respectively. By using the term "existential," we wish to emphasize that this satisfaction and this fear are of a higher order than ordinary emotions. Unlike the latter, they are detached from any specific instances or episodes; instead, they respond to the identity of the self rooted broadly in these specific stances or episodes in social life. In general, both the higher-order satisfaction in interdependence and social engagement and the higher-order fear of excessive social disengagement will characterize those with an interdependent construal of self, whereas the higher-order satisfaction in independence and social disengagement and the higher-order fear of excessive social engagement will be more typical of those with an independent construal of self. For the interdependent self, the cultural nightmare is to be excluded; for the independent self, it is not to be noticed, or to be so engaged that one is merely a cog in a giant wheel (Markus & Kitayama, 1991a). And such higher-order satisfaction and fear may serve as strong motivators or regulators of a variety of social behaviors.

SOCIAL FUNCTIONS OF EMOTIONS: A CROSS-CULTURAL ANALYSIS

When Do We Feel "Unconditionally Good"?

To examine existential satisfaction or generic, high-order happiness, we carried out a number of studies on the links between positive feelings and self-esteem. Generic positive feelings are assumed to result either from emotions of social engagement (for those with interdependent selves) or from emotions of social disengagement (for those with independent selves). In the previously mentioned study on emotional experience in Japan and the United States (Kitayama et al., 1994), we explored this issue by including in the study some positive emotions that are general in their social orientations, such as calm, relaxed, and elated feelings. In addition, happiness was examined in Japan.[2] These positive feelings are quite general in the range of social situations to which they can be applied—much more so than the positive emotions with specific social orientation of the self as engaged (e.g., friendly feelings) or disengaged (e.g., pride). We hypothesized, therefore, that the generic positive emotions feel "unconditionally good" (at least with respect to the social orientation dimension) to a degree that friendly feelings and pride do not. We then hoped to analyze the nature of circumstances in which individuals feel these "unconditionally good" emotional states across cultures.

The MDS analysis reported earlier (Figures 18.1A and 18.1B) demonstrated that socially engaged positive emotions and socially disengaged positive emotions form distinct clusters in both cultures. Hence, we averaged the reported frequencies of experiencing positive emotions of each kind, and correlated the mean frequency of experiencing these emotions with each of the generic positive emotions tested here. The correlations are summarized in Table 18.1. In Japan, all the generic positive emotions consistently had very high correlations with the socially engaged positive emotions, but the corresponding correlations with the socially disengaged positive emotions were much weaker. This pattern was completely reversed in the United States: The socially disengaged positive emotions had much higher correlations with each of the three generic positive emotions tested here than did the socially engaged positive emotions. This can be interpreted to mean that in Japan generic happiness is more clearly associated with social engagement, whereas in the United States happiness is more clearly related to disengagement. (Notice, however, that in the U.S. data the correlations between the positive engaged emotions and the generic positive positive feelings were still substantial—a point to which we return later.) These findings are mirrored in Figures 18.1A and 18.1B, which show that the generic feelings formed a cluster in each case, but the location of this cluster was different for each culture. As we expected, for Japan the generic positive feelings were located in the quadrant of socially engaged positive emotions, but for the United States they were found in the quadrant of socially disengaged positive emotions.

TABLE 18.1. Correlations between Generic Positive Feelings and Positive Emotions Varying in Social Orientation (Disengaged and Engaged) in Two Cultures

	Japan		United States	
	Men	Women	Men	Women
Correlation between the positive disengaged emotions and:				
Elated feelings	.39	.30	.58	.62
Relaxed feelings	.25	.06	.66	.68
Calm feelings	.15	.10	.61	.59
Happiness	.34	.27	—	—
Combined	.29	.13	.58	.49
Correlation between the positive engaged emotions and:				
Elated feelings	.80	.81	.06	.30
Relaxed feelings	.71	.68	.33	.30
Calm feelings	.54	.46	.38	.29
Happiness	.81	.79	—	—
Combined	.57	.58	.35	.37

Note. From Kitayama, Markus, and Kurokawa (1994).

"Self-Esteem" and Emotion

A construct that is central in personality and social psychology and that is directly related to the notion of "feeling good" is self-esteem. In the current literature, "self-esteem" is operationalized as the total of good feelings directed to the self—that is, the sum of positive socially disengaged and "self-conscious" emotions (e.g., pride) (for reviews, see Epstein, 1973; Harter & Marold, 1991; Rosenberg, 1979). Thus, the most widely used scale of self-esteem (devised by Rosenberg, 1979) carries items such as "I feel that I'm a person of worth," "I feel that I have a number of good qualities," "I feel I do not have much to be proud of" [a reverse item], and the like. Because feeling good about one's own internal attributes (experiencing socially disengaged positive feelings, such as pride) is only one of many potential ways in which one can "feel good," self-esteem as defined in this current literature is a more restricted construct than the generic happiness or existential satisfaction we have described here.

In what follows, we use the term "self-esteem" in its restricted, more conventional sense and distinguish it from existential satisfaction. Our findings reviewed above indicate that "self-esteem" (as a sum of socially disengaged positive feelings) was closely related to existential satisfaction only among independent selves. Among interdependent selves, it was the nature of social relationships (as revealed in the experience of socially engaged positive emotions) that had a direct impact on the generic positive feelings. "Self-esteem" therefore may be less central among interdependent individuals. It is our hypothesis that just as "self-esteem" is central to the affirmation of the identity of the self as independent, "esteem" or satisfaction with one's social relationships may be pivotal to the affirmation of the identity of the self as interdependent. Bluntly put, what the esteemed inner attributes of the self are to independent selves may be what the esteemed social relationships are to interdependent selves.

This does not imply, however, that "self-esteem" is totally unimportant among interdependent selves, let alone nonexistent. Because we know that socially disengaged (or "self-conscious") positive emotions (e.g., pride) can be identified in many cultures, we also expect that cultural categories analogous to this Western construct of "self-esteem" can be found across a wide range of cultures. In Japan, for example, there is a commonly used notion of *jison-shin,* which literally means "the feeling of self-respect." Our argument does imply, however, that the structure of "self-esteem" and its broader functions in social life may vary considerably across cultures (Kitayama, Markus, & Lieberman, 1994). More specifically, among interdependent cultures, self-esteem may be less central in constructing the self, and it may be more interpersonally based than is the case in independent cultures. Interdependent selves may be more likely to use interpretations of the situation or expectations held by relevant others in determining their own performance or behavior. As a consequence, their success or failure (and hence "self-esteem") may depend primarily on the standards or criteria held by the relevant others or the perceived expectations of these others. By contrast, independent selves may mostly use their own interpretations and construals of the relevant situation and the task to determine their own performance. Consequently, their perception of success or failure in a given situation (and hence "self-esteem") may depend primarily on their own standards or criteria of excellence in the task.

In our initial exploration of this issue, we (Kitayama, Markus, Sugiman, Takagi, & Matsumoto, 1992) asked both Japanese and U.S. undergraduates to list either (1) as many situations as possible, up to 30 different ones, in which their self-esteem (*jison-shin* in Japanese) was enhanced (the "success" condition); or (2) as many situations as possible in which their self-esteem was impaired (the "failure" condition). In both cultures, subjects were tested in small groups of 3 to 15 individuals; they were given 25 minutes for this listing task. More than 90% of the listed situations could be reliably coded into one of three generic categories: self-appraisal, other-appraisal, or social comparison. "Self-appraisal" refers to situations in which self-esteem is influenced as a result of one's own actions or characteristics and/or one's own evaluation of these actions or characteristics. The typical example is to succeed or fail to achieve one's own goals. "Other-appraisal" includes cases in which self-esteem is influenced as a result of other people's behavior to the self or their evaluation of the self. The typical example is to receive positive or negative remarks from friends. Finally, "social comparison" involves evaluation of the self's attributes, behavior, or performance alongside those of others. In general, we predicted that in the United States self-appraisals should be more prominent than other-appraisals, whereas in Japan other-appraisals should be more important than self-appraisals.

The proportions of each category for the two cultures are summarized in Table 18.2. There are three important findings. First, both U.S. and Japanese subjects used many more self-appraisals than other-appraisals in the success condition. Second, in the failure condition there was a striking

TABLE 18.2. Percentage of the Situations Generated by Japanese and U.S. Respondents in Each of Three Categories: Self-Appraisal, Other-Appraisal, and Social Comparison

	Self-appraisal	Other-appraisal	Social comparison
Japan			
Success	52.3	27.1	16.6
Failure	28.4	52.2	14.3
United States			
Success	56.1	27.9	4.8
Failure	45.5	38.4	9.1

Note. From Kitayama, Markus, Sugiman, Takagi, and Matsumoto (1992).

difference between the two cultures: Whereas the U.S. subjects used more self-appraisals than other-appraisals, Japanese subjects used far more other-appraisals than self-appraisals. Third, although social comparisons were a minor determinant of self-esteem in both cultures, they were relatively more prominent in Japan than in the United States. In short, these data showed, as predicted, that among those with predominantly independent selves (i.e., in the United States), self-appraisals were far more common than other-appraisals. Among those with predominantly interdependent selves (i.e., in Japan), however, other-appraisals were more prominent, especially in assessing failure.

If, as in the U.S. case, "self-esteem" depends primarily on one's own appraisal of the self, it may be relatively easy to maintain or enhance it by, say, defining, revising, or even contriving the current situation in a self-serving manner. Consistent with this analysis, it has been repeatedly found that "self-esteem," as measured by the currently available instruments, is in general significantly lower in many non-Western populations than in Western populations (e.g., Crocker, Luhtanen, Blaine, & Broadnax, in press; Diener & Diener, 1993). Furthermore, a number of studies in North America have demonstrated what may be called a "self-serving bias" in social judgment (e.g., Gilovich, 1983; Harter, 1990; Lau, 1984; Miller, 1986; Wylie, 1979; Whitely & Frieze, 1985; Zuckerman, 1979). Individuals tend to take credit for success and to discount their failure by explaining it in terms of external factors. They also think that a certain domain is important to themselves if they succeed in that domain; if they fail, the personal importance of the domain is discounted (Brown & Taylor, 1991). And a vast majority of people in the United States tend to believe that they are better than average in a variety of different areas (e.g., Myers, 1987).

If, however, "self-esteem" is socially afforded and constrained rather than individually constructed and controlled, many of the self-serving biases demonstrated in the United States may not be manifested in Japan (Kitayama et al., 1994). Available evidence suggests that this in fact is the case. In one study, we asked U.S. and Japanese undergraduates to estimate the proportion of students in their respective universities who were better than themselves in a variety of different domains (Markus & Kitayama, 1991b). Our sample was fairly representative of the population in each university. As a result, to the extent that each respondent made the estimate without any systematic bias, the overall mean estimate should converge to 50%. In the U.S. sample, we found the overall means (varying between 30% and 40%) to be significantly less than 50%, suggesting that they, as a group, were biased to emphasize that they were uniquely good. In the Japanese sample, however, we failed to find any evidence whatever for such an effect. The averages converged to 50% in most of the domains examined. Similar

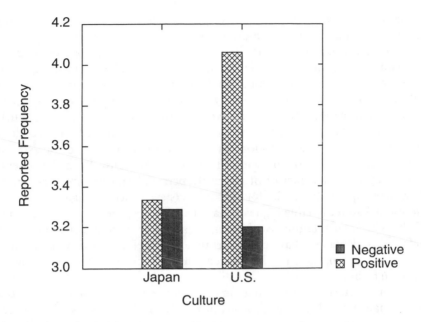

FIGURE 18.2. Differences in the reported frequency of experiencing positive versus negative emotions in Japan and the United States.

findings have also been reported by Heine and Lehman (1994; see Markus & Kitayama, 1991a, for a review).

Additional evidence was obtained in the aforementioned study on emotional experience in Japan and the United States (Kitayama et al., 1993). Although the general structure of emotional experience was quite similar across cultures (Figures 18.1A and 18.1B), there was considerable cultural difference in the frequency of experiencing the emotions. The most powerful effect concerned the dominant evaluation (positive vs. negative) of emotion. As shown in Figure 18.2, in the United States positive emotions were reportedly experienced far more frequently than negative emotions, but this difference was entirely absent in Japan. These findings suggest a strong motivation to elaborate and emphasize positive emotional experience in the United States, but not in Japan.

Interestingly, this effect was observed for socially engaged emotions as well. Thus, it was the U.S. rather than the Japanese subjects who reportedly experienced such engaged emotions as friendly feelings and feelings of respect most frequently. This finding might seem to contradict our hypothesis that many people in the United States strive primarily for social disengagement. This curious finding, however, may suggest that the exact manner in which socially engaged emotions are constructed is quite different

458   CROSS-CULTURAL PERSPECTIVES

in the respective cultures. Specifically, from an interdependent (i.e., Japanese) perspective, these engaged emotions arise in a mutually engaging social relationship, in which the participants exchange mutually positive appraisals. Thus, one cannot feel "truly" friendly or respectful without recognizing reciprocation of similar appraisals from the others. In interdependent cultures, therefore, positive socially engaged feelings (as well as "self-esteem") may be socially and collectively afforded and constrained to a much larger extent than may be the case in independent cultures. In independent cultures, these engaged emotions may also arise as a result of one's own positive appraisal of others without reciprocal response from the others; thus, they may be a matter of primarily personal and private experience. This may explain, first, why for U.S. subjects even socially engaged positive emotions had reasonably high correlations with the generic positive feelings (Table 18.1). Furthermore, without many social or external constraints, our U.S. respondents may have consequently elaborated any positive emotional states (either engaged or disengaged), insofar as they afforded generic positive feelings.

This pattern suggests that among people in the United States, the maintenance of self-esteem depends primarily on the self's own interpretations of the relevant situation, its own standards or criteria for excellence, and so on. The system of self-esteem maintenance, in other words, is relatively autonomous. Thus, one can self-servingly and self-protectively choose the most convenient one of several potentially possible interpretations of a situation, or can adopt evaluative criteria that emphasize certain domains of self-evaluation over others. Furthermore, the experience of socially disengaged positive emotions is highly self-affirming for those with independent selves. Hence, there is likely to emerge an endless elevation of self-esteem based on a variety of cognitive maneuvers, especially in the absence of any reality check.

By contrast, among people in Japan, evaluation of the self (especially evaluation of failures) is derived from opinions, evaluations, or expectations held by relevant others. The system of self-esteem maintenance, in other words, is interpersonally more constrained. Furthermore, the experience of socially disengaged positive emotions is not especially self-affirming for those with interdependent selves. Hence, there is neither high motivation nor enough realistic means to engage in cognitive protection or enhancement of "self-esteem."

CONCLUSIONS

In this chapter we have presented a cultural view of emotion. Emotions are action-oriented, script-like structures that simultaneously respond both to the external situation and to internal sensations (cf. Kitayama & Markus, 1994). Emotional experience is both constituted by and constitutive of social relationships. From this point of view, emotions should differ in accordance with one major dimension of the social content—namely, the assumption and practice of independence or of interdependence. We have argued and presented evidence that emotions in fact vary in the degree either to which they engage and connect the self in ongoing relationships, and thereby promote the interdependence of the self with others (social engagement), or to which they disengage and separate the self from such relationships, and thereby promote the independence of the self from the relationships (social disengagement). We have suggested that "self-conscious" emotions and "other-conscious" emotions have remarkably divergent social functions along this social orientation dimension. We have also pointed out that taking this social dimension into account makes it possible to shed some new light on cross-culturally divergent organizations of emotional processes.

Specifically, experiencing a socially disengaged (or engaged) emotion will signal further disengagement (or engagement) of the self from (with) relevant others. This anticipated disengagement (engagement) of the self may then be either self-affirming (thus resulting in a generic happiness—existential satisfaction) or self-threatening (thus resulting in a generic fear of obscuring or losing the self), depending on the dominant identity of the self as independent or interdependent. This point has been illustrated with our own work on generic positive feelings and "self-esteem."

The present analysis may entail additional implications. For example, Tangney, Wagner, Fletcher, and Gramzow (1992) have examined U.S. respondents and found that shame is often readily transformed into anger. We suggest that this transformation may be a culturally scripted, and thus culturally shared, collective strategy of defending the identity of the self as independent. In U.S. culture, with its dominant construal of the self as independent, the experience of shame—characterized by social engagement with a complete loss of personal control—may lend itself to a strong fear or anxiety of a higher order (existential fear). One strategy to reduce this existential fear without distorting the dominant evaluation associated with the current situation (i.e., negative) is to cognitively reframe or even socially and behaviorally manage the situation so as to redirect the negative affect away from the self to others, thus producing a more self-affirming state of social disengagement.

We further speculate that the collective strategy of self-defense involving the transformation of shame to anger may be relatively uncommon in other, more interdependent cultures, where social engagement does not pose as much threat to the self as in U.S. culture. Moreover, it would seem reasonable that in these cultures, socially disengaged emotions (e.g., pride and anger), rather than shame, may pose an important threat to self-identity and thereby may initiate analogous strategies of self-defense. It is not unreasonable, for example, to expect that these socially disengaged emotions may be effectively transformed into some other emotional states of a socially engaging nature. A recent observation by White (1989) in the Solomon Islands provides one illustration. He describes a collectively shared social ritual seemingly designed to change a "dangerous" emotion of anger arising from a dispute in a village to collective sadness. Similarly, Menon and Shweder (1994) provide a convincing ethnographic case that in Hindu India, an emotion of *lajya* (glossed as shame) is experienced as a highly desirable state of social engagement that functions primarily as a check against a burst of anger.

Despite these initial suggestions, the currently available empirical evidence about culture-specific organizations of emotion and defense strategies is still rudimentary and largely limited to a few isolated examples. Yet further work along this line seems crucial in advancing the understanding of emotion as a sociocultural product and process. And the current analysis based on the social orientation of emotion, in conjunction with an analysis of cultural structures in terms of two central social tasks of independence and interdependence, may prove to be useful in this endeavor.

ACKNOWLEDGMENT

The present work was supported by a National Science Foundation grant (BNS-9010754). We would like to thank Stephen Ahadi, Joe Dien, Angela Simon, and June Tangney for their helpful comments on an early draft of this chapter.

NOTES

1.   Hence, in the United States the intentions to be socially engaged are often highly valued and highlighted at the level of individual consciousness. For example, Howard and Kitayama (1992) examined free self-descriptions of U.S. undergraduates, and found that interdependence-related traits were six to eight times as likely to appear in these self-descriptions as independence-related traits. This was the case despite the fact that these two types of traits were roughly equally available in both the English language and each subject's memory. Similarly, Schwartz (1992) reports a close association between values of independence and prosocial values. This somewhat paradoxically strong endorsement of prosocial values in the United States may reflect the hierarchical organization of an independent culture, where tasks of interdependence are defined primarily as individual-level activities, and therefore are neither prescribed nor enforced collectively.

2.   Happiness was not tested in the United States, because "feeling happy for someone" was included in the U.S. list as one of the socially engaged positive emotions.

REFERENCES

Averill, J. R. (1982). *Anger and aggression: An essay on emotion.* New York: Springer-Verlag.

Benedict, R. (1946). *The chrysanthenum and the sword: Patterns of Japanese culture.* Boston: Houghton Mifflin.

Berman, J. J. (Ed.). (1989). *Nebraska Symposium on Motivation: Vol. 37. Cross-cultural perspectives.* Lincoln: University of Nebraska Press.

Block, J. (1957). Studies of the phenomenology of emotions. *Journal of Abnormal and Social Psychology, 54,* 358–363.

Bruner, J. (1990). *Acts of meaning.* Cambridge, MA: Harvard University Press.

Bush, L. E., II. (1973). Individual differences multidimensional scaling of adjectives denoting feelings. *Journal of Personality and Social Psychology, 25,* 50–57.

Crocker, J., Luhtanen, R., Blaine, B., & Broadnax, S. (in press). Collective self-esteem and psychological well-being among white, black, and Asian college students. *Personality and Social Psychology Bulletin.*

Davidson, R. J., & Cacioppo, J. T. (1992). New developments in the scientific study of emotion: An introduction to the special section. *Psychological Science, 3,* 21–22.

de Rivera, J., & Grinkis, C. (1986). Emotions as social relationships. *Motivation and Emotion, 10,* 351–369.

Derryberry, D., & Tucker, D. M. (1991). The adaptive base of the neural hierarchy: Elementary motivational controls on network function. In R. Dienstbier (Ed.), *Nebraska Symposium on Motivation: Vol. 38. Perspectives on motivation* (pp. 289–342). Lincoln: University of Nebraska Press.

Diener, E., & Diener, M. (1993). *Cross-cultural correlates of life satisfaction and self-esteem.* Unpublished manuscript, University of Illinois, Urbana–Champaign.

Dittman, A. T. (1972). *Interpersonal messages of emotion.* New York: Springer.

Doi, L. T. (1973). *The anatomy of dependence.* Tokyo: Kodansha.

Ekman, P. (1984). Expression and the nature of emotion. In K. Scherer & P. Ekman (Eds.), *Approaches to emotion* (pp. 319–344). Hillsdale, NJ: Erlbaum.

Epstein, S. (1973). The self-concept revisited, or a theory of a theory. *American Psychologist, 28,* 405–416.

Fiske, A. P. (1991). *Making up society: The four basic relational studies.* New York: Free Press.

Frijda, N. H. (1969). Recognition of emotion. In L. Berkowitz (Ed.), *Advances in experimental social psychology* (Vol. 4, pp. 167–223). New York: Academic Press.

Gilovich, T. (1983). Biased evaluation and persistence in gambling. *Journal of Personality and Social Psychology, 40,* 797–808.

Harter, S. (1990). Causes, correlates and the functional role of global self-worth: A life span perspective. In R. J. Sternberg & J. Kolligian, Jr. (Eds.), *Competence considered* (pp. 67–97). New Haven, CT: Yale University Press.

Harter, S., & Marold, D. B. (1991). A model of the determinants and mediational role of self-worth: Implications for adolescent depression and suicidal ideation. In G. R. Goethals & J. Strauss (Eds.), *Multidisciplinary perspectives on the self* (pp. 66–92). New York: Springer-Verlag.

Heine, S. J., & Lehman, D. R. (1994). *Cultural variation in unrealistic optimism: Is the West more invulnerable than the East?* Unpublished manuscript, University of British Columbia, Vancouver, British Columbia, Canada.

Holland, D., & Quinn, N. (1987). *Cultural models in language and thought.* Cambridge, England: Cambridge University Press.

Howard, S., & Kitayama, S. (1992). *Structural differences between independence and interdependence as American cultural values.* Proceedings of the conference on emotion and culture, University of Oregon, Eugene, OR.

Kemper, T. D. (1978). *A social interaction theory of emotions.* New York: Wiley.

Kitayama, S., & Markus, H. R. (Eds.). (1994). *Emotion and culture: Empirical studies of mutual influence.* Washington, DC: American Psychological Association Press.

Kitayama, S., Markus, H. R., & Kurokawa, M. (1994). *Cultural views of self and emotional experience. Does the nature of good feelings depend on culture?* Unpublished manuscript, Kyoto University, Kyoto, Japan.

Kitayama, S., Markus, H. R., & Lieberman, C. (1994, May). *Self-esteem and the collective construction of social reality: Implications for culture, self, and emotion.* Paper presented at the NATO advanced research workshop on everyday conceptions of emotions, Almagro, Spain.

Kitayama, S., Markus, H. R., Sugiman, T., Takagi, H., & Matsumoto, H. (1992). *Culture and self-esteem.* Paper presented at the biennial meeting of the International Society of Cross-Cultural Studies, Liege, Belgium.

Lau, R. R. (1984). Dynamics of the attribution process. *Journal of Personality and Social Psychology, 46,* 1017–1028.

LeDoux, J. E. (1987). Emotion. In F. Plum (Ed.), *Handbook of physiology: Section 1. The nervous system.* (Vol. 1, pp. 419–459). Bethesda, MD: American Physiological Society.

Lutz, C. (1988). *Unnatural emotions: Everyday sentiments on a Micronesian atoll and their challenge to Western theory.* Chicago: University of Chicago Press.

Lutz, C., & White, G. M. (1986). The anthropology of emotions. *Annual Review of Anthropology, 15,* 405–436.

Markus, H. R., & Kitayama, S. (1991a). Culture and the self: Implications for cognition, emotion, and motivation. *Psychological Review, 98,* 224–253.

Markus, H. R., & Kitayama, S. (1991b). Cultural variation in self-concept. In G. R. Goethals & J. Strauss (Eds.), *Multidisciplinary perspectives on the self* (pp. 18–48). New York: Springer-Verlag.

Markus, H. R., & Kitayama, S. (1992). The what, why, and how of cultural psychology: A review of Shweder's *Cultural psychology: Thinking through cultures. Psychological Inquiry, 3,* 357–364.

Mehrabian, A., & Russell, J. A. (1974). *An approach to environmental psychology.* Cambridge, MA: MIT Press.

Menon, U., & Shweder, R. A. (1994). Kali's tongue: Cultural psychology and the power of shame in Orissa, India. In S. Kitayama & H. R. Markus (Eds.), *Emotion and culture: Empirical studies of mutual influence.* Washington, DC: American Psychological Association Press.

Miller, J. B. (1986). *Toward a new psychology of women* (2nd ed.). Boston: Beacon Press.

Myers, D. (1987). *Social psychology* (2nd ed.). New York: McGraw-Hill.

Riesenzein, R., & Hoffman, T. (1990). An investigation of dimensions of cognitive appraisal in emotion using the repertory grid technique. *Motivation and Emotion, 14,* 1–26.

Rosenberg, M. (1979). *Conceiving the self.* New York: Basic Books.

Rosenberger, N. R. (Ed.). (1993). *Japanese sense of self.* New York: Cambridge University Press.

Russell, J. A. (1980). A circumplex model of affect. *Journal of Personality and Social Psychology, 39,* 1161–1178.

Sampson, E. E. (1985). The decentralization of identity: Toward a revised concept of personal and social order. *American Psychologist, 40,* 1203–1211.

Sampson, E. E. (1988). The debate on individualism: Indigenous psychologies of the individual and their role in personal and societal functioning. *American Psychologist, 43,* 15–22.

Schwartz, S. (1992). Universals in the content and structures of values: Theoretical advances and empirical tests in 20 countries. In M. Zanna (Ed.), *Advances in experimental social psychology* (Vol. 25, pp. 16– 65). San Diego: Academic Press.

Shaver, P., Schwartz, J., Kirson, D., & O'Connor, C. (1987). Emotion knowledge: Further exploration of a prototype approach. *Journal of Personality and Social Psychology, 52,* 1061–1086.

Shweder, R. A. (1991). *Cultural psychology: Thinking through cultures.* Cambridge, MA: Harvard University Press.

Shweder, R. A., & Bourne, E. J. (1984). Does the concept of the person vary cross-culturally? In R. A. Shweder & R. A. LeVine (Eds.), *Culture theory: Essays on mind, self, and emotion* (pp. 158–199). Cambridge, England: Cambridge University Press.

Smith, C. A., & Ellsworth, P. C. (1985). Patterns of cognitive appraisal in emotion. *Journal of Personality and Social Psychology, 48,* 813–838.

Steele, C. (1988). The psychology of self-affirmation: Sustaining the integrity of the self. In L. Berkowitz (Ed.), *Advances in experimental social psychology* (Vol. 21, pp. 181–227). San Diego: Academic Press.

Tangney, J. P., Wagner, P., Fletcher, C., & Gramzow, R. (1992). Shamed into anger? The relation of shame and guilt to anger and self-reported aggression. *Journal of Personality and Social Psychology, 62,* 669–675.

Tomkins, S. S. (1963). *Affect, imagery, and consciousness: Vol. 2. The negative affects.* New York: Springer.

Triandis, H. C. (1989). The self and social behavior in differing cultural contexts. *Psychological Review, 96,* 506–520.

White, G. M. (1989). Moral discourse and the rhetoric of emotions. In C. A. Lutz & L. Abu-Lushod (Eds.), *Language and the politics of emotion* (pp. 46–68). Cambridge, England: Cambridge University Press.

Whitely, B. E., & Frieze, I. H. (1985). Children's causal attributions for success and failure in achievement settings: A meta-analysis. *Journal of Educational Psychology, 77,* 608–616.

Wiggins, J. S. (1979). A psychological taxonomy of trait-descriptive terms: The interpersonal domain. *Journal of Personality and Social Psychology, 37,* 395–412.

Wylie, R. (1979). *The self-concept: Vol. 2. Theory and research on selected topics.* Lincoln: University of Nebraska Press.

Zajonc, R. B., Murphy, S. T., & Inglehart, M. (1989). Feeling and facial efference:

Implications of the vascular theory of emotion. *Psychological Review, 96,* 395–416.

Zuckerman, M. (1979). Attribution of success and failure revisited, or: The motivational bias is alive and well in attribution theory. *Journal of Personality, 47,* 245–287.

19

Cultural Determinants in Experiencing Shame and Guilt

HARALD G. WALLBOTT
KLAUS R. SCHERER

The aim of this chapter is twofold: first, to examine whether the self-reflective emotions shame and guilt differ with respect to subjective experience; second, to test for cultural differences in the experience of shame and guilt. After some theoretical approaches attempting to differentiate between these two self-conscious emotions are presented, and possible cultural influence factors on the experience of emotion are discussed, data from a cross-national questionnaire study of 2,921 subjects from 37 countries are presented. We analyze shame–guilt differences with respect to the evaluation of emotion-eliciting situations, causality attributions, reported physiological symptoms, and expressive reactions, and a number of other characteristics of subjective emotional experience. We also analyze the influence of the predominance of certain values in cultures on shame and guilt experiences.

Given the problems (to be discussed below) with separating shame from guilt on the basis of theoretical criteria, the approach taken in the present chapter is a strictly empirical one. We attempt to study the differences between shame and guilt experiences and possible effects of cultural differences by analyzing emotional experiences of shame and guilt as labeled and reported by subjects in different countries. We do not restrict ourselves to specific hypotheses that could be developed from one or another of the

465

theories presented below. Instead, we try to address the following questions in an empirical fashion, relying on a rather large empirical data base:

- Does the subjective experience of shame and guilt differ with respect to evaluations of the eliciting situations and with respect to emotional reactions?
- Are there differences among cultures in the experience of shame and guilt? If so, what underlying factors can be identified to group or classify cultures with respect to these differences?

ARE SHAME AND GUILT PRIMARY EMOTIONS?

Many disciplines are concerned with the emotions of shame and guilt. Moral theorists, philosophers, and theologians examine the important role of these two emotions in social conduct or in the "process of civilization." Anthropologists describe the function of these two emotions in different societies, to the point of classifying cultures with respect to the differential importance of these emotions into "shame cultures" and "guilt cultures" (see below). Psychologists discuss whether or not shame and guilt are primary emotions, and what antecedents and reactions accompany these states. However, despite the large amount of literature on this topic, the differential definition of both states remains fuzzy. We mention just a few attempts here:

1. *Shame and guilt as symptoms of an underlying variable.* Some authors claim that shame has to be considered as just a symptom of the more fundamental emotion of guilt (Carroll, 1985). Guilt, in turn, is considered as a specific type of anxiety—either anxiety stimulated by the fear of conscience, before an act has been committed, or anxiety stimulated by an enraged conscience following an action (Carroll, 1985).

2. *Shame and guilt as not primary emotions.* Others (e.g., Ortony, 1987) discuss the multifaceted meaning of guilt (e.g., guilt in the legal sense vs. "feeling guilty"), and arrive at the conclusion that guilt should not be considered a primary emotion. Ekman (1972) considers neither shame nor guilt to be a primary emotion, because no specific facial expressions for these two states have been identified.

3. *Shame and guilt as primary emotions.* For Izard (1977), on the other hand, shame is a primary emotion that is caused by intense attention toward the self, especially its shortcomings and deficits. This conceptualization is related to Buss's (1980) distinction between public self-consciousness and private self-consciousness—that is, whether the focus of attention is directed toward the self (similar to Duval & Wicklund's [1972] concept of objective self-awareness) or is directed toward other persons' reactions to and perceptions of the self or its behavior. Similarly, Modigliani (1971) conceptualizes shame (or embarrassment) as an acute momentary loss of self-esteem. Darwin (1872/1965) described specific reaction patterns accompany-

ing the two emotions (especially shame). Here are a few citations for shame: "blinking the eyelids" (p. 321), "restless movements in the eyes, eyes averted or cast down" (p. 321, 329), "little cough" (p. 32), "turning away the whole body, more especially the face" (p. 320), "avert, bend down" (p. 328), "awkward, nervous movements" (p. 329), and "blushing" (pp. 69, 329).

PROPOSED DIFFERENCES BETWEEN SHAME AND GUILT

In an attempt to study differences between shame and guilt, Wicker, Payne, and Morgan (1983) found that shame seems to be a more intense emotion than guilt in being related to feelings of weakness, helplessness, and a strong (negative) effect on self-esteem. One criterion for distinguishing between these emotions thus seems to be the intensity of the emotional experience. This criterion may be doubted, because it implies that quantitative changes in emotion qualitatively differentiate them. Furthermore, it is not clear at which point on the intensity continuum the qualitative jump from guilt to shame should occur.

One popular distinction between shame and guilt is based on contrasting external and internal sanctions. This view has been advanced especially by anthropologists like Margaret Mead (1937) and Ruth Benedict (1946). Mead defined such sanctions as "mechanisms by which conformity is obtained, by which desired behavior is induced, and undesired behavior prevented" (1937, p. 493). "Shame cultures" are said to regulate the behavior of their members via external sanctions. In "guilt cultures," on the other hand, such sanctions are internalized; guilt can therefore be elicited in situations where no other persons are present, or even when no other people know about the event. Thus, shame cultures regulate social conduct via compliance and external pressure on the individual, whereas guilt cultures do the same via internalization (in psychoanalytic terms, the superego). Johnson et al. (1987, p. 359) summarize this view in stating, "[Shame] results from the existence of a real or imagined audience (or observer) of one's misdeed, while guilt generally is defined as a feeling of negative self-regard associated with the real or imagined commission of an act, without any need for an audience." In the anthropological literature, there is a definite tendency to identify "primitive" cultures as shame cultures and "modern" Western cultures as guilt cultures.

Though this distinction may seem plausible, it can be criticized for a number of reasons (see Piers & Singer, 1971). First, shame may also occur when no audience is physically present. Second, some "internal" sanctions associated with guilt, such as fear of loss of status or loss of love, seem very closely related to shame sanctions. Third, there is strong empirical evidence that the "sense of guilt is to be found in most, if not all cultures" (Piers & Singer, 1971, p. 85; see also Heider, 1991). Thus, a distinction between the two emotions based solely on the location of sanctions seems to be inadequate.

Piers and Singer (1971) propose another approach to distinguishing between shame and guilt. On the basis of psychoanalytic theory, they characterize shame as the "anxiety aroused by failure to live up to internalized parental ideas under the unconscious threat of abandonment" and guilt as the "anxiety aroused by transgression of internalized parental prohibitions under the unconscious threat of mutilation" (p. 97). Thus, guilt is characterized by a transgression of rules and norms, whereas shame is experienced when certain goals or standards are not reached. In psychoanalytic terms, shame is a result of the conflict between the ego and the ego ideal. Guilt, on the other hand, is seen as arising out of a conflict between the ego and the superego. This conceptualization seems quite straightforward, especially from a psychoanalytic point of view. But we might argue that the distinction becomes somewhat vague, if we consider, for instance, that reaching or fulfilling goals and standards may be a rule or norm within an individual, a group, or even a culture. Not fulfilling standards should result in shame, according to Piers and Singer (1971), but if "fulfilling standards" is a norm, the resulting emotion should be guilt. In fact, psychoanalysis does not totally separate the superego from the ego ideal, and sometimes even considers the ego ideal a part of the superego (see Laplanche & Pontalis, 1967); this makes it difficult to predict shame and guilt.

We have mentioned three criteria discussed in the literature as being relevant to the distinction between shame and guilt: intensity; external versus internal sanctions; and transgression of norms versus not reaching standards. All of these approaches may be criticized for different reasons. But, irrespective of the specific definitions of these emotions, it should be clear from our discussion that the experience of both shame and guilt requires the attainment of a specific developmental stage with appropriate cognitive abilities. Thus, it is not surprising that some studies indicate that shame and guilt experiences (contrary to the experiences of other primary emotions, such as joy, sadness, or anger) appear only at later stages of development—specifically, between 3 and 5 years of age, when the necessary structures of self-identity, superego, the understanding of social norms and rules, and achievement motivation are developed (cf. Buss, 1980). This in turn suggests that the experience of shame and guilt should differ depending on cultural factors, such as reliance on social norms, group pressures, or educational techniques.

THE SEARCH FOR CULTURAL INFLUENCE FACTORS

In the study of differences among cultures, it is increasingly obvious that psychologically relevant dimensions should be identified to serve as independent variables in this research (Sears, 1970; Foschi & Hales, 1979; Jahoda, 1980; Hofstede & Bond, 1984). Furthermore, it seems important not just to compare two cultures (often selected either randomly or according to a researcher's personal connections and acquaintanceships), but instead to base cross-cultural comparisons on several cultures varying on several relevant dimensions (Hofstede & Bond, 1984). Most cross-cultural studies on shame and guilt are restricted to very few cultures (see Johnson et al., 1987; Lebra, 1973; Bierbrauer, in press). We do not discuss the thorny issue of cross-national versus cross-cultural research here; as will be seen below, we (and others) are clearly comparing countries rather than cultures. However, we do believe that cultural differences are involved; in consequence, we use the term "cultures" for simplicity's sake throughout.

One approach might be to study "objective characteristics" of specific cultures—for instance, the gross national product per inhabitant—as potential determinants of emotional experiences (see Wallbott & Scherer, 1988). Another approach might be to study "subjective dimensions" of cultures—for instance, shared attitudes and values within cultures. Though a number of such approaches have been suggested (e.g., Parsons & Shils, 1951; Peabody, 1985; Dahrendorf, 1969; Freeman & Winch, 1957; Witkin & Berry, 1975), only the classification proposed by Hofstede (1984) has been adopted in a considerable number of cross-cultural studies. By questionnaire studies of values shared within cultures, Hofstede arrived at four dimensions on which cultures may vary:

- "Power distance," which, according to Hofstede and Bond (1984), is "the extent to which the less powerful members of institutions and organizations accept that power is distributed unequally" (p. 419).
- "Uncertainty avoidance," which is "the extent to which people feel threatened by ambiguous situations and have created beliefs and institutions that try to avoid these" (Hofstede & Bond, 1984, p. 419).
- "Individualism versus collectivism," which refers to whether "people are supposed to look after themselves and their immediate family only" or whether "people belong to in-groups or collectivities which are supposed to look after them in exchange for loyalty" (Hofstede & Bond, 1984, p. 419).
- "Masculinity versus femininity," which refers to whether in a society "success, money, and things" are valued, or whether "caring for others and the quality of life" are honored (Hofstede & Bond, 1984, p. 420).

Though these value dimensions concerning cultures were based on a rather specific sample (employees of a large international corporation), evidence for their validity has been found in a number of studies. Using another value survey by Rokeach (1973), Hofstede and Bond (1984) found that the cultural dimensions obtained with this different measurement instrument very closely resembled the dimensions obtained by Hofstede. Similarly, Triandis, Bontempo, Betancourt, Bond, and Leung (1986) found conclusive evidence for the dimension of individualism versus collectivism. Gudykunst and Ting-Toomey (1988) reanalyzed some of our data collected on subjective emotional experience (Scherer, Wallbott, & Summerfield, 1986) and reported that emotional experiences are related in part to Hofstede's cultural dimensions.

Leung and Bond (1982) found that the distribution of outcomes in groups was affected by the dimension of individualism–collectivism. Gudykunst and Nishida (1986) showed that the dimension of masculinity–femininity played a major role in the perception of opposite-sex relationships, and determined the amount of self-disclosure in interactions. Finally, Gudykunst, Yang, and Nishida (1987) found differences among public self-consciousness, private self-consciousness, and social anxiety, depending on a culture's position on Hofstede's dimensions. They reported that the dimension of uncertainty avoidance was crucial: In public self-consciousness, for instance, a U.S. sample had higher scores then a Korean sample, which in turn had higher scores than a Japanese sample. On the other hand, Japanese subjects had higher private self-consciousness scores than the Korean and U.S. samples.

Given the pattern of theoretical expectations described above, it might be predicted that people in collectivistic societies should experience more shame than guilt, whereas people living in more individualistically oriented societies should experience more guilt than shame (Bierbrauer, in press; Triandis et al., 1986). In addition, Argyle (1986) has reported that in Japan and Hong Kong (generally considered to be collectivistic societies), compared to Italy and Great Britain (more individualistic societies), the "rules" of obedience to authority, saving face, group harmony, and restraining emotional expression are very important. This could also affect shame and guilt experiences. Finally, as it is known that people from cultures high in uncertainty avoidance tend to express their emotions more openly (Gudykunst & Nishida, 1986), it might be predicted that shame and guilt experiences in general should be more pronounced in such cultures, compared to cultures low in uncertainty avoidance. Together with the other findings reported above, this suggests the use of Hofstede's dimensions and data in studying possible cross-cultural differences in shame and guilt experiences. Though more recent attempts have been made to refine the Hofstede dimensions (Hui, 1988), the data reported by Hofstede are still based on the largest sample ($n = 40$) of cultures.

OUR EMPIRICAL DATA BASE

The data to be presented here were collected in a large-scale cross-cultural study in 37 countries (for preliminary reports of the data for 27 countries, see

Wallbott & Scherer, 1986, 1988). Subjects in the different cultures were given a questionnaire, asking them to recall situations in which they had experienced the emotions of joy, sadness, fear, anger, disgust, shame, and guilt, respectively (the complete questionnaire is reproduced in Scherer, 1988a). After a free description of the situations remembered, subjects had to answer 15 questions concerning the situation and their reactions. Topics covered by the questions included subjects' evaluation of the situation; their attribution of causation; physiological symptoms experienced and various reactions expressed during the emotion; intensity and duration of the emotional experience; and the amount of control used to regulate the emotional experience. There were also a number of questions addressing results of stimulus evaluation checks (as proposed by Scherer, 1984, 1986a) of the event, such as its expectedness, intrinsic pleasantness, goal conduciveness, perceived coping potential, fairness, morality, and effects on self-esteem and interpersonal relationships (for details, see Wallbott & Scherer, 1986.) Again, data from 37 countries (total $n = 2,921$ subjects) were gathered, with an average of about 80 student subjects per country. Here, only the data for shame and guilt are used to investigate empirically the questions put forward above.

In order to allow the use of parametric statistical techniques, some of the variables collected in the questionnaire had to be recoded; this was particularly the case for the physiological symptoms and expressive reactions. Recoding was performed by counting the number of symptoms or reactions mentioned by a respondent for each of a number of categories that had been formed on the basis of theoretical considerations. Generally, only the results for these recoded variables are reported in the following sections.

For physiological symptoms, categories were based partly on the distinction between ergotropic and trophotropic systems as proposed by Gellhorn (1967; comparable to a sympathetic–parasympathetic distinction) and partly on the discussion of these symptoms and the underlying mechanisms in the relevant psychophysiological literature. Ergotropic symptoms (scored from 0 to 4) included change in breathing, heart beating faster, muscles tensing/trembling, and perspiring/moist hands. As trophotropic symptoms (scored from 0 to 3), lump in throat, stomach troubles, and crying/sobbing were counted. Felt temperature was recoded as follows: feeling cold/shivering (−1), feeling warm/pleasant (+1), and feeling hot/cheeks burning (+2) (0 was assigned when no temperature symptom was mentioned).

For expressive behavior, four composite variables were coded. Approach behavior ranged from withdrawing (−1) to moving toward (+1) people and things (0 was assigned when no movement category was mentioned). Nonverbal behavior (scored from 0 to 6) included laughing/smiling, crying/sobbing, other facial expression change, screaming/yelling, other voice changes, and changes in gesturing (crying/sobbing was used as an indicator both of trophotropic arousal and of nonverbal behavior activity). Paralinguistic behavior (scored from 0 to 3) included speech melody change, speech disturbances, and speech tempo change. (Laughing/smiling was analyzed as a separate variable, because it was rather often mentioned by our subjects as a prime symptom of shame.) For verbal behavior, for which respondents could check the categories "silence, short utterance, one or two sentences, lengthy utterance," a variable with scores from 0 (silence) to 3 (lengthy utterance) was constructed via recoding the category checked into the appropriate value for the variable.

The questions concerning attributed responsibility for the eliciting event were recoded (1–4) in such a way that a small value would indicate more internal attributions, while a large value would indicate more external attributions (1 = self; 2 = relatives, friends, colleagues; 3 = strangers, authorities; 4 = natural/supernatural forces, fate, chance). Coping ability ranged from low (1 = feeling powerless, 2 = trying to escape the situation) to medium (3 = pretending that nothing important had happened, 4 = no action necessary) to high coping potential (5 = positive influence on the situation.

We should remind readers that the data we bring to bear here on the two issues under discussion (differences between shame and guilt, and cultural influences on shame and guilt) are based on subjective self-reports on personal shame and guilt experiences as obtained via questionnaires. The use of such reports unquestionably involves a number of problems (memory effects, social desirability, availability heuristics, etc.). We have discussed both the advantages and disadvantages of collecting self-reports of emotional experiences in detail elsewhere, and do not expand on this issue in the present context (see Wallbott & Scherer, 1985, 1989).

DIFFERENCES IN THE SUBJECTIVE EXPERIENCE OF SHAME AND GUILT ACROSS CULTURES

As a first step in the analysis, matched tests were used to compare shame and guilt experiences for the major variables of emotional experience studied. Because the samples studied were very large, and because 21 dependent variables were tested, only results exceeding a significance level of $p < .002$ are reported here (Bonferroni correction: significance level $p = .05/21$ comparisons results approximately in $p = .002$; see Harris, 1975). This correction ensured that the significant differences between shame and guilt were substantial, though the differences when one looks at the means may sometimes seem rather small. The results are presented in Table 19.1.

The statistical analysis revealed several significant differences between guilt and shame. The shame experiences described by our subjects lay further in the past than their guilt experiences, which—following the logic put forward by Scherer (1986b)—might indicate that the persons in our sample experienced guilt more frequently than shame. Furthermore, guilt was a longer-lasting emotion than shame for our subjects. No differences were found with respect to the felt intensity of the two emotions.

Concerning the reported amount of control of the emotional experi-

TABLE 19.1. Differences between Shame and Guilt Experiences for All Composite Variables (Matched t Tests Based on 2,921 Subjects from 37 Countries)

Variable	Means		t	df	p
	Shame	Guilt			
Subjective feeling					
Time distance	2.95	2.76	7.83	2,710	.001
Duration	2.63	3.09	16.25	2,715	.001
Intensity	2.59	2.59	0.07	2,717	n.s.
Control attempts	2.28	2.07	10.63	2,549	.001
Relationship effects	1.75	1.78	1.41	1,968	n.s.
Physiological symptoms					
Ergotropic arousal	1.04	0.83	8.58	2,920	.001
Trophotropic arousal	0.44	0.56	7.56	2,916	.001
Temperature	0.74	0.26	20.81	2,920	.001
Motor expression patterns					
Approach behavior	−0.21	−0.15	4.28	2,920	.001
Laughing/smiling	0.14	0.04	13.85	2,919	.001
Nonverbal behavior	0.94	0.81	6.43	2,919	.001
Paralinguistic behavior	0.36	0.33	2.13	2,919	n.s.
Verbal behavior	0.42	0.41	0.46	2,919	n.s.
Evaluation of situation					
Expectation	1.49	1.59	5.13	2,511	.001
Unpleasantness	2.80	2.80	0.03	2,567	n.s.
Influence on plans	2.32	2.33	0.69	1,808	n.s.
Unfairness	1.77	1.77	0.20	1,664	n.s.
Immorality	1.94	2.03	4.46	1,929	.001
Positive self-esteem	1.46	1.44	1.24	2,186	n.s.
Attribution of causality	1.64	1.47	6.21	2,380	.001
Coping attempts	3.13	3.23	2.65	2,685	n.s.

ences, we found that attempts at hiding or controlling the feeling were much stronger when subjects were experiencing shame than when they were experiencing guilt. It seems, then, that shame and the events eliciting this emotion are much more closely linked to social regulation or control than are guilt experiences. No differences were found for the effects of both emotions on self-esteem or social relationships; both emotions were being seen as having rather negative effects.

With respect to physiological symptoms, a number of significant differences were found. Shame was characterized by *more* reported ergotropic arousal than guilt, but *less* trophotropic arousal. Furthermore, in terms of felt temperature shame was a much "hotter" emotion (probably an indicator of blushing as a prime symptom of shame).

Expressive reactions also distinguished the two emotions. Nonverbal reactions, particularly laughing and smiling, were reported more frequently for shame. In addition, shame compared to guilt was characterized by more avoidance behavior. No significant differences were found with respect to verbal and paralinguistic reactions. These patterns indicate that shame experiences are characterized by stronger withdrawal tendencies and greater expressive activity than are experiences of guilt.

With respect to the stimulus evaluation checks proposed by Scherer (1984, 1986a), no differences between guilt and shame were found for intrinsic pleasantness (both emotional experiences appeared to be very unpleasant), for conduciveness to goal attainment or need satisfaction (both shame and guilt situations hindered goals and frustrated desires to a considerable degree), or for coping potential (which was rather high for both emotions). However, during guilt experiences the eliciting situation was expected or anticipated to a larger degree than during experiences arousing shame (indicating the "acute," sudden character of shame experiences).

With respect to the attribution of causality for the eliciting events, the differences indicated that shame experiences were elicited significantly more often by other people or by external sources, whereas guilt experiences were to a very large extent attributed to the self. This is consistent with the idea that guilt is caused by internal sanctions, whereas shame is caused by external sanctions emanating from other people or institutions.

With respect to the external standards checks, behaviors arousing guilt feelings were judged to more immoral or improper than behaviors eliciting shame feelings. No difference was found for the fairness of the situation. Thus, we may conclude that, as proposed by some theorists, guilt experiences are elicited by behaviors perceived to be very "immoral" (transgression of norms and rules; Piers & Singer, 1971), whereas for shame experiences the "inappropriateness" aspect (not satisfying standards) is more important.

The overall pattern of results concerning the differences in subjective self-reports of shame and guilt indicates that the two emotions differ quite markedly. It is interesting to note that two of the major theoretical distinctions in the literature—internal versus external sanctions, and transgression of rules versus not reaching standards—would appear to be supported by our data, but that the notion of possible intensity differences failed to find support.

So far we have not considered possible cultural differences in the experience of the two emotions (as reflected, for example, in the proposed distinction between shame cultures and guilt cultures). In the remainder of this chapter, we examine the cross-cultural differences found in our data set.

EMPIRICAL EVIDENCE FOR THE INFLUENCE OF CULTURAL FACTORS ON SHAME AND GUILT EXPERIENCES

Of our sample of 37 cultures, 24 were also included in Hofstede's study (1984). Two-way mixed analyses of variance (ANOVAs) were computed using emotion (shame vs. guilt; repeated measures) and value dimensions (three groups: high, medium, low on each of the four value dimensions of countries, according to Hofstede's classifications) as factors. Rather than using means across country samples for the emotion data, we used all subjects in the respective samples. In this way, significant effects provided a stronger test, because within-country sample variance was taken into account. All of our countries that were also included in Hofstede's (1984) analyses were grouped into high, medium, and low groups for each dimension. The sample composition for Hofstede's four value dimensions is reported in Table 19.2.

Given our theoretical analysis, one important dimension with respect to shame and guilt should be individualism versus collectivism. The results of the two-way ANOVAs (emotion × individualism–collectivism) are presented in Table 19.3, together with the main effects for the individualism–collectivism dimension (for the main effects for emotion, see Table 19.1). In the following analyses a number of variables reported in Table 19.1 are not mentioned, in case no dimension main effects or significant interactions (dimension × emotion) were found. As above, only results exceeding a significance level of $p < .002$ (Bonferroni correction) are reported.

Individualism–collectivism had a considerable influence on emotional

TABLE 19.2. Country Samples Classified as High, Medium, or Low According to Hofstede's (1984) Data on His Four Value Dimensions

High	Medium	Low
Individualism versus collectivism[a]		
(Hofstede scores > 69)	(Hofstede scores = 41–68)	(Hofstede scores = 1–40)
United States	Germany	Brazil
France	Switzerland	Venezuela
Australia	Austria	Chile
Netherlands	Finland	Hong Kong
New Zealand	Spain	Yugoslavia
Italy	Israel	Portugal
Norway	India	Mexico
Sweden	Japan	Greece
(Total n = 596)	(Total n = 746)	Total n = 650)
High versus low power distance		
(Hofstede scores > 62)	(Hofstede scores = 36–62)	(Hofstede scores = 1–35)
Portugal	Spain	Germany
Yugoslavia	Italy	Switzerland
Chile	Netherlands	Austria
Mexico	Greece	Israel
India	Japan	New Zealand
Brazil	United States	Sweden
Hong Kong	Australia	Norway
France		Finland
Venezuela		
(Total n = 715)	(Total n = 711)	(Total n = 566)

High versus low uncertainty avoidance

(Hofstede scores > 82)	(Hofstede scores = 55–81)	(Hofstede scores = 1–54)
Greece	Germany	Sweden
Portugal	Switzerland	Netherlands
Yugoslavia	Austria	Hong Kong
Japan	Finland	India
France	Italy	United States
Chile	Israel	Australia
Mexico	Brazil	New Zealand
Spain	Venezuela	Norway
(Total n = 793)	(Total n = 615)	(Total n = 584)

Masculinity versus femininity[b]

(Hofstede scores > 62)	(Hofstede scores = 42–61)	(Hofstede scores = 1–42)
Japan	France	Sweden
Germany	Greece	Norway
Austria	Israel	Netherlands
Venezuela	India	Finland
Italy	Hong Kong	Spain
Switzerland	Brazil	Portugal
United States	Australia	Yugoslavia
Mexico	New Zealand	Chile
(Total n = 859)	(Total n = 557)	(Total n = 576)

[a]For individualism versus collectivism, high means individualistic and low means collectivistic.
[b]For masculinity versus femininity, high means masculine and low means feminine.

experiences, as the rather large number of main effects indicates. In collectivistic as compared to individualistic cultures, shame *and* guilt experiences were less recent, were less expected, were less immoral, and had fewer negative influences both on self-esteem and on relationships. These differences indicate that shame and guilt were more infrequent and unexpected, but have fewer negative consequences for the individual in the collectivistic cultures. Furthermore, in these cultures both emotions were accompanied more often by laughing/smiling, but less often by verbal behavior.

When we looked at the interactions between cultural value dimension (individualism vs. collectivism) and emotion (shame vs. guilt), a rather coherent picture emerged. A number of such significant interactions pointed to the same conclusion: Shame experiences in collectivistic cultures differed from shame experiences in individualistic cultures, as well as from guilt experiences in both types of cultures. Shame was experienced as being of comparatively short duration in collectivistic cultures, was felt as less immoral, and was frequently accompanied by laughing and smiling. Furthermore, shame in collectivistic cultures was characterized by the highest felt temperature and by very low trophotropic arousal. Thus, in the

TABLE 19.3. Differences between Shame and Guilt in Relation to the Individualism–Collectivism Dimension

Variable	Means						Main effect for dimension		Interaction (emotion × dimension)	
	Shame			Guilt						
	Indiv.	Medium	Collec.	Indiv.	Medium	Collec.	F	p	F	p
Subjective feeling										
Time distance	2.95	2.78	3.03	2.62	2.62	2.87	12.67	.001	2.94	n.s.
Duration	2.65	2.35	2.42	2.97	3.02	3.14	3.65	n.s.	11.78	.001
Relationship effects	1.66	1.76	1.87	1.72	1.77	1.87	12.62	.001	0.66	n.s.
Physiological symptoms										
Trophotropic arousal	0.52	0.39	0.42	0.55	0.59	0.63	1.07	n.s.	7.44	.001
Temperature	0.66	0.87	0.90	0.31	0.19	0.29	3.62	n.s.	12.84	.001
Motor expression patterns										
Laughing/smiling	0.10	0.15	0.22	0.06	0.04	0.04	8.63	.001	18.08	.001
Verbal behavior	0.46	0.42	0.39	0.49	0.40	0.34	10.86	.001	2.14	n.s.
Evaluation of situation										
Expectation	1.58	1.54	1.45	1.71	1.66	1.51	15.53	.001	0.84	n.s.
Immorality	2.07	1.81	1.74	1.99	2.09	1.99	8.95	.001	19.97	.001
Positive self-esteem	1.35	1.45	1.62	1.40	1.41	1.50	16.35	.001	5.81	n.s.

Note. Effects are only mentioned where either the dimension main effect or the dimension × emotion interaction reached significance, and where one of these reached $p < .002$.

477

collectivistic societies shame experiences seemed to be much more "typical" for the general shame profile (compare Table 19.1) than the ones reported by subjects from individualistic societies, which to a larger degree resembled those events reported as typical guilt situations in both types of societies.

In Table 19.4 similar analyses for the dimension of high versus low power distance are presented. Again, a large number of main effects for the dimension emerged. In cultures high in power distance (i.e., cultures with acceptance of unequal distribution of power), the emotional experiences were less recent and of lower intensity. Furthermore, the emotional experiences were accompanied by more laughing/smiling, but reduced verbal behavior. In high-power-distance cultures the events were significantly less expected, but were perceived as being less immoral and less unpleasant, and were accompanied by fewer negative influences on self and relationships. In high-power-distance cultures, therefore, shame and guilt seemed to be less negative experiences than in low-power-distance cultures.

The significant interactions between emotion and high versus low power distance were mostly attributable (as in the case of individualism–collectivism) to the differences in shame experiences between high- and low-power-distance cultures. Shame in high-power-distance cultures was accompanied by very high temperature and a considerable amount of laughing/smiling, but was not very unpleasant. Again, it seems that subjects from high-power-distance cultures reported genuine shame experiences, whereas the shame experiences of subjects from low-power-distance cultures were more similar to reported guilt experiences.

The results for the dimension of high versus low uncertainty avoidance are reported in Table 19.5. In cultures high in uncertainty avoidance (i.e., cultures with rigid beliefs and institutions to avoid ambiguity), the emotions were accompanied by higher felt temperature, more laughing/smiling, and more nonverbal expression in general. The results concerning paralinguistic and verbal behavior were not very conclusive, because the medium group reported the highest values, which was also true for the amount of trophotropic arousal. The events were seen as less immoral, with fewer negative influences on self-esteem and on relationships, in high-uncertainty-avoidance cultures. Again, the main effects for the dimension with respect to coping ability and unpleasantness were not conclusive, because the medium group reported the lowest values in coping ability and the highest values in unpleasantness.

As before, a number of these main effects for the value dimension are mediated by significant interactions between emotion and dimension, indicating that most interactions were attributable to shame experiences in high-uncertainty-avoidance cultures. In these cultures, shame was of shorter duration than shame experiences in low-uncertainty-avoidance cultures or guilt experiences in both types of cultures; in addition, it was accompanied by the highest felt temperature, the most laughing/smiling, and the least trophotropic arousal reported. Moreover, the shame-eliciting event was seen

TABLE 19.4. Differences between Shame and Guilt in Relation to the High versus Low Power Distance Dimension

Variable	Means						Main effect for dimension		Interaction (emotion × dimension)	
	Shame			Guilt						
	High	Medium	Low	High	Medium	Low	F	p	F	p
Subjective feeling										
Time distance	3.02	2.83	2.90	2.87	2.58	2.66	12.03	.001	0.94	n.s.
Intensity	2.50	2.49	2.65	2.57	2.45	2.62	7.08	.001	1.87	n.s.
Relationship effects	1.88	1.75	1.63	1.90	1.72	1.75	17.45	.001	3.15	n.s.
Physiological symptoms										
Temperature	0.83	0.93	0.66	0.26	0.26	0.27	4.77	n.s.	8.19	.001
Motor expression patterns										
Approach behavior	−0.15	−0.23	−0.26	−0.14	−0.15	−0.20	6.32	.002	1.74	n.s.
Laughing/smiling	0.21	0.15	0.10	0.05	0.05	0.04	11.55	.001	12.51	.001
Verbal behavior	0.40	0.43	0.44	0.34	0.41	0.48	6.97	.001	2.81	n.s.
Evaluation of situation										
Expectation	1.43	1.56	1.58	1.50	1.71	1.67	20.84	.001	1.40	n.s.
Unpleasantness	2.76	2.70	2.87	2.84	2.74	2.80	12.44	.001	6.66	.001
Immorality	1.74	1.86	2.06	1.97	2.05	2.06	12.36	.001	6.01	n.s.
Positive self-esteem	1.63	1.41	1.36	1.52	1.41	1.37	23.47	.001	3.62	n.s.

Note. Effects are only mentioned where either the dimension main effect or the dimension × emotion interaction reached significance, and where one of these reached $p < .002$.

479

TABLE 19.5. Differences between Shame and Guilt in Relation to the High versus Low Uncertainty Avoidance Dimension

Variable	Means						Main effect for dimension		Interaction (emotion × dimension)	
	Shame			Guilt						
	High	Medium	Low	High	Medium	Low	F	p	F	p
Subjective feeling										
Duration	2.31	2.39	2.77	3.06	3.12	2.94	5.97	n.s.	27.14	.001
Relationship effects	1.85	1.74	1.67	1.83	1.79	1.72	8.73	.001	0.87	n.s.
Physiological symptoms										
Trophotropic arousal	0.38	0.50	0.47	0.62	0.68	0.46	8.35	.001	13.07	.001
Temperature	0.99	0.80	0.60	0.22	0.27	0.31	6.86	.001	25.71	.001
Motor expression patterns										
Laughing/smiling	0.21	0.15	0.09	0.04	0.04	0.05	11.70	.001	13.82	.001
Nonverbal behavior	0.94	1.10	0.76	0.77	0.98	0.65	31.14	.001	0.70	n.s.
Paralinguistic behavior	0.39	0.46	0.27	0.30	0.45	0.25	21.78	.001	2.16	n.s.
Verbal behavior	0.39	0.48	0.40	0.35	0.47	0.41	11.16	.001	1.10	n.s.
Evaluation of situation										
Unpleasantness	2.71	2.86	2.75	2.81	2.87	2.70	16.74	.001	6.73	.001
Immorality	1.72	1.86	2.07	2.03	2.00	2.04	12.01	.001	15.11	.001
Positive self-esteem	1.55	1.50	1.33	1.44	1.42	1.43	6.58	.001	10.33	.001
Coping ability	3.16	2.90	3.14	3.23	3.04	3.30	8.63	.001	0.39	n.s.

Note. Effects are only mentioned where either the dimension main effect or the dimension × emotion interaction reached significance, and where one of these reached $p < .002$.

as less immoral, was not very unpleasant, and was accompanied by fewer negative effects on self-esteem in high- than in low-uncertainty-avoidance cultures. Taken together, these differences indicate that shame was more typical of the general shame pattern reported above in high-uncertainty-avoidance cultures than in low-uncertainty-avoidance countries, whereas for guilt the differences attributable to this dimension were weaker.

The masculinity–femininity dimension, finally, seemed to be the least important of Hofstede's dimensions with respect to emotional experiences of shame and guilt in our sample. Only a few significant effects were found. The one significant main effect for the value dimension (longest duration of the emotions in the medium group) was difficult to interpret, and the one significant interaction between emotion and dimension (for felt temperature) indicated that shame in masculine cultures was different from shame experiences in feminine cultures *and* from guilt experiences in both types of cultures.

To sum up, it seems that "typical" shame experiences (as characterized by short duration, high ergotrophic arousal, unexpectedness, etc.; see above) are typical of collectivistic, high-power-distance, and high-uncertainty-avoidance cultures, whereas shame experiences in individualistic, low-power-distance, and low-uncertainty-avoidance cultures resemble the "typical" guilt pattern to a larger degree. The dimension of masculinity–femininity does not seem to play an important rule with respect to experiential differences of shame and guilt.

DISCUSSION

Our results indicate that there are differences in shame and guilt experiences, depending on culturally shared values. The interactions between emotion and value dimension for individualism–collectivism show that shame is a rather acute, short-lived emotional experience in collectivistic cultures (shorter duration, less trophotropic arousal, less immorality involved, fewer negative influences on self-esteem and on relationships, more laughing/smiling, and higher felt temperature) compared to individualistic cultures. Basically similar differences have been found between high- and low-power-distance cultures, and between high- and low-uncertainty-avoidance cultures. For guilt, on the other hand, differences attributable to the value dimensions are much less pronounced. Cultural differences in shame are such that "real" shame with the characteristic experiential features described above is reported in collectivistic, high-power-distance, and high-uncertainty-avoidance cultures, whereas "guilt–shame" (i.e., shame experiences with features very similar to those of guilt experiences) is predominant in individualistic, low-power-distance, and low-uncertainty-avoidance cultures. The latter cultures may be considered as "guilt cultures," where shame turns to guilt, or where shame experiences at least involve a rather large number of guilt components.

If we consider the country samples that tended to be individualistic, low in power distance, and low in uncertainty avoidance (such as Sweden, Norway, Finland, New Zealand, and the United States), the patterns found may be attributable to a "white, Anglo-Saxon/Nordic" way of living and thinking—in short, the "Protestant ethic" (Weber, 1904; see also McClelland, 1961), which seems to mingle each self-reflexive emotion with guilt. Countries in our research that tended to be collectivistic, high in power distance, and high in uncertainty avoidance included Mexico, Venezuela, India, Brazil, France, Chile, Spain, Greece, and Portugal—in other words, countries that are not considered to share the "Protestant ethic." Here, shame still seems to be an emotion in its own right. In Piers and Singer's (1971) terms, this would imply that in "Protestant ethic" cultures the superego is the crucial psychological factor, turning self-conscious emotional experiences into guilt experiences.

The results of our study indicate that the effects of Hofstede's value dimensions on shame in particular are rather similar for power distance, uncertainty avoidance, and individualism–collectivism. From a methodological point of view, it should be stressed that this communality in results can certainly be attributed in part to the fact that the groups of country samples selected for the comparisons overlapped to a large degree—that is, that the *same* countries were high, for instance, in power distance and in uncertainty avoidance. This may have been a result of the culture-sampling restrictions imposed upon us (additional samples we have collected, such as samples from African countries, were not represented in Hofstede's sample, and thus could not be used here for the cross-cultural comparisons). Or it could be a result of the fact that the four dimensions Hofstede (1984) identified are not independent of one another. This issue obviously requires further analysis.

On the whole, our findings imply that the focus of a society on certain shared values is related to emotional experiences to a considerable degree, particularly with respect to certain emotions that depend on the compatibility of behavior with external and internal standards, such as shame and guilt (see Scherer, 1986a, 1988b). Our findings partly confirm anthropological observations (e.g., Benedict, 1946; Mead, 1937), which would suggest that shame experiences are more predominant in "primitive" cultures, whereas guilt experiences are more intense and more frequent in "modern" countries (though of course truly "primitive" cultures were not part of our samples). Our data suggest that less norm-guided and more "open" cultures (low in power distance and uncertainty avoidance), which stress individualism, result in a predominance of guilt experiences in their members, whereas more "closed" societies, which espouse more collectivistic values, induce shame experiences that are rather different from guilt experiences.

In summary, two findings seem to be of importance:

1. The reaction patterns and feeling characteristics of shame and guilt differ to a considerable degree, with shame being a more "ergotropic" emotion (with higher felt temperature and more nonverbal expression) and guilt being a more "trophotropic" emotion. A number of other differences between these two emotions indicate that guilt in fact is a more "internal" emotional experience, often caused by the self, whereas shame is often caused by "external" factors. Other data indicate that, as Piers and Singer (1971) discussed, shame may be related to not achieving goals, while guilt seems to be related to transgression of social norms.

2. Shame experiences in particular seem to vary cross-culturally. Important factors in this respect are culturally shared norms, such as orientation of a society more toward individualistic values or more toward collectivistic values. Comparisons indicate that individualism tends to be associated with shame experiences that are rather similar to guilt, while collectivism tends to result in shame and guilt experiences that are rather distinct. In a recent study, Bierbrauer (in press) using a different approach with three samples (German subjects, Lebanese and Kurdish asylum seekers in Germany) arrived at a somewhat similar conclusion.

In general, it was demonstrated that some of the differences between shame and guilt experiences are related to cultural value dimensions and that the analysis of the emotional experience data by taking these value dimensions into account results in a rather coherent picture of differences between shame and guilt. These findings highlight the importance of developmental and socialization factors in the experience of the two emotions studied. Different cultural values shared within a society should influence socialization techniques to a large degree (see McClelland, 1961), and these differential socialization techniques would appear to lead to either a predominance of guilt with no "real" shame experiences in one type of culture (the "Protestant ethic" cultures) and to very distinct shame and guilt experiences in the other type of culture.

One could argue that culture and cultural norms determine or even "construct" emotional experiences (see Averill, 1980; Gergen, 1985; Harré, 1986; Lutz & White, 1986), but we should not forget that in turn emotions may contribute to the fuzzy set we call "culture." Employing Hofstede's classification of cultures on the dimensions of power distance, uncertainty avoidance, individualism–collectivism, and masculinity–femininity here to analyze our large cross-cultural data set on emotional experiences is just a start, but the results are encouraging. Although we have demonstrated some relationships between the two factors of emotion and culture, the causality of these relationships remains to be studied in much more detail.

ACKNOWLEDGMENTS

The following collaborators in the intercultural studies reported in this chapter have conducted the research in the respective countries. They have also contributed important suggestions to the overall design of the research program, and must be considered as coauthors. They are listed in alphabetical order, together with the university where each conducted the study: Elisha Babad, Hebrew University of Jerusalem, Israel; Eva Baenninger-Huber, University of Zurich, Switzerland; Cleve Barlow, University of Auckland, New Zealand; Marek Cielecki, University of Warsaw, Poland; Cindy Gallois, University of Queensland, Australia; Jo Kleiven, Oppland Regional College, Norway; Jacques Cosnier, University II of Lyon, and Monique Alles-Jardel, University of Provence, Aix-en-Provence, France; Britt-Marie Drottz, University of Göteburg, Sweden; Heiner Ellgring, Free University of Berlin, Germany; Alfonso Jimenez-Fernandez and Jose Miguel Fernandez-Dols, Autonoma University of Madrid, Spain (J. M. Fernandez-Dols in addition helped in collecting the data in Costa Rica, Honduras, Mexico, Guatemala, Venezuela, Chile, and El Salvador; within these countries, we extend our thanks to: Mirta Gonzalez [Costa Rica], Otto E. Gilbert [Guatemala], Isabel de Villanueva [Honduras], Rolando Diaz-Loving [Mexico], Ignacio Martin [El Salvador], Angelica Gonzalez and Gonzalo Zaror [Chile], and Pedro R. Rodriguez [Venezuela]); Tsutomu Kudoh, University of Osaka, Japan; Hing-Keung Ma, Chinese University of Hong Kong, Hong Kong; David Matsumoto, University of California at Berkeley, United States; Silvia Maurer-Lane and Silvia Friedman, Catholic University of Sao Paulo, Brazil; Gerold Mikula, University of Graz, Austria; Alastair Mundy-Castle, University of Lagos, Nigeria; Rauni Myllyniemi, University of Helsinki, Finland; Usha S. Naidu, Tata Institute of Social Sciences, Bombay, India; Vladimir Nesic, University of Nis, Yugoslavia; S. Nyandia-Bundy and R. P. Bundy, University of Zimbabwe, Zimbabwe; Robert F. Norton, American University of Beirut, Lebanon; Dimitra Papadopoulou and D. Markoulis, University of Thessaloniki, Greece; Karl Peltzer, University of Malawi, Malawi; Catherine Peng, University of Oxford, England, who collected the data in the People's Republic of China; Pio Ricci-Bitti and Dino Giovannini, University of Bologna, Italy; Luis Soczka and Constanza Paul, University of Porto, Portugal; Velina Topalova, Bulgarian Academy of Sciences, Bulgaria; Ad Vingerhoets and J. Hendriksen, Catholic University of Nijmegen, Netherlands; and C. Westenholz-Bless, University of Zambia, Zambia.

REFERENCES

Argyle, M. (1986). Rules for social relationships in four cultures. *Australian Journal of Psychology, 38,* 309–318.
Averill, J. R. (1980). A constructivist view of emotion. In R. Plutchik & H. Kellerman (Eds.), *Emotion: Theory, research, and experience* (Vol. 1, pp. 305–340). New York: Academic Press.
Benedict, R. (1946). *The chrysanthenum and the sword.* Boston: Houghton Mifflin.
Bierbrauer, G. (in press). Reactions to violation of normative standards: A cross-cultural analysis of shame and guilt. *International Journal of Psychology.*
Buss, A. H. (1980). *Self-consciousness and social anxiety.* San Francisco: W. H. Freeman.

Carroll, J. (1985). *Guilt: The gray eminence behind character, history, and culture.* London: Routledge & Kegan Paul.

Dahrendorf, R. (1969). *Society and democracy in Germany.* Garden City, NY: Doubleday.

Darwin, C. (1965). *The expression of the emotions in man and animals.* Chicago: University of Chicago Press. (Original work published 1872)

Duval, S., & Wicklund, R. A. (1972). *A theory of objective self-awareness.* New York: Academic Press.

Ekman, P. (1972). Universals and cultural differences in facial expression of emotion. In J. K. Cole (Ed.), *Nebraska Symposium on Motivation* (Vol. 19 pp. 207–283). Lincoln: University of Nebraska Press.

Foschi, M., & Hales, W. H. (1979). The theoretical role of cross-cultural comparisons in experimental social psychology. In L. H. Eckensberger, W. J. Lonner, & Y. H. Poortinga (Eds.), *Cross-cultural contributions to psychology* (pp. 244–254). Lisse, The Netherlands: Swets & Zeitlinger.

Freeman, L. C., & Winch, R. F. (1957). Social complexity: An empirical test of a typology of societies. *American Journal of Sociology, 62,* 461–466.

Gellhorn, E. (1967). *Principles of autonomic–somatic integrations.* Minneapolis: University of Minnesota Press.

Gergen, K. J. (1985). The social constructionist movement in modern psychology. *American Psychologist, 40,* 266–275.

Gudykunst, W. B., & Nishida, T. (1986). The influence of cultural variability on perceptions of communication behavior associated with relationship terms. *Human Communication Research, 13,* 147–166.

Gudykunst, W. B., & Ting-Toomey, S. (1988). Culture and affective communication. *American Behavioral Scientist, 31,* 384–400.

Gudykunst, W. B., Yang, S.-M., & Nishida, T. (1987). Cultural differences in self-consciousness and self-monitoring. *Communication Research, 14,* 7–34.

Harré, R. M. (Ed.). (1986). *The social construction of emotions.* Oxford. Blackwell.

Harris, R. J. (1975). *A primer of multivariate statistics,* New York: Academic Press.

Heider, K. G. (1991). *Landscapes of emotion.* Cambridge, England· Cambridge University Press.

Hofstede, G. (1984). *Culture's consequences: International differences in work-related values.* Beverly Hills, CA: Sage.

Hofstede, G., & Bond, M. H. (1984). Hofstede's culture dimensions: An independent validation using Rokeach's value survey. *Journal of Cross-cultural Psychology, 15,* 417–433.

Hui, C. H. (1988). Measurement of individualism–collectivism. *Journal of Research in Personality, 22,* 17–36.

Izard, C. E. (1977). *Human emotions.* New York: Plenum Press.

Jahoda, G. (1980). Theoretical and systematic approaches in cross-cultural psychology. In H. C. Triandis & W. W. Lambert (Eds.), *Handbook of cross-cultural psychology: Vol. 1. Perspectives* (pp. 69–141). Boston: Allyn & Bacon.

Johnson, R. C., Danko, G. P., Huang, Y., Park, J. Y., Johnson, S. B., & Nagoshi, C. T. (1987). Guilt, shame and adjustment in three cultures. *Personality and Individual Differences, 8,* 357–364.

Laplanche, J., & Pontalis, J. B. (1967). *Vocabulaire de la psychanalyse.* Paris: Presses Universitaires de France.

Lebra, T. S. (1973). The social mechanism of guilt and shame: The Japanese case. *Anthropological Quarterly, 44,* 241–255.

Leung, K., & Bond, M. H. (1982). How Chinese and Americans reward task-related contributions: A preliminary study. *Psychologia, 25,* 32–39.

Lutz, C., & White, G. M. L. (1986). The anthropology of emotions. *Annual Review of Anthropology, 15,* 405–436.

McClelland, D. C. (1961). *The achieving society.* Princeton, NJ: Van Nostrand.

Mead, M. (1937). *Cooperation and competition among primitive peoples.* New York: McGraw-Hill.

Modigliani, A. (1971). Embarrassment, facework, and eye contact: Testing a theory of embarrassment. *Journal of Personality and Social Psychology, 11,* 15–24.

Ortony, A. (1987). Is guilt an emotion? *Cognition and Emotion, 1,* 283–298.

Parsons, T., & Shils, E. A. (1951). *Toward a general theory of action.* Cambridge, MA: Harvard University Press.

Peabody, D. (1985). *National characteristics.* Cambridge, England: Cambridge University Press.

Piers, G., & Singer, M. B. (1971). *Shame and guilt.* New York: Norton.

Rokeach, M. (1973). *The nature of human values.* New York: Free Press.

Scherer, K. R. (1984). On the nature and function of emotion. In K. R. Scherer & P. Ekman (Eds.), *Approaches to emotion* (pp. 293–318). Hillsdale, NJ: Erlbaum.

Scherer, K. B. (1986a). Vocal affect expression: A review and a model for future research. *Psychological Bulletin, 99,* 143–165.

Scherer, K. R. (1986b). Emotion experiences across European cultures: A summary statement. In K. R. Scherer, H. G. Wallbott, & A. B. Summerfield (Eds.), *Experiencing emotion: A cross-cultural study* (pp. 173–189). Cambridge, England: Cambridge University Press.

Scherer, K. R. (Ed.). (1988a). *Facets of emotion: Recent research.* Hillsdale, NJ: Erlbaum.

Scherer, K. R. (1988b). Criteria for emotion–antecedent appraisal: A review. In V. Hamilton, G. H. Bower, & N. H. Frijda (Eds.), *Cognitive perspectives on emotion and motivation.* (pp. 89–126). Dordrecht, The Netherlands: Nijhoff.

Scherer, K. R., Wallbott, H. G., & Summerfield, A. R. (Eds.). (1986). *Experiencing emotion: A cross-cultural study.* Cambridge, England: Cambridge University Press.

Sears, R. R. (1970). Transcultural variables and conceptual equivalence. In I. Al-Issa & W. Dennis (Eds.), *Cross-cultural studies of behavior* (pp. 164–174). New York: Holt, Rinehart & Winston.

Triandis, H. C., Bontempo, R., Betancourt, H., Bond, M., Leung, K. (1986). The measurement of the etic aspects of individualism and collectivism across cultures. *Australian Journal of Psychology, 38,* 257–267.

Wallbott, H. G., & Scherer, K. R. (1985). Differentielle Situations und Reaktionscharakteristika in Emotionserinnerungen: Ein neuer Forschungsansatz. *Psychologische Rundschau, 36,* 83–101.

Wallbott, H. G., & Scherer, K. R. (1986). How universal and specific is emotional experience? Evidence from 27 countries on five continents. *Social Science Information, 25,* 763–795.

Wallbott, H. G., & Scherer, K. R. (1988). Emotion and economic development: Data and speculations concerning the relationship between emotional experience and socio-economic factors. *European Journal of Social Psychology, 18,* 267–273.

Wallbott, H. G., & Scherer, K. R. (1989). Assessing emotion by questionnaire. In R. Plutchik & H. Kellermann (Eds.), *Emotion: Theory, research, and experience* (Vol. 4, pp. 55–82). New York: Academic Press.

Weber, M. (1904). *The Protestant ethic and the spirit of capitalism.* New York: Scribner's.

Wicker, F. W., Payne, G. C., & Morgan, R. D. (1983). Participant descriptions of guilt and shame. *Motivation and Emotion, 7,* 25–39.

Witkin, H. A., & Berry, J. W. (1975). Psychological differentiation in cross-cultural perspective. *Journal of Cross-Cultural Psychology, 6,* 4–87.

20

Self-Conscious Emotions, Child Rearing, and Child Psychopathology in Japanese Culture

KAZUO MIYAKE
KOSUKE YAMAZAKI

In this chapter, we first review the role of self-conscious emotions (specifically, shame, guilt, embarrassment, and shyness) in Japanese culture, particularly as they are involved in child rearing. We then show how they relate to some of the most common forms of psychological and psychopathological problems in Japanese children and adolescents, such as *taijin-kyohfu* (delusional social phobia), school refusal, and violence in the home.

SHAME, GUILT, AND THE PSYCHOLOGICAL CHARACTERISTICS OF THE JAPANESE

In discussing the psychological problems facing children in any particular society, one must first take into account the issue of mental structure as determined by the traditional culture of the country in question, and that of mental structure as it stands wavering in the wake of the drastic changes in modern-day society.

Quite a number of cross-cultural studies have been undertaken to date on the relationship between Japanese culture and the psychological characteristics of the Japanese. Ruth Benedict (1946) pointed out in her book *The*

Chrysanthemum and the Sword that the Japanese culture is not a *tsumi* (guilt) culture, but is one based on *haji* (shame). In other words, European cultures are based on the understanding that people must take final responsibility for their actions before God, who is regarded as the single absolute being; this renders each individual acutely aware of his or her own guilt. On the other hand, Japan is a realm of multivariate gods, lacking a single absolute being; thus, being shamed in front of others (*haji-o-kaku*) is regarded as the most powerful driving force for the Japanese.

Of course, many questions have been raised regarding Benedict's theory, because her study was based on a restricted group of Japanese under peculiar circumstances and not on a representative group of people. For example, the following can be said in response to her view that the Japanese do not possess a universalistic form of ethics such as that found in the Western world, and that a situationalistic and particularistic form of ethics and the concept of *haji* are all that they have. Benedict indicated that *haji* is a reaction to criticism by others—that the Japanese feel *haji* in instances when they are ridiculed and rejected in front of others, or when they come to believe they have been so ridiculed. This observation is actually right on target, because *haji* in our country, on which so much emphasis has come to be placed in modern times, has always been about being laughed at.

An unpublished survey of our college students about the situations in which they were *hazukashii* (embarrassed) revealed that most of them felt so when they were "ridiculed in front of others," when they "failed to perform well in front of others," when they "did things which were different from others," when "they were the only one who could not do something," and when their "secrets were revealed in front of others." As such, what these college students held in common as consciousness of *haji* was what arose as the result of the perception that they were being looked upon with ridicule, disdain, or rejection; this falls squarely into Benedict's category of *haji* (shame). This type of *haji* is probably that which arises from recognition that one is inferior among one's reference group as defined by the ego ideal.

However, responses indicative of a different type of *haji* could be seen in the same group of college students. This is the case in which one is embarrassed without recognition that one is inferior in comparison to others. Examples of this in our sample were concepts such as "What I am doing might be childish and crass for my age," or "I am not giving all I can and am only dodging the issue." This type of *haji* probably arises from recognition of having breached the boundaries of the reference group as defined by the superego. The eyes of others do not intervene in this type of *haji*, but one nevertheless feels as if one is being watched by others. In this context, Benedict's theory that *haji* as experienced by the Japanese is solely situationalistic and particularistic does not hold.

From another angle, Chie Nakane (1970) has pointed out as a characteristic of Japanese society that the *tate* (vertical) structure, in which ties between diverse elements are established precisely for their diversity, is particularly strong, whereas the *yoko* (horizontal) relationship, wherein like elements are bonded together for their similarities, is so weak as not to be socially functional. Yuji Aida (1972) has pointed out that within the Japanese consciousness, there exists an *omote* (front, facade) culture and an *ura* (back, inner truth) culture; *omote* and *ura* culture is defined as the product of human and social relations on a private or anti-establishmentarian level. He adds that in the consciousness of many Japanese, the *ura* culture is the more dominant, and the *omote* culture is regarded as a superficial world. Takeo Doi (1986) has discussed this distinction between *ura* and *omote,* as well as that between *tatemae* (outward appearance, the publicly enunciated principle) and *honne* (inner reality, the privately held feeling), from a psychiatric standpoint, clarifying the structure of *amae* (propensity to depend upon another's presumed indulgence) peculiar to the Japanese.

But among the many theories on the Japanese like those cited above, that put forth by Hiroshi Minami (1983) is of particular interest in terms of the psychological problems harbored by Japanese children. He points out that the presence of ego uncertainty resulting from lack of proper identity is a notable characteristic of mental structure among the Japanese. This ego uncertainty appears in such passive aspects as weakness, timidity, constraint, and resignation on the one hand; on the other hand, it creates consideration and kindness, and as an individual tries to overcome the uncertainty it produces an intricately intertwined combination of favorable behavior, appearing as engrossment, studiousness, positive ambition, and flexibility. Minami states that within the ego or self-consciousness, there is an active subjective self and a passive self. Furthermore, within the passive self there exist two aspects—the inner passive self, which arises out of introspection and evaluation of one's own inner self, and an outer passive self, which is what one perceives oneself to be as seen by others. For instance, when children are regularly reprimanded for not doing well by their parents or teachers, an outer passive self in which they feel they are perceived as inferior is soon created, and the feelings of inferiority give rise to an unstable active subjective self. In that state, the children lack confidence in the ability of their active self to make decisions, giving rise to uncertainty and ego insufficiency. Such uncertainty in the active self in turn brings on uncertainty in the inner passive self, making them feel things such as "I don't think I can do this" or "I am a failure."

In order to alleviate the various anxieties arising from such ego uncertainty, the Japanese utilize the following defense mechanisms. The first is to try to resolve the anxiety by harboring dependence upon some group—that is, to have a sense of common destiny. The second one is "ranking-consciousness," or consciousness of how one is being evaluated by others, as seen in obsessively held everyday behavior such as greetings, exchange of business cards, and gift giving. The third is the attempt to attain ego certainty through changing one's behavior to fit some mold, which appears as conformity, uniformity, and perfectionism.

Obsessive tendencies and overconsciousness of eye contact, reported to be relatively common among the Japanese, may be regarded as products of the aforementioned defense mechanisms and may be seen only in certain situations. People overly conscious of eye contact worried about the ambiguity of evaluations being given them by others do not become conscious of eye contact in intimate settings such as the family, where they generally know how they are evaluated, and in anonymous group settings of random people, where they need not know or worry about how others see them. On the other hand, in settings involving intermediate levels of exchange, such as those between students and teachers, workers and their superiors, and colleagues, overconsciousness of eye contact is strongly manifested.

A further characteristic, which may be regarded as the fourth method of resolving anxiety stemming from ego uncertainty, consists of the multifacetedness, ambiguity, and flexibility of the Japanese. In this respect, the fact that the Japanese go by what can best be described as "circumstantialism" in modes of living, religion, culture, and all other aspects of life cannot be overlooked. In other words, the Japanese while possessing a uniformity-oriented perfectionalistic aspect are also adept at adapting oneself to group movement, embracing diverse cultures and ways of thinking. For instance, they have a way of accepting Western modes of living (e.g., carpets and beds) with no resistance to coexist with the Japanese style of living (e.g., tatami-mats and futon bedding). They also show great enthusiasm for participating in native religious celebrations (i.e., religions other than the one they personally follow) thereby mixing with great agility varying cultures and modes of thinking, creating a characteristically Japanese culture and way of thought.

In addition, as a fifth method, behaving so as not to be laughed at by others is accorded considerable importance. "Not becoming a laughingstock of society" is emphasized in all aspects of education—in the home, in school, and in regional society. Being laughed at creates *haji,* and avoiding such situations has become the moral law of the Japanese. Failing or making mistakes in front of others will result in having to endure embarrassment. However, standing out from the crowd (e.g., being the only one in formal dress at a casual gathering) will also bring about embarrassment. Technically, the former situation may be interpreted as shame and the latter as embarrassment, but what is common to both is the fact that unwanted attention is focused upon the subject. Hence, the Japanese end up taking care not to stand out from the crowd at all times, in order to avoid being embarrassed in front of others. Not standing out, not becoming an issue, has come to be regarded as a great virtue in group situations. In other words, it can be said that the Japanese are a people who deeply value uniform harmony within a group—who go through life with diffidence, always withholding themselves in deference to others.

Now let us review the feeling of *tsumi* (guilt) among the Japanese. Ruth Benedict (1946) stated that the Japanese lack the sense of *tsumi*, but ethnologist Kunio Yanagida (1970) states otherwise. According to him, the word *tsumi* frequently appears as part of the active vocabulary of evaluation among the Japanese. For example, to perform *tsumi*-producing acts is to do something sinful and cruel; to do something *tsumi* is to be merciless.

Hiroko Hara and Hiroshi Wagatsuma (1974) see significance in the peculiarly Japanese sense of *tsumi*, which is the concept of "having grown up hurting one's parents, particularly the mother, in the process" (p. 172; our translation). They indicate that the reason why Japanese children come to accord special significance to the hurt experienced by parents, which easily leads to feelings of *tsumi*, is the tendency toward moral masochism present in Japanese mothers. "Moral masochism" is the control of another person's behavior through killing or hurting oneself, producing feelings of *tsumi* in the other, and resulting in the other person's changing to suit one's needs. A survey of Thematic Apperception Test (TAT) responses by the Japanese (Devos & Wagatsuma, 1961) indicated a very large percentage of cases presenting the following theme:

> A son becoming delinquent and turning to misdeeds. He causes troubles with the neighbors. Lecturing him does no good. The mother loses weight from worry, becomes ill, and eventually dies. The son then becomes penitent and in tears, reforms, works hard, and becomes an asset to society. (p. 1217)

When parents become hurt and take such moral masochistic action, *tsumi* is produced within children who love their parents; because of the *tsumi*, the children eventually come to act exactly as their parents wish them to behave. It is believed that this *tsumi*, driving the Japanese to redemptive behavior, forms the basic drive behind the needs for achievement and accomplishment. Such drives, while appearing to work positively, also contribute to the often-cited fact that the Japanese are not adept at enjoying life; enjoyment is sometimes only the consequence of actions taken as a last resort.

However, things do not always turn out as intended. Some time ago, failure to atone for one's sins was frequently followed by suicide. Today, this failure can be regarded as leading to feelings of self-abandonment ("I am a failure as a human being") and to even greater delinquency; thus, feelings of *tsumi* are only reinforced. And this phenomenon is not unrelated to other problem behaviors exhibited by Japanese adolescents, which are discussed later on.

These psychological characteristics of the Japanese affect the mental state of children and adolescents in various manners, giving rise to many unique psychopathological phenomena (Yamazaki, Inomata, & Mackenzie, 1987).

SHAME, GUILT, EMBARRASSMENT, SHYNESS, AND CHILD-REARING PRACTICES

When the Japanese scold their children, they use phrases such as "If you do such things, people will laugh at you"; "if a boy cries like that, his friends will laugh at him"; or "If you don't behave well at school, I [the mother] will be too embarrassed to see your teacher." In an unpublished recent study of ours, 52 out of 84 mothers with children aged 5–6 indicated that they had used such phrases before. Parents try to make the children aware and conscious of the "eyes" of other people—other children, friends, and teachers. The purpose is to teach them the importance of *sekentei* (social appearance). In this case, *sekentei* is the eyes of the people who watch the actions and abilities of the children. In other words, it is a sort of "measuring community" or a watchful normative presence. The Japanese have learned what is "shameful" through discipline by internalizing the concept of *sekentei*. In our country, the socialization of shame is an important part of discipline.

In general, the characteristic of this type of discipline is indirect rather than direct use of negative words of rejection or reprimand. In experiments involving infants, we often find that when a child becomes fussy and the experiment does not proceed smoothly, the mother will become embarrassed, although she will rarely scold the child. Moreover, at the end of the experiment, the mother will apologize to the experimenter for not having been able to cooperate because the child did not behave as expected. Although mothers do not necessarily expect children to learn through observing their behavior, it is likely that this behavior will influence the children.

The main concern of Japanese mothers is whether their children will behave properly outside the home, will not upset others, and will not become objects of ridicule. However, the mothers are also worried that if they directly reprimand their children, it will affect the emotional tie between them and the children. Therefore, they use *soto* (out, outsiders, public), meaning other people, teachers, and friends, as opposed to *uchi* (in, members of the family, private), when they scold their children. During experiments, we often observe U.S. mothers verbally encouraging their children to perform, praising and commending them when the children are able to work out a given task. However, this behavior is not often observed among Japanese mothers. Japanese mothers, at most, give subtle nonverbal expressions. The mothers are probably afraid that behavior such as open encouragement and praise will lead to excessive independence on the children's part. On the other hand, the shaming technique is believed to strengthen mother–child interdependence.

Self-conscious emotions, especially shame, are believed to appear when the concept of "me" and "self" is distinguished from "others" at about the age of 2. Shyness, which is slightly different in meaning from shame, is often observed among Japanese children at an earlier stage of about 18 months. However, a large number of mothers consider stranger anxiety in 8-month-olds as shyness, and in interviews indicate that children display shyness at even earlier stages. We conducted interviews (Kanaya, Bradshaw, Campos, & Miyake, 1992) with 43 Japanese mothers and 15 U.S. mothers of 5-month-old infants. The items covered in the interview included the following:

1. Can you list for us the emotions your baby has shown since he or she was born?
2. I want to ask you how each emotion was shown, at what age it appeared, and in what situation it was elicited. (Mothers were also asked about emotions that were not mentioned spontaneously in their response. Happiness, anger, sadness, fear, surprise, disgust, interest, displeasure, shyness, and guilt were the emotions addressed.)

There were no distinct differences between the U.S. and Japanese mothers with regard to the basic emotions, such as happiness, anger, sadness, fear, surprise, and disgust. Neither U.S. nor Japanese mothers cited shyness, shame, or guilt spontaneously in response to the first question. However, for the second question, 47% of the Japanese mothers and 13% of the U.S. mothers responded that shyness was shown, and 5% of the Japanese mothers and 7% of the U.S. mothers responded that shame was shown. There were no mothers in either group who responded that guilt was shown.

Even though it is probably justifiable to consider shyness as a part of stranger anxiety appearing at about 18 months, as indicated above, nearly half of the Japanese mothers considered it to have been apparent at 5 months. It can be speculated that Japanese children, reared by mothers who are overly sensitive to shyness, develop shyness from an early stage, and that this is followed by embarrassment and shame, in comparison to U.S. children.

In several of our laboratory experiments involving infants and mothers in Japan, we experienced more difficulty in obtaining valid data from successful experimentation than researchers in the United States generally encounter. In some cases, the percentage of successful experiments did not reach 50%. One of the reasons for the failure was the open concern exhibited by many mothers, even before entering the lab, about being observed and whether their children would do well in the experiment. For these mothers, the lab setting was the "public" itself, making them conscious of the eye of the observer. Many mothers came dressed in their Sunday best. Furthermore, the mothers' display of shyness and embarrassment enhanced their children's anxiety and fussiness. Some mothers were embarrassed and ashamed that they were not able to cooperate, and therefore would not accept remuneration. This type of behavior is repeated in other public situations as the children grow older, and probably cannot be separated from the development of shame in the children. In any case, the behavior mentioned above is a serious problem in cross-cultural studies on emotions involving experimental paradigms. Obviously, there are biases in the Japanese samples.

TAIJIN-KYOHFU, OR DELUSIONAL SOCIAL PHOBIA

As mentioned before, the psychological characteristics of the Japanese are epitomized by the *haji* and *ura* cultures, strong *tate* and *amae* structural ties, and reference group dependence. The Japanese attempt to interpret other persons' intentions nonverbally through their expressions and mannerisms; shy away from precise verbal criticism that might do decisive damage to their opponents; and display a tendency to resort to unspoken consent for effecting smooth interpersonal relationships. Because of this, the distance in interpersonal relationships becomes critical, and maintaining a "reasonable distance" becomes indispensable in casual relationships beyond those with members of the family and close friends. And *taijin-kyohfu* is an excellent depiction of this psychological characteristic of the Japanese in accentuated (psychopathological) form.

The Concept of *Taijin-Kyohfu*

Case reports on *sekimen-kyohfu* (erythrophobia) originated in Europe at the beginning of the 20th century. Pierre Janet (1908) regarded the phenomenon as *la phobie des situations sociales,* but the concept was soon replaced by those of *die soziale Angst* (social unrest) and social neurosis. With regard to *taijin-kyohfu,* reportedly occurring in particularly large numbers in Japan, Shoma Morita stated in 1921 that "erythrophobia, i.e. phobia of interpersonal relations, is a manifestation of embarrassment" (p. 23; our translation). Thereafter, many studies have been conducted on the various manifestations of *taijin-kyohfu,* and detailed records have been kept on the characteristic symptoms of *sekimen-kyohfu* (fear of blushing), *shisen-kyohfu* (fear of eye contact), *jikoshuu-kyohfu* (fear of one's body odors), *shuukei-kyohfu* (fear of body dysmorphia), and others. The connotations carried by these phobias are fairly distinct from those of the phobias as noted in the Western countries, and the usual German and English terminology is very often insufficient for portraying the conditions accurately. Here again, the *haji* (shame) and *tsumi* (guilt) peculiar to the Japanese are important.

Rene Spitz (1965) regards stranger anxiety as a developmental milestone, appearing at about 8 months of age. But in Japan, the term *hitomishiri* (stranger anxiety or people-shyness) is often employed in speaking of adults. As stated before, the Japanese feel *haji* when given the special attention of others, whether it is negative or positive. For example, about 70% of ordinary college students have indicated that they feel embarrassment when they "fall in front of others," when "they are the only one dressed differently," when "the door closes on them when trying to board a train," and when they are "praised by the teacher in front of others." Such tendencies have also been recognized in children. In a comparative study on embarrassment among elementary school children in the United States and Japan, Eiko Hashimoto (1988) obtained significantly higher responses from Japanese children for these items: "Being dressed differently from others," "Not doing as well in studies as one's friends," "Wearing socks or clothing that are torn," and "Eating meals in other people's homes." Such responses are very precise reflections of the psychological characteristics of the Japanese, shaped within the psychological framework of *sekentei* (social appearance) and *haji* (shame), as can be seen in the regular use of such terms as "present an ill figure" or "save appearances" in daily situations. And these particular psychological characteristics are closely related to the fact that cases of *taijin-kyohfu* are abundant in Japan.

Kunio Yanagida (1976) has made an interesting comment with regard to the gaze of the Japanese. He notes that there are a great number of bashful people in Japan. For people having led an un-self-conscious existence among familiar people to meet the gaze of strangers for the first time is something that requires a large degree of courage. In the company of friends, they are most often capable of looking at or looking back at strangers without much ado, but on their own, they cannot help casting down their eyes, resorting to the passive role of being looked at. He states that the Japanese have always needed to consciously call up courage so as not to be deflected or defeated by the gaze of others. Hence, *niramekko* (staring down) has become a form of play for children, arising out of the need to strengthen one's gaze from childhood. This is of interest in terms of the ethnological background to *shisen-kyohfu* (fear of eye contact) as it exists in Japan.

Symptoms of *Taijin-Kyohfu*

The typical course of *taijin-kyohfu* can generally be summarized as follows. A certain degree of cohesion is maintained in the family environment from infancy, and the subjects' mothers or surrogate figures are very often full of love and affection and look after the subjects well. Raised somewhat overprotectively, the subjects are generally good-natured, showing traces of *amae*, and frequently appearing more childish than their age. However, being honest and incapable of wrongdoing, they are most often active and bright as well as competitive, at least before onset of the disorder. At the same time, they appear to be adaptable (at least on the surface) and considerate of the feelings of others, are liked by others in turn, and have strong desires to be liked and accepted by others.

Onset usually comes between junior high school and the beginning of college, without any substantial trigger. The subjects voice a variety of complaints: "My face reddens," "My eyes move of their own accord so that I end up looking at someone," "My features become frozen," "I end up smiling unintentionally," "My nose is crooked and ugly," "My voice trembles," and "My body emits odors" (sweat, flatulence, underarm odor, semen). They also complain of bodily sensations accompanying these complaints (e.g., heat or flushing of the face). Moreover, they insist with confidence that they know instinctively and with certainty that their faces are flushed because of the way other persons will unconsciously run their hands over their own faces, or that their eyes have an unpleasant cast because of the way other persons will subtly lower their eyes, or that their bodies are emitting some odor because of the way others touch their noses or clear their throats. These subjects will sense the presence of odor through another person's cough even at times when their own noses cannot detect any smell. In other words, they observe themselves through other persons' eyes, ears, and noses; sensing that they represent repugnant entities in other persons' minds, they live in fear of the actions of others, such as face rubbing, looking down, nose touching, and coughing, which are believed to arise as manifestations of disgust.

Such subjects end up constantly wary of the expressions and behavior of those around them. Seeing themselves reflected therein, they seek help from physicians or plastic surgeons, trying to alter their appearance in any way possible. Their complaints, delivered with gross confidence, can also be called delusional. For this reason, although the subjects will go through much moaning and groaning, the prognosis is actually quite good. For example, the belief that they are emitting sweaty smells may not change; in time, however, people will appear to clear their throats less around them, they will pick up interests elsewhere in work and play, and the degree of disablement they feel in getting through life will gradually subside.

Itaru Yamashita (1993) has summarized the four principal characteristics of *taijin-kyohfu* as follows:

1. Patients have a delusional belief in the existence of serious shortcomings in themselves.

2. The existence of such shortcomings is intuitively perceived by patients from the behavior and actions of others around them.

3. These defects make others feel unpleasant and therefore should be corrected or removed by all means.

4. There are no other mental symptoms appearing in patients with *taijin-kyohfu*.

The onset of *taijin-kyohfu* can be triggered by some trivial incident against the backdrop of the characteristic over-self-consciousness of adolescence. Those with *taijin-kyohfu* are most distressed by situations in which contact between personalities are not deep but not altogether superficial, involving people with whom psychological distance is subject to change. Sensitive to such boundaries in psychological distance, they immediately come to harbor ideas of reference upon sensing any change, and become trapped by *taijin-kyohfu*. The development up to onset of *taijin-kyohfu* in relation to such circumstances, from the viewpoint of interpersonal communication, may be interpreted as follows: In interpersonal relationships in the process of development, there are matters that cannot be communicated directly. Children are forced to learn to "pretend" to know, or, in other words, to learn the art of "silent agreement." In the acquisition of such skills (exceeding the normal level of communication), the aforementioned typically Japanese notions of conformity, uniformity, and perfectionism create a variety of conflicts, in turn producing the various psychopathological phenomena seen in older children and adolescents.

Family Environment and Personality Characteristics of *Taijin-Kyohfu* Cases

As suggested above, a common factor in the family environment of *taijin-kyohfu* patients is overprotection, with children being reared with great care. For this reason, the subjects generally have positive feelings about their parents or surrogate figures. In other words, such subjects in infancy have mothers who are full of love and affection, although strict; they expect their children to fulfill a certain image; and narcissistic feelings of wishing to be treasured by the mothers are visible in the children. Mother–child separation is not complete, and strong dependence upon the mothers can be seen. Upon reaching school age, the subjects feel bewildered in dealing with children their own age; instead of employing their increasing interpersonal experience in making appropriate adjustments in the mother–child relationship or family dynamics, they seek a superficial solution by attempting to be "good" children. This form of problem solving through identification with an idealized self, in what could be termed the "golden years" for the subjects (from infancy through the early years in school), becomes impossible in practice upon reaching adolescence. Made aware through some trivial incident of their own awkward behavior in an impossible situation, and the attitudes of those watching them, they lose sight of how to deal with people and become anxious in relating to others.

Most *taijin-kyohfu* patients have great consideration for the feelings and emotions of others, and will go to extraordinary lengths to think in terms of other persons. At the same time, they possess such traits as a "goody-goody" conscience, pride, and a need to come up first. Positive tendencies such as being bright, active, carefree, cheerful, and diligent in work exist alongside passive tendencies such as diffidence, shyness, and timidity.

Hence, raised in homes with strong overprotective overtones, these children want to be considerate of the feelings of others, while also strongly wishing to be liked by them. As a result, they are beset by a peculiar vicious circle in terms of human relations upon being thrown into the midst of Japanese society, with its emphasis on such concepts as *haji, tatemae, menboku* (face), group identification, perfectionism, and the importance of human relations with proximal persons. All of this results in the subjects' being crushed by doubt and anxiety, and their attempts to rationalize those fears bring with them an obsessive *taijin-kyohfu*. Thus, *taijin-kyohfu* is a neurotic manifestation deeply rooted in Japanese culture; although it is also seen in some other countries in Asia, it is believed to be rare in the Western nations.

SCHOOL REFUSAL

Apart from *taijin-kyohfu*, in which "reasonable distance" within interpersonal relations is the issue in point, another phenomenon representing an exaggeration of typical Japanese psychological characteristics is that of "school refusal." Within the group-dependent and perfectionistic society of Japan, children are often expected to act in a uniform manner. The era of rapid economical growth starting in the 1950s brought with it a rapid rise in rate of school enrollment, producing a uniformly higher-education-oriented society with total disregard for the individuality of children.

The Connotations of School Refusal in Japan

Let us review the issue of "school refusal"—a vivid reflection of the effects of Japanese culture, and of the social and economic situation of the country, on the minds of children. It is a vital issue symbolically encompassing the full spectrum of psychological problems harbored by children, highlighting the discord brought about by the one-sided demands made upon children by Japanese society, school, and parents.

In Japan, case reports started appearing in early 1955, and various terms (e.g., "prolonged absenteeism," "neurotic school refusal," and "school phobia") have been employed to describe the phenomenon. Presently, "school refusal" has become the most prevalent term, and the phenomenon is regarded as a neurotic manifestation; however, the terms "school dislike" and "school nonattendance" are also used from time to time. A key point here is that "school refusal" is not listed as a separate diagnostic classification in international diagnostic criteria. In other words, "school refusal" is a neurotic manifestation with refusal to go to school as the chief complaint, but the diverse psychological and psychopathological backgrounds of children displaying the phenomenon do not permit it to be assimilated into a single disorder classification.

The Ministry of Education has been conducting surveys on "dislike of school" from 1966. The 1991 survey (Monbasho, 1992) revealed the numbers of children absent from school for over 30 days per year for "disliking school" as being 12,637 in elementary school (0.14% of all elementary school children), and 54,112 in junior high (1.04% of all junior high students). In recent decades, greater numbers of elementary school children are being affected; along with the tendency for increasingly younger age groups to be affected, it is characteristic that many of those children are manifesting neurotic symptoms such as obsessive states, apocleisis, and hyperphagia.

In the 1989 survey (Monbasho, 1990), the direct trigger precipitating school refusal among elementary school children was found in the home in 36.2%, in school life in 26.8%, and in personal problems in 21.0%. Among junior high school students, school causes were cited in 44.5%, home causes in 27.9%, and personal causes in 18.2%. A breakdown of these figures revealed the following among elementary school cases: problems in parent–child relationships (18.4%), problems within the individual (12.9%), drastic changes in the family environment (11.4%), and problems pertaining to relations with friends (10.8%). Among junior high school students, the breakdown was as follows: academic problems (17.6%), problems pertaining to relations with friends (16.0%), problems in parent–child relationships (12.9%), problems within the individual apart from illness (10.5%), and drastic changes in the family environment (8.4%). In any case, the question of why the neurotic manifestation of refusing to appear in the school setting is on the rise is certainly cause for a review of the fundamental question of how school education in modern-day Japan ought to be.

The Origins of School Refusal

It can be said that separation–individuation as described by Margaret Mahler (1968) has not been carried out successfully among the Japanese, leaving them with what can probably be best described as a "symbiotic self," without the establishment of a "self" in the Western sense. The ego ideal of the Japanese is a reciprocal entity, and fulfilling one's responsibilities and obligations among family, group members, and friends is a matter of great importance. In other words, the successful maintenance of ties between oneself and others is the required form of conduct. The act of going to school is accompanied by certain obligations, incurring strong tensions. In the family, a child is looked after, cherished and recognized by the parents in exchange for being a "good child" from the parents' point of view—being compliant, loyal, and dependent. A similar reciprocal relationship is sought in the school setting between a child and his or her teachers and friends. And when for some reason the maintenance of such reciprocal relationships becomes impossible, children recognize it as a failure on their part and come to harbor emotions leading to *haji*.

What needs to be considered in this context is why so many children attempt to express the conflicts in their minds by not going to school, while, on the other hand, parents and teachers suddenly panic when the children cease going to school, and lose direction in how to deal with the situation. Children with problems of a psychological nature exhibit various symptoms as a way of making the adults around them aware of their problems and of seeking their help. The cards they can play to accomplish this should be numerous, but why is it that the act of not going to school alone has become the trump card for this purpose in Japan? It is an indisputable fact that changes in family dynamics, the hostile environment created by the structure of our higher-education-oriented society, and complex problems inherent in the state of our overly uniform school education are all deeply related to the drastic increase in school refusal.

The factors involved in school refusal are complex, and a variety of reasons for it may be found. Notably, however, children refusing school incorporate parents and teachers, home and school as domineering others into their egos; with their egos overwhelmed by these domineering entities, they willingly submit to suppression of their own egos, creating fake social egos tailored to the expectations of others. It can be said that this very condition is one large reason driving them to obsessiveness. Here again, the peculiar psychological characteristics of the Japanese, such as *haji*, feelings of group identification, and perfectionism are closely reflected, casting strong obsessive overtones upon school refusal as it exists in our country (Yamazaki, Inomata, Makita, & Mackenzie, 1992).

VIOLENCE IN THE HOME

"Violence in the home" in Japan denotes a condition in which children perpetrating acute violence toward parents, siblings, and sometimes grandparents in the home exhibit no problem behavior whatsoever elsewhere. This is believed to be a phenomenon unique to Japan. Generally, such children meekly follow their parents' wishes in infancy, and are much loved as "good" children; one day, however, they turn with violence against their parents or siblings for some trivial reason and thereafter continue to bully their family members as if they were brutal tyrants. They may destroy all the furniture in the house with a bat, break windows, and strike and kick principally their mothers. The fathers may reprimand the children for their violence, but do not attempt to deal with it seriously, depending upon others to intervene. The families, unable to continue living at home, may sometimes move out to a nearby inn, but even then hesitate to seek help from a medical institution.

Demanding the impossible from their parents, these children use failure to meet their wishes as the perfect excuse to rationalize their behavior, and go about smirking as they coldly view their parents in their bewilderment at what to do. They ignore normal living patterns, spend their days in a self-centered way, and come to exhibit life rhythms in which their days and nights are inverted. However, such subjects do harbor guilt feelings regarding their violent behavior and feel the need to rationalize these, so that even while being violent, they exhibit wheedling behavior like that of small

children, especially toward their mothers. As such, they appear as if they
have split personalities.

Shinichiro Wakabayashi (1989) has pointed out a number of personality
tendencies characterizing children who exhibit violence in the home; among
these are punctiliousness, perfectionism, overt obsession in many ways (e.g.,
needing to do their homework scrupulously), inferiority in linguistic expression, and very limited friendships. Such children, restrained by their parents
from infancy, strive obsessively to meet the level of their parents' expectations, but come to learn that it is impossible to fulfill their parents' demands
completely. Wishing to attain the impossible, they gradually become conscious of the gap, which gives rise to anxiety. Unequipped to express their
doubts verbally, and unable to distract themselves through play with friends,
they are forced to limit their interaction to family members, and attempts
to assert themselves are channeled through violence alone. It appears almost
as if they fear retaliation from their parents if they do *not* continue being
violent.

There is a tendency among Japanese parents to place large demands
upon their children in terms of achievement and accomplishment from early
infancy, so that for the children to live up to their parents' expectations in
itself denotes winning their parents' love and belief in them. Hence, should
a child be unable to meet parental demands, that child is highly shamed.
This follows because the failure of the child is also regarded as an
embarrassment for the parents and family, given the reciprocal nature of
their relationship. Violence in the home, as it exists in Japan, is in a way
symbolic of the exclusiveness of the Japanese home as well as of the
psychological absence of the father; it may well be that those children who
can express only aggression toward their mothers are really not capable of
forming interpersonal relationships with anyone except them. In any case,
the peculiarly Japanese concept and structure of *amae* (dependence upon
the supposed indulgence of others) seems to be construed as "Both parents
and home are mine" in the minds of such children (Yamazaki, 1979).

CONCLUSION

School refusal, violence in the home, and *taijin-kyohfu* have a number of
issues in common. Children unable to fully enjoy a stable parent–child
relationship in infancy, and nurtured in a perfectionist environment, may
break apart within the uniformity-based school system and come to refuse
school; on the other hand, they may attempt to confirm their own existence
through violence against other members of the family. Or, in the case of
taijin-kyohfu, they fear interaction with others at a time when they most
need to experience various human relationships and establish their own
identity, and come to exhibit a variety of problem behaviors symbolically.
All these problems are believed to reflect a refusal to develop by children

and adolescents in the very process of development; they also illustrate the way in which the many distortions in present-day Japanese society are molding the minds of young people, producing in turn the many forms of problem behavior.

REFERENCES

Aida, Y. (1972). *Nihonjin no ishiki kozo* [*The conscious structure of the Japanese*]. Tokyo: Kodansha Gendai-Shinsho.

Benedict, R. (1946). *The chrysanthemum and the sword: Patterns of Japanese culture*. Boston: Houghton Mifflin.

Devos, G., & Wagatsuma, H. (1961). Value attitudes toward role behavior of women in two Japanese villages. *American Anthropologist, 63,* 1204–1230.

Doi, T. (1986). *The anatomy of self: The individual versus society* (M. A. Harbison, Trans.). Tokyo: Kodansha International.

Hara, H., & Wagatsuma, H. (1974). *Shitsuke* [*Bringing up a child*], Tokyo: Kohbundoh.

Hashimoto, E. (1988). A cross-cultural study of the intensity of the emotion of shame/embarrassment: American, Iranian and Japanese children. *Seibojyogakuin Tankidaigaku Kiyo, 17,* 55–60.

Janet, P. (1903). *Les obsessions et la psychasthenie* (2 vols.). Paris: Félix Alcan.

Kanaya, Y., Bradshaw, D., Campos, J., & Miyake, K. (1992). Japanese and American mothers perceiving and evaluating their 5-month-old infants' emotional expression. In K. Miyake (Ed.), *Research and Clinical Center for Child Development annual report 1990–1991* (pp. 41–51). Sapporo: Hokkaido University.

Mahler, M. (1968). *On human symbiosis and the vicissitudes of individuation.* New York: International Universities Press.

Minami, H. (1983). *Nihonteki jiga* [*The Japanese self*]. Tokyo: Iwanami Shinsho.

Monbasho (Ministry of Education). (1990). Gakkoh kihon chosa [*General statistics on schooling 1989*]. Tokyo: Author.

Monbasho (Ministry of Education). (1992). Gakkoh kihon chosa [*General statistics on Schooling 1991*]. Tokyo: Author.

Morita, S. (1921). *Shinkeishitsu oyobi shinkeisuijyaku no ryoho* [*Therapies for Morita's shinkeishitsu and psychasthenia*]. Tokyo: Shinkeishitsu-Kenkyukai.

Nakane, C. (1970). *Japanese society.* Tokyo: Charles E. Tuttle.

Spitz, R. (1965). *The first year of life.* New York: International Universities Press.

Wakabayashi, S. (Ed.). (1989). *Jido-seinen-seishinka* [*Child and adolescent psychiatry*]. Tokyo: Kongoshuppan.

Yamashita, I. (1993). *Taijin-kyofu or delusional social phobia.* Sapporo: Hokkaido University Press.

Yamazaki, K. (1979). Transition of the father's role in Japanese family and culture. In K. Miyake (Ed.), *Research and Clinical Center for Child Development annual report 1978–1979* (pp. 43–53). Sapporo: Hokkaido University.

Yamazaki, K., Inomata, J., & Mackenzie, J. A. (1987). Self-expression, interpersonal relations, and juvenile delinquency in Japan. In C. M. Super (Ed.), *The role of culture in developmental disorders* (pp. 179–204). New York: Academic Press.

Yamazaki, K., Inomata, J., Makita, K., & Mackenzie, J. A. (1992). Japanese culture and neurotic manifestation in childhood and adolescence. In C. Chiland & J.

G. Young (Eds.), *New approaches to mental health from birth to adolescence* (pp. 384–391). New Haven, CT: Yale University Press.

Yanagida, K. (1970). *Teihon Yanagida Kunio shu* [*The authentic text: Works of Kunio Yanagida*] (Vol. 30). Tokyo: Chikuma-Shobo.

Yanagida, K. (1976). *Meiji-Taisho shi: Sesohron* [*The history of the Meiji and Taisho era: A phase of life*]. Tokyo: Kodansha.

APPENDIX

Self-Conscious Emotions: Measures and Methods

This volume has highlighted numerous new and exciting lines of research associated with self-conscious emotions. The recent vast increase in empirical research in this area is due, in part, to the development of a number of new methods for assessing self-conscious affect. This appendix provides a partial list of the measurement methods and techniques employed by the contributors to this volume.

MEASURES OF SHAME AND GUILT

Measure: Clown Doll Paradigm
Authors: Barrett, K. C., & Zahn-Waxler, C.

Brief Description: A brief situation is presented in which a toddler (age 17 months to 36 months) is led to believe that he/she has broken a clown rag doll that is "the experimenter's favorite." Responses to this situation can be used to dichotomize children into those showing a shame-relevant pattern (avoiders) or a guilt-relevant pattern (amenders).

Source: Barrett, K. C., Zahn-Waxler, C., & Cole, P. M. (1993). Avoiders vs. amenders: Implications for the investigation of guilt and shame during toddlerhood? *Emotion and Cognition, 7,* 481–505.

Further information available from: Karen C. Barrett, PhD, Dept. of HDFS, Colorado State University, Fort Collins, CO 80523.

Measure: Personal Feelings Questionnaire 2 (PFQ 2)
Author: Harder, D. W.

Brief Description: A 22 item paper-and-pencil measure of shame-proneness and guilt-proneness, appropriate for adults 18 years and over.

Further information available from: David W. Harder, PhD, Department of Psychology, Tufts University, Medford, MA 02155-2334.

Measure: Shame–Pride Behavioral Codes
Authors: Lewis, M., & Alessandri, S.

Brief Description: Eighteen behavioral codes used to assess presence or absence of shame and pride in preschool-aged children.

Source: Lewis, M., Alessandri, S., & Sullivan, M. W. (1992). Differences in shame and pride as a function of chidren's gender and task difficulty. *Child Development, 63, 630–638.*

Measure: Pride and Sorry Representation Scales
Authors: Mascolo, M., & Fischer, K.

Brief Description: The scales are comprised of procedures for administering 10 story stems to assess children's developing understanding of events that evoke proud and sorry feelings. In a pretend play scenario, the administrator uses dolls and props to model a set of proud and sorry reactions in increasingly complex social situations. A variety of probes are used to assess children's understanding of each proud or sorry reaction. The scale is applicable to children between the ages of 2 and 4, although additional stories can be added to extend the scale to older children.

Further information available from: Michael F. Mascolo, PhD, Department of Psychology, Merrimack College, North Andover, MA 01845.

Measure: Questionnaire from the International Survey on Emotion Antecedents and Reactions (ISEAR)
Authors: Scherer, K., & Wallbott, H. G.

Brief Description: A questionnaire concerning physical, affective, cognitive, expressive, and situational factors associated with seven key emotions: Joy, fear, anger, sadness, disgust, shame, and guilt.

Source: Further details on this instrument can be found in Scherer, K. R. (Ed.). (1988). *Facets of Emotion.* Hillsdale, NJ: Erlbaum.

Further information available from: Klaus Scherer, FPSE, University of Geneva, 9, Route de Drize, CH-1227 Coronge-Geneva.

Measure: Children: Child Reaction and Attribution Survey (C-CARS)
Authors: Stegge, H., & Ferguson, T. J.

Brief Description: A paper-and-pencil measure consisting of eight written and illustrated situations where a child is depicted as violating standards of conduct. For each situation children rate three responses reflecting guilt, shame, and externalization. Justifications for each emotion are coded according to the use of coping mechanisms. The measure can be completed in a group situation by children 9 years old and up; individual interviews can be used with younger children. A version consisting of positive situations, assessing pride, shame, guilt, and externalization is available in Dutch.

Further information available from: Heddy Stegge, MA, Free University Amsterdam, van der Boechorststraat 1, 1081 BT Amsterdam, The Netherlands.

Measure: Test of Self-Conscious Affect (TOSCA)
Authors: Tangney, J. P., Wagner, P. E., & Gramzow, R.

Brief Description: A scenario-based paper-and-pencil measure of shame-proneness and guilt-proneness, appropriate for adults 18 years and over. Shame and guilt scales are each composed of 15 items (10 in connection with negative events, 5 in connection with ostensibly positive events).

Further information available from: June Price Tangney, PhD, Department of Psychology, George Mason University, Fairfax, VA 22030.

Measure: Test of Self-Conscious Affect for Adolescents (TOSCA-A)
Authors: Tangney, J. P., Wagner, P. E., Gavlas, J., & Gramzow, R.

Brief Description: A scenario-based paper-and-pencil measure of shame-proneness and guilt-proneness, appropriate for adolescents ages 12 to 18. Shame and guilt scales are each composed of 15 items (10 in connection with negative events, 5 in connection with ostensibly positive events).

Further information available from: June Price Tangney, PhD, Department of Psychology, George Mason University, Fairfax, VA 22030.

Measure: Test of Self-Conscious Affect for Children (TOSCA-C)
Authors: Tangney, J. P., Wagner, P. E., Burggraf, S. A., Gramzow, R., & Fletcher, C.

Brief Description: A scenario-based paper-and-pencil measure of shame-proneness and guilt-proneness, appropriate for children ages 8 to 12. Shame and guilt scales are each composed of 15 items (10 in connection with negative events, 5 in connection with ostensibly positive events).

Further information available from: June Price Tangney, PhD, Department of Psychology, George Mason University, Fairfax, VA 22030.

SOCIALIZATION OF SHAME AND GUILT

Measure: Expectations Sort for Parents (ESP)
Author: Ferguson, T. J.

Brief Description: A Q-sort measure assessing parents' expectations of how their child ideally would be or behave (ideals), parents' expectations of how their child ought to be or behave (oughts), and parents' perceptions of how their child actually is or behaves. Seventy negatively worded items reflecting four domains (morally appropriate behavior, respect for others' rights and requests, age-appropriate self-regulation, and stereotypically desirable characteristics) are sorted three times (one each for ideal, ought, and actual).

Further information available from: Tamara J. Ferguson, PhD, Department of Psychology, Utah State University, Logan, UT 84322.

Measure: Parents: Child Reaction and Attribution Survey (P-CARS)
Authors: Ferguson, T. J., & Stegge, H.

Brief Description: A paper-and-pencil measure consisting of eight situations where a parent's child is depicted as either violating standards of conduct (negative version) or upholding these same standards (positive version). For each situation, parents rate 26 items pertaining to their own emotional reaction (e.g., anger, embarrassment, disappointment), the personal validity of the situation, and the parent's use of inductive, love withdrawal, and power assertive techniques. A retrospective version for use with college-age students is also available.

Further information available from: Tamara J. Ferguson, PhD, Department of Psychology, Utah State University, Logan Utah 84322.

Measures: Socialization of Moral Affect—Parent of Preschoolers Form (SOMA-PP); Socialization of Moral Affect—Parent of Children Form (SOMA-PC)
Authors: Rosenberg, K. L., Tangney, J. P., Denham, S., Leonard, A. M., & Widmaier, N.

Brief Description: A scenario-based paper-and-pencil measure of specific parental behaviors thought to be influential to the development of children's shame-prone and guilt-prone styles. The measure consists of 18 (8 positive and 10 negative) situations depicting childrens' success, failure, and transgression behaviors, and subsequent parental responses. The 11 parental behavior scales are: love withdrawal; power assertion; victim-focused induction; parent-focused induction; disgust–teasing–contempt; conditional approval of behavior; focus on behavior; focus on person; public humiliation; neglect–ignoring of positive behaviors; and teaching reparation. Two forms are available—one for parents of preschool-age children and another for parents of children ages 8 to 12.

Further information available from: June Price Tangney, PhD, Department of Psychology, George Mason University, Fairfax, VA 22030.

Measure: Socialization Of Moral Affect—Child Form (SOMA-C)
Authors: Rosenberg, K. L., Tangney, J. P., Denham, S., Leonard, A. M., & Widmaier, N.

Brief Description: A scenario-based paper-and-pencil measure of specific parental behaviors thought to be influential to the development of shame-prone and guilt-prone styles in children ages 8 to 12. The measure consists of 18 (8 positive and 10 negative) situations depicting childrens' success, failure, and transgression behaviors, and subsequent parental responses. The 11 parental behavior scales are: love withdrawal; power assertion; victim-focused induction; parent-focused induction; disgust–teasing–contempt; conditional approval of behavior; focus on behavior; focus on person; public humiliation; neglect–ignoring of positive behaviors; and teaching reparation. Children rate how likely they believe their mother or father would be to react in the depicted ways. A companion videotape shows a "mother" and a "father" acting out each response item, and children follow along and mark their answers on the questionnaire.

Further information available from: June Price Tangney, PhD, Department of Psychology, George Mason University, Fairfax, VA 22030.

MEASURES OF EMBARRASSMENT

Measure: Embarrassability Scale
Author: Modigliani, A.

Brief Description: A 26 item paper-and-pencil measure of adults' susceptibility to embarrassment.

Source: Leary, M. R. (1991). Social anxiety, shyness, and related constructs. In J. Robinson, P. Shaver, & L. Wrightsman (Eds.), *Measures of personality and social psychological attitudes* (pp. 161–194). New York: Academic Press.

Measure: Embarrassment Behavioral Codes
Authors: Lewis, M., Stanger, C., Sullivan, M. W., & Weiss, M.

Brief Description: Facial and behavioral codes used to assess occurrence of embarrassment in preschool-age children.

Source: Lewis, M., Stanger, C., Sullivan, M. W., & Weiss, M. (1989). Self development and self conscious emotions. *Child Development, 60,* 146–156.

MEASURES OF PRIDE

Measure: Shame–Pride Behavioral Codes
Authors: Lewis, M., & Alessandri, S.

Brief Description: Eighteen behavioral codes used to assess presence or absence of shame and pride in preschool-age children.

Source: Lewis, M., Alessandri, S., & Sullivan, M. W. (1992). Differences in shame and pride as a function of children's gender and task difficulty. *Child Development, 63,* 630–638.

Measure: Pride and Sorry Representation Scales
Authors: Mascolo, M., & Fischer, K.

Brief Description: The scales are comprised of procedures for administering 10 story stems to assess children's developing understanding of events that evoke proud and sorry feelings. In a pretend play scenario, the administrator uses dolls and props to model a set of proud and sorry reactions in increasingly complex social situations. A variety of probes are used to assess children's understanding of each proud or sorry reaction. The scale is applicable to children between the ages of 2 and 4, although additional stories can be added to extend the scale to older children.

Further information available from: Michael F. Mascolo, PhD, Department of Psychology, Merrimack College, North Andover, MA 01845.

Measure: Test of Self-Conscious Affect (TOSCA)
Authors: Tangney, J. P., Wagner, P. E., & Gramzow, R.

Brief Description: A scenario-based paper-and-pencil measure of Alpha Pride (pride in self) and Beta Pride (pride in behavior), appropriate for adults 18 years and over. Alpha Pride and Beta Pride scales are each composed of five items.

Further information available from: June Price Tangney, PhD, Department of Psychology, George Mason University, Fairfax, VA 22030.

Measure: Test of Self-Conscious Affect for Adolescents (TOSCA-A)
Authors: Tangney, J. P., Wagner, P. E., Gavlas, J., & Gramzow, R.

Brief Description: A scenario-based paper-and-pencil measure of Alpha Pride (pride in self) and Beta Pride (pride in behavior), appropriate for adolescents ages 12 to 18. Alpha Pride and Beta Pride scales are each composed of five items.

Further information available from: June Price Tangney, PhD, Department of Psychology, George Mason University, Fairfax, VA 22030.

Measure: Test of Self-Conscious Affect for Children (TOSCA-C)

Authors: Tangney, J. P., Wagner, P. E., Burggraf, S. A., Gramzow, R., & Fletcher, C.

Brief Description: A scenario-based paper-and-pencil measure of Alpha Pride (pride in self) and Beta Pride (pride in behavior), appropriate for children ages 8 to 12. Alpha Pride and Beta Pride scales are each composed of five items.

Further information available from: June Price Tangney, PhD, Department of Psychology, George Mason University, Fairfax, VA 22030.

AUTHOR INDEX

Abrams, S., 413
Abramson, L.Y., 348
Achenbach, T.M., 124
Agnoli, F., 37, 39
Aida, Y., 490
Ainsworth, M.D.S., 12, 52
Alessandri, S.M., 50, 81, 84, 85, 178, 192, 208
Allinsmith, W., 305
Altucher, N., 307, 312
American Psychiatric Association, 292, 347
Amsel, A., 199
Amsterdam, B.K., 205, 207
Angyal, A., 358
Apsler, R., 327, 333
Arend, R., 52
Argyle, M., 470
Arluke, A., 336
Armon-Jones, C., 66
Aronfreed, J., 175, 176, 305
Arsenio, W.F., 180
Asendorpf, J.B., 151, 158, 328
Astington, J.W., 221
Atkinson, J., 237
Ausubel, D.B., 302, 313
Ausubel, D.P., 175, 176, 177
Averill, J.R., 125, 261, 439, 483
Ayoub, C., 105

Bailey, R., 185
Baillargeon, R., 49, 71
Baldwin, J., 238
Balkin, J., 369, 379
Barden, R.C., 180, 233
Barlow, D.H., 114, 115, 117, 119, 120, 125, 131, 132, 133, 136, 176, 313, 344, 357, 358, 360
Barnett, M.A., 52, 162
Barone, P., 326
Barrett, D.E., 48

Barrett, J.C., 178
Barrett, K., 240
Barrett, K.C., 3, 4, 5, 6, 26, 27, 28, 35, 36, 38, 39, 42, 45, 48, 55, 65, 66, 68, 84, 93, 101, 106, 120, 145, 153, 154, 161, 165, 175, 375
Basch, F., 371
Baston, C.D., 129, 130, 156
Baston, J.G., 130
Baudonniere, P.M., 151
Baumeister, R.F., 255, 256, 257, 258, 259, 262, 263, 266, 267, 268, 269, 309, 318
Baumrind, D., 53
Beavin, J., 395
Beck, A.T., 281, 348, 353, 360, 378
Bell, R.Q., 159
Benedict, R., 27, 39, 55, 136, 445, 467, 482, 488, 492
Benes, F., 5
Benesh-Weiner, M., 233
Bennett, M., 323, 326
Bergman, A., 30, 50
Berman, J.J., 440
Berry, J.W., 469
Bertenthal, B.L., 70, 94, 95
Betancourt, H., 470
Bidell, T., 72, 73
Bidell, T.R., 71, 72
Bierbrauer, G., 469, 470, 483
Bilmes, M., 369
Binder, J., 373, 374
Biringen, Z., 162, 428
Bischof-Kohler, D., 151
Black, M.S., 306, 307
Blackwell, J., 250
Blaine, B., 456
Blatt, S., 348
Blehar, M., 12
Block, J., 446
Block, J.H., 145

SUBJECT INDEX